Other Information Security Study Guides from Sybex

IAPP CIPP / US Certified Information Privacy Professional Study Guide, 2nd Edition — ISBN 978-1-394-28490-0, January 2023

IAPP CIPM Certified Information Privacy Manager Study Guide — ISBN 978-1-394-15380-0, January 2023

ISC2 CISSP Certified Information Systems Security Professional Official Study Guide, 10th Edition — ISBN 978-1-394-25469-9, June 2024

CISM Certified Information Security Manager Study Guide — ISBN 978-1-119-80193-1, May 2022

ISC2 CCSP Certified Cloud Security Professional Official Study Guide, 3rd Edition — ISBN 978-1-119-90937-8, October 2022

CISA®

Certified Information Systems Auditor

Study Guide

Covers 2024–2029 Exam Objectives

Peter H. Gregory, CISA, CISSP

Mike Chapple, Ph.D., CISA, CISSP

Published by John Wiley & Sons, Inc., Hoboken, New Jersey.
Published simultaneously in Canada and the United Kingdom.

ISBNs: 9781394288380 (paperback), 9781394288403 (ePDF), 9781394288397 (ePub)

For general information on our other products and services, please contact our Customer Care Department within the United States at (800) 762-2974, outside the United States at (317) 572-3993. For product technical support, you can find answers to frequently asked questions or reach us via live chat at https://sybexsupport.wiley.com.

Wiley also publishes its books in a variety of electronic formats. Some content that appears in print may not be available in electronic formats. For more information about Wiley products, visit our website at www.wiley.com.

Library of Congress Control Number: 2024942279

Cover image: © Jeremy Woodhouse/Getty Images
Cover design: Wiley

SKY10090948_111424

To my grandchildren – may they grow up in a safer world.
—Peter

To my wife, Renee. We are a quarter century into this adventure together and yet we still find ourselves standing on the precipice of change. Here's to what's next!
—Mike

Acknowledgments

Books like this involve work from many people, and as authors, we truly appreciate the hard work and dedication that the team at Wiley shows. We would especially like to thank our acquisitions editor, Jim Minatel, who jumped through some incredible hoops to make this project possible.

We also greatly appreciated the editing and production team for the book, including Christine O'Connor, the managing editor, who brought years of experience and great talent to the project; Archana Pragash, the production editor who kept the train on the tracks, guided us through layouts, formatting, and final cleanup to produce a great book; Bobby Rogers and Jessica Chang, the technical editors, who provided insightful advice and gave wonderful feedback throughout the book. We would also like to thank the many behind-the-scenes contributors, including the graphics, production, and technical teams who make the book and companion materials into a finished product.

Shahla Pirnia, Mike's technical editor at `CertMike.com`, was instrumental in helping us get all of the details straightened out as we prepared the manuscript.

Our agent, Carole Jelen of Waterside Productions, continues to provide us with wonderful opportunities, advice, and assistance throughout us writing career.

Finally, we would like to thank our families, who supported us through the late evenings, busy weekends, and long hours that a book like this requires to write, edit, and get to press.

About the Authors

Peter H. Gregory, CISSP, CISM, CISA, CRISC, CIPM, CDPSE, CCSK, DRCE, A/CCRF, A/CCRP, is the author of more than 60 books on security and technology, including *Solaris Security* (Prentice Hall, 2000), *The Art of Writing Technical Books* (Waterside Productions, 2022), *CISM Certified Information Security Manager All-In-One Exam Guide* (McGraw-Hill, 2022), *Chromebook For Dummies* (Wiley, 2023), and *Elementary Information Security* (Jones & Bartlett Learning, 2024).

Peter is a career technologist and a security executive at a regional telecommunications provider. Before this, he held security leadership positions at Optiv Security (`www.optiv.com`) and Concur Technologies (`www.concur.com`). Peter is an advisory board member for the University of Washington and Seattle University for education programs in cybersecurity. He is a graduate of the FBI Citizens Academy.

Peter resides in Central Washington State and can be found at `www.peterhgregory.com`.

Mike Chapple, PhD, CISA, is the author of over 50 books, including the best-selling *ISC2 CISSP Certified Information Systems Security Professional Official Study Guide* (Sybex, 2024) and the *ISC2 CISSP Official Practice Tests* (Sybex, 2024). He is a cybersecurity professional with 25 years of experience in higher education, the private sector, and government.

Mike currently serves as Teaching Professor in the IT, Analytics, and Operations department at the University of Notre Dame's Mendoza College of Business, where he teaches undergraduate and graduate courses on cybersecurity, data management, and business analytics.

Mike previously served as executive vice president and chief information officer of the Brand Institute, a Miami-based marketing consultancy. Mike also spent four years in the information security research group at the National Security Agency and served as an active-duty intelligence officer in the U.S. Air Force.

Mike earned both his BS and PhD degrees from Notre Dame in computer science and engineering. Mike also holds an MS in computer science from the University of Idaho and an MBA from Auburn University. Mike holds the Certified Information Systems Auditor (CISA), Cybersecurity Analyst+ (CySA+), Security+, Certified Information Security Manager (CISM), Certified Cloud Security Professional (CCSP), and Certified Information Systems Security Professional (CISSP) certifications.

Learn more about Mike and his other security certification materials at his website, `https://CertMike.com`.

About the Technical Editors

Bobby E. Rogers is a senior cybersecurity professional with over 30 years in the field. He serves as a cybersecurity auditor and virtual Chief Information Security Officer (vCISO) for a variety of clients. He works with a major engineering company in Huntsville, Alabama, helping to secure networks and manage cyber risk for its customers. In addition to numerous educational institutions, Bobby's customers have included the U.S. Army, NASA, the State of Tennessee, and private/commercial companies and organizations. Bobby's specialties are cybersecurity engineering, security compliance, and cyber risk management, but he has worked in almost every area of cybersecurity, including network defense, computer forensics and incident response, and penetration testing.

He has narrated and produced over 30 computer training videos for several training companies. He is the author of McGraw-Hill Education's "CompTIA CySA+ Cybersecurity Analyst Certification Passport (Exam CS0-002)," 1st Edition, "CISSP Passport," 1st Edition, coauthor of "Certified in Risk and Information Systems Control (CRISC) All-in-One Exam Guide," 1st and 2nd editions, and contributing author/ technical editor for the popular "CISSP All-in-One Exam Guide," (7th, 8th, and 9th editions).

Jessica Chang is a licensed CPA in the state of Colorado with over 15 years of public accounting and general accounting experience in multiple leadership roles. She has worked in various industries, from telecommunications, hospitality, real estate, and e-commerce and has served as the chief audit executive for multiple companies.

Contents at a Glance

Contents

Introduction

Congratulations on choosing to become a Certified Information Systems Auditor (CISA). Whether you have worked for several years in the field of information systems auditing or have just recently been introduced to the world of controls, assurance, and security, don't underestimate the hard work and dedication required to obtain and maintain CISA certification. Although ambition and motivation are essential, the rewards of being CISA certified can far exceed the effort.

You probably never imagined you would find yourself working in the world of auditing or looking to obtain a professional auditing certification. Perhaps the increase in legislative or regulatory requirements for information system security led to your introduction to this field. Or possibly you noticed that CISA-related career options are increasing exponentially and you have decided to get ahead of the curve. You aren't alone; since the inception of CISA certification in 1978, more than 200,000 professionals worldwide reached the same conclusion and have earned this well-respected certification. Welcome to the journey and the amazing opportunities that await you.

We have put together this information to help you understand the commitment needed, prepare for the exam, and maintain your certification. Not only is it our wish that you prepare for and pass the exam with flying colors, but we also provide you with the information and resources to maintain your certification and to represent yourself and the professional world of information system (IS) auditing proudly with your new credentials.

ISACA (formerly known as the Information Systems Audit and Control Association) is a recognized leader in the areas of control, assurance, and IT governance. Formed in 1967, this nonprofit organization represents more than 180,000 professionals in more than 188 countries. ISACA administers several exam certifications, including:

- Certified Information Systems Auditor (CISA)
- Certified Information Security Manager (CISM)
- Certified in Risk and Information Systems Control (CRISC)
- Certified Data Privacy Solutions Engineer (CDPSE)
- Certified in Governance of Enterprise IT (CGEIT)
- Certified Cybersecurity Operations Analyst (CCOA)

The certification program has been accredited under ISO/IEC 17024:2012, which means that ISACA's procedures for accreditation meet international requirements for quality, continuous improvement, and accountability.

If you're new to ISACA, we recommend that you tour the organization's website (www.isaca.org) and become familiar with the guides and resources available. In addition, if you're near one of the 225 local ISACA chapters in 99 countries worldwide, consider reaching out to the chapter board for information on local meetings, training days, conferences, or study sessions. You may be able to meet other IS auditors who can give you additional insight into the CISA certification and the audit profession.

Established in 1978, the CISA certification primarily focuses on audit, controls, assurance, and security. It certifies the individual's knowledge of testing and documenting IS controls and their ability to conduct formal IS audits. Organizations seek qualified personnel for assistance with developing and maintaining strong control environments. A CISA-certified individual is a great candidate for these positions.

If you're preparing to take the CISA exam, you'll undoubtedly want to find as much information as you can about information systems and auditing. The more information you have at your disposal, the better off you'll be when attempting the exam. This study guide was written with that in mind. The goal was to provide enough information to prepare you for the test, but not so much that you'll be overloaded with information that's outside the scope of the exam.

This book presents the material at an intermediate technical level. Experience with and knowledge of security and auditing concepts will help you get a full understanding of the challenges you'll face as an information systems auditor.

We've included review questions at the end of each chapter to give you a taste of what it's like to take the exam. We recommend that you check out these questions first to gauge your level of expertise. You can then use the book mainly to fill in the gaps in your current knowledge. This study guide will help you round out your knowledge base before tackling the exam.

If you can answer 80 percent or more of the review questions correctly for a given chapter, you can feel safe moving on to the next chapter. If you're unable to answer that many correctly, reread the chapter and try the questions again. Your score should improve.

 Don't just study the questions and answers! The questions on the actual exam will be different from the practice questions included in this book. The exam is designed to test your knowledge of a concept or objective, so use this book to learn the objectives behind the questions.

The CISA Exam

The CISA exam is designed to be a vendor-neutral certification for information systems auditors. ISACA recommends this certification for those who already have experience in auditing and want to demonstrate that experience to current and future employers.

The exam covers five major domains:

1. Information Systems Auditing Process
2. Governance and Management of IT
3. Information Systems Acquisition, Development and Implementation
4. Information Systems Operations and Business Resilience
5. Protection of Information Assets

These five areas include a range of topics, from enterprise risk management to evaluating cybersecurity controls. They focus heavily on scenario-based learning and the role of the information systems auditor in various scenarios. There's a lot of information that you'll need to learn, but you'll be well rewarded for possessing this credential. ISACA reports that the average salary of CISA credential holders is over $145,000.

The CISA exam includes only standard multiple-choice questions. Each question has four possible answer choices and only one of those answer choices is the correct answer. When you're taking the test, you'll likely find some questions where you think multiple answers might be correct. In those cases, remember that you're looking for the *best* possible answer to the question!

The exam costs $575 for ISACA members and $760 for non-members. More details about the CISA exam and how to take it can be found at:

`www.isaca.org/credentialing/cisa`

You'll have four hours to take the exam and will be asked to answer 150 questions during that time period. Your exam will be scored on a scale ranging from 200 to 800, with a passing score of 450.

> ISACA frequently does what is called *item seeding*, which is the practice of including unscored questions on exams. It does so to gather psychometric data, which is then used when developing new versions of the exam. Before you take the exam, you will be told that your exam may include these unscored questions. So, if you come across a question that does not appear to map to any of the exam objectives—or for that matter, does not appear to belong in the exam—it is likely a seeded question. You never really know whether or not a question is seeded, however, so always make your best effort to answer every question.

Taking the Exam

Once you are fully prepared to take the exam, you can visit the ISACA website to register. Currently, ISACA offers two options for taking the exam: an in-person exam at a testing center and an at-home exam that you take on your own computer through a remote proctoring service.

In-Person Exams

ISACA partners with PSI Exams testing centers, so your next step will be to locate a testing center near you. In the United States, you can do this based on your address or your zip code, while non-U.S. test takers may find it easier to enter their city and country. You can search for a test center near you at the PSI Exams website:

`https://home.psiexams.com/#/test-center?p=Z97SE74H`

Now that you know where you'd like to take the exam, simply set up a PSI testing account and schedule an exam on their site.

On the day of the test, bring a government-issued identification card or passport that contains your full name (exactly matching the name on your exam registration), your signature, and your photograph. Make sure to show up with plenty of time before the exam starts. Remember that you will not be able to take your notes, electronic devices (including smartphones and watches), or other materials in with you.

At-Home Exams

ISACA also offers online exam proctoring. Candidates using this approach will take the exam at their home or office and be proctored over a webcam by a remote proctor.

Due to the rapidly changing nature of the at-home testing experience, candidates wishing to pursue this option should check the ISACA website for the latest details.

After the CISA Exam

Once you have taken the exam, you will be notified of your score immediately, so you'll know if you passed the test right away. You should keep track of your score report with your exam registration records and the email address you used to register for the exam.

Meeting the Experience Requirement

The CISA program is designed to demonstrate that an individual is a qualified information systems auditor. That requires more than just passing a test—it also requires real hands-on work experience.

The basic CISA work experience requirement is that you must have five years of work experience in information systems auditing, controls, assurance, or security. If the work you do aligns with any of the job practice statements found later in this introduction, that experience likely qualifies.

If you're a current information systems auditor or cybersecurity professional, you may find it easy to meet these requirements. If you don't yet meet the experience requirement, you may still take the exam and then you'll have five years to gain the experience and become fully certified after passing the test.

There are some waivers available that can knock 1, 2, or 3 years off your experience requirement:

- If you hold an associate's degree in any field, you qualify for a 1-year waiver.
- If you hold a bachelor's, master's, or doctoral degree in any field, you qualify for a 2-year waiver.
- If you hold a master's degree in information systems or a related field, you qualify for a 3-year waiver.
- If you hold full certification from the Chartered Institute of Management Accountants (CIMA), you qualify for a 2-year waiver.
- If you are a member of the Association of Chartered Certified Accountants (ACCA), you qualify for a 2-year waiver.

NOTE These waivers may not be combined. You may only use *one* of these waiver options against your certification requirements.

You must have earned all of the experience used toward your requirement within the 10 years preceding your application or within 5 years of the date you pass the exam.

Maintaining Your Certification

Information systems auditing is a constantly evolving field with new threats and controls arising regularly. All CISA holders must complete continuing professional education on an annual basis to keep their knowledge current and their skills sharp. The guidelines around continuing professional education are somewhat complicated, but they boil down to two main requirements:

- You must complete 120 hours of credit every three years to remain certified.

- You must have a minimum of 20 hours of credit every year during that cycle.

You must meet both of these requirements. For example, if you earn 120 credit hours during the first year of your certification cycle, you still must earn 20 additional credits in each of the next 2 years.

Continuing education requirements follow calendar years, and your clock will begin ticking on January 1 of the year after you earn your certification. You are allowed to begin earning credits immediately after you're certified. They'll just count for the next year.

There are many acceptable ways to earn CPE credits, many of which do not require travel or attending a training seminar. The important requirement is that you generally do not earn CPEs for work that you perform as part of your regular job. CPEs are intended to cover professional development opportunities outside of your day-to-day work. You can earn CPEs in several ways:

- Attending conferences

- Attending training programs

- Attending professional meetings and activities

- Taking self-study courses

- Participating in vendor marketing presentations

- Teaching, lecturing, or presenting

- Publishing articles, monographs, or books

- Participating in the exam development process

- Volunteering with ISACA

- Earning other professional credentials

- Contributing to the profession

- Mentoring

For more information on the activities that qualify for CPE credits, visit this site:

www.isaca.org/credentialing/how-to-earn-cpe

Study Guide Elements

This study guide uses a number of common elements to help you prepare. These include the following:

Summaries   The Summary section of each chapter briefly explains the chapter, allowing you to easily understand what it covers.

Exam Essentials   The Exam Essentials focus on major exam topics and critical knowledge that you should take in to the test. The Exam Essentials focus on the exam objectives provided by ISACA.

Chapter Review Questions   A set of questions at the end of each chapter will help you assess your knowledge and if you are ready to take the exam based on your knowledge of that chapter's topics.

Additional Study Tools

This book comes with a number of additional study tools to help you prepare for the exam. They include the following.

Go to www.wiley.com/go/Sybextestprep to register and gain access to this interactive online learning environment and test bank with study tools.

Sybex Test Preparation Software

Sybex's test preparation software lets you prepare with electronic test versions of the review questions from each chapter, the practice exam, and the bonus exam that are included in this book. You can build and take tests on specific domains, by chapter, or cover the entire set of CISA exam objectives using randomized tests.

Electronic Flashcards

Our electronic flashcards are designed to help you prepare for the exam. Over 100 flashcards will ensure that you know critical terms and concepts.

Glossary of Terms

Sybex provides a full glossary of terms in PDF format, allowing quick searches and easy reference to materials in this book.

Bonus Practice Exams

In addition to the practice questions for each chapter, this book includes two full 150-question practice exams. We recommend that you use them both to test your preparedness for the certification exam.

Like all exams, the Certified Information Systems Auditor from CISA is updated periodically and may eventually be retired or replaced. At some point after CISA is no longer offering this exam, the old editions of our books and online tools will be retired. If you have purchased this book after the exam was retired or are attempting to register in the Sybex online learning environment after the exam was retired, please know that we make no guarantees that this exam's online Sybex tools will be available once the exam is no longer available.

CISA Exam Objectives

ISACA publishes relative weightings for each of the exam's objectives. The following lists the five CISA domains and the extent to which they are represented on the exam.

Domain	% of Exam
1. Information Systems Auditing Process	18%
2. Governance and Management of IT	18%
3. Information Systems Acquisition, Development and Implementation	12%
4. Information Systems Operations and Business Resilience	26%
5. Protection of Information Assets	26%

CISA Certification Exam Objective Map

The CISA exam covers two different types of objectives: job practice areas and supporting tasks. We recommend that instead of focusing on these objectives in the order they appear in the exam objectives that you instead learn them in the order they are presented in this book. In our experience preparing students for certification exams, we've found that approaching these topics in a more logical order will better prepare you for the exam.

If you're looking for where we've covered a specific objective in the book, use the following two lists to find the appropriate chapter.

Job Practice Areas	Chapter
Domain 1: Information Systems Auditing Process	
A. Planning	
1. IS Audit Standards, Guidelines, and Codes of Ethics	2
2. Business Processes	2
3. Types of Controls	2

Domain 5: Protection of Information Assets

How to Contact the Publisher

If you believe you have found a mistake in this book, please bring it to our attention. At John Wiley & Sons, we understand how important it is to provide our customers with accurate content, but even with our best efforts an error may occur.

To submit your possible errata, please email it to our Customer Service Team at wileysupport@wiley.com with the subject line "Possible Book Errata Submission."

Assessment Test

1. Seth's organization recently experienced a security incident where an attacker was able to place offensive content on the home page of his organization's website. Seth would like to implement a series of security controls to prevent this type of attack from occurring in the future. What goal of information security is Seth most directly addressing?

   A. Integrity

   B. Availability

   C. Nonrepudiation

   D. Confidentiality

2. Domer Delectables is a U.S. publicly traded company. They are currently undertaking a significant IT project that will redesign their access control systems. What is the best role for Internal Audit in this project?

   A. Develop procedures

   B. Design controls

   C. Provide feedback on control design

   D. Implement controls

3. Jen is building a series of controls for her organization's information security program and is categorizing those controls by type. She is updating the organization's firewall to include next-generation capabilities. What type of control is she working on?

   A. Detective

   B. Preventive

   C. Compensating

   D. Deterrent

4. Belinda recently assumed the CISO role at a publicly traded company. She is sorting through the corporate governance model and identifying the roles that different people and groups play in the organization. Which one of the following roles has ultimate authority for the corporation?

   A. CEO

   B. CIO

   C. Board

   D. Board chair

5. Brandon leads the information security team for a large organization and is working with the software development team to provide them with application security testing services. He would like to document roles and responsibilities of the two teams in a written agreement with the leader of the development team. What type of agreement would be most appropriate?

    A. MOU

    B. SLA

    C. BPA

    D. MSA

6. Monica is conducting a quantitative risk assessment of the risk that a fire poses to her organization's primary operating facility. She believes that a serious fire would destroy 50 percent of the facility, causing $10 million in damage. She expects that a fire of this nature would only occur once every 50 years, on average. What is the AV in this scenario?

    A. $200,000

    B. $5 million

    C. $10 million

    D. $20 million

7. After assessing the risk of fire, Monica decides to install new sprinkler systems throughout the facility to reduce the likelihood of a serious fire. What type of risk treatment action is she taking?

    A. Risk avoidance

    B. Risk acceptance

    C. Risk transference

    D. Risk mitigation

8. Kevin is conducting a SWOT analysis for his organization's IT program. He is especially proud of the talented and diverse team that exists within his organization. Where would he place this quality on the SWOT matrix?

    A. Upper-left quadrant

    B. Upper-right quadrant

    C. Lower-left quadrant

    D. Lower-right quadrant

9. Peihua is reviewing the organizing documents for an organization's IT program as she prepares for an audit. She comes across a document that outlines the parameters under which the organization will function. What type of document is she reviewing?

    A. Charter

    B. Scope statement

    C. Business purpose statement

    D. Statement of authority

10. Fred is helping his boss develop a set of metrics for the organization's security program. After consulting the ITIL framework used by his organization, he decides to track the number of major security incidents that occur each year. What type of metric is this?

    A. KGI

    B. KPI

    C. KSI

    D. KRI

11. Roberta is tasked with detecting whether fraud is occurring in sales commission processing. She selects records looking for cases of fraud. What type of sampling is she using?

    A. Statistical sampling

    B. Stratified sampling

    C. Attribute sampling

    D. Discovery sampling

12. Michael is leading a software development project and is currently in the testing phase. He has completed the unit testing for various modules and is about to proceed with system testing. Which statement best describes the primary focus of system testing in this context?

    A. System testing is primarily concerned with verifying the individual functions of the application as specified in the functional requirements.

    B. System testing focuses on verifying that different modules or components work together correctly and includes testing interfaces and data migration.

    C. System testing is an informal testing phase where developers manually check the code for errors before deployment.

    D. System testing involves end users performing tests to ensure the application meets their needs and requirements.

13. What is a primary advantage of using prototyping as a software development methodology?

    A. It ensures that all functional requirements are addressed, even those unknown to users.

    B. It reduces the risk of the application being developed incorrectly by involving users continuously.

    C. It allows the prototype to be used in production environments without further development.

    D. It eliminates the need for formal documentation and user feedback.

14. Cindy is concerned that users in her organization might take sensitive data and email it to their personal email accounts for access after they leave the organization. Which one of the following security technologies would best protect against this risk?

    A. Firewall

    B. IPS

    C. DLP

    D. Configuration management

15. Andrea is placing a new server onto her organization's network. The server is a web server that will be accessible only by internal employees. What network zone would be the most appropriate location for this server?

A. Internet

B. Intranet

C. Extranet

D. DMZ

16. Tech Solutions is a growing software development company. Recently, they have implemented a companywide documented software development process that all teams are required to follow. This process includes detailed guidelines for each stage of development, and the teams consistently use this process for all projects. However, the company has not yet started measuring the effectiveness or efficiency of the process, nor are there any formal metrics in place to monitor defects.

Based on the SEI CMM, at which level of maturity is Tech Solutions currently operating?

A. Repeatable

B. Defined

C. Managed

D. Optimizing

17. Jen is conducting a financial audit of a large multinational corporation. In reviewing payroll transactions, she notes that a team of five employees was accidentally underpaid by 10 percent on their overtime hours for the past year. What statement best describes the impact of this discovery on the audit?

A. This is a legal violation and must be immediately reported to governmental authorities.

B. This error may cause a significant impact on the financial statements and should be reported as an audit finding.

C. This issue indicates potential fraud and should be investigated further to determine if there are broader implications.

D. This finding is immaterial.

18. Norma is evaluating the security of a web-based system. She determines that the system verifies that dates fall within a logical range before accepting them as input to the system. What term best describes this technique?

A. Input authorization

B. Input validation

C. Logical redundancy

D. Error handling

19. Wally is assessing the controls used to protect his organization against the risk of data loss. Which one of the following controls would be the best defense against the accidental deletion of data by an authorized user?

A. RAID 1

B. RAID 5

C. Backups

D. Access controls

20. Melissa is preparing to test her organization's disaster recovery plan. During the test, she will activate the organization's backup processing facility and use it to process data as a test, but normal operations will continue in the primary facility. What type of test is she running?

A. Parallel test

B. Cutover test

C. Simulation test

D. Walk-through

Answers to Assessment Test

1. **A.** The three main goals of information security are confidentiality, integrity, and availability, so we can eliminate nonrepudiation right away. There is also no indication that there was any disclosure of sensitive information, so we can also eliminate confidentiality. It is possible that we could consider this an availability breach if the attacker made legitimate information unavailable, but integrity is a better answer here, because the attacker definitely altered the content of the website without authorization. You'll find a thorough discussion of the goals of an information security program in Chapter 7.

2. **C.** Any Internal Audit function should not design or implement controls or procedures, other than those in its own department. Internal Audit may, however, opine on the design of controls for their suitability to achieve control objectives and auditability. Internal Audit cannot play a design role in any process or control that it may later be required to audit. You'll find a discussion of the roles of auditors in Chapter 2.

3. **B.** Firewalls are best described as preventive controls because their purpose is to block an attack from succeeding. Detective controls seek to identify attacks that are taking place, and though a firewall can detect some attacks, this is not the primary purpose of the device. Firewalls may also serve as compensating controls in a regulatory environment, but there is no indication in this question that the firewall is being used as a compensating control. Firewalls are not normally visible to an attacker until after they have attempted an attack, so they cannot serve as deterrent controls. You'll find a discussion of control categories and types in Chapter 7.

4. **C.** The board of directors, acting as a group, has ultimate authority over the organization. They are elected by the shareholders who own the company and serve as the owner's representatives. They delegate much of their authority to the chief executive officer (CEO) but retain ultimate control. You'll learn more about corporate governance models in Chapter 1.

5. **A.** In this case, Brandon needs an agreement with another internal organization. These types of agreements most commonly take the form of memoranda of understanding (MOU). More formal master service agreements (MSAs) and service level agreements (SLAs) are normally used with external service providers. Business partnership agreements (BPAs) are used when two organizations are entering into a joint effort. You'll learn more about different agreement types in Chapter 1.

6. **D.** The asset value (AV) is the total value of the asset being analyzed. In this case, we know that the data center would be 50 percent destroyed by a fire and that the damage caused by the fire would be valued at $10 million. We can then work backward to determine that if $10 million is 50 percent of the asset value, then the asset value is $20 million. You'll learn more about quantitative risk assessment in Chapter 1.

7. **D.** Monica is seeking to reduce the likelihood and/or impact of a risk. Therefore, she is engaging in risk mitigation activity. Risk avoidance involves changing business practices to make a risk irrelevant. Risk acceptance involves continuing business activities in the face of a risk. Risk transference involves shifting some of the impact of a risk to a third party, such as an insurance company. You'll learn more about risk treatment options in Chapter 1.

8. A. This is an example of a strength. It is an internal force that is positive. Therefore, it would be placed in the upper-left quadrant. The upper-right quadrant is for internal negative forces, or weaknesses. The lower-left quadrant is for external positive forces, or opportunities. The lower-right quadrant is for external negative forces, or threats. You'll find more information about SWOT analyses in Chapter 7.

9. A. Peihua is drafting the organization's IT charter. This is the organizing document for the program, and it outlines the parameters under which the program will function. This is a tricky question because the scope statement, business purpose statement, and statement of authority are all common elements of the charter. You'll learn more about the organizing documents for an IT program in Chapter 1.

10. B. This metric is directly out of the ITIL framework's nine key performance indicators (KPIs) for a security program. KPIs are metrics that demonstrate the success of the program in achieving its objectives and are a look at historical performance. Key goal indicators (KGIs) are similar but track progress toward a defined goal and there is no clear goal in this scenario. Key risk indicators (KRIs) look forward at risks that may jeopardize future security. You'll learn more about these metrics in Chapter 4.

11. D. When a set of records is too large for an auditor to examine each one, the auditor must choose a sampling technique to select the records to examine. Discovery sampling is used to detect fraud. Statistical sampling employs a strictly random selection of records. Stratified sampling is used to select samples with, for example, low, moderate, and high dollar figures. Attribute sampling involves an examination of one or more values to understand control performance, such as the time required to patch a system. You'll find a discussion of sampling strategies in Chapter 2.

12. B. System testing focuses on verifying that different modules or components work together correctly and includes testing interfaces and data migration. This phase ensures that the integrated system functions as intended and all parts interact properly, which is crucial after unit testing individual modules.

    Verifying the individual functions of the application as specified in the functional requirements is the primary focus of unit testing, not system testing.

    An informal testing phase where developers manually check the code for errors before deployment refers to ad hoc or informal testing, which is not structured like system testing.

    End users performing tests to ensure the application meets their needs and requirements is characteristic of user acceptance testing (UAT), which follows system testing. You'll learn about these testing methodologies in Chapter 3.

13. B. Prototyping reduces the risk of the application being developed incorrectly by involving users continuously. This user involvement helps ensure that the development team receives ongoing feedback, which can be used to make necessary adjustments early in the development process, leading to a product that better meets user needs and expectations.

    Ensuring that all functional requirements are addressed, even those unknown to users, is not a primary advantage of prototyping since unknown requirements can still be missed.

Allowing the prototype to be used in production environments without further development is inaccurate because prototypes are typically not fully developed or tested for production use; they serve primarily as models for feedback and iterative development.

Eliminating the need for formal documentation and user feedback is incorrect since prototyping often relies on user feedback and may still require documentation to guide the development process and ensure all aspects are covered.

You'll find a discussion of prototyping in Chapter 3.

14. C. While it is possible that any security technology could play an indirect role in preventing the unauthorized exfiltration of information, data loss prevention (DLP) technology is specifically designed to protect against this threat, so that is the best possible answer to this question. You'll learn more about DLP and other security technologies in Chapter 7.

15. B. Servers intended for internal use only should be placed on the intranet, where they are accessible only to other internal systems. The DMZ would be an appropriate location for this server if it permitted public access. An extranet would be appropriate if the server was being accessed by business partners. The Internet is generally never a good location for a server. You'll learn more about firewalls and security zones in Chapter 7.

16. B. Tech Solutions is currently operating at the Defined level. At this level, the organization has established standardized and documented processes for software development that all teams follow consistently. These processes are described in detail and provide guidelines for each stage of development.

The Repeatable level is characterized by basic project management practices, but processes are not standardized across the organization. Teams may have their own practices that are not consistent companywide.

The Managed level involves measuring the effectiveness and efficiency of the processes, with formal metrics in place to monitor defects and performance, which Tech Solutions has not yet implemented.

The Optimizing level focuses on continuous process improvement through quantitative feedback and innovative practices, which also requires established metrics and measurements, and Tech Solutions has not yet reached this stage. You'll learn more about the SEI CMM in Chapter 3.

17. D. Despite the fact that Jen has discovered a situation that should be corrected, the fact that five employees were underpaid is not going to meet the materiality threshold for a large corporation. Therefore, it will likely have no impact on the results of the financial audit and should not be reported as a finding. Jen should report it to management but is under no obligation to report to any government authorities on this matter. There is no evidence of fraud in this case. You'll learn about materiality in Chapter 2.

18. B. Input validation ensures that data meets specific criteria before it is accepted into the system, including verifying that dates fall within a logical range, which prevents invalid or malicious data from causing errors or vulnerabilities.

Input authorization pertains to ensuring that only authorized personnel can enter data into the system, involving user access controls and approvals, rather than validating the correctness of the data itself.

Logical redundancy refers to the duplication of critical components or functions within a system to increase reliability, which is unrelated to the process of validating input data.

Error handling involves the actions taken by a system when input validation fails, such as rejecting invalid data or requesting re-input, but it does not describe the process of checking that the input data is correct. You'll learn more about input validation in Chapter 3.

19. C. Backups allow the organization to recover data that was accidentally deleted. RAID technology is used to protect against the failure of a hard drive and would not protect against the loss of data by user action. Access controls would be effective to prevent an unauthorized user from deleting data but would not stop an authorized user from doing so. You'll learn more about data protection controls in Chapter 6.

20. A. This type of test, where the alternate processing facility is activated but the primary site retains operational control, is known as a parallel test. In a cutover test, the primary site is shut down and operational control moves to the alternate site. Simulations and walk-throughs do not affect normal operations and do not activate the alternate site. You'll learn more about business continuity and disaster recovery programs and testing in Chapter 6.

Chapter

1

IT Governance and Management

THE CERTIFIED INFORMATION SYSTEMS AUDITOR (CISA) OBJECTIVES REPRESENT 18% OF THE MATERIAL COVERED ON THE EXAM AND INCLUDE:

✓ **Domain 2: Governance & Management of IT**

  A. IT Governance

    1. IT Governance and IT Strategy

    2. IT-Related Frameworks

    3. IT Standards, Policies, and Procedures

    4. Organizational Structure

    5. Enterprise Architecture

    6. Enterprise Risk Management

    7. Maturity Models

    8. Organization

  B. IT Management

    1. IT Resource Management

    2. IT Service Provider Acquisition and Management

    3. IT Performance Monitoring and Reporting

    4. Quality Assurance and Quality Management of IT

Supporting Tasks

    5. Evaluate the IT strategy for alignment with the organization's strategies and objectives.

    6. Evaluate the effectiveness of IT governance structure and IT organizational structure.

    7. Evaluate the organization's management of IT policies and practices.

8. Evaluate the organization's IT policies and practices for compliance with regulatory and legal requirements.

10. Evaluate the organization's risk management policies and practices.

15. Evaluate whether IT supplier selection and contract management processes align with business requirements.

22. Evaluate IT operations to determine whether they are controlled effectively and continue to support the organization's objectives.

37. Provide consulting services and guidance to the organization in order to improve the quality and control of information systems.

IT governance should be the wellspring from which all other IT activities flow.

Properly implemented, governance is a process whereby senior management exerts strategic control over business functions through policies, objectives, delegation of authority, and monitoring. Governance is management's control over all other IT processes to ensure that IT processes continue to meet the organization's business objectives effectively.

Business alignment is a critical characteristic of IT governance. IT's primary mission should be the support of the overall business mission, goals, and objectives. The alignment of IT to the business must be intentional and deliberate for IT and the organization to succeed.

Organizations usually establish governance through an IT steering committee that is responsible for setting long-term IT strategy and by making changes to ensure that IT processes continue to support IT strategy and the organization's needs. This is accomplished through the development and enforcement of IT policies, requirements, and standards.

IT governance typically focuses on several key processes, such as personnel management, sourcing, change management, financial management, quality management, security management, and performance optimization. Another key component is the establishment of an effective organization structure and clear statements of roles and responsibilities. An effective governance program will use a balanced scorecard (BSC) or other means to monitor these and other key processes, and through a process of continuous improvement, IT processes will be changed to remain effective, to support ongoing business needs, and to respond to existing and emerging risks.

IT Governance Practices for Executives and Boards of Directors

Governance starts at the top, and a proper "tone at the top" is crucial for effective governance and oversight.

Whether the organization has a board of directors, council members, commissioners, or some other top-level governing body, governance begins with the establishment of top-level objectives and policies that are translated into more actions, policies, processes, procedures, and other activities downward through each level in the organization.

This section describes governance practices recommended for IT organizations, including a strategy-developing committee, measurement via the BSC, and security management.

 NOTE   Governance is not merely an IT practice. Rather, governance is practiced in the business apart from IT to facilitate management's control over all aspects of business operations, including IT.

IT Governance

The purpose of IT governance is to align IT with the strategies and objectives of the organization. The term IT governance refers to a collection of top-down activities intended to control the IT organization from a strategic perspective to ensure that the IT organization supports the business. The artifacts and activities that flow out of healthy IT governance include the following:

- **Policy:** At a minimum, IT policy should directly reflect the mission, objectives, and goals of the overall organization.

- **Priorities:** Priorities in the IT organization should flow directly from the organization's mission, objectives, and goals. Whatever is most important to the organization as a whole should be important to IT as well.

- **Standards:** The technologies, protocols, and practices used by IT should reflect the organization's needs. On their own, standards help to drive a consistent approach to solving business challenges; the choice of standards should facilitate solutions that meet the organization's needs in a cost-effective and secure manner.

- **Resource management:** The budget, personnel, equipment, and other resources are planned, selected, managed, and measured to ensure that the IT organization has the ability to meet its objectives.

- **Vendor management:** The suppliers and service providers that IT selects should reflect IT and business priorities, standards, and practices.

- **Program and project management:** IT programs and projects should be organized and performed in a consistent manner that reflects IT and business priorities and supports the business.

While IT governance contains the elements just described, strategic planning is also a key component of governance. Strategy development is discussed in the next section.

IT Governance Frameworks

Every organization may have a unique mission, objectives, goals, business models, tolerance for risk, and so on, but organizations need not invent governance frameworks from scratch to manage their IT and business objectives. Several good frameworks can be adapted to meet organizations' needs, including the following:

- **COBIT 2019:** This IT management framework was developed by the IT Governance Institute and ISACA. COBIT's five domains are:
  - Evaluate, Direct, and Monitor
  - Align, Plan, and Organize
  - Build, Acquire, and Implement
  - Deliver, Service, and Support
  - Monitor, Evaluate, and Assess
- **ISO/IEC 27001:** This is the well-known international standard for top-down information security management. In the context of IT security governance, most important here are the requirements in ISO/IEC 27001, not the security controls that appear in its appendix. This is a good opportunity to point out that governance frameworks and control frameworks are not the same thing.
- **ITIL:** Formerly an acronym for IT Infrastructure Library, ITIL is a framework of processes for IT service delivery. ITIL was originally sponsored by the UK Office of Government Commerce to improve its IT management processes, but it is now owned by an organization named AXELOS. The international standard, ISO/IEC 20000, is adapted from ITIL.
- **ISO/IEC 38500:** This international standard on corporate governance of IT is suitable for small and large organizations in the public or private sector.
- **COSO:** This framework was developed by the Committee of Sponsoring Organizations of the Treadway Commission to combat internal fraud. COSO is a framework of internal controls, mainly targeting financial accounting systems and implicitly underlying relevant IT controls.

These and other frameworks are discussed in greater detail in Appendix A.

Digital Transformation

The phenomenon known as digital transformation represents the trend of increasing reliance of businesses on information technology. DX, as it is sometimes known, surpasses the mere support of business processes with information technology, but also includes business processes entirely based on IT. This trend underscores the need for information system (IS) auditors, and even the digital transformation of IS auditing itself.

IT Strategy Committee

In organizations where IT plays a significant strategic business role, the board of directors should have an IT strategy committee, consisting of members of the board who have experience in technology issues. This group will advise the full board of directors on strategies to enable better IT support of the organization's overall strategy and objectives.

The IT strategy committee can meet with the organization's top IT executives to impart the board's wishes directly to them. This works best as a two-way conversation, where IT executives can inform the strategy committee of their status on major initiatives, as well as on challenges and risks. This ongoing dialogue can take place as often as needed, usually once or twice a year.

Readers should note that this suggestion of the IT strategy committee communicating with IT management is not an attempt to circumvent communications through intermediate layers of management. Those individuals should be included in this conversation as well.

The Balanced Scorecard

The *balanced scorecard (BSC)* is a management tool that is used to measure the performance and effectiveness of an organization. The BSC is used to determine how well an organization can fulfill its mission and strategic objectives, and how well it is aligned with overall organizational objectives.

In the BSC, management defines key performance indicators (KPIs) in each of four perspectives:

- **Financial:** Key financial items measured include the cost of strategic initiatives, support costs of key applications, and investment.
- **Customer:** Key measurements include the satisfaction rate with various customer-facing aspects of the organization.
- **Internal business:** Measurements of activities that the organization must perform as the essential components of the business that drive customer satisfaction.
- **Innovation and learning:** Measurements of activities that drive the company's future success, including new product development and continuous product improvement.

Each organization's BSC will represent a unique set of measurements that reflects the organization's type of business, business model, and style of management.

The Standard IT Balanced Scorecard

The BSC should be used to measure overall organizational effectiveness and progress. A similar scorecard, the standard IT balanced scorecard (IT-BSC), can be used specifically to measure IT organization performance and results.

Like the BSC, the standard IT-BSC has four perspectives:

- **Business contribution:** Key indicators here are the perception of IT department effectiveness and value as seen from other (non-IT) corporate executives.

- **User:** Key measurements include end-user satisfaction rate with IT systems and the IT support organization. Satisfaction rates of external users should be included if the IT department builds or supports externally facing applications or systems.

- **Operational excellence:** Key measurements include the number of support cases, amount of unscheduled downtime, and defects reported.

- **Innovation:** This includes the rate at which the IT organization uses newer technologies to increase IT value and the amount of training made available to IT staff.

The IT-BSC should flow directly out of the organization's overall BSC. This will ensure that IT will align itself with corporate objectives. Although the perspectives between the overall BSC and the IT-BSC vary, the approach for each is similar, and the results for the IT-BSC can "roll up" to the organization's overall BSC.

Information Security Governance

Security governance is the collection of management activities that establishes key roles and responsibilities, identifies and treats risks to key assets, and measures key security processes. Depending on the structure of the organization and its business purpose, information security governance may be included in IT governance, or security governance may stand on its own (but if so, it should still be linked to IT governance so that these two activities are kept in sync). Security governance helps to align information security with the organization's strategies and objectives.

The main roles and responsibilities for security should be as follows:

- **Board of directors:** The board is responsible for establishing the tone for risk appetite and risk management in the organization. To the extent that the board of directors establishes business and IT security, so, too, should the board consider risk and security in that strategy. The board is accountable to shareholders for the overall performance of the firm, including the satisfaction of information security obligations.

- **Steering committee:** The security steering committee should establish the operational strategy for security and risk management in the organization. This includes setting strategic and tactical roles and responsibilities in more detail than was done by the board of directors. The security strategy should be in harmony with the strategy for IT and the business overall. The steering committee should also ratify security policy and other strategic policies and processes developed by the chief information security officer.

- **Chief information security officer (CISO):** The CISO should be responsible for developing security policy; conducting risk assessments; developing processes for risk management, vulnerability management, incident management, identity and access management, security awareness and training, third-party risk management, and compliance management; and informing the steering committee and board of directors of incidents and new or changed risks. In some organizations, this is known as the chief information risk officer (CIRO).

> Some organizations may employ a chief security officer (CSO) who is responsible for logical security as described in the CISO role, as well as physical security, including workplace and personnel safety, physical access control, and investigations.

- **Chief information officer (CIO):** The CIO is responsible for overall leadership of the IT organization, including IT strategy, development, operations, and service desk. In some organizations the CISO or another top-ranking security individual reports to the CIO, while in other organizations they are peers.

- **Management:** Every manager in the organization should be at least partially responsible for the conduct of their employees. This approach helps to establish a chain of accountability from the top of the organization all the way down to individual employees.

- **Internal audit:** Internal auditors are responsible for providing independent and objective assurance that the organization is achieving its stated objectives.

- **All employees:** Every employee in the organization should be required to comply with the organization's security policy, as well as with security requirements and processes. All senior and executive management personnel should demonstrably comply with these policies as an example for others.

Security governance is not only for the identification and enforcement of applicable laws, regulations, and other legal requirements, but also for the fulfillment of goals and objectives, as well as management, monitoring, and enforcement of policies and processes.

Security governance should also make it clear that compliance with policies is a condition of employment; employees who fail to comply with policy are subject to discipline or termination of employment.

Where Should the CISO Report?

A great debate rages on in the cybersecurity community about where the CISO should fit within an organization. Some argue that the CISO should report to the CIO, while others insist they be peers reporting to the CEO. While there is no right answer for all organizations, many organizations choose to divide security responsibilities. In such an arrangement, the CISO might oversee governance, policy, investigations, and risk. The CIO may oversee a security operations function that carries out daily operational tasks. This approach has the benefit of allowing the CISO to oversee governance efforts with independence from the IT organization while the CIO can lead a team responsible for end-to-end technical operations.

Reasons for Security Governance

Organizations are dependent on their information systems. This has progressed to the point where organizations—including those whose products or services are not information-related—are completely dependent on the integrity and availability of their information systems to continue operations; this is the trend of digital transformation. Security governance, then, is needed to ensure that the probability and impact of security-related incidents are minimized and do not threaten critical systems and their support of the ongoing viability of the organization.

Security Governance Activities and Results

Within an effective security governance program, the organization's management will see to it that information systems necessary to support business operations will be adequately protected. Following are some of the activities that will take place:

- **Risk management:** Management will ensure that risk assessments will be performed to identify risks in information systems. Follow-up actions—primarily, risk treatment—will be carried out that will reduce the risk of system failure and compromise to acceptable levels that align with the organization's risk appetite or risk tolerance.
- **Process improvement:** Management will ensure that key changes will be made to business processes that will result in security improvements.
- **Incident response:** Management will implement incident response procedures that will help to avoid incidents, reduce the impact and probability of incidents, and improve response to incidents so that their impact on the organization is minimized.
- **Improved compliance:** Management will be sure to identify all applicable laws, regulations, and standards and carry out activities to confirm that the organization is able to attain and maintain compliance.
- **Business continuity and disaster recovery planning:** Management will define objectives and allocate resources for the development of business continuity and disaster recovery plans.
- **Third-party risk management:** With increased reliance on external service providers, management will direct the assessment and management of third-party service providers that process and store critical information and perform critical functions for the organization.
- **Effectiveness measurement:** Management will establish processes to measure key security events such as incidents, policy changes and violations, audits, and training.
- **Resource management:** The allocation of labor, budget, and other resources to meet security objectives will be monitored by management.
- **Improved IT governance:** An effective security governance program will result in better strategic decisions in the IT organization that keep risks at an acceptably low level.

These and other governance activities are carried out through planned interactions among key business and IT executives at regular intervals. Meetings will include a discussion of effectiveness measurements, recent incidents, recent audits, and risk assessments. Other discussions may include such things as changes to the business, recent business results, and any anticipated business events such as mergers or acquisitions.

There are two key results of an effective security governance program:

- **Increased trust:** Customers, suppliers, and partners trust the organization to a greater degree when they see that security is managed effectively.

- **Improved reputation:** The business community, including customers, investors, and regulators, will hold the organization in higher regard.

IIA Three-Lines Model

The Institute of Internal Auditors (IIA) uses a three-lines model to describe how assurance and governance exist in an organization.

In this model, the board of directors is accountable to stakeholders for overseeing the organization. The board delegates responsibility to both management and the internal audit department.

Management is responsible for taking actions to manage risk and achieve the organization's objectives. Management reports to the board and coordinates with the internal audit department.

Internal audit is responsible for providing independent assurance. The internal audit department also reports to the board and coordinates with management.

IT Strategic Planning

A good strategic planning process answers the question of what should we do? Although IT organizations require personnel who perform the day-to-day work of supporting systems and applications, some IT personnel need to spend at least part of their time developing plans for what the IT organization will be doing two, three, or even five years into the future.

Strategic planning needs to be part of a formal, iterative planning process, not an ad hoc, chaotic activity. Specific roles and responsibilities for planning need to be established, and those individuals must carry out planning roles as they would any other responsibility. A part of the struggle with the process of planning stems from the fact that strategic planning is partly a creative endeavor that includes analysis of reliable information about future technologies and practices, as well as a development of long-term strategic plans for the organization itself.

In a nutshell, the key question is this: In five years, when the organization will be performing specific activities in a particular manner, how will IT systems enable and support those activities?

But it's more than just understanding how IT will support future business activities. Innovations in IT may help to shape what activities will take place, or at least how they will take place. On a more down-to-earth level, IT strategic planning is about the ability to provide the capability and capacity for IT services that will match the levels of and the types of business activities that the organization expects to achieve at certain points in the future. In other words, if organizational strategic planning predicts specific transaction volumes (as well as new types of transactions) at specific points in the future, the job of IT strategic planning will be to ensure that cost-effective IT systems of sufficient processing capacity will be up and running to support those features and workloads. As digital transformation sweeps across industries, increasingly, IT does not merely support a business process; IT is a business process.

Discussion of new business activities, as well as the projected volume of current activities at certain times in the future, is most often discussed by a steering committee.

The IT Steering Committee

A *steering committee* is a body of senior managers or executives that meets from time to time to discuss high-level and long-term issues in the organization. An IT steering committee will typically discuss the future state of the organization and how the IT organization will evolve to meet the organization's needs. A steering committee will typically consist of senior-level IT managers as well as business unit leaders, and key internal customers or constituents. This provider-customer dialogue will help to ensure that IT, as the organization's technology service arm, will fully understand the future vision of the business (in business terms) and be able to support future business activities in terms of capacity, cost-effectiveness, and the ability to support new activities that do not yet exist.

 The IT steering committee also assesses results of recent initiatives and major projects to gain a high-level understanding of past performance in order to shape future activities. The committee also needs to consider industry trends and practices, risks as defined by internal risk assessments, and current IT capabilities.

The role of the IT steering committee is depicted in Figure 1.1.

A steering committee's mission, objectives, roles, and responsibilities should be formally defined in a written charter. Steering committee meetings should be documented and minutes published.

The steering committee needs to meet regularly to consider strategic issues and make decisions that translate into actions, tasks, and projects in IT and elsewhere.

FIGURE 1.1 The IT steering committee synthesizes a future strategy using several inputs.

Organization Mission and Objectives

Risks

Long-Term Objectives

Industry Trends

Current IT Capabilities

Past Results

Steering Committee

Long-Term IT Strategy

Policies

Practices

Standards

Not all organizations have an IT steering committee. The role is sometimes filled by key senior staff members, with or without an official charter. And in some organizations, the role is not filled at all; as a result, the IT organization is more likely to be directionless and not aligned to the business.

The IT steering committee differs from the IT strategy committee discussed earlier. The steering committee is an internal committee consisting of managers and other stakeholders who are employees of the organization. The strategy committee is a committee of the board of directors.

Policies, Processes, Procedures, and Standards

Policies, processes, procedures, and standards define IT organizational behavior and uses of technology. They are part of the written record that defines how the IT organization performs the services that support the organization.

Policy documents should be developed and ratified by IT management and should be reviewed annually. Policies state only what must be done (or not done) in an IT organization. They should not state how something must be done (or not done). That way, a policy document will be durable—meaning it may last many years with only minor edits from time to time.

IT policies typically cover many topics, including the following:

- **Roles and responsibilities:** These will range from general to specific, usually by describing each major role and responsibility in the IT department and then specifying which position is responsible for it. IT policies will also make general statements about responsibilities that all IT employees will share.

- **Development and acquisition practices:** IT policy should define the processes used to acquire, develop, and implement software for the organization. Typically, IT policy will require a formal development methodology that includes a few specific ingredients, such as quality review and the inclusion of security requirements and testing.

- **Operational practices:** IT policy defines the high-level processes that constitute IT's operations. This will include service desk, backups, system monitoring, metrics, and other day-to-day IT activities.

- **IT processes, documents, and records:** IT policy will define other important IT processes, including incident management, project management, vulnerability management, and support operations. IT policy should also define how and where documents such as procedures and records will be managed and stored.

IT policy, like any other organization policy, is generally focused on what should be done and on what parties are responsible for different activities. However, policy generally steers clear of describing how these activities should be performed. That, instead, is the role of procedures and standards, discussed later in this section.

The relationship between policies, processes, procedures, and standards is shown in Figure 1.2.

FIGURE 1.2   Policies, processes, procedures, and standards

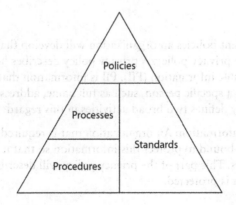

Information Security Policy

The *information security policy* defines how an organization will protect its important assets and respond to threats and incidents. Like IT policy, information security policy defines several fundamental principles and activities:

- **Roles and responsibilities:** Security policy should define specific roles and responsibilities, including the roles of specific positions in the organization as well as the responsibilities of all staff members.

- **Risk management:** Security policy should define how the organization identifies, manages, and treats risks. An organization should perform periodic risk assessments and risk analysis, which will lead to decisions about risk treatment for specific risks that are identified, and which align with established risk tolerance levels.

- **Security processes:** Security policy should define important security processes, such as vulnerability management and incident management, and incorporate security into other business processes, such as software development and acquisition, vendor selection and management, and employee screening and hiring.

- **Acceptable use:** Security policy should define the types of activities and behaviors that are acceptable and those that are not.

The best practice for information security policy is the definition of a top-down, management-driven information security program that performs periodic risk assessments to identify and focus on the most important risks in the organization. Roles and responsibilities define who is responsible for carrying out these activities. Executive management should have visibility and decision-making power, particularly in the areas of policy review and risk treatment.

It is generally accepted that security policy and security management should be separate from IT policy and IT management. This permits the security organization function to operate outside of IT, thereby permitting security to be objective and independent of IT. This puts security in a better position to be able to assess IT systems and processes objectively without fear of direct reprisal.

Privacy Policy

One of the most important policies an organization will develop that is related to information security is a privacy policy. A privacy policy describes how the organization will treat personally identifiable information (PII). PII is information that is considered private because it can be tied to a specific person, such as full name, address, and Social Security number. A privacy policy defines two broad activities in this regard:

- **Protecting private information:** An organization that is required to collect, store, or transmit PII is duty-bound to protect this information so that it is not disclosed to unauthorized parties. This part of the privacy policy will describe what information is obtained and how it is protected.

- **Handling private information:** Aside from the actual protection of PII, some organizations may, in the course of their business activities, transmit some or all of this information to other parts of the organization or to other organizations. A privacy policy is typically forthright about this internal handling and sharing with third parties. Further, a privacy policy describes how the information is used by the organization and by other organizations to which it is transmitted. The privacy policy typically describes how a private citizen may confirm whether their PII is stored by the organization, whether it is accurate, and how the citizen can arrange for its removal if they wish.

Many countries have privacy laws that require an organization to have a privacy policy and to enact safeguards to protect private information.

Data Classification Policy

A *data classification policy* defines degrees of sensitivity for various types of information used in the organization. A typical data classification policy will define two or more (but rarely more than five) data classification levels, such as the following:

- Top Secret
- Secret
- Sensitive
- Public

Along with defining levels of classification, a data classification policy will define policies and procedures for handling information in various settings at these levels. For instance, a data classification policy will state the conditions at each level in which sensitive information may be emailed, faxed, stored, transmitted, or shipped. Note that some methods for handling may be forbidden, such as emailing a Top Secret document over the Internet.

Leaders should ensure that the data classification program and practices align with the organization's data governance program, privacy program, policies, and applicable external requirements.

Exam Tip

While the CISO is responsible for establishing the organization's data classification policy, it is usually the responsibility of a document owner to classify and mark a document correctly. It is then the responsibility of any party who uses a document to handle it according to its classification level. All personnel who work with the document are responsible for handling it according to the classification policy.

System Classification Policy

A data classification policy may specify levels of security for systems storing classified information. A system classification policy will establish levels of system security that correspond to levels of data classification. Such a policy will help the organization to be more deliberate in its system hardening standards so that the most sensitive information will be stored only on systems with the highest levels of hardening (often, those higher levels of hardening are more costly and time-consuming to manage; otherwise, an organization might just make all of its systems highly sensitive).

Site Classification Policy

A *site classification policy* defines levels of security for an organization's work sites. This policy sets levels of physical security that correspond to one or more factors:

- Criticality of staff who work at the site
- Criticality or value of business processes performed at the site
- Value of assets located at the site
- Sensitivity or value of data stored or processed at the site
- Siting risks associated with a site (human-made or natural hazards)

Based on the classification of a site, an organization may have additional security controls, such as video surveillance, guards, fences, visitor controls, and so on. Just as it does not make sense to protect all data at a single level, it also is sensible to have the appropriate level of physical security at each site according to the information, equipment, or activity that takes place there.

Access Control Policy

An *access control policy* defines the need for specific processes and procedures related to the granting, review, and revocation of access to systems and work areas. This policy will state which roles are permitted to manage access controls, what levels of approval are required for access requests, how often access reviews will take place, and what access control records will be kept.

Often, there will be a linkage between a data classification policy and an access control policy. This is because access controls protecting the most sensitive information should usually be stricter than access controls protecting less sensitive information.

Mobile Device Policy

A *mobile device policy* defines the use of mobile devices and personally owned devices in the context of business operations and access to business information and information systems. This policy will state the types of devices that may be permitted, the rules and conditions of their use, and the responsibilities of device owners and users. A mobile device policy often addresses the business rules related to the use of bring your own device (BYOD) that allow employees to use personally owned devices such as smartphones to access and manage business information.

Social Media Policy

A *social media policy* defines employees' use of social media. Generally, this encompasses online behavior and employees' online representations of their personal and professional conduct. A social media policy may include the following components:

- **Personal social media:** Policy may limit the posting of content that could put the employee or the organization in a bad light.
- **Professional social media:** Policy may address or restrict how employees describe their positions and activities in the workplace.
- **Disclosure of company information:** Policy may restrict the types of information that employees are permitted to disclose to the public.

Although organizations generally don't try to restrict employees' use of social media, organizations use social media policy to reaffirm their ownership of official information about the organization.

Other Policies

Organizations may have additional technology-related policies, including the following:

- **Equipment control and use:** Policy may address the appropriate use of IT and other equipment, perhaps including equipment assigned to employee use in the field.
- **Data destruction:** Policy defines acceptable and required methods for the disposal of information when it's no longer needed.
- **Moonlighting:** Policy addresses matters regarding outside employment, such as employees who have a second job or who perform volunteer work.
- **Intellectual property:** Policy addresses matters related to the ownership of intellectual property that is created, accessed, or used.
- **Use of portable storage devices:** Policy addresses the use of portable storage devices to prevent the removal of sensitive information from the organization or the introduction of malware.

Processes and Procedures

Process and procedure documents, sometimes called standard operating procedures (SOPs), describe in step-by-step detail how IT processes and tasks are performed. Formal procedure documents ensure that tasks are performed consistently and correctly, even when performed by different IT staff members.

In addition to the actual steps in support of a process or task, a procedure document needs to contain several pieces of metadata:

- **Document (or process) ownership:** The document should contain the name of the person or department responsible for its review, revision, and publication.

- **Document revision information:** The procedure document should contain the name of the person who wrote the document and the person who made the most recent changes to the document. The document should also include the name or location where the official copy of the document can be found.

- **Review and approval:** The document should include the name of the manager who last reviewed the procedure document, as well as the name of the manager (or higher) who approved the document.

- **Dependencies:** The document should specify which other procedures are related to each procedure. This includes other procedures that are dependent on a procedure, and any other procedures that each procedure depends on. For example, a document that describes the database backup process will depend on database management and maintenance documents; documents on media handling will depend on this document.

IT process and procedure documents are not meant to be a replacement for vendor task documentation. For instance, an IT department does not necessarily need to create a document that describes the steps for operating a data storage device when the device vendor's instructions are available and sufficient. Also, IT procedure documents need not be remedial and include every specific keystroke and mouse click; they can usually assume that the reader has experience in the subject area and needs to know how things are done in this organization only. For example, a procedure document that includes a step that involves the modification of a configuration file does not need to include instructions on how to operate a text editor.

 An IT department should maintain a catalog of its procedure documents to facilitate convenient document management. This will permit IT management to better understand which documents are in its catalog, when each was last reviewed and updated, and which will be impacted by specific IT or business changes.

Standards

IT standards are official, management-approved statements that define the technologies, protocols, suppliers, and methods that are used by an IT organization. Standards help drive consistency across the IT organization, which will make the organization more cost-efficient and cost-effective.

An IT organization will have different types of standards, including these:

- **Technology/product standards:** These standards specify what software and hardware technologies or products are used by the IT organization. Examples include operating systems, database management systems, application servers, storage systems, backup media, and so on.

- **Protocol standards:** These standards specify the protocols that are used by the organization. For instance, an IT organization may opt to use Transmission Control Protocol/Internet Protocol (TCP/IP) v6 for its internal networks, Cisco gateway routing protocols (GRPs), Transport Layer Security (TLS) for secure transmission of data, Secure Shell (SSH) for device management, and so forth.

- **Supplier standards:** These define which suppliers and vendors are used for various types of supplies and services. Using established suppliers can help the IT organization through specially negotiated discounts and other arrangements.

- **Methodology standards:** These refer to practices used in various processes, including software development, system administration, network engineering, and end-user support.

- **Configuration standards:** These standards refer to specific detailed configurations that are to be applied to servers, database management systems, end-user workstations, network devices, and so on. This enables users, developers, and technical administrative personnel to be more comfortable with IT systems, because the systems will be consistent with one another. This helps reduce unscheduled downtime and improves quality.

- **Architecture standards:** These standards refer to the technology architecture at the database, system, or network level. An organization may develop reference architectures for use in various standard settings. For instance, a large retail organization may develop specific network diagrams to be used in every retail location, down to the colors of wires to use and how equipment is situated on racks or shelves.

- **Security standards:** These standards apply to security-specific technologies, mechanisms, and controls. Examples include encryption algorithm or strength, password complexity, or requirements for multifactor authentication. The standards ensure that an organization meets the requirements to protect information, ensure compliance with governance, and reduce risk.

Standards enable the IT organization to be simpler, leaner, and more efficient. IT organizations with effective standards will have fewer types of hardware and software to support, which reduces the number of technologies that must be managed by the organization. An organization that standardizes on one operating system, one database management system, and one server platform need only build expertise in those technologies. This enables the IT organization to manage and support the environment more effectively than if many different technologies were in use.

Enterprise Architecture

Enterprise architecture (EA) is both a business function and a technical model. In terms of a business function, the establishment of an EA consists of activities that ensure that important business needs are met by IT systems overall. EA may also involve the construction of a model that is used to map business functions into the IT environment and IT systems in increasing levels of detail so that IT professionals can more easily understand the organization's technology architecture at any level.

The Zachman Framework

The *Zachman* enterprise architecture framework, established in the late 1980s, continues to be the dominant EA standard today. Zachman likens IT EA to the construction and maintenance of an office building: at a high (abstract, not number of floors) level, the office building performs functions such as containing office space. As we look into increasing levels of detail in the building, we encounter various trades (steel, concrete, drywall, electrical, plumbing, telephone, fire control, elevators, and so on), each with its own specifications, standards, regulations, construction and maintenance methods, and so on.

In the Zachman framework, IT systems and environments are described at a high, functional level, and then in increasing detail, encompassing systems, databases, applications, networks, and so on. The Zachman framework is illustrated in Table 1.1.

TABLE 1.1 Zachman framework showing IT systems in increasing levels of detail

	Data	Functional (Application)	Network (Technology)	People (Organization)	Time	Strategy
Scope	List of datasets important in the business	List of business processes	List of business locations	List of organizations	List of events	List of business goals and strategy
Enterprise Model	Conceptual data/object model	Business process model	Business logistics	Workflow	Master schedule	Business plan
Systems Model	Logical data model	System architecture	Detailed system architecture	Human interface architecture	Processing structure	Business rule model
Technology Model	Physical data/class model	Technology design	Technology architecture	Presentation architecture	Control structure	Rule design
Detailed Representation	Data definition	Program	Network architecture	Security architecture	Time definition	Rule speculation
Function Enterprise	Usable data	Working function	Usable network	Functioning organization	Implemented schedule	Working strategy

While the Zachman framework enables an organization to peer into cross-sections of an IT environment that support business processes, the model does not convey the relationships between IT systems. Data flow diagrams, discussed in the next section, are instead used to depict information flows.

The U.S. government takes EA quite seriously. All U.S. government agencies are required to develop EA and use it in their strategic planning activities. Often the DoD Architecture Framework (DoDAF) is used for this purpose.

Data Flow Diagrams

Data flow diagrams (DFDs) are frequently used to illustrate the flow of information between IT applications. Like the Zachman model, a DFD can begin as a high-level diagram, where the labels of information flows are expressed in business terms. Written specifications about each flow can accompany the DFD; these specifications would describe the flow in increasing levels of detail, all the way to field lengths and communication protocol settings.

Similar to Zachman, DFDs enable nontechnical business executives to understand the various IT applications and the relationships between them. A typical DFD is shown in Figure 1.3.

FIGURE 1.3   A typical DFD shows the relationship between IT applications.

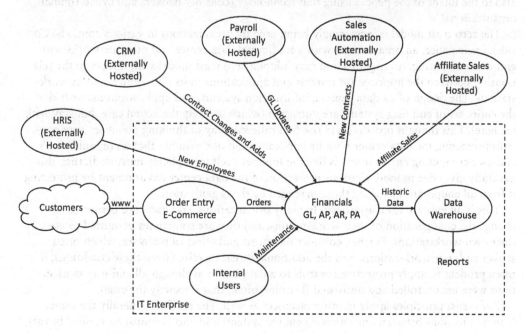

Data Storage Diagrams

A counterpart to data flow diagrams are depictions (visual or tabular) or data storage diagrams. These depict data at rest across the enterprise. The purpose of data storage diagrams (or data storage catalogs) is to document the intended and expected instances of stored information in the organization.

Data storage diagrams document the structured data that resides in an organization. The term "structured data" refers to the fact that data in this instance resides in formal management systems (often, database management systems, or DBMSs) that have a structured design, usually known as a schema. Contrast structured data to unstructured data, which is the data that resides in network file shares and end-user workstations in a mostly or entirely ad hoc fashion. Unstructured data often exists as a result of the ability of business applications to produce extracts and reports, which users create, download, and store on their local workstations or on network file shares.

Zero Trust

Zero trust is an architectural philosophy wherein one or more portions of an environment are considered untrusted. The first such model is the greater Internet itself: networks and workstations external to an organization (on the Internet) are not controlled by the organization and, hence, are untrusted. This model applies not only to the technology in place, but also to the intent of the people using that technology (consider hackers and cybercriminal organizations).

The zero trust model is increasingly being used by organizations in various contexts. Consider, for instance, an organization with a traditional data center and office networks with end-user computing. An organization may adopt a zero trust model with respect to the relationship between the information systems and applications in its data center, and its workstations. The design of its data centers, information systems, and applications assumes that the entire set of end-user systems are untrusted (which is rarely the actual case, but stay with me here). This thought process gives rise to a different way of thinking about security controls protecting the data center with its applications; if one assumes that an organization's end-user computing environment is like the Internet itself (completely untrusted), then this naturally gives rise to more rigorous protection of the data center environment by protecting it from all endpoints, including those managed by the organization.

This is an entirely valid approach. In many organizations, end users are permitted to change the configuration of their workstations, and they are sometimes permitted to use their own workstations. Further, consider the threat and effect of malware, which often strikes end-user workstations, and the additional threat therein. Given these conditions, it is often prudent to apply protective controls to a data center as though all end-user workstations were uncontrolled and untrusted (because, often, that is exactly the case).

Zero trust principles apply in other instances as well. The result is generally the same: Communications between one environment (or system) and another must be verified in various ways to ensure that no unplanned or hostile activities can interfere with computing and business operations.

Applicable Laws, Regulations, and Standards

Organizations need to identify all of the laws, regulations, and standards that are applicable to their operations. As IT has become more critical for organizations in many industry sectors, many nations and local governments have enacted new laws and regulations concerning the processing and protection of information.

The board of directors, strategy committee, or chief legal counsel should appoint an executive to be responsible for identifying all potentially applicable laws, regulations, and standards. This appointee should then consult with inside or outside legal counsel to determine their scope and applicability.

Once applicable laws and regulations have been identified, the organization needs to determine how they affect the following:

- **Enterprise architecture:** Laws, regulations, and standards may require that organizations use specific IT components or configurations that affect the organization's EA.

- **Controls:** Laws and regulations may require that additional controls be enacted or existing controls be changed.

- **Business processes:** Laws and regulations may require that the organization perform certain tasks that may affect processes.

- **Personnel:** Laws and regulations may require that certain personnel possess specific qualifications, certifications, or licenses.

Many factors will determine whether specific requirements are applicable to an organization, including these:

- Type of data that is stored, processed, or transmitted by the organization's systems
- Industry sector
- Location and management of stored, processed, or transmitted data
- Location of the owner(s) and steward(s) of stored, processed, or transmitted data

Organizations may also be required to comply with specific standards. For example, organizations that process, store, or transmit payment card numbers may be required to comply with the Payment Card Industry Data Security Standard (PCI DSS), even though there may be no laws requiring organizations to do so.

Risk Management

Organizations need to understand the internal activities, practices, and systems, as well as threats, that are introducing risk into their operations. The span of activities that seek, identify, and manage these risks is known as risk management. Like many other processes, risk management is a life cycle activity that has no beginning and no end. It's a continuous and phased set of activities that includes the examination of processes, records, systems, and external phenomena in order to identify risks. This is continued by an analysis that examines a range of solutions for reducing risk, followed by formal decision making that brings about a resolution to risks.

Risk management needs to support the overall business objectives. This support will include the adoption of a risk appetite that reflects the organization's overall approach to risk. For instance, if the organization is a conservative financial institution, the organization's risk management program will probably adopt a position of being risk averse. Similarly, a high-tech startup organization that, by its very nature, is comfortable with overall business risk will probably be less averse to risks identified in its risk management program.

Regardless of its overall risk appetite, when an organization identifies risks, the organization can take one of four possible actions:

- **Accept:** The organization accepts the risk as is.

- **Mitigate (or reduce):** The organization acts to reduce the level of risk.

- **Transfer (or share):** The organization shares the risk with another entity, often an insurance company.

- **Avoid:** The organization discontinues the activity associated with the risk.

These choices are known as risk treatments. Often, a particular risk will be treated with a blended solution that consists of two or more of the actions just listed.

This section dives into the details of risk management, risk analysis, and risk treatment.

Governance, Risk, and Compliance

Governance, risk, and compliance (GRC) is an integrated approach that ensures organizations achieve their objectives, manage uncertainty, and act with integrity. It encompasses three interrelated disciplines: governance, risk management, and compliance.

Governance refers to the frameworks, policies, and procedures that senior management and the board of directors use to exert strategic control over business operations. It ensures that IT aligns with the organization's goals and objectives. Effective governance involves establishing clear roles and responsibilities, setting objectives, monitoring performance, and ensuring accountability.

Risk management involves identifying, assessing, and prioritizing risks followed by coordinated efforts to minimize, monitor, and control the probability or impact of unfortunate events. The goal is to ensure that risks are managed within the organization's risk appetite.

Compliance ensures that an organization adheres to legal, regulatory, and industry standards. It involves not only meeting external requirements but also adhering to internal policies and procedures.

The Risk Management Program

An organization that operates a risk management program should establish principles that will enable the program to succeed. These may include the following:

Objectives   The risk management program must have a specific purpose; otherwise, it will be difficult to determine whether the program is successful. Example objectives include reducing the number of industrial accidents, reducing the cost of insurance premiums, and reducing the number or severity of security incidents. If objectives are measurable and specific, then the individuals who are responsible for the risk management program can focus on its objectives to achieve the best possible outcome.

Scope   Management must determine the scope of the risk management program. This is a delicate undertaking because of the many interdependencies found in IT systems and business processes. However, in an organization with several distinct operations or business units (BUs), a risk management program could be isolated to one or more operational arms or BUs. In such a case, where there are dependencies on other services in the organization, those dependencies can be treated like external service providers (or customers).

Authority   The risk management program is formally authorized or led by one or more executives in the organization. It is important to know who these individuals are and their levels of commitment to the program.

Roles and Responsibilities   The program clearly identifies the specific job titles involved in risk management along with their respective roles and responsibilities. It should be clear which individuals are responsible for which activities in the program.

Resources   The risk management program, like other activities in the business, requires resources to operate. This will include a budget for salaries as well as for workstations, software licenses, and possibly travel.

Policies, Processes, Procedures, and Records   The various risk management activities, such as asset identification, risk analysis, and risk treatment, along with some general activities such as recordkeeping, should be included in business records.

An organization's risk management program should be documented in a charter. A charter is a formal document that defines and describes a business program and becomes a part of the organization's record.

The risk management life cycle is depicted in Figure 1.4.

The Risk Management Process

Risk management is a life cycle set of activities used to identify, analyze, treat, and monitor risks. These activities are methodical and, as mentioned in the previous section, should be documented so that they will be performed consistently and in support of the program's charter and objectives.

FIGURE 1.4   The risk management life cycle

The risk management process is part of a larger risk framework, such as ISACA's Risk IT Framework, whose components are:

- **Risk governance:** This includes integration with the organization's enterprise risk management (ERM) process, the establishment and maintenance of a common risk view, and the ability to ensure that business decisions include the consideration of risk.

- **Risk evaluation:** This includes asset identification, risk analysis, and the maintenance of a risk profile.

- **Risk response:** This includes the management and articulation of risks and the response to events.

Exam Tip

CISA candidates are not required to memorize the Risk IT Framework, but familiarity with its principles is important.

Asset Identification

The risk management program's main objective (whether formally stated or not) is the protection of the organization and its assets. These assets may be tangible or intangible, physical, logical, or virtual. Some examples of assets include the following:

- **Buildings and property:** These assets include structures and other improvements.

- **Equipment:** This can include machinery, vehicles, and office equipment such as copiers and fax machines.

- **IT equipment:** This includes computers, printers, scanners, tape libraries (the devices that create backup tapes, not the tapes themselves), storage systems, network devices, and phone systems.

- **Supplies and materials:** These can include office supplies as well as materials that are used in manufacturing.

- **Records:** These include business records, such as contracts, video surveillance tapes, visitor logs, and much more.

- **Information:** This includes data in software applications, documents, email messages, and files of every kind on workstations and servers.

- **Intellectual property:** This includes an organization's trade secrets, designs, architectures, software source code, processes, and procedures.

- **Personnel:** In a real sense, an organization's personnel are the organization. Without its staff, the organization cannot perform or sustain its processes.

- **Reputation:** One of the intangible characteristics of an organization, reputation is the individual and collective opinion about an organization in the eyes of its customers, competitors, shareholders, and the community.

- **Brand equity:** Similar to reputation, this is the perceived or actual market value of an individual brand of product or service that is produced by the organization.

Grouping Assets

For risk management purposes, an electronic inventory of assets will be useful in the risk management life cycle. It is not always necessary to list each individual asset; often, it is acceptable to instead list classes or groups of assets as a single asset entity for risk management purposes. For instance, a single entry for laptop computers may be preferred over listing every laptop computer; this is because the risks for all laptop computers are roughly the same (ignoring behavior differences among individual employees or employees in specific departments). This eliminates the need to list them individually.

Similarly, groups of IT servers, network devices, and other equipment can be named instead of all of the individual servers and devices, again because the risks for each of them will usually be similar. One reason to create multiple entries for servers, however, might be their physical location or their purpose; servers in one location may have different risks than servers in another location, and servers containing high-value information will have different risks than servers that do not contain high-value information.

Sources of Asset Data

An organization that is undergoing its initial risk management cycle may need to build its asset database from scratch. Management will need to determine where this initial asset data will come from, such as the following:

- **Financial system asset inventory:** An organization that keeps all of its assets on the books will have a wealth of asset inventory information. It may not be entirely useful, however; asset lists often do not include the location or purpose of the asset and whether it is still in use. Correlating a financial asset inventory to assets in actual use may consume more effort than the other methods for creating the initial asset list.

However, for organizations that have a relatively small number of highly valued assets (for instance, a rock crusher in a gold mine or a mainframe computer), knowing the precise financial value of an asset is highly useful because the actual depreciated value of the asset is used in the risk analysis phase of risk management. Knowing the depreciated value of other assets is also useful, as this will figure into the risk treatment choices that will be identified later.

Financial records that indicate the value of an asset do not include the value of information stored on (or processed by) the asset or the revenue earned through operation of the asset (or the financial consequences of its loss).

- **Interviews:** Discussions with key personnel for purposes of identifying assets are usually the best approach. However, to be effective, several people usually need to be interviewed to be sure to include all relevant assets.

- **IT systems portfolio:** A well-managed IT organization will have formal documents and records for its major applications. Although this information may not encompass every single IT asset in the organization, it can provide information on the assets supporting individual applications or geographic locations.

- **Online data:** An organization with numerous IT assets (systems, network devices, and so on) can sometimes utilize the capability of local online data to identify those assets. For instance, a systems or network management system often includes a list of managed assets, which can be a good starting point when creating the initial asset list.

- **Asset management system:** Larger organizations may find it more cost-effective to use an asset management application dedicated to this purpose, rather than rely on lists of assets from other sources.

Organizations need to keep in mind that some information assets will physically reside in service provider environments (mainly, information assets). For example, cloud service providers may be a critical portion of the IT infrastructure and the assets that organizations have deployed in the cloud should be included in the inventory.

Collecting and Organizing Asset Data

It is rarely possible to take (or create) a list of assets from a single source. Rather, more than one source of information is often needed to be sure that the risk management program has identified at least the important, in-scope assets that it needs to worry about.

As a part of IT governance, management needs to determine which person or group is responsible for maintaining an asset inventory.

It is usually useful to organize or classify assets. This will help to get the assets under study into smaller chunks that can be analyzed more effectively. There is no single way to organize assets, but here are a few ideas:

- **Geography:** A widely dispersed organization may classify its assets according to their locations. This will aid risk managers during the risk analysis phase, since many risks are geographic-centric, particularly natural hazards. Mitigation of risks is often geography based; for instance, it's easier to put a fence around one data center than to put up fences around buildings in every location.

- **Business process:** Because some organizations rank the criticality of their individual business processes, it can be useful to group assets according to the business processes that they support. This helps in the risk analysis and risk treatment phases, because assets supporting individual processes can be associated with business criticality and treated appropriately.

- **Organizational unit:** In larger organizations, it may be easier to classify assets according to the organizational units they support.

- **Sensitivity:** Usually ascribed to information, sensitivity relates to the nature and content of that information. Sensitivity usually applies in two ways: to an individual, where the information is considered personal or private, and to an organization, where the information may be considered a trade secret. Sometimes sensitivity is somewhat subjective and arbitrary, but often it is defined in laws and regulations.

- **Regulation:** For organizations that are required to follow government or private regulation regarding the processing and protection of information, it will be useful to include data points that indicate whether specific assets are considered in scope for specific regulations. This is important because some regulations specify how assets should be protected, so it's useful to be aware of this during risk analysis and risk treatment.

There is no need to choose which of these methods will be used to classify assets. Instead, an IT analyst should collect several points of metadata about each asset (including location, process supported, and organizational unit supported). This will enable the risk manager to sort and filter the list of assets in various ways to better understand which assets are in a given location or which ones support a particular process or part of the business.

    Organizations should consider managing information about assets in a fixed-assets application.

Risk Analysis

Risk analysis is the activity in a risk management program where individual risks are identified. A risk consists of the intersection of threats, vulnerabilities, probabilities, and impact. In its simplest terms, risk is described in the following formula:

$$Risk = Probability \times Impact$$

This means that the level of risk facing an organization is determined by how likely it is that the risk will occur (probability) and how bad the situation will be if it does occur (impact).

You can use this equation literally by calculating risk, which is known as quantitative risk analysis. You may use it conceptually to ensure that you are considering all subjective factors during a qualitative risk analysis.

Other definitions of risk include the following:

- The combination of the probability of an event and its consequence (source: ISACA Cybersecurity Fundamentals Glossary)

- The probable frequency and probable magnitude of future loss (source: "An Introduction to Factor Analysis of Information Risk (FAIR)," Risk Management Insight, LLC)

- The potential that a given threat will exploit vulnerabilities of an asset or group of assets and thereby cause harm to the organization (Source: ISO/IEC 27005)

These definitions convey essentially the same message: The amount of risk is directly proportional to the probability of occurrence and the impact that a risk would have if realized.

A risk analysis consists of identifying threats and their impact of realization against each asset. It usually also includes a vulnerability analysis, where assets are studied to determine whether they are vulnerable to identified threats. The sheer number of assets may make this task appear daunting; however, threat and vulnerability analyses can usually be performed against groups of assets. For instance, when identifying natural and human-made threats against assets, it often makes sense to perform a single threat analysis against all of the assets that reside in a given location. After all, the odds of a volcanic eruption are the same for any of the servers in the room—the threat need not be called out separately for each asset.

Threat Analysis

The usual first step in a risk analysis is to identify threats against an asset or group of assets. A threat is an event that, if realized, would bring harm to an asset and, hence, to the organization. Often called threat modeling, a typical approach is to list all of the threats that have some realistic opportunity of occurrence; those threats that are highly unlikely to occur can be left out. For instance, the listing of meteorites, tsunamis in landlocked regions, and wars in typically peaceful regions will just add clutter to a risk analysis.

A more reasonable approach in a threat analysis is to identify all of the threats that a reasonable person would believe could occur, even if the probability is low. For example, include flooding when a facility is located near a river, hurricanes for an organization located along the southern or eastern coast (and inland for some distance) of the United States, or a terrorist attack in practically every major city in the world. All of these would be considered reasonable in a threat analysis.

It is important to include the entire range of both natural and human-made threats. The full list could approach or even exceed 100 separate threats. The categories of possible threats include these:

- **Severe storms:** These includes tornadoes, hurricanes, windstorms, ice storms, and blizzards.

- **Earth movement:** This includes earthquakes, landslides, avalanches, volcanoes, and tsunamis.

- **Flooding:** This includes both natural and human-made situations.

- **Disease:** This includes sickness outbreaks and pandemics, as well as quarantines that result.

- **Fire:** This includes forest fires, range fires, and structure fires, all of which may be natural or human-caused.

- **Labor:** This includes work stoppages, protests, and strikes.

- **Violence:** This includes riots, looting, terrorism, and war.

- **Malware:** This includes all kinds of viruses, worms, Trojan horses, rootkits, ransomware, and associated malicious software.

- **Hacking attacks:** These include automated attacks (think of an Internet worm that is on the loose) as well as targeted attacks by employees, former employees, or criminals.

- **Hardware failures:** These include any kind of failure of IT equipment or failures of related environmental equipment, such as heating, ventilation, and air conditioning (HVAC).

- **Software failures:** These can include any software problem that precipitates a disaster.

- **Utilities:** These include electric power failures, water supply failures, and natural gas outages, as well as communications outages.

- **Transportation:** This includes airplane crashes, railroad derailments, ship collisions, and highway accidents.

- **Hazardous materials:** This includes chemical spills. The primary threat here is direct damage by hazardous substances, casualties, and forced evacuations.

- **Criminal activity:** This includes extortion, embezzlement, theft, vandalism, sabotage, and hacker intrusion. Note that company insiders can play a role in these activities.

- **Errors:** These include mistakes made by personnel that result in disaster situations.

Alongside each threat that is identified, the risk analyst assigns a probability or frequency of occurrence. For a quantitative risk analysis, this will be a numeric value, expressed as a probability of one occurrence within a calendar year. For example, if the risk of a flood is 1 in 100, it would be expressed as 0.01, or 1 percent. In a qualitative risk analysis, probability is expressed as a ranking; for example, Low, Medium, and High; or it can be expressed on a subjective numeric scale ranking the probability from 1 to 5.

An approach for completing a threat analysis is to:

- **Perform a geographic threat analysis for each location:** This will provide an analysis on the probability of each type of threat against all assets in each location.

- **Perform a logical threat analysis for each type of asset:** This provides information on all of the logical (that is, not physical) threats that can occur to each asset type.

For example, the risk of malware on all assets of one type is probably the same, regardless of the assets' locations.

- **Perform a threat analysis for each highly valued asset:** This will help to identify any unique threats that may have appeared in the geographic or logical threat analysis, but with different probabilities of occurrence.

Threat Forecasting Data Is Sparse

One of the biggest problems with information security–related risk management is the lack of reliable data on the probability of many types of threats. While the probability of some natural threats can sometimes be obtained from local disaster response agencies, the probabilities of most other threats are difficult to predict accurately.

The difficulty in predicting security events sits in stark contrast to volumes of available data related to automobile and airplane accidents, as well as human life expectancy. In these cases, insurance companies have been accumulating statistics on these events for decades, and the variables (for instance, tobacco and alcohol use) are well-known. On the topic of cyber-related risk, there is a general lack of reliable data, and the factors that influence risk are not well-known from a statistical perspective. It is for this reason that risk analysis still relies on educated guesses for the probabilities of most events. But given the recent surge in popularity for cyber insurance, the availability and quality of cyberattack risk factors may soon be more accurately determined.

Vulnerability Identification

A vulnerability is a weakness or absence of a protective control that increases the probability of one or more threats occurring. A vulnerability analysis is an examination of an asset to discover weaknesses that could lead to a higher than normal rate of occurrence or potency of a threat.

Here are some examples of vulnerabilities:

- Missing or inoperative antivirus software
- Outdated and unsupported software in use
- Missing security patches
- Weak password settings
- Missing or incomplete audit logs
- Inadequate monitoring of event logs
- Weak or defective application session management

- Building entrances that permit tailgating
- Insufficient coverage of video surveillance

In a vulnerability analysis, the risk manager needs to examine the asset itself as well as all of the protective measures that are—or should be—in place to protect the asset from relevant threats.

Vulnerabilities are usually ranked by severity. Vulnerabilities are indicators that show the effectiveness (or ineffectiveness) of protective measures. For example, an antivirus program on a server that updates its virus signatures once per week might be ranked as a medium vulnerability, whereas the complete absence (or malfunction) of an antivirus program on the same server might be ranked as a high vulnerability. Severity is an indication of the likelihood that a given threat might be realized. This is different from impact, which is discussed later in this section.

Probability Analysis

For any given threat and asset, the probability that the threat will actually be realized needs to be estimated. This is often easier said than done, as there is a lack of reliable data on security incidents. A risk manager will need to perform some research and develop a best guess based on any available data.

Impact Analysis

A threat, when actually realized, will have some effect on the organization. Impact analysis is the study of estimating the impact of specific threats on specific assets.

In impact analysis, it is necessary for the analyst to understand the relationship between an asset and the business processes and activities that the asset supports. The purpose of impact analysis is to identify the impact on business operations or business processes. This is because risk management is not an abstract identification of abstract risks, but instead a search for risks that have real impact on business operations.

In an impact analysis, the impact can be expressed as a rating such as H-M-L (High-Medium-Low) or as a numeric scale, and it can also be expressed in financial terms. But what is also vitally important in an impact analysis is the inclusion of a statement of impact for each threat. Example statements of impact include "inability to process customer support calls" and "inability for customers to view payment history." Statements such as "inability to authenticate users" may be technically accurate, but they do not identify the business impact.

 NOTE   Because of the additional time required to quantify and develop statements of impact, impact analysis is usually performed only on the highest ranked threats on the most critical assets.

Qualitative Risk Analysis

A qualitative risk analysis is an in-depth examination of in-scope assets with a detailed study of threats (and their probability of occurrence), vulnerabilities (and their severity), and statements of impact. The threats, vulnerabilities, and impact are all expressed in qualitative terms such as High-Medium-Low or in quasi-numeric terms such as a 1–5 numeric scale.

The purpose of qualitative risk analysis is to identify the most critical risks in the organization based on these rankings.

Qualitative risk analysis does not get to the issue of "how much does a given threat cost my business if it is realized?"—neither does it mean to do this. The value in a qualitative risk analysis is the ability to identify the most critical risks quickly without the additional burden of identifying precise financial impacts.

The individual(s) performing risk analysis may want to include threat–vulnerability pairing as well as asset–threat pairing. These techniques may help a risk analyst better understand the probability or impact of specific threats.

 Organizations that do need to perform quantitative risk analysis often begin with qualitative risk analysis to determine the highest-ranked risks that warrant the additional effort of quantitative analysis.

Quantitative Risk Analysis

Quantitative risk analysis is a risk analysis approach that uses numeric methods to measure risk. Quantitative risk analysis offers statements of risk in terms that can be easily compared with the known values of their respective assets. In other words, risks are expressed in the same units of measure as most organizations' primary unit of measure: financial.

Despite this, quantitative risk analysis must still be regarded as an effort to develop estimates, not exact figures. Partly this is because risk analysis is a measure of events that may occur, not a measure of events that do occur.

Standard quantitative risk analysis involves the development of several figures:

- **Asset value (AV):** This is the value of the asset, which is usually (but not necessarily) the asset's replacement value.

- **Exposure factor (EF):** This is the financial loss that results from the realization of a threat, expressed as a percentage of the asset's total value. Most threats do not completely eliminate the asset's value; instead, they reduce its value. For example, if a construction company's $500,000 earth mover is destroyed in a fire, the equipment will still have salvage value, even if that is only 10 percent of the asset's value. In this case, the EF would be 90 percent. Note that different threats will have different impacts on EF, because the realization of different threats will cause varying amounts of damage to assets.

- **Single loss expectancy (SLE):** This value represents the financial loss when a threat is realized one time. SLE is defined as AV × EF. Note that different threats have a varied impact on EF, so those threats will also have the same multiplicative effect on SLE.

- **Annualized rate of occurrence (ARO):** This is an estimate of the number of times that a threat will occur per year. If the probability of the threat is 1 in 50, then ARO is expressed as 0.02. However, if the threat is estimated to occur four times per year, then ARO is 4.0. Like EF and SLE, ARO will vary by threat.

- **Annualized loss expectancy (ALE):** This is the expected annualized loss of asset value due to threat realization. ALE is defined as SLE × ARO.

Risk managers should take extra care to develop the best possible estimate for ARO, based on whatever data is available. Sources for estimates include:

- History of event losses in the organization
- History of similar losses in other organizations
- History of dissimilar losses
- Best estimates based on available data

When the analyst is performing a quantitative risk analysis for a given asset, the ALE for all threats can be added together. The sum of all ALEs is the annualized loss expectancy for the total array of threats. A particularly high sum of ALEs would mean that a given asset is confronted with a lot of significant threats that are more likely to occur. But in terms of risk treatment, ALEs are better off left as separate and associated with their respective threats.

Developing Mitigation Strategies

An important part of risk analysis is the investigation of potential solutions for reducing or eliminating risk. This involves understanding specific threats and their impact (EF) and likelihood of occurrence (ARO). Once a given asset and threat combination has been baselined (i.e., the existing asset, threats, and controls have been analyzed to understand the threats as they exist at a given point in time), the risk analyst can then apply various hypothetical means for reducing risk, documenting each one in terms of its impact on EF and ARO.

For example, suppose a risk analysis identifies the threat of attack on a public web server. Specific EF and ARO figures have been identified for a range of individual threats. Now the risk analyst applies a range of fixes (on paper), such as an application firewall, an intrusion prevention system (IPS), and a patch management tool. Each solution will have a specific and unique impact on EF and ARO (these are all estimates, of course, just like the estimates of EF and ARO on the initial conditions); some will have better EF and ARO figures than others. Each solution should also be rated in terms of cost (financial or H-M-L) and effort to implement (financial or H-M-L).

Developing mitigation strategies is the first step in risk treatment, where various solutions are put forward, each with its cost and impact on risk.

While security analysts may have the responsibility for documenting vulnerabilities, threats, and risks, it is senior management's responsibility (through the security steering committee) to formally approve the treatment of risk. Risk treatment is discussed later in this chapter.

Risk Analysis and Disaster Recovery Planning

Disaster recovery planning (DRP) and business continuity planning (BCP) utilize risk analysis to identify risks that are related to business resilience and the impact of disasters. The risk analysis performed for DRP and BCP is the same risk analysis that is discussed in this chapter—the methods and approach are the same, although the overall objectives are somewhat different.

Business continuity planning and disaster recovery planning are discussed in detail in Chapter 6, "Business Continuity and Disaster Recovery."

High-Impact Events

The risk manager is likely to identify one or more high-impact events during the risk analysis. These events, which may be significant enough to threaten the very viability of the organization, require risk treatment that warrants executive management visibility and belongs in the categories of business continuity planning and disaster recovery planning. These topics are discussed in detail in Chapter 6.

Risk Treatment

When risks to assets have been identified through qualitative and/or quantitative risk analysis, the next step in risk management is to decide what to do about the identified risks. During risk analysis, one or more potential solutions may have been examined, along with their cost to implement and their impact on risk. In risk treatment, a decision about whether to proceed with any of the proposed solutions (or others) is needed.

Risk treatment pits available resources against the need to reduce risk. In an enterprise environment, not all risks can be mitigated, because there are not enough resources to treat them all. Instead, a strategy for choosing the best combination of solutions that will reduce risk by the greatest possible margin is needed. For this reason, risk treatment is often more effective when all the risks and solutions are considered together, instead of considering each one separately. Then they can be grouped, compared, and prioritized.

When risk treatment is performed at the enterprise level, risk analysts and technology architects can devise ways to bring about the greatest possible reduction in risk. This can be achieved through the implementation of solutions that will reduce many risks for many assets at once. For example, a firewall can reduce risks from many threats on many assets; this will be more effective than individual solutions for each asset.

So far, we have been talking about risk mitigation as if it were the only option available when handling risk. But there are actually four primary ways to treat risk: mitigation, transfer, avoidance, and acceptance. And there is always some leftover risk, called residual risk. These approaches are discussed next.

Risk Mitigation

Risk mitigation, or risk reduction, involves the implementation of some solution that will reduce an identified risk. For instance, the risk of advanced malware being introduced on to a server can be mitigated with advanced malware prevention software or a network-based IPS. Either of these solutions would constitute mitigation of this risk on a given asset, and either solution would effectively mitigate the risk depending on the enterprise-level resource allocation.

An organization usually decides to implement some form of risk mitigation only after performing some cost analysis to determine whether the reduction of risk is worth the expenditure of risk mitigation.

Back to the term solution, as mentioned here. Readers should not automatically think of new devices, systems, or features such as firewalls, IPSs, antivirus software, data loss prevention systems, or other hardware or software products. Instead, a solution may be as simple as an update to a written policy, a configuration change, or the modification of a firewall rule, or it may be as complex as network segmentation that could take many months to implement. A solution could also be to monitor the risk to assess what the appropriate response could be if the risk were to materialize in a significant quantitative or qualitative way (for instance, monitoring for key cybersecurity intrusions and then choosing to implement mitigating measures if the threat level increases).

Risk Transfer

Risk transfer, or risk sharing, means that some or all of the risk is being transferred to some external entity, such as an insurance company or business partner. When an organization purchases an insurance policy to protect an asset against damage or loss, the insurance company is assuming part of the risk in exchange for payment of insurance premiums.

The details of a cyber-insurance policy need to be carefully examined to ensure that any specific risk is transferable to the policy. Cyber-insurance policies typically have exclusions that limit or deny payment of benefits in certain situations. Additionally, cyber risk insurance or other insurance policies can be contingent on the underwritten entity having proper risk mitigation and control activities in place as defined in the policy.

 Organizations considering cyber-insurance policies should carefully read the terms and conditions of such policies to ensure the selection of an appropriate policy. Some policies assume and require that the organization have specific measures in place. Further, policies have exclusions that must be well understood. Some organizations are denied benefits from malware attacks that insurance companies claim are acts of war, a common exclusion.

Risk Avoidance

In *risk avoidance,* the organization abandons the potential risk activity altogether, effectively taking the asset out of service so that the threat is no longer present. In another scenario, the organization may decide that the risk of pursuing a given business activity is too great so that specific activity is completely avoided. This can sometimes be illustrated through organizational efforts to minimize the amount of old software or hardware within the IT environment by replacing it with newer equipment.

> Organizations do not often back away completely from an activity because of identified risks. Generally, this avenue is taken only when the risk of loss is great and the perceived probability of occurrence is high.

Risk Acceptance

Risk acceptance occurs when management is willing to accept an identified risk as is, with no effort taken to reduce it. Risk acceptance also takes place (sometimes implicitly) for residual risk, after other forms of risk treatment have been applied. It is important through governance policies and procedures for the organization to have a consistent approach to risk acceptance.

Residual Risk

Residual risk is the risk that is left over from the original risk after some of the risk has been removed through mitigation or transfer. For instance, if a particular threat had a probability of 10 percent before risk treatment and 1 percent after risk treatment, the residual risk is that 1 percent left over. This is best illustrated by the following formula:

$$\text{Original Risk} - \text{Mitigated Risk} - \text{Transferred Risk} = \text{Residual Risk}$$

It is unusual for risk treatment to eliminate risk altogether; rather, various controls are implemented that remove some of the risk. Often, management implicitly accepts the leftover risk; however, it's a good idea to make that acceptance of residual risk more formal by documenting the acceptance in a risk management log or decision log.

Compliance Risk

Organizations that perform risk management are generally aware of the laws, regulations, and standards they are required to follow. For instance, U.S.-based banks, brokerages, and insurance companies are required to comply with the Gramm–Leach–Bliley Act (GLBA), and organizations that store, process, or transmit credit card numbers are required to comply with PCI DSS (Payment Card Industry Data Security Standard). Health care providers and insurers in the United States are required to comply with the Health Insurance Portability and Accountability Act (HIPAA). The European General Data Protection Regulation (GDPR) has an especially long reach, applying to organizations throughout the world that store and process personally identifiable information about European Union (EU) citizens.

GDPR, GLBA, HIPAA, PCI DSS, and other regulations often state in specific terms what controls are required in an organization's IT systems. This brings to light the matter of compliance risk. Sometimes, the risk associated with a specific control (or lack of a control) may be rated as a low risk, either because the probability of a risk event is low or because the impact of the event is low. However, if a given law, regulation, or standard requires that the control be enacted anyway, the organization must consider the compliance risk. The risk of noncompliance may result in fines or other sanctions against the organization, which may (or may not) have consequences greater than the actual risk.

The result of this is that organizations sometimes implement specific security controls because they are required by laws, regulations, or standards—not because their risk analysis would otherwise compel them to do so.

IT Management Practices

The primary services in the IT organization typically are development, operations, and support. These primary activities require the support of a second layer of activities that together support the delivery of primary IT services to the organization. The second layer of IT management practices consists of the following:

- Personnel management
- Sourcing
- Third-party service delivery management
- Change management
- Financial management
- Quality management
- Portfolio management
- Controls management
- Security management
- Performance and capacity management

Some of these activities the IT organization undertakes itself, whereas some are usually performed by other parts of the organization. For instance, most of the personnel management functions are typically carried out by a human resources department. This is another essential reason for the existence of an organizationwide IT steering committee that is represented by members of other departments such as human resources. This enables the entire spectrum of IT management to be centrally controlled even when other departments perform some IT management functions.

Personnel Management

Personnel management encompasses many activities related to the status of employment, training, and the acceptance and management of policy. These personnel management activities ensure that the individuals who are hired into the organization are suitably vetted, trained, and equipped to perform their functions. It is important that they are provided with the organization's key policies so that their behavior and decisions will reflect the organization's needs.

Hiring

The purpose of the employee hiring process is to ensure that the organization hires persons who are qualified to perform their stated job duties and that their personal, professional, and educational histories are appropriate. The hiring process includes several activities necessary to ensure that candidates being considered are suitable.

Background Verification

Various studies suggest that 30 to 80 percent of employment candidates exaggerate their education and experience on their résumé, and some candidates commit outright fraud by providing false information about their education or prior positions. Because of this, employers need to perform their own background investigation on an employment candidate to obtain an independent assessment of the candidate's true background.

Employers should examine the following parts of a candidate's background prior to hiring:

- **Employment background:** The employer should check at least two years back, although five to seven years is needed for mid- or senior-level personnel.

- **Education background:** The employer should confirm that the candidate has earned the degrees or diplomas listed on their résumé. There are many "diploma mills," enterprises that will print a fake college diploma for a fee.

- **Military service background:** If the candidate served in any branch of the military, this must be verified to confirm whether the candidate served at all, whether they received relevant training and work experience, and whether their discharge was honorable or otherwise.

- **Professional licenses and certifications:** If a position requires that the candidate possess licenses or certifications, these need to be confirmed, including whether the candidate is in good standing with the organizations that manage those licenses and certifications.

- **Criminal background:** The employer needs to investigate whether the candidate has a criminal record. In countries with a national criminal registry, such as the National Crime Information Center (NCIC) in the United States, this is simpler than in countries that have no nationwide criminal records database. Some industrialized countries do not permit criminal background checks (believe it or not).

- **Credit background:** Where permitted by law, the employer may want to examine a candidate's credit and financial history. There are two principal reasons for this type of check: First, a good credit history indicates the candidate is responsible, while a poor credit history may be an indication of irresponsibility or poor choices (although in many cases a candidate's credit background is not entirely their own doing); second, a candidate with excessive debt and a poor credit history may be considered a risk for embezzlement, fraud, or theft.

- **Terrorist association:** Some employers want to know whether a candidate has documented ties with terrorist organizations. In the United States, an employer can request verification of whether a candidate is on one of several lists of individuals and organizations with whom U.S. citizens are prohibited from doing business. Lists are maintained by the Office of Foreign Assets Control (OFAC), by a department of the U.S. Treasury, and by the U.S. Bureau of Industry and Security.

- **References:** The employer may want to contact two or more personal and professional references—people who know the candidate and will vouch for their background, work history, and character.

 In many jurisdictions, employment candidates are required to sign a consent form that will allow the employer (or a third-party agent acting on behalf of the employer) to perform the background check.

Employers also frequently research a candidate's background through word-of-mouth inquiries, Internet searches, and social media. Much useful information can be obtained that can help an employer corroborate information provided by a candidate.

Background checks are a prudent business practice to identify and reduce risk. In many industries, they are a common practice or even required by law. And in addition to performing a background check at the time of hire, many organizations perform them annually for employees in high-risk or high-value positions.

Employee Policy Manuals

Sometimes known as an employee handbook, an employee policy manual is a formal statement of the terms of employment, facts about the organization, benefits, compensation, conduct, and other policies.

Employee handbooks are often the cornerstone of corporate policy. A thorough employee handbook usually covers a wide swath of territory, including the following topics:

- **Welcome:** This welcomes a new employee into the organization, often in an upbeat letter that makes the new employee glad to have joined the organization. This may also include a brief history of the organization.

- **Policies:** These are the most important policies in the organization, which include security, privacy, code of conduct (ethics), and acceptable use of resources. In the United States and other countries, the handbook may also include antiharassment and other workplace behavior policies.

- **Compensation:** This describes when and how employees are compensated.
- **Benefits:** This describes company benefit programs.
- **Work hours:** This discusses work hours and basic expectations for when employees are expected to report to work and how many hours per week they are expected to work.
- **Dress code:** This provides a description and guidelines for required attire in the workplace.
- **Performance review:** This describes the performance review policy and program that is used periodically to evaluate each employee's performance.
- **Promotions:** This describes the criteria used by the organization to consider promotions for employees.
- **Time off:** This describes compensated and uncompensated time off, including holidays, vacation, illness, disability, bereavement, sabbaticals, military duty, and leaves of absence.
- **Security:** This discusses basic expectations on the topics of physical security and information security, as well as expectations for how employees are expected to handle confidential and sensitive information.
- **Regulation:** If the organization is subject to regulation, this may be mentioned in the employee handbook so that employees will be aware of this and conduct themselves accordingly.
- **Safety:** This discusses workplace safety, which may cover evacuation procedures, emergency procedures, permitted and prohibited items and substances (for example, weapons, alcoholic beverages, other substances and items), procedures for working with hazardous substances, and procedures for operating equipment and machinery.
- **Conduct:** This covers basic expectations for workplace conduct, both with fellow employees and with customers, vendors, business partners, and other third parties.
- **Discipline:** Organizations that have a disciplinary process usually describe its highlights in the employee handbook.

Employees are often required to sign a statement that affirms their understanding of and compliance with the employee handbook. Many organizations require that employees sign a new copy of the statement on an annual basis, even if the employee handbook has not changed. This helps to affirm for employees the importance of policies contained in the employee handbook.

Initial Access Provisioning

New employees may need access to office locations, computers, networks, and/or applications to perform their required duties. This will necessitate the provisioning of access to one or more buildings and to computer or network user accounts, as required to perform their work-related tasks.

An access-provisioning process should be used to determine which access privileges a new employee should be given. A template of job titles and access privileges should be set up in advance so that management can easily determine which access privileges any new employee will receive. Even with such a plan, each new employee's manager should formally request that these privileges be set up for new employees.

Job Descriptions

A *job description* is a formal document that describes the roles, responsibilities, and experience required. Each position in an organization, from chief executive officer to office clerk, should have a formal job description.

Job descriptions should also state that employees are required to support company policies, including but not limited to security and privacy, code of conduct, and acceptable use policies. By listing these in a job description, an employer is stating that all employees are expected to comply with these and other policies.

 Employers usually are required to include several boilerplate items or statements (such as equal opportunity clauses) in job descriptions to conform to local labor and workplace safety laws.

Employee Development

Once hired into the organization, employees will require training in the organization's policies and practices so that their contributions will be effective and further the organization's goals. Regular evaluations will help employees to focus their long-term efforts on personal and the organization's goals and objectives.

Training

To be effective, employees need to receive periodic training. This includes:

- **Skills training:** Employees should learn how to use tools and equipment properly. In some cases, employees are required to receive training and prove competency before they are permitted to use some tools and equipment. Sometimes this is required by law.

- **Practices and techniques:** Employees need to understand how the organization uses its tools and equipment for its specific use.

- **Policies:** Organizations often impart information about their policies in the context of training. This helps the organization make sure that employees comprehend the material.

Performance Evaluation

Many organizations utilize a performance evaluation process to examine each employee's performance against a set of expectations and objectives. A performance evaluation program also helps to shape employees' behavior over the long term and helps them to reflect on how their efforts contribute toward the organization's overall objectives. A performance evaluation is frequently used to determine whether (and by how much) an employee's compensation should be increased.

Career Path

In many cultures, employees believe that they can be successful if they understand how they can advance within the organization. A career path program can help employees understand what skills are required for other positions in the organization and how they can strive toward positions that they desire in the future.

Mandatory Vacations

Some organizations, particularly those that deal with high-risk or high-value activities, require mandatory vacations of one week or longer for some or all employees. This practice can accomplish three objectives:

- **Cross-training:** An absence of one week or longer will force management to cross-train other employees so that the organization is less reliant on specific individuals.

- **Audit:** A minimum absence gives the organization an opportunity to audit the absent employee's work to make sure that the employee is not involved in any undesired behavior.

- **Reduced risk:** Knowing that they will be away from their day-to-day activities for at least one or two contiguous weeks each year, employees are less apt to partake in prohibited activities that could be discovered by colleagues or auditors during their absence.

Termination

When an employee leaves an organization, these actions need to take place:

Physical access to all work areas must be immediately revoked.   Depending on the sensitivity of work activities in the organization, the employee may also need to be escorted out of the work area and have their personal belongings gathered by others and delivered to the departed employee's residence.

Each of the employee's computer and network access accounts must be locked.   The purpose of this action is to protect the integrity of business information by permitting only authorized employees to access it. Locking computer accounts also prevents other employees from accessing information using the former employee's credentials.

WARNING   The issue of whether a former employee's account should be removed or merely disabled depends on the nature of the application or system. In some cases, the record of actions taken by employees (such as an audit log) depends on the existence of the employee's ID on the system; if a former employee's ID is removed, then those audit records may not properly reference who is associated with them.

If the organization chooses to disable rather than remove computer or network accounts for terminated employees, those accounts must be restricted in a way that positively prohibits any further access. For instance, merely changing the passwords of terminated accounts to "locked" would be considered a highly unsafe practice in the event that anyone discovers the password. If changing the account's password is the only way to disable it, then a long and highly random password must be used and then forgotten so that even the account administrator cannot use it.

In some jurisdictions, employers may be required to permit former employees to be able to access their compensation and tax records.

Transfers and Reassignments

In many organizations, employees will move between positions over time. These position changes are not always upward through a career path, but can be lateral moves from one type of work to another.

Unless an organization is very careful about its access management processes and procedures, employees who transfer and are promoted tend to accumulate access privileges. This happens because a transferring employee's old privileges are not revoked, even though those privileges are no longer needed. Over a period of years, an employee who is transferred or promoted can accumulate many excessive privileges that can indicate significant risk should the individual choose to perform functions in the applications that they are no longer officially authorized to use. This phenomenon is sometimes known as accumulation of privileges or privilege creep.

Privilege creep happens frequently in company accounting departments. An individual, for example, can move from role to role in the accounting department, all the while accumulating privileges that eventually result in the ability for that employee to defraud their employer by requesting, approving, and disbursing payments to themselves or to accomplices. Similarly, this can occur in an IT department, when an employee transfers from the operations department to the software development department (which is a common career path). Unless the IT department deliberately removes the transferring employee's prior privileges, it will end up with an employee who is a developer with access to production systems—a red flag to auditors who examine roles and responsibilities.

Contractor Management

For years, HR organizations refused to have anything to do with workers who were not employees of the organization. From the perspective of access management, this usually resulted in substandard practices for managing temporary workers, bringing increased risk to organizations. Thankfully, the tide is turning, and HR organizations are beginning to embrace the management of temporary workers. In part, this is because modern HR information systems are easily able to distinguish employees from all types of temporary workers. Still, because of their often itinerant nature, temporary workers must be properly and accurately tracked. In the realm of access controls in sensitive environments, this represents an important risk reduction factor. Best practice would be to have both contractors and employees follow similar policies and processes, especially when they are involved in higher-risk areas of the organization.

Sourcing

Sourcing refers to the choices that organizations make when selecting the personnel who will perform functions and where those functions will be performed. Sourcing options include the following:

- **Insourced:** The organization hires employees to perform work. These workers can be full-time, part-time, or temporary.
- **Outsourced:** The organization uses contractors or consultants to perform work.
- **Hybrid:** The organization can utilize a combination of insourced and outsourced workers.

Next, the options include where personnel will perform tasks:

- **On-site:** Personnel work at the organization's worksite(s).
- **Off-site, local:** Personnel are not located on-site, but are near the organization's premises, usually in or near the same community.
- **Off-site, remote:** Personnel are in the same country, but not near the organization's premises.
- **Offshore:** Personnel are located in a different country.
- **Nearshore:** Outsourced personnel are located in a nearby country.
- **Onshore:** Outsourced personnel are located in the same country.

 Organizations are often able to work out different combinations of insourced or outsourced personnel and where they perform their work. For instance, an organization can open its own office in a foreign country and hire employees to work there; this would be an example of offshore insourcing. Similarly, an organization can use contractors to perform work on-site; this is on-site outsourcing.

Insourcing

Insourcing, which is the practice of hiring employees for long-term work, is discussed earlier in this chapter in the "Personnel Management" section.

Outsourcing

Outsourcing is the practice of using contractors or consultants to perform work for the organization. An organization will decide to outsource a task, activity, or project for a wide variety of reasons:

Project duration   An organization may require personnel only for a specific project, such as the development of or migration to a new application. Often, an organization will opt to use contractors or consultants when it cannot justify hiring permanent workers.

Skills   An organization may require personnel with certain hard-to-find skills but may not need them on a full-time basis. Persons with certain skills may command a higher salary than the organization is willing to pay, and the organization may not have sufficient work to keep such a worker interested in permanent employment.

Variable demand   Organizations may experience seasonal increases and decreases of demand for certain workers. Organizations often cannot justify hiring full-time employees for peak demand capacity, when at other times, those workers will not have enough work to keep them busy and productive. Instead, organizations will usually staff for average demand and augment staff with contractors for peak demand.

High turnover   Some positions, such as IT helpdesk and call center positions, are inherently high-turnover positions that are costly to replace and train. Instead, an organization may opt to outsource some or all of the personnel in these positions.

Focus on core activities   An organization may concentrate on hiring for positions related to its core purpose and to outsource functions that are considered "overhead." For instance, an organization that produces computer hardware products may elect to outsource its IT computer support department so that it can focus on its product development and support.

Financial   A decision to outsource may be based primarily on financial issues. Usually, an organization seeking to reduce costs of software development and other activities will outsource and offshore these activities to service organizations located in other countries.

Complete time coverage   An organization that needs to have personnel available around the clock may choose to outsource part of that function to personnel at work centers in other time zones.

An organization that chooses to hire employees only in its core service areas can outsource many of its noncore functions, including these:

- **IT helpdesk and support:** This is often a high-turnover function, as well as variable in demand, making it a good candidate for outsourcing.
- **Software development:** An organization that lacks employees with development and programming skills can elect to have contractors or consultants perform this work.

- **Software maintenance:** An organization may choose to keep its developers and analysts focused on new software development projects and to leave maintenance of existing software to contractors.

- **Customer support:** An organization may choose to outsource its telephone and online support to personnel or organizations in countries with lower labor costs.

> Although outsourcing decisions appear, on the surface, to be economically motivated, some of the other reasons stated here may be even more important in some organizations. For example, the flexibility afforded by outsourcing may help to make an organization more agile, which may improve quality or increase efficiency over longer periods.

Outsourcing Benefits

Organizations that are considering outsourcing need to weigh the benefits and the costs carefully to determine whether the effort to outsource will result in measurable improvement in processing, service delivery, or finances. In the 1990s, when many organizations rushed to outsource development and support functions to operations in other countries, they did so with unrealistic short-term gains in mind and without adequately considering all of the real costs of outsourcing.

Outsourcing can bring many benefits:

- **Available skills and experience:** Organizations that may have trouble attracting persons with specialized skills often turn to outsourcing firms with highly skilled personnel who can ply their trade in a variety of client organizations.

- **Economies of scale:** Often, specialized outsourcing firms can achieve better economies of scale through discipline and mature practices that organizations are unable to achieve.

- **Objectivity:** Some functions are better done by outsiders. Personnel in an organization may have trouble being objective about some activities, such as process improvement and requirements definition. Also, auditors frequently must be employed by an outside firm to achieve sufficient objectivity and independence.

- **Reduced costs:** When outsourcing involves offshore personnel, an organization may be able to lower its operating costs and improve its competitive market position, usually through currency exchange rates and differences in the standards of living in headquarters versus offshore countries.

When an organization is making an outsourcing decision, it needs to consider these advantages together with the risks that are discussed in the next section.

Risks Associated with Outsourcing

Although outsourcing can bring many tangible and intangible benefits to an organization, it is not without certain risks and disadvantages. Naturally, when an organization employs outsiders to perform some of its functions, it relinquishes some control. The risks of outsourcing include these:

- **Higher-than-expected costs:** Reduced costs were the main driver for offshore outsourcing in the 1990s. However, many organizations failed to anticipate all the operational realities. For instance, when outsourcing to overseas operations, IT personnel back in U.S.-based organizations may have to make many more expensive overseas trips than expected. Also, changes in international currency exchange rates can transform this year's bargain into next year's high cost.

- **Poor quality:** The outsourced work product may be lower in quality than the product created when the function was performed in-house.

- **Poor performance:** The outsourced service may not perform as expected. The capacity of networks or IT systems used by the outsourcing firm may cause processing delays or longer-than-acceptable response times.

- **Loss of control:** An organization that is accustomed to being in control of its workers may undergo a loss of control of its outsourced workers. Making small adjustments to processes and procedures may be more time-consuming or may increase costs.

- **Employee integrity and background:** It may be decidedly more difficult to determine the integrity of employees in an outsourced situation, particularly when the outsourcing is taking place offshore. Some countries, even where outsourcing is popular, lack the support of nationwide criminal background checks and other means for making a solid determination on an employee's background.

- **Loss of competitive advantage:** If the services performed by the outsourcing firm are not flexible enough to meet the organization's needs, this can result in the organization losing some of its competitive advantage. For example, suppose an organization outsources its corporate messaging (email and other messaging) to a service provider. Later, the organization wants to enhance its customer communication by integrating its service application with email. The email service provider may be unable or unwilling to provide the necessary integration, which will result in the organization losing a competitive advantage.

- **Errors and omissions:** The organization performing outsourcing services may make serious errors or may fail to perform essential tasks. For instance, an outsourcing service may suffer a data security breach that may result in the loss or disclosure of sensitive information. This can be a disastrous event when it occurs within an organization's four walls, but when it happens in an outsourced part of the business, the organization may find that the lack of control will make it difficult to take the proper steps to contain and remediate the incident. If an outsourcing firm has undergone a security breach or similar incident, it may put its own interests first and only secondarily watch out for the interests of its customers.

- **Vendor failure:** The failure of the organization to provide outsourcing services may result in increased costs and delays in service or product delivery.

- **Differing mission and goals:** An organization's employees are going to be loyal to its mission and objectives. However, the employees in an outsourced organization usually have little or no interest in the hiring organization's interests; instead, they will be loyal to the outsourcing provider's values, which may at times be in direct conflict. For example, an outsourcing organization may place emphasis on maximizing billable hours, while the hiring organization emphasizes efficiency. These two objectives conflict with each other.

- **Difficult recourse:** If an organization is dissatisfied with the performance or quality of its outsourced operation, contract provisions may not sufficiently facilitate any remedy. If the outsourced operation is in a foreign country, applying remediation in the court system may also be futile.

- **Lowered employee morale:** If an organization chooses to outsource work and lays off some full-time workers, employees who remain may be upset because some of their colleagues have lost their jobs as a result of the outsourcing. Further, remaining employees may fear that their own jobs may soon be outsourced or eliminated. They may also believe that their organization is more interested in saving money than in taking care of its employees. Personnel who have lost their jobs may vent their anger at the organization through a variety of harmful actions that can threaten assets or other workers.

- **Audit and compliance:** An organization that outsources a part of its operation that is in scope for applicable laws and regulations may find it more challenging to perform audits and achieve compliance. Audit costs may rise, as auditors need to visit the outsourced work centers. Requiring the outsourced organization to make changes to achieve compliance may be difficult or expensive.

- **Applicable laws:** Laws, regulations, and standards in headquarters and offshore countries may impose requirements on the protection of information that can complicate business operations or enterprise architectures.

- **Cross-border data transfer:** Governments around the world are paying attention to the flow of data, particularly the sensitive data of their citizens. Many countries have passed laws that attempt to exert control over data about their citizens when it is transferred out of their jurisdictions.

- **Time zone differences:** Communications will suffer when an organization outsources some of its operations to offshore organizations that are several time zones distant. It will be more difficult to schedule telephone conferences if there is very little overlap between work hours in each time zone. It will take more time to communicate important issues and to make changes.

- **Language and cultural differences:** When outsourcing crosses language and cultural barriers, it can result in less than optimal communication and results. The outsourcing customer will express its needs through its own language and culture, and the outsourcing provider will hear those needs through its own language and culture. Both sides may be thinking or saying, "They don't understand what we want" and "We don't understand what they want." This can result in unexpected differences in work produced by the outsourcing firm. Delays in project completion or delivery of goods and services can occur as a result.

- **Political conditions:** When offshoring labor and when using foreign workers with work visas, changes in political conditions can result in restrictions of the use of foreign workers, wherever they are working. For example, restrictions on certain types of work visas for foreign workers have forced some organizations to change their strategies for attracting offshore talent.

 Some of the risks associated with outsourcing are intangible or may lie outside the bounds of legal remedies. For instance, language and time zone differences can introduce delays in communication, adding friction to the business relationship in a way that may not be easily measurable.

Mitigating Outsourcing Risk

The only means of exchange between an outsourcing provider and its customer organization are money and reputation. In other words, the only leverage that an organization has against its outsourcing provider is the withholding of payment and communicating the quality (or lack thereof) of the provider's services to other organizations. This is especially true if the outsourcing crosses national boundaries. Therefore, an organization that is considering outsourcing must carefully consider how it will enforce contract terms so that it receives the goods and services that it is expecting.

Many of the risks of outsourcing can be remedied through contract provisions. Here are some of the remedies:

- **Service level agreement (SLA):** The contract should provide details for every avenue of work performance and communication, including escalations and problem management.

- **Quality:** Depending on the product or service, this may translate into an error or defect rate, a customer satisfaction rate, or system performance.

- **Security policy and controls:** Whether the outsourcing firm is safeguarding the organization's intellectual property, keeping business secrets, or protecting information about its employees or customers, the contract should spell out the details of the security controls that it expects the outsourcing firm to maintain. The organization should also require periodic third-party audits and the results of those audits. The contract should contain a "right to audit" clause that allows the outsourcing organization to examine the work premises, records, and workpapers on demand.

- **Business continuity:** The contract should require the outsourcing firm to have reasonable measures and safeguards in place to ensure resilience of operations and the ability to continue operations with minimum disruption in the event of a disaster.

- **Employee integrity:** The contract should define how the outsourcing firm will vet its employees' backgrounds so that it is not inadvertently hiring individuals with a criminal history and so employees' claimed education and work experience are proven genuine.

- **Ownership of intellectual property:** If the outsourcing firm is producing software or other designs, the contract must define ownership of those work products and whether the outsourcing firm may reuse any of those work products for other engagements.

- **Roles and responsibilities:** The contract should specify in detail the roles and responsibilities of each party so that each will know what is expected of them.

- **Schedule:** The contract must specify when and how many items of work product should be produced.

- **Regulation:** The contract should require both parties to conform to all applicable laws and regulations, including but not limited to intellectual property, data protection, and workplace safety.

- **Warranty:** The contract should specify terms of warranty so that there can be no ambiguity regarding the quality of goods or services performed.

- **Dispute and resolution:** The contract should contain provisions that define the process for handling and resolving disputes.

- **Payment:** The contract should specify how and when the outsourcing provider will be paid. Compensation should be tied not only to the quantity but also to the quality of work performed. The contract should include incentive provisions for additional payment when specific schedule, quantity, or quality targets are exceeded. The contract should also contain financial penalties that are enacted when SLA, quality, security, audit, or schedule targets are missed.

The terms of an outsourcing contract should adequately reward the outsourcing firm for a job well done, which should include the prospect of earning additional contracts as well as referrals that will help it to earn outsourcing contracts from other customers.

Outsourcing Governance

You cannot outsource accountability. Outsourcing is a convenient way to transfer some operations to an external organization, thereby allowing the outsourcing organization to be more agile and allowing the outsourcing organization to improve focus on core competencies. Although senior managers can transfer these activities to external organizations and even specify rewards for good performance and penalties for substandard performance, those senior managers are still ultimately accountable for the delivery of these services, whether they are outsourced or performed by internal staff.

In the context of outsourcing, the role of governance must be expanded to include the aggregation of activities that control the work performed by external organizations. Governance activities may include the following:

Contracts   The overall business relationship between the organization and its service providers should be defined in detailed legal agreements. The terms of legal agreements should define the work to be done (in general), the expectations of all parties, service levels, quality, the terms of compensation, and remedies in case expectations fail to be met. Appropriate levels of management must approve the content in contracts.

Work Orders   Sometimes called statements of work (SOWs), work orders describe in greater detail the work that is to be performed. While contracts are seldom changed, work orders operate in short-term intervals and are specific to currently delivered goods or services. Like contracts themselves, work orders should include precise statements regarding work output, timeliness, quality, and remedies.

Service Level Agreements   These documents specify service levels in terms of the quantity of work, quality, timeliness, and remedies for shortfalls in quality or quantity.

Change Management   A formal method is needed so that changes in delivery specifications can be formally controlled.

Security   If the service provider has access to the organization's records or other intellectual property, the organization will require that specific security controls be in place. In higher-risk situations, the organization will want to validate periodically that the service provider's security controls are effective.

Quality   Minimum standards for quality should be expressed in detail so that both service provider and customer have a common understanding of the expected quality of work to be performed.

Metrics   Often, the outsourcing organization will want to actively measure various aspects of the outsourced activity to gain short-term visibility into work output as well as the ability to understand long-term trends.

Audits   The outsourcing organization may require that audits of the outsourced work be performed. These audits may be performed by a competent third party, by an independent security consulting firm, or by the customer. Often, an outsourcing organization will negotiate a "right to audit" clause in the contract but will exercise this only if the organization encounters irregularities or issues related to the work performed.

Depending on the nature of specific outsourcing arrangements, the preceding activities may be combined or performed separately.

Benchmarking

Benchmarking measures a process to compare its performance and quality against the same process in other organizations. Its purpose is to discover opportunities for improvement that may result in lower costs, fewer resources, and higher quality.

In the context of outsourcing, benchmarking can be used to measure the performance of an outsourced process against the same process performed by other outsourcing firms, as well as to compare it with the same process performed internally by other organizations. The objective is the same: to learn whether a particular outsourcing solution is performing effectively and efficiently.

Third-Party Service Delivery Management

Service delivery management is the institution of controls and metrics to ensure that services are performed properly and with a minimum of incidents and defects. When activities are transferred to a service provider, service delivery management has some added dimensions and considerations.

When service delivery management is used to manage an external service provider, the service provider is usually required to maintain detailed measurements of its work output. The organization utilizing an external service provider also needs to maintain detailed records of work received, and it should perform its own defect management controls to ensure that the work performed by the service provider meets quality standards. Problems and incidents encountered by the organization should be documented and transmitted to the service provider to improve quality.

These activities should be included in the SLA or in the contract to ensure that the customer will be able to impose financial penalties or other types of leveraging on to the service provider to improve quality while maintaining minimum work output.

Service delivery standards related to IT service management are defined in the international standard ISO/IEC 20000:2018. Relevant controls from this standard can be used to impose a standard method for managing service delivery by the service provider.

Third-party risk management (TPRM) is a similar activity with regard to the management of service providers. TPRM is discussed in detail in Chapter 7, "Information Security Management."

SaaS, IaaS, and PaaS Considerations

Organizations such as SaaS (software-as-a-service), IaaS (infrastructure-as-a-service), and PaaS (platform-as-a-service) provide cloud-based application or computing resources to clients that cannot justify building their own.

SaaS is an arrangement in which an organization obtains a software application for use by its employees, where the software application is hosted by the software provider as opposed to the customer organization. IaaS is an arrangement in which an organization rents IT infrastructure from a service provider. PaaS is a service that enables organizations to deploy applications without having to deal with underlying infrastructure such as servers and database management systems.

The primary advantages of using SaaS, IaaS, and PaaS as opposed to self-hosting are as follows:

- **Capital savings:** The SaaS/IaaS/PaaS provider makes its software, infrastructure, or platform resources available to its customers on its own servers, thereby eliminating a customers' need to purchase dedicated hardware and software.

- **Labor savings:** The SaaS/IaaS/PaaS provider performs many administrative functions, including typical administrative tasks such as applying software or operating system patches, managing performance and capacity, upgrading software, and troubleshooting.

In addition to the advantages outlined here, the use of SaaS/IaaS/PaaS providers can also assist a company in risk management, as discussed previously, by transferring key risks to the service provider.

An organization that is considering an SaaS, an IaaS, or a PaaS provider for one of its environments will need to ensure that the provider has adequate controls in place to protect the organization's data. Specifically, an organization needs to understand the security responsibility model thoroughly to determine which controls are performed by the service provider and which have to be implemented by the organization. Further, the provider should have controls in place that will prevent one customer from being able to view the data associated with a different customer.

An organization can consider the SaaS/IaaS/PaaS provider to be similar to other service providers. Generally, methods used to determine the integrity and quality of the SaaS/IaaS/PaaS provider would be the same as those used with other service providers.

Business Process-as-a-Service

As the cybersecurity skills shortage widens, service organizations are developing numerous business process-as-a-service offerings to help businesses continue critical security processes. Examples of new service offerings include identity-as-a-service, vulnerability management-as-a-service, and patch management-as-a-service. One of the first "as-a-service" offerings was security event monitoring, which is still popular.

Change Management

Change management is a business process that is used to control changes made to an IT environment. A formal change management process consists of several steps that are carried out for each change:

1. Request.
2. Review.
3. Approve (or deny).
4. Perform.
5. Verify.
6. Back out (when verification of a successful change fails).

Each step in change management includes recordkeeping. Change management is covered in detail in Chapter 3, "IT Life Cycle Management."

Financial Management

Sound financial management is critical in any organization. Because IT is a cost-intensive activity, it is imperative that the organization be well managed, with short-term and long-term budget planning, and that it track actual spending.

One area where senior management needs to make strategic financial decisions in IT is the manner in which it acquires software applications. At the steering committee level, IT organizations carefully need to weigh "make versus buy" with their primary applications. This typically falls into three alternatives:

- **Develop the application:** The organization develops the application using in-house or contracted software developers, designers, and analysts.

- **Purchase the application:** The organization licenses the application from a software vendor and installs it on servers that it leases or purchases.

- **Rent the application:** This generally refers to the cloud computing or SaaS model, whereby the cloud/application service provider hosts the application on its own premises (or in an Internet data center) and the organization using the software pays either a fixed fee or an on-demand fee. The purchasing organization will have no capital cost for servers and little or no development cost (except, possibly, for interfaces to other applications).

The choice that an organization makes is not just about the finances, but is also concerned with the degree of control that the organization requires.

IT financial management is about not only applications, but also the other services that an IT organization provides. Other functions such as service desk, PC build and support, email, and network services can likewise be insourced or outsourced, each with financial and other implications.

Many larger organizations employ a "chargeback" feature for the delivery of IT services. In this method, an IT organization charges (usually through budget transfers but occasionally through real funds) for the services that it provides. The advantage to chargeback is that the customers of the IT organization are required to budget for IT services and are less likely to make frivolous requests of IT, since every activity has a cost associated with it. Chargeback may also force an IT organization to be more competitive, as chargeback may invite IT customers to acquire services from outside organizations and not from the internal IT organization. Chargeback can thus be viewed as outsourcing to the internal IT organization.

Quality Management

Quality management refers to the methods by which business processes are controlled, monitored, and managed to bring about continuous improvement. The scope of a quality management system in an IT organization may cover any or all of the following activities:

- Software development
- Software acquisition
- Service desk

- IT operations
- Security

The components that are required to build and operate a quality management system are as follows:

- **Documented processes:** Each process that is part of a quality management system must be fully documented. This means that all of the tasks, notifications, records, and data flows must be fully described in formal process documents that are themselves controlled.

- **Key measurements:** Each process under quality management must have some key measurement points so that management will be able to understand the frequency and effort expended for the process. Measurement goes beyond simply tallying and must include methods for recognizing, classifying, and measuring incidents, events, problems, and defects.

- **Management review of key measurements:** Key measurements need to be regularly analyzed and included in status reports that provide meaningful information to various levels of management. This enables management to understand how key processes are performing and whether they are meeting management's expectations.

- **Audits:** Processes in a quality management system should be periodically measured by internal or external auditors to ensure that they are being operated properly. These auditors need to be sufficiently independent of the processes and of management itself so that they can objectively evaluate processes.

- **Process changes:** When key measurements suggest that changes to a process are needed, a business or process analyst will make changes to the design of a process. Examples of process changes include the addition of data fields in a change request process, the addition of security requirements to the software development process, or a new method for communicating passwords to the users of newly created user accounts.

 An organization should document and measure its quality management processes, just as it does with all of the processes under its observation and control. This will help to confirm whether the quality management system itself is effective.

ISO/IEC 9000

Established in the 1980s, the ISO/IEC 9000 family of standards remains the gold standard for quality management systems.

Organizations that implement the ISO/IEC 9001:2015 standard can voluntarily undergo regular external audits by an accredited firm to earn an ISO/IEC 9001:2015 certification. More than one million ISO/IEC 9001 certificates have been issued to organizations around the world since 1987.

ISO/IEC 9000 began as a manufacturing product quality standard. While many manufacturing firms are certified to ISO/IEC 9000, the standard is growing in popularity among service providers and software development organizations.

ISO/IEC 20000

Many IT organizations have adopted ITIL IT service management processes as a standard framework for IT processes. Organizations that desire a certification can be evaluated by an accredited external audit firm to confirm that they conform to the ISO/IEC 20000 IT Service Management standard. ISO/IEC 20000 supersedes the earlier BS 15000 standard.

The ITIL 4 framework consists of 34 management practices in three categories:

- General Management Practices
- Service Management Practices
- Technical Management Practices

The ITIL 4 framework consists of four dimensions:

- Organization and People
- Value Streams and Processes
- Partners and Suppliers
- Information and Technology

ITIL's management practices constitute an effective framework for IT's primary function: delivering valuable services to enable key organizational processes.

Portfolio Management

Portfolio management refers to the systematic management of IT projects, investments, and activities. The purpose of portfolio management is to measure the value derived from IT projects, investments, and activities and to make adjustments periodically to maximize that value for the organization.

The principles of IT portfolio management are similar to those of financial investment portfolio management. All of the activities in IT are treated like investments, with a careful look at the value they bring to the organization.

Mature organizations that practice IT portfolio management typically develop three portfolios:

- Project portfolio
- Infrastructure portfolio
- Application portfolio

The items in these portfolios are measured, examined, and scrutinized for their continuing contribution to, and alignment with, the organization's mission and main objectives. Management can make periodic adjustments to the level of resources associated with IT projects and activities to maximize value to the organization.

Controls Management

IT organizations employ controls to ensure specific outcomes within business processes, IT systems, and personnel. Better organizations adopt one of several standard frameworks of controls and then periodically assess risk and control performance, resulting in changes to controls as well as the addition or removal of controls.

Controls are generally enacted as a result of one or more of the following:

- **Policies:** Controls can be established to ensure compliance to a policy and to measure a policy's effectiveness.
- **Regulations:** Organizations often establish controls to ensure compliance with regulations.
- **Requirements:** Legal or operational requirements, such as terms and conditions in contracts with customers or suppliers, compel an organization to enact controls to ensure compliance.
- **Risks:** An internal or external risk assessment may compel an organization to enact controls to reduce risks to acceptable levels.
- **Incidents:** A compelling incident or event may prompt an organization to enact controls to prevent similar incidents from recurring.

It is not enough for organizations to develop and implement controls. Organizations need to examine controls periodically to determine whether they are operating properly and ensuring their intended outcomes. The entire discipline of internal and external audit is brought to bear on the subject of control examination and effectiveness. The process and practice of audits is explored in detail in Chapter 9, "Conducting a Professional Audit."

Well-known control frameworks include:

- **COBIT 2019:** Developed by ISACA, COBIT 2019 is a general-purpose IT controls framework.
- **NIST 800-53:** Developed by the National Institute of Standards and Technology (NIST), NIST 800-53 is a comprehensive set of security and privacy controls for information systems. This framework has been adopted by many government and nongovernment organizations.
- **NIST Cybersecurity Framework (CSF) 2.0:** This framework organizes controls into six functions: Govern, Identify, Protect, Detect, Respond, and Recover. CSF also serves as a guide for organizations to determine their security maturity.
- **ISO/IEC 20000:** This is the international standard with its roots in the ITIL, the framework of IT service management.
- **ISO/IEC 27002:** This is the international standard framework of IT security controls, and it is widely adopted worldwide.
- **PCI DSS 4.0 (Payment Card Industry Data Security Standard):** This is the IT security controls framework required for systems and networks that store, process, or transmit credit and debit card data.

- **HIPAA (Health Insurance Portability and Accountability Act) Security Rule:** This is the framework of controls required for organizations that store, process, or transmit electronic patient health information (ePHI).

- **Center for Internet Security (CIS) Critical Security Controls:** Originally developed by the SANS Institute, CIS Critical Security Controls consist of 18 controls. As an integral part of information security and IT audit, these controls are discussed throughout this book.

Security Management

Security management refers to several key activities that work together to identify risks and risk treatment for the organization's assets. In most organizations these activities include:

Security Governance   This is the practice of setting organizational security policy and then taking steps to ensure that the policy is followed. Security governance also is involved with the management and continuous improvement of other key security activities discussed in this section.

Risk Assessment   This is the practice of identifying key assets in use by the organization and identifying vulnerabilities in, and threats against, each asset. This is followed by the development of risk treatment strategies that attempt to mitigate, transfer, avoid, or accept identified risks.

Incident Management   This practice is concerned with the planned response to security incidents when they occur in the organization. An incident is defined as a violation of security policy; such an incident may be minor (such as a user choosing an easily guessed password) or major (such as a hacking attack and theft of sensitive information). Aspects of incident management include computer forensics (the preservation of evidence that could be used in later legal action) and the involvement of regulatory authorities and law enforcement.

Vulnerability Management   This is the practice of proactively identifying vulnerabilities in IT systems, as well as in business processes, that could be exploited to the detriment of the organization. Activities that take place in vulnerability management include security scanning, vulnerability assessment, code review, patch management, and reviewing threat intelligence and risk advisories issued by software vendors and security organizations.

Identity and Access Management   These practices are used to control which persons and groups may have access to which applications, assets, systems, workplaces, and functions. Identity management is the activity of managing the identity and access history of each employee, contractor, temporary worker, supplier worker, and, optionally, customer. These records are then used as the basis for controlling which workplaces, applications, IT systems, and business functions each person is permitted to use.

Compliance Management   Security management should be responsible for knowing which laws, regulations, standards, requirements, and legal contracts the organization is required to comply with. Verification of compliance may involve internal or external audits and other activities to confirm that the organization is in compliance with all of these legal and other requirements.

Third-Party Risk Management   This is the practice of identifying and managing risks associated with third-party organizations that store, process, or transmit sensitive information on behalf of the organization. Activities include up-front due diligence and periodic assessment of critical control effectiveness and overall business risk.

Business Continuity and Disaster Recovery Planning   These practices enable the organization to develop response plans in the event that a disaster should occur that would otherwise threaten the ongoing viability of the organization. Business continuity and disaster recovery planning is covered in detail later in this chapter.

Control frameworks for security management include:

- **ISO/IEC 27001 requirements:** The first half of the ISO/IEC 27001 standard contains a set of requirements that describe a scalable and flexible information security management system (ISMS) that is based on a life cycle of risk assessment, controls examination, and controls development, with an overarching theme of executive oversight and control.

Performance and Capacity Management

Performance optimization is concerned with the continual improvement of IT processes and systems. This set of activities is concerned not only with financial efficiency, but also with the time and resources required to perform common IT functions. The primary objective of IT performance optimization is to ensure that the organization is getting the maximum benefit from IT services for the lowest possible expenditure of resources.

An organization that measures process performance is more apt to recognize opportunities for making improvements to business processes. Organizations that reach a level of process maturity that includes measurement and feedback will be able to adopt a culture of continuous improvement. Then management can track improvement opportunities and assign resources accordingly.

Performance optimization is considered a rather mature approach to the management of IT processes and systems. It requires mature processes with key controls and measurement points, and it is one of the natural results of effective quality management. An organization that is not already monitoring and managing its processes is probably not ready to undertake performance optimization. See the earlier section, "Quality Management," for more information on this perspective.

Performance optimization is a complicated undertaking, because IT systems and processes usually change frequently over time; it can be difficult to attribute specific changes in systems or processes to changes in performance metrics.

Maturity models such as Capability Maturity Model Integration (CMMI) can be used to determine the level of an organization's processes. CMMI focuses on whether an organization's processes have a level of maturity associated with measurement and continuous improvement.

The COBIT 2019 framework also contains facilities to identify and measure KPIs, with the aim of enabling continuous improvement to processes and technology. The COBIT framework contains 40 governance and management objectives, along with the means for any individual organization to determine how much (and what kind of) control is appropriate for the organization, based on its business objectives and how IT supports them.

A typical organization will not have the same level of maturity across all of its departments and processes. Instead, some processes and departments will be more mature than others, often by a wide variance.

Benchmarking

An organization may decide to benchmark its key processes. Benchmarking is a process of performing a detailed comparison of a business process (or system, or almost any other aspect of an organization) with the same process in other organizations. This will help an organization better understand how similar organizations are solving similar business problems, which could lead the organization to enact process improvements on its own.

In the past, it was common for organizations to benchmark the overall cost of information technology or information security. Today, however, IT and security costs are more ambiguous, particularly considering the trend of outsourcing business and IT services to third parties. Hence, it has become more useful to benchmark process maturity or risk appetite as a way of comparing an organization to its peers.

Organization Structure and Responsibilities

Organizations require structure to distribute responsibility to groups of people with specific skills and knowledge. The structure of an organization is depicted in an organization chart (org chart). Figure 1.5 shows a typical IT organization chart.

Organizing and maintaining an organization structure requires that many factors be considered. In most organizations, the org chart is a living structure that changes from time to time, based on several conditions, including the following:

▪ **Short- and long-term objectives:** Organizations sometimes move departments from one executive to another so that departments that were once far from each other (in terms of the org chart structure) will be near each other. This provides new opportunities for developing synergies and partnerships that did not exist before the reorganization. These organizational changes are usually performed to help an organization meet new objectives that were less important before and that require new partnerships and teamwork.

FIGURE 1.5 Typical IT organization chart

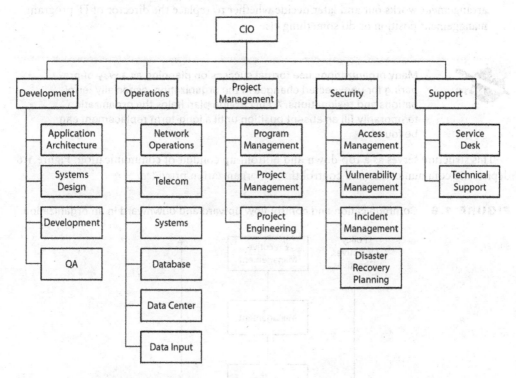

- **Market conditions:** Changes in market positions can cause an organization to realign its internal structure to strengthen itself. For example, if a competitor lowers its prices based on a new sourcing strategy, an organization may need to respond by changing its organizational structure to put experienced executives in charge of specific activities.

- **Regulations:** New laws, regulations, or standards may induce an organization to change its organizational structure. For instance, an organization that becomes highly regulated may elect to move its security and compliance group away from IT and place it under the legal department, since compliance has much more to do with legal compliance than industry standards.

- **Attrition and available talent:** When someone leaves the organization or moves to another position within the organization, particularly in positions of leadership, a space opens in the org chart that often cannot be filled right away. Instead, senior management will temporarily change the structure of the organization by moving the leaderless department under the control of someone else. Often, the decisions of how to change the organization will depend on the talent and experience of existing leaders, in addition to each leader's workload and other factors. For example, if the director of IT program management leaves the organization, the existing department could temporarily be placed under the IT operations department, in this case because the director of IT operations used to run IT program management. Senior management can see how that arrangement works out and later decide whether to replace the director of IT program management position or do something else.

 Many organizations use formal succession planning as a way of preparing for unexpected changes in the organization, especially terminations and resignations. A succession plan helps the organization temporarily fill an absent position until a long-term replacement can be found.

This structure serves as a top-down and bottom-up conduit of communication. Figure 1.6 depicts the communication and control that an organization provides.

FIGURE 1.6   Communication and control flow upward and downward in an organization.

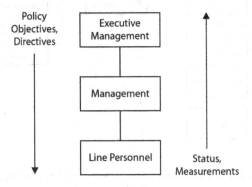

Roles and Responsibilities

The topic of roles and responsibilities is multidimensional; it encompasses positions and relationships on the organization chart, it defines specific job titles and duties, and it denotes generic expectations and responsibilities regarding the use and protection of assets.

Individual Roles and Responsibilities

Several roles and responsibilities fall upon all individuals throughout the organization:

- **Board of directors:** The organization's governing body is legally responsible for overseeing the organization's activities, as well as the selection, support, and review of the chief executive. In private industry, boards are composed of the organization's senior executives as well as executives from other firms, including firms with a significant investment in the organization. In government, directors are often elected. Increasingly, directors are held to a higher standard of personal responsibility regarding the management and outcomes of the organizations they lead.

- **Executive management:** The most senior managers and executives in an organization are responsible for developing the organization's mission, objectives, and goals, as well as policy. Executives are responsible for enacting security policy, which defines (among other things) the protection of assets.

- **Owner:** An owner is an individual (usually but not necessarily a manager) who is the designated owner-steward of an asset. Depending on the organization's security policy, an owner may be responsible for the maintenance and integrity of the asset, as well as for deciding who is permitted to access the asset. If the asset is information, the owner may be responsible for determining who can access and make changes to the information.

- **Manager:** Managers are, in the general sense, responsible for understanding the organization's policies and procedures and making them available to their staff members. They should also, to some extent, be responsible for their staff members' behavior.

- **User:** Users are individuals (at any level of the organization) who use assets in the performance of their job duties. Each user is responsible for how they use the asset, and each user does not permit others to access the asset in the user's name. Users are responsible for performing their duties lawfully and for conforming to organization policies.

These generic roles and responsibilities should apply across the org chart to include every person in the organization. Persons in these roles may be full-time or part-time employees, or they may be temporary workers such as contractors and consultants.

The roles and responsibilities of executives, owners, managers, and users should be formally defined in an organization's security policy.

Job Titles and Job Descriptions

A job title is a label that is assigned to a job description. A job title denotes a position in the organization that has a given set of responsibilities and that requires a certain level and focus of education and prior experience. A job description is a list of those responsibilities and required education and experience.

Exam Tip

The CISA exam may present questions that address proper procedures for the audit of a specified job title. When considering your response, think about the job role assigned to the specific title rather than focusing on the title itself. Questions that address job titles are intended to examine your understanding of their related roles—an example being the network management role associated with the network engineer title.

An organization with a program of career advancement may have a set of career paths or career ladders that model how employees may advance. For each job title, a career path will show the possible avenues of advancement to other job titles and the experience required to reach those job titles.

Job titles in IT have matured and are quite consistent across organizations. This consistency helps organizations in several ways:

- **Recruiting:** When the organization needs to find someone to fill an open position, the use of standard job titles will help prospective candidates more easily find positions that match their criteria.

- **Compensation baselining:** Because of the chronic shortage of talented IT workers, organizations are forced to be more competitive when trying to attract new workers. To remain competitive, many organizations periodically undertake a regional compensation analysis to understand the levels of compensation paid to IT workers in other organizations. The use of standard job titles makes the task of comparing compensation far easier.

- **Career advancement:** When an organization uses job titles that are consistent in the industry, IT workers have a better understanding of the functions of positions within their own organizations and can more easily plan how they can advance.

The remainder of this section includes many IT job titles with a short description (not a full job description by any measure) of the function of that position.

Virtually all organizations also include titles that denote the level of experience, leadership, or span of control in an organization. These titles may include executive vice president, senior vice president, vice president, executive director, senior director, director, general manager, senior manager, manager, and supervisor. Larger organizations will use more of these and possibly additional titles such as regional manager, district manager, group manager, or area manager.

Executive Management

Executive managers are the chief leaders and policymakers in an organization. They set objectives and work directly with the organization's most senior management to help make decisions affecting the future strategy of the organization:

- **CIO (chief information officer):** This is the title of the topmost leader in a larger IT organization.

- **CTO (chief technical officer):** This position is usually responsible for an organization's overall technology strategy. Depending on the purpose of the organization, this position may be separate from IT.

- **CRO (chief risk officer):** This position is responsible for all aspects of risk, including information risk, business risk, compliance risk, and market risk. This role is separate from IT.

- **CSO (chief security officer):** This position is responsible for all aspects of security, including information security, physical security, and possibly executive protection (protecting the safety of senior executives). This role is separate from IT.

- **CISO (chief information security officer):** This position is responsible for all aspects of information-related security. This usually includes incident management, disaster recovery, vulnerability management, and compliance. This role is usually separate from IT.

- **CIRO (chief information risk officer):** This position is responsible for all aspects of information-related risk management. The CIRO position symbolizes the risk management emphasis of information security.

- **CPO (chief privacy officer):** This position is responsible for the protection and use of personal information. This position is present in organizations that collect and store sensitive information for large numbers of persons.

- **CCO (chief compliance officer):** This position has broad responsibility for compliance, including information protection and privacy. Organizations under a heavy regulatory burden employ a CCO, who is responsible for compliance across a broad spectrum of regulations and requirements.

- **CAIO (chief artificial intelligence officer):** This position is responsible for the strategy, implementation, and governance of artificial intelligence technologies and systems within the organization. The CAIO ensures that AI initiatives align with business goals and regulatory requirements.

Software Development

Those in positions in software development are involved in the design, development, and testing of software applications:

- **Systems architect:** This position is usually responsible for the overall information systems architecture in the organization. This may or may not include overall data architecture as well as interfaces to external organizations.

- **Systems analyst:** A systems analyst is involved with the design of applications, including changes in an application's original design. This position may develop technical requirements, program design, and software test plans. In cases where organizations license applications developed by other companies, systems analysts design interfaces to other applications.

- **Software engineer/developer:** This position develops application software. Depending on the level of experience, persons in this position may also design programs or applications. In organizations that utilize purchased application software, developers often create custom interfaces, application customizations, and custom reports.

- **Software tester:** This position tests changes in programs made by software engineers/developers.

Data Management

Those in positions in data management are responsible for developing and implementing database designs and for maintaining databases:

- **Data manager:** This position is responsible for data architecture and data management in larger organizations.

- **Data scientist:** This position is responsible for employing scientific methods to gain knowledge from data.

- **Big data architect:** This position develops data models and data analytics for large, complex datasets.

- **Database architect:** This position develops logical and physical designs of data models for applications. With sufficient experience, this person may also design an organization's overall data architecture.

- **Database administrator (DBA):** This position builds and maintains databases designed by the database architect and those databases that are included as a part of purchased applications. The DBA monitors databases, tunes them for performance and efficiency, and troubleshoots problems.

- **Database analyst:** This position performs tasks that are junior to the database administrator, carrying out routine data maintenance and monitoring tasks.

Exam Tip

The roles of data manager, data scientist, big data architect, database architect, database administrator, and database analyst are distinct from the data owner. The former are IT department roles for managing data technology, whereas the data owner role governs the business use of data in information systems.

Network Management

Those in positions in network management are responsible for designing, building, monitoring, and maintaining voice and data communications networks, including connections to outside business partners and the Internet:

- **Network architect:** This position designs data and voice networks and designs changes and upgrades to networks as needed to meet new organization objectives.

- **Network engineer:** This position implements, configures, and maintains network devices such as routers, switches, firewalls, and gateways.

- **Network administrator:** This position performs routine tasks in the network such as making configuration changes and monitoring event logs.

- **Telecom engineer:** This position works with telecommunications technologies such as telecom services, data circuits, phone systems, conferencing systems, and voicemail systems.

Systems Management

Those in positions in systems management are responsible for architecture, design, building, and maintenance of servers and operating systems. This may include desktop operating systems as well.

- **Systems architect:** This position is responsible for the overall architecture of systems (usually servers), which includes both the internal architecture of a system and the relationship between systems. This position is usually also responsible for the design of services such as authentication, email, and time synchronization.

- **Systems engineer:** This position is responsible for designing, building, and maintaining servers and server operating systems.

- **Storage engineer:** This position is responsible for designing, building, and maintaining storage subsystems.

- **Systems administrator:** This position is responsible for performing maintenance and configuration operations on systems.

Operations

Those in positions in operations are responsible for day-to-day operational tasks that may include networks, servers, databases, and applications:

- **Operations manager:** This position is responsible for overall operations that are carried out by others. Responsibilities include establishing operations shift schedules, ensuring compliance with operational policies, and managing operational budgets.

- **Operations analyst:** This position may be responsible for the development of operational procedures; examining the health of networks, systems, and databases; setting and monitoring the operations schedule; and maintaining operations records.

- **Controls analyst:** This position is responsible for monitoring batch jobs, data entry work, and other tasks to make sure that they are operating correctly.

- **Systems operator:** This position is responsible for monitoring systems and networks, performing backup tasks, running batch jobs, printing reports, and other operational tasks.

- **Data entry:** This position is responsible for keying batches of data from hard copy or other sources.

- **Media manager:** This position is responsible for maintaining and tracking the use and whereabouts of backup tapes and other media.

Security Operations

Those in positions in security operations are responsible for designing, building, and monitoring security systems and security controls to ensure the confidentiality, integrity, and availability of information systems:

- **Security architect:** This position is responsible for the design of security controls and systems such as authentication, audit logging, intrusion detection systems (IDSs), IPSs, and firewalls.

- **Security engineer:** This position is responsible for building and maintaining security services and systems that are designed by the security architect.

- **Security analyst:** This position is responsible for examining logs from firewalls, intrusion detection and prevention systems, and audit logs from systems and applications. This position may also be responsible for issuing security advisories to others in IT.

- **Access administrator:** This position is responsible for accepting approved requests for user access management changes and performing the necessary changes at the network, system, database, or application level. Often, this position is carried out by personnel in network and systems management functions; only in larger organizations is user account management performed in the security or even in a separate user access department.

- **Security auditor:** This position is responsible for performing internal audits of IT controls to ensure that they are being operated properly.

The security auditor position needs to be carefully placed in the organization so that persons in this role can be objective and independent from the departments they audit. In U.S. public companies and other organizations, the internal audit function often reports directly to the audit committee of the board of directors.

Service Desk

Those in positions at the service desk are responsible for providing frontline support services to IT and IT's customers:

- **Service desk manager:** This position serves as a liaison between end users and the IT service desk department.

- **Helpdesk analyst:** This position is responsible for providing frontline user support services to personnel in the organization.

- **Technical support analyst:** This position is responsible for providing technical support services to other IT personnel and perhaps to IT customers.

Quality Assurance

Those in positions in quality assurance are responsible for developing IT processes and standards and for measuring IT systems and processes to confirm their accuracy:

- **QA manager:** This position is responsible for facilitating quality improvement activities throughout the IT organization.

- **QC manager:** This position is responsible for quality control through the testing of IT systems and applications to confirm whether they are free of defects.

Other Roles

Other roles in IT organizations include:

- **Vendor manager:** This position is responsible for maintaining business relationships with external vendors, measuring their performance, and handling business issues.

- **Project manager:** This position is responsible for creating project plans and managing IT projects.

Segregation of Duties

Information systems often process large volumes of information that is often highly valuable or sensitive. IT organizations should take measures to ensure that individuals do not possess sufficient privileges to carry out potentially harmful actions on their own. Checks and balances are needed so that high-value and high-sensitivity activities involve the coordination of two or more authorized individuals. The concept of segregation of duties (SOD), sometimes known as separation of duties, ensures that single individuals do not possess excess privileges that could result in unauthorized activities such as fraud or the manipulation, exposure, or compromise of sensitive data.

The concept of SOD has long been established in organization accounting departments, where, for instance, separate individuals or groups are responsible for the creation of vendors, the request for payments, and the remittance of payments. Since accounting personnel frequently handle checks, currency, and other payment instruments, the principles and practices of SOD controls in accounting departments are the norm.

IT departments are lagging behind somewhat, because the functions in IT are less often involved in direct monetary activities, except in some industries such as banking. But thanks to financial scandals in the 1980s and 1990s that involved the illicit manipulation of financial records and the emergence of new laws such as Sarbanes–Oxley, the need for full and formal IT-level SOD is now well recognized.

WARNING   In its most basic form, the rule of segregation of duties specifies that no single individual should be permitted or be able to perform high-value, high-sensitivity, or high-risk actions. Instead, two or more parties must be required to perform these functions.

Segregation of Duties Controls

Preventive and detective controls should be implemented to manage SOD matters. In many organizations, both the preventive and detective controls will be manual, particularly when it comes to unwanted combinations of access between different applications. However, in some transaction-related situations, controls can be automated, although they may still require intervention by others.

Examples of SOD controls include the following:

- **Transaction authorization:** Information systems can be programmed or configured to require two (or more) persons to approve certain transactions. Many of us see this in retail establishments, where a manager is required to approve a large transaction or a refund. In IT applications, transactions meeting certain criteria (for example, exceeding normally accepted limits or conditions) may require a manager's approval to be able to proceed.

- **Split custody of high-value assets:** Assets of high importance or value can be protected using various means of split custody. For example, a password to an encryption key that protects a highly valued asset can be split in two halves—one half assigned to two persons, and the other half assigned to two persons—so that no single individual knows the entire password. Banks do this for central vaults, where a vault combination is split into two or more pieces so that two or more people are required to open it.

- **Workflow:** Applications that are workflow-enabled can use a second (or third) level of approval before certain high-value or high-sensitivity activities can take place. For example, a workflow application that is used to provision user accounts can include extra management approval steps in requests for administrative privileges.

- **Periodic reviews:** IT or internal audit personnel can periodically review user access rights to identify whether any SOD issues exist. The access privileges for each worker can be compared against an SOD control matrix. Table 1.2 shows an example matrix.

When SOD issues are encountered during a review, management will need to decide how to mitigate the matter. The choices for mitigating an SOD issue include:

- **Reduce access privileges:** Management can reduce individual user privileges so that the conflict no longer exists.

- **Introduce a new control:** If management has determined that a person needs to retain privileges that are viewed as a conflict, then new preventive or detective controls need to be introduced that will prevent or detect unwanted activities. Examples of mitigating controls include increased logging to record the actions of personnel, improved exception reporting to identify possible issues, reconciliations of datasets, and external reviews of high-risk controls.

In addition to mitigating the SOD issue on a go-forward basis, a review should be performed to ensure that the SOD issue was not maliciously or unintentionally exploited.

An organization should periodically review its SOD matrix, particularly if new roles or high-value applications are added or changed.

Maintaining an Existing Program

Once an organization has an existing information security program, information security managers must operate and maintain that program. This involves monitoring the program to ensure that it remains in alignment with business objectives and the information security strategy as well as providing regular reporting to stakeholders.

TABLE 1.2 Example segregation of duties matrix identifying forbidden combinations of privileges (designated by an X)

	Management	Systems Analyst	SW Developer	SW Test	DB Admin	Systems Admin	Network Admin	Security Admin	Systems Operator	Helpdesk
Management	OK	OK	X	X	X	X	X	X	X	X
Systems Analyst	OK	OK	OK	X	X	X	X	X	X	X
SW Developer	X	OK	OK	X	X	X	X	X	X	X
SW Test	X	X	X	OK	X	X	X	X	X	X
DB Admin	X	X	X	X	OK	OK	X	X	X	X
Systems Admin	X	X	X	X	OK	OK	X	X	OK	X
Network Admin	X	X	X	X	X	X	OK	X	X	X
Security Admin	X	X	X	X	X	X	X	OK	X	X
Systems Operator	X	X	X	X	X	OK	X	X	OK	OK
Helpdesk	X	X	X	X	X	X	X	X	OK	OK

Metrics and Monitoring

Organizations evaluate their security programs through the use of metrics that assess the efficiency and effectiveness of critical security controls. Metrics are measurements that provide insight into the health of a security program both at a single point in time and on a long-term basis.

It's critical that organizations define the metrics and performance measurements they will use in advance of reporting the data. This ensures the integrity of the process and prevents cherry-picking of favorable results for reporting purposes.

Security programs use three primary types of metrics to demonstrate their effectiveness and the state of the organization's security controls. These key indicators offer program management and operational metrics that evaluate the effectiveness and efficiency of the information security program:

- Key performance indicators (KPIs) are metrics that demonstrate the success of the security program in achieving its objectives. KPIs are mutually agreed-upon measures that evaluate whether a security program is meeting its defined goals. Generally speaking, KPIs are a look back at historical performance, providing a measuring stick to evaluate the past success of the program.

- Key risk indicators (KRIs) are measures that seek to quantify the security risk facing an organization. KRIs, unlike KPIs and key goal indicators (KGIs), are a look forward instead of back. They attempt to show how much risk exists that may jeopardize the future security of the organization.

Key Performance Indicators (KPIs)

Every organization will have to define its own KPIs, but the Information Technology Infrastructure Library (ITIL) framework provides a good starting point. They offer nine KPIs that security programs may choose to leverage:

- Percentage of the decrease in security breaches reported to the service desk
- Percentage of the decrease in the impact of security breaches
- Percentage of the increase in SLAs with appropriate security clauses
- Number of preventive security measures the organization implemented in response to security threats
- Amount of elapsed time between the identification of a security threat and the implementation of an appropriate control
- Number of major security incidents
- Number of security incidents that created service outages or impairments
- Number of security test, training, and awareness events that took place
- Number of shortcomings identified during security tests

Key Risk Indicators (KRIs)

KRIs also must be customized to the needs of the organization. ISACA recommends selecting KRIs based on four criteria:

- The potential impact of the KRI, or the likelihood that the indicator will identify potential risks that are significant to the business
- The effort required to implement, measure, and support the indicator on an ongoing basis
- The reliability of the indicator as a good predictor of risk
- The sensitivity of the indicator, meaning that it is able to accurately capture variances in the risk

Selecting and monitoring a strong set of KPIs and KRIs provides business and technology leaders with a solid assessment of the state of their security programs.

Reporting

Information security managers are responsible not only for developing and monitoring the key metrics of their security programs, but also for ensuring that key stakeholders remain aware of the program's status.

One common mistake made by information security managers is to develop a dashboard or web page with updated metrics and then simply inform stakeholders that they may view those metrics whenever they like. This approach may seem open and transparent, but it suffers from two major drawbacks:

- Stakeholders who are not involved in security on a day-to-day basis are unlikely to revisit the site unless prompted to do so periodically.
- Providing metrics is only one piece of the picture. Security managers should also provide context around those metrics to explain changes and update stakeholders on the progress of the program.

Managers should compile and present reports to key stakeholders on the activities, trends, and overall effectiveness of the information security program and underlying business processes. They may do this using formal written reports, in-person or recorded briefings, and/or informal email updates. In most cases, managers will use a mixture of these methods in a manner that is appropriate for the needs and culture of their organization.

Auditing IT Governance

IT governance is more about business processes than it is about technology. This will make audits of IT governance rely more on interviews and documentation reviews than on inspections of information systems. Effective or ineffective IT governance is discernible in interviews of IT personnel as well as of business customers and end users.

Exam Tip

Governance questions on the exam will consider ISACA's COBIT strategies as the standard but will be generic enough in nature to ensure that an understanding of other common IT governance methods will remain applicable to the test-taker. Focus here on the measures and instruments used to validate the governance model.

Problems in IT governance will manifest themselves through a variety of symptoms:

- **Discontent among staff or end users:** Burned-out or overworked IT staff, low IT morale, high turnover, and malaise among end users about IT-supported systems can indicate an IT department that lacks maturity and is falling behind on its methodology or is applying Band-Aid fixes to systems.

- **Poor system performance:** Excessive incidents of unscheduled downtime, a large backlog of support tasks, and long wait times indicate a lack of attention to the quality of applications.

- **Nonstandard hardware or software:** A mix of hardware or software technologies among applications or end-user systems may indicate a lack of technology standards or the failure to enforce standards that are already in place.

- **Project dysfunction:** An IT department suffering from late projects, aborted projects, and budget-busting projects indicates a lack of program and project management discipline.

- **Highly critical personnel:** A disproportionate overreliance on a few IT personnel indicates that responsibilities are not fairly apportioned over the entire IT staff. This may be a result of a lack of training, unqualified personnel, or high turnover.

Auditing Documentation and Records

The heart of an IT audit is the examination of documentation and records. They tell the story of IT control, planning, and day-to-day operations. When auditing IT governance, the IS (information systems) auditor will need to review many documents:

- **IT charter, strategy, and planning:** These documents will indicate management's commitment to IT strategic planning as a formally required activity. Other documents that should be requested include IT steering committee meeting agendas, minutes, and decision logs.

- **IT organization chart and job descriptions:** These documents give an indication of the organization's level of maturity regarding the classification of employees and their specific responsibilities. An org chart also depicts the hierarchy of management and control. Job description documents describe detailed responsibilities for each position in the IT organization. An IS auditor's interviews should include some inquiry into the actual skills and experience of IT personnel to determine whether they correspond to their respective job descriptions.

- **HR/IT employee performance review process:** The IS auditor should review the process and procedures used for employee performance reviews. In particular, the IS auditor should view actual performance goals and review documents to see how well individual employees' goals align with IT department objectives. Further, any performance problems identified in performance reviews can be compared with documents that describe the outcomes of key IT projects.

- **HR promotion policy:** It will be helpful for the IS auditor to determine whether the organization has a policy (written or not) of promoting from within. In other words, when positions become available, does the organization first look within its ranks for potential candidates, or are new hires typically outsiders? This will influence both employee morale and the overall effectiveness of the IT organization.

- **HR manuals:** Documents such as the employee handbook, corporate policies, and HR procedures related to hiring, performance evaluation, disciplinary action, and termination should exist; reflect regular management reviews; and reflect practices that meet the organization's business needs.

- **Life cycle processes and procedures:** Processes such as the software development life cycle and change management should reflect the needs of IT governance. The IS auditor should request records from the SDLC (specifically, documents that describe specific changes to IT systems and supporting infrastructure) and change management process to see how changes mandated at the steering group level are carried out.

- **IT operations procedures:** IT operations process documents for activities such as service desk, monitoring, and computer and network operations should exist. The IS auditor should request records for these activities to determine whether these processes are active.

- **IT procurement process:** An IT organization needs to take a consistent and effective approach to the procurement process. The process should reflect management's attention to requirements development, bidding, vendor selection, and due diligence so that any supplier risks are identified and mitigated in the procurement phase and reflected in the service agreement contract. The goods and services provided by suppliers should be required to adhere to the organization's IT policies, processes, and standards; exceptions should be handled in an exception process. Records should exist that reflect ongoing attention to this process.

- **Quality management documents:** An IT organization that is committed to quality and improvement will have documents and records to support this objective.

- **Business continuity and disaster recovery documents:** These include documents such as the business impact assessment, critical assessment, and statements of impact, as well as evidence of periodic updates to recovery documentation and regular testing. Audits of business continuity and disaster recovery planning are covered in Chapter 6.

Another indication of a healthy governance system is evidence of regular review and update of all of these documents. Best practice would be to perform an annual review. Often this is found in each document's modification history, but it may also be present in a separate document management system.

Like any other facets of an audit, the IS auditor needs to conduct several interviews and walkthroughs to gain a level of confidence that these documents reflect the actual management and operations of an IT organization. These interviews should include staff from all levels of management, as well as key end users who can also attest to IT's organization and commitment to its governance program and the maturity of its processes.

The IS auditor should also review the processes related to the regular review and update of IT governance documents. Regular reviews attest to active management involvement in IT governance. The lack of recent reviews might suggest that management began a governance program but subsequently lost interest in it.

Auditing Contracts

The IS auditor who is examining IT governance needs to examine the service agreements between the organization and its key IT-related suppliers. Contracts should contain several items:

- **Service levels:** Contracts should contain a section on acceptable service levels and the process followed when service interruptions occur. Service outages should include an escalation path so that management can obtain information from appropriate levels of the supplier's management team.

- **Quality levels:** Contracts should contain specifications on the quality of goods or services delivered, as well as remedies when quality standards are not met.

- **Right to audit:** Contracts should include a right-to-audit clause that permits the organization to examine the supplier's premises and records upon reasonable notice.

- **External audits:** Contracts should include provisions that require the supplier to undergo appropriate and regular external audits. Audit reports should be available upon request, including remediation plans for any significant findings found in audits.

- **Conformance to security policies:** Suppliers should be required to provide goods or services that can meet the organization's security policies. For instance, if the organization's security policy requires specific password-quality standards, then the goods or services from suppliers should be able to meet those standards.

- **Protection and use of sensitive information:** Contracts should include detailed statements that describe how the organization's sensitive information will be protected and used. This is primarily relevant in an online, SaaS, or application service provider (ASP) model, where some of the organization's data will reside on systems or networks that are under the control of a supplier. The contract should include details that describe how the supplier tests its controls to ensure that they are still effective. Third-party audits of these controls may also be warranted, depending on the sensitivity of the information in question.

- **Compliance with laws and regulations:** Contracts should require that the supplier conform to all relevant laws and regulations, including those that the organization itself is required to comply with; in other words, compliance with laws and regulations should flow to and include suppliers. For example, if a health care organization is required to comply with HIPAA, any suppliers that store or manage the organization's health care–related information must also be required to be in compliance with HIPAA regulations.

- **Incident notification:** Contracts should contain specific language that describes how incidents are handled and how the organization is notified of incidents. This includes not only service changes and interruptions, but also security incidents. The supplier should be required to notify the organization within a specific period, and also required to provide periodic updates as needed.

- **Source code escrow:** If the supplier is a software organization that uses proprietary software as a means for providing services, the supplier should be required to deposit its software source code regularly into a software escrow. A software escrow firm is a third-party organization that will place software into a vault and release it to customer organizations in the event of the failure of the supplier's business.

- **Liabilities:** Contracts should clearly state which parties are liable for which actions and activities. They should further specify the remedies available should any party fail to perform adequately.

- **Termination terms:** Contracts should contain reasonable provisions that describe the actions to be taken if the business relationship is terminated.

Although the IS auditor may not be required to understand the nuances of legal contracts, the auditor should look for these sections in contracts with key suppliers. The IS auditor should also look for other contractual provisions in supplier contracts that are specific to any unique or highly critical needs that are provided by a supplier.

Auditing Outsourcing

When an auditor is auditing an organization's key processes and systems, those processes and systems that are outsourced require just as much (if not more) scrutiny than if they were performed by the organization's own staff using its own assets. However, it may be difficult to audit the services provided by a third-party supplier, for several reasons:

- **Distance:** The supplier may be located in a remote region, and travel to the supplier's location may be costly.

- **Lack of audit contract terms:** The organization may not have a clause in its contract with the supplier that requires cooperation with auditors. While it may be said that the organization should have negotiated a right-to-audit clause, this point may be moot at the time of the audit.

- **Lack of cooperation:** The supplier might not cooperate with the organization's auditors. Noncooperation takes many forms, including taking excessive time to return inquiries and providing incomplete or inadequate records. An audit report may include one or more findings (nonconformities) related to the lack of cooperation; this may provide sufficient leverage to force the supplier to improve its cooperation or for the organization to look for a new supplier.

In an ideal situation, a supplier undergoes regular third-party audits that are relevant to the services provided and the supplier makes those audit results available on request. It is also important for an organization to have controls and review procedures for any out-sourced processes.

Summary

IT governance is the top-down management and control of an IT organization. Governance is usually undertaken through a steering committee that consists of executives from throughout the organization. The steering committee is responsible for setting overall strategic direction and policy, ensuring that IT strategy is in alignment with the organization's strategy and objectives. The wishes of the steering committee are carried out through projects and tasks that steer the IT organization toward strategic objectives. The steering committee can monitor IT progress through a balanced scorecard.

The IT steering committee is responsible for IT strategic planning. The IT steering committee will develop and approve IT policies and appoint managers to develop and maintain processes, procedures, and standards, all of which should align with one another and with the organization's overall strategy.

Security governance is accomplished using the same means as IT governance; it begins with board-level involvement that sets the tone for risk appetite and is carried out through the chief information security officer (CISO) or chief information risk officer (CIRO), who develops security and privacy policies as well as strategic security programs, including incident management, vulnerability management, and identity and access management.

Enterprise architecture provides a meaningful way to depict complex IT environments in functional terms. The Zachman Framework is most often used to represent IT architecture in various layers of detail. Similarly, data flow diagrams illustrate the relationship between IT applications.

Risk management is the practice of identifying key assets and the vulnerabilities they may possess and the threats that may harm them if permitted. This is accomplished through a risk assessment that identifies assets, threats, and vulnerabilities in detail, and is followed by specific risk treatment strategies used to mitigate, transfer, avoid, or accept risks.

A risk assessment may be qualitative, where threats and risks are labeled on scales such as "high," "medium," and "low"; or it may be quantitative, where risks are expressed in financial terms.

Key management practices will help ensure that the IT organization will operate effectively. These practices include personnel management, which encompasses the hiring, development, and evaluation of employees, as well as onboarding and offboarding processes, and development of the employee handbook and other policies. Another key practice area is sourcing, which is the management of determining where and by whom key business processes will be performed; the basic choices are insourced or outsourced and on-site or off-site. The third key practice area is change management, the formal process whereby changes are applied to IT environments in a way that reduces risk and ensures highest reliability. The next practice area is financial management, a key area, given that IT organizations are cost-intensive and require planning and analysis to guarantee the best use of financial resources. Another practice area is quality management, where processes are carefully measured and managed so that they may be continuously improved over time. Another practice is portfolio management, which is the systematic management of IT projects, investments, and activities. The next key practice is controls management, which is oversight of the life cycle of activities related to the creation, measurement, and improvement of controls. The next practice area is security management, which encompasses several activities, including risk assessments, incident management, vulnerability management, access and identity management, compliance management, business continuity planning, and performance and capacity management.

The IT organization should have a formal management and reporting structure, as well as established roles and responsibilities and written job descriptions. Roles and responsibilities should address the need for segregation of duties to ensure that high-value and high-risk tasks are carried out by two or more persons and recorded.

Exam Essentials

Know how metrics are used to assess the efficiency and effectiveness of the information security program. Key performance indicators (KPIs) are metrics that demonstrate the success of the security program in achieving its objectives. KPIs look at historical performance. Key goal indicators (KGIs) measure progress toward defined goals. Key risk indicators (KRIs) try to quantify the security risk facing an organization. KRIs look forward at future potential risks.

Understand the roles and responsibilities for IT governance. IT executives and the board of directors are responsible for imposing an IT governance model encompassing IT strategy, information security, and formal enterprise architectural mandates. Strategic planning is accomplished by a steering committee, addressing the near-term and long-term requirements aligning business objectives and technology strategies.

Know the role that governance documents play in an organization. Policies, procedures, and standards enable validation of business practices against acceptable measures of regulatory compliance, performance, and standard operational guidelines.

Describe the purpose of a risk management program.   Risk management involves the identification of potential risks and the appropriate responses for each risk based on impact assessment using qualitative and/or quantitative measures for an enterprise-wide risk management strategy.

Know the responsibilities of IT managers.   Assigned IT management roles ensure that resource allocation, enterprise performance, and operational capabilities coordinate with business requirements by validating alignment with standards and procedures for change management and compliance with sourcing, financial, quality, and security controls.

Describe the purpose of an organizational structure.   Formal organizational structure ensures alignment between operational roles and responsibilities within the enterprise, where a separation of duties ensures individual accountability and validation of policy alignment between coordinated team members.

Understand the role of auditing in the IT governance process.   Regular auditing of the IT governance process ensures alignment with regulatory and business mandates in the evolving enterprise by ensuring that all documentation, contracts, and sourcing policies are reviewed and updated to meet changes in the living enterprise.

Review Questions

1. IT governance is most concerned with:
   A. Security policy
   B. IT policy
   C. IT strategy
   D. IT executive compensation

2. What is one of the advantages of outsourcing?
   A. It permits the organization to focus on core competencies.
   B. It results in reduced costs.
   C. It provides greater control over work performed by the outsourcing agency.
   D. It eliminates segregation of duties issues.

3. An external IS auditor has discovered a segregation of duties issue in a high-value process. What is the best action for the auditor to take?
   A. Implement a preventive control.
   B. Implement a detective control.
   C. Implement a compensating control.
   D. Document the matter in the audit report.

4. An organization has chosen to open a business office in another country where labor costs are lower and has hired workers to perform business functions there. This organization has:
   A. Outsourced the function
   B. Outsourced the function offshore
   C. Insourced the function on-site
   D. Insourced the function at a remote location

5. A company has been experiencing high IT staff turnover, long wait times for support, and discontent among end users regarding IT-supported systems. For an IT auditor, which of the following would be the most appropriate initial action to investigate these issues?
   A. Review the IT department's project management methodologies.
   B. Conduct interviews with IT personnel and end users.
   C. Analyze the organization's hardware and software standards.
   D. Evaluate the company's business continuity and disaster recovery plans.

6. An organization needs to better understand whether one of its key business processes is effective. What action should the organization consider?
   A. Audit the process.
   B. Benchmark the process.
   C. Outsource the process.
   D. Offshore the process.

7. Annualized loss expectancy (ALE) is defined as:

    A. Single loss expectancy (SLE) × annualized rate of occurrence (ARO)

    B. Exposure factor (EF) × the annualized rate of occurrence (ARO)

    C. Single loss expectancy (SLE) × the exposure factor (EF)

    D. Asset value (AV) × the single loss expectancy (SLE)

8. A quantitative risk analysis is more difficult to perform because:

    A. It is difficult to get accurate figures on the impact of a realized threat.

    B. It is difficult to get accurate figures on the probability of specific threats.

    C. It is difficult to get accurate figures on the value of assets.

    D. It is difficult to calculate the annualized loss expectancy of a specific threat.

9. During an IT governance audit, you notice that several projects have been aborted and many others have exceeded their budgets. Which document would most likely provide insight into the underlying causes of these project dysfunctions?

    A. IT procurement process records

    B. IT organization chart and job descriptions

    C. IT steering committee meeting agendas and minutes

    D. HR promotion policy documents

10. What is the purpose of a balanced scorecard?

    A. Measures the efficiency of an IT organization

    B. Evaluates the performance of individual employees

    C. Benchmarks a process in the organization against peer organizations

    D. Measures organizational performance and effectiveness against strategic goals

11. An organization has discovered that some of its employees have criminal records. What is the best course of action for the organization to take?

    A. Terminate the employees with criminal records.

    B. Immediately perform background checks, including criminal history, on all existing employees.

    C. Immediately perform background checks, including criminal history, on all new employees.

    D. Immediately perform background checks on those employees with criminal records.

12. What are the options for risk treatment?

    A. Risk mitigation, risk reduction, and risk acceptance

    B. Risk mitigation, risk reduction, risk transfer, and risk acceptance

    C. Risk mitigation, risk avoidance, risk transfer, and risk acceptance

    D. Risk mitigation, risk avoidance, risk transfer, and risk conveyance

13. An IS auditor is examining the IT standards document for an organization that was last reviewed two years earlier. What is the best course of action for the IS auditor?

    A. Locate the IT policy document and see how frequently IT standards should be reviewed.

    B. Compare the standards with current practices and make a determination of adequacy.

    C. Report that IT standards are not being reviewed often enough.

    D. Report that IT standards are adequate.

14. What is the most important step in the process of outsourcing a business function?

    A. Developing a business case

    B. Measuring the cost savings

    C. Measuring the change in risk

    D. Performing due diligence on the external service provider

15. An organization has published a new security policy. What is the best course of action for the organization to undertake to ensure that all employees will support the policy?

    A. The company CEO should send an email to all employees, instructing them to support the policy.

    B. The company should provide training on the new security policy.

    C. The company should publish the policy on an internal website.

    D. The company should require all employees to sign a statement agreeing to support the policy.

16. After completing the first year of his security awareness program, Charles reviews the data about how many personnel completed training compared to how many were assigned the training to determine whether he hit the 95 percent completion rate he was aiming for. What is this type of measure called?

    A. A KPI

    B. A metric

    C. An awareness control

    D. A return on investment rate

17. An accounting employee at Doolittle Industries was recently arrested for participation in an embezzlement scheme. The employee transferred money to a personal account and then shifted funds around between other accounts every day to disguise the fraud for months. Which one of the following controls might have best allowed the earlier detection of this fraud?

    A. Separation of duties

    B. Least privilege

    C. Defense in depth

    D. Mandatory vacation

18. Sally is developing a set of metrics that will help her organization assess changes in the threat environment and adjust their security program accordingly. What type of metrics is she developing?

   A. KMIs

   B. KGIs

   C. KRIs

   D. KPIs

19. The Acme Widgets Company is putting new controls in place for its accounting department. Management is concerned that a rogue accountant may be able to create a new false vendor and then issue checks to that vendor as payment for services that were never rendered. What security control can best help prevent this situation?

   A. Mandatory vacation

   B. Separation of duties

   C. Defense in depth

   D. Job rotation

20. Bob is developing a set of measures designed to evaluate how well the information security program in his organization is functioning. He will provide monthly reporting on these metrics, looking back at the program's functioning over the past month. What term best describes these metrics?

   A. KMIs

   B. KGIs

   C. KRIs

   D. KPIs

Chapter

2

The Audit Process

THE CERTIFIED INFORMATION SYSTEMS AUDITOR (CISA) OBJECTIVES REPRESENT 18% OF THE MATERIAL COVERED ON THE EXAM AND INCLUDE:

✓ **Domain 1: Information Systems Auditing Process**

A. Planning

    1. IS Audit Standards, Guidelines, and Codes of Ethics

    2. Business Processes

    3. Types of Controls

    4. Risk-Based Audit Planning

    5. Types of Audits and Assessments

B. Execution

    1. Audit Project Management

    2. Sampling Methodology

    3. Audit Evidence Collection Techniques

    4. Data Analytics

    5. Reporting and Communication Techniques

    6. Quality Assurance and Improvement of the Audit Process

Supporting Tasks

    1. Plan audit to determine whether information systems are protected, controlled and provide value to the organization.

    2. Conduct audit in accordance with IS audit standards and a risk based IS audit strategy.

    3. Communicate audit progress, findings, results and recommendations to stakeholders.

    4. Conduct audit follow-up to evaluate whether risks have been sufficiently addressed.

36. Utilize data analytics tools to streamline audit processes.

39. Evaluate potential opportunities and threats associated with emerging technologies, regulations and industry practices.

The topics in this chapter represent 18 percent of the CISA examination.

The information system (IS) audit process is the procedural and ethical structure used by auditors to assess and evaluate the effectiveness of the IT organization and how well it supports its overall goals and objectives. The audit process is backed up by the Information Technology Audit Framework (ITAF) and the ISACA code of ethics. The ITAF ensures that auditors will take a consistent approach from one audit to the next throughout the entire industry. This will help advance the entire audit profession and facilitate its gradual improvement over time.

Audit Management

An organization's audit function should be managed so that an audit charter, strategy, and program can be established, audits can be performed, recommendations can be enacted, and auditor independence can be assured throughout. The audit function should align with the organization's mission and goals, and the risk assessment process should work well alongside IT governance and operations.

The Audit Charter

As with any formal, managed function, the audit function should be defined and described in a charter document. The charter should clearly define roles and responsibilities consistent with ISACA audit standards and guidelines, including but not limited to ethics, integrity, and independence. The audit function should have sufficient authority so that its recommendations will be respected and implemented, but not so much power that the audit tail will wag the IS dog. An audit charter would also include statements about scope, both in terms of business units and business lines, and also about applicable regulations. For instance, an audit charter in a U.S. public company would include financially relevant systems for Sarbanes–Oxley compliance but may exclude PCI DSS.

 For additional guidance, the IS auditor can use ISACA audit standard 1001, Audit Charter, and guideline 2001, Audit Charter.

The Audit Program

The *audit program* describes the audit strategy and plans, including scope, objectives, resources, and procedures, used to evaluate controls and deliver an audit opinion. It could be said that an audit program is the plan for conducting audits over a given period.

In this case, the term *program* is intended to evoke a similar "big picture" point of view as the term *program manager* does. A program manager is responsible for performing several related projects in an organization. Similarly, an audit program is a plan for conducting several audits, types of audits, or audits of varying scope in an organization.

Strategic Audit Planning

The purpose of audit planning is to determine the activities that need to take place in the future, including an estimate of the resources (tools, budget, and staff) required to support those activities. Audit planning is just project planning for audit projects or related to audits. Annual audit plans should be shared with the applicable governing body and should align closely with an organization's short- and long-term strategic goals.

Factors That Affect an Audit

As with security planning, audit planning must consider several factors:

- **Organization's strategic goals and objectives:** The organization's overall goals and objectives should flow down to individual departments and their support of these goals and objectives. These goals and objectives will translate into business processes, technology to support business processes, controls for both the business processes and technologies, and audits of those controls. This is depicted in Figure 2.1.

FIGURE 2.1   The organization's goals and objectives translate into audit activities.

- **New organization initiatives:** Closely related to goals and objectives are new initiatives that organizations often undertake, including new products, new services, or new ways of delivering existing products and services.

- **Mergers and acquisitions:** Recent mergers and acquisitions can throw a wrench into any audit program when organizations have been grafted together; business integration objectives, no matter how simple or extensive, are also affected. A merged organization is a moving target, and planning must be done carefully to factor in business conditions during the audit.

- **Market conditions:** Changes in the product or service market may impact auditing. For instance, in a market where security is becoming more important, market competitors could decide to undergo audits voluntarily to show that their products or services are safer or better than those from competing organizations. Other market players may need to follow suit for competitive parity. Changes in the supply or demand of supply-chain goods or services can also affect audits.

- **Changes in technology:** Enhancements in the technologies that support business processes may affect business or technical controls, affecting audit procedures for those controls. An organization that moves its applications or services from on-premises locales to the cloud is a good example.

- **Changes in regulatory requirements:** Changes in technologies, markets, or security-related events can result in new or changed regulations. Maintaining compliance may require changes to the audit program. In the 20 years preceding the publication of this book, many new information security–related regulations have been passed or updated, including the Gramm–Leach–Bliley Act (GLBA), the Sarbanes–Oxley Act (SOX), the Health Insurance Portability and Accountability Act (HIPAA), the European General Data Protection Regulation (GDPR), the European Union AI Act, as well as national and state laws related to information security and privacy. Additionally, the U.S. Securities and Exchange Commission (SEC) has adopted rules that require public companies to disclose cybersecurity governance and risk management policies and procedures as well as require disclosure if an organization experiences a material cybersecurity incident.

- **Changes in standards and frameworks:** Changes in applicable standards and frameworks may directly or indirectly impact an organization's operations. Examples include PCI DSS, ISO 27001, NIST CSF, NIST SP 800-53, and NIST SP 800-171, all of which are revised from time to time. Organizations are often required to implement one or more of these standards, resulting in occasional changes in processes, procedures, configurations, and even architecture.

- **Artificial intelligence (AI):** The emergence of publicly available large language model (LLM) AI systems is revolutionizing how information workers and corporate employees work. Services like OpenAI's ChatGPT and Microsoft Copilot bring unparalleled analytical abilities to end users, making them more efficient at many tasks, while also introducing emerging risk areas that need to be addressed by various organizations.

All the changes listed here usually translate into new business processes or changes in existing business processes. Often, changes to information systems and changes to the controls supporting systems and processes are also involved.

Changes in Audit Activities

External factors may affect auditing in the following ways:

- **New internal audits:** Business and regulatory changes sometimes compel organizations to audit more systems or processes. For instance, SOX requires that U.S. publicly traded companies perform internal audits of IT systems that support financial business processes.

- **New external audits:** New regulations or competitive pressures could introduce new external audits. For example, virtually all banks and many merchants and service providers must undergo external Payment Card Industry Data Security Standard (PCI DSS) audits.

- **Market competition:** In certain industries, such as financial services, service providers are voluntarily undertaking new audits such as SOC 1 (SSAE 18 in the United States and ISAE 3402 elsewhere), SOC 2, TrustArc (formerly TRUSTe), HITECH (in the health care industry), and ISO/IEC 27001 certification, partly to support marketing claims that their security is superior to that of their competitors.

- **Increase in audit scope:** The scope of existing internal or external audits could increase to include more systems, processes, or business units.

- **Impacts on business processes:** This could take the form of additional steps in processes or procedures, or additions/changes in recordkeeping or record retention.

- **Changes in audit standards:** Also undergoing continuous improvement, general and specific audit rules occasionally change, which may alter sampling methodologies as well as audit procedures. For example, the PCI DSS 4.0 update requires penetration tests to include network segmentation validation, which can significantly increase costs and the time required for penetration testing.

- **Emergence of LLM AI systems:** The use of AI in some processes and procedures is bringing AI systems into scope (or at least into consideration). Further, many auditors use AI to augment staff auditors' capabilities.

Resource Planning

At least once per year, management needs to consider all internal and external factors affecting auditing to determine the resources required to support these activities. Resources will primarily consist of the budget for external audits and staff for internal audits. External audits also require staff resources to meet with external auditors and provide evidence.

Additional external audits usually require additional staff hours to meet with external auditors; discuss scope; coordinate meetings with process owners and managers; discuss audits with process owners and managers; discuss audit findings with auditors, process owners, and management; and organize remediation work.

Internal and external audits usually require information systems to track audit activities and store evidence. Additional audit activities may require additional capacity on these systems or new systems altogether.

Additional internal audits require all these factors, plus time for performing the internal audits themselves. All these details are discussed in this chapter and throughout this book.

Audit and Technology

ISACA auditing standards require that the auditor retain technical competence. As technology and business process innovation continue, auditors need to continue learning about new technologies, how they support business processes, and how they are controlled. As with many professions, IS auditors must undergo hours of continuing education to stay current with technological changes.

Ways that an IS auditor can update their knowledge and skills include the following:

- **ISACA training and conferences:** As the developer of the CISA certification, ISACA offers many valuable training and conference events, including:

  - ISACA North America and ISACA Europe Conferences

  - Governance, Risk, and Control (GRC) Conference

  - CMMI Conference

- **ISACA chapter training:** Many ISACA chapters offer training events so local members can acquire new knowledge and skills close to where they live.

- **University courses:** These can include both for-credit and noncredit classes on new technologies. Some universities offer certificate programs on many new technologies, which can boost an auditor's knowledge, skills, and confidence.

- **Vocational–technical training:** Many organizations offer training in information technologies, including ACI Learning, Udemy, SANS Institute, ISC2, CompTIA, ISSA, and ISACA.

- **Training webinars:** These events are usually focused on a single topic and last from one to three hours. ISACA and many other organizations offer training webinars, which are especially convenient because they require no travel, and many are provided at no cost.

- **Other security association training:** Many other security-related trade associations offer training, including ISSA (International Systems Security Association), SANS Institute, ISC2, and IIA (The Institute of Internal Auditors). Training sessions are offered online, in classrooms, and at conferences.

- **Security conferences:** Several security-related conferences include lectures and training. These conferences include those hosted by RSA, SANS, ISSA, ISC2, Gartner, and SecureWorld Expo. Many local ISACA, ISSA, and ISC2 chapters organize local conferences that include training.

Exam Tip

ISACA requires CISA certification holders to undergo at least 120 hours of training every three years (and a minimum of 20 hours per year) to maintain their certification. "Introduction" provides more information on this requirement.

Audit Laws and Regulations

Laws and regulations are some of the primary reasons organizations perform internal and external audits. Regulations on industries generally translate into additional effort on the part of target companies to track and verify their compliance. Tracking and verification are undertaken via internal auditing; new regulations sometimes require external audits. Moreover, while other factors, such as competitive pressures, can compel an organization to begin or increase auditing activities, this section discusses laws and regulations that require auditing.

Digital Transformation Brings New Regulation

Automating business processes with information systems is still a relatively new phenomenon. Modern businesses have been around for the past two or three centuries, but information systems have played a significant role in business process automation for only about the past 20 years. Before that time, most information systems supported business processes, but only in an ancillary way. Automation of entire business processes is still relatively young, and so many organizations have messed up in such colossal ways that legislators and regulators have responded with additional laws and regulations to make organizations more accountable for the security and integrity of their information systems.

Almost every industry sector is subject to laws and regulations that affect organizations' use of information and information systems. These laws are concerned primarily with one or more of the following characteristics and uses of information and information systems:

- **Security:** Some information in information systems is valuable and/or sensitive, such as financial and medical records. Many laws and regulations require such information to be protected so that unauthorized parties cannot access it, and they require that information systems be free of defects, vulnerabilities, malware, and other threats.

- **Integrity:** Some regulations are focused on the integrity of information to ensure that it is correct and that the systems it resides on are free of vulnerabilities and defects that could make or allow improper changes.

- **Privacy:** Many information systems store information that is considered private. This includes financial records, medical records, and other information about people. The extraterritorial nature of some privacy laws extends their reach and scope beyond the borders of the nations that enact them.

Computer Security and Privacy Regulations

This section contains several computer security and privacy laws in the United States, Canada, Europe, and elsewhere. The laws here fall into one or more of the following categories:

- **Computer trespass:** Some of these laws extend the concept of trespass to computers and networks, making it illegal to access a computer or network without explicit authorization.

- **Protection of sensitive information:** Many laws require the protection of sensitive information, and some include required public disclosures in the event of a security breach.

- **Collection and use of information:** Several privacy laws define the boundaries regarding the collection and acceptable use of information, particularly private information.

- **Offshore data flow:** Some security and privacy laws place restrictions or conditions on the flow of sensitive data (usually about citizens) out of a country.

- **Law enforcement investigative powers:** Some laws clarify and expand the search and investigative powers of law enforcement.

- **Artificial intelligence:** The emergence of generally available AI systems in 2022 has sparked the enactment of laws governing their use. A noteworthy example is the European Union AI Act, enacted in 2024.

The consequences of the failure to comply with these laws vary. Some laws have penalties written in as a part of the law; however, the absence of an explicit penalty doesn't mean there aren't any! Some of the results of failing to comply are as follows:

- **Damage to reputation:** Failure to comply with some laws can make front-page news, resulting in a reduction in reputation and loss of business. For example, if an organization suffers a security breach and is forced to notify customers, word may spread quickly and be picked up by news media outlets, further spreading the bad news.

- **Loss of competitive advantage:** An organization with a reputation for sloppy security may begin to see its business diminish and move to its competitors. A record of noncompliance may also result in difficulty winning new business contracts.

- **Government sanctions:** Breaking many federal laws may result in sanctions from local, regional, or national governments, including the loss of the right to conduct business.

- **Lawsuits:** Civil lawsuits from competitors, customers, suppliers, and government agencies may result from breaking some laws. Plaintiffs may file lawsuits against an organization even if there are other consequences. Large-scale violations sometimes lead to costly class action lawsuits.

- **Fines:** Monetary consequences are frequently the result of breaking laws.

- **Prosecution:** Many laws have criminalized behavior such as computer trespassing, stealing information, or filing falsified reports to government agencies. Executives and board members are sometimes found to be personally liable for security violations. Breaking some laws may result in imprisonment.

Knowledge of these consequences incentivizes organizations to develop management strategies to comply with the laws that apply to their business activities. These strategies often result in the development of controls that define required activities and events, plus analysis and internal audit to determine whether the controls effectively keep the organization in compliance with those laws. Although organizations often initially resist undertaking these additional activities, they usually accept them as a requirement for doing business and seek ways of making them more cost-efficient in the long term.

Determining Applicability of Regulations

An organization should take a systematic approach to determine the applicability of regulations and the steps required to comply with applicable regulations.

Determining applicability often requires the assistance of legal counsel, preferably an expert on government regulations and organizational experts familiar with the organization's practices.

Next, the language in the applicable law or regulation needs to be analyzed, and a list of compliant and noncompliant practices must be identified. These are then compared with the organization's practices to determine which practices are compliant and which are not. Those practices that are not compliant need to be corrected; one or more accountable individuals should be appointed to determine what is required to achieve and maintain compliance.

Another approach is to outline the required (or forbidden) practices specified in the law or regulation and then "map" the organization's relevant existing activities into the outline. Where gaps are found, the organization must develop or change processes or procedures to bring the organization into compliance.

PCI DSS: A Highly Effective Non-law

The Payment Card Industry Data Security Standard (PCI DSS) is a data security standard developed by a consortium of the major credit card brands: Visa, MasterCard, American Express, Discover, and JCB. These brands have the contractual right to levy fines and impose sanctions, such as losing the right to issue credit cards, process payments, or accept credit card payments. PCI DSS has gotten much attention, and by many accounts, it has been more effective than many state and national laws.

Regulations Are Not Always Clear

Sometimes, the effort to determine what's needed to achieve compliance is substantial. For instance, when the Sarbanes–Oxley Act was signed into law, virtually no one knew precisely what companies had to do to achieve compliance. Guidance from the Public Company Accounting Oversight Board was not published for almost a year. It took another two years before audit firms and U.S. public companies became familiar and comfortable with the basic approach to achieving compliance with the act.

Similarly, organizations still need to determine what actions they are required to take to be compliant with the European General Data Protection Regulation (GDPR) as well as the California Consumer Privacy Act (CCPA) and the California Privacy Rights Act (CPRA). Primarily, this is because laws state *what* must be done, but not *how* it must be done.

U.S. Regulations

Selected security and privacy laws and standards applicable in the United States include the following:

- Privacy Act of 1974
- Counterfeit Access Device and Computer Fraud and Abuse Act, 1984
- Computer Fraud and Abuse Act (CFAA) of 1984—This is a key law used to prosecute attackers for trespassing, malware, denial of service, and the trafficking of stolen passwords. CFAA has been amended several times.
- Electronic Communications Privacy Act (ECPA) of 1986
- Computer Matching and Privacy Protection Act of 1988
- Communications Assistance for Law Enforcement Act (CALEA) of 1994
- Economic and Protection of Proprietary Information Act of 1996
- National Infrastructure Protection Act of 1996
- Health Insurance Portability and Accountability Act (HIPAA) of 1996—Directed to the health care industry, HIPAA adds security and privacy requirements for the protection of health care–related personally identifiable information (PII) known as electronic protected health information (ePHI).
- Economic Espionage Act (EEA), 1996
- No Electronic Theft (NET) Act, 1997
- Digital Millennium Copyright Act (DMCA), 1998—This law extends the reach of copyright protection, most notably in recorded music.
- Children's Online Privacy Protection Act (COPPA) of 1998

- Identity Theft and Assumption Deterrence Act of 1998
- Gramm–Leach–Bliley Act (GLBA) of 1999—Directed to the financial services industry, GLBA adds privacy and safeguarding provisions to customer information.
- Cyberspace Electronic Security Act of 1999
- Federal Energy Regulatory Commission (FERC) with its legally binding standards
- Uniting and Strengthening America by Providing Appropriate Tools Required to Intercept and Obstruct Terrorism (USA PATRIOT) Act of 2001 (expired in 2015, succeeded by the USA Freedom Act)
- Sarbanes–Oxley Act of 2002
- Cyber Security Enhancement Act (CSEA) of 2002
- Federal Information Security Management Act (FISMA) of 2002
- Controlling the Assault of Non-Solicited Pornography and Marketing (CAN-SPAM) Act of 2003
- California privacy law SB 1386 of 2003—The first such U.S. state privacy regulation; similar laws in most other states are excluded from this list.
- Identity Theft and Assumption Deterrence Act of 2003 (revised)
- Basel II, 2004, an international accord
- Payment Card Industry Data Security Standard (PCI DSS), 2004; updated 2022
- North American Electric Reliability Corporation (NERC), 1968/2006, with its legally binding standards
- Red Flags Rule, 2008
- Health Information Technology for Economic and Clinical Health Act (HITECH) of 2009
- Executive Order (EO), "Improving Critical Infrastructure Cybersecurity," 2013
- USA Freedom Act, 2015
- Cybersecurity Information Sharing Act (CISA) of 2015
- New York Department of Financial Services (NYDFS) Cybersecurity Regulation (2017, updated in 2022)
- Executive Order (EO), "Improving the Nation's Cybersecurity," 2021
- SEC Rules on Cybersecurity Risk Management, Strategy, Governance, and Incident Disclosures, 2023

Canadian Regulations

Selected security and privacy laws and standards in Canada include:

- Interception of Communications (Section 184 of the Canada Criminal Code)
- Unauthorized Use of Computer (Section 342.1 of the Canada Criminal Code)

- Privacy Act, 1983
- Personal Information Protection and Electronic Documents Act (PIPEDA), 2000
- Protecting Canadians from Online Crime Act, 2014
- Digital Privacy Act, 2015

European Regulations

Selected security and privacy laws and standards from Europe include the following:

- Convention for the Protection of Individuals with Regard to Automatic Processing of Personal Data, 1981, Council of Europe
- Computer Misuse Act (CMA), 1990, UK
- Directive on the Protection of Personal Data (95/46/EC), 2003, European Union
- Data Protection Act (DPA) 1998, UK
- Regulation of Investigatory Powers Act 2000, UK
- Anti-Terrorism, Crime, and Security Act 2001, UK
- Privacy and Electronic Communications Regulations 2003, UK
- Fraud Act 2006, UK
- Police and Justice Act 2006, UK
- European General Data Protection Regulation (GDPR), 2016
- Data Protection Act 2018, UK—This is the UK's version of GDPR.
- European Union AI Act, 2024

Other Regulations

Selected security and privacy laws and standards from the rest of the world include:

- Cybercrime Act, 2001, Australia
- Information Technology Act, 2000, India
- Cybersecurity Law, 2017, China

ISACA Auditing Standards

ISACA has published its Information Technology Audit Framework in the ITAF: A Professional Practices Framework for IS Audit/Assurance (currently in its fourth edition and free of charge at www.isaca.org/ITAF). ITAF consists of the ISACA Code of Professional Ethics, IS audit and assurance standards, IS audit and assurance guidelines, and IS audit and assurance tools and techniques. This section discusses the Code of Professional Ethics, standards, and guidelines. The relationship between them is illustrated in Figure 2.2.

FIGURE 2.2   Relationship between ISACA audit standards, audit guidelines, and Code of Professional Ethics

Audit Guidelines
(optional)

Audit Standards
(mandatory)

Code of Ethics
(mandatory)

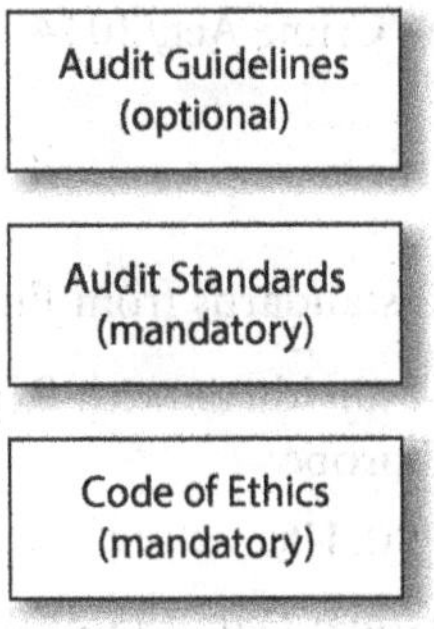

Exam Tip

ISACA does not require CISA candidates to memorize ITAF, but they should understand its importance and purpose.

ISACA Code of Professional Ethics

Like many professional associations, ISACA has published a Code of Professional Ethics. The purpose of the code is to define principles of professional behavior based on the support of standards, compliance with laws and standards, and the identification and defense of the truth.

Audit and IT professionals who earn the CISA certification must sign a statement declaring their support of the ISACA Code of Professional Ethics. If someone who holds the CISA (or any other ISACA certification) is found to violate the code, they may be disciplined and possibly lose their certification. The full text of the ISACA Code of Professional Ethics can be viewed at https://www.isaca.org/code-of-professional-ethics.

Exam Tip

The CISA candidate is not expected to memorize the ISACA Code of Professional Ethics, but must understand and be familiar with it.

ISACA Audit and Assurance Standards

The *ISACA audit and assurance standards* framework, known as the Information Technology Audit Framework (ITAF), defines minimum standards of performance related to security, audits, and the actions that result from audits. This section lists the standards and paraphrases each.

The full text of these standards is available at www.isaca.org/standards.

Exam Tip

ISACA does not require CISA candidates to memorize frameworks or audit standards, but they should understand its importance and purpose.

1001, Audit Charter

Audit activities in an organization should be formally defined in an audit charter. This should include statements of scope, responsibility, and authority for conducting audits. Senior management should support the audit charter through direct signature or by linking the audit charter to corporate policy.

1002, Organizational Independence

The IS auditor's placement in the command-and-control structure of the organization should ensure that the IS auditor can act independently.

1003, Auditor Objectivity

Behavior of the IS auditor should be independent of the auditee. The IS auditor should take care to avoid even the appearance of impropriety.

1004, Reasonable Expectation

IS auditors and assurance professionals shall have a reasonable expectation that an audit engagement can be completed according to ISACA and other audit standards, that the audit scope enables completion of the audit, and that management understands its obligations and responsibilities.

1005, Due Professional Care

IS auditors and assurance professionals shall exercise due professional care, including but not limited to conformance with applicable audit standards.

1006, Proficiency

IS auditors and assurance professionals shall possess adequate skills and knowledge on the performance of IS audits and of the subject matter being audited and shall continue in their proficiency through regular continuing professional education and training.

1007, Assertions

IS auditors and assurance professionals shall review audit assertions to determine whether they are capable of being audited, and whether the assertions are valid and reasonable.

1008, Criteria

IS auditors and assurance professionals shall select objective, measurable, and reasonable audit criteria.

1201, Risk Assessment in Planning

The IS auditor should use a risk-based approach when deciding which controls and activities to audit and the level of effort to be expended in each audit. These decisions should be documented in detail to avoid any appearance of partiality and shared with applicable governing bodies as needed.

A risk-based approach looks not only at security risks, but at overall business risk. This will include operational risk and may include aspects of financial risk.

1202, Audit Scheduling

The IS auditor should establish a strategic audit plan including short-term (within the year) and long-term (multiple years) audits and other activities.

1203, Engagement Planning

IS auditors shall perform audit planning work to ensure that the scope and breadth of an audit is sufficient to meet the organization's needs, that it is in compliance with applicable laws, and that it is risk-based.

1204, Performance and Supervision

IS auditors shall conduct an audit according to the plan and on schedule; shall supervise audit staff; shall accept and perform audit tasks only within their competency; and shall collect appropriate evidence, document the audit process, and document findings.

1205, Evidence

The IS auditor should gather sufficient evidence to develop reasonable conclusions about the effectiveness of controls and procedures. The IS auditor should evaluate the sufficiency and integrity of audit evidence, and this evaluation should be included in the audit report.

Audit evidence includes the procedures performed by the auditor during the audit, the results of those procedures, source documents and records, and corroborating information. Audit evidence also includes the audit report.

1206, Using the Work of Other Experts

An IS auditor should consider using the work of other auditors when and where appropriate. Whether an auditor can use the work of other auditors depends on several factors, including:

▪ The relevance of the other auditors' work

- The qualifications and independence of the other auditors
- Whether the other auditors' work is adequate (this will require an evaluation of at least some of the other auditors' work)
- Whether the IS auditor should develop additional test procedures to supplement the work of another auditor(s)

If an IS auditor uses another auditor's work, their report should document which portion of the audit work was performed by the other auditor, as well as an evaluation of that work.

1207, Irregularities and Illegal Acts

IS auditors should have a healthy but balanced skepticism regarding irregularities and illegal acts: The auditor should recognize that irregularities and/or illegal acts could be ongoing in one or more of the processes that they are auditing. They should recognize that management may or may not be aware of any irregularities or illegal acts.

The IS auditor should obtain written attestations from management that state management's responsibilities for the proper operation of controls. Management should disclose to the auditor any knowledge of irregularities or illegal acts.

If the IS auditor encounters material irregularities or illegal acts, they should document every conversation and retain all evidence of correspondence. The IS auditor should report any matter of material irregularities or illegal acts to management. If material findings or irregularities prevent the auditor from continuing the audit, the auditor should carefully weigh their options and consider withdrawing from the audit. The IS auditor should determine if they are required to report material findings to regulators or other outside authorities. If the auditor is unable to report material findings to management, they should consider withdrawing from the audit engagement.

1401, Reporting

The IS auditor should develop an audit report that documents the process followed, inquiries, observations, evidence, findings, conclusions, and recommendations from the audit. The audit report should follow an established format that includes a statement of scope, period of coverage, recipient organization, controls or standards that were audited, and any limitations or qualifications. The report should contain sufficient evidence to support the findings of the audit.

1402, Follow-up Activities

After the completion of an audit, the IS auditor should follow up at a later time to determine if management has taken steps to make any recommended changes or apply remedies to any audit findings.

ISACA Audit and Assurance Guidelines

ISACA *audit and assurance guidelines* contain information that helps the auditor understand how to apply ISACA audit standards. These guidelines are a series of articles that clarify the meaning of the audit standards. They cite specific ISACA IS audit standards and COBIT controls and provide specific guidance on various audit activities. Last updated in 2020, ISACA audit guidelines offer insight into why each guideline was developed and published.

The full text of these guidelines is available at www.isaca.org/itaf.

2001, Audit Charter

This guideline provides information on the following IS audit standards topics:

- Mandate
- Contents of the audit charter

2002, Organizational Independence

This guideline provides information on the following IS audit standards topics:

- Position in the enterprise
- Reporting level
- Assessing independence

2003, Auditor Objectivity

This guideline provides information on the following IS audit standards topics:

- Conceptual framework
- Threats and safeguards
- Managing threats
- Nonaudit services or roles
- Nonaudit services or roles that do not impair independence
- Nonaudit services or roles that do impair independence
- Audit charter and nonaudit services/advisory roles
- Reporting

2004, Reasonable Expectation

This guideline provides information on the following IS audit standards topics:

- Standards and regulations
- Scope
- Scope limitations
- Information
- Acceptance of a change in engagement terms
- Other considerations

2005, Due Professional Care

This guideline provides information on the following IS audit standards topics:

- Professional skepticism and competency
- Application
- Life cycle of the engagement
- Communication
- Obtaining and managing information
- Other considerations

2006, Proficiency

This guideline provides information on the following IS audit standards topics:

- Professional competence
- Evaluation
- Reaching the desired level of competence
- Other considerations

2007, Assertions

This guideline provides information on the following IS audit standards topics:

- Assertions
- Subject matter criteria
- Assertions developed by third parties
- Conclusion and report
- Other considerations

2008, Criteria

This guideline provides information on the following IS audit standards topics:

- Selection and use of criteria
- Suitability
- Acceptability
- Source
- Change in criteria during the audit engagement

2201, Risk Assessment in Planning

This guideline provides information on the following IS audit standards topics:

- Risk assessment of the IT audit plan
- Risk assessment methodology
- Risk assessment of individual engagements
- Audit risk
- Inherent risk
- Control risk
- Detection risk
- Other considerations

2202, Audit Scheduling

This guideline provides information on audit scheduling:

- Developing and maintaining an audit schedule
- Audit schedule and engagement planning

2203, Engagement Planning

This guideline provides information on the following IS audit standards topics:

- Objectives
- Scope and business knowledge
- Risk-based approach
- Documenting the audit engagement project plan and audit program
- Changes during the course of the audit

2204, Performance and Supervision

This guideline provides information on the following IS audit standards topics:

- Performing the work
- Roles and responsibilities, knowledge and skills
- Supervision
- Evidence
- Documenting
- Findings
- Other considerations

2205, Evidence

This guideline provides information on the following IS audit standards topics:

- Types of evidence
- Obtaining evidence

- Evaluating evidence
- Preparing audit documentation
- Other considerations

2206, Using the Work of Other Experts

This guideline provides information on the following IS audit standards topics:

- Considering the use of work of other experts
- Assessing the adequacy of other experts
- Planning and reviewing the work of other experts
- Evaluating the work of other experts
- Additional test procedures
- Audit opinion or conclusion
- Other considerations

2207, Irregularities and Illegal Acts

This guideline provides information on the following IS audit standards topics:

- Irregularities and illegal acts
- Responsibilities of management
- Responsibilities of practitioners
- Irregularities and illegal acts during engagement planning
- Designing and reviewing engagement procedures
- Responding to irregularities and illegal acts
- Internal reporting
- External reporting
- Other considerations

2401, Reporting

This guideline provides information on the following IS audit standards topics:

- Required contents of the audit engagement report
- Subsequent events
- Additional communication
- Other considerations

2402, Follow-up Activities

This guideline provides information on the following IS audit standards topics:

- Follow-up process
- Management's proposed actions

- Assuming the risk of not taking corrective action
- Follow-up procedures
- Timing and scheduling of follow-up activities
- Nature and extent of follow-up activities
- Deferring follow-up activities
- Form of follow-up responses
- Follow-up by practitioners on external audit recommendations
- Reporting of follow-up activities

Relationship Between Standards and Guidelines

The ISACA audit standards and guidelines have been written to assist IS auditors with audit- and risk-related activities. They are related to each other in this way:

- Standards are statements that all IS auditors are expected to follow, and they can be considered a rule of law for auditors.

- Guidelines help IS auditors better understand how ISACA standards can be implemented.

The ISACA Code of Professional Ethics encompasses the standards and guidelines for proper professional behavior.

Risk Analysis

In the context of an audit, a risk analysis is an activity used to determine the areas that warrant additional examination and analysis.

Without a risk analysis, an IS auditor is likely to follow their "gut instinct" and apply additional scrutiny in areas where they feel risks are higher. Alternatively, an IS auditor may give all areas of an audit equal weighting, putting equal resources into low-risk and high-risk areas. Either way, the result is that an IS auditor's focus is not necessarily on the areas where risks really are higher. This results in a potential disservice to the audit client.

Better audits are risk-driven. Some risk analysis methods are performed to determine which controls, activities, processes, or locations warrant additional attention and to determine the areas deemed lower risk, requiring less attention. The factors that contribute to a risk determination include:

- Value or criticality of a process, system, or business unit
- Focus of regulatory burden

- History of security events
- Results of prior audits

> Although the performance of a risk analysis is less empirical than, say, observing a system to determine whether it has specific configuration settings, assessing risk based on a risk analysis is likely more consistent than assessing it based on gut instinct. The ISACA Risk IT Framework, discussed later, details performing risk analysis.

Auditors' Risk Analysis and the Corporate Risk Management Program

Risk analysis carried out by IS auditors is distinct from risk analysis performed as part of the corporate risk management program, which uses different personnel for differing reasons. Table 2.1 compares IS audit and IS management risk analysis.

TABLE 2.1   Comparison of IS audit and IS management risk analysis

Activity	IS audit focus tendency	IS management focus tendency
Perspective	Objective	Subjective
Focus of risk assessment	All areas of potential risk	Existing controls
Identify a high risk in an existing control	Additional audit scrutiny on the control during the audit	Continue operating control
Identify a high risk; no existing control	Additional audit scrutiny on the activity as though control exists; recommend creation of control	Create and operate control*

*Many organizations do not look for risks outside of their control frameworks; this can result in risks that are overlooked altogether.

> In Table 2.1, we are not attempting to show a polarity of focus and results, but instead a tendency for focus based on the differing missions and objectives of IS audit and IS management.

The ISACA Risk IT Framework

Auditors' risk analysis and corporate risk management can be performed using the ISACA Risk IT Framework. This framework, depicted in Figure 2.3, approaches risk from the enterprise perspective, encompassing all types of business risk, including IT risk.

FIGURE 2.3 The ISACA Risk IT Framework high-level components

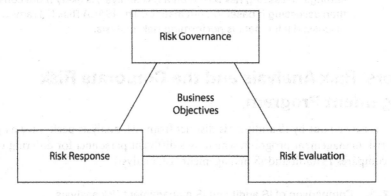

 Although the Risk IT Framework is a stand-alone standard, it is fully incorporated into the COBIT 2019 controls framework.

The Risk IT Framework consists of three primary activities:

- **Risk governance:** Ensure that IT risk is integrated into the organization's enterprise risk management (ERM) program.

- **Risk evaluation:** Provide a framework of processes for performing risk assessments against business assets and explain them in business terms.

- **Risk response:** Provide a framework of processes for responding to identified risks through reporting and risk treatment.

Like other business frameworks, the Risk IT Framework contains detailed top–down explanations of business processes. It includes references to COBIT, ISACA audit standards, and Val IT—another ISACA framework concerned with achieving business value from IT investments.

The Risk IT Framework is integrated into COBIT 2019 and available from ISACA at `www.isaca.org/cobit`.

Exam Tip
ISACA does not require CISA candidates to memorize the Risk IT Framework, but you should understand its importance and purpose.

Evaluating Business Processes

The first phase of a risk analysis is an evaluation of business processes to determine the purpose, importance, and effectiveness of business activities. Though parts of a risk analysis may focus on technology, remember that technology exists to support business processes, not the other way around.

When a risk analysis starts with a focus on business processes, it is appropriate that the auditor consider the entire process and not just the technology that supports it. When an auditor examines business processes, they must obtain all available business process documentation, including the following:

- **Charter or mission statement:** Often, an organization will develop and publish a high-level document that describes the process in its most basic terms. This usually includes why the process exists and how it contributes to the organization's overall goals and objectives.

- **Process architecture:** A complex process may have several procedures, flows of information (in electronic form or otherwise), internal and external parties that perform functions, assets that support the process, resources required, and the locations and nature of records. In a strictly IT-centric perspective, this would be a data flow diagram or an entity-relationship diagram, but starting with either would be too narrow a focus. Instead, it is necessary to look at the entire process, taking the broadest view of its functions and connections with other processes and parties.

- **Procedures:** Looking closer at the process will reveal individual procedures—documents that describe the individual steps taken to perform activities that are part of the overall process. Procedure documents usually describe who (if not by name, then by title or department) performs what functions with what tools or systems. Procedures will cite business records that may be faxes, reports, databases, phone records, application transactions, and so on.

- **Records:** Business records contain the events that take place within a business process. Records will take many forms, such as faxes, computer reports, electronic worksheets, database transactions, receipts, canceled checks, and email messages.

- **Information system support:** When processes are supported by information systems, the auditor must examine all available documents that describe information system(s) that support business processes. Examples of documentation are architecture diagrams, requirements documents (used to build, acquire, or configure the system), computer-run procedures, network diagrams, database schemas, and so on.

In addition to reviewing documentation, the auditor must interview personnel involved with each process to describe their understanding of the process, its procedures, and other relevant details. The auditor can then compare individual descriptions with details in process and procedure documents. This will help the auditor understand how processes and procedures are performed consistently and harmoniously with documentation.

Once the IS auditor has obtained business documents and interviewed personnel, they can identify and understand any risk areas in the process.

The risk analysis method described here is similar to the risk analysis during a disaster recovery project's business impact assessment phase, covered in Chapter 5, "IT Infrastructure."

Identifying Business Risks

Identifying business risks is partly analytical and based on the auditor's experience and judgment. An auditor will usually consider both within the single activity of risk identification.

An auditor will usually perform a threat analysis to identify and catalog risks. A threat analysis is an activity whereby the auditor considers a large body of possible threats and selects those that have some reasonable possibility of occurrence, however small. In a threat analysis, the auditor will consider each threat and document some facts about each, including:

- Probability of occurrence: This may be expressed in qualitative (high, medium, low) or quantitative (percentage or number of times per year) terms. The probability should be as realistic as possible, recognizing that actuarial data on business risk is difficult to obtain and interpret. An experienced auditor's judgment is required to establish a reasonable probability.

- Impact: This is a short description, from a few words to a couple of sentences, of the results if the threat is actually realized.

- Loss: This is usually a quantified and estimated loss should the threat actually occur. This figure might be a loss of revenue per day (or week or month) or the replacement cost for an asset, for example.

- Possible mitigating controls: This is a list of one or more countermeasures that can reduce the probability, impact, or both.

- Potential for transfer: This is an analysis of the potential for transferring risk to another party, such as an insurance company, software-as-a-service (SaaS) vendor, or business process outsourcer (BPO).

- Countermeasure cost and effort: The cost and effort to implement each countermeasure should be identified, either with a high, medium, or low qualitative figure or a quantitative estimate.

- Updated probability of occurrence: With each mitigating control, a new probability of occurrence should be cited. A different probability, one for each mitigating control, should be specified.

- Updated impact: With each mitigating control, a new impact of occurrence should be described. The impact may be the same for specific threats and countermeasures, but for some threats, it may be different. For example, for a threat of fire, a mitigating control may be an inert gas fire suppression system. The new impact (probably just downtime and cleanup) will differ significantly from the initial impact (probably water damage from a sprinkler system).

The auditor will put all this information into a chart (or electronic spreadsheet) to permit further analysis and establish conclusions—primarily, which threats are most likely to occur, and which have the greatest potential impact on the organization.

Because auditors are not usually expected to suggest solutions to risks, they sometimes forego countermeasures analysis. A more likely outcome is the identification of high-risk controls that warrant additional audit scrutiny and potential remediation. To ensure that the auditors view risk consistent with the rest of the organization, periodic alignment on risk tolerance, risk impact, and other factors is best practice to ensure that the auditor is focusing on the highest-risk areas of the company.

 Establishing a list of threats, along with their probability of occurrence and impact, depends heavily on the IS auditor's experience and the resources available to them.

Risk Mitigation

The actual mitigation of risks addressed in the risk assessment is the implementation of one or more of the countermeasures identified in the risk assessment. In simple terms, mitigation could be as easy as a minor adjustment in a process or procedure, or it could be a significant project to introduce new controls in the form of system upgrades, new components, or new procedures.

When the IS auditor conducts a risk analysis before an audit, risk mitigation may take the form of additional audit scrutiny of specific activities during the audit. Such subsequent analysis will give the IS auditor additional insight into the effectiveness of high-risk controls; a control that the auditor identified as high-risk could end up performing well, whereas other, lower-risk activities could actually cause control failures. Determining which of the two represents a higher risk to the organization requires further analysis.

Additional audit scrutiny could take several forms, including one or more of the following:

- More time spent in inquiry and observation
- More personnel interviews
- Higher sampling rates
- Additional tests
- Performing some control activities again to confirm accuracy or completeness (known as reperformance)
- Corroboration interviews
- Peer reviews of audit work

Countermeasures Assessment

Depending on the severity of an identified risk, mitigation could also take the form of countermeasures (controls and other safeguards implemented to reduce a threat or vulnerability), even before (or despite the results of) the audit itself. The countermeasure may be major or minor, and the time and effort required to implement it could range from almost trivial to a significant project.

The cost and effort required to implement a countermeasure should be determined before it is implemented. It probably does not make sense to spend $10,000 to protect an asset worth $100—unless, of course, there was considerable revenue or organizational reputation also associated with that $100 asset.

 The effort required to implement a countermeasure should be commensurate with the risk reduction expected from the countermeasure. If the cost and effort seem high, especially compared to the value of the asset being protected, a quantified risk analysis may be needed.

Monitoring

After implementing countermeasures, the IS auditor must reassess the controls through additional testing. If the control includes self-monitoring or measuring, the IS auditor should examine those records to determine whether the countermeasures have any effect.

The auditor may need to repeat audit activities to determine the effectiveness of countermeasures. For example, additional samples selected after the countermeasure is implemented can be examined, and the rate of exceptions can be compared to periods before the countermeasure's implementation.

Using AI and ML in Support of Audits

AI (artificial intelligence) and ML (machine learning) systems are proving to be quite helpful in making information workers more effective and/or efficient in their routine work. IS auditors familiar with LLM AI systems such as ChatGPT, Copilot, Gemini, and Claude would benefit from their use in IS audits during planning, prioritization, analysis, and reporting. Before using AI or ML in support of audits, IS auditors should consider the following:

- Before using AI/ML systems to assist with audit operations, IS auditors need to be mindful of their organization's AI policy, to ensure that the use of AI/ML systems is safe, legal, ethical, and unbiased, and does not compromise the confidentiality of information. IS auditors should ensure the integrity of information input to an AI system (thereby avoiding "garbage in, garbage out").

- Fact-check all outputs from an AI system to ensure accuracy and completeness.

- Keep a "human in the loop" when an AI system makes decisions, such as sample selection.

- Use only those AI/ML algorithms that are "explainable," so that both auditor and auditee understand the output from AI/ML systems.
- Confirm that policy in both the audit organization and the audit client organization permits the use of AI/ML, and with what stipulations.
- Confirm that any use of AI in any particular audit is permitted.
- Disclose to auditees all uses of AI/ML in audits.

The use of AI and ML in support of IS auditing brings several benefits, including:

- Fraud and anomaly detection
- Rapid transaction sampling
- Rapid analysis of samples
- Analysis of large datasets
- Rapid report creation and report QA

Controls

Controls are the policies, procedures, mechanisms, systems, and other measures designed to reduce risk and assure desired outcomes. An organization develops controls to ensure that its business objectives will be met, risks will be reduced, and errors will be prevented or corrected.

Controls are used in two primary ways in an organization: They are created to ensure the occurrence of desired events and to help prevent unwanted events.

Control Classification

Several types, classes, and categories of controls are discussed in this section. Figure 2.4 depicts this control classification.

FIGURE 2.4 Control classification shows types, classes, and categories of controls.

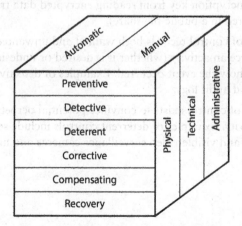

Types of Controls

The three types of controls are physical, technical, and administrative:

- **Physical:** These types of controls exist in the tangible, physical world. Examples of physical controls are video surveillance, bollards, and fences.

- **Technical:** Sometimes called logical controls, these controls are implemented as information systems and are usually intangible. Examples of technical controls are encryption, computer access controls, and audit logs.

- **Administrative:** Also referred to as managerial controls, these are the policies and procedures that require or forbid certain activities. Examples of an administrative control are change management procedures and a policy prohibiting personal use of corporate information systems.

Exam Tip

ISACA does not expressly use the terms "type," "class," or "category" to describe and distinguish the variety of controls and their essential characteristics. These terms are used in this book to highlight the multidimensional nature of controls and how they can be understood and classified. Like other constructs, these models better enable us to envision how controls operate and are used.

Classes of Controls

There are six classes of controls:

- **Preventive:** This type of control is used to prevent the occurrence of an unwanted event. Examples of preventive controls are computer login screens (which prevent unauthorized persons from accessing information), keycard systems (which prevent unauthorized persons from entering a building or workspace), and encryption (which prevents persons lacking an encryption key from reading encrypted data transmitted over an open network or stored in a public file share).

- **Detective:** This type of control records both wanted and unwanted events. A detective control cannot enforce an activity (whether it is desired or undesired) but can only record whether and how the event occurred. Examples of detective controls include video surveillance and audit logs.

- **Deterrent:** This type of control exists to convince potential perpetrators not to perform some unwanted activity. Examples of deterrent controls include security guards, guard dogs, warning signs, and visible video surveillance cameras and monitors.

Auditors and security professionals usually prefer preventive controls over detective controls, because preventive controls actually block unwanted events. Likewise, auditors prefer detective controls to deterrent controls, because detective controls record events whereas deterrent controls do not. However, there are often circumstances where cost, resources, or technical limitations force an organization to accept a detective control when it would prefer a preventive one. For example, there is no practical way to build a control to prevent criminals from entering a bank. Still, a detective control (video surveillance) would record what they did after their arrival.

- **Corrective:** This type of control is activated (manually or automatically) after an unwanted event has occurred. An example of a corrective control is improving a process that was found to be defective.

- **Compensating:** This type of control is enacted because some other direct control cannot be used. For example, a video surveillance system can be a compensating control when it is implemented to compensate for the lack of a more robust detective control, such as a keycard access system. A compensating control addresses the risk related to the original control. The PCI DSS requires compensating controls when a control cannot be implemented for business, technical, or economic reasons.

- **Recovery:** This type of control is used to restore the state of a system or asset to its pre-incident state. An example of a recovery control is using a tool to remove a virus from a computer.

Auditors need to understand one key difference between preventive and deterrent controls: A deterrent control requires knowledge of the control by the potential violator, and it works only if they know it exists; a preventive control works regardless of whether the potential violator is aware of it.

In a well-designed control environment, there should be a mixture of preventive and detective controls, especially in new and emerging risk areas in cybersecurity. Due to the continuous evolution of cybercriminals, it is important for an organization to establish both preventive controls to prevent a breach and detective controls to the extent that the preventive controls are not adequate or do not effectively prevent a breach.

Many controls can be included in more than one class. For example, a video surveillance camera can be considered both a detective control (because it is part of a system that records events) and a deterrent control (because its visibility is designed to discourage persons from committing unwanted acts). Also, an audit log can be considered both a detective and a compensating control—detective because it records events and compensating because it may compensate for the lack of more robust preventive control, such as user IDs and password access control. In addition, the organization of controls described in this section does not follow any published standard.

Categories of Controls

There are two categories of controls:

- **Automatic:** This type of control performs its function with little or no human judgment or decision making. Examples of automatic controls include a login page on an application that cannot be circumvented and a security door that automatically locks after someone walks through the doorway.

- **Manual:** This type of control requires a human to operate it. It may be subject to a higher rate of errors than an automatic control. An example of a manual control is a monthly review of computer user activity.

> IS auditors and security professionals often prefer automatic controls to manual ones, because automatic controls are typically more reliable and less prone to error. However, there are often circumstances in which an organization must settle for a manual control because of cost or some other factor, such as the requirement for human decision and intervention, perhaps during an emergency or disaster.

Internal Control Objectives

Internal control objectives are statements of desired states or outcomes from business operations. Example control objectives include:

- Protection of IT assets
- Accuracy of transactions
- Confidentiality and privacy
- Availability of IT systems
- Controlled changes to IT systems
- Compliance with corporate policies
- Compliance with applicable laws, regulations, and standards

Control objectives are the foundation for controls. For each control objective, one or more controls will exist to ensure the realization of the control objective. For example, the "Availability of IT Systems" control objective will be met with several controls, including:

- IT systems will be continuously monitored, and any interruptions in availability will result in alerts sent to appropriate personnel.
- IT systems will have resource-measuring capabilities.
- IT management will review capacity reports monthly and adjust resources accordingly.
- IT systems will have antimalware controls that are monitored by appropriate staff.

Together, these four (or more) controls contribute to the overall control objective of IT system availability. Similarly, the other control objectives will have one or more controls to ensure their realization.

 Control objectives should be established before the controls themselves.

IS Control Objectives

IS control objectives resemble ordinary control objectives but exist in the context of information systems. Examples of IS control objectives include:

- Protection of information from unauthorized personnel
- Protection of information from unauthorized modification
- Integrity of operating systems
- Controlled and managed changes to information systems
- Controlled and managed development of application software

An organization may have several additional IS control objectives on other essential topics such as malware, availability, and resource management.

Like ordinary control objectives, IS control objectives will be supported by one or more controls.

Exam Tip

CISA candidates are not required to memorize COBIT or other frameworks, but familiarity with them will help the CISA candidate understand how they contribute to effective IT governance and control.

The COBIT 2019 Controls Framework

To ensure that IT is aligned with business objectives, the COBIT 2019 controls framework of five principles and 40 control objectives is an industry-wide standard. The six principles are:

- Provide Stakeholder Value
- Holistic Approach
- Dynamic Governance Systems
- Governance Distinct from Management

- Tailored to Enterprise Needs

- End-to-End Governance System

COBIT 2019 contains more than 1,200 control activities to support these principles.

Established in 1996 by ISACA and the IT Governance Institute, COBIT is the result of industry-wide consensus by managers, auditors, and IT users. Today, COBIT 2019 is accepted as a best-practices IT process and control framework.

Starting with version 5 and continuing with COBIT 2019, COBIT has absorbed ISACA's Risk IT Framework and Val IT Framework.

General Computing Controls

An IS organization supporting many applications and services will generally have some controls specific to each application. However, it will also have a set of controls, usually called general computing controls (GCCs), that apply to all its applications and services.

An organization's GCCs are general and are often implemented in different ways on different information systems, based on their individual capabilities and limitations, as well as applicability. Examples of GCCs include:

- Applications require unique user IDs and strong passwords.

- Passwords are encrypted while stored and transmitted and are not displayed.

- Highly sensitive information, such as bank account numbers, is encrypted when stored and transmitted.

- All administrative actions are logged, and logs are protected from tampering.

Readers familiar with information systems technology will realize that these GCCs will be implemented differently across different types of information systems. Specific capabilities and limitations, for example, will result in somewhat different capabilities for password complexity and data encryption. Unless an organization uses really old information systems, the preceding four GCCs can be implemented everywhere in an IS environment. How they are implemented is the subject of the next section.

IS Controls

GCCs are implemented across a variety of information technologies. Each GCC is mapped to a specific IS control on each system type, where it is implemented. In other words, IS controls describe the implementation details for GCCs.

For example, a GCC for password management can be implemented through several IS controls—one for each type of technology platform in use in the organization: One for a central authentication service, one for Linux servers, one for network devices, and one for each application that performs its own access management. Those specific IS controls would describe implementation details that reflect the capabilities and limitations of each respective platform.

Performing an Audit

An audit is a systematic and repeatable process whereby a competent and independent professional evaluates one or more controls, interviews personnel, obtains and analyzes evidence, and develops a written opinion on the effectiveness of the control(s).

An IS audit is an audit of information systems and the processes that support them. An IS auditor interviews personnel, gathers and analyzes evidence, and delivers a written opinion on the effectiveness of controls implemented in information systems.

An auditor cannot just begin an audit. Instead, audits need to be planned events. Formal planning is required that includes the following:

- **Purpose:** The IS auditor and the auditee must establish a reason why an audit is to be performed. The purpose of a particular audit could be to determine the level of compliance with a specific law, regulation, standard, or contract. Another reason could be determining whether specific control deficiencies identified in past audits have been remediated. Another reason is to determine the level of compliance with a new law or standard the organization may be subject to in the future. It is also becoming increasingly common for an audit to benchmark a specific area of an organization against industry peers, especially in areas such as cybersecurity.

- **Scope:** The auditor and the auditee must also establish the scope of the audit. The audit's purpose often makes the scope evident, but not always. Scope may be multidimensional; it could be a given period (records spanning a start date and end date may comprise the body of evidence), geography (systems in a particular region or locale), technology (systems using a specific operating system, database, application, or other aspect), business process (systems that support specific processes such as accounting, order entry, or customer support), or segment of the organization.

- **Risk analysis:** To know which areas require the greatest amount of attention, the IS auditor needs to be familiar with the levels of risk associated with the domain being audited. Two perspectives of risk may be needed: First, the IS auditor needs to know the relative levels of risk among the different aspects of the domain being audited so that audit resources can be allocated accordingly. For example, suppose the audit is on an enterprise resource planning (ERP) system, and the auditor knows that the accounts receivable function has been problematic in the past. In that case, the IS auditor may want to devote more resources and time to the accounts receivable function than others. Second, the IS auditor needs to know about the absolute level of risk across the entire domain being audited. For example, if this is an audit to determine compliance with new legislation, the overall risk could be very high if the consequences of noncompliance are high. Both aspects of risk enable the IS auditor to plan accordingly.

- **Audit standards and procedures:** The purpose and scope of the audit may help identify the standards and define the procedures that will be required to perform the audit. Requirements for a compliance audit, for example, may involve specific rules on sample sizes and sampling techniques or call for auditors with specific qualifications to perform the audit. A compliance audit may also specify criteria for determining whether a particular finding constitutes a deficiency. There may also be rules for materiality, a topic discussed later in this chapter.

- **Resources:** The IS auditor must determine what resources are needed and available for the audit. In an external audit, the auditee (which is a client organization) may have a maximum budget figure available. For an external or internal audit, the IS auditor needs to determine the number of staff hours required and the various skills required. Other resources that may be necessary include specialized tools to gather or analyze information obtained from information systems—for example, an analysis program to process the roles and permissions in a database management system to identify high-risk areas. To a great degree, the purpose and scope of the audit will determine the resources required to complete it.

- **Schedule:** The IS auditor needs to develop an audit schedule that will allow enough time for interviews, data collection and analysis, and report generation. However, the schedule could also be a constraint, meaning the audit must be complete by a certain date. If the IS auditor is given a deadline, they will need to see how the audit activities can fit within that period. If the date is too aggressive, the IS auditor will need to discuss the matter with the auditee to make the required scope, resources, or schedule adjustments.

Chapter 9, "Conducting a Professional Audit," is devoted to a pragmatic approach to conducting professional audits.

Audit Objectives

Audit objectives are the specific goals of an audit. Generally, the objective of an audit is to determine whether controls exist and are effective in some specific aspect of an organization's business operations. An audit is generally performed as required by regulations, compliance, or legal obligations. It may also be performed as the result of a serious incident or event to ensure that post-incident improvements have been implemented and are effective.

Depending on the subject and nature of the audit, the auditor may personally examine the controls and related evidence, or the auditor may instead focus on the business content processed by the controls. In other words, if the focus of an audit is an organization's accounting system, the auditor may focus on financial transactions in the system to see how they affect financial bookkeeping. The auditor could also focus on the IS processes that support the operation of the financial accounting system. Formal audit objectives should make a distinction so that the auditor understands the objectives. This tells the auditor what to examine during the audit. Of course, knowing the type of audit to be undertaken helps, too; this is covered in the next section.

Types of Audits

The scope, purpose, and objectives of an audit will determine the type of audit that will be performed. IS auditors need to understand each type of audit, including the procedures that are used for each:

- **Operational audit:** This type of audit is an examination of the existence and effectiveness of IS controls, security controls, or business controls. The focus of an operational audit is usually the operation of one or more controls; it could concentrate on the IS management of a business process or the business process itself. The scope of an operational audit is shaped to meet audit objectives. Do note that, in this context, an operational audit is the audit of a business process supporting the information system, not the business process supported by the information system. The latter would not be an IS audit but an audit of a business process.

- **Financial audit:** This type of audit examines the organization's accounting system, including accounting department processes and procedures. The typical objective is to determine whether business controls are sufficient to ensure the integrity of financial statements.

- **Integrated audit:** This type of audit combines an operational audit and a financial audit for the auditor to gain a complete understanding of the entire environment's integrity. Such an audit will closely examine accounting department processes, procedures, records, and the IS applications that support the accounting department. Virtually every organization uses a computerized accounting system for the management of its financial records; the computerized accounting system and all the supporting infrastructure (database management system, operating system, networks, workstations, and so on) will be examined to determine whether the IS department has the entire environment under adequate control. This is the most common audit for U.S. publicly traded companies.

- **IS audit:** This type of audit is a detailed examination of most or all of an IS department's operations. It examines IT governance to determine whether IS is aligned with overall organizational goals and objectives. The audit also closely examines all major IT processes, including service delivery, change and configuration management, security management, systems development life cycle, business relationship and supplier management, and incident and problem management. This audit will determine whether each control objective and control is effective and operating properly.

- **Administrative audit:** This type of audit is an examination of operational efficiency within some segment of the organization.

- **Compliance audit:** This type of audit is performed to determine the level and degree of compliance to a law, regulation, standard, or internal control. If a particular law or standard requires an external audit, the compliance audit may have to be performed by approved or licensed external auditors; for example, a U.S. public company financial audit must be performed by a public accounting firm, and a PCI audit must be performed by a licensed QSA (qualified security assessor). If, however, the law or standard does not explicitly require audits, the organization may still want to perform one-time or regular audits to determine the level of compliance with the law or standard. Internal or external auditors may perform this type of audit, typically performed to help management better understand the level of compliance risk.

- **Forensic audit:** This type of audit is usually performed by an IS auditor or a forensic specialist in support of an anticipated or active legal proceeding. To withstand cross-examination and avoid having evidence ruled inadmissible, a forensic audit requires strict procedures, including preserving evidence and a chain of custody of evidence.

- **Fraud audit:** This audit is designed to reveal fraud and other business irregularities.

- **Functional audit:** This audit examines a software product to verify its functionality claims and compliance with requirements. It can be performed before or after a software product is leased or purchased.

- **Service provider audit:** Because many organizations outsource critical activities to third parties, these third-party service organizations will often undergo one or more external audits to increase customer confidence in the integrity of the third-party organization's services. In the United States, a System and Organization Controls (SOC) audit can be performed on a service provider's operations, and the audit report can be transmitted to customers of the service provider. The SOC standard was developed by the American Institute of Certified Public Accountants (AICPA) to audit third-party service organizations that perform financial services on behalf of their corporate customers.

Internal and External Audits

The terms "internal audit" and "external audit" refer to the relationship between auditor and auditee, not the types of audits discussed in this section.

- **Internal audit:** This audit is performed by personnel employed or contracted by the auditee organization. Internal auditors typically still have a degree of independence due to their locations on the organizational chart.

- **External audit:** This audit is performed by auditors who are not auditee employees. Typically, external auditors are employees of an audit firm.

Of course, there is some gray area here; in a large organization such as a holding company, auditors who are employees of the holding company may be considered external auditors to the auditee.

Also, some organizations outsource the internal audit function, which means that the persons performing internal audits are not the organization's employees, but consultants or contractors in a co-sourcing relationship. This can be a source of confusion, based on appearances. What matters here is the specific audit function and how it is carried out, not so much whether the persons performing it are employees.

- **Pre-audit:** While not technically an audit, a pre-audit is a readiness examination of business processes, IS systems, and business records in anticipation of an upcoming audit. Usually, an organization undergoes a pre-audit to better understand its compliance with a law, regulation, or standard before an actual compliance audit. An organization can use the results of a pre-audit to implement corrective measures, thereby improving the outcome of the real audit.

Compliance vs. Substantive Testing

IS auditors need to understand the distinction between compliance testing and substantive testing. These two types of testing are defined here:

- **Compliance testing:** This type of testing is used to determine whether control procedures have been appropriately designed and implemented and are operating correctly. For example, an IS auditor may examine business processes, such as the systems development life cycle, change management, or configuration management, to determine whether information systems environments are appropriately managed. Auditors use the term "test of design" to indicate an examination of the design of a process or control, but falling short of an examination of its effectiveness.

- **Substantive testing:** This type of testing is used to determine the accuracy and integrity of transactions that flow through processes and information systems. For instance, an IS auditor may create test transactions and trace them through the environment, examining them at each stage until completion.

IS audits sometimes involve both compliance testing and substantive testing. The established audit objectives will determine whether compliance testing, substantive testing, or both will be required.

Audit Methodology and Project Management

Like any business endeavor that involves developing a plan, identifying resources, and establishing scope, procedures, and records, audits are projects that need to be managed as such. The reasons for employing formal project planning for audits include:

- Development and management of a schedule and timelines
- Identification of resources and their availability
- Management of turnaround time for documentation and evidence requests
- Management of the time required for analysis and report writing
- Management of the time required for audit client report review, response, acceptance, and closure

Project management principles and methodologies should be used throughout an audit, including periodic status meetings and status reports, tracking of schedule and activities, and retention of records.

Auditors only sometimes make good project managers. This may be the best reason to employ the services of project managers during more extensive audits.

Audit Methodology

An *audit methodology* is the set of procedures used to accomplish a set of audit objectives. An organization that regularly performs audits should develop formal methodologies to ensure consistency, even when carried out by different personnel.

Here are the phases of a typical audit methodology:

Audit Subject   Determine the business process, information system, or other domain to be audited. For instance, an IS auditor might be auditing an IT change control process, an IT service desk ticketing system, or the activities performed by a software development department.

Audit Objective   Identify the purpose of the audit. For example, the audit may be required by a law, regulation, standard, or business contract. It may also be needed to determine compliance with internal control objectives and measure control effectiveness.

Type of Audit   Identify the type of audit to be performed. It may be an operational audit, financial audit, integrated audit, administrative audit, compliance audit, forensic audit, fraud audit, or security provider audit.

Audit Scope   The audit's business process, department, or application subject should be identified. Usually, a span of time needs to be identified so that activities or transactions during that period can be examined.

The subject of an audit is a broad definition, whereas the scope further defines precisely which processes, locations, and systems will be audited.

Pre-Audit Planning   Here, the auditor needs to obtain information about the audit that will enable them to establish the audit plan. Information needed includes:

- Location or locations that need to be visited
- A list of the applications to be examined
- The personnel to be interviewed
- The technologies supporting each application
- Policies, standards, and diagrams that describe the environment and its requirements
- Business records created by business processes and supporting systems
- Information about business processes supported by one or more systems

This and other information will enable the IS auditor to determine the resources and skills required to examine and evaluate processes and information systems. The IS auditor will be able to establish an audit schedule and will have a good idea of the types of evidence that are needed. The IS auditor may be able to make advance requests for certain other types of evidence even before the on-site phase of the audit begins.

For an audit with a risk-based approach, the auditor has a couple of options:

- Precede the audit with a risk assessment to determine which processes or controls warrant additional scrutiny.
- Gather information about the organization and historical events to discover risks that warrant additional audit scrutiny.

Audit Statement of Work   For an external audit, the IS auditor may need to develop a statement of work or an engagement letter that describes the audit purpose, scope, duration, and costs. The auditor may require written approval from the client before audit work can officially begin.

Audit Procedures Development   Using information obtained regarding audit objectives and scope, the IS auditor can now develop procedures for this audit. For each objective and control to be tested, the IS auditor can specify the following:

- A list of people to interview
- Inquiries to make during each interview
- Documentation (policies, procedures, and other documents) to be requested during each interview
- Audit tools to use
- Sampling rates and methodologies
- How and where evidence will be archived
- How evidence will be evaluated
- How findings will be reported

Communication Plan   The IS auditor will develop a communication plan to keep the IS auditor's management and the auditee's management informed throughout the audit project. The communication plan may contain one or more of the following:

- A list of evidence requested, usually in the form of a PBC (provided by client) list, typically a worksheet that lists specific documents and records, and the names of personnel who can provide them (or who provided them in a prior audit)
- Regular written status reports of activities performed since the last status report, upcoming activities, and any significant findings that may require immediate attention
- Audit progress, issues, and other matters that may be discussed in person or via conference call in regular status meetings
- Contact information for both IS auditor and auditee so that both parties can contact each other quickly if needed

Report Preparation   The IS auditor needs to develop a plan for preparing the audit report. This plan should include the report's format and content, as well as how findings will be established and documented.

The IS auditor must ensure that the audit report complies with all applicable standards, including ISACA IS audit standards.

If the audit report requires internal review, the IS auditor will need to identify the parties who will perform the review and ensure that they will be available when the IS auditor expects to complete the final draft of the audit report.

Wrap-up   The IS auditor needs to perform several tasks after the audit, including the following:

- Deliver the report to the auditee.
- Schedule a closing meeting so that the audit results can be discussed with the auditee and the IS auditor can collect feedback.
- For external audits, send an invoice to the auditee.
- Collect and archive all workpapers. Enter their existence in a document management system to retrieve them later, if needed, and to ensure their destruction when they have reached the end of their retention life.
- Update PBC documents if the IS auditor anticipates the audit will be performed again.
- Collect feedback from the auditee and convey it to audit staff as needed.

Post-audit Follow-up   After a given period (which could range from days to months), the IS auditor should contact the auditee to determine what progress the auditee has made on the remediation of any audit findings. There are several good reasons for doing this:

- It establishes a tone of concern for the auditee organization (and an interest in its success) and demonstrates that the auditor is taking the audit process seriously.
- It helps to establish a dialogue whereby the auditor can help auditee management work through any needed process or technology changes because of the audit.
- It helps the auditor understand management's commitment to the audit process and continuous improvement.
- For an external auditor, it improves goodwill and the prospect of repeat business.

An audit methodology is a process. Like any process, it should be documented in its entirety, and process documents should be reviewed periodically.

Audit Evidence

Evidence is information collected by the auditor during the audit project. The IS auditor uses the contents and reliability of the evidence obtained to reach conclusions on the effectiveness of controls and control objectives. The IS auditor needs to understand how to evaluate various types of evidence and how (and if) it can be used to support audit findings.

The auditor will collect many kinds of evidence during an audit, including:

- Observations
- Written notes
- Correspondence
- Independent confirmations from other auditors, customers, and/or vendors of the organization
- Internal process and procedure documentation
- Business records

When the IS auditor examines the evidence, they must consider several characteristics of the evidence that will contribute to its weight and reliability. These characteristics include the following:

- **Independence of the evidence provider:** The IS auditor needs to determine the independence of the party providing evidence. The auditor will place more weight on evidence provided by an independent party than on evidence provided by the auditee. For instance, phone and banking records obtained directly from phone and banking organizations will be given more credence than an organization's records (unless original statements are also provided). Some auditees may be able and inclined to "doctor" audit evidence, giving the appearance of process effectiveness.

- **Qualifications of the evidence provider:** The IS auditor needs to consider the qualifications of the person providing evidence. This is particularly true when evidence is in the form of highly technical information, such as source code, system configuration settings, or database extracts. The quality of the evidence will rest partly upon the evidence provider's ability to explain the source of the evidence, how it was produced, and how it is used. Similarly, the auditor's qualifications come into play, as they will need to be able to understand the nature of the evidence thoroughly and be familiar enough with the technology to determine its veracity. Some auditees like to "snowball" auditors by providing irrelevant or incomplete evidence, potentially to avoid disclosing details about ineffective controls.

- **Objectivity:** Objective evidence may be considerably more reliable than subjective evidence. An audit log, for instance, is entirely objective, whereas an auditee's description or opinion of the audit log is less objective.

- **Timing:** The IS auditor needs to understand the availability of evidence in the systems being audited. Certain log files, extract files, debug files, and temporary files that may be of value during the examination of the system may be available only for short periods before they are recycled or removed. Often, intermediate files are not backed up or retained for long periods. For instance, Dynamic Host Configuration Protocol (DHCP) lease logs may be available only for a few hours or days. When tracing transactions through a system during substantive testing, an IS auditor must understand early what files or intermediate data should be retrieved to analyze the data later after those intermediate files have been cycled out.

 The IS auditor must understand the sufficiency of evidence thoroughly gathered using ISACA audit standards 1203, Performance and Supervision, and 1205, Evidence.

Gathering Evidence

The IS auditor must understand and be experienced in the methods and techniques used to gather evidence during an audit. The methods and techniques used most often in audits include the following:

- **Organizational chart review:** The IS auditor should request a current organizational chart and the job descriptions of key personnel. This will help the auditor understand the management, control, and reporting structures within the organization.

- **Review of department and project charters:** These documents describe the roles and responsibilities of the IT organization overall, as well as for specific departments within IT. The charters for any recent significant projects should also be requested to understand newer objectives that could represent adjustments in organizational behavior. Suppose the audit is going to focus on applications used by other departments. In that case, the auditor should request those departments' charters and descriptions, which will help the auditor better understand those departments' functions, roles, and responsibilities. Without a formal charter, the auditor must interview personnel to gain a consistent view of a department's or project's purpose, roles and responsibilities, and authority.

- **Review of third-party contracts and service level agreements (SLAs):** Even if they are not a focus of the audit, certain third-party contracts and SLAs may provide additional insight into the workings and culture of the IS organization and specific systems and business processes.

- **Review of IS policies and procedures:** The auditor should obtain and review IS policies and process and procedure documents related to the audit. This will help the auditor better understand the tone and direction set by management and provide information about how well organized the IS organization is.

- **Review of the risk register (also known as a risk ledger):** The auditor should obtain the organization's risk register, which will provide insight into the kinds of risks the organization has identified.

- **Review of incident log:** The auditor should obtain the organization's security incident log. This will help the auditor understand the types of security incidents, including those involving in-scope processes and systems.

- **Review of IS standards:** The auditor should obtain any IS standards documents to learn about current policies for vendors, products, methods, languages, and protocols in use. The auditor should also review process and documentation standards to see how consistently the organization follows them; this will provide valuable insight into the discipline of the organization.

> **NOTE**   The IS auditor should pay attention to what IS charters, policies, and procedure documents say and don't say. They should perform corroborative interviews to determine whether these documents define the organization's behavior or if they're just window dressing. This will help the auditor understand the organization's maturity, a valuable insight that will be helpful when writing the audit report.

- **Review of IS system documentation:** The subject of the audit (directly or indirectly) is an IS application; the auditor should obtain much of the project documentation that chronicles the development or acquisition of the system. This may include the following:
  - Feasibility study
  - Functional, technical, and security requirements
  - Requests for proposals (RFPs)/requests for information (RFIs)
  - Responses from vendors (at least the one chosen)
  - Evaluation of vendor responses
  - System design documentation, including data flow diagrams, entity-relationship diagrams, database schema, and so on
  - Test plans and results
  - Implementation guides and results
  - User manuals
  - Operations manuals
  - Business continuity plans
  - Changes made since the initial release
  - Incidents and events
  - Reports of system stability, capacity, and availability

- **Personnel interviews (walk-throughs):** The IS auditor should conduct walk-through interviews with key personnel who can describe the system's function, design, use, and operation. Rather than assume that all acquired documentation is complete and accurate, the auditor should ask open-ended questions to gain additional insight into how well the system operates and how accurately the documentation describes the system in use and its operation. The auditor should develop questions in advance to keep the interview on track and ensure all topics are covered. The auditor should carefully select key questions and ask them of more than one individual to compare answers, thus providing more insight.

 Some organizations coach their auditee personnel so they do not provide any more than the minimum amount of information. An experienced auditor should recognize this and may need to get creative (without compromising ethics standards!) to get to key facts and circumstances. The IS auditor must always be polite, friendly, and professional and request the cooperation of each interviewee. They must always be truthful and never threaten any interviewee.

- **Reperformance:** When practical, an auditor will create transactions to be executed by the process being audited to confirm that the process produces expected results. Sometimes, however, reperformance is not feasible; in this case, the auditor must critically observe planned/routine transactions to confirm the expected results.

- **Passive observation:** When an IS auditor is embedded in an organization, people will "let their guard down" after they are accustomed to their presence. The auditor may be able to observe people being themselves and possibly hear or see clues that will provide clear insights into the organization's culture and tone.

Observing Personnel

An auditor is often required to obtain and understand process documentation and to be able to make judgments about the effectiveness of the process. Usually, the auditor will have to collect evidence in the form of observations to see how consistently a system's process documentation is followed. Following are some of the techniques used in observing personnel:

- **Real tasks:** The auditor should request to see some IS functions being carried out. For example, suppose an auditor is examining user access management processes. In that case, they should request to observe the people who manage user accounts to see how they perform their tasks. The auditor should compare the steps taken against procedure documentation and observe the configuration settings the interviewee has made to determine whether they are being done according to procedure documents.

- **Skills and experience:** The auditor should ask each interviewee about their career background to determine the interviewee's level of experience and maturity. This will help the auditor understand whether key responsibilities are in the hands of personnel who can handle them.

- **Security awareness:** The IS auditor should observe personnel to determine whether they follow security policies and procedures. The auditor can casually ask interviewees what they know about security procedures to determine whether the security awareness program is effective. This should implicitly be a part of every audit, even if not explicitly included in the scope. Major deviations from policy or common sense could constitute deficiencies.

- **Segregation of duties:** The IS auditor should observe personnel to determine whether adequate segregation of duties is in place. Lapses could include a user account administrator creating or changing a user account without official approval, or a systems engineer making a quick change on a system without going through the change management process, or bypassing technical controls.

An experienced IS auditor will have a well-developed "sixth sense," an intuition about people that can be used to understand the people who execute procedures.

 Many organizations have adopted a work-from-home (WFH) practice that has resulted in their employees working from home part-time or full-time; further, many employees do not reside in the organization's business locations. Hence, observing personnel often means observing them remotely through videoconferencing. Auditors must ask their auditees to show and explain what they are doing.

Sampling

Sampling is a technique used when testing an entire population of transactions is not feasible. The objective of sampling is to select a portion of a population so that the characteristics observed will reflect those of the entire population.

There are several sampling methods, including:

- **Statistical sampling:** The IS auditor uses a technique of random or semi-random selection that will statistically reflect the entire population. The auditor will have to determine the size of the sample (usually expressed as a percentage of the entire population) so that the results obtained through testing will statistically reflect the entire population, where each event in the population has an equal chance of being selected.

- **Judgmental sampling (aka nonstatistical sampling):** The IS auditor judgmentally and subjectively selects samples based on established criteria such as risk or materiality. For instance, when reviewing a list of user accounts to examine, the auditor can purposely select those whose accounts represent higher risk than others in the population.

- **Attribute sampling:** This technique is used to study the characteristics of a given population to answer the question, "How many?" The auditor selects a statistical sample and then examines the information. A specific attribute is chosen, and the samples are examined to see how many items have the characteristic and how many do not. For example, an auditor may test a list of terminated user accounts to see how many were terminated within 24 hours and how many were not. This is used to determine statistically the rate at which terminations are performed within 24 hours among the entire population.

- **Variable sampling:** A statistical technique is used to determine the characteristics of a given population to answer the question, "How much?" For example, an auditor who wants to know the total value of an inventory can select a sample and then statistically determine the total value in the entire population based on the total value of the sample.

- **Stop-or-go sampling:** This technique is used to permit sampling to stop at the earliest possible time. The IS auditor will use this technique when they believe the overall population is at low risk and has a low rate of exceptions in the overall population.

- **Discovery sampling:** This technique is used when an IS auditor tries to find at least one exception in a population. When the auditor examines a population in which even a single exception would represent a high-risk situation (such as embezzlement or fraud), they will recommend a more intensive investigation to determine whether additional exceptions exist.

- **Stratified sampling:** Here, the event population is divided into classes, or strata, based on the value of one of the attributes. Then, samples are selected from each class, and results are developed from each class or combined into a single result. An example of where this could be used is a selection of purchase orders (POs), where the IS auditor wants to make sure that some of the extremely high-value and low-value POs will be selected to determine whether any statistical difference exists in the results in different classes.

When performing sampling, the IS auditor should understand several terms related to aspects of statistical sampling techniques:

- **Confidence coefficient:** Sometimes known as the reliability factor or confidence level, this is expressed as a percentage, which is the probability that the sample selected represents the entire population. A confidence coefficient of 95 percent is considered high.

- **Sampling risk:** This is equal to one hundred minus the confidence coefficient percentage. For example, if a given sample has a confidence coefficient of 93 percent, the risk level is 7 percent (100 percent – 93 percent = 7 percent).

- **Precision:** This represents how closely the sample represents the entire population. A low-precision figure means high accuracy, and a high-precision figure means low accuracy. A smaller sample increases the precision, but the risk of exceptions in the entire population is higher.

- **Expected error rate:** This is an estimate that expresses the percentage of errors that may exist in the entire population. When the expected error rate is higher, the sample needs to be higher (because a population with a high rate of errors requires greater scrutiny). If the expected error rate is low, the sample can be smaller.

- **Sample mean:** This is the sum of all samples divided by the number of samples. This equals the average value of the sample.

- **Sample standard deviation:** This is a computation of the variance of sample values from the sample mean and measures the "spread" of values in the sample.

- **Population standard deviation:** This computes the variance of values from the mean within the entire evidence population. All other factors being equal, a larger population standard deviation means the auditor should select a larger set of samples.

- **Tolerable error rate:** This is the highest number of errors that can exist without a result being materially misstated.

 Part of the body of evidence in an audit is a description of how a sample was selected and why the particular sampling technique was used.

Agile Auditing

When we hear or see the term "agile," we generally think of the well-known iterative systems development methodology. However, some agile concepts can be applied to audits, making them more efficient and cost-effective.

Regarding development methodologies, traditional audit projects resemble the "waterfall" model, in which each major phase is completed before the start of the next phase. Agile audits, on the other hand, are more iterative, with lighter up-front planning and audit results available earlier.

While the overall scope and high-level plan of an audit are specified up front, the theme of "plan and discover as you go" reflects agile methodology versus "plan every detail before any audit activity begins," which describes traditional auditing.

 Regardless of the audit methodology chosen, ISACA IS audit standards are mandatory and must be followed.

Reliance on the Work of Other Auditors

Audit departments and external auditors, like other IT service organizations, are challenged to find qualified audit professionals who understand all aspects of organizational technologies in use. Increased specialization in IT results in auditors having increased technical knowledge in certain areas and fewer auditors with all the necessary expertise to perform an audit. Third-party service providers usually do not permit customers to audit them; instead, they rely on external auditors to conduct audits and make those audit reports available to customers. These and other factors are increasing pressure on organizations to outsource some auditing tasks (or entire audits) to third-party organizations and rely on audit reports from other sources.

When considering reliance on other auditors, you must examine many potential issues, including the following:

- Laws, regulations, standards, or contracts that may place restrictions on the use of third-party auditors

- Impact on risk

- Costs and the overhead required to manage external auditors
- Impact on audit schedule and reporting
- Impact on general and professional liability
- Audit standards and methodologies used by the third-party auditor
- Competence and experience of the third-party auditor
- Independence and objectivity of internal versus external auditors
- Methods for communication of audit issues and results
- Access by a third-party auditor to internal records and systems
- Protection and privacy of information made available to external auditors
- Background checks, nondisclosure, and other agreements for third-party audit personnel
- Audit management controls used to manage external audit activities
- Compliance and/or compatibility with audit standards, regulations, and stipulations

---

Reliance on Third-Party Audit Reports

Another familiar setting for reliance on third-party auditors occurs when an organization chooses to rely on audit reports for an external service provider rather than audit the external service provider directly. A typical example is an organization that hires a payroll services provider that has its own SOC 1 audit performed by qualified audit firms. The organization's auditors will likely rely on the payroll service provider's SOC 1 audit rather than audit the payroll service provider directly.

From the service provider's point of view, the cost to commission a SOC 1 audit and make the audit report available to its clients is less than the cost for even a small percentage of its customers to perform their own audits of the service provider's business.

IS auditors should be familiar with ISACA audit guideline 2206, Using the Work of Other Experts, and audit standard 1203, Performance and Supervision, to properly manage the work performed by external auditors.

Audit Data Analytics

Data analytics techniques enable IS auditors to select and analyze potentially large datasets and use these techniques to determine control effectiveness. In the context of IS audits, data analytics represents a variety of computational techniques used to analyze larger volumes of audit data to assist IS auditors in determining control effectiveness. This section describes these techniques.

The term "data analytics" may invoke visions of big data and data lakes used to obtain and analyze audit data, and this may be the situation at times. However, often there are far simpler situations where computational assistance is used to process data. For example, programmatically cross-referencing badge access records with system login data can help auditors detect potentially fraudulent user logins.

Audit data analytics can be performed using computer-assisted audit tools such as generalized audit software and continuous auditing. We will discuss these topics next.

Computer-Assisted Audit Techniques and Automated Workpapers

When auditing complex information systems, IS auditors often need to obtain sample data from systems with various operating systems, database management systems, record layouts, and processing methods. Auditors are turning to computer-assisted audit techniques (CAATs) to help them examine and evaluate data across these complex environments.

CAATs come in a variety of forms:

- **Direct extracts from database management systems:** With off-the-shelf systems such as Oracle Financials and PeopleSoft Financials, auditors can obtain extracts from databases supporting these and other packaged applications and perform independent analysis of the data. Analytics software can then be run against extracted data to identify transaction exceptions or fraud.

- **Test transactions:** For standard financial and business management applications, auditors can prepare test transactions that will produce known, expected results. Such tests can determine the integrity of transaction processing by comparing test results with expected results.

- **Debugging and scanning software:** Tools that reveal the details of transactions and data flow can help auditors better understand how transactions are processed by a system, to opine on their integrity and accuracy. Scanning software can identify specific data in database management systems and unstructured data stores. Security-scanning software can be used to identify known vulnerabilities in target systems. Code-scanning software can examine application source code to help reveal vulnerabilities and poor coding practices, such as embedding login credentials in source code.

- **Test scripts:** These are tools that perform a variety of functions. An auditor can provide them and run them on target systems. Such tools can reveal configuration details in operating systems, database management systems, and applications. Test scripts can also examine a broad array of automated controls.

When using CAATs, auditors need to document the evidence they obtain from systems and be able to link it to business transactions. Often, auditors will have to obtain several other items, including:

- Application source code
- Online reports that correlate captured data to transactions and results
- Database schemas

- Data flow diagrams (DFD) and flowcharts
- Sample reports
- Operations procedures

Auditors should be able to stitch all these pieces back together to show a complete picture of the details behind business transactions.

Protecting Automated Workpapers

CAATs help IS auditors by making sampling easier and capturing data with varying degrees of persistence in an organization's business application environment. That captured data will often be considered part of the body of workpapers. Like the systems that are targets of audits, audit data needs to be protected to ensure its integrity. Controls such as the following need to be enacted to safeguard automated workpapers:

- **Access control:** Only authorized persons (ideally, only the auditor) should have read access to automated workpapers.

- **Protection from tampering and damage:** Automated workpapers must be protected so that no one can change them, remove them, or threaten their integrity.

- **Backup:** Automated workpapers should be included in data backups.

- **Encryption:** Automated workpapers should be encrypted if they contain sensitive information. Effective key management procedures and controls must be in place.

Generalized Audit Software

IS auditors can use generalized audit software (GAS) to read and access data directly from database platforms and flat files. They can independently and directly acquire sample data from databases, which they can then analyze on a separate system. GAS can select samples, select data, and perform analysis on data. This can help the auditor better understand key datasets in a system and assist them in determining the integrity and accuracy of a system and the business transactions it supports.

Continuous Auditing

CAATs can also be used as part of a continuous audit approach, where samples are obtained automatically over long periods instead of during audit engagements. This represents a paradigm shift from the traditional model of periodic sampling and reporting. To be truly effective, continuous auditing should include the following:

- Frequent notifications to auditors and control owners on audit results
- Triggers to notify auditors and control owners of control failures and other exceptions

There are several types of continuous auditing:

- **Audit hooks:** These components in software applications are used to provide additional transaction monitoring and create alerts when certain events occur, such as a potentially fraudulent transaction.

- **Integrated test facility (ITF):** In a software application, additional "dummy" test records will be processed alongside actual business transactions. These additional records are usually created by auditors and are introduced during normal production transaction processing.

- **Continuous and intermittent simulation (CIS):** This technique involves connecting to a live production environment. When new transactions are introduced, they are simulated in a transaction simulator and executed in the live environment. The results of the simulation are compared to the actual transaction. In CIS, it is unnecessary to simulate every transaction; instead, a sampling technique is used to simulate selected transactions.

- **Systems control audit review file and embedded audit modules (SCARF/EAM):** This involves developing and embedding specialized audit software directly into production applications. This audit software can perform various functions, including selecting transactions to audit, additional logging, and additional checks.

Additional guidance on using CAATs and continuous auditing is in ISACA auditing guideline 2205, Evidence.

 NOTE IS auditors should ensure that the effort required to set up the CAAT environment doesn't exceed the effort required by other methods for sampling and analysis.

Reporting Audit Results

The work product of an audit project is the audit report, a written report that describes the entire audit project, including audit objectives, scope, controls evaluated, opinions on the effectiveness and integrity of those controls, and recommendations for improvement.

Although an IS auditor or audit firm will generally use a standard format for an audit report, some laws and standards require that particular reports contain specific information or be presented in a particular format. Still, some variance is expected in the structure and appearance of audit reports created by different audit organizations.

The auditor is typically asked to present findings in a closing meeting, where they can explain the audit and its results and be available to answer questions about it. The auditor may include an electronic presentation to guide the discussion of the audit.

Structure and Contents

Although there are often different methods for presenting audit findings, as well as regulations and standards that require specific content, an audit report will generally include several elements:

- **Cover letter:** The cover letter briefly describes the audit, its scope and purpose, and the auditor's findings. Often, this letter is used alone as evidence to other organizations that the audit took place.

- **Introduction:** The introduction describes the contents of the audit report.

- **Summary:** The executive summary briefly describes the audit, its purpose and scope, and the auditor's findings and recommendations.

- **Description of the audit:** The report includes a high-level description of the audit, its purpose, and its objectives.

- **Listing of systems and processes examined:** The report should contain a list of systems, applications, and business processes that were examined.

- **Listing of interviewees:** The report should contain a complete list of interviewees, including when they were interviewed, and topics discussed.

- **Listing of evidence obtained:** A detailed list of all evidence obtained, from whom, and when it was obtained is included. Electronic evidence should be described, including the time it was acquired, the system it was obtained from, and the method used to obtain it. The names of any staff members who assisted should be included.

- **Explanation of sampling techniques:** Each time the auditor performs any sampling, the techniques used should be described.

- **Description of findings and recommendations:** Detailed explanations describe the effectiveness of each control, based on evidence and the auditor's judgment. Exceptions are described in detail to demonstrate that they occurred. Information in this section may be organized according to criticality, technology in use, or business function, or it may be organized by several of these. Some audit reports do not include recommended remediation to avoid the appearance of influencing the organization in a consultative manner.

The IS auditor creating the report must ensure it is balanced, reasonable, and fair. The report should list the deficiencies and the controls that were found to be operating effectively.

The IS auditor also needs to take care when describing recommendations, realizing that any organization can produce a finite amount of change in a given period. If the audit report contains many findings, the auditor must recognize that the organization may only be able to remediate some issues after the next audit cycle. Instead, the organization will need to understand which findings should be remediated first—the audit report should provide this guidance through severity ratings on individual findings or groups of findings.

It is typically not the auditor's role to describe how an audit finding should be remediated. Auditee management decides the method(s) used to apply remediation.

Evaluating Control Effectiveness

When developing an audit report, the auditor needs to communicate the effectiveness of controls to the auditee. This reporting is often needed at several layers; for instance, the auditor may provide more detailed findings and recommendations to control owners, whereas the report for senior management may contain only the significant findings.

> ### Audit Reports Should Not Contain Surprises
>
> In a collaborative relationship between auditor and auditee, there should be a level of candor and trust so that the auditee understands where things stand throughout the audit. At the end of the audit, when the auditor presents the audit results to management, those in management should already know with reasonably good (but not necessarily absolute) accuracy what the audit report will contain.
>
> This is not to say that auditee management will be happy with the audit results. Certainly, if the report contains deficiencies, management, in its spirit of continuous improvement and quality, should not be satisfied with a less-than-perfect audit result. The point here is that auditors should not necessarily conceal their findings until the report is delivered.

One method that auditors frequently use is the development of a matrix of all audit findings, where each audit finding is scored on a criticality scale. This helps the auditor to illustrate the audit findings that are the most important and those that are less important, in the auditor's opinion. The auditor can also report on cases where an ineffective control is mitigated (fully or partially) by one or more compensating controls. For example, a system may not be able to enforce password complexity (for example, requiring upper- and lowercase letters, plus numbers and special characters), but this can be compensated for by using longer-than-usual passwords and perhaps even more frequent expiration times.

 When developing the audit report, the IS auditor should review ISACA auditing standard 1401, Reporting, and guideline 2401, Reporting, to ensure it is complete and accurate.

Other Audit Topics

This section includes essential discussions on topics related to IS audits. Topics discussed here include:

- Detecting fraud and other irregularities
- Audit risk and materiality
- Auditing and risk assessments

Detecting Fraud and Other Irregularities

Fraud is defined as an intentional deception made for personal gain or to damage another party. In corporate information systems and IS auditing, fraud is an act whereby a person discovers and exploits a weakness in a process or system for personal gain or satisfaction. An irregularity is an event that represents actions contrary to accepted practices or policy.

Management is responsible for implementing controls to prevent, deter, and detect fraud. However, no system or process is without weaknesses—worse yet, if two or more employees agree to a conspiracy to defraud the organization, the conspirators may steal from or harm the organization, at least temporarily.

Although detecting fraud and irregularities is undoubtedly not the IS auditor's primary responsibility, an IS auditor indeed has many opportunities to discover exploitable weaknesses in processes and systems that could be used to defraud the organization. The IS auditor will occasionally discover evidence of fraud while examining transaction samples during substantive testing.

When the auditor detects signs of fraud or irregularities, they should carefully evaluate these findings and then communicate them to the appropriate authorities. Precisely whom they contact will depend on the nature and structure of the organization and whether there is regulatory oversight of the organization and/or the auditor. The auditor must be extremely careful when reporting findings within the organization because the auditee could be the perpetrator or associated with the perpetrator. This logic may prompt the auditor to report findings directly to the audit committee, thereby bypassing all potential perpetrators in the organization (usually, members of the audit committee are not employees in the organization, have no role in the organization's operations, and hence are probably not among the culprits).

The auditor may be compelled to report irregularities to industry regulators or law enforcement if the organization has no audit committee or similar overseeing body.

When the auditor represents an external audit organization, they often discuss weakness, irregularity, or actual fraud with selected members of the organization to confirm their observations and agree on a plan for notifying the auditee or outside authorities.

Communication of the weakness, actual fraud, or irregularity typically begins with a phone call or face-to-face conversation, followed by a formal written letter. This will satisfy the need to inform the auditee quickly (via the phone call) and formally (via the written letter).

Audit Risk and Materiality

What if material errors in business processes remain undetected by the IS auditor? There are several ways in which this can occur, including the following:

- **Control risk:** This is the risk that a material error exists that will not be prevented or detected by the organization's control framework. For example, a manual control designed to detect unauthorized changes in an information system may fail if the person who reviews logs overlooks significant errors, irregularities, or fraud.

- **Detection risk:** This is the risk that an IS auditor will overlook errors or exceptions during an audit. Detection risk should be a part of the IS auditor's risk assessment that is carried out at the beginning of an audit; this would help the auditor focus on controls that require additional scrutiny (meaning higher sampling rates) and thereby improve the chances of detecting errors.

- **Inherent risk:** This is the risk that material weaknesses exist in business processes, and that there are no compensating controls to aid in their detection or prevention. Inherent risks exist independent of the audit.
- **Sampling risk:** This is the risk that the sampling technique will not detect transactions that are not in compliance with controls.
- **Overall audit risk:** This is the summation of all the residual risks discussed in this section.

In financial audits, materiality is established as a dollar amount threshold that is calculated in one of several possible ways, including a percentage of pretax income, a percentage of gross profit, a percentage of total assets, a percentage of total revenue, a percentage of equity, or blended methods using two or more of these.

When an auditor examines transactions and controls during an audit, a finding can be classified as a material weakness if the dollar amount of the exceptions exceeds the materiality threshold. There is, however, some latitude (more in some cases and less in others) in the auditor's judgment as to whether a finding is material.

In an IS audit, the controls being examined usually do not have dollar figures associated with them, and deficiencies are not measured against materiality thresholds in the same way. Instead, materiality in an IS audit occurs when a control deficiency (or combination of related control deficiencies) makes it possible for serious errors, omissions, irregularities, or illegal acts to occur due to the deficiency or deficiencies. Here, more than in a financial audit, the judgment of the IS auditor is critical in determining whether a finding is material.

Auditing and Risk Assessments

When assessing the effectiveness of controls in an organization, the IS auditor should take the time to understand how the organization approaches risk assessment and risk treatment.

Risk Assessment

Organizations should periodically undertake risk assessments to identify areas of risk that warrant management attention and response. A risk assessment should identify, prioritize, and rank risks. The subject of risk assessment should be those business processes and supporting information systems and infrastructures that are central to the organization's mission.

After the auditor identifies risks, the risk assessment should include one or more potential remedies, each analyzing the cost and effort required to implement it and the estimated reduction, transfer, avoidance, or acceptance of risk. When these remedies and their impact (regarding risk reduction) are ranked, the result should be a list of the organization's most effective initiatives for reducing risk. An effective risk assessment approach would be when the standard risk managing departments are aligned on strategy and approach, including internal audit, compliance, risk, and security functions.

There are two types of risk assessment: qualitative and quantitative. A qualitative risk assessment rates risks as high-medium-low or on a simple numeric scale such as 1–5 or 1–10, whereas a quantitative risk analysis rates risks in terms of actual probabilities and costs.

A quantitative risk assessment is considerably more difficult and time-consuming to perform, since it can be difficult to ascertain reasonable probabilities of threats and their financial impact. However, when seriously considering measures to reduce risk in the highest-risk areas in the assessment, the auditor will find that it sometimes makes sense to perform some quantitative risk assessment to verify which investments will make the most difference.

Risk Treatment

Once risks have been identified, risk treatment involves the decisions made and subsequent actions taken to address them. There are four possible avenues for risk treatment:

- **Risk reduction:** Sometimes known as risk mitigation, risk reduction involves changing processes, procedures, systems, or controls to reduce the probability or impact of a threat. For example, suppose the risk assessment identifies a threat of a SQL injection attack on an application. In that case, the organization can reduce risk by implementing an application firewall to block such attacks.

- **Risk transfer:** This typically involves insurance, which can compensate the organization for the financial losses or damages that would occur if the threat were realized. For example, the organization can transfer the risk of a denial-of-service attack by purchasing a cyber-insurance policy that would compensate it should an attack occur. Risk can also be transferred through business process outsourcing (BPO) and software-as-a-service (SaaS) when the service provider agrees to own related risks.

- **Risk avoidance:** Here, the organization will cease the activity associated with the risk. For instance, if the risk assessment identifies risks associated with implementing an e-commerce capability, the organization may abandon this idea, thereby avoiding e-commerce–related risks.

- **Risk acceptance:** In this case, the organization believes that the risk is acceptable and that no measures need to be taken to reduce the risk. Note that risks should not be accepted in perpetuity, but for a finite amount of time, such as one year, when the risk will be analyzed again and brought up for risk treatment.

Rarely does an organization make a decision that fits entirely within a single risk treatment category. Instead, risk treatment is usually a blended approach, where, for instance, measures are taken to reduce risk; however, even a combination of measures rarely eliminates all risk—there is usually some risk left over after some risk treatment is performed. This leftover risk is known as residual risk. And like the remaining dirt that can't be picked up with a broom and dustpan after a few successive attempts, the leftover risk is usually accepted.

Control Self-Assessment

Control self-assessment (CSA) is a methodology used by an organization to review key business objectives, risks related to achieving these objectives, and the key controls designed to manage those risks. The primary characteristic of a CSA is that the organization takes the initiative to self-regulate rather than engage outsiders, who may be experts in auditing but not in the organization's mission, goals, and culture.

Examples of CSA include:

- **Sarbanes–Oxley mandated internal audit:** U.S. public companies are required to implement an internal audit function that examines financial controls.

- **PCI Self-Assessment Questionnaire:** The Payment Card Industry requires all merchants and service providers to comply with the PCI DSS; organizations whose transaction volumes are below set thresholds can self-assess with a Self-Assessment Questionnaire (SAQ).

- **Voluntary internal audit:** Better that organizations realize that cybersecurity controls are essential to protecting their ongoing business and undertake voluntary internal audits, not because a law or regulation requires them to, but because they understand it's a suitable method for ensuring their controls remain effective.

CSA Advantages and Disadvantages

Like almost any business activity, CSA has several advantages and disadvantages that the IS auditor and others should be familiar with. This will help the organization make the most of this process and avoid common problems.

The advantages of CSA include:

- Risks can be detected earlier, because subject matter experts are involved earlier.

- Internal controls can be improved promptly.

- CSA leads to greater ownership of controls through involvement in their improvement.

- CSA leads to improved employee awareness of controls through involvement in their improvement.

- CSA may help improve relationships between departments and auditors.

The disadvantages of CSA include:

- CSA could be mistaken by employees or management as a substitute for an internal audit.

- CSA may be considered extra work and dismissed as unnecessary.

- Employees may attempt to cover up shoddy work and misdeeds.

- CSA may be considered an attempt by the auditor to shrug off responsibilities.

- Lack of employee involvement would translate to little or no process improvement.

The CSA Life Cycle

Like most continuous improvement processes, the CSA process is an iterative life cycle. The phases are as follows:

- **Identify and assess risks:** Operational risks are identified and analyzed.

- **Identify and assess controls:** Controls to manage risks are identified and assessed. If any controls are missing, new controls are designed and implemented.

- **Develop questionnaire or conduct workshop:** An interactive session is conducted to discuss risks and controls. If attending personnel are distributed across several locations, a conference call can be convened, or a questionnaire may be developed and sent to them.

- **Analyze completed questionnaires or assess workshop:** If a workshop was held, the workshop results are assessed to see what good ideas for remediation emerged. If a questionnaire is distributed, the results are analyzed to identify good risk remediation ideas.

- **Control remediation:** Using the best ideas from the workshop or questionnaire, controls are designed or altered to better manage specific risks.

- **Awareness training:** This activity is carried out through every phase of the life cycle to keep personnel informed about the various activities.

The CSA life cycle is illustrated in Figure 2.5.

FIGURE 2.5 The control self-assessment life cycle

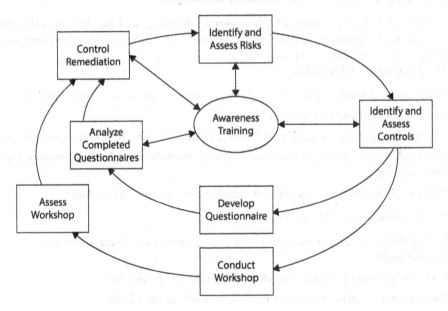

Self-Assessment Objectives

The primary objective of CSA is to transfer some of the responsibility for overseeing and monitoring control performance to the control owners. The IS auditor's role is not diminished because the IS audit still needs to test control effectiveness periodically. Still, control owners will play a more active role in auditing their controls.

Another objective of CSA is the long-term reduction in exceptions. As control owners assume more responsibility for the performance of their controls, they will strive to avoid situations where IS auditors identify exceptions. CSA gives control owners an opportunity and a process for housecleaning and improving audit results.

 NOTE The IS auditor should be involved in CSA to ensure that the CSA process is not hijacked by efficiency zealots who try to remove the controls from processes because they do not understand their significance.

Auditors and Self-Assessment

IS auditors should be involved in CSA processes that various departments conduct. The role of an IS auditor should be that of an objective subject matter expert who can guide discussions in the appropriate direction so that controls will receive the right kind of development over time.

IS auditors should resist taking too large a role in CSA, however. Responsibility for control development and maturation should lie within the department that owns the CSA process. However, if a department is new at conducting CSA, it may take some time before they are confident and competent enough to take full ownership and responsibility for the process.

Implementation of Audit Recommendations

Internal and external audits identify potential opportunities to improve control objectives, activities, and related processes. The handoff point between the completion of the audit and the auditee's assumption of control is in the portion of the audit report containing findings and recommendations. These are the imperatives the auditor recommends the auditee perform to improve the control environment.

The auditee is responsible for the implementation of audit recommendations. However, there is some sense of shared responsibility with the auditor, as the auditor seeks to understand the auditee's business to develop recommendations that can reasonably be undertaken and completed. In a productive auditor–auditee relationship, the auditor will develop recommendations using the fullest possible understanding of the auditee's business environment, capabilities, and limitations—in essence, saying, "Here are my recommendations to you for reducing risk and improving controls." The auditee, having worked with the auditor to understand their methodology and conclusions, and having been understood by the auditor, will accept the recommendations and take full responsibility for them—in essence, saying, "I accept your recommendations and will implement them." This is the spirit and intent of the auditor–auditee partnership.

In some auditor–auditee relationships, auditors do not include recommendations in their audit reports. This is often because auditors are not permitted to influence auditee business decisions. Put another way, auditors can tell an auditee organization what control exception to fix but not how to fix the control exception.

Audit Quality Assurance

An organization's auditors function as a quality assurance (QA) feedback mechanism, ensuring the integrity and effectiveness of business processes and information systems. The organization needs to monitor the audit program to ensure it continues driving quality into organization processes and systems. QA activities may include the following:

- **QA activities in some or all audits:** Prior to issuing a completed audit report to the auditee, the complete audit should be reviewed by qualified personnel, to ensure that the audit approach, methodologies, sampling, evidence requested, interpretation of evidence, and reporting are free from errors and inconsistencies. Better audit firms have formal QA procedures, and in some industries, external bodies perform QA for some or all audits conducted by an audit firm.

- **Auditor training and development:** Information technology and cybersecurity tools, techniques, products, standards, and regulations evolve rapidly. Thus, staff auditors and managers need to undertake training and pursue certifications in various relevant topics to remain current and effective.

- **Audit program oversight:** In U.S. public companies, the audit committee of the board of directors oversees and supervises the audit program. In organizations without a board of directors, company leadership must establish a supervising committee to oversee the audit program. A supervising committee should have some knowledgeable and objective outsiders to avoid unethical manipulation of the audit function.

The activities described above should be subject to formal monitoring so that the audit program's competence and independence are periodically observed, and corrective actions taken when necessary.

Summary

An organization's audit function should be defined and described in a charter. The audit program and strategy should support the organization's mission and objectives and facilitate business development and growth.

Auditors need to establish and maintain technical competence to evaluate technical controls effectively and identify technical control risks. They will need to attend periodic training in the technologies in use by the organization and in emerging technologies that the organization may use in the future.

Auditors should be aware of new laws, regulations, and standards that apply to the organizations they are auditing.

The ISACA Code of Professional Ethics defines the standards of behavior and conduct for IS auditors. The ISACA auditing standards framework defines mandatory audit standards, as well as guidelines that contain suggestions for implementing the standards. All persons holding the CISA designation must uphold the ISACA Code of Professional Ethics; violations will result in investigations and possible disciplinary actions, including expulsion.

ISACA audit standards, guidelines, and procedures provide a framework for developing an IT assurance program. The Information Technology Audit Framework (ITAF) is a complete IT assurance and audit framework that borrows elements from COBIT and ISACA audit standards, guidelines, and procedures.

IS auditors may need to perform a risk analysis as an integral part of an audit project to identify risk areas requiring additional resources. The risk analysis's results will help the auditor build a complete audit plan that includes the appropriate level of activities to be carried out during the audit.

The ISACA Risk IT Framework provides a set of processes for performing risk governance, risk evaluation, and risk response.

AI and ML can streamline audits by automating sampling, analysis, reporting writing, and other tasks. Auditors need to be aware of organizational policy and applicable laws, regulations, and standards that govern the use of AI.

IS auditors generally develop and follow an audit methodology, which ensures consistent, repeatable audits from start to finish. Often, the type of and reason for an audit will determine the methodology to be used.

Internal controls are the policies, procedures, mechanisms, systems, and other means designed to reduce risk and facilitate the achievement of business objectives. Controls are classified in several ways that describe how they are intended to control behaviors and outcomes.

Internal control objectives are statements of desired states and outcomes in the organization. They are supported by one or more controls that ensure the realization of control objectives. Controls should be measurable and are defined and enforced with processes, procedures, or automatic mechanisms within information systems. IS control objectives resemble internal control objectives but are focused on the desired states and outcomes within the context of information systems.

General computing controls (GCCs) are applied across an entire IS environment. An organization will likely have additional controls applied to individual applications or components in the environment.

An audit is the planned, methodical evaluation of controls and control objectives. A key activity is the identification and acquisition of evidence that supports the operation of controls and helps the auditor confirm the effectiveness of a control.

Evidence is information collected by the auditor during the audit. The reliability and relevance of evidence help the auditor reach sound conclusions about the effectiveness of controls and control objectives.

Sampling is the technique used when testing an entire population of transactions is not feasible. Sampling techniques must be carefully considered to represent the entire population accurately.

Agile auditing is an iterative audit methodology that may be more efficient and get audit results into the hands of control and process owners sooner than with traditional methodology.

Auditors frequently find that they must rely on the work of other auditors. A common example is service providers undertaking SOC 1 or SOC 2 audits and distributing those audit reports to their business customers. PCI DSS is another standard that includes reliance on other auditors.

Computer-assisted audit techniques (CAATs) automate the sampling and analysis of information in complex application environments. They can help auditors analyze and correlate data in ways that would be too difficult to do manually. Continuous auditing consists of samples automatically gathered over long periods.

The audit report is the work product of the audit project. It contains a summary, a description of the evidence gathered, and findings, conclusions, and potential recommendations.

In IS audits, materiality is the threshold where control deficiencies make it possible for serious errors, omissions, irregularities, or illegal acts to occur.

A control self-assessment (CSA) is an activity used by organizations to take ownership of controls and improve the implementation of controls through workshops and other activities.

Exam Essentials

Be able to explain the various categories of controls.   Controls are categorized in several ways. Detective and preventive refer to whether a control can prevent unwanted outcomes or merely detect them. Controls can be categorized as automatic or manual, which refers to whether a control is automated or must be invoked manually. Controls can be categorized as deterrent, which usually means the control is visible and exists to discourage violations. Controls can be categorized as corrective, compensating, and/or recovery, all related to actions taken when things go wrong. Finally, controls often have multiple categories. For example, a security-controlled door lock can be considered automatic, preventive, and deterrent.

Know the various techniques used in sampling.   When a set of records is too large for an auditor to examine each one, the auditor must choose a sampling technique to select the records to examine. Statistical sampling employs a strictly random selection of records. Discovery sampling is used to detect fraud. Stratified sampling is used to select samples with, for example, low, moderate, and high dollar figures. Attribute sampling involves an examination of one or more values to understand control performance, such as the time required to patch a system. Judgmental sampling is used when auditors select samples manually based on established criteria.

Be familiar with ISACA audit standards and audit guidelines.   ISACA audit standards are considered mandatory whenever a CISA-certified individual plans or performs audits. The standards are a set of audit rules that auditors must follow. ISACA audit guidelines provide additional guidance to auditors and are considered optional.

Audit plans should be at least partially risk-driven.   IS auditors generally put more audit resources into higher-risk processes and controls. The relative risk level can be determined from an up-front risk assessment, the results of prior audits, recent security events or incidents, the introduction of new processes or systems, new laws and regulations, or any combination of these factors.

AI and ML provide needed assistance to auditors examining large datasets.   Artificial intelligence (AI) and machine learning (ML) tools can streamline auditors' study of large datasets, saving time and providing additional insights. Auditors must first ensure that the use of AI/ML tools is permitted by policy and applicable laws and does not endanger the confidentiality of sensitive information.

The auditor–auditee relationship should be collaborative, not adversarial.   Too many organizations see auditors as nit-picking adversaries who point out every flaw. While it is true that the auditors' role is to objectively opine on the effectiveness of controls, a preferred mindset is to consider auditors as collaborators or partners rather than enemies.

Review Questions

1. An IS auditor is planning an audit project and needs to know which areas represent the highest risk. What is the best approach for identifying these risk areas?

   A. Perform the audit; control failures will identify the areas of highest risk.

   B. Perform the audit and then perform a risk assessment.

   C. Perform a risk assessment first, and then concentrate control tests in high-risk areas identified in the risk assessment.

   D. Increase sampling rates in high-risk areas.

2. An auditor has detected potential fraud while testing a control objective. What should the auditor do next?

   A. Notify the audit committee.

   B. Conduct a formal investigation.

   C. Report the fraud to law enforcement.

   D. Report the suspected fraud to management.

3. The possibility that a process or procedure will be unable to prevent or detect serious errors and wrongdoing is known as:

   A. Detection risk

   B. Inherent risk

   C. Sampling risk

   D. Control risk

4. The categories of risk treatment are:

   A. Risk reduction, risk transfer, risk avoidance, and risk acceptance

   B. Risk avoidance, risk transfer, and risk mitigation

   C. Risk avoidance, risk reduction, risk transfer, risk mitigation, and risk acceptance

   D. Risk avoidance, risk treatment, risk mitigation, and risk acceptance

5. An IS auditor needs to perform an audit of a financial system and wants to trace individual transactions through the system. What type of testing should the auditor perform?

   A. Discovery testing

   B. Statistical testing

   C. Compliance testing

   D. Substantive testing

6. An IS auditor is auditing the change management process for a financial application. The auditor has two primary pieces of evidence: change logs and a written analysis of the change logs performed by a generative AI system. Which evidence is best and why?

    A. The change log is best because it is subjective.

    B. The written analysis is best because it interprets the change log.

    C. The change log is best because it is objective and unbiased.

    D. The written analysis is best because it is objective.

7. Under which circumstances should an auditor use subjective sampling?

    A. When the population size is low

    B. When the auditor believes that specific transactions represent higher risk than most others

    C. When the risk of exceptions is low

    D. When statistical sampling cannot be performed

8. An IS auditor has discovered a high-risk exception during control testing. What is the best course of action for the IS auditor to take?

    A. Immediately perform mitigation.

    B. Include the exception in the report and mark the test as a control failure.

    C. Immediately inform the auditee of the situation.

    D. Immediately inform the audit committee of the situation.

9. What is the appropriate role of an IS auditor in a control self-assessment?

    A. The IS auditor should participate as a subject matter expert.

    B. The IS auditor should act as facilitator.

    C. The IS auditor should not be involved.

    D. The IS auditor should design the control self-assessment.

10. Which of the following would not be useful evidence in an IS audit?

    A. Personnel handbook

    B. Organization mission statement and objectives

    C. Organizational chart

    D. Organization's history

11. An auditor has discovered that automated workpapers were configured with read/write permissions for database administrators. What actions should the auditor take?

    A. Simply continue to rely on the automated workpapers.

    B. Note an exception and continue to rely on these automated workpapers.

    C. Recommend that permissions on automated workpapers be changed so that no personnel have write access and so that this data may be relied on in the future.

    D. Notify the board of directors or the audit committee.

12. During an audit, an auditor has discovered a process that is being performed consistently and effectively, but the process lacks procedure documentation. What action should the auditor take?

    A. Document the process.

    B. Find that the process is effective but recommend that it be documented.

    C. Write the procedure document for the auditee and include it in audit evidence.

    D. Find that the process is ineffective.

13. During audit planning, an auditor has discovered that a key business process in the auditee organization has been outsourced to an external service provider. Which option should the auditor consider?

    A. Audit the external service provider or rely on an SSAE 16 audit report if one is available.

    B. Audit the external service provider.

    C. Determine that the business process is not effective.

    D. Request that the external service provider submit its internal audit workpapers.

14. Why should an auditor prefer bank statements over a department's own business records that list bank transactions?

    A. Bank statements can be provided in electronic format.

    B. Bank statements contain data not found in internal records.

    C. Bank statements are usually easier to obtain.

    D. Bank statements are independent and objective.

15. Which of the following statements is true about ISACA audit standards and guidelines?

    A. ISACA audit standards are mandatory, whereas ISACA audit guidelines are optional.

    B. ISACA audit standards are optional, whereas ISACA audit guidelines are mandatory.

    C. ISACA audit standards and guidelines are mandatory.

    D. ISACA audit standards and guidelines are optional.

16. When planning an audit project, all of the following should be established prior to the start of the project, *except*:

    A. Audit schedule

    B. Purpose

    C. Sampling technique

    D. Audit scope

17. An organization has outsourced the operation of its ERP system to an external service provider. Which audits should the organization expect to receive from the service provider periodically upon request?

    A. SOC 1 and SOC 2 Type I

    B. SOX

    C. SOC 2 Type II

    D. SOC 1 and SOC 2

18. An auditor is examining the population of transactions in a business process. The auditor wants to select samples until an exception is found. What sampling technique is the auditor using?

   A. Exception

   B. Discovery

   C. Stop-or-go

   D. Judgmental

19. An IS auditor is auditing an accounting system and is looking for evidence of accounting fraud. Which sampling technique should the auditor use?

   A. Discovery

   B. Variable

   C. Detective

   D. Stratified

20. An auditor wants to use AI/ML tools in an examination of a large dataset to identify anomalies. In what conditions may the auditor use these tools?

   A. The use of AI for this purpose is allowable by policy, is legal, and is ethical.

   B. The use of AI for this purpose is allowable by policy.

   C. The use of AI for this purpose is legal and ethical.

   D. The use of AI for this purpose is the most efficient.

Chapter

3

IT Life Cycle Management

THE CERTIFIED INFORMATION SYSTEMS AUDITOR (CISA) OBJECTIVES REPRESENT 12% OF THE MATERIAL COVERED ON THE EXAM AND INCLUDE:

✓ **Domain 3: Information Systems Acquisition, Development, & Implementation**

  A. Information Systems Acquisition and Development

      1. Project Governance and Management

      2. Business Case and Feasibility Analysis

      3. System Development Methodologies

      4. Control Identification and Design

  B. Information Systems Implementation

      1. Testing Methodologies

      2. Configuration and Release Management

      3. System Migration, Infrastructure Deployment and Data Conversion

      4. Post-implementation Review

  Supporting Tasks

      9. Evaluate IT resource and portfolio management for alignment with the organization's strategies and objectives.

      16. Evaluate the organization's project management policies and practices.

      17. Evaluate controls at all stages of the information systems development lifecycle.

18. Evaluate the readiness of information systems for implementation and migration into production.

19. Conduct post-implementation review of systems to determine whether project deliverables, controls and requirements are met.

The topics in this chapter represent 12 percent of the CISA examination.

Organizations employ business processes to organize the tasks related to the development and maintenance of application software and the supporting IT infrastructure. Business processes provide constraint and management control for high-value activities such as the acquisition, development, and maintenance of software and infrastructure, and these processes also provide the structure for projects and project management.

Organizations, for the most part, have undergone significant transformation in the past decade with regard to the nature of their business software applications. In the past, organizations developed or acquired software applications, heavily customized them with an internal staff of programmers, and operated them in on-premises data centers (once known as computer rooms). Contrast to today, where most organizations employ software-as-a-service (SaaS) business applications with integrations among them, and with few, if any, software developers on staff. The emphasis on the software development life cycle has now given way to the systems development (really, acquisition) life cycle.

Many organizations recognize that business processes themselves have the same intricacies as software and that life cycle management is appropriate for, and similar to, the life cycle for software development. They also realize that business processes and application software are often tightly coupled and must often be managed as complex, multifaceted single entities.

IS auditors should pay particular attention to an organization's methodologies and practices for the acquisition, development, and management of software, infrastructure, and business processes. This is valuable information regarding the effectiveness of an organization's life cycle management and helps auditors determine how well the organization develops requirements and can transform them into applications and infrastructure that effectively support key business processes.

In addition to auditing the organization's development processes, auditors must audit software applications. Areas of particular interest include controls that govern input, processing, and output, as well as the application's ability to perform calculations correctly and maintain the integrity of data that is being accessed by many users simultaneously.

Benefits Realization

Benefits realization is the result of strategic planning, process development, and systems development, which all contribute toward a launch of business operations to reach a set of business objectives. This chapter focuses on process and systems acquisition and development, which are used to build the engine of business operations. Audits of these activities provide objective views of their effectiveness. Benefits realization is depicted in Figure 3.1.

FIGURE 3.1   Benefits realization

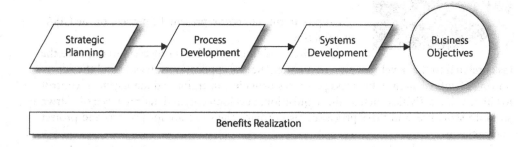

Portfolio and Program Governance and Management

A *program* is an organization of many large, complex activities and can be thought of as *a set of projects that work to fulfill one or more key business objectives or goals*. A program is generally a multiyear effort that consists of many complex projects, each with its own project manager, project schedule, budget, and participants.

A program is usually run by a *program manager* who has oversight over all the projects in the program. Figure 3.2 shows the relationship between a program manager and the projects that they manage.

Like a single project, a program has a defined scope, budget, resources, and a schedule. Program management also helps to organize and coordinate the operation of its projects, identify dependencies between them, manage conflicts and issues, and manage common and shared resources used by project teams.

Starting a Program

When an organization sets objectives and goals that will be realized through a program, a number of activities usually take place:

- **Development of a program charter:** A *charter* is a formal document that defines the objectives of a program, its main timelines, the sources of funding, the names of its principal leaders and managers, and the names of the business executive or executives who are sponsoring the program.

- **Identification of available resources:** Senior management must identify the resources that will be used by the program. These will include funding, personnel, and business assets such as information systems and other equipment.

The charter and resources provide the direction and the means to begin a program that will move the business closer to realizing its objectives.

FIGURE 3.2 A program manager oversees several projects.

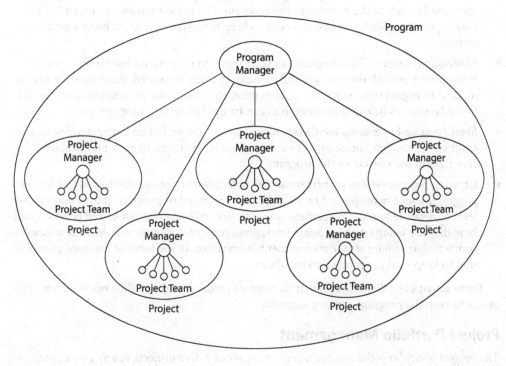

Titles vs. Roles

Many middle and senior managers are program managers, even if they don't have "program manager" in their title or job description. Any manager who is responsible for the execution of multiple concurrent projects, particularly if those projects are helping the organization get closer to common objectives, is a program manager.

Running a Program

After a program has been launched, the program manager needs to manage it actively to ensure that the program is on track and fulfilling its objectives. Some of the activities required may include the following:

- **Monitoring project schedules:** Each of the projects running in the program will have its own schedule. The program manager will need to examine these schedules periodically to understand how each is progressing. This often requires the program manager to communicate frequently with program participants and project managers to get up-to-date statuses on project tasks.

- **Managing project budgets:** The program manager needs to monitor and manage spending by each of the projects in the program. The program manager may need to make spending adjustments periodically to keep the overall program budget under control.

- **Managing resources:** The program manager needs to understand how resources are being used across all the projects and to make changes as needed. Resources are scarce in most IT organizations, so this requires creativity; often, the program manager needs to *find* resources before those resources can be used to further program goals.

- **Identifying and managing conflicts:** Individual projects will often encounter resource conflicts—sometimes projects will vie for the same resources, or they may require resources in use outside of the program.

- **Creating program status reports for senior management:** As executive sponsors for the program, senior management needs to be kept informed of program status, in whatever level of detail required. Often, these status reports will describe issues and conflicts and how they are being resolved. Sometimes, however, status reports will describe unresolved conflicts that require senior management intervention in the form of resource prioritization to keep vital programs moving ahead.

These activities enable management to measure progress and to adjust resources and priorities to keep the program running smoothly.

Project Portfolio Management

The *project portfolio* is the organization's entire set of active projects at any given time. Unlike a program, where projects are related and support a common objective, a portfolio of projects is simply *all* the active projects, which may support many different and even unrelated objectives and be part of different programs.

An organization needs to maintain a collection of information about all its projects in a central location. Having this information will help a senior manager or executive quickly view high-level information about all the active projects in the organization. Often, this information will be stored electronically in a form that will enable an executive to sort and filter company projects in various ways. Here's some of the information that may be maintained in this portfolio of projects:

- Executive sponsor
- Program manager
- Project manager
- Start and end dates
- Key milestones
- Names of participants
- Objectives or goals that the project supports
- Budget

- Resources used
- Dependencies

Ease of access to project and program portfolios helps management better understand what activities are taking place and the resources that each is consuming.

Business Case and Feasibility Analysis Development

The prevalent point of view is that IT exists in support of business objectives. Given this assumption, every IT project should directly or indirectly result in tangible business benefits, regardless of how technical or abstract any particular IT project may be.

Before any IT project is permitted to begin, a *business case* for the project is developed. The purpose of a business case is to explain the benefits to the business that will be realized as a result of the project.

The development of a business case will normally follow a feasibility study. A *feasibility analysis* defines the business problem and describes potential solutions. It is possible, however, that none of the solutions will result in a benefit for the business. For example, each may be too costly or may incur excessive risk. However, the business case should go beyond the feasibility analysis in terms of business benefits and include actual figures for costs and benefits.

A typical business case is a written document that includes:

- **Business problem:** This is a description of the business problem in qualitative and quantitative terms.
- **Feasibility analysis results:** The business case should include results of the feasibility analysis if one was performed.
- **High-level project plan:** This should include a timeline and the number of persons required.
- **Budget:** This should include the cost to execute the project as well as costs associated with the solution.
- **Metrics:** The business case should include information on how business benefit will be measured, as well as expected before-and-after measurements. Estimates should be backed up by examples of the benefits of similar projects in the organization or in other organizations.
- **Risks:** The business case should include any risks that may occur, as well as how those risks can be mitigated. These risks may be market risks or financial risks.

Some organizations make the development of a business case the first phase in the actual project; however, this arrangement may be self-serving, as the project team may be taking the point of view of justifying the continuation of the project instead of focusing on whether the project will actually benefit the business. The development of a business case should be performed in an objective manner by persons who do not benefit from the result.

The start of a project is not the only time to assess the project's business case and decide whether to undertake the project. At key milestones throughout the project, the business case should be reevaluated. As a project unfolds, often situations develop that could not be anticipated earlier, and these situations sometimes result in added risks, costs, or other changes. For this reason, the business case should be reconsidered throughout the project so that senior management can determine whether or not the project should continue.

Decisions on whether to continue a project should be made not only by those people who benefit from the project, but also by other stakeholders who can be more objective. Otherwise, there is a risk that projects will be continued for their own sake instead of for the good of the business.

Measuring Business Benefits

In the mid-to-late 20th century, information technology was primarily used to automate tasks, and in that era it was fairly easy to measure the benefits derived from IT. Often, measuring the benefits was a matter of comparing the cost and time spent to perform tasks manually versus the cost and time spent to automate those tasks. Digital transformation (sometimes abbreviated as DX) refers to the integration of digital technology into all areas of a business, fundamentally changing how you operate and deliver value to customers. Information technology's role today is digital transformation, which provides benefits that are not easily measured and often not short-term in nature.

For example, an organization that invests in a new customer relationship management (CRM) application may do so to improve its customer service in measurable ways. Shortly after implementing a CRM system, productivity may actually decrease until individuals and teams learn how to operate and fully utilize the new system. But customer satisfaction may improve in future quarters. A year or more may be required to determine whether improvements in customer satisfaction is a blip or an actual upward trend attributable to the new CRM. The new system can also help the organization improve its products and services; the benefits from these improvements may not be experienced for years after implementation of the new CRM.

Measuring business benefits requires that the organization select key performance indicators (KPIs) and measure them formally and accurately over the long term. When new projects and programs are considered, business benefits should be estimated and measurements should be taken before and after the project has completed to validate whether the project's predictions were valid. The nature of the project may require months or even years of measurements to validate project results.

Major projects should include post-implementation reviews that take place long after the project's completion (as long as 24 months, or even longer) to determine whether trends in key metrics changed as predicted.

Business case development should include a description of the business benefits that are expected from the completed project, including how those benefits will be measured. These key metrics should be decided before the project begins. If key metrics are not being measured, those measurements should begin as soon as possible so that the organization will have enough "before-and-after" metrics to determine whether the project has benefited the organization or not.

 An organization that does not agree on key metrics is in danger of setting self-fulfilling metrics later on as a way of justifying the project, regardless of whether it actually benefits the organization.

In the spirit of continuous improvement, careful analysis of key metrics long after a project has been completed should lead the organization to consider additional improvements in its processes and technologies. Organizations may wish to benchmark against other firms to identify best practices and other opportunities for improvement.

Finally, organizations that modernize business processes with automation often enjoy unexpected benefits, including insight gained through business analytics or business intelligence (BI), such as customer buying trends that could not have been known before. Additionally, the incorporation of artificial intelligence (AI) into business processes can further enhance these benefits by providing advanced data analysis, predictive insights, and improved decision-making capabilities. This use of analytics also leads to a more effective control environment by replacing error-prone manual processes with efficient, automated techniques.

Project Management

The preceding section on benefits realization is concerned with the high-level view across many projects. This section on project management takes a closer look at the management of individual projects.

A *project* is a coordinated and managed sequence of tasks that results in the realization of an objective or goal. The effort may be performed by a single individual or by many. A project's duration may be a few days or as long as two years or more.

Organizing Projects

Projects should be organized in a methodical way that supports the organization's objectives. Management should formally approve projects, which should be documented in a consistent manner.

In addition to being a collection of organized activities, a project has a social context and culture. A project consists of a project team that includes the people who perform tasks for the project. The project manager may have several different types of relationships to the project team:

- **Supervisor:** In this case, the project manager directly supervises the employees on the project team. This may occur in several different ways:

  - The project team consists of individuals from the same department and the department manager serves as the project manager. The team members already report to the department/project manager.

  - Employees assigned to the project are moved so that they report directly to the project manager for the duration of the project and then return to their original assignments at the conclusion of the project. This is commonly done when employees are dedicated 100 percent to a project.

- **Matrix manager:** In this case, individuals have two different reporting relationships. They have a permanent reporting relationship in their functional area and a temporary reporting relationship to the project manager. The functional and project manager either collaborate on performance reviews and other management issues or they each separately evaluate employees. This approach is commonly used when individuals work on a project for a portion of their time while they continue having responsibilities in their functional department.

- **Influencer:** The project manager has no direct management over project team members. The project manager must practice the art of influence and persuasion over the project team members to keep the project moving. This is a very difficult way for project managers to function.

 Although a project may have a formal plan and schedule, it's the people on the project team who help a project reach its objectives. Paying attention to the human side of projects is just as important as the project objectives themselves.

Initiating a Project

The formal project launch occurs when the project has been approved by the IT steering committee or a similar oversight body. Management will appoint a project manager as well as all project team members.

Management also needs to establish priorities for the team and for each team member. Because most or all project team members will probably have other work responsibilities, management must be very clear on where project activities fall on the work priority list.

In addition, management must express its support for the project schedule and important project milestones so that all project team members are aware of management's objectives for timely project completion. This will help to motivate project team members to start and complete tasks on time.

> A project kickoff meeting is an effective way to convey these messages; management can gauge project team members' interest by studying their body language. A meeting is also an effective way to discuss issues and answer questions in real time.

Prior to the launch of a project, management should also discuss the upcoming project with individuals to learn their opinions regarding the makeup of the project team and its prospects for success.

Developing Project Objectives

The specific objectives of a project must be established and documented before the project begins. In fact, project objectives should be a part of the project's description when the project is being considered for approval by the IT steering committee. Project objectives should be specific, measurable, achievable, relevant, and time-bound (SMART). They should support and relate to business objectives and to the organization's key performance indicators.

Here are some example project objectives:

- Reduce customer service call wait time by 70 percent.

- Reduce implementation time for new customers by 5 days.

- Reduce annual data storage system cost by 20 percent.

Additional objectives that are not a project's key objectives may also be developed; these objectives may clarify a project's purpose or the manner in which it will be performed. As much as possible, these objectives should be defined during the project planning effort. Changes to project objectives that occur during the project implementation may result in *scope creep* that delays the project and/or jeopardizes project success.

Object Breakdown Structure

As a part of the project objectives, a project manager may develop an *object breakdown structure (OBS)*, which represents the components of the project in graphical or tabular form. An OBS can help management and project team members better visualize the scope and objectives of the project. An example OBS appears in Figure 3.3.

An OBS is a visual or structural representation of the system, software, or application, in a hierarchical form, from high level to fine detail. An OBS is not a schematic, architecture, or data flow diagram, although one or more of these may also need to be developed, either as a part of the design or as a tool to help project participants better understand the overall system.

Work Breakdown Structure

Another common method for depicting a project is the *work breakdown structure (WBS)*. This is a logical representation of the high-level and detailed tasks that must be performed to complete the project. A WBS used for this purpose can also be used as the basis for the creation of the project schedule. An example WBS is shown in Figure 3.4.

FIGURE 3.3   An object breakdown structure helps participants understand project scope and objectives.

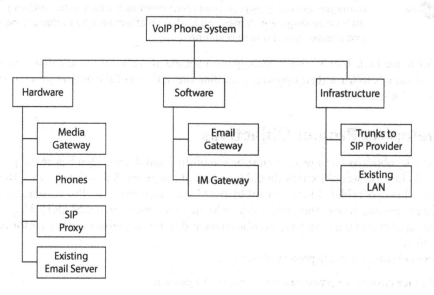

FIGURE 3.4   A work breakdown structure depicts a project's tasks.

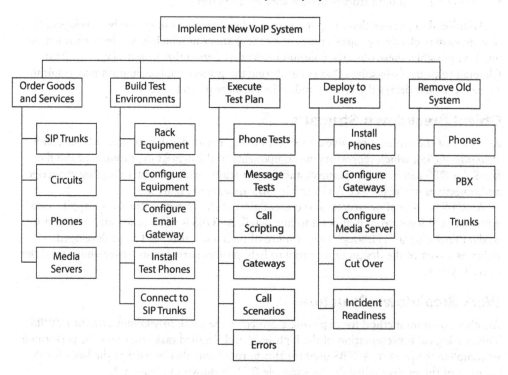

The WBS created in this phase will be simpler than the full-fledged project plan, which will include the resources required to perform each task, task dependencies, and schedules.

In simpler projects, the WBS and the project plan are one and the same. Or, put another way, the WBS can be the *start* of the project plan, containing all the tasks that need to be included in the project plan. With tools like WBS Planner (www.wbsplanner.com), the WBS is the list of tasks in the left column, and the project plan is that same list when it also contains dependencies, dates, resources, and other details. Project planning is discussed in more detail later in this section.

Managing Projects

Projects should be managed by a project manager. The project manager is responsible for performing several activities:

- **Building and managing the project schedule:** The project manager may have developed the original project schedule, and they will be responsible for maintaining the schedule throughout the life of the project. As tasks are completed early, on time, or late, this will impact the rest of the project schedule, and the project manager will have to make adjustments to take into account these scheduling variations. In addition to changes in timing, other types of changes in the schedule will be required, including new tasks, new dependencies, and other unforeseen matters that could affect the schedule.

- **Recording task completion:** As tasks progress and are completed, the project manager must keep the project schedule up-to-date. The project schedule must accurately reflect the status of each task.

- **Running project meetings:** The project manager organizes regular meetings of project participants where project status and issues are discussed. The project manager facilitates project meetings to make sure that the meeting agenda is followed. The project manager is also responsible for sending meeting agendas, meeting minutes, and other updates to the project team.

- **Tracking project expenditures:** The project manager is responsible for tracking and reporting on project costs.

- **Communicating project status:** The project manager is responsible for communicating project status to project team members and also to management. A project status report will include details on task statuses and on whether the project is still on schedule and on budget, as well as a list of open and closed issues.

The project manager needs to be a highly organized, methodical individual who is detail oriented and a good communicator and negotiator. While knowledge of the technologies in a project is useful, of utmost importance are the project manager's people skills, which enable the manager to work effectively with project team members and to be an effective facilitator and problem solver.

Project Roles and Responsibilities

Formal roles and responsibilities need to be established so that projects will be well organized and will have the greatest possible chance of success. Defined roles and responsibilities ensure that important tasks are known to all project participants. Typical roles and responsibilities include:

- **Senior management:** Support the approval of the project, its funding, and resource allocation.

- **IT steering committee:** Commission the feasibility study, approve the project, assign IT and business resources to the project, and approve the project schedule. Periodically review project status and progress. Take corrective action when necessary—for example, when priorities conflict.

- **Project manager:** Develop the detailed project plan, identify and indicate dependencies, and estimate the time required to complete each task. Track progress at the task level. Call regular project meetings where project status and issues are discussed among project team members. Track spending and other resource allocation. Publish status reports to project team members and to senior management.

- **Project team members:** Participate in all project team meetings; complete tasks on time; identify issues and communicate them to the project manager; look for opportunities to optimize tasks, reduce necessary resources, and improve the project.

- **End-user management:** Assign staff to the project team and support the development of business requirements, test cases, test data, and system testing.

- **End users:** Contribute to business requirements, test cases, use cases, test data, and test systems, and report test results to the project manager. Participate in acceptance testing and provide accurate, timely results.

- **Project sponsor:** Define project objectives, provide budget and other resources, and work with the project manager and other management stakeholders to ensure that the project delivers the desired outcomes.

- **Systems development management:** Provide adequate hardware, software, tools, and resources to facilitate development. Assign competent, trained developers to the project, and support their participation in the project.

- **Systems developers:** Develop software and systems that conform to functional requirements, good coding practices, and organizational IT standards. Perform unit, program, and system testing as required. Ensure that software and systems are free of software bugs, vulnerabilities, and security issues that could result in undesired activities such as a break-in or disclosure of sensitive information. Develop operational procedures.

- **Quality assurance team:** Review the results and deliverables throughout the project to determine whether the project deliverables are in compliance with project requirements and any applicable regulatory requirements and other legal obligations.

- **Security manager:** Provide security requirements, privacy requirements, regulatory requirements, audit requirements, test plans, and test cases. Ensure that the system meets organizational controls and audit requirements. Perform security testing. Report test results to the project manager.

- **IT operations team:** Provide operational requirements, review operational procedures, and participate in acceptance testing. Participate in system implementation, and operate the system after implementation. Report post-implementation problems to the project manager and developers.

- **IS auditor:** Subsequently audit the systems and processes built or changed in the project. Act in an advisory role and as a controls expert. The auditor should not otherwise act as a decision maker on the project team. The involvement of the auditor early on in the project will help to avoid any potential pitfalls after the project has commenced and/or finished.

In smaller organizations, one person may have two or more project roles. In larger organizations (or large projects in any size organization), each role may be assigned to one person, a group, or even an entire team.

Project Planning

The term *project planning* refers to the activities related to the development and management of a project. The project manager is responsible for identifying all the activities required for the project, the sequence in which they must be performed, dependencies between tasks, the resources required, and the priorities of tasks and resources. The project manager will also be expected to determine how the project can make the most efficient use of resources and the shortest amount of time in which the entire project can be completed.

The RACI Matrix

Many organizations have adopted the RACI model for establishing responsibilities within projects as well as in other contexts. The four roles in the RACI model are presented here in hierarchical order (indicating why this model is sometimes called ARCI):

- **Accountable:** Usually a single individual who is accountable for the success of a project.

- **Responsible:** One or more individuals who are responsible for completing tasks in a project.

- **Consulted:** One or more individuals who may need to be consulted on various matters throughout a project. These are typically subject matter experts.

- **Informed:** One or more individuals who need to be informed.

Program managers and project managers often publish RACI charts so that all project participants know the responsibilities for each project team member.

Project planning encompasses many detailed activities:

- **Task identification:** One of the first steps in the development of a project plan is identifying all the tasks that must be performed to complete the project. This is often accomplished using a project management tool that can be used to build a detailed WBS. When completed, a WBS is a structural decomposition of the work necessary to complete the entire project, task by task, bit by bit.

- **Task estimation:** Once the project planner has identified all of the tasks required to complete the project, the next step is determining how much time and effort each task requires. There are a couple of different ways to measure this: actual effort and elapsed time. For example, it may take a painter one hour to paint a room, but there is also preparation and cleanup time to consider, and it may take four hours for the paint to dry (though while the paint is drying, the painter can be doing other tasks). Often, it is necessary to know how many hours or days of work are required for one or more persons to perform a task, but knowing elapsed time is critical also. The work breakdown structure (WBS) is useful during this process.

- **Task resources:** It is necessary to know what resources are required to perform a task. Resources include people (and not just any people—often a given task must be performed by specific people), equipment, consumable resources, outside professional services, materials, software licenses, and so on.

- **Task dependencies:** Often in a project there will be tasks that cannot be started until other tasks have been completed. Project managers must discern all of the dependencies between projects so that project teams don't run into unexpected obstacles.

- **Milestone tracking:** In larger projects, it is a good idea to identify milestones. Milestones are significant events in the project when major phases have been completed. Example milestones are completion of the design, completion of software development, completion of network wiring, and completion of software testing. Often management will want to schedule a project review meeting when these milestones have been completed; such reviews give management an opportunity to make go/no-go decisions on whether the project should be permitted to continue, or to see whether any lingering issues should first be addressed before the project is continued.

- **Task tracking:** When a project is in progress, the project manager must accurately track the status and progress of every task. They also must look toward the short-term and long-term futures, anticipate future resource needs, and make sure that tasks that have not started yet will be able to start without undue delays.

One of the most common pitfalls in project planning is the failure to identify task resources and dependencies properly. Sometimes a project planner will have "optimized" a project plan, only to find that many tasks that could be done concurrently must be done consecutively. This happens, for instance, when several tasks that are slated to be done in parallel must all be performed by the same individual. For example, five tasks that take one day each were scheduled to all take place on the same day, but it turns out that the same person is required to perform all of those tasks; this results in those tasks being completed one day after another, requiring five days in all.

Estimating and Sizing Software Projects

Several tools and methods can be used to estimate the amount of effort required to complete tasks in a software project. Tools and methodologies can make the task of estimating work more accurate, because they rely on techniques that have been proven over the long run. Also, tools and methodologies like the following can reduce the time required to perform the estimating work.

Using the OBS   The OBS can be useful to depict the system and its components visually, particularly in complex projects where the tasks, costs, and other aspects of the project are not immediately evident. Object breakdown structures were described in more detail earlier in this chapter in the section "Developing Project Objectives."

Using the WBS   The WBS is a great way to get to the tasks in a complex project. A project manager or planner can decompose large efforts into smaller and smaller pieces, down to the task level.

Using Source Lines of Code   Sizing for software projects has traditionally relied on *source lines of code* (SLOC) estimates. Experienced systems analysts could make rough estimates on the numbers of lines of code required for a given software project. Then, using results from past projects, the analyst could make an accurate estimate for the time required to develop a program based on its length. A similar measuring unit is kilo lines of code (KLOC).

SLOC and KLOC offer the advantages of being quantitative and somewhat repeatable for a given computer language such as COBOL, Fortran, or BASIC. However, these methods are falling out of favor because many of the languages in use today are not textual in nature.

The most direct replacements for SLOC/KLOC are methods that estimate the effort required to program a form, page, window, report, cell, widget, file, or calculation. For example, the programming effort for a web application would be tied to the number of forms, pages, and windows in a web application and the number of fields and variables in each.

An analogy between the older and newer methods for estimating source code is to estimate the time required to develop engineering drawings for an automobile. Old methods would rely on the weight (number of pounds, akin to the number of lines of code) of the car. Newer methods rely on the number of individual features (engine size, number of doors, seats, lights, accessories, and so on).

Using Constructive Cost Model The *Constructive Cost Model (COCOMO)* method for estimating software development projects was developed in the aerospace industry in the 1970s and represented an advancement in the ability to estimate the effort required to develop software. Three levels of COCOMO were developed: Basic COCOMO, Intermediate COCOMO, and Detailed COCOMO. Only Basic COCOMO is described here.

Basic COCOMO uses a minimal number of inputs:

KLOC The number of lines of code (in thousands)

Complexity Rating The rating for the project, expressed as "organic" (a smaller project with experienced software engineers and less-than-rigid requirements), "semi-detached" (a larger project with a mix of rigid and semi-rigid requirements), or "embedded" (a large project with highly specific and restrictive requirements)

Equations in Basic COCOMO are:

$$E = a(KLOC)^b$$

$$D = c(E)d$$

$$P = E / D$$

where the values a, b, c, and d are taken from Table 3.1, and

E = Effort required in person-months

D = Development time in months

P = Number of people required

TABLE 3.1 COCOMO weighting factors

Project type	a	b	c	d
Organic	2.4	1.05	2.5	0.38
Semi-detached	3.0	1.12	2.5	0.35
Embedded	3.6	1.20	2.5	0.32

Let's look at two examples. First, a software project that has 32,000 lines of code and is classified as organic. Using the COCOMO estimating model, this effort will require 91.3 person-months, 13.9 months of elapsed time, and seven people.

In a second example, a software project requires 186,000 lines of code and is classified as embedded. Using the formulas here, this project will require 1,904 person-months, 28 months of elapsed time, and 68 people. This is a large project!

Using Function Point Analysis *Function point analysis* (FPA) is a time-proven estimation technique for larger software projects. Developed in the 1970s, it looks at the number of application functions and their complexity. FPA is not hindered by specific technologies or measuring techniques (such as lines of code), so it is more adaptable for today's graphical user interface (GUI)-based software.

In FPA, the analyst studies the detailed design specifications for an application program and counts the number of user inputs, user outputs, user queries, files, and external interfaces. The analyst then selects a complexity weighting factor for each of those five points. The number of inputs, outputs, queries, files, and interfaces are multiplied by their respective complexity weights, and those products are added together. The sum is called the number of unadjusted *function points (FPs)* for the program.

A *value adjustment factor (VAF)* is then determined for the application; this factor will raise or lower the function points based on 14 criteria that address various aspects of application complexity. The total number of unadjusted function points is multiplied by the VAF to yield the total adjusted function points.

A sample FPA calculation table appears in Table 3.2.

TABLE 3.2   Using FPA to Estimate Effort Required to Develop Complex Applications

Parameter	Count	Weighting			Results
		Simple	Average	Complex	
# of user inputs	_____	× 3	× 4	× 6	= _____
# of user outputs	_____	× 4	× 5	× 7	= _____
# of user queries	_____	× 3	× 4	× 6	= _____
# of files opened	_____	× 7	× 10	× 15	= _____
# of external interfaces	_____	× 5	× 7	× 10	= _____
				Total Unadjusted Function Points	= _____
				Multiplied by Value Adjustment Factor	× _____
				Total Adjusted Function Points	= _____

The only disadvantage of FPA is that the value of an FP for a program does not directly specify the time required to develop it. However, an organization that has used FPA in the past will probably have a pretty good idea of the number of person-hours or person-months each FP requires.

Considering Other Costs   In addition to person-months, other costs will need to be considered in a software project, including:

Development, Modeling, and Testing Tools   The project may require new tools for developers or additional licenses if there are more developers working on the project than the number of available licenses.

Workstations   Developers, testers, or users may require additional (or more powerful) workstations.

Servers   The project may require additional servers or upgrades to existing servers. Servers may be needed for production and for development and testing purposes.

Software Licenses   This includes licenses for operating systems, database management systems, application software, virtual network devices, and possibly more.

Network Devices   The project may require additional network devices (whether physical or virtual) such as switches, routers, or firewalls to tie everything together.

Storage   The system may require more storage than was estimated.

Connectivity   Higher-capacity network connections might be required.

Training   Developers or testers may need training on the use of their tools, and users may need training regarding the use of new software.

Equipment   This could include office equipment such as copiers, and just about anything else.

Travel   Staff, trainers, consultants, suppliers, and others may need to travel to various locations throughout the project.

Additional costs associated with a project may be specific to certain industries, regulations, or locales.

Scheduling Project Tasks

When the project manager or planner has established the complete breakdown of tasks and has determined resources, dependencies, and levels of effort for each, they can create the actual project schedule. Tools such as Trac, Microsoft Planner, Microsoft Project, and many others will automatically assign dates to tasks once their duration, dependencies, and resources are identified.

After the planner/manager has entered all the tasks into a project planning tool, they will probably discover that the end date of the project (as calculated by the tool) is long after the date that senior management has defined as the end of the project.

This is where a good project planner/manager begins to earn their compensation.

This is a critical phase in the project, when the project manager begins to analyze the project plan and look for ways to shorten the overall duration. Methods for optimizing project duration and squeezing the project into management-supplied constraints include:

- **Shorten task duration:** The project manager should consult with subject matter experts who provided time estimates for each task and see whether those estimates were high. A good project manager presses for details as they ask the expert to justify the time frames on the plan.

- **Reduce dependencies:** The project manager can consult with subject matter experts to find ways to reduce dependencies, which can enable more tasks to run in parallel (which is okay as long as there aren't multiple tasks stacking up on individual resources or teams).

- **Identify critical paths:** The project manager can perform critical path analysis (discussed in more detail later in this section). This will help to point out which parts of the project may need additional scrutiny.

There are a number of tools available to assist with this work. Let's take a look at a few of the most common ones.

Gantt Chart   A *Gantt chart* is a visual representation of a project in which individual tasks occupy rows on a worksheet and horizontal time bars depict the time required to complete each task relative to other tasks in the project. A Gantt chart can also show schedule dependencies and percentage of completion of each task. A sample Gantt chart is shown in Figure 3.5.

Program (or Project) Evaluation and Review Technique   A *program (or project) evaluation and review technique* (which is nearly always known just as PERT) chart provides a visual representation of project tasks, timelines, and dependencies. A PERT chart shows project tasks from left to right in time sequence, with connectors signifying dependencies. An example PERT chart is shown in Figure 3.6.

Critical Path Methodology (CPM)   A PERT chart helps to illustrate how a project is a "network" of related and sequenced tasks. In this network, it is possible to draw "paths" through ordered tasks from the beginning to the end of the project.

When a PERT chart includes notation regarding the elapsed time required for each task, you can follow each path through the network and add the elapsed time to get a total time for each path.

A project's *critical path* is that path through the PERT chart with the highest total elapsed time.

FIGURE 3.5 A Gantt chart illustrates task duration, schedule dependencies, and percentage of completion.

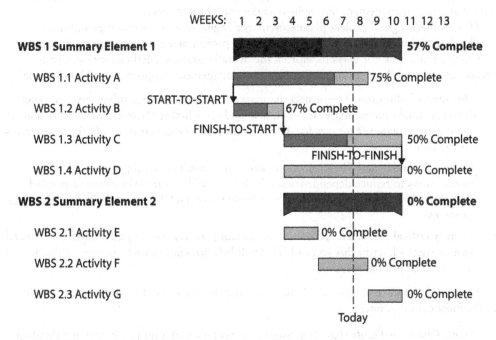

It is important to identify the critical path in a project, because this enables the project manager to understand which tasks are most likely to impact the project schedule and to determine when the project will finally conclude. When a project manager knows which tasks are on the critical path, they can perform analysis and attempt to improve the project plan through one of the following:

Start critical tasks earlier. If a critical-path task on a project can be started earlier, this will directly affect the project's end date. To be able to start a task earlier, it may be necessary to change the way that earlier dependent tasks are performed. For example, a Unix system administrator can be brought into a project a week earlier to begin critical tasks such as building servers.

Reduce dependencies. If earlier tasks in the project can be changed, it may be possible to remove one or more dependencies that will enable critical tasks to begin (and hence, end) earlier. For example, the "Install operating system" task depends on an earlier task, "Purchase server." If the organization has an available server in-house, the project does not need to wait to order, purchase, and receive a server. By using an in-house server, the "Install operating system" task can be started earlier.

Apply more resources to critical tasks. Some labor-intensive tasks can be completed more quickly if more resources are available to assist with them.

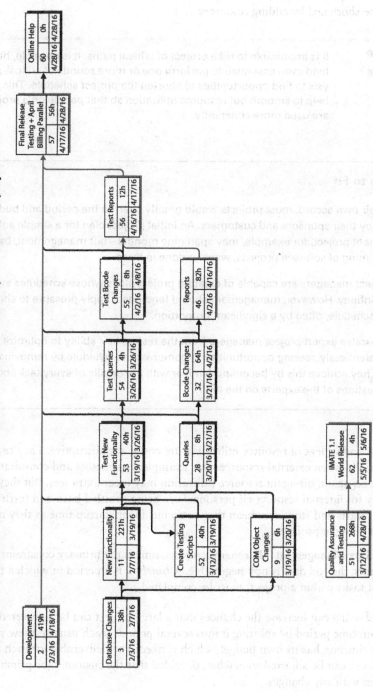

FIGURE 3.6 A PERT chart helps to visualize time sequence and dependencies in a project.

(Image courtesy of Digital Aardvark, Inc.)

An experienced project manager will be able to identify the types of tasks that can be shortened by adding resources.

It is impossible to rid a project of critical paths. It is possible, however, (and even essential) to perform one or more rounds of critical-path analysis to find opportunities to shorten the project schedule. This can also help to smooth out resource utilization so that people on a project team are used more constantly.

Squeeze to Fit

Left to their own accord, most projects would greatly overrun the period and budget intended by their sponsors and customers. An initial project plan for a simple software development project, for example, may span nine months—but management, being astute with the timing of software projects, wants it done in three.

Most project managers are capable of creating project plans whose schedules extend practically to infinity. However, management should (and does) apply pressure to shorten a project's schedule, often by a significant proportion.

What separates expert project managers from the rest is their ability to optimize a project plan by relentlessly seeking opportunities to compress the schedule by removing dependencies. They achieve this by becoming familiar with the details of every task and by asking tough questions of the experts on the team.

Peaks and valleys of resource utilization are costly and disruptive. They're more costly especially when external resources (for example, contractors and consultants) are used, since on-again, off-again resource utilization may incur extra fees. But they can also be costly for internal resources if personnel are being shuttled back and forth between projects. Starts and stops can mean that personnel incur startup time as they move back and forth between projects.

Timebox Management   For many projects, time is the primary constraint, and in such projects, the end date is non-negotiable. A *timebox* is a period in which a project (or a set of tasks within a project) must be completed.

Timeboxing can increase the chances that a large project can be completed within a certain time period by splitting it into several periods (each usually a few weeks long). Each timebox has its own budget, which is fixed. The deliverable for each timebox, however, can be adjusted somewhat, provided that the customer (or primary end user) agrees with any changes.

Timeboxing overcomes problems of procrastination and projects whose timelines slip. One characteristic of software developers is a tendency to strive for perfection on a project. The result of this tendency is that developers will complete a task and then repeatedly "preen" the output, which takes considerable extra time with little tangible benefit.

A Project of Sprints

Many organizations are organizing their IT projects using agile methodology, which is not used just for software development anymore—in fact, many projects are broken down into one-to-four–week sprints. It's been recognized that sprints help a project team focus on intermediate goals and achieve them in short periods of time.

Project Records

Projects need to have written records of their proceedings, from project inception to shutdown. The purpose of these records is to help project managers and other project team members keep track of the details related to the project during its lifetime and beyond.

The types of records that most often need to be kept for a project include:

- **Project plans:** This includes initial project plans as well as the records used to track task scheduling and completion.

- **Project changes:** Proposed and approved (as well as rejected) changes to the project schedule, deliverables, budget, and so on need to be recorded.

- **Legal documents:** Contracts, proposals, and statements of work (SOWs) that are a part of the project should be recorded. Internal and external SLAs fit in this category also.

- **Meeting agendas and minutes:** This includes issues, decisions, and other matters encountered and discussed from week to week.

- **Resource consumption:** Purchase orders, invoices, and receipts for equipment, supplies, and services should be recorded. This may also include time sheets and invoices for employees, contractors, consultants, and other service providers.

- **Task information:** Details associated with the performance and/or completion of project tasks should be recorded.

- **Draft and final deliverables:** Any work products that are produced as a part of the project need to be retained. If there are any approvals associated with final versions of deliverables, these need to be retained as well.

Good, Cheap, Fast: Pick Any Two

Experienced project managers are—consciously or unconsciously—aware of the Good-Cheap-Fast triad in project management. For any project, for the characteristics Good, Cheap, and Fast, management may choose which two characteristics are the most desirable. Whichever two they select, the third characteristic will take an inverse trend.

These are the principles:

- If a project is Good and Cheap, it will not be Fast.
- If a project is Good and Fast, it will not be Cheap.
- If a project is Cheap and Fast, it will not be Good.

While these statements are not absolute, they are reasonable principles to keep in mind when managing issues that affect budget, schedule, and the quality of the project's outcome.

Project Documentation

Virtually every IT project needs to include documentation that describes the system or application that is built or modified. Documentation helps a wide audience with many aspects of an application, including:

- **Users:** End users of applications need to understand how the systems are supposed to be used. This includes the operation of all user interfaces, the business meaning of application controls, and how to solve typical problems and issues.

- **Support:** If end-user support is provided, these individuals need to know how to guide users through typical and not-so-typical problems and how to fix common problems.

- **IT operations:** System operators who monitor and operate systems and applications need to know what they are supposed to do. This can include application, database, operating system, or device monitoring; problem identification and resolution; backups; system recovery; and daily or weekly tasks.

- **Developers:** Detailed descriptions of the system will help current and future IT workers understand how the system works. Descriptions of the inner workings of individual programs, components, and tools; internal and external data flows; interfaces; and state diagrams will help developers and engineers understand a system so that they can more easily support problems and make future changes.

- **Auditors:** IT and business auditors who audit the systems, applications, or the business process(es) supported by the system need to know how the system works. This includes business controls such as access controls and the enforcement of business rules, as well as the manner in which business information is stored and processed.

- **Configuration management:** This includes information on the methods to be used to manage and record configuration changes in the system and in the supporting infrastructure and services.

- **Security:** This includes information on controls within and around the system that protect it, as well as event logging and incident response procedures.

- **Disaster recovery and business continuity planning:** If the system supports a business process that is in scope for business continuity planning or disaster recovery planning, a complete set of documentation is required that describes system recovery and emergency operations.

- **Management:** Company management needs to understand how systems support critical business functions, as well as information about the internal and external resources required to build and support the system.

 NOTE For software projects where existing systems are being updated, all of the existing documents associated with the system need to be reviewed and updated.

Project Change Management

When a project is launched, company management has agreed to sponsor and allocate resources to the project based on the objectives of the project at its onset. As a project is launched, and as it progresses week by week, the project manager and team will meet regularly to discuss the schedule and any issues that arise that were unanticipated at the start of the project.

While managing the project schedule, a project manager could be tempted to adjust the end date on a task that is running late to adjust affected downstream tasks. However, doing so may affect the budget or the final project deliverable. Management might not appreciate the project manager making arbitrary changes to the project schedule without asking for permission. If management permits this degree of latitude from the project manager, it is likely that the schedule will continue to slip here and there, significantly affecting the final completion date as well as the budget and resource utilization. This type of change cannot be permitted to take place.

Issues that affect the overall project schedule, deliverables, resources, and budget need to be formally identified and submitted for approval through a formal change process. Management needs to establish parameters for changes to budget, schedule, deliverables, and resources. For example, any proposed project change that results in a change of budget or final delivery date would need to be approved by management. The procedure for making changes to the project should be done in two basic steps:

1. The project team, together with the project manager, should identify the specific issue, its impact on the project, and their proposed remedy. This information should be packaged into a formal request.

2. This change request should be presented to management, either in one of the regular project meetings or in a separate meeting that includes the project manager, any relevant project team members (experts in the specific matter to be discussed), and members of senior management—preferably those who are sponsoring the project. The proposed change and its impact on the project should be discussed, and management should make a decision on whether to approve the change.

It should be evident that not every small change needs to go through this process. A spending increase of $10 is hardly a reason to call a management review, but an increase of $50,000 done without any review may make management fuming mad. Management needs to set some parameters so that change reviews will take place only when changes exceed any set thresholds.

Smaller changes in schedule and budget can be made a part of a regular project status report that should be sent to management and project sponsors. Smaller issues of changes to budget, schedule, and resources can be highlighted so that management is aware of these less significant changes.

 Tracking changes in a project is as important as tracking the project's activities. Only by tracking project changes such as schedule, resource, and cost adjustments can the project manager and senior management understand the status of a project at any given time.

Project Closure

When the developed or updated application is completed, the system will be handed over to users (as applicable) and support staff. Before the project team disbands, some project closure activities need to take place:

- **Project debrief:** Here, project team members conduct an honest assessment of the performance of the project. Every aspect of the project is considered: project management, management support, team member participation, user participation, tools and technologies, issues and how they were managed, and turnover. Lessons on what went well and what did not are included.

- **Project documentation archival:** All of the records associated with the project are archived for future reference. This includes project plans, correspondence, meeting agendas and minutes, budgets, drawings, specifications, requirements, documentation, and practically everything else.

- **Management review:** This is similar to the project debrief and may be the same activity or something different from the project debrief. Management provides the same kind of feedback on the performance of the project that project team members do themselves.

- **Training:** Users, operators, support, and analysts need to be trained on the new or changed system. In some cases, this should be handled prior to project closure, particularly if users will be using the system before that time.

- **Formal turnover to users, operations, and support:** When the project is completed, the project team formally relinquishes control of all the elements of the project. Responsibility for managing and operating the application is transferred to IT operations and support. Responsibility for using the application is transitioned to business owners and end users.

Project Management Methodologies

Planning, initiating, and managing a project is a complex undertaking, and many different types of projects are undertaken, even within an individual organization. Several project management methodologies are in use. These methodologies differ in approach, documentation, and management techniques.

Project Management Body of Knowledge (PMBOK) Guide

The *PMBOK Guide* is a widely used standard that defines the essentials of project management. PMBOK is based on 12 project delivery principles:

- Stewardship
- Team
- Stakeholders
- Value
- Holistic Thinking
- Quality
- Complexity
- Leadership
- Tailoring
- Opportunities and Threats
- Adaptability and Resilience
- Change Management

   Project performance domains represent a group of related activities that are critical for the effective delivery of project outcomes. These domains emphasize outcomes over processes and are organized into eight categories:

- Team
- Stakeholders
- Life cycle
- Planning
- Navigating Uncertainty and Ambiguity

- Delivery
- Performance
- Project Work

The project delivery principles and performance domains in PMBOK 7th Edition are interdependent and mutually reinforcing. The principles offer a foundational mindset and behavior framework, whereas the performance domains provide a structured approach to achieving project outcomes. Together, they guide project managers in delivering successful projects by focusing on value, quality, stakeholder engagement, adaptability, and continuous improvement.

The PMBOK is described in a publication called *A Guide to the Project Management Body of Knowledge,* published by the Project Management Institute (PMI).

Projects in Controlled Environments

Projects IN Controlled Environments (PRINCE2®) is a project management framework that was developed by the UK Office of Government Commerce and is now managed by Axelos. PRINCE2® 7 is a process-driven framework with the following characteristics:

PRINCE2 Core Principles   The core principles of PRINCE2® form the foundation on which the framework is built. These principles are essential for ensuring the success and effectiveness of projects:

- Continued business justification
- Defined roles and responsibilities
- Focus on products
- Learn from experience
- Manage by exception
- Manage by stages
- Tailor to suit the project environment

PRINCE2 Themes   PRINCE2® themes address various aspects of project management, providing a comprehensive approach to handling different project elements:

- Business case
- Change
- Organization
- Plans
- Progress

- Quality
- Risk

PRINCE2 Processes   PRINCE2® processes provide a step-by-step approach to managing projects, ensuring that all aspects are addressed systematically:

- Starting up a project
- Initiating a project
- Directing a project
- Managing a stage boundary
- Controlling a stage
- Managing product delivery
- Closing a project

Each of these processes has its own structure and additional detail that describe steps and required activities. The PRINCE2® 7 method that integrates principles, themes, and processes is depicted in Figure 3.7.

FIGURE 3.7   The PRINCE2 method integrates principles, themes, and processes.

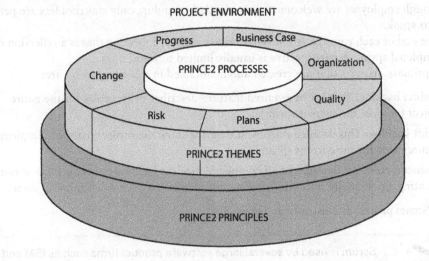

 PRINCE2 is the de facto project management framework in the United Kingdom and several other countries. PRINCE2 is available from www.axelos.com/best-practice-solutions/prince2.

Scrum

Scrum is an iterative and incremental process most commonly used to manage an agile software development effort. Scrum defines three stakeholder roles:

- **Product owner:** The customer or the customer's representative who speaks for the customer.

- **Scrum Master:** The project manager or team leader who facilitates the Scrum process.

- **Developers:** The team members who create the product.

A typical Scrum team is just five to nine members. Larger projects are organized into a Scrum of Scrums that scales upward to include hundreds of programmers.

A typical Scrum project consists of a *sprint,* a focused effort to produce some portion of the total project deliverable. A sprint usually lasts from two to four weeks.

The project team meets every day in a meeting called the *daily Scrum* (or the daily standup) that lasts no more than 15 minutes. It is called a *standup* because participants usually stand (it helps the meeting go faster). The Scrum Master leads the meeting and asks three questions of each team member:

1. What have you done since yesterday?

2. What are you planning to do by tomorrow?

3. What obstacles are preventing you from completing your work?

Although employees are welcome to join the daily standup, only stakeholders are permitted to speak.

At the end of each sprint, a *sprint retrospective* is held, a meeting that is a reflection of the just-completed sprint. A retrospective is usually limited to four hours.

The primary artifacts that are created and maintained in a Scrum project are:

- **Product backlog:** This list of required features describes deliverables for the entire project (not just the current sprint).

- **Sprint backlog:** This detailed document describes how the project team will implement requirements for the current sprint.

- **Product increment:** The sum of all completed product backlog items during a sprint, representing a potentially releasable product that meets the team's definition of done.

The Scrum process is illustrated in Figure 3.8.

 Scrum is used by several large software product firms such as IBM and Microsoft.

Lean

You should think of *lean* more as an approach than as a process like waterfall or Scrum. Lean focuses on efficiency; it starts by identifying value and then achieves it through the mindset of continuous improvement and elimination of waste.

FIGURE 3.8 The Scrum process consists of one or more sprints that produce project deliverables every two to four weeks.

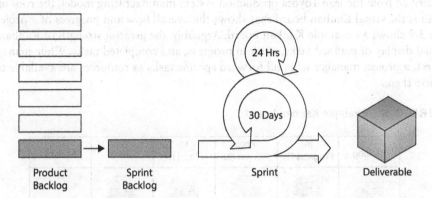

Product   Sprint   Sprint   Deliverable
Backlog   Backlog

Lean was derived from the *lean manufacturing* methodology that originated in the Japanese manufacture of Toyota automobiles, which focused on the elimination of waste without sacrificing value.

The principles of lean are as follows:

- Eliminate waste.
- Amplify learning.
- Decide as late as possible.
- Deliver as fast as possible.
- Empower the team.
- Build integrity in.
- Optimize the whole.

Agile

Like lean, *agile* is more of an approach than a methodology or a process. The agile manifesto describes four principles:

- Individuals and interactions over processes and tools
- Working software over comprehensive documentation
- Customer collaboration over contract negotiation
- Responding to change over following a plan

Agile is mainly known as an iterative technique used to move a project toward success. Pundits would call agile a development process without a master plan, but with iterative plans instead. Like an artist rendering a painting, the artist adds basic shapes and hues, continually adding detail and touching up until the piece is finished.

Kanban

Also derived from the lean Toyota production system manufacturing model, the root of Kanban is the visual Kanban board that shows the overall flow and progress of a project. Figure 3.9 shows an example Kanban board. Arguably, the greatest strength of Kanban is its visual display of planned tasks, work in progress, and completed tasks. While managing a project, a project manager will pull forward specific tasks as resources are available to complete them.

FIGURE 3.9   Example Kanban board

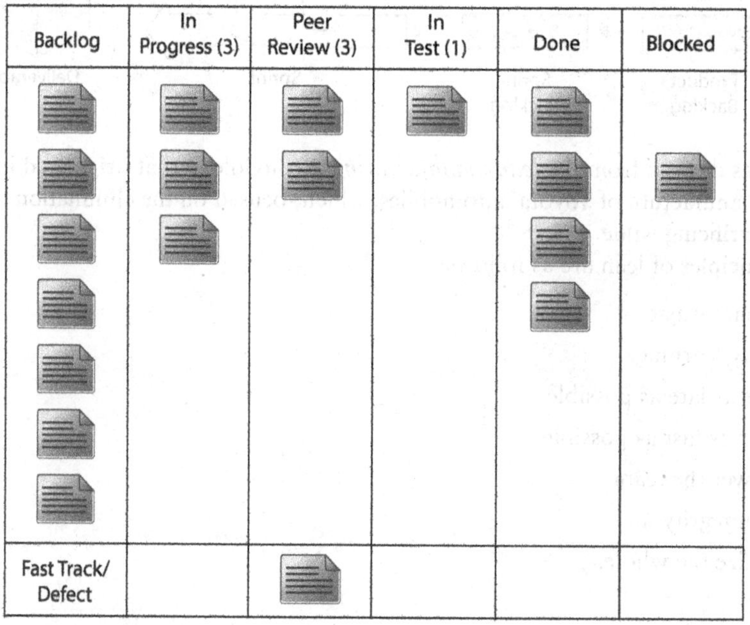

Backlog	In Progress (3)	Peer Review (3)	In Test (1)	Done	Blocked

Scrumban

As the name suggests, *Scrumban* is a combination of Scrum and Kanban methodologies. Scrumban has the structure of Scrum with the flexibility of Kanban. Scrumban is suitable for Kanban-oriented teams that need more structure, or for Scrum teams that need more flexibility.

Extreme Programming

Extreme programming (XP) is an iterative development methodology used primarily in software development projects. Extreme programming has a set of values that are similar to Scrum:

- Simplicity
- Communication
- Feedback
- Respect
- Courage

Figure 3.10 depicts an XP workflow. More information on XP is available at www
.extremeprogramming.org.

FIGURE 3.10   Extreme programming process flow

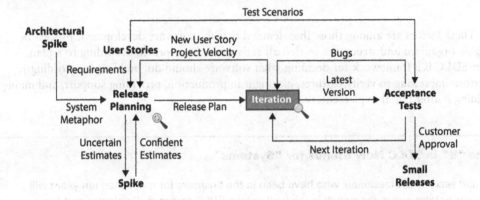

Systems Development Methodologies

Developing and maintaining information systems is a complex undertaking that requires a great deal of structure, organization, and discipline. Application software and other systems are used to automate or support key business processes. Organizations rely heavily on applications to be operating properly, on demand, and with sufficient capacity.

Designing, developing, and using information systems requires a diverse array of skills that are typically held by people located throughout an organization. These diverse skills are applied by persons with different levels and styles of education, and in the workplace, these different groups of people are sometimes suspicious of one another and believe that the others do not really understand "the way things ought to be." This is a part of the human dynamic that affects the performance of project teams and influences the outcome of larger development projects.

System development projects are expensive. Given the cost of developers, project managers, software tools, and computer hardware, even a "small" project can easily cost many tens of thousands of dollars, and large projects can cost several million.

Management wants the project to finish on time and on budget, and users want the software to operate as promised. Shareholders want the entire development process to be efficient and effective.

Exam Tip

The CISA exam may include multiple questions related to the SDLC or its business process equivalent, the Business Process Life Cycle (BPLC), covered later in this chapter. Familiarity with the phases of the SDLC is key to your success with these questions.

These factors are among those that demand that the software development process be highly organized and structured so that all activities are performed according to a plan. The SDLC is a framework for deciding what software should do, building it accordingly, performing testing to verify features, placing it in production, providing support, and maintaining it after initial implementation.

The "S" in SDLC Now Stands for "Systems"

IT and security professionals who have been in the business for more than ten years will sooner or later notice the switch in the well-known SDLC acronym. Originally, and for decades, SDLC referred to the "software development life cycle," for many organizations developed their own business applications and spent considerable effort maintaining and customizing those applications over many years.

Two changes have occurred. First, fewer organizations develop their own business application software, and instead purchase off-the-shelf applications or (more often) subscribe to software-as-a-service (SaaS) services for their primary business applications. Second, the SDLC redundant has been expanded to encompass projects such as the development of infrastructure. Hence, the "S" in SDLC has been changed to "systems" to represent a broader perspective than just that of software applications.

SDLC Methodology Phases

The *systems development life cycle* describes the end-to-end process for developing and maintaining software and systems. A common structure for SDLC is a *waterfall*-style framework that consists of several distinct phases:

- Feasibility study
- Requirements definition
- Design
- Development
- Testing
- Implementation
- Post-implementation

Organizations often employ a "gate process" approach to their SDLC by requiring that a formal review be held at the conclusion of each phase before the next phase is permitted to begin. The review is usually a formal meeting where project managers and other participants describe the status of the project; management, if satisfied that the current phase of the project has been completed successfully and that all requirements have been met, will permit the project to proceed to the next phase.

In addition to the waterfall SDLC model, iterative and spiral models are used in SDLC processes. The iterative and spiral models both operate in (visually) circular modes, as opposed to the linear waterfall model.

The *spiral* model consists of the development of requirements, design, and one or more prototypes, followed by additional requirements and design phases until the entire design is complete. Similarly, the development in the *iterative* model goes through one or more loops of planning, requirements, design, coding, and testing until development and implementation are considered complete.

The *DevOps* model is also often used for systems development processes. DevOps is an iterative development and operations model that is discussed later in this chapter.

SDLC in this section is described from the waterfall model's perspective. The activities discussed in this section in the waterfall model are quite similar to those in the iterative and spiral models.

Pre-SDLC: Software and Business Capabilities Imagined

The first phase of the SDLC is the *feasibility study*. But how does the feasibility study get started? It does not create itself; instead, the feasibility study is started as a result of some pre-SDLC event.

An instantiation of the SDLC is created when management has decided that some new software application is needed, or some significant changes are needed in an existing application. By "instantiation" I mean that management has decided to initiate the process to develop or update a software application. Management makes such a decision as a response to an event, which could be any of the following:

- **Changes in market conditions:** For example, the entrance of a new competitor or the development of a new product or service feature by a competitor may spur management to respond by matching the competitor's capabilities. A competitor can also create a new market through innovation in products or services; this kind of a move sometimes needs to be answered by making a change to maintain parity with the competitor. Or *your* organization may be the one that creates a new market through some groundbreaking innovation in the way that it does business or in what it delivers to its customers.

- **Changes in costs or expenses:** Dramatic shifts in capital or expense costs may force an organization to make changes. For instance, higher fuel costs may prompt the organization to reduce field service calls, but doing so might require better remote diagnostic and self-healing capabilities. In the 1990s, the shift to software development outsourcing required transformations in development methodologies that prompted organizations to make or buy better defect-management applications. And dropping telecommunications costs and higher bandwidth meant that online service providers began to ratchet up their offerings, most of which required enhancements to existing online service applications, and sometimes brand-new ones.

- **Changes in regulation:** The rise in dependence on technology has resulted in some negative events, which in turn resulted in new legislation or changes in existing legislation. Examples of relatively recent and updated regulation include Sarbanes–Oxley; GLBA (Gramm–Leach–Bliley Act); HIPAA (Health Insurance Portability and Accountability Act); FERC/NERC (regulations from the Federal Energy Regulatory Commission and the North American Electric Reliability Corporation); USA PATRIOT Act (Uniting and Strengthening America by Providing Appropriate Tools Required to Intercept and Obstruct Terrorism Act of 2001), which has been updated by the USA Freedom Act; European General Data Protection Regulation (GDPR); PCI DSS (Payment Card Industry Data Security Standard); and many others. Many of these regulations require organizations to implement additional safeguards, controls, and recordkeeping to information systems. Sometimes this results in an organization opting to discontinue use of an older information system in favor of making or buying a newer application that can more effectively comply with applicable laws.

- **Changes in risk:** New types of vulnerabilities are discovered with regularity, and new threats are developed in response to vulnerabilities as well as changes in economic conditions and organizational business models. In other words, hackers find new ways to try to attack systems for profit within the growing cybercriminal enterprises of the world. Applications that were considered safe just a few years ago are now known to be too vulnerable to operate. Reducing risk sometimes means making changes to application logic, and sometimes it requires that an application be discontinued altogether.

- **Changes to business processes:** Many types of changes to business processes will require organizations to alter their business applications so that they continue to support those processes. For example, a change in the way that purchase orders are requested and approved may require changes to the financial accounting application.

- **Changes to legal agreements:** Changes in the legal agreements between organizations can compel an organization to make changes to its software applications. There are several possible reasons for this, including changes in risks or regulations imposed upon customer or partner organizations.

- **Changes in customer requirements:** Changes like those just discussed will often prompt customer organizations to ask for new features or for changes in existing features in the products and services they buy. Often this requires changes in processes and applications to meet these customers' needs.

It is important to understand that *innovation* is also a valid and frequent reason that an organization chooses to make changes to a software application. Generally, this means that an organization has developed new features or methods in a software application in an attempt to gain a competitive advantage.

 Internal and external events prompt management to action by initiating changes in business processes, product designs, service models, and, frequently, the software applications that are used to support and manage them. What begins as an informal discussion turns to more formal actions and, finally, to the initiation of a project to make changes.

Feasibility Study

The *feasibility study* is the first formal phase in the SDLC. The feasibility study is an intellectual effort that seeks to determine whether a specific change or set of changes in business processes and underlying applications is practical to undertake.

Capital and money are the fuel and lubricant for an organization. Often the purpose of a feasibility study is not to answer the question, "Can a specific type of change be made to the business?" but rather, "Is a specific type of change to the business feasible from a cost and benefit perspective?" In other words, the feasibility study is an analysis of proposed changes to business processes and supporting applications, including the costs associated with making those changes and the benefits that are expected as a result of those changes. While there is often a qualitative aspect in the feasibility study, there is almost always a quantitative aspect that states, "These specific changes will cost XXX to build, YYY to maintain, and are anticipated to make a ZZZ impact on revenue."

Organizations don't always make changes to business processes to increase revenue or reduce costs. However, revenue and costs are nearly always the quantitative elements that receive attention. For example, if an organization is enacting changes to processes and systems to remain compliant with regulations, management is still going to be interested in the cost and revenue impact that the changes will bring about.

A feasibility study often will propose two or more approaches to a particular challenge. For instance, if a project has been initiated as a result of changes in market conditions, the purpose of the feasibility study may be to explore various ways to respond to those market conditions; for each way to respond, there may be two, three, or more ways to implement the change by using a variety of technologies or approaches. For example, when a ride-sharing service seeks ways of expanding its markets, it considers developing additional services such as the delivery of restaurant meals, flowers, and other goods.

The feasibility study should also include the following considerations:

- Time required to develop or acquire software (or to make changes) and whether the solution can be developed or acquired within that time frame
- A comparison between the cost of developing the application versus buying one
- Whether an existing system can meet the business need
- Whether the application supports strategic business objectives
- Whether a solution can be developed (or acquired) that is compatible with other IT systems
- The cost of building interfaces between the new system and other existing systems
- The impact of the proposed changes to the business regarding regulatory compliance
- Whether future requirements can be met by the system
- Whether an innovative change will result in an increase in market share

A feasibility study should seek to uncover every reasonable issue and risk that will be associated with the new system. The study should have the appearance and form of impartiality and should not reflect the biases and preferences of those who are taking part in the feasibility study or its outcome.

A feasibility study may also include or reference a formal business plan for the proposed new activity. A *business plan* is a formal document that describes the new business activity, its contribution and impact to the organization, resources required to operate the activity, benefits from operating the activity, and risks associated with the activity.

 When the feasibility study has been completed, a formal management review should take place so that senior management fully understands the results and recommendations of the study and can determine whether the project should proceed or whether any changes to the plan should take place.

Requirements Definition

Requirements describe necessary characteristics of a new application or of changes being made to an existing application. They describe how the application should work as well as the technologies that it should support. The types of requirements used in software projects are as follows:

- Business functional requirements
- Technical requirements and standards
- Security and regulatory requirements
- Disaster recovery and business continuity requirements
- Privacy requirements

These types of requirements are described as follows:

Business Functional Requirements   Nearly every software project will include *functional requirements*. These are statements that describe required characteristics that the software must have to support business needs. This includes both the way that the software accepts, processes, and produces information, and how users interact with the software in terms of technology, appearance, and user interface function.

Functional requirements should be a part of new software acquisitions as well as modifications or updates to software.

Example functional requirements resemble the following:

- Application supports payroll tax calculations for U.S. federal, states, counties, and cities

- Application supports payment by credit card, electronic check, and virtual currency

- Application encrypts credit card numbers, Social Security numbers, and driver's license numbers in storage and when transmitted

Notice that the preceding examples do not specify *how* the application is to accomplish these things. Business requirements are interested in *what* the application does; the application architect or designer will determine *how* the application will support those requirements.

In a few circumstances, new business requirements are not needed for a software modification. For example, if a software interface is being upgraded, an existing software program may need to be modified to work with the new interface. A change like this should be transparent to users, and the software should not differ in the way that it supports existing business requirements. So, in a way, it can be argued that business requirements apply even in this case: the program will still be required to adhere to existing business functional requirements.

It is not unusual for a formal requirements document to span many hundreds of pages. This will be the case especially for larger and more complex applications such as customer relationship management (CRM), enterprise resource planning (ERP), manufacturing resource planning (MRP), or service management systems.

Technical Requirements and Standards   To help the organization remain efficient, any new application or system should use the same basic technologies that are already in use (or that are planned on being used in the long term). The details related to maintaining the consistency that is required constitute the majority of technical requirements and standards.

An organization of any appreciable size should have formal technical standards in place. These standards are policy statements that cite the technologies, protocols, vendors, and services that make up the organization's core IT infrastructure. The purpose of standards is to increase technological consistency throughout the entire IT infrastructure, which helps to simplify the environment and reduce costs. Standards should include the following:

- Server hardware, virtualization platform, virtual machine, operating system, and operating system configuration
- Server tools and services
- Application programming interfaces (APIs)
- Database and storage management systems
- Network architecture, communications protocols, and services
- Authentication and authorization models and protocols
- Security architecture, hardening, configuration, and algorithms
- Software development methodologies, tools, languages, and processes
- User applications and tools
- Any other standards that describe methodologies, technologies, or practices

When an organization is considering the acquisition of a new system, the requirements for the new system should include the organization's IT and security standards. This will help the organization select a system that will have the lowest possible impact on capital and operational costs over the lifetime of the system.

Besides IT standards, many additional technical requirements will define the desired new system. These requirements will describe several characteristics of the system, including:

- How the system will accept, process, and output data
- Specific data layouts for interfaces to other systems
- Support of specific modules or tools that will supplement or support application functions (e.g., the type of tax table that will be used in an invoicing or payroll system)
- Language support
- Specific middleware support
- Client platform support

NOTE   The entire body of technical requirements should accomplish two sweeping objectives: ensure that the new system will blend harmoniously with the existing environment, and ensure that the new system will operate as required at the technical level.

Security and Regulatory Requirements   Security control requirements must be developed to ensure that the new application will contain appropriate controls and characteristics that will protect sensitive information and comply with applicable regulations.

Security and regulation are sometimes strange bedfellows, and sometimes they are symbiotic. It is often better to split security and regulatory requirements into two separate sections. However, security and regulation are often mashed together, since the majority of recent applicable regulations seem to be security-related.

NOTE   We have kept these two topics together because We suspect that most readers expect to find security and compliance together, but We recommend you separate them, because many security requirements are not associated with regulations, and because many regulations are not security related. In the following, We will keep them separated.

Organizations should have an existing *security requirements document* that can be readily applied to any systems development or acquisition project. These requirements should describe the business and technical controls that address several security topics, including the following:

- **Authentication:** This broad category includes many specific requirements related to the manner in which application users authenticate to the system. For systems that perform autonomous authentication, this will include all of the password quality requirements (minimum length, expiration, complexity, and so on), account lockout settings, password reset procedures, user account provisioning/deprovisioning, and user ID standards. Authentication standards may also include requirements for machine and system accounts in support of automated functions in the application. For applications that use a network-based authentication service such as LDAP (Lightweight Directory Access Protocol), Kerberos, or a single sign-on (SSO) solution, security requirements should describe how the application must interface with a network authentication service.

- **Authorization:** This category includes requirements related to the manner in which different users are granted access to different functions and data in the application. Authorization requirements may include the way in which roles are established, maintained, and audited. An organization may require that the application support a number of *roles*, which are templates that contain authorization details that can be applied to a user account.

- **Access control:** This category has to do with how the application is configured to permit access to users and/or roles. Unlike authorization, which is about assigning roles to users, access control is concerned with assigning access permissions to objects such as application functions and data. Depending on the way in which an application is designed, permissions assignment may be user-centric, object-centric, or both.

- **Encryption:** Encryption is used to hide data that, for whatever reason, may exist in "plain sight" in some contexts and yet must still be protected from those who do not have authorization to access it. Encryption standards fall into two broad categories: (1) data requiring encryption in certain settings and contexts, and with certain encryption algorithms and key lengths; and (2) key management to be handled in specific ways that permit the application to be operated similarly to other applications in the IT environment.

- **Data validation:** Applications should not blindly trust all input data to be properly formed and formatted. Instead, an application should perform validation checks against input data, whether a user types in input data on an application input form or the application receives the data via a batch feed from a trusted source. Data validation includes not only input data, but also the results of intermediate calculations and output data. Requirements should also specify what the application should do when it encounters data that fails a validation check.

- **Audit logging:** This is the characteristic whereby the application creates an electronic record of events. These events include changing application configuration settings, adding and deleting users, changing user roles and permissions, resetting user login credentials, changing access control settings, and, of course, the actions and transactions that the application is designed to handle. Requirements about audit logging will be concerned with the configuration that is used to control the types of events that are written to an audit log, as well as the controls used to protect the audit log from tampering (which, if permitted, could enable someone to "erase their tracks").

- **Security operational requirements:** Management of passwords, encryption keys, event logs, patching, and other activities is required to maintain an application's confidentiality, integrity, and availability.

- **Misuse and abuse requirements:** This category needs to include the full range of use (and misuse) cases through which a user may—deliberately or not—misuse or abuse the application. This includes malicious input and other methods that may cause the application to malfunction, resulting in an escalation of privilege, exposure of—or tampering with—sensitive data, and exhaustion of system resources. The list of requirements should not merely match the capabilities of any automated or manual testing tools used by the organization.

Disaster Recovery and Business Continuity Requirements

Applications that do—or may in the future—support critical business functions included in an organization's disaster recovery plans need to have certain characteristics. Depending on specific recovery targets specified for the business process supported by the application, these requirements may include the ability for the application to run in the public cloud, on a server cluster, on a virtual machine, or in a load-balanced mode; to support data replication; to facilitate rapid recovery from backup tape or database redo logs; or to be installed on a cold recovery server without complicated, expensive, or time-consuming software licensing issues. Requirements could also dictate the ability for the application to be easily recovered from a server or virtual machine image on a storage area network (SAN), to operate correctly in a virtual server environment, and to operate correctly in a cloud environment such as AWS or Azure. An application might also be expected to work with a different brand or version of the database management system or to coexist with other applications, even though it may usually be configured to run on a server by itself.

Privacy Requirements   In the broadest sense, privacy is about three distinctly different issues. First, privacy has to do with the protection of personally sensitive information so that it cannot be accessed by unauthorized parties. This aspect of privacy neatly falls into the umbrella of security; security requirements can be developed that require access controls or encryption of personal information.

The second aspect of privacy is the prevention of proliferation and misuse of personally sensitive information. This has a lot less to do with security and more to do with how the organization treats and uses sensitive information and whether it permits this information to be passed on to other organizations for their own purposes. In this regard, privacy is about business functionality that is specifically related to how the application handles personal information.

Finally, privacy is about individual control over personal data. Data subjects should have the right to know how their data is being collected, maintained, used, and shared. Personal information should only be handled with notice to and consent of the data subject; data subjects should have the ability to withdraw that consent at any time.

For example, if an application includes canned reports about customers, and those reports are sent to third parties, those reports should be configurable so that they can contain (or omit) certain fields. For instance, customers' dates of birth may be omitted from a report that is sent to a third-party organization to reduce the possibility of the third party using or abusing information to the detriment of individual customers. The rule in this case is this: "You can't abuse or misuse information you do not possess or cannot access." Indeed, regulations such as the European GDPR require that organizations collect sensitive data only as required to perform services, and that they retain the data for only as long as it is needed.

Increasingly, privacy is addressed by regulation, so an organization may choose to classify privacy requirements in a privacy section or in a regulations section.

Organizing and Reviewing Requirements   In a software project in which many individuals are contributing requirements, the project manager or another person should track each requirement back to a specific individual so that person can justify or explain those requirements if needed.

When all requirements have been collected and categorized, the project manager should check with each contributor to make sure that each requirement is actually a *requirement* and not merely a "nice-to-have" feature. Perhaps each requirement can be weighted or ranked in order of importance. This will help, especially in a request for proposal (RFP) situation, where analysts need to evaluate suppliers' conformance to individual requirements. This helps project personnel determine which vendors are best able to meet the requirements that matter most.

The teams that develop requirements need to ensure that requirements are measurable. The reason for this is that the requirements developed in this phase of the project should flow directly into user acceptance testing plans (for functional requirements) and system testing plans (for technical requirements).

The RFP Process   The vast majority of mainstream business functions, such as accounting, customer relationship management, incident management, sales force management, and enterprise resource planning, can be handled exceedingly well using cloud-based software-as-a-service (SaaS) and common off-the-shelf (COTS) software. Advances in SaaS and COTS software have resulted in most IT organizations needing to develop only custom interfaces between SaaS or COTS applications and specialized programs that cannot be readily obtained. Thus, the SDLC process can be morphed somewhat to accommodate the fact that most big software projects are a matter of leasing or buying, not making. The result is the ever popular RFP activity used to communicate requirements and solicit proposals from vendors. Typical steps in the RFP process are:

Research   Personnel in the organization may need to learn more about available applications and solutions so that they can develop better requirements that will more closely align with business needs.

Requirements   This trend makes the development of good requirements much more important, because the matching of different vendors' software products with business and technical requirements depends mostly on requirements. The software that is obtained is configurable only to a point, and it probably will not be able to perform other functions so easily. In an environment where a business analyst or project manager realizes that some requirements were omitted, if the organization wrote its own software, then it might be fairly easy to change the application. If, on the other hand, some important requirements were omitted and a product selection was made in the absence of those requirements, the organization may have to live without the functionality related to those requirements. It's kind of like specifying a four-passenger automobile because you forgot about that fifth family member; now that you've got the car, it's more difficult to make a change.

Vendor Financial Stability   When an organization is considering purchasing or licensing software from a software vendor, the organization should examine the financial stability of the vendor. This is done as a way of determining whether the vendor is likely to be in business in the future. If the vendor's financial fundamentals are unhealthy, then purchasing software from this vendor is a risky proposition, since the vendor may not be in business in the future. This would probably require the organization to change its software in another expensive application migration that could have been avoided.

Product Roadmap   Although the software vendor may be healthy, it's also important to understand the vendor's long-term vision for its product. This includes not only business functionality but also the technical platforms that will be supported in the future. In this regard, it is also useful to know whether any of the vendors being considered can be deemed to be market leaders or market followers. If the organization shopping for software is likewise a market leader, it may make more sense to select a market-leading company that will be able to keep up with the organization's own vision and market leadership.

Experience   It's important to understand how much experience a prospective vendor has. A suitable vendor should have many years of experience developing software for the solution that the organization is trying to solve. This will help to clarify whether the vendor has been in the business of developing this particular type of software for a long time or has only recently entered the market. Deep experience will give confidence that the vendor has experience helping its customers solve the types of business problems that its software is designed to solve, whereas a company with little experience will probably have more difficulty helping its customers solve even simpler business problems, not to mention unusual or complex problems. You do not want to be in the position of calling the software vendor to ask, "Hi, we have a new kind of problem that we need to solve," only to receive the answer, "Well, we won't be able to be of much help because we're new at this ourselves."

Vision   Even for a software product as mundane as one for accounting, it is important to know each vendor's vision for how it aims to innovate and to approach business problems in the future. If a vendor's vision varies widely from your organization's vision, perhaps that particular vendor is not the best choice. Although difference in vision should rarely disqualify a vendor entirely, it should be just one more variable to consider in the long equation of vendor selection.

Multitenant Data Protection and Data Segregation   For SaaS applications, it is important for those service providers to enact strict controls so that users in one customer organization are not able to access other customers' data, even in cases of software defects and intrusions.

References   When an organization is considering leasing or purchasing software from an outside vendor, it is wise to discuss the vendor and its services with at least two or three reference customers. We suggest that a standard questionnaire be developed before any vendor contacts are made. A questionnaire will help the project manager or business analyst to collect the same information from each reference customer. This will help the organization more easily compare reference information that has been collected from several reference clients. Questions asked of reference clients fall into several areas:

Satisfaction with Implementation   If the software vendor will be helping with software implementation, ask reference clients about the quality of this effort. Find out what kinds of specific issues came up and how the vendor managed them.

Satisfaction with Migration   If the software vendor is going to be assisting with migrating business functionality to the new software application, ask each reference client about the quality of this effort. Whether it went well or not so well, get the names of specific personnel so that your organization can (if feasible) ask that certain vendor staff be there to support migration.

Satisfaction with Support   Find out from each reference client whether they are satisfied with each vendor's support organization. See if the support organization provides timely, high-quality, and consistently good service.

Satisfaction with Long-Term Roadmap   Ask the reference client if they are satisfied with each vendor's long-term product roadmap. Ask what strengths and weaknesses are in the roadmap.

What Went Well   Find out each vendor's strengths and try to determine if those strengths are associated with individual vendor employees or with the vendor overall. Ask if the reference client would choose the vendor again and why (or why not).

What Did Not Go So Well   Ask the reference client what parts of their software project did not go so well. Find out if the reference client believes their experience to be associated with one specific vendor employee or the entire company as a whole.

Other Questions   Finally, ask each vendor's reference client if they have any other useful information that has not been discussed. Sometimes you'll find out about a completely different set of activities that were associated with the vendor's migration.

Evaluation   When you have received RFP responses from each vendor, you can begin to chart the responses in a multicolumn spreadsheet, with each vendor's responses in a separate column. You can even score each response with a Low-Medium-High rating, and use that to see how the vendors rank in terms of requirements and references. If you can reduce the field of potential vendors to the top two or three vendors, you may choose to evaluate their products in your IT environment for a time. This means installing the software in your organization to try out with some users. The evaluation should be highly scripted—not to "win" or "lose," but to verify systematically that the software performs as claimed and that the vendor's responses to your functional requirements are credible. If the software operates differently from their claims in the RFP responses, it's time either to ask hard questions or to disqualify the vendor for stretching the truth and move on.

Vendor Support   Success with a given vendor's software product can rest on vendor support alone. Specifically, if there are problems and support is of insufficient quality, the project can stall or even fail. Support quality has a few dimensions to it, including timeliness, quality, and speed to escalation. If a vendor falls short in any of these areas, then that choice may have more risk.

Source Code Escrow   When an organization develops its own software, of course the software is already in the organization's custody. However, when a third-party vendor develops the software, the customer probably does not have a copy of it. Under ordinary business conditions, this is acceptable. However, should the vendor fail, the vendor will be unable to maintain the software and the organization would be stuck with a software package without source code or programmers to support it. Source code escrow is a viable solution to this problem, and it works like this: The software vendor sends an electronic copy of its source code to a third-party software escrow firm, which keeps control of the software. If, however, the software vendor goes out of business, the organization will be able to obtain a copy of the vendor's software for support purposes. This is a bad-case scenario, but it's better than the worst-case scenario, where the software vendor goes out of business and the organization has no source code at all.

Selection   After the organization has narrowed the search down to two or three vendors, it's time to do more critical thinking, discussing, and identifying of the primary strengths, weaknesses, and differentiators between the vendor finalists. The RFP team should make a recommendation to management on its choice, explaining why this particular vendor should be chosen over the others. The final decision on a software vendor should be made by management, with the RFP team being a consultative body. Remember that senior management will be making a business decision that partly considers the technology and partly considers the value proposition (the value derived from a given expenditure).

Contract Negotiation   When the selection is made, the contract between the organization and the software vendor needs to be negotiated. There are plenty of ways that the software vendor can be held accountable in terms of delivering and supporting software that meets the business's needs. However, the organization purchasing the software will also likely have obligations of its own. I recommend that you *not* tell the other vendor finalists that they are out of the game too soon. If contract negotiations with the first-choice vendor do not proceed well, it may be smart to begin negotiations with one of the other finalists (management should decide which vendor). Contract negotiation should be left to the lawyers. However, lawyers on each side will often consult with IT experts or management to make sure that sections of contract language accurately describe systems, controls, security, and any other matters that lawyers may not have expertise in.

Closing the RFP   When the RFP process has concluded, the project team can begin preparations for testing and implementing the software. For obvious reasons, the design and development phases of the SDLC process are usually skipped altogether, unless the organization needs to build some custom interfaces or other programs that will enable the acquired software to work in the environment.

Request for Information   A request for information (RFI) is similar to a request for proposal (RFP) in that organizations are soliciting information from one or more vendors or service providers. Compared to an RFP, an RFI is lightweight, as it requests information about vendors' products and services with no stated intent to purchase any services or products.

An RFI might precede a planned purchase, or it could precede an RFP. Mainly, the purpose of an RFI is to help individuals in an organization learn more about specific vendors or the products or services they sell.

Design

When all functional, technology, security, privacy, regulatory, and other requirements have been finalized, design of the application can begin. It is assumed that a high-level design was developed in the feasibility study, since an elementary design is necessary to estimate costs to compute the financial viability of the application—but, if not, the high-level design should be developed first.

The design effort should be a top-down process, starting with the major components of the application and then decomposing each module into increasingly detailed pieces.

It's difficult to say whether a data flow diagram (DFD), entity relationship diagram (ERD), or some other high-level depiction of the application should be developed first. This will depend partly upon the nature of the application and partly on the experience of the developers, analysts, and designers. Regardless, design should start at a high level and graduate to levels of increasing complexity, to the point where database designers and developers have sufficient detail to begin development.

Project team members who represent business owners/operators/customers should review the application design to confirm that the analysts' and designers' concept of the application agrees with that of the business owners. Reviews should be done at each level of design, not just at the top level. Business experts should be able to read and understand both a high-level design and a detailed design and to confirm whether the design is appropriate or not.

Design review by customers can be a step in the process where business customers and designers do not see eye to eye and where they might disagree on the design; any disagreements can be attributed either to differences in the understanding of technology or to practical versus abstract thinking. To end the design review prematurely could have costly consequences. The potential consequences of failing to come to an agreement on design are vividly depicted in the classic illustration shown in Figure 3.11.

FIGURE 3.11   The potential consequences of failing to agree on design

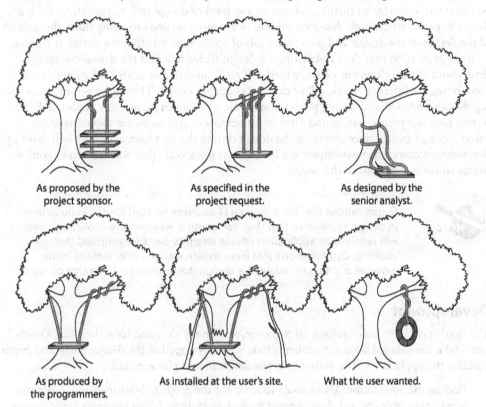

As proposed by the
project sponsor.

As specified in the
project request.

As designed by the
senior analyst.

As produced by
the programmers.

As installed at the user's site.

What the user wanted.

Key activities in the software design phase include:

- The use of a structured software design tool or methodology that records details of data flow and processing flow from high levels to detail levels
- Generalized and detailed database design at the logical and physical levels
- Storyboards showing user interaction with the application
- Details on reports that can be generated by the application

The application design effort should also include the development of test plans that will be used during the development and test phases of the project. Test plans need to be developed no later than the design phase, because developers will need to perform unit testing during development as a way of verifying that they have coded software modules properly (and they may need to consult test plan documents for confirmation that they are developing software correctly). If test plans are not developed until the test phase, developers will have to figure out tests on their own, or they might not perform enough testing, which will result in many more defects being discovered during the formal testing phase of the project.

When design reviews have concluded that the design is complete, a "design freeze" should be instituted, whereby no further changes to any level of design will be permitted. With a design freeze in effect, both designers and users are more inclined to really think through all of the details of the design and do a better job of confirming whether the design is correct.

An organization that does not institute a design freeze will find the design changing throughout the development phase, which will result in different parts of the application conforming to different "versions" of the ever-changing design. This will result in chaos during the development and testing phases and is sure to result in many more reported defects during user acceptance testing and after implementation. Management should strongly assert a design freeze, since changing the design during the development phase will drive up development costs when developers are forced to rework code that was written in conformance to earlier versions of the design.

Organizations that have internal IT auditors on staff should include them in design reviews so that they can confirm whether the application design will result in an application whose integrity can be confirmed through auditing. Organizations that incur external audits may want to invite external auditors to review the design documents for this same purpose.

Development

The developers have been waiting all this time, and finally they can have their fun. Developers take the detailed design documents that were developed in the design phase and begin building the application. The activities in the development phase include:

- **Coding the application:** Using tools selected for the project, developers will build the application code. Newer development tools may include design elements, code generators, debuggers, or testing tools that will make developers more productive.

- **Developing program- and system-level documents:** During development, developers document technical details such as program logic, data flows, and interfaces. This aids other developers later on when modifications to the application are needed.

- **Developing user procedures:** As they develop user interfaces, developers can write the procedure documents and help text that application users will read. In a more extensive, formal environment, developers may write the essential core of these documents, which will be completed by tech writers. But an even better idea may be this: end-user documentation is written by tech writers who derive procedures from requirements; then the software developers will use technical requirements and the completed end-user documentation to guide them on development of end-user software.

- **Working with users:** As they develop the parts of the application that interface with users, developers will need to work with them to ensure that the forms, screens, and reports that they build will meet users' needs.

Let's examine the tools and techniques commonly used in software development.

Application Programming Languages   An organization that is considering an application development project has to make several strategic decisions regarding the technologies and techniques that will be used to perform the development and to operate the completed application.

Among those choices is the programming language(s) that will be used to write the application. Rarely does an organization have a wide-open choice of languages; rather its choices will be constrained by several factors, including:

Standards   The organization's preferences for specific brands of computer hardware, operating systems, and databases will limit available languages to those that are available on its chosen application platform.

Available Expertise   Preferences will be further limited by available programming experience among staff or contracted developers. After the application has been developed and placed in use, the organization will need to make periodic changes; an experienced developer will be needed for that task as well.

Context and Practicality   For a given hardware and software environment, the nature of the application will make some of the available languages more desirable and others less so. For instance, an organization wants to write a professional-services invoicing application in a Unix environment where assembler, C, C++, C#, and Java are the available languages. Chances are good that assembler will be eliminated, because assembler is a poor choice for application development. Instead, C++, C#, or Java is likely to be chosen. Similarly, mobile applications on the Android platform are likely to be written in Java, and applications for iOS are likely to be written in Swift.

Another factor that will influence language selection is the availability of development and testing tools. With nearly as much scrutiny as for the application features themselves, the organization should carefully select an application development environment if it does not already have one (or if it has determined that its present capabilities are insufficient).

Requirements for a development environment must include functions that will permit developers to write software code that can meet functional requirements for the application itself. If, for example, functional requirements specify a high degree of accuracy in a way that requires a high volume of test cases, a development environment that can help to automate testing will enable developers to perform this rigorous testing more easily.

Development in a Software Acquisition Setting   In a software acquisition situation where an organization is purchasing or leasing software instead of developing it in-house, development activities may still be required. In a software acquisition project, software development is often needed to facilitate several needs:

Customizations   Larger off-the-shelf applications make accommodations for customizations that must be developed. These customizations can take many forms, including application code modules, XML documents, and configurations.

Integration with Other Systems   Applications rarely stand alone. Instead, they accept data from various sources and, in turn, provide data to other systems. Sometimes "bridge programs" or integration gateways need to be written that serve to move and transform data from one environment to another.

Authentication   In an effort to improve security or make application adoption easier, organizations often desire that new applications use a system- or network-based authentication service. The primary advantage to this approach is that users do not need to remember yet another user ID and password. An application's authentication can often be tied to LDAP or Microsoft Active Directory, or it can be part of a federated identity environment.

Reports   Complex applications may have a report writer module that is used to create custom reports. Depending on the underlying technology, a developer may be needed to develop these reports. Even if a report authoring tool is intuitive and easy to use, a developer may still be needed to help users design reports.

An organization that is considering acquiring software should develop and enforce policies regarding the extent to which customizations will be permitted. Customizations can be costly when off-the-shelf software upgrades take place, because they may need to be rewritten to work with the upgraded software. The cost savings of using off-the-shelf software can be negated by the additional time required to manage and upgrade customizations.

Debugging   The first and most crucial part of software testing is performed by the developers themselves during development. *Debugging* is the process of testing software code to make sure that it operates properly and is free of defects. The testing that a developer performs is called *unit testing*; this means that the individual modules (units) that developers create are tested on their own. Wider-scale testing is usually performed by others later on in the development cycle.

The objectives of debugging include the following:

Correct Operations   Software developers need to make sure that software modules are manipulating data and performing calculations correctly.

Proper Input Validation   All input fields and input records should perform detailed checks on all input data to prevent errors and tampering. Manipulation of input data is one of the principal forms of application abuse and a significant cause of security incidents.

Proper Output Validation   Modules must perform output validation to ensure that output data is within bounds. Output validation is one way to detect malfunctions that occur in an application module.

Proper Resource Usage   Modules should be tested to make sure that they utilize resources such as memory correctly. Modules should properly request and relinquish resources so that malfunctions such as memory leaks do not occur.

While it is tempting to gloss over debugging and unit testing, the effort usually pays big dividends by streamlining the integration effort and reducing the number of defects in system testing. Defects that could have been found during debugging usually take more resources to find during system testing, because a defect must first be isolated to a specific section of code before it can be diagnosed and corrected.

Source Code Management   In any size development effort, whether the development team is one developer or 250 developers, an organization should use a source code repository tool. Such a tool has several purposes:

Protection   A source code management tool often includes access controls so that only authorized personnel are permitted to access application source code. This helps to protect the organization's intellectual property and to prevent other persons from learning the secrets of the application's inner workings or performing unauthorized changes to source code, either of which could lead to fraud or misuse of the application later on.

Control   A source code management system utilizes "checkout" and "check-in" functions so that only one developer at a time may work on a specific part of the application. This helps to ensure the integrity of the application's source code.

Version Control   A source code management system tracks each version of the code as it is checked in by developers. The system tracks the changes made from version to version and can show the differences in code between versions, and it also permits the reversion to an older version if application problems arise later on.

Recordkeeping   A source code management system maintains records related to checkouts, check-ins, and modifications to source code. This makes it possible for management to know what changes are being made to source code and who is making those changes.

Organizations that outsource some of their software development to third parties need to determine the business rules regarding those outsiders' access to source code. Some portions of a software application may be considered intellectual property or may constitute trade secrets. Further, there may be sections that are security-related. In such cases, organizations should consider enacting and enforcing business rules that restrict outsourced developer access to these more sensitive portions of code.

Source code management is not an activity that is limited to the period when the application is first developed; on the contrary, source code management is a vital activity that must continue throughout the lifespan of the application.

Testing Methodologies

During the requirements, design, and even development phases of a software project, various project team members develop specific facts and behavioral characteristics about the application. Each of those characteristics must be verified before the application is approved for production use. This concept is depicted in a V-model in Figure 3.12. The V-model is sometimes used to depict the increasing levels of detail and complexity in the SDLC.

FIGURE 3.12   Requirements and design characteristics must all be verified through testing.

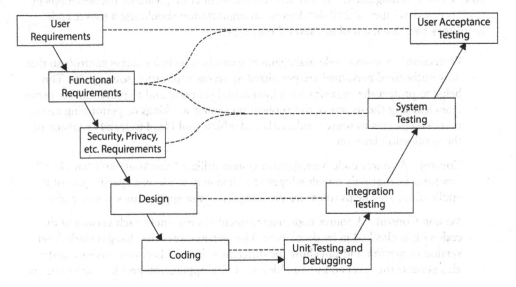

The stages of testing in a software development project are unit testing, system testing, functional testing, and user acceptance testing. Each stage is addressed in turn following a brief overview of test plans.

Test Plans   Before testing can take place, it is first necessary to create test plans. Testing, at the overall project level and at the detail level, should be a methodical and repeatable process, not subject to the skills and experience of any individuals who are performing tests.

To a great extent, test plans are going to be derived directly from requirements that were developed prior to development taking place. There may, however, be other sources or types of testing that may not be explicitly stated in requirements, including:

- Adequacy of business use cases
- Resistance against misuse and abuse cases
- The degree to which a program's operation and functions are self-evident to the user

Because of the volume and/or complexity of test cases, it may be necessary to create test plans. Test plans may be developed for several reasons, including:

- Volume of tests needed to be distributed to several individuals in some logical manner
- Testing performed by one or more outside parties or organizations
- Tests allocated based on the availability of individual testers or test teams
- Tests allocated based on the knowledge or skills of individual testers or test teams
- Tests allocated based on the tools required to perform testing (for example, workload testing or security defect testing)

Unit Testing   Unit testing is usually performed by developers during the coding phase of the software development project. When each developer is assigned the task of building a section of an application, the specifications that are given to the developer should include test plans or test cases that the developer will use to verify that the code works properly. This is true regardless of whether the part of the application that the developer is working on will be seen and used by end users or will be buried deep within the bowels of the application and never seen by anyone.

In a formal development environment, the unit test plans should be precise and list each test that the developer should undertake. The developer then performs each of the tests and records the results (usually the actual output) of the test. Those test results are then archived so that they can be referred to later if needed.

The archiving of unit testing records sometimes proves valuable when later phases of testing are taking place and some problem is found. Developers trying to isolate the cause of later testing problems can refer back to test plans and results at the unit testing phase to see whether the test plans and other unit-testing activities were performed correctly, or whether they contained appropriate test cases. This evidence can save the project team a lot of time by eliminating the need to repeat unit testing.

Unit testing should be a part of the development of each module in the application. When a developer is assigned a programming task in a software development project, unit testing should be performed immediately after coding and debugging have taken place. In some organizations, developers work in pairs—the senior developer writes code, and the junior developer performs testing. This gives junior programmers an opportunity to learn more about advanced programming by observing the senior developer and by testing his or her code.

It can be easily argued that unit testing for a software module should not be performed by the developer who wrote the module. The developer may be under time pressure to complete development and testing and may overlook test cases or gloss over errors as irrelevant. Also, a developer can be too familiar with their code to be capable of objectively testing it. The methodology of "written by one and tested by another" has the advantage of objective testing, but it can be more difficult to carry out in smaller organizations where only a single developer may be writing all of the code.

System Testing   As various parts of the application are developed and unit-tested, they will be installed into a test environment. When a sufficient number of modules or components has been completed, it will eventually become possible to begin end-to-end (or at least partial end-to-end) testing. In this way, it will be possible to test several components as a whole to verify whether they work together properly.

System testing includes *interface testing* to confirm that the application is communicating properly with other applications. This will include real time interfaces as well as batch processing.

System testing also includes *migration testing*. When one application is replacing another, data from the old application is often imported into the new application to eliminate the need for both old and new applications to function at the same time. Migration testing ensures that data is being properly formatted and imported into the new application. This testing is often performed several times in advance of the real, live migration at cutover time.

As with unit testing, system testing should have pre-prepared test plans that were developed at the system design phase. And as with unit testing, system testing should probably not be performed by the developers who developed the modules under test or by the integrators who set them up in the test environment. Further, system testing results should be formally documented and archived in case they are needed later.

Functional Testing   *Functional testing* is primarily concerned with the verification of functional requirements that were developed earlier in the application project.

Each functional requirement must be expressed in a way that makes it inherently verifiable. When each functional requirement is developed, one or more tests should also be developed, which are conducted during the functional testing phase of the project.

Functional tests should be formally recorded, including test input and test results. All of this should be archived in case it's needed if the application is suspected of malfunctioning. Often functional test results can verify whether the malfunction was present during the functional testing before the application went live.

User Acceptance Testing   Before business users will formally approve and begin using a new (or updated) application, often a formal phase called *user acceptance testing (UAT)* is performed. UAT should consist of a formal, written body of specific tests that permits application users to determine whether the application will operate properly.

The detailed output of user acceptance testing should be archived, as it may be needed in the future.

UAT is often a stage in the acceptance of leased or purchased software, as well as in software that is developed by a third-party organization. User acceptance testing is the formal test that determines whether the customer organization will accept (and pay for, as the case may be) the application and begin formal use of it.

Acceptance criteria for UAT should be developed by end users and not by developers or designers; otherwise, internal or external customers are liable to end up with software that does not function as desired or expected.

Quality Assurance Testing

Quality assurance testing (QAT) is a formal verification of system specifications and technologies. Users are usually not involved in QAT; instead, this testing is typically performed by IT or IS departments.

Like UAT, QAT should be a "gatekeeper" test in any situation where the organization is purchasing off-the-shelf software or the application software is being developed by an external organization. The results of QAT should also determine whether the organization will formally accept and pay for the application.

Implementation

Implementation is the phase of the project in which the completed application software is placed into the production environment and started.

Implementation must be started before UAT and QAT begin. UAT and QAT should be performed on the production environment that is anticipated to become the in-use production environment once approvals to use the application are obtained.

From the very day that construction of the implementation environment begins, that environment should be as controlled as a production environment. This means that all changes to the environment should go through a change management process. Also, administrative access to the production environment should be restricted to those personnel who will be supporting the environment after it goes live. The implementation timeline, in relation to other phases of the software development project, is depicted in Figure 3.13.

Because the production environment is the environment where UAT and QAT testing usually takes place, this environment must be pristine and free from the possibility of being accessed by developers and other personnel.

FIGURE 3.13 Implementation involves preparing the production environment prior to UAT and QAT.

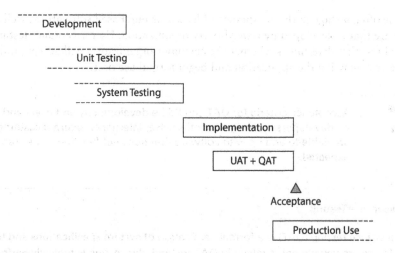

Implementation Planning   Implementation is a complicated undertaking that requires advance planning. Some activities may have a long lead time associated with them, requiring some implementation activities to begin during development or earlier.

Prepare physical space for on-premises production systems.   For organizations implementing an application on physical servers, an existing data center may be used for an application's servers and other equipment. But if there isn't room, or if an existing data center's available space is insufficient, the organization may need to consider expanding an existing data center or consider a colocation center.

Build production systems.   The actual servers that the application will use must be built and configured. If the organization does not have the necessary servers available, the hardware systems must be leased or purchased; depending on the type of hardware, considerable lead time may be required. If the public cloud will be used, the organization needs to select a public cloud vendor (this should be done at design time, or earlier!) and implement server operating systems there. Once the hardware or virtualization platform is available, personnel will need to install and configure operating systems and possibly other subsystems such as database management systems or application management systems. Supporting infrastructure such as routers, switches, firewalls, and so forth must also be implemented at this time.

Prepare virtual machines for cloud-based production systems.

For an organization deploying its application in an infrastructure-as-a-service (IaaS; discussed later in the chapter), virtual machines need to be acquired and configured.

Install application software.

Once the systems are ready for the application software, it can be installed and configured.

Migrate the data.

For environments in which an existing application will be retired, data from the former environment usually needs to be transferred to the new environment. Often this procedure requires the development of one or more custom programs to extract, convert, and insert the data into the new environment. This procedure is usually performed more than once: it must be rehearsed at least one time to make sure that it works properly. Also, migrated data is often needed for functional testing, UAT, and training before the actual cutover.

As each phase of implementation is completed, the newly completed component should be locked down immediately and treated as though it is already in production. Usually this is the only way to ensure the integrity of the entire environment.

Training   The success of the entire software development project hinges on the knowledge and skills of several different people in the organization. The following are among those who may need training:

End Users   Personnel who will be using the application need to be trained so that they will know how to operate it properly.

Customers   If outside customers will be using the new application, they will need an appropriate amount of information so that they will understand how to use it. In other cases, customers will not be using the application directly, but a new application can still influence how they interact with the organization. If customer service or sales personnel are using a new application for taking orders or for looking up customer data, they may be asking different questions or presenting different information to the customer.

Support Staff   Personnel who provide customer service to users and customers need to be trained in the workings of the application, as well as on administrative "back office" tools that they may use to assist users.

Trainers   Organizations that employ a training organization will need to "train the trainers" so that, in turn, they will be able to train users and customers correctly.

The purpose of an application may require that others also receive training. This could include internal or external auditors, or regulators who have oversight over the organization.

Data Conversion and System Migration   In the context of the SDLC, the purpose of a data migration is to transfer data from an older, soon-to-be-retired system to a new system. Depending on the nature of the old and new applications, the purpose of the data migration may be to make historical records that originated in the older system available in the newer system.

In some cases, an organization will continue to keep the older application running to facilitate access to historical data. In some circumstances, it may require fewer resources to keep the old application running than to migrate the historical data to the new application.

Data migration often requires the development of programs that extract data from the old application, perform required transformations, and then format the data and import it into the new application. This is frequently a complex task, as there may be differences so significant between the data models of the old and new applications that the meaning of stored data differs between them. In some cases, it will be necessary to create some parts of the database in the new application by extracting data from the old application and then performing calculations to create the data necessary in the new. Careful analysis is required in all cases to make sure that the *meaning* of data in each application is known so that the migration will be done properly. Following are some techniques and considerations that ensure a successful migration:

Record Counts   Programs or utilities should be used to count the number of records in counterpart tables in the old and new environments. This will confirm the completeness of the migration programs that move data from the old environment to the new one.

Batch Totals   Data records with numeric values can be added together in the old and new databases. This will help to confirm the integrity of key data elements in the old and new environments.

Checksums   Programs that compute checksums can be run against old and new databases to ensure the accuracy of migrated data. Programmers do need to be aware of the methods used to store data, which could lead to differences in checksums. For instance, an address field in one application may pad the field with spaces, but in the other it may be padded with nulls. Also, the way that dates are stored can vary between applications. Although using checksums can be valuable, programmers and analysts must be familiar with any differences in data representation between the old and new environments.

Like other software projects, the migration programs themselves must be carefully designed and tested, and the results of tests must be analyzed to make sure that they are working properly. Often it is necessary to perform a test migration—well in advance of the scheduled cutover date—to give enough time to make sure that the migration programs have been properly written.

Cutover   When the production system has been constructed, applications loaded, data migrated, and all testing performed and verified, the project team has reached the cutover milestone. Often, management review and approval are required to verify that all necessary steps have been completed correctly.

Depending on the nature of the application as well as external influences such as regulation or business requirements, an organization may transfer processing to the new environment in one of several ways:

Parallel Cutover   The organization may operate both the old and new applications in parallel for a time, making careful comparisons between old and new to ensure that the new application is working properly.

Geographic Cutover   In an application used throughout large geographic regions, such as a retail point-of-sale application, the organization may migrate individual locations to the new application instead of moving all locations at one time.

Module-by-Module Cutover   The organization may migrate different parts of the application at different times. In a financial management application, for instance, the organization could move accounts receivable to the new environment, later move accounts payable, and still later move general ledger. During and between each of these phases, the organization must keep track of exactly which business information resides in which system and reconcile information in different systems to ensure that it is complete and accurate.

All-at-Once Cutover   An organization may elect to migrate the entire environment at one time.

The project team must analyze all available methods for a cutover and choose the method that will balance risk, efficiency, and cost-effectiveness.

Analysts may discover problems in data in the old environment that necessitate a cleanup be performed prior to the migration or as a part of the migration. Examples of the types of problems that can be found include duplicate records, incomplete records, or records that contain values that violate one or more business rules. Analysts who discover data inconsistencies such as these need to alert the project team to the matter and then help the project team decide how to remedy the situation.

Rollback Planning   Sometimes an organization will migrate an application from an old environment to a new one, and shortly afterward will discover a serious problem in the new environment that requires a return to the old environment. *Rollback planning* is a safety net that provides a last-resort path away from a situation where the organization cannot continue using the new environment.

A rollback is a serious undertaking and would be considered only when there is a problem in the new environment that is so serious that it cannot be easily remedied. However, rollback planning is recommended in environments where the availability and integrity of an application is critical to the organization, even if a rollback is never needed.

Post-Implementation

The software project is not completed when the application cutover has taken place. Several activities still must take place before the project is closed. These final tasks include the following:

Post-Implementation Review   After the implementation of a new application, one or more formal reviews need to take place. The purpose of these reviews is to collect all known open issues and to identify and discuss the performance of the project. Because the organization is likely to undertake similar projects in the future, it is a valuable use of time to identify what parts of the project went well and what could have been done better. The implementation review should consider:

System Adequacy   The project team should work with the users of the new system and collect issues and comments, which are then discussed in the implementation review. Any issues requiring further attention should be identified.

Security Review   The system's access controls and other security controls should be discussed and any issues or problems identified.

Privacy Review   The system's privacy features and controls need to be discussed and any problems identified.

Audit Review   The system's ability to be audited, as well as any early audit results, need to be discussed.

Issues   All known problems regarding the new environment should be identified. This should include user feedback, operations feedback, and the accuracy and completeness of documentation and records. The project team needs to discuss each issue and assign it to one or more individuals who will address and remedy it.

Return on Investment   If the purpose for implementing the application was to establish or improve return on investment (ROI) or efficiency, then initial measurements need to be taken. The project team needs to recognize that several business cycles may be required before an accurate ROI can be determined.

More than one post-implementation review may be needed. To hold a single post-implementation review shortly after going live and then calling it good is probably inadequate for most organizations. Instead, a series of reviews may be needed, perhaps stretching over years.

IS auditors should be involved in every phase of the SDLC, including post-implementation reviews, to ensure that the application is functioning according to whatever control or regulatory requirements are attended to by auditors. Auditor feedback must be included in the body of issues and comments that is reviewed in the initial and subsequent reviews.

Software Maintenance   Immediately after implementation, the application enters the maintenance phase. From this point forward, all changes to the environment must be performed under formal processes, including incident management, problem management, defect management, vulnerability management, change management, and configuration management. All of these processes should have been developed and modified as necessary to accommodate the new application when cutover was completed.

Software Development Risks

Software development is not a risk-free endeavor. Even when management provides adequate resources for a software development project and supports a viable methodology, there are still many more paths to failure than to success.

Some of the specific risks that are associated with software development projects are as follows:

- **Application inadequacy:** The application may fail to support all business requirements. During the requirements and specifications phases of a software development project, some business requirements may have been overlooked, disregarded, misunderstood, or unappreciated. Whatever the reason, an application that falls short of meeting all business requirements may, as a result, be underutilized or even abandoned.

- **Security and privacy defects:** The application may contain security or privacy defects that permit various forms of misuse and abuse, including denial of service, escalation of privilege, data disclosure, and data corruption.

- **Project risk:** If the application development (or acquisition) project is not well run, the project may exceed spending budgets, time budgets, or both. This may result in significant delays and even abandonment of the project altogether if management has considered the project a failure.

- **Business inefficiency:** The application may fail to meet business efficiency expectations. In other words, the application itself may be difficult to use, it may be exceedingly slow, or business procedures may require additional manual work to meet business needs. This can result in critical business tasks taking too long or requiring additional resources to complete.

- **Market changes:** Between the time that a software development project is approved and when it is completed, sudden or unexpected changes in market conditions can spell disaster for the project. For instance, drastic supply or price shocks in a macro environment can have an adverse effect on costs that may make a new business activity no longer viable. Changes in the market can also result in reduced margins on products and services, which can turn the ROI of a project upsidedown.

Management is responsible for the business decisions that it makes; in ideal situations, management makes these decisions with sufficient information at hand. Usually, however, there are always unknowns that may lead to challenges later in the project.

Alternative Software Development Approaches and Techniques

For decades, the waterfall approach to software development was the de facto model used by most organizations. Breakthroughs and changes in technology in the 1970s and 1980s have led to new approaches in software development that can be every bit as effective as the waterfall model and, in many cases, more efficient and faster.

DevOps

DevOps is the growing movement that utilizes agile development methodology coupled with tighter integration of development teams, software QA, and IT operations. DevOps isn't complete without tools facilitating more effective (often automated) testing.

In DevOps, the lines between software development, QA, and IT operations are somewhat blurred. It is essential for organizations to ensure that access control models and capabilities continue to support regulatory and compliance requirements such as:

- **Data segregation:** Developers should never have access to production data.

- **Separation of duties:** Critical processes such as change control still require administrative and technical controls so that no one person (such as a developer) can make unauthorized changes in production environments or promote their own code into production.

The relationship between development, software QA, and IT operations is depicted in Figure 3.14.

FIGURE 3.14   DevOps is the integration of development, software QA (testing), and IT operations.

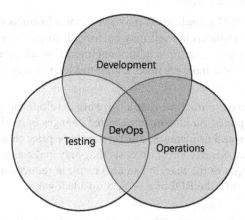

DevSecOps

DevSecOps is an offshoot of (others would say an improvement to) DevOps. DevSecOps represents the best of DevOps and includes security design and testing capabilities that are a part of the rapid development and automated testing process. Often, static and/or dynamic code-scanning capabilities are integrated into the software build environment so that security defects are identified as soon as possible. Further automated testing can be performed on production environments to reveal exploitable defects that can be remediated by developers in subsequent sprints.

Agile Development

Agile development is a software development model and is referred to as an alternate methodology that is appropriate for some organizations. The agile methodology utilizes the Scrum project methodology that is discussed in detail earlier in this chapter. In an agile development project, a larger development team is broken up into smaller teams of five to nine developers and a leader, and the project deliverables are broken up into smaller pieces that can each be attained in just a few weeks.

Prototyping

Application *prototyping* is a methodology whereby rapidly developed application prototypes are developed with user input and continuous involvement. In this method, users work closely with developers who build specific components in short periods and solicit frequent user feedback.

The primary advantage of prototyping is that the risks of the application turning out all wrong are reduced because users are constantly involved and can head off an incorrect approach before more time is wasted.

The main disadvantage of prototyping is that the system is developed based only on what the user sees and knows; other functional requirements that users may be unaware of may go unaddressed, resulting in a system with inadequate controls and resilience. Another disadvantage occurs when the organization allows the use of the prototype in a production environment before it is a mature product, rather than waiting on a mature, fully tested version.

Rapid Application Development

Rapid application development (RAD) is a response to the slower and more structured application development methodologies (such as waterfall) that were developed in the 1970s. RAD is characterized by the following activities and features:

- Small development teams consisting of highly experienced developers and analysts
- The development of prototypes
- Development tools that integrate data design, data flow, user interface, and prototyping
- A central repository for software components with an emphasis on code reusability
- Design and prototype analysis sessions with end users
- Tight time frames

RAD can almost be thought of as a 1960s-era protest of the political and business establishment. In most cases, it takes the opposite approach to software development from the then-traditional and time-proven (but also inefficient and time-consuming) development models created in the decades before.

Data-Oriented System Development

Data-oriented system development (DOSD) is, as the name suggests, a data-centric software development methodology. In DOSD, data is the central focus, the "hub of the wheel" as it were, and the other development activities occur as a result of data analysis and design.

DOSD is utilized in some of the larger information processing environments that are interconnected by many organizations. For instance, airline reservations systems, merchant and payment processing systems, securities trading systems, medical records processing systems, and cloud-based platform-as-a-service (PaaS) vendors such as SalesForce.com and Concur all have well-defined data models and transaction interfaces. Organizations that want to participate in these larger systems will build their own applications that are focused on the published data interfaces on the systems they want to connect to.

DOSD can be applied to environments that use batches of transactions that are, for example, transmitted and processed in bulk, as well as transactions that are performed in real time, such as airline reservations or securities trading.

Object-Oriented System Development

Object-oriented (OO) system development is a world unto itself that contains an entire vocabulary to describe objects and many other software components. It is so different from traditional structured programming (such as Fortran, BASIC, and C) that it has its own languages and even databases if you want to implement one.

Entire books (and even series of books) have been written on OO development and technology. We will summarize the basic vocabulary and activities here.

The basic unit of OO technology is the *class*. A class describes the characteristics of an object, including its attributes, properties, fields, and the methods it can perform.

The instantiation of a class is called an *object*. You could think of a class as stored code and configuration, and when it's running, the part that is running is the object.

A *method* refers to the actions that an object can perform. If, for instance, an object is written to calculate the interest on a loan, the method is the software code in the object that performs the calculation. In other programming languages, subroutines and functions are basically the same thing as a method in OO.

Objects routinely employ another technique known as *encapsulation*. This is a common practice whereby any particular method may call other methods to perform its work. This is similar to a function calling another function. The point of encapsulation in OO is that the software developer does not need to know anything about the implementation details of a method, including whether it calls other methods.

Earlier I mentioned a class. OO frequently has a hierarchy of classes. A class can belong to a parent class, and in turn, a class can contain subclasses. But parent classes and subclasses are not just ways of arranging or storing classes. Instead, the relationship of classes is functional. The attributes of a parent class are passed down through *inheritance*.

Earlier I stated that when a class is instantiated, it becomes an object. Depending on the data that is passed on to the object, it may behave in different ways. This characteristic is known as *polymorphism*. For example, a class that computes shipping charges will behave in different ways, depending on the source and destination addresses as well as on special circumstances such as customers. In this case, polymorphism is not just about the rate that is chosen for shipping, but possibly other objects will be called, such as objects to handle customs, taxes, or hazardous materials declarations.

OO programming and operational environments will have one or more *class libraries*. These take many forms, depending on the operating system, languages, and subsystems that are in use. For instance, in the Java language, class libraries are stored in JAR (Java ARchive) files that are located on the system where programs can refer to them when needed.

Component-Based Development

Component-based development is an approach that reflects the software architecture of an application. Here, an application environment will be made up of several independent components, often located on different physical or virtual systems, which work together.

For example, a large application environment may consist of a group of centrally located servers that process primary transactions. These servers may contain interfaces, using standard interface technologies such as CORBA (Common Object Request Broker Architecture), RPC (Remote Procedure Call), or SOA (Service-Oriented Architecture), with which other parts of the overall application environment may communicate. For instance, auxiliary components such as batch input and output, data warehouses, static table updates (such as tax or shipping rates), and client programs may all be independent applications that communicate with the core system.

 In a component-based environment, some components may be systems that are owned and operated by other organizations. This is especially true of modern distributed applications, PaaS environments, and web-based mash-ups, where applications may include components from external applications.

Web-Based Application Development

The creation of the HTML content-display standard and the HTTP communications protocol has revolutionized application development. The web browser is ubiquitous and has become the universal client platform that is not unlike an intelligent display terminal from earlier eras.

The web, as it is popularized now, came along just in time; two-tier and three-tier client-server computing, the great new application development paradigm that was developed in the 1990s, was not living up to its promise, particularly in the areas of performance and upkeep of client software. Web software has dramatically simplified software development from the perspective of the user interface (UI); though the developer has a little less control over what and how data will be displayed on a user workstation, the trade-off in not having to maintain client-side software is viewed as acceptable.

From a development methodology perspective, web application development can be performed within virtually all of the development frameworks, including waterfall, DevOps, agile, RAD, DOSD, and OO (all discussed in this chapter). Primarily it's the target technology that differentiates web-based application development from its alternatives.

Important standards have been developed that facilitate communications between web-based applications, including JSON-RPC, SOAP (Simple Object Access Protocol), and Web Services Description Language (WSDL). JSON-RPC is an XML (Extensible Markup Language)-based protocol coded in JavaScript Object Notation (JSON) used by a client system to request a method of a remote system.

SOAP is an XML-based application programming interface (API) specification that facilitates real time communications between applications using the HTTP and HTTPS protocols. Functionally, SOAP operates similarly to RPC, wherein one application transmits a query to another application, and the other application responds with a query result. SOAP messages are based on the XML standard.

WSDL serves as a specification repository for the SOAP services available in a particular environment. This permits an application to discover what services are available on an application server.

Reverse Engineering

Reverse engineering is the process of analyzing a system to see how it functions, usually as a means for developing a similar system or for learning about how the system works. Reverse engineering usually requires tools that examine computer binary code and that build a programming language equivalent.

Reverse engineering can help to speed up a development project where an organization needs to build an application that is similar to another in its possession that exists in binary format only. Without reverse engineering, the organization would have to spend additional time in the software design and development phases of the project.

This practice is usually forbidden in software license agreements, because using it would reveal protected intellectual property that could economically damage the original software maker.

 Reverse engineering is a standard technique used in malware analysis to understand how the malware works.

System Development Tools

Application developers can create source code using tools ranging from simple text editors to advanced tools such as computer-aided software engineering and fourth-generation languages (4GLs). While there's little reason to discuss text editors such as vi, Notepad, or Emacs, advanced development tools are worth your attention and are discussed in this section.

Integrated Development Environment

Integrated development environments (IDEs) are a class of desktop software development tools that incorporates source code editing, source code version control, compilation, and debugging in a single tool. An IDE enables a developer to write, test, and debug code without having to switch between programs.

IDEs typically have multiple windows, or panes, that enable the software developer to view and edit code, run code and observe execution, and view the source code library. Other functions may be available as well.

Some IDEs have connectivity to external tools such as source code scanning tools that look for security defects.

Computer-Aided Software Engineering

Computer-aided software engineering (CASE) represents a broad variety of tools used to automate various aspects of application software development. CASE tools cover three basic realms of development:

- **Upper CASE:** Upper CASE tools are essential for the initial planning and design stages of a software project. They help in creating a blueprint of the system, which guides the development process.

- **Lower CASE:** Lower CASE tools facilitate the transition from design to actual software creation and maintenance. They streamline coding, testing, and deployment activities.

- **Integrated CASE:** Integrated CASE tools offer a seamless environment that bridges the gap between upper- and lower-CASE tools. They provide comprehensive support throughout the software development life cycle.

These terms are loosely used to classify various CASE tools. Some CASE tools are strictly upper CASE, whereas others include lower CASE and/or integrated CASE, but many cover the entire range of functionality and can be used to capture specifications, create data structure and flow diagrams, define program functions, and generate source code.

CASE tools do not usually create source code that is ready for implementation and testing. Instead, they are used to create the majority (in the best cases) of code for a given program; then the developer(s) would add details and specific items that the CASE tool did not cover. CASE tools are not used to replace the work of a developer, but to help make the coding part of a development project take less time, to improve consistency, and to enhance program quality.

CASE tools often contain *code generators* that create the actual program source code.

NOTE   CASE tools do not eliminate the need for any of the essential phases of the SDLC. With or without CASE tools, it is still necessary for a project team to create requirements, specifications, and design. CASE does help to automate some of these activities, however.

Fourth-Generation Languages

Fourth-generation languages, or 4GLs, comprise a variety of tools that are used in the development of applications or that are parts of the applications themselves.

4GLs are most often used as adjuncts to applications rather than for their core functionality. For instance, 4GLs are useful for report generators, query generators, and other higher-level functions. 4GLs are typically designed for use by nontechnical users who have few or no programming skills. 4GLs can also be used by developers as code generators.

Acquiring Cloud-Based Infrastructure and Applications

Organizations often choose to acquire a business application that is hosted in a cloud or SaaS environment, as opposed to hosting the application on their own systems. This section discusses issues that organizations should understand when considering this option.

The common options available for cloud-based application environments are:

- **Software-as-a-service:** An application service provider is hosting its application software on its own infrastructure, often located in a data center and used by several customers. Users access the application in much the same way that they would if the application were hosted within the organization's own IT environment.

- **Infrastructure-as-a-service:** A cloud service provider is providing an environment in which its customers build and operate virtual machines. While the client organization is relieved of the burden of purchasing network, system, and storage hardware, it still needs to create a network architecture, security architecture, systems architecture, and application architecture, and it must install and manage operating systems, virtual network devices such as switches and routers, and virtual security tools such as firewalls, intrusion prevention systems, and data loss prevention systems.

- **Platform-as-a-service:** A cloud service provider is providing an application-based or data-based platform on which customers can develop and/or integrate their applications. PaaS services are typically organized around a business theme—for example, Salesforce.com for sales enablement or Concur.com for expense and travel management.

Regardless of the cloud model that is chosen, the organization needs to understand many details that are related to the manner in which the cloud provider provides its services to the organization. Some of these details are:

- **Access control:** The cloud service provider must have an effective access control plan to ensure that only authorized personnel have access to infrastructure components and virtual machines. Often, the organization using cloud services will manage access control in upper layers (such as in operating systems, database management systems, and applications that it may install and maintain on cloud servers), whereas the cloud provider will manage access control in lower levels (such as in virtual machine hypervisors and via physical access).

- **Environment segregation:** The cloud service provider must effectively separate systems and data between customers so that no cloud customer is able to access systems and data of other customers.

- **Physical security:** The cloud services provider must provide adequate physical security so that only authorized personnel will have physical access to all cloud environment infrastructure and facilities.

- **Regulation:** The cloud service provider must provide controls that will meet all applicable regulatory needs for its customers.

- **Privacy:** The cloud service provider (and, indeed, the organization using cloud services) must implement safeguards to ensure appropriate protection and handling of personally identifiable information (PII) stored in cloud environments.

- **Legal jurisdiction:** The cloud service provider and its customers must have a firm understanding regarding the physical location of stored data, relative to the location of the owner(s) of that data. This will enable legal counsel to understand the applicability of security and privacy laws governing the use of stored data. This is particularly important in the context of data privacy and data sovereignty laws.

- **Availability:** The cloud services provider must deliver availability of services to customers at a level to meet customers' expectations. This applies not only to the steady availability of services, but also to on-demand availability.

- **Audit:** Many standards, regulations, and legal agreements require some level of auditing of systems, applications, and their supporting controls. The cloud environment must be verifiable in this regard.

Figure 3.15 shows a typical cloud responsibility model that illustrates which party is responsible for implementing and operating which aspects of security in a cloud environment.

FIGURE 3.15   Typical cloud responsibility model

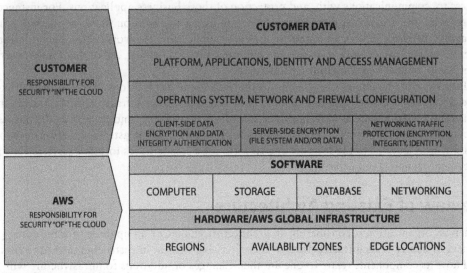

Image source: Amazon Web Services

The Cloud Security Alliance (https://cloudsecurityalliance.org) is
a high-quality resource for controls and guidance for cloud services providers as well as organizations using cloud-based services.

Infrastructure Development and Deployment

Infrastructure is used to connect applications to users and to other applications. Infrastructure is composed of the networks, servers, storage systems, and other facilities that support the use of applications.

While an organization may be able to acquire off-the-shelf or SaaS software for many of its core business activities, infrastructure is almost always custom-architected and integrated for the organization. Whereas software applications are like the tools in the hand of an astronaut, the infrastructure is like the astronaut's glove, which must be tailor-made to fit each astronaut's hand. Infrastructure needs to conform to the organization's geography, business model, security requirements, regulatory requirements, and culture.

Formal processes are required to design and develop infrastructure that is sure to meet the organization's needs. This section describes the detailed process of the infrastructure development life cycle that is needed to ensure that the infrastructure will adequately support the use of applications and other IT facilities and tools.

In the context of business applications and information systems, infrastructure is the collection of networks, network services, devices, facilities, and system software that facilitate access to, communications with, and protection of those business applications. For instance, a user who wants to access a business application uses a workstation that is connected to a local area network (LAN). To access the business application, the workstation communicates over networks formed with routers, switches, firewalls, and cabling. All of that "in-between" equipment and cabling constitutes infrastructure.

Infrastructure facilitates the communication and use of applications. Without infrastructure, applications cannot function or be accessed by users. Since infrastructure is so vital, its construction and maintenance require the same level of formality and process as the business applications that it supports. In newer organizations, however, infrastructure serves only to connect workstations to the Internet and to facilitate a few business location services such as document scanning and printing.

Review of Existing Architecture

When an organization is considering an architecture change or an upgrade to some component or aspect of its infrastructure, it must first review what infrastructure already exists and how its components relate to one another. Changes or additions to infrastructure will be most effective when existing infrastructure is carefully analyzed. This permits the organization to make necessary additions and changes that will be most effective and at the lowest possible cost. Characteristics of existing architecture that need to be considered include the following:

- Physical security, size, weight, and power requirements for on-premises environments
- Compatibility with virtualization platforms for cloud-based environments
- Compatibility with existing infrastructure and infrastructure that will be acquired in the future
- Operations and support
- Security architecture and operations

Requirements

The next step in any addition or upgrade of infrastructure is the development of requirements. As with the SDLC, it is essential to know precisely what is expected of the infrastructure in terms of specific features and capabilities. An analyst or project team should develop specific requirements in a number of categories:

- **Business functional requirements:** These specify what the addition or change to the infrastructure is expected to do. For instance, networks or network services will be expected to support new or improved communications between users and applications, remote access, communications to service providers, or services between applications. Or segmentation may be planned to isolate a cardholder environment from the rest of the environment.
- **Technical requirements and standards:** These specify which technologies and standards must be followed for the new infrastructure. Additions or changes to infrastructure should support existing protocol and services standards such as TCP/IP, LDAP (used for authentication and authorization), product standards for devices such as routers and switches, and other standards that will permit the new infrastructure to work harmoniously with existing infrastructure with the smallest possible increases in support costs. Technical requirements for infrastructure should also include performance requirements such as availability, latency, and throughput so that the infrastructure will have the capacity to support all needed business functions.
- **Interoperability:** These requirements ensure that additions or upgrades will work in harmony with existing components and systems in an organization's environment.
- **Security and regulatory requirements:** These requirements specify how information is protected from unauthorized third parties. Examples include firewalls to limit access, intrusion detection systems to create alerts of possible tampering, and encryption to protect information from eavesdropping and interception.
- **Privacy requirements:** These requirements specify how information is protected and handled to limit the use of personal information to officially sanctioned purposes.

Design

Additions and changes to existing infrastructure (or even to brand-new infrastructure) must be designed, and that design must be validated by subject matter experts. An infrastructure design may also include the use of specific protocols or services for authentication, routing, encryption, device management, and administrative support. When an environment is being expanded or upgraded, generally the new components will need to work with the same support and management methods that are used for existing infrastructure, except when the infrastructure change has to do with a change in these features.

The design should be detailed enough so that a network or systems engineer can determine the logical and physical components that are needed and can configure them to support business needs. If software or hardware vendors will be asked to make suggestions on the components required for the infrastructure, then the design must be detailed enough so that they can make appropriate recommendations that will meet business needs.

 With enough detail in business and technical requirements and sufficient discipline, any two qualified engineers should be able to take requirements and arrive at the same design result. Architecture and design are not so much about creativity as they are the development of a solution that will meet business needs.

Procurement

More often than not, additions or changes to infrastructure involve the procurement of infrastructure hardware and/or software.

Request for Proposal

Any significant expansion or upgrade to infrastructure may require the use of a *request for proposal (RFP)*. This is a formal process whereby the organization gathers all business and technical requirements and forwards them to several qualified vendors, who produce formal written proposals that include detailed information on the equipment and services required to perform the upgrade. Some organizations require the RFP process to be used for any purchases that exceed a set amount.

When the project team receives RFP responses, the responses must be evaluated to determine which vendors are capable of meeting the organization's business and technical needs. The project team may also need to evaluate one or more of the vendors' solutions to "see for themselves" whether each vendor's proposed solution will successfully meet the organization's needs.

The *request for information (RFI)* process is similar to that of RFP, except that the primary request is not for business proposals, but instead for information that will help the organization select solutions.

Evaluation

If the project team will be evaluating potential solutions, the team will need to provide whatever facilities are required to house the equipment or software. The project team will also need to take whatever time is required to test the components to determine whether they can support business needs. This may require the team to provide other equipment to set up an end-to-end test.

Each of the business and technical requirements needs to be verified. This will require that one or more project team members work with the equipment being evaluated to see how that equipment works. A test checklist should be developed that has a one-to-one correspondence to each business and technical requirement. This will permit project team members to rate each feature from each vendor in an objective manner.

Testing

Before new infrastructure—or significant changes to existing infrastructure—can be made available for production users, the infrastructure should be formally and thoroughly tested. This helps to confirm that the infrastructure was built correctly and that it will be reliable and secure.

Each functional and technical requirement that was developed earlier needs to be systematically verified. This means that a detailed test plan needs to be developed that uses functional and technical requirements as a source. For instance, if a technical standard requires a specific routing protocol configuration setting, then a network engineer on the project team needs to verify whether network devices support that feature (a matter such as this should have been settled during requirements development).

Most organizations do not have a test network environment that completely mirrors their production network. This means that some of the testing needs to be creative, and some testing and verification can't be done until implementation time. The project team will need to discuss the hard-to-test characteristics of the new infrastructure and decide the best course of action that facilitates the greatest amount of testing and the lowest risk of project failure. In other words, the results of some testing won't be known until the new infrastructure goes live.

Tests that cannot be done until implementation will become part of the verification that implementation was performed correctly.

Proof of Concept

Because integration issues are often complex, organizations are turning to the *proof of concept* to evaluate a proposed new technology or system. In a proof of concept, the organization asks an infrastructure vendor, value-added reseller, or consultant to set up components in the organization's environment and perform some simple integrations with existing systems. This helps the organization to better understand the likely answer to the question, "Will this new technology work in *our* environment?" before committing to a particular solution.

The project team should carefully plan the proof of concept so that key features can be demonstrated. A proof of concept is usually performed over a relatively short period, and only a small proportion of integration will be performed. Also remember that the vendor is providing the proof-of-concept hardware and resources without compensation (but with the hope that its solution will be chosen); there is only so much that a vendor will be willing to do for free. Of course, the vendor or an integrator will be able to provide additional integrations for a fee. This is why it is important to identify the key, measurable objectives before the proof of concept is carried out.

Implementation

When evaluation and testing are complete and all obstacles and issues have been satisfied, the new infrastructure (or changes to existing infrastructure) can be implemented. This may involve the physical installation of cabling, devices, and other components, as well as the use of common carrier facilities such as communications circuits. In an implementation, the infrastructure is all assembled, tested, and placed into production use.

Maintenance

Infrastructure requires periodic maintenance, usually in the form of software and hardware upgrades and configuration changes to accommodate changes in the business and technical environments. These changes should be controlled through change management and configuration management processes that are described in detail earlier in this chapter and in the following section.

Maintaining Information Systems

The job is only half done when an application or system has been implemented. Like any system with moving parts (whether real or virtual), information systems and the environments that support them require frequent maintenance. There are dual aspects to system maintenance: business processes and changes to technology. This is embodied in the change management and configuration management processes discussed here.

Change Management

Change management is a formal process whereby every proposed and required change to an environment must be formally requested, reviewed, and approved before it is made. The purpose of change management—which is also known as *change control*—is to identify and reduce risks associated with changes to an IT environment. Change management also helps to reduce unscheduled downtime in an environment. The typical components in a change management process are:

- **Change request:** The requestor describes, in structured detail, the desired change. The change request should include the business reason for the change, a procedure for making the change, who will make the change, and who will verify the change (this should be two different individuals or groups); a procedure for verifying that the change was made properly, when the change will be made, and a plan for backing out of the change if it is unsuccessful; and results from test implementations in a testing environment. The request should be distributed to all stakeholders to give them time to read and understand the change.

- **Change review:** A quorum of stakeholders (usually called the *change advisory board*, or CAB) meets to discuss the requested change. The person or group proposing the change should describe the change and why it is being made, and they should be able to answer questions from others about the change and its impact. If the stakeholders agree that the change may proceed, the change is approved.

- **Perform the change:** The person or team slated to perform the change does so at the agreed-upon date and time, using instructions that were agreed upon in the review phase of the change. Results from the change are recorded and archived.

- **Verify the change:** Any necessary tests are performed to verify that the change was executed properly and that it has produced the desired result. If the change takes too long, or if the change cannot be successfully verified, the organization "backs out" of the change according to the agreed-upon procedure.

- **Emergency changes:** When the performance of a change cannot wait until the next scheduled change review, organizations usually provide a process whereby developers or engineers are permitted to make an emergency change. Typically, some management approval is still required; personnel should never be permitted to make changes and then inform others after the fact. Emergency changes still need to be formally reviewed in a change review to ensure that all stakeholders understand what change was made to the environment. A long-term goal that should be realized from managing emergency changes is the reduction in the need to make emergency changes, but a change plan should provide enough information to enable the organization to anticipate situations and manage them proactively if they do occur.

 NOTE The change management process should be formalized and include a documented process, procedures, forms, and recordkeeping.

Unauthorized Changes

Organizations need to have tools and methods in place to detect unauthorized changes that are made to systems, and to respond to those changes. Two avenues of action need to take place: first is the behavioral aspect, whereby management discusses the unauthorized changes with the person(s) who made them; second, the impact of those unauthorized changes needs to be understood and appropriate actions taken as a result.

Controls should be in place to prevent unauthorized changes from occurring. These controls include:

- **Segregation of duties:** Critical activities such as application software changes should be apportioned among a group of individuals so that no single individual is able to make key changes. For instance, only developers should have access to source code and be able to make changes to a staging area. Next, only authorized personnel should be able to read changes from a staging area and place those changes into production. No single person should be able to do all of these things.

- **Application code review:** Before checking in any change to application code, an independent review should be performed to ensure that only approved changes are being made.

- **Least privilege access:** Only those personnel who have a need to access and make changes to a system should be able to do so. For example, developers should not be able to make changes to production systems.

- **File integrity monitoring:** Production systems should be equipped with file integrity monitoring (FIM) software that automatically detects and reports changes to files on a system. This will help to detect changes that may have been made without formal approval.

- **File activity monitoring:** Production systems should be equipped with file activity monitoring (FAM) software that automatically detects and reports activities on sensitive files. Generally, FAM tools are used to detect access to operating system files that are usually accessed infrequently. Such access can be an indicator of compromise or of unauthorized activity by trusted insiders.

Configuration Management

Configuration management (CM) is the combination of a business recordkeeping process and automated tool(s) where the configuration of components in an IT environment is independently recorded. This activity has many potential benefits:

- **Recovery:** When configuration information for IT systems is stored independent of the systems themselves, CM information can be used to recover a system or device in the event of a malfunction or failure.

- **Consistency:** Often, automated tools are used to manage systems and devices in an environment. A CM tool can help an organization drive consistency into the configuration of its systems and devices. This consistency will simplify administration, reduce mistakes, and result in less unscheduled downtime.

- **Troubleshooting:** When unexpected behavior and unplanned outages occur, information in a CM system can help with troubleshooting the problem.

Configuration management and change management processes together can help to reduce errors by requiring approval for changes and then by recording them when they are completed.

Controlling and Recording Configuration Changes

While CM is usually considered a means for recording changes made to a system, it can also be used to control those changes. Typically, this is achieved through the use of tools that control system configuration and through system access controls that prohibit changes that circumvent those tools.

Automated tools are almost always used for CM. These tools include a *configuration management database (CMDB)* that serves as a repository for every component in an environment and that contains information on every configuration change made to those components. The more sophisticated CM tools also permit their operator to revert a given component to a configuration that existed at any time in the past.

Configuration Management and Change Control

While controlling and recording changes in an environment is highly valuable for some organizations, configuration management is not a substitute for the change management process. Instead, configuration management is the means by which change management–approved changes are carried out and recorded on systems. Change management is the review and approval of changes, while configuration management is used to perform and record changes.

Business Processes

Organizations that are mature in their thinking and practices will treat their business processes almost like they do their software; both are carefully designed, constructed, operated, and measured, and any changes that are made for either one should be formally considered. Ongoing processes are measured, and continuous improvement and optimization are carried out over time.

Both software and processes should be considered as structured and procedural. The primary difference between the two is that software directs the processing of information in computers, whereas processes (usually) direct the activities of personnel.

Organizations that understand this type of approach to processes will control their processes like they control their software: through a life cycle.

The Business Process Life Cycle and Business Process Reengineering

Like software, business processes should not be constructed on a whim, but instead should be carefully planned, designed, and constructed, with the involvement of all concerned parties in the organization. These activities are a part of the *business process life cycle (BPLC)*.

The most important component in the business process life cycle is *business process reengineering (BPR)*, which is the set of activities related to the process of making changes to business processes.

A *process* is a set of procedures that achieves some business purpose or objective. These procedures should be formally documented and usually will require recordkeeping of the activities controlled by the process. The procedures will help ensure that the activities are carried out correctly and consistently. The records produced help to document the activities that occurred as the process was carried out over and over. Depending on the nature of the process, the records serve as tangible evidence that each activity occurred at specific dates and times, by specific personnel, using specific resources. Records also record details about activities such as money spent, products or services processed or sold, and names of customers or others. Records are also used to create statistics about the process that help management understand how well the process is performing and how it is contributing to overall business goals.

There should be a process to control the creation of new processes as well as changes to existing processes. This process is remarkably similar to the SDLC (since software and processes are similar, this should be of little surprise) and consists of the following major steps:

- **Feasibility study:** This effort determines the viability of a new process or a change in an existing process. The amount of rigor needed here is proportional to the impact of the new or changed process.

- **Requirements definition:** This formal record details the process that must be included in the new or changed process. All stakeholders should contribute to the requirements definition process and review to ensure that everyone understands the details of the process.

- **Design:** When requirements are completed, the process can be designed. Depending on the nature of the process, this may include descriptions of activities performed by various personnel; the business equipment, assets, or materials used; and the specific involvement of customers, partners, and suppliers.

- **Development:** The details of the process are developed, using all of the requirements and design as a guide. This will include detailed procedures, templates for recordkeeping, and whatever other details are required.

- **Testing:** When procedures have been developed, they are then tested to ensure their accuracy and suitability. Detailed test plans need to be developed that have a one-to-one correspondence to each of the requirements developed in that earlier phase.

- **Implementation:** When the process has been perfected through testing, it is ready to be implemented. This means using the process in actual business operations with real equipment, people, materials, and money.

- **Monitoring:** The process needs to be continually monitored (primarily through its recordkeeping) so that management can manage resource allocation in support of process operations and to determine whether the process is performing against stated goals.

- **Post-implementation:** After the process has been implemented, one or more formal reviews need to take place to review the development process itself as well as the new (or changed) process. Depending on the size, impact, and scope of the process, several reviews may be required, possibly over several years, to measure the effectiveness of the process and its results.

The reality in business today is that information systems and applications are used to support most business processes. This means that software development and process development often occur side by side and must be coordinated so that software applications meet the needs of the business processes that they support.

As organizations began to understand that business processes can be designed, developed, and improved like software, the term *business process reengineering* as a beneficial activity came into being in 1990. A common pitfall occurs when new system implementations happen without BPR. This can lead to over-customization of the software package, causing the system to be harder to support over the long term.

Business process management (BPM) is more often used to describe ongoing process improvement. A formal discipline of its own, BPM is a "Plan-Do-Check-Act" continuous improvement cycle described in the preceding paragraphs and illustrated in Figure 3.16.

FIGURE 3.16   The business process management life cycle

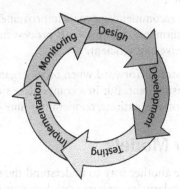

Benchmarking a Process

Benchmarking describes the activity of continuous process improvement. The purpose of benchmarking is to compare key measurements in a business process to the same measurements performed by other organizations, particularly those that are considered to be top performers.

Typically, the steps in process benchmarking are as follows:

- **Plan:** A critical process is selected and measurement techniques are identified. If the process has been through at least one improvement cycle, metrics may be available;

otherwise, the team will need to determine how the process is measured in terms of throughput, cost, and quality.

- **Research:** The team collects information about the target process over time. The team also identifies other organizations whose similar processes can be monitored and measured.

- **Measure and observe:** The benchmarking team collects actual measurements on other organizations' processes. In "friendly" situations, the team will be able to visit the organizations and be permitted to collect measurements openly. In "unfriendly" situations, the team will need to make indirect measurements using whatever information is readily, legally, and ethically available. The team will also need to collect qualitative data about the processes that it is measuring in the other organizations so that it can understand how the other organizations' processes are performed.

- **Analyze:** The team compares measurements of its own processes against those of the other organizations. Often the team will need to adjust measurements to account for known differences. Then the team will identify differences in metrics between its organization and those of the other organizations.

- **Adapt:** Here the team needs to understand the fundamental reasons why other organizations' measurements are better than its own. The team will need to understand not only the quantitative differences, but also the qualitative differences, between its organization's processes and the other organizations' processes to see how the other organizations achieve their metrics.

- **Improve:** Finally, the team recommends process improvements in its own organization. Management makes commitments to improve its process in specific ways to help its process to become more effective and efficient.

Benchmarking is relatively straightforward when other organizations are cooperative with regard to observation and measurement. But in a competitive situation, market rivals are unlikely to cooperate, and in some situations, cooperation may even be considered illegal.

Capability Maturity Models

Capability maturity models are another way to understand the effectiveness of an organization's business processes, particularly its software development processes. Three software development maturity models are discussed in this section.

Software Engineering Institute Capability Maturity Model

Developed at Carnegie Mellon University and now a part of ISACA, the Software Engineering Institute Capability Maturity Model (SEI CMM, often referred to as the CMM) is a conceptual model that helps an organization better understand the maturity of its own processes. This is a necessary step if an organization wants to improve its processes, particularly if the organization is not precisely sure how to begin this improvement.

The SEI CMM defines five levels of maturity:

1. **Initial:** This level has no process, no procedures, and no consistency. Success, when it is attained, is achieved through brute force and luck.

2. **Repeatable:** At this level of maturity, there is some consistency in the ways that individuals perform tasks from one time to the next, as well as some management planning and direction to ensure that tasks and projects are performed consistently.

3. **Defined:** The organization has developed a sitewide, documented software development process that is used for all development projects.

4. **Managed:** At this level, the documented software development process includes key measurement points used to measure effectiveness, efficiency, and defects. These measurements are performed and reported to management as a part of the life cycle.

5. **Optimizing:** At this highest level of maturity, the organization has instituted metrics-driven process improvement techniques to bring about continuous improvement in its SDLC.

Considerable effort is required for an organization to ascend from one level to the next. This model helps an organization better understand its current level of maturity and the process changes needed to improve its maturity over time.

How Mature Should We Be?

Confusion abounds on the topic and discussions on process maturity, and few organizations have the right perspective. Here's the myth: Better-run organizations will aspire to improve their business processes until they are at the optimizing level—the top level in the CMM. Instead, consider this: In most organizations, a maturity level of around 3 is sufficient, for the long term. Organizations in some industries such as banking and aerospace should be closer to, or even a little beyond, level 4, managed. Few organizations should aspire to level 5, optimizing. The reason for this is that the cost of operations to rise from level 3 to level 4 is considerable, and for most organizations the amount of risk reduction does not warrant the expense.

The best way for organizations to approach process maturity is to determine the aspirational maturity level of each important business process—not merely a big average figure. In each organization, some processes need to be more mature, and others can acceptably be less mature. Organizations should ask two questions about each business process: How precisely should this business process be run, and should we collect measurements on this process so that we can manage and improve it?

ISO/IEC 25019, Systems and Software Engineering

International standard ISO/IEC 25019:2023 is used to evaluate the quality of systems and software. This standard classifies systems and software quality within a set of three main characteristics:

- Beneficialness
- Freedom from risk
- Acceptability

ISO/IEC 33001, Information Technology—Process Assessment

International standard ISO/IEC 33001:2015 is a maturity model for business processes. ISO/IEC 33001 is an introduction to the ISO/IEC 330XX family of process assessment standards and how they work together.

NIST Cybersecurity Framework (CSF)

The *National Institute of Standards and Technology (NIST)* is responsible for developing cybersecurity standards across the U.S. federal government. The guidance and standard documents they produce in this process often have wide applicability across the private sector and are commonly referred to by nongovernmental security analysts due to the fact that they are available in the public domain and are typically of very high quality.

In 2024, NIST released version 2.0 of its Cybersecurity Framework (CSF) designed to assist organizations attempting to meet one or more of the following three objectives:

- Describe the current or target cybersecurity posture of part or all of an organization, determine gaps, and assess progress toward addressing those gaps.
- Identify, organize, and prioritize actions for managing cybersecurity risks that align with the organization's mission, legal and regulatory requirements, and risk management and governance expectations.
- Provide a common language for communicating inside and outside the organization about cybersecurity risks, capabilities, needs, and expectations.

The NIST framework includes three components:

- The Framework Core, shown in Figure 3.17, is a set of six security functions that apply across all industries and sectors: govern, identify, protect, detect, respond, and recover. The framework then divides these functions into categories, subcategories, and informative references. Figure 3.18 shows a small excerpt of the framework detail in completed form, looking specifically at the Identify (ID) function and the Asset Management category. If you would like to view a fully completed matrix, see the NIST document Framework for Improving Critical Infrastructure Cybersecurity at https://nvlpubs.nist.gov/nistpubs/cswp/nist.cswp.04162018.pdf.

FIGURE 3.17   NIST Cybersecurity Framework Core Structure

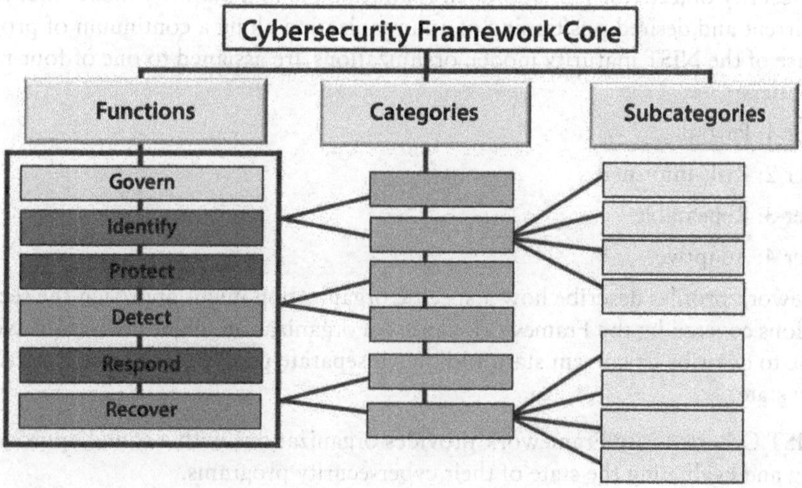

Source: The NIST Cybersecurity Framework (CSF) 2.0, National Institute of Standards and Technology (https://nvlpubs.nist.gov/nistpubs/CSWP/NIST.CSWP.29.pdf)

FIGURE 3.18   Asset Management Cybersecurity Framework

IDENTIFY (ID): The organization's current cybersecurity risks are understood

- **Asset Management (ID.AM):** Assets (e.g., data, hardware, software, systems, facilities, services, people) that enable the organization to achieve business purposes are identified and managed consistent with their relative importance to organizational objectives and the organization's risk strategy

  o **ID.AM-01:** Inventories of hardware managed by the organization are maintained

  o **ID.AM-02:** Inventories of software, services, and systems managed by the organization are maintained

  o **ID.AM-03:** Representations of the organization's authorized network communication and internal and external network data flows are maintained

  o **ID.AM-04:** Inventories of services provided by suppliers are maintained

  o **ID.AM-05:** Assets are prioritized based on classification, criticality, resources, and impact on the mission

  o **ID.AM-07:** Inventories of data and corresponding metadata for designated data types are maintained

  o **ID.AM-08:** Systems, hardware, software, services, and data are managed throughout their life cycles

Source: The NIST Cybersecurity Framework (CSF) 2.0, National Institute of Standards and Technology (https://nvlpubs.nist.gov/nistpubs/CSWP/NIST.CSWP.29.pdf)

- The Framework Implementation assesses how an organization is positioned to meet cybersecurity objectives. This approach is an example of a maturity model that describes the current and desired positioning of an organization along a continuum of progress. In the case of the NIST maturity model, organizations are assigned to one of four maturity model tiers:
  - Tier 1: Partial
  - Tier 2: Risk-Informed
  - Tier 3: Repeatable
  - Tier 4: Adaptive
- Framework profiles describe how a specific organization might approach the security functions covered by the Framework Core. An organization might use a framework profile to describe its current state and then a separate profile to describe its desired future state.

The NIST Cybersecurity Framework provides organizations with a sound approach to developing and evaluating the state of their cybersecurity programs.

Managing Third Parties

The suppliers, vendors, service providers, and business partner organizations that assist the organization in the realization of its objectives are known as *third parties*. The standard of due care for the management of third parties requires that organizations carefully examine each third party during the selection process and thereafter. In response to the trend of outsourcing IT services to third-party organizations, the standard of due care has been steadily increasing. This is necessary to maintain risk parity so that organizations have a reasonable amount of visibility into cyber risk matters.

Risk Factors

The range and type of involvement of a third party in an organization's development and delivery of its products or services may vary widely. This means that the risks associated with individual third parties will also vary. Accordingly, the activities that an organization will need to undertake at the onset of each third-party relationship, and periodically thereafter, will also differ.

Examples of the factors that influence risk levels include the following:

- Does the third party assist in the design, development, or operations of important information systems?
- Does the third party have access to sensitive data?
- Is sensitive data transmitted to the third party for processing?

- Do members of the third-party organization have access to the organization's work centers?

- Are any of the activities performed by the third party in scope for laws, regulations, standards, or contracts with other parties?

The answers to these and other questions help organizations better understand various aspects of cybersecurity risk associated with each third-party organization.

Onboarding and Due Diligence

An organization typically embarks on a search of third-party service providers to find one or more candidate service providers. The organization will develop objectives and requirements and use these in an evaluation process to determine how successfully each candidate service provider will be able to assist the organization to fulfill its business objectives.

Often, organizations will conduct a formal RFP or RFI process, in which formal business and technical requirements are developed and sent to each candidate service provider. Those service providers will then respond to each requirement. The RFP process is described in more detail earlier in this chapter.

After vetting candidate service providers and making a final selection, the organization should determine the level and type of up-front and periodic (typically quarterly or annual) due diligence that will take place. These activities should be described in legal agreements between the organization and the chosen third party.

Classification

Organizations with more than just a few third-party service providers should establish a *risk-tiering scheme* to separate the third parties into similar risk groups. The purpose of this tiering is to serve as a part of a larger program of third-party risk management whereby the organization will determine various types of due diligence for third parties at each risk level. An example tiering scheme is depicted in Table 3.3. This is a simplistic example; organizations need to develop their own criteria to determine the number and type of risk levels and rules to select a risk tier for each third party.

TABLE 3.3 Third-party risk tiers

Classification	Access to client data	Access to source code	Access to facilities
High	Y	Y	Y
Medium	N	N	Y
Low	N	N	N

Assessment

All third parties need to be periodically assessed, but not all assessments are the same. After risk tiering is used to determine the risk level for each third party, the activities to assess each third party are established. These activities correspond to risk levels; a simplistic example scheme of risk levels and assessments is shown in Table 3.4.

TABLE 3.4 Assessment techniques for each level of risk

Classification	High	Medium	Low
Full Questionnaire	Y	Y	N
Limited Questionnaire	N	N	Y
On-site Visit	Y	N	N
Penetration Test	Y	N	N

Remediation

Organizations should expect that the initial and ongoing processes of conducting due diligence on its third-party service providers are not going to proceed perfectly. Occasionally, an organization will discover that the third party is not performing all of the required or desired activities to its liking. At times, these deficiencies may put the organization in jeopardy with regulators.

For example, an organization may require its top-tier service providers to use two-factor authentication for all remote access; an organization may, through the use of questionnaires or a site visit, discover that the third party is not using two-factor authentication for remote access. The organization may consider this a serious deficiency and must decide a course of action. Remediation can range from cessation of the relationship to acceptance of the risk. Neither of these is reasonable, but instead the organization generally will seek some middle ground whereby it will compel the third party to enact two-factor authentication for remote access within a reasonable period of time.

In situations where the third party is unable or unwilling to remediate a deficiency, the organization will need to consider its options carefully and find a path of action that brings together the right level of risk and continued business.

Risk Reporting

As personnel periodically assess third parties, a bigger picture can begin to form. Often, metrics or a risk dashboard are presented to senior management so that management can understand where the risk "hot spots" are, as well as trends in third-party risk. This information helps management decide how to manage this important aspect of cybersecurity risk over time.

Application Controls

Software applications accept, process, store, and transmit information. Unless specifically programmed and configured, software applications lack the ability to properly distinguish valid and reasonable data from that which is not. Controls are necessary to ensure that information at each stage of processing retains its required integrity.

Exam Tip

Exam questions may present a more complex situation than simple input, process, and output controls. Few business processes exist in a vacuum, so many process controls also need to have the full set of internal input, process, and output controls for each subprocess. Test-takers should watch for questions that address application controls that may deal with subprocess requirements, or in which the output of one process is presented as the input for the process under review (affecting which set of controls is appropriate to the question).

While marked differences exist in the architecture of software applications, the typical approach to controls is to apply these controls at the point of entry, processing, and exit. In other words, controls around input data, processing, and output data are needed.

Input Controls

Data that is presented to an application as input data must be validated for authorization, reasonableness, completeness, and integrity. Several controls must be implemented to ensure these points.

Input Authorization

All data that is input into a system must be authorized by management. The method of authorization can take many forms:

- **User access controls:** Only approved personnel, such as system operators, input clerks, business analysts, and customer service representatives, are permitted to log in and use applications. Each user must have unique login credentials.

- **Entity access controls:** Only authorized organizations are permitted to log in and access business applications. Entities in each such organization (including users, service accounts, and hosts) are required to have unique login credentials.

- **Workstation identification:** Only approved terminals and workstations are permitted to be used to input transactions. Identification can take many forms, including electronic serial number, network address, or digital certificate.

- **Approved transactions and batches:** Through manual signature, online approval, and other means, management and other approved personnel perform necessary checks and verifications before individual transactions and batches of transactions are permitted to be input and processed.

- **Source documents:** In some settings, data can be input only from existing source documents. This can include mailed invoices, checks, receipts, or forms filled in by customers. Source documents themselves should be controlled so that they cannot be altered, misplaced, or removed.

 Well-designed applications include audit logs that record when specific data was input, how it was input, and who authorized its input. This permits an organization to research matters when a question arises regarding the source of specific input data after the fact.

Input Validation

The process of *input validation* is used to make sure that the types and values of information are appropriate and reasonable. The types of input validation include:

- **Type checking:** Each input field should be programmed to accept only the type of data that is appropriate for the field. For instance, a numeric field should contain only numeric digits, and a name field should contain only alphabetic characters.

- **Range and value checking:** Input fields need to validate the range and value of characters. For instance, the day field in a date should only accept figures 1 through 31, and the month field 1 through 12. Even more intelligent checking is often warranted; for example, a date field often should be a date that is only in the past, or the future, or even a specific range of the past or future. Other examples include only valid zip or postal codes, only valid telephone numbers, and only valid IP addresses. In some cases, input data must match values in a table of data stored in the application; for instance, only valid city, state, or country codes; telephone area codes; or valid Universal Product Codes (UPCs).

- **Existence:** This simple check confirms that each input field actually contains data.

- **Consistency:** This check compares related data from different input fields. For instance, a zip code value in an input field can be validated by comparing it to the range of allowed zip codes for the city and state values.

- **Length:** Programs must validate the length of input data in an input field. Fields such as names and addresses are often limited to, say, 30 characters. This is especially important on interactive programs where intruders may attempt buffer overflow attacks in an attempt to cause the program to malfunction.

- **Check digits or hash totals:** Numeric values such as bank account numbers can be verified for integrity by recalculating their check digits or hash totals.
- **Spelling:** Input fields that are supposed to contain common words can be spell-checked.
- **Unwanted characters:** Input fields should filter out unwanted characters that could be a result of mistyping. However, unwanted characters can also be a sign of a software malfunction (on a system that is the source of input data) or of an attempted intrusion.
- **Batch controls:** Batches of data should include calculations and counts to ensure the integrity and completeness of a batch of data. Some available methods include transaction counts, control totals (the numeric sum of one or more numeric fields in all of the batch records), and hash totals (a computed "sum" of all of the input fields, regardless of their actual type).

Input validation is certainly necessary on user input forms in applications where users are filling in online forms. However, input validation is just as necessary on batch input and other automated functions; errors in other systems may occur that can cause input data to be entered into the wrong fields, and failure to validate input data can result in inappropriate data being input and stored in a system, which can lead to other problems later.

Input Validation as Achilles Heel

In many, or dare I say most, organizations, insufficient input validation is the nexus for many critical system vulnerabilities and breaches (for example, SQL injection and buffer overflow conditions). With alarming regularity, we learn of critical vulnerabilities in commercial software products and systems such as buffer overflow and cross-site scripting. These vulnerabilities exist as a result of insufficient input validation.

Error Handling

As software programs perform all of the input validation checking described earlier, these programs must be programmed or configured to take specific actions when any of the input validations fail. There are many possible responses, depending on the type of data being input as well as the method of input:

- **Batch rejection:** For input batches, if the transaction count, control totals, or hash totals of a batch do not agree with expected values, the entire batch should be rejected. Usually the application software will have no way to determine what exactly is wrong with the batch, so the only reasonable course of action is to reject the entire batch, which will require data control analysts to examine the batches to see what went wrong.
- **Transaction rejection:** For individual input transactions, whether automated or user input, the software application can reject the transaction.

- **Hold in suspense:** The entire batch will be held in suspense so that the error(s) in the batch can be corrected and the batch can be rerun.

- **Request re-input:** An interactive user program can request that the user re-input the entire form or just the specific field that appears to be incorrect.

When an application rejects input, in most cases the application will need to create a log entry, an error report, or another record of the rejected input so that data analysts will know that an error occurred and take steps to correct it. If the application does not create a record of the error, analysts are apt to believe that all data was input successfully, which could lead to problems later on when those invalid transactions cannot be found anywhere in the system. A lack of such records makes detailed troubleshooting far more difficult.

Processing Controls

It is necessary to ensure that data in a system retains its integrity. All new data that is created—for instance, as a result of calculations—must be checked for reasonableness to ensure that calculations are working properly and that bad information or program code is not creeping in through some other means. The controls used to ensure that data in the system retains its integrity are discussed in this section.

Editing

In many types of applications, data that is initially input into the system will be changed from time to time. For example, a subscriber's email or mailing address may change, or a bank account number, passport number, or license plate number may change. Often these changes are performed either directly by customers or by a customer service representative during a telephone conversation. Sometimes these changes are made automatically as a result of trusted and validated data arriving from other sources.

Whenever values are changed, the new values must be validated before they are accepted and stored; otherwise, problems may ensue later on. The types of validation checks performed during editing are similar to those performed during initial input, described earlier in this section.

Calculations

When application programs are performing calculations, the results of those calculations need to be validated for accuracy and reasonableness to verify that the application is performing calculations properly. Several techniques are used to validate calculations:

- **Run-to-run totals:** This validates that specific stored or calculated data values retain their values throughout the steps in a transaction. This helps to ensure that no errors, tampering, or software malfunctions have occurred.

- **Limit checking:** Results of specific calculations can be checked for upper and lower limits. Calculation results that exceed predetermined limits can be rejected.

- **Batch totals:** When data is processed in batches, batch totals that are calculated at the beginning of the batch can be recalculated at the end of processing for the batch to ensure the integrity of the batch data.
- **Manual recalculation:** An analyst or clerk can recalculate certain transaction calculations manually, and those manual calculation results can be verified or keyed into the application.
- **Reconciliation:** When a set of records is processed that results in the creation of a second set of records—or the next stage of calculation results—totals from the old to new batches may need to be calculated to ensure that processing was done correctly and that no data corruption or calculation errors occurred.
- **Hash values:** The values in selected sets of numeric or text fields can be rehashed at various stages of calculations to verify that they have not been altered or tampered with.

Data File Controls

When processing is performed on data stored in data files, several types of controls are needed to ensure the security and integrity of those data files. Some of the controls available are:

- **Data file and database security:** Access controls can be configured so that only authorized users or processes are permitted to access data files and databases.
- **Error handling:** Erroneous transactions that need to be corrected or re-input should be checked by personnel other than those who originally keyed them.
- **Failure monitoring:** If data transfer jobs fail, administrators should be informed of the failure and investigate the impact on data integrity.
- **Internal and external labeling:** Labeling on removable storage media is vital to ensure that the correct volume (whether tape, disc, or other storage medium) has been loaded.
- **Data file version:** The version of a data file should be independently verified to ensure that the proper file is being processed. This would, for example, help to prevent processing yesterday's file twice.
- **Source files:** Data input at the beginning of a processing run should be retained for a minimum period in case a batch needs to be rerun many days or weeks later.
- **Transaction logs:** Log files containing transactions should be retained for a minimum period in support of later troubleshooting or the investigation of data errors weeks or months later. In addition, compliance obligations may require retaining logs for a longer period of time than needed for operational purposes.

Processing Errors

Errors that occur during processing must be recorded in a log file or other output medium that will be examined by personnel. All errors need to be addressed, whether through rekeying of errant data, rerunning failed batch runs, correcting data transmission errors, or other means.

Processing errors that occur in interactive programs may display an error message to the user. Depending on the type of program, the user may have an opportunity to correct or rekey information.

Output Controls

Applications accept input data, perform calculations, and produce output data. The results of final calculations and transformations need to be checked for reasonableness and validity. Several types of output controls are available, depending on the type of activity and data.

Controlling Special Forms

Some calculation outputs are printed on special physical forms, such as checks, warrants, invoices, and certificates. These forms should be serialized and kept in a locked cabinet. In high-value situations, these forms should be kept in dual custody, where two individuals are required in order to access them.

A forms log should be maintained to account for the use of forms. This log should be examined frequently to ensure that forms are used only for their stated purpose and that all are accounted for.

Checks, warrants, bonds, and other negotiable instruments must be secured at all times to ensure that all are accounted for and properly handled. Just as with electronic data, physical forms must be inventoried and accounted for at each stage of processing and handling.

Signature devices and stamps, when used, must be secured at all times. They should be stored in locations separate from checks and certificates and should be under the control of separate individuals.

Report Distribution and Receipt

Application processing often results in the creation of reports that are sent to authorized personnel in paper or electronic form. Often these reports will contain sensitive information, which requires that the reports be safeguarded at all times in any form.

Reports that are printed and later delivered may need to be placed in tamper-proof or tamper-evident envelopes. Reports that remain in electronic form may need to be encrypted or password-protected. Reports that are transmitted over public networks need to be encrypted. If recipients send electronic reports to printers, special safeguards may be required so that sensitive data is not left on printers for others to view.

Reconciliation

Numeric and financial data on reports may need to be reconciled to input data, data from intermediate calculations, or control totals. This activity, when required, should be documented and logged.

Retention

Reports are sometimes the only human-readable data available during each business cycle. Whether reports deal with research, reference, or statutory requirements, it is often necessary to retain them for a minimum period of up to several years. Reports containing sensitive data will need to be physically safeguarded to prevent access by unauthorized personnel.

> Output controls are just as vital as input controls, because the outputs from one system do not necessarily become the inputs to another system that the organization has control over. Sometimes, one system's output will become another system's inputs where little or no input validation takes place.

Auditing the Systems Development Life Cycle

Audits of the processes used to create and maintain software will assist the organization in knowing how effective these processes are. This provides the organization with valuable information that can be used to make its processes more effective. If the IS auditor examines only an organization's applications and controls but not the processes used to create them, then the root cause of endemic problems in applications and processes may be unknowable.

Exam Tip

The exam will expect you to have a general understanding of the details of each type of audit practice. Focus on the type of documentation and the mechanism for validation of each as you review this section. Watch for exam questions that begin with phrases such as "During the design phase . . ." or similar terminology to guide your response.

Auditing Program and Project Management

The IS auditor who is auditing an organization's program and project management is verifying whether the organization's projects are adequately controlled. Controls in project management ensure the integrity of the organization's projects so that the systems and processes that are built actually support the requirements that are supported and agreed to by management.

The activities that the IS auditor should review when auditing project management include:

- Oversight by senior management and any steering committee(s)
- Risk management techniques used in the project

- Processes and methodologies used to build project plans
- Methods for dealing with issues
- Management of costs
- Status reporting to management
- Project change control
- Project recordkeeping, including decisions, approvals, resource utilization, and costs

Auditors should not only inquire about these activities but should also review documentation to ensure that it provides adequate evidence that these activities occurred throughout the project life cycle.

Auditing the Feasibility Study

IS auditors should audit any feasibility studies that occur at the beginning of major projects. The activities that IS auditors should review include:

- Budgets and cost justifications, and whether they can be independently verified
- Criticality of the project and/or the criticality of the business process supported by the project
- Alternatives that were considered, including the feasibility that existing systems could be used in support of the business need
- Reasonableness of the solution that was chosen and implemented

Auditing Requirements

An IS auditor should audit a project's requirements and the process that was used to develop them. The IS auditor needs to review several aspects of requirements:

- Identify all of the personnel who contributed requirements and determine whether this body of personnel actually represents all true stakeholders.
- Interview several of the requirements contributors to gain a better understanding of whether contributors' requirements were included and whether they were altered without their knowledge.
- Identify any ranking or alteration of requirements that may have occurred without the knowledge of those who contributed them.
- Perform some reasonableness checking of requirements to see if they support the project described in the feasibility stage.
- Determine whether the final body of requirements was approved by management.

Auditing Design

The IS auditor should audit the design and specifications that were developed during a project. During the audit, the IS auditor should consider whether:

- The design actually reflects and supports requirements and the feasibility study.
- The design contains sufficient detail to enable application developers to produce software that will unambiguously meet the organization's requirements and business needs.
- The design was adequately reviewed and was approved by management.
- The design will reasonably result in a successful implementation that meets the users' needs.
- Testing and UAT (user acceptance testing) plans and criteria were developed by this phase in the project.

Auditing Software Acquisition

For software development projects where the organization acquires software from an outside vendor, an IS auditor should audit several aspects and activities in the acquisition stage of the project. The IS auditor should consider whether:

- The organization performed a formal RFP or RFI process.
- All requirements were transferred to the RFP or RFI document.
- Suitable vendors were considered and their responses were properly analyzed against each of the requirements.
- The vendor that was selected could support a majority of the requirements.
- The organization did reference checking, evaluation, and/or pilot evaluation before purchase.
- The contract contains clauses that reasonably protect the organization in the event the software or the vendor fails to perform adequately.
- The contract was reviewed by the organization's legal department before being signed.

Auditing Development

For software development projects where the organization develops software on its own, the IS auditor should consider whether:

- The developers were adequately trained and experienced in the languages and tools used in the project.
- The chosen design and development tools were adequate for the project.

- The chosen computer language and other related technologies were adequate for the project.
- The application contains adequate controls to ensure proper operation, recordkeeping, and support of business processes.
- Controls used to protect source code are adequate.
- The application was written in support of stated requirements.
- The application has adequate input, processing, and output controls.
- The application performs calculations correctly.
- The application produces adequate transaction and audit logs.

Auditing Testing

Software that is developed within the organization or acquired from an outside vendor needs to be tested to ensure that it meets the organization's requirements. When auditing software testing, the IS auditor should consider whether:

- All test plans were developed during the requirements and design phases.
- Test plans reflect the entirety of requirements and design elements.
- All tests were performed and verified successfully.
- Actual test results are available for review as well as contact information for personnel who performed testing.
- Test results have been archived for later research if needed.
- Parallel tests were needed and, if so, were performed appropriately.
- UAT was performed, and the results of those tests are available.

Auditing Implementation

Implementation should be performed only after all testing has been successful and all issues identified during testing have been resolved. When auditing implementation, the IS auditor should consider whether:

- Management approved the implementation.
- The system was implemented using established change control procedures.
- The system was administratively locked down before implementation, thereby preventing tampering by any developer or other persons who do not have authorization to access production systems.
- Data conversions were performed in a controlled manner, including controls to ensure correct conversion processing.

Auditing Post-Implementation

The IS auditor should audit all post-implementation activities, considering whether:

- A post-implementation review took place and, if so, whether the review was documented and actions taken.
- The application supports the entire body of requirements established during the project.
- The application is being measured to verify whether it is meeting established performance and ROI targets.
- Excessive changes were made to the system after implementation, which could be an indicator of inadequate requirements or testing.
- Excessive unscheduled downtime or errors occurred, which could be an indicator of inadequate requirements or testing.
- Control balances indicate that the application is performing properly.

Auditing Change Management

Change management is the management process whereby all changes to an environment are controlled. The IS auditor should consider whether:

- A change management policy and process exists and is followed in practice.
- Adequate records exist that indicate how much the change management process is followed.
- The number of emergency changes indicates inadequate requirements or testing.
- Proposed changes contain implementation procedures, back-out procedures, and test results.
- Minutes are kept of change management meetings.
- Emergency changes are adequately reviewed.

Auditing Configuration Management

Configuration management involves controlling, configuring, and recording configuration changes to information systems. When auditing configuration management, the IS auditor should consider whether:

- Configuration management policies and controls exist and are followed.
- Configuration management tools are used to control and/or record changes made to systems.
- Changes are approved through the change management process.
- Configuration management tools are able to verify the integrity of systems and whether discrepancies are identified and resolved.

Auditing Business Controls

Business controls are points in time during business processes where key activities occur. The IS auditor needs to identify the key processes in an organization and understand the controls that are in place—or that should be in place—that govern the integrity of those processes.

Many business controls are supported by IT applications, but the auditor also needs to take a business process perspective and understand the control points from a strictly process viewpoint. This is necessary because, although controls may be automated by applications, personnel are still in control of and responsible for the correct operation of business processes. Further, processes, even when partly or entirely automated, must be monitored and managed by staff or management. And these processes must be documented—itself an important control.

For the IS auditor to overlook business controls and focus only on IT applications would be a disservice to the organization, because the auditor could miss the obvious control points in key business processes. Remember that the IT system is not the process; instead, the IT system *supports* the process.

Auditing Application Controls

Application controls ensure that only valid data enters a system through input controls, that calculations yield only valid results, and that output data is valid. The IS auditor needs to examine system documentation to understand internal and external data flows and calculations. The IS auditor also needs to examine system records to ensure that all changes made to the system were authorized. Several aspects of application activity need to be examined; these are described in the remainder of this section.

Transaction Flow

The IS auditor should audit an application and follow transactions from end to end. The IS auditor should consider whether:

- Any data flow diagrams or flowcharts exist that describe data flow in the transaction, and whether such diagrams or flowcharts correctly identify the flow of data.

- Any data items in the transaction were altered in the data flow, and, if so, where alterations occurred and whether audit log entries recorded those changes, including who or what made them.

Observations

During an audit of information systems, the IS auditor should make several observations, including whether:

- Any segregations of duties (SODs) are established in terms of the entire transaction process flow.
- Input data is validated, and how the validation is performed.
- Input data is authorized, and how the authorization is documented.
- Any balancing or reconciliation is performed to ensure data integrity.
- Any errors occur, how they are detected, and how they are handled.
- Reports and other outputs are generated, controlled, protected, examined, and acted upon and that they contain complete and accurate data.

Data Integrity Testing

Data integrity testing is used to confirm whether an application properly accepts, processes, and stores information. Data integrity tests will determine whether there are any failures or errors in input, processing, or output controls in an application. The IS auditor should perform several tests on the application, in each case attempting to input data that is invalid or unreasonable to determine whether the application properly rejects such data. The auditor should also attempt to have the application perform calculations that should result in errors or exceptions—for example, a calculation result that should be rejected.

The IS auditor should test not only the stated input, calculation, and output rules for data integrity, but they should also assess the efficacy of the rules themselves. For example, an auditor should determine whether the absence of a rule forbidding the entry of negative hours in a time-reporting system constitutes a deficiency in the application's rules.

Testing Online Processing Systems

Online processing systems are characterized by their ability to process transactions for many users simultaneously. An online application must be able to compartmentalize each user's work so that the users do not interfere with one another, even if two or more users are attempting to read or update the same records. A typical database management system (DBMS) will be able to enforce record locking, and an application must have logic to deal with locked records gracefully and according to established business rules.

Business records and transactions in DBMSs are usually made up of rows in several different tables. *Referential integrity* is the characteristic that requires that the DBMS maintain the parent-child relationships between records in different tables and prohibit activities such as deleting parent records and transforming child records into orphans. Application logic must be designed to prevent these situations and other types of "collisions" and deadlocks that can occur when many users are performing different tasks in an application. The characteristic of *atomicity* states that a complex transaction, which could consist of simultaneous actions on many records in many different tables, is performed as a single unit of work: either it will all be completed properly or none of it will be completed. This helps to ensure the integrity of all data in the DBMS.

The IS auditor will need a complete understanding of the inner workings of an application, including the actions of different transactions on the underlying DBMS. Then the auditor will need to stage a number of different tests to see how the application handles situations that may challenge the integrity of business information. Examples include:

- Having two different users try to open the same transaction to update it

- Having one user try to remove the transaction while another user is trying to update it

- Having two different users open related records in a database, and then having one of the users attempt to remove records that the other user is viewing

These are simple examples, but they should serve to illustrate the need for the IS auditor to determine whether the application properly manages business records.

Auditing Applications

Applications must never be assumed to perform all of their input, processing, and output perfectly. This must be the mindset of the IS auditor: that every important function of applications must be verified to be operating correctly and completely.

Many techniques are available for auditing IT applications, including:

- **Transaction tracing:** The IS auditor enters specific transactions and then carefully examines the application, data, and reports to see how the transaction is represented and processed in the application.

- **Test batches:** The IS auditor creates a batch of test transactions with expected outcomes and directs that they be processed by the system and their results compared against what is expected.

- **Software mapping:** The application software is traced during execution to determine whether there are any unused sections of code. Unused code could signify faulty program logic, obsolete code, or backdoors.

- **Baselining:** This process uses sets of input data (batch- or key-processed by the system) with known results. After system changes, the same sets of data are processed again to determine whether the expected results have changed.

- **Parallel testing:** Programs that simulate the application's function are used to process real data to determine whether results vary from the production system.

It is not suggested that an IS auditor employ all of these methods, but they should select those that will be most effective at verifying correct and complete processing at key points in an application.

Continuous Auditing

Continuous auditing permits the IS auditor to conduct audits of an online environment in a way that is less disruptive to business operations. Instead of more costly and invasive audits, IS auditors can test systems while they are running and with minimum or no involvement from IT staff. Continuous auditing techniques, also known as *computer-assisted audit techniques* (CAATs), are especially useful in applications such as an e-commerce operation with no paper audit trail. Several techniques are available to perform online auditing:

- **Audit hooks:** Special audit modules are placed in key points in an application and are designed to trigger if a specific audit exception or special condition occurs. This can alert auditors to the situation, permitting them to decide whether additional action is required.

- **Systems Control Audit Review File and Embedded Audit Modules (SCARF/EAM):** Special audit software modules are embedded in the application; these modules perform continuous auditing and create an independent log of audit results.

- **Integrated test facility (ITF):** This permits test transactions to be processed in a live application environment. A separate test entity is required, however, so that test data does not alter financial or business results (because the test data does not present actual transactions).

- **Continuous and intermittent simulation (CIS):** The application contains an audit software module that examines online transactions. When a transaction meets audit criteria, the transaction is processed by the application and is also processed by a parallel simulation routine, and the results of the two are compared. These results are logged so that an auditor may examine them at a later time and decide whether any action is required based on the results.

- **Snapshots:** This technique involves the use of special audit modules embedded in an online application that samples specific transactions. The modules make copies of key parts of transactions, often by copying database records and storing them independently. This enables an auditor to trace specific transactions through an application to view the state of transactions as they flow through the application.

- **Online inquiry:** An auditor has the ability to query the application and/or its database to retrieve detailed information on specific transactions or groups of transactions. The auditor typically must have an intimate knowledge of transaction and data structures to make use of this technique.

Auditing Third-Party Risk Management

Auditing third-party risk management involves careful examinations of policy and process documents as well as business records to determine whether all of the organization's third parties are represented in the organization's third-party risk management program. Several techniques and activities are available, including:

- **Completeness of third-party population:** When examining other activities in the business, auditors should determine third parties that are working with the organization and verify whether these third parties are a part of the organization's third-party risk process.

- **Risk criteria:** Auditors should examine stated risk criteria to determine whether they are measurable and complete, and whether they reflect risks present in the organization.

- **Legal agreements:** Auditors should examine legal agreements with third parties to see what security-related controls and obligations are required of each third party. The auditors should determine whether contract language adequately covers business risks and whether that language corresponds to any specific risks identified in the initial vetting of a third party.

- **Third-party classification:** Auditors should examine the classification of third parties and determine whether they were classified properly, according to the organization's risk-tiering scheme (as covered earlier in the chapter in the section "Classification"). While the organization may have latitude for making exceptions (rating third parties higher risk or lower risk than usual), these exceptions should be documented and reasonable.

- **Examination of questionnaires:** Auditors should examine the various questionnaires that are sent to third parties to determine whether the contents and subject matter in the questionnaires cover risks adequately.

- **Questionnaire processing:** Auditors should examine questionnaires returned from third parties and look for responses that warrant attention or response. Auditors should follow the remediation process and see what actions were performed when third parties failed to answer questions or provided answers that warrant action. There should be a complete record of action from a returned questionnaire to remediation and issue closure.

Summary

Organizations should have processes and procedures in place to manage the development, acquisition, and maintenance of software applications and supporting infrastructure. These processes ensure that all of the activities related to additions and changes to software applications are performed consistently and that all necessary considerations are included and documented.

Program management is the oversight of several projects and project teams. A program manager oversees project managers who manage individual projects in a program that contributes to an organization's objective. The program manager's oversight includes monitoring project schedules, budgets, resource allocation, conflicts, and the preparation of status reports for senior management. Another form of program management involves the management of a *project portfolio*, which is a collection of all of the active projects, regardless of whether they contribute to a single corporate objective or to many.

Management should approve any new project only after a valid business case has been developed, reviewed, and approved. A *business case* describes the business problem, the results of any feasibility studies, a project plan, a budget, and related risks. The project will be approved only if there is a reasonable expectation of business benefits; a business case should include one or more ways in which the outcome of the project can be measured so that management can determine whether the project resulted in actual business benefit.

Projects require formal planning that includes the development of a project schedule, creation of methods for estimating the time required for individual tasks, management of budgets and resources, methods for identification and resolution of issues and conflicts, management of project records, and creation of status reports for management. Changes to projects should be managed through a formal review and approval process. Project debriefs or reviews should take place when projects conclude so that the organization can identify lessons learned that will help improve future projects.

Software development and acquisition should be managed through a *systems development life cycle* (SDLC) or similar process. The SDLC is a rigorous set of activities that help ensure that new applications will meet the organization's business needs. The phases of the SDLC are a feasibility study, requirements definition, design, development, testing, implementation, and post-implementation. These phases are all formally documented, reviewed, and measured.

The feasibility study and requirements definition phases help a project team develop a highly detailed set of specifications that developers can use to build the application. An organization that is purchasing off-the-shelf software can use requirements to make sure that the most appropriate software product will be selected.

The testing phase ensures that the application that was developed or acquired will actually perform as required. A test plan should be formally developed; this plan should be a direct derivation from formal requirements that were developed earlier in the project; essentially, every requirement must be measurable and confirmed during testing. Other critical activities in a software and systems development project include data migration (where data is transferred from an older application to the new application), training (for users, operations, and technical support staff), and implementation of the new software application.

Some alternatives to the traditional SDLC process include agile development, prototyping, rapid application development (RAD), data-oriented system development (DOSD), object-oriented (OO) system development, component-based development, web-based development, and reverse engineering.

Acquiring cloud-based applications requires the same steps as software acquisition, although additional considerations need to be managed, including access control, environment segregation, and legal jurisdiction.

Change management and configuration management processes are used to manage changes to existing applications and infrastructure. Change management is a formal process whereby desired changes are planned, tested, and reviewed prior to implementation. Configuration management is a process (usually supported by automated tools) of recording configuration information in operating systems, software environments, and applications.

Like software applications and infrastructure, business processes should also be managed by a life cycle process that includes feasibility studies, requirements definition, business process engineering, testing, and implementation. Often, business processes are tightly coupled to software applications; frequently, changes to one will necessitate changes in the other.

Software applications should be equipped with controls that ensure the integrity of information and the integrity of processing and applications. These controls include input validation, processing validation, and output validation, all of which ensure that the data in the application is of the proper type and within required numeric ranges.

IS auditors who audit life cycle management activities need to obtain and examine documents that describe program and project management processes, charters, and records. They must understand the processes that are used to develop and acquire software applications and supporting infrastructure, as well as the processes used to maintain them. IS auditors have to understand the processes that are in place and to examine records to help determine whether the processes are followed and effective.

Third parties should be assessed for risk and their compliance with the organization's requirements. Organizations with many third parties should establish a risk-tiering scheme and enact periodic assessment procedures commensurate with each level of risk. IS auditors need to audit an organization's third-party risk program to ensure that all third parties are included in the program, that third parties are correctly classified, and that issues are remediated. Metrics and specific issues on third-party risk should be reported to senior management.

Exam Essentials

Understand how organizations realize business benefits.   Benefits realization is the result of strategic planning, process development, and systems development, which all contribute toward a launch of business operations to reach a set of business objectives.

Know the project management strategies and their impact on program execution.   Project management strategies guide program execution through the organization of resources and development of clear project objectives. Management of the project schedule, roles, change management, and subsequent completion or closure criteria determine the outcome of each project. Many project management methodologies exist to guide project expectations, requirements, and completion criteria.

Explain the systems development life cycle (SDLC) and its importance in application software creation. The systems development life cycle (SDLC) defines a subset of project management focusing on the requirements for the creation, implementation, and maintenance of application software. The SDLC relies on a sequence of events that may occur one time or cyclically as part of a formal continual improvement process. The SDLC phases include a feasibility study, definition of requirements, design, development, testing, implementation, and post-implementation.

Describe the role of enterprise infrastructure in facilitating application access and its development process. Application access is facilitated by the enterprise infrastructure, which is in turn developed, implemented, and maintained through a process similar to the SDLC. Infrastructural development begins with a review of existing infrastructure elements, matching each to identified requirements to produce the initial design. After procurement to meet design requirements, the activities of testing, implementation, and post-implementation follow similarly to the SDLC.

Understand post-implementation maintenance of information systems. Post-implementation maintenance of information systems includes both change and configuration management strategies to ensure the enterprise remains aligned with business requirements and practices.

Explain the business process life cycle (BPLC) and business process reengineering (BPR). The business process life cycle (BPLC) and business process reengineering (BPR) aid in coordinating business processes using a sequence of events similar to that of the SDLC focused on business process creation, implementation, and maintenance. Benchmarking facilitates continuous improvement within the BPLC, while capability maturity models can enable point-in-time assessment of business process and information system capability alignment.

Know the importance of application controls and their role in information systems. Application controls limit information system access at the point of entry (input controls), during consumption (process controls), and at the point of expression (output controls).

Describe the process of auditing the enterprise's development life cycle. Auditing each element of the enterprise's development life cycle validates alignment between business and regulatory controls against process and functional control strategies and standards. The auditor should be familiar with the project management strategy in place within an enterprise to ensure that both the elements and the process used to develop each are properly aligned with business process requirements.

Explain the importance of auditing application controls and the role of CAATs. Auditing application controls validates the proper operation of input, process, and output controls by following transaction flow from initiation through conclusion and performing data integrity testing appropriate to the application design. Computer-assisted audit techniques (CAATs) systems are particularly useful for the continuous audit of application controls.

Review Questions

1. What testing activities should developers perform during the development phase?
   A. Security testing
   B. Integration testing
   C. Unit testing
   D. Developers should not perform any testing

2. The purpose of function point analysis (FPA) is to:
   A. Estimate the effort required to develop a software program.
   B. Identify risks in a software program.
   C. Estimate task dependencies in a project plan.
   D. Inventory inputs and outputs in a software program.

3. A project manager needs to identify the tasks that are responsible for project delays. What approach should the project manager use?
   A. Function point analysis
   B. Gantt analysis
   C. Project evaluation and review technique
   D. Critical path analysis

4. A software developer has informed the project manager that a portion of the application development is going to take five additional days to complete. The project manager should:
   A. Inform the other project participants of the schedule change.
   B. Change the project schedule to reflect the new completion time.
   C. Create a project change request.
   D. Adjust the resource budget to account for the schedule change.

5. The phases and their order in the systems development life cycle are:
   A. Requirements definition, feasibility study, design, development, testing, implementation, post-implementation
   B. Feasibility study, requirements definition, design, development, testing, implementation, post-implementation
   C. Feasibility study, requirements definition, design, development, testing, implementation
   D. Requirements definition, feasibility study, development, testing, implementation, post-implementation

6. Which personnel should be involved in the requirements phase of a software development project?

    A. Systems administrators, network administrators, and software developers

    B. Developers, analysts, architects, and users

    C. Security, privacy, and legal analysts

    D. Representatives from each software vendor

7. The primary source for test plans in a software development project is:

    A. Requirements

    B. Developers

    C. End users

    D. Vendors

8. The primary purpose of a change management process is to:

    A. Record changes made to systems and infrastructure.

    B. Review and approve proposed changes to systems and infrastructure.

    C. Review and approve changes to a project schedule.

    D. Review and approve changes to application source code.

9. What is the purpose of a capability maturity model?

    A. To assess the experience of software developers

    B. To assess the experience of project managers

    C. To assess the integrity of application software

    D. To assess the maturity of business processes

10. The purpose of input validation checking is to:

    A. Ensure that input values are within acceptable ranges.

    B. Ensure that input data contains the correct type of characters.

    C. Ensure that input data is free of hostile or harmful content.

    D. Ensure all of the above.

11. An organization is considering the acquisition of enterprise software that will be hosted by a cloud services provider. What additional requirements need to be considered for the cloud environment?

    A. Logging

    B. Access control

    C. Data segregation

    D. Performance

12. System operators have to make an emergency change in order to keep an application server running. To satisfy change management requirements, the systems operators should:

    A. Document the steps taken.

    B. Fill out an emergency change request form.

    C. Seek approval from management before making the change.

    D. Do all of the above.

13. A global organization is planning the migration of a business process to a new application. What cutover methods can be considered?

    A. Parallel, geographic, module by module, or all at once

    B. Parallel, geographic, or module by module

    C. Parallel, module by module, or all at once

    D. Parallel, geographic, or all at once

14. The purpose of developing risk tiers in third-party management is to:

    A. Determine whether to perform penetration tests.

    B. Satisfy regulatory requirements.

    C. Determine the appropriate level of due diligence.

    D. Determine data classification requirements.

15. The reason that functional requirements need to be measurable is:

    A. Developers need to know how to test functional requirements.

    B. Functional tests are derived directly from functional requirements.

    C. To verify correct system operation.

    D. To measure system performance.

16. Which project management approach involves employees having both a permanent reporting relationship in their functional area and a temporary reporting relationship to the project manager?

    A. Supervisor

    B. Influencer

    C. Functional manager

    D. Matrix

17. What is the primary purpose of the benchmarking process in business?

    A. To identify risks in business processes

    B. To improve communication within the organization

    C. To compare key measurements in a business process to those of top-performing organizations

    D. To develop new business strategies

18. Which component of the NIST Cybersecurity Framework (CSF) describes the set of six security functions that apply across all industries and sectors?

   A. Framework Implementation

   B. Framework Profiles

   C. Framework Core

   D. Maturity Model Tiers

19. A project team has completed the development of a new software application. During the testing phase, they need to verify that all requirements are met and that the application performs as expected according to the specifications. The project manager has instructed the team to simulate various user scenarios and ensure each function of the application works correctly as described in the requirements document. Which stage of testing is the team conducting?

   A. Unit testing

   B. System testing

   C. Functional testing

   D. User acceptance testing

20. A company is transitioning to a DevOps model to improve collaboration between development and operations teams. The goal is to create a more iterative and continuous integration/continuous delivery (CI/CD) pipeline to enhance the efficiency and reliability of software deployments. Which of the following benefits is the company most likely aiming to achieve with this transition?

   A. Reduced project costs by minimizing the number of developers required

   B. Improved time-to-market by enabling faster and more frequent software releases

   C. Increased security by isolating development and operations environments

   D. Enhanced customer satisfaction by reducing the number of features in each release

Chapter

4

IT Service Management

THE CERTIFIED INFORMATION SYSTEMS AUDITOR (CISA) OBJECTIVES REPRESENT 26% OF THE MATERIAL COVERED ON THE EXAM AND INCLUDE:

✓ **Domain 4: Information Systems Operations & Business Resilience**

  A. Information Systems Operations

    1. Data Governance

    2. Systems Performance Management

    3. Problem and Incident Management

    4. Change, Configuration, Release, and Patch Management

    5. IT Service Level Management

    6. Database Management

  Supporting Tasks

    12. Evaluate the monitoring and reporting of IT key performance indicators (KPIs).

    14. Evaluate whether the business case for proposed changes to information systems meet business objectives.

    20. Evaluate whether IT service management practices align with business requirements.

    24. Evaluate database management practices.

    25. Evaluate data governance policies and practices.

    26. Evaluate problem and incident management policies and practices.

27. Evaluate change, configuration, release and patch management policies and practices.

38. Identify opportunities for process improvement in the organization's IT policies and practices.

Together, the topics in Chapter 5, "IT Infrastructure," Chapter 6, "Business Continuity and Disaster Recovery," and this chapter represent 26 percent of the CISA examination. IT organizations are effective if their operations are effective. Management needs to be in control of information systems operations, which means that all aspects of operations need to be measured, those measurements and reports reviewed, and management-directed changes carried out to ensure continuous improvement.

IT organizations are service organizations—they exist to serve the organization and support its business processes. IT's service management operations need to be well-designed, adequately measured, and reviewed by management.

Information Systems Operations

IS operations encompass the day-to-day control of the information systems, applications, and infrastructure that support organizational objectives and processes. IS operations consist of several sets of activities, which include management and control of operations:

- Systems performance management
- Problem and incident management
- Change, configuration, release, vulnerability, and patch management
- Operational log management
- IT operations and exception handling
- IT service level management
- Data governance and management
- Financial management
- Quality assurance
- Security management
- Media control

These activities are discussed in detail in the remainder of this chapter, following a brief overview describing how IS operations need to be managed and controlled.

Don't get too hung up on the terms "IS operations" versus "IT operations"; often, they are considered synonymous.

Management and Control of Operations

All the activities that take place in an IT department should be managed and controlled, meaning all actions and activities performed by operations personnel should be a part of a control, procedure, process, or project that has been approved by management. Processes, procedures, and projects should have sufficient recordkeeping so that management can understand the status of these activities. They should be documented in a manner so that someone else would be able to reperform the activity and arrive at the same result.

Management is ultimately responsible for all activities in an IS operations department. The primary high-level management activities that govern IS operations are:

- **Development of processes and procedures:** Every repetitive activity performed by any operations personnel should be documented as a *process* or *procedure*. This means that documents that describe each step of every process and procedure need to be developed, reviewed, approved by management, and made available to operations staff.

- **Development of standards:** From the way that operations perform tasks to the brands and technologies used, *standards* drive consistency in everything that IS operations does.

- **Resource allocation:** Management is responsible for allocating resources that support IS operations, including labor, technology, and budget. Resource allocation should align with the organization's mission, goals, and objectives.

- **Process management:** All IS operations processes should be measured and managed to ensure that processes are performed properly, accurately, and within time and budget targets.

Systems Performance Management

Also referred to by ISACA as systems availability and capacity management, this set of activities is performed to ensure that IT systems are performing correctly and with sufficient capacity to support business processes.

Availability Management

The goal of availability management is to sustain IT service availability in support of organizational objectives and processes. The availability of IT systems is governed by the following:

- **Effective change management:** When changes to systems and infrastructure are properly vetted through a change management process, changes (including request, review, approval, and testing) are less likely to result in unanticipated downtime.

- **Effective system testing:** When system changes are made according to a set of formal requirements, review, and testing, the system is less likely to fail and become unavailable.

- **Resilient architecture:** When an environment's overall architecture is designed from the beginning to be highly reliable, it will be more resilient and more tolerant of individual faults and component failures.

- **Serviceable components:** When the individual components of an environment can be effectively serviced by third-party service organizations, those components will be less likely to fail unexpectedly.

 Organizations typically measure availability as a percentage of uptime of an application or service. Another common measure is the number of minutes of unscheduled downtime per month.

Capacity Management

Capacity management is a set of activities that confirms that sufficient capacity exists in IT systems and IT processes to meet service needs. Primarily, an IT system or process has sufficient capacity if its performance falls within an acceptable range, as specified in service level agreements (SLAs).

Capacity management is not just a concern for current needs; it must also consider future needs. This is attained through several activities, including:

- **Periodic measurements:** Systems and processes need to be regularly measured so that trends in usage can be used to predict future capacity needs. Measurements taken may include:
  - CPU utilization
  - Storage utilization (memory and hard drive/SSD)
  - Network utilization
  - Number of processes and users
  - Number of virtual machines and containers
  - System or device temperature
- **Considering planned changes:** Planned changes to processes and IT systems may impact the predicted workload.
- **Understanding long-term strategies:** Changes in the organization, including IT systems, business processes, and organizational objectives, may impact workloads, requiring more (or less) capacity than would be extrapolated through simpler trend analysis.
- **Changes in technology:** Several factors may influence capacity plans, including the expectation that computing and network technologies will deliver better performance in the future and that trends in technology usage may influence how end users use technology.

Events, event logging, and operational response to events are discussed later in this chapter.

Linkage to Financial Management

One of the work products of capacity management is a projection for the acquisition of additional computer or network hardware (whether physical devices or virtual in-the-cloud workloads) to meet future capacity needs. This information needs to be part of budgeting and spending management processes.

Linkage to Service Level Management

If there are insufficient resources to handle workloads, capacity issues may result in SLA violations. Overburdened systems and processes will result in longer response times. In some cases, systems may stop responding altogether.

Linkage to Incident and Problem Management

Systems with severe capacity issues may take excessive time to respond to user requests. In some cases, systems may malfunction, or users may give up. Often, users will call the service desk, resulting in the logging of incidents and problems.

System and Security Monitoring

Information systems, applications, and supporting infrastructure must be monitored to ensure that they continue to operate as required.

Monitoring tools and programs enable IT operations staff to detect when software or hardware components are not operating as planned. The IT operations staff must also make direct observations to detect some problems. The types of errors that should be detected and reported include:

- System errors
- Program errors
- Communications errors
- Operator errors

Simply put, any event representing unexpected or abnormal activity should be recorded so that management and customers may become aware of it. This requires that incident and problem management processes be developed. Incident and problem management are discussed in detail in the later section, "Problem and Incident Management."

Many organizations perform several types of security monitoring as a part of their overall strategy to prevent and respond to security incidents. The types of monitoring that an organization may perform include:

- Firewall exceptions
- Intrusion prevention system (IPS) alerts

- Data loss prevention (DLP) system alerts
- Cloud access security broker (CASB) alerts
- File integrity monitoring (FIM) alerts
- File activity monitoring (FAM) alerts
- User access management system alerts
- Network anomaly alerts
- Web content filtering system alerts
- Endpoint management system alerts
- Vendor security advisories
- Third-party security advisories
- Threat intelligence advisories
- Work center access system alerts
- Video surveillance system alerts

IT business processes also need to be monitored. Process monitoring is discussed in Chapter 2, "The Audit Process," and Chapter 3, "IT Life Cycle Management."

Problem and Incident Management

Problem and incident management are the two main business processes employed to deal with unplanned events in IT operations.

Incident Management

ITIL defines an *incident* as "an unplanned interruption to an IT service or reduction in the quality of an IT service. Failure of a configuration item that has not yet affected service is also an incident—for example, failure of one disk from a mirror set."

Thus, an incident may be any of the following:

- Service outage
- Service slowdown
- Service malfunction
- Software bug

Regardless of the cause, incidents result from failures or errors in any component or layer of IT infrastructure.

In ITIL terminology, if the incident has been experienced before and its root cause is known, this is a *known error*. If the service desk can access the catalog of known errors, this may result in more rapid resolution of incidents, resulting in less downtime and inconvenience. Change management and configuration management processes are used to modify and fix the system temporarily or permanently.

If the incident's root cause is not known, the incident may escalate to a *problem*, which is discussed in the next section.

The topic of security incident response is fully explored in Chapter 7, "Information Security Management."

IT Infrastructure Library, Not Just for the United Kingdom

Although ITIL has roots in the UK, it has become an international standard. This is partly due to ITIL being adopted by the International Organization for Standardization (ISO)/ International Electrotechnical Commission (IEC) in the ISO/IEC 20000 standard, and IT management practices are becoming more standardized and mature.

Problem Management

When several incidents have occurred that appear to have the same or a similar root cause, a problem is occurring. ITIL defines a *problem* as "a cause of one or more incidents."

The overall objective of problem management is the reduction in the number and severity of incidents. Problem management can also include some proactive measures, including system monitoring to measure system health and capacity management that will help forestall capacity-related incidents.

Examples of problems include:

- A server that has exhausted available resources that result in similar, multiple errors (which, in ITSM terms, are known as *incidents*)
- A software bug in a service that is noticed by and affects many users
- A chronically congested network that causes the communications between many IT components to fail

Like incidents, when the root cause of a problem has been identified, the change management and configuration management processes will be enacted to make temporary and permanent fixes.

Service Desk

Often known as the helpdesk or call center, the IT service desk function handles incidents and service requests on behalf of internal IT customers by acting as a single point of contact. The service desk performs end-to-end management of incidents and service requests (at least from the customer's perspective). It is responsible for communicating status updates and reports to customers for matters that take more time to resolve.

The service desk can also serve as a collection point for other ITSM processes, such as incident management, problem management, change management, configuration management, service level management, availability management, and other ITSM functions.

Service Continuity Management

Service continuity management is the set of activities concerned with the organization's ability to continue providing services, primarily when a natural or human-made disaster has occurred. Service continuity management is ITIL parlance for the more common terms *business continuity planning* and *disaster recovery planning*.

Business continuity and disaster recovery are discussed in Chapter 6.

Change, Configuration, Release, and Patch Management

Several IT processes are used to manage various changes to IT infrastructure. These processes include change management, configuration management, release management, and patch management.

Change Management

Change management is the set of processes that ensures all changes performed in an IT environment are controlled and performed consistently. ISACA's CMMI defines change management as a "methodical approach for controlling and implementing changes in a planned and structured manner." ITIL defines change management as follows: "The goal of the change management process is to ensure that standardized methods and procedures are used for efficient and prompt handling of all changes, to minimize the impact of change-related incidents upon service quality, and consequently improve the day-to-day operations of the organization."

The main purpose of change management is to ensure that all proposed changes to an IT environment are vetted for suitability and risk. It also ensures that changes will not interfere with each other, with other planned or unplanned activities, or with business processes supported by IT systems. To be effective, each stakeholder should review all changes so that every perspective of each change is properly reviewed.

A typical change management process is a formal "waterfall" process that includes the following steps:

1. **Proposal or request:** The person or group performing the change announces the proposed change. Typically, a change proposal contains a description of the change, the change procedure, the IT components that are expected to be affected by the change,

a verification procedure to ensure that the change was applied properly, a backout procedure in the event the change cannot be applied (or failed verification), and the results of tests that were performed in a test environment. The proposal should be distributed to all stakeholders several days before its review.

2. **Review:** This is typically a meeting or discussion about the proposed change, where the personnel performing the change can discuss the change and answer stakeholders' questions. Since the change proposal was sent out earlier, each stakeholder should have had an opportunity to read about the proposed change before the review. Stakeholders can discuss any aspect of the change during the review. The stakeholders may agree to approve the change, or they may request that it be deferred or that some aspect of the proposed change be altered.

3. **Approval:** When a change has been formally approved in the review step, the person or group responsible for change management recordkeeping will record the approval, including the names of the individuals who consented to the change. If, however, a change has been deferred or denied, the person or group that proposed the change will need to make alterations to the proposed change so that it will be acceptable, or they can withdraw the change altogether.

4. **Implementation:** The actual change is implemented per the procedure described in the change proposal. Here, the personnel identified as the change implementers perform the actual change to the IT system(s) identified in the approved change procedure.

5. **Verification:** After the implementers have completed the change, they will perform the verification procedure to ensure that the change was implemented correctly and produced the desired result. Generally, the verification procedure will include one or more steps that involve gathering evidence (and directions for confirming a correct versus an incorrect change) that shows the change is correct. This evidence will be filed with other records related to the change and may be useful in the future if there is any problem with the system where this change is suspected as a part of the root cause.

6. **Post-change review:** Some or all changes in an IT organization will be reviewed after the change is implemented. In this activity, the personnel who made the change discuss the change with other stakeholders to learn more about the change and whether any updates or future changes may be needed.

These activities should be part of the duties of a *change control board*, a group of IT stakeholders, and every group affected by changes in IT applications and supporting infrastructure.

The change management process is like the system development life cycle (SDLC) in that it consists of life cycle activities that systematically enact changes to an IT environment.

Change Management Records

Most or all the activities related to a change should include updates to business records so that all the facts related to each change are captured for future reference. In even the smallest

IT organization, too many changes occur over time to expect that anyone will be able to recall facts about each change later on. Records that are related to each change serve as a permanent record.

Emergency Changes

Though most changes can be planned using the change management process described here, there are times when IT systems need to be changed right away. Most change management processes include a process for emergency changes that details most of the steps in the non-emergency change management process, but they are performed in a different order. The steps for emergency changes are:

- **Emergency approval:** When an emergency arises, the staff members attending to the emergency should still seek management approval for the proposed change. This approval may be done by phone, in person, or in writing (typically email). If the approval was by phone or in person, email or other follow-up communication is usually performed. Certain members of management should be designated in advance who can approve these emergency changes.
- **Implementation:** Staff members perform the change.
- **Verification:** Staff members verify that the change produced the expected result, involving other staff members or end users.
- **Review:** The emergency change is formally reviewed. This review may be performed alongside non-emergency changes with the change control board, which is the same group of individuals who discuss non-emergency changes.

Like non-emergency changes, emergency changes should be fully documented, with records available for future reference. It is also best practice to have a clear definition of an emergency change, as a lack of planning and foresight should not be considered an emergency.

Linkage to Problem and Incident Management

Often, changes are made because of an incident or problem. Emergency and non-emergency changes should reference specific incidents or problems so that those incidents and problems may be properly closed once verification of their resolution has been completed.

Configuration Management

Configuration management (CM) is the process of recording the configuration of IT systems. ISACA defines configuration management as "the control of changes to a set of configuration items over a system life cycle." Each IT asset is known in ITSM parlance as a *configuration item (CI)*. CIs usually include the following:

- **Hardware complement:** This includes the hardware specifications of each system (such as CPU speed, amount of memory, firmware version, adapters, and peripherals).
- **Hardware configuration:** Settings at the hardware level may include boot settings, adapter configuration, and firmware settings.

- **Operating system version and configuration:** This includes versions, patches, and many operating system configuration items that impact system performance and functionality.

- **Software versions and configuration:** Software components such as database management systems, application servers, and integration interfaces often have many configuration settings of their own.

Organizations with many IT systems may automate the CM function with tools used to record and change configuration settings automatically. These tools help streamline IT operations and make it easier for IT systems to be more consistent. The database of system configurations is called a *configuration management database (CMDB)*.

Linkage to Problem and Incident Management

An intelligent problem and incident management system can access the CMDB to help IT personnel determine whether incidents and problems are related to specific configurations. This can be a valuable aid to those seeking to determine a problem's root cause.

Linkage to Change Management

Many configuration management tools can detect system configuration changes automatically. With some change and configuration management systems, it is possible to correlate changes detected by a configuration management system with changes approved in the change management process. Further, many changes approved by the change management process can be performed by configuration management tools, which can be used to push changes out to managed systems.

Release Management

Release management is the ITIL term used to describe the portion of the SDLC where changes in applications and other information systems are placed into production and made available for production use. The release management process is used to control the changes that are made to software programs, applications, and environments.

The release process is used for several types of changes to a system, including the following:

- **Incident and problem resolution:** Also known as *bug fixes*, these types of changes are made in response to an incident or problem, where it has been determined that a change to application software is the appropriate remedy.

- **Enhancements:** New functions in an application are created and implemented. Customers may have requested these enhancements, or they may be a part of the long-range vision on the part of the software program designers.

- **Subsystem patches and changes:** Changes in lower layers in an application environment may require a testing level similar to what is used when changes are made to the application itself. Examples of changes are patches, service packs, and version upgrades to operating systems, database management systems, application servers, and middleware.

The release process is a sequential process—that is, each change that is proposed to an information system will be taken through each step in the release management process. In many applications, changes are usually assembled into a "package" for process efficiency purposes; discussing and managing groups of changes is more effective than managing individual changes.

Typical SDLC process steps precede the steps in a typical release process:

1. **Feasibility study:** This study seeks to determine the expected benefits of a program, project, or change to a system.

2. **Requirements definition:** Each software change is described in terms of a feature description and requirements. The *feature description* is a high-level description of a change to software that may explain the change in business terms. *Requirements* are detailed statements that describe a change in enough detail for a developer to make changes and additions to application code that will provide the desired functionality. Often, end users will be involved in developing requirements so that they may verify that the proposed software change is what they really desire.

3. **Design:** After requirements have been developed, a programmer/analyst or application designer will create a formal design. This will usually involve changes to existing design documents and diagrams for an existing software application. Still, new applications must be created from scratch or copied from similar designs and modified. Regardless, the design will have sufficient detail to permit a programmer or software engineer to complete development without having to discern the meaning of requirements or design.

4. **Development:** When the requirements definition and design have been completed, reviewed, and approved, programmers, software engineers, or other IT engineers begin development. This involves actual coding in the chosen computer language with approved development tools and the creation or update of ancillary components, such as a database design or application programming interface (API). Developers will often perform their own *unit testing*, when they test individual modules and sections of the application code to ensure it works properly. In other cases, development will consist of planned configuration changes, patch application, or module upgrades to an information system.

5. **Testing:** When the developers have finished coding and unit testing (or other engineers have completed their initial work), a more formal and comprehensive test phase is performed. Here, analysts, dedicated software or systems testers, and perhaps end users, will test all the new and changed functionality to confirm whether it performs according to requirements. Depending on the nature of the changes, some *regression testing* is also performed; this means that functions confirmed to be working properly in prior releases are tested again to ensure that they continue to work as expected. Testing is performed according to formal, written test plans designed to confirm that every requirement is fulfilled. Formal test scripts are used, and the results of all tests should be recorded and archived. The testing that users perform is usually called *user acceptance testing (UAT)*. Automated test tools are often used, making testing more accurate and efficient. After testing, a formal review and approval are required before the process can continue.

6. **Implementation:** When testing has been completed, the changes are implemented on production systems. Here, developers hand off the completed software or system changes to operations personnel, who install it according to instructions created by developers. This could also involve using tools to make changes to data and database design, operating systems, or network devices, to accommodate changes in the system. When changes are completed and tested, the release itself is carried out with these last two steps:

   a. **Release preparation:** When UAT and regression testing have been completed, reviewed, and approved, a release management team will begin to prepare the new or changed system for release. Depending on the system's complexity and the change itself, release preparation may involve not only software (or another component) installation but also the installation or change to database design, operating systems, network devices, and perhaps even customer data. Hence, the release may involve developing (or engineering) and testing data conversion tools and other required programs so that the new or changed system will operate properly. As with testing and other phases, full testing records and implementation of release preparation details need to be captured and archived.

   b. **Release deployment:** When release preparation is completed (and perhaps reviewed and approved), the release is installed on the target system(s). Personnel deploying the release will follow the release procedure, which may involve using tools that will modify the target system at the operating system, database, or other level; any required data manipulation or migration; and installing the actual software. The release procedure will also include verification steps that will be used to confirm the correct installation of all components.

7. **Post-implementation:** After implementing system changes, a post-implementation review takes place to examine system adequacy, security, ROI, and any issues encountered during implementation.

Release management is the proverbial "tip of the iceberg," with the entire subject of systems and software life cycle development discussed in Chapter 3.

Utilizing a Gate Process

Many organizations use a "gate process" approach in their release management process, meaning each step undergoes formal review and approval before the next step is allowed to begin. For example, a formal design review will be performed and attended by end users, personnel who created requirements and feature description documents, developers, and management. If the design is approved, development may begin. However, if questions or concerns are raised during the design review, the design may need to be modified and reviewed before development is allowed to begin.

Agile processes utilize gates as well, although the flow of agile processes is often parallel rather than sequential. The concept of formal reviews is the same, regardless of the SDLC process in use.

Vulnerability Management

Vulnerability management is the set of actions related to identifying and remedying exploitable vulnerabilities in systems, applications, and devices. Like other processes, vulnerability management is a life cycle process with several activities:

- **Vulnerability identification:** Vulnerabilities are identified in one of two ways. First, an advisory from a vendor or non-vendor source may announce a vulnerability, which often contains details that enable organizations to confirm their existence and understand the level of effort required to exploit the vulnerability, as well as the likely result. Second, a routine security scan may detect a vulnerability that often involves a misconfiguration or a missing patch.

- **Risk analysis:** IT or security personnel need to understand the vulnerability and determine the impact of a threat event that exploits it. Often, personnel seek to know the severity level of the vulnerability in their organization.

- **Mitigation:** Using established change management and configuration management tools and practices, IT or security personnel will mitigate the vulnerability by applying a patch or altering a configuration setting.

- **Confirmation and closure:** After the vulnerability has been remediated, IT or security personnel take steps to confirm that the vulnerability no longer exists. The matter is then closed.

Organizations often establish SLAs to ensure remediation is performed within a schedule. Typically, a critical vulnerability should be closed within 30 days, and a highly critical vulnerability within 7 days.

Effective vulnerability management is one of the most critical cybersecurity practices. Organizations that practice effective vulnerability management have a lower probability of security incidents and breaches.

Patch Management

Patch management is the set of activities concerned with the application of security patches and functionality patches to information systems, software applications, network devices, and other types of systems and devices. Patch management is considered a subset of vulnerability management, which is concerned with security patches as well as configuration settings.

When software defects (bugs) are identified in applications, systems, and devices, the manufacturer of these products will produce one or more pieces of software code and insert the code into a "package" that the system or device can use to install the patch.

Like other IT processes, patch management is a life cycle process with these activities:

- Obtain vendor and non-vendor advisories that describe the defect and how it can be mitigated.

- Perform risk analysis to determine the applicability and urgency of installing the patch.

- Apply the patch in a test environment and perform a suitable degree of regression testing to ensure that the patch does not produce any unintended consequences.

- Use the change control and configuration management processes to schedule and record the details of the patch installation to production systems.

- Perform vulnerability scanning or other means to confirm the correct installation of patches.

As described, the installation of security and functionality patches should be performed *proactively* by IT personnel who manage the various types of systems and devices where patches are applied. That way, vulnerability scanning fulfills the role of quality assurance to confirm that all systems that must be patched are successfully patched.

Operational Log Management

IT systems, applications, network devices, and other types of systems have event logs and/or audit logs that record many events. The log entries contain important operational and/or security-related information, some of which warrant response by IT or security personnel.

A typical log entry contains the following:

- Date and time the event occurred

- Type of event that occurred

- Details of the event, which may include user IDs, process names, device names, file or directory names

- Source of the event

- Outcome of the event

IT systems and devices typically store an event or audit log in the local filesystem. Permissions of the audit log prevent tampering with its contents, stopping someone from trying to conceal their actions. However, log entries are often transmitted over the network to a centralized event log collection system, discussed later in this section.

Types of Log Entries

IT systems, applications, and devices can generate numerous types of log entries, including:

- **Authentication:** This includes successful and unsuccessful login attempts, and may include geographic location data if available.

- **Access control:** This can include successful and unsuccessful attempts by users to access objects.

- **Permission changes:** This may include access rights to system files and objects, as well as changes to the privileges of user accounts.

- **Tampering:** This includes events representing suspected tampering of configuration settings detected by a file integrity monitoring (FIM) or file activity monitoring (FAM) tool.

- **Configuration change:** This includes changes in configuration settings. Log entries will often include the old and new settings.

- **System resources and functions:** This is a broad category of system and device resource utilization, including CPU, memory, filesystems, and networks.

- **Errors:** This is another broad category of events representing malfunctions and other mishaps.

- **Firewall:** This includes instances of dropped packets and changes in firewall rules and other settings.

- **Database:** This is a special type of log, sometimes called a replay log, in which all changes to data fields (and permissions and other things) are recorded. Generally, these logs reside within the database management system itself, and often, these log entries are not sent to a centralized log management system because of their high volume.

Log Management

In even the smallest IT environments, the volume of log data is too great for human review. Many organizations will implement a security information and event management (SIEM) system that automatically collects log entries from systems in the environment. A SIEM will perform event correlation to piece together potentially complex events and generate alerts so that IT and security personnel can take appropriate action.

We explore this topic in considerable detail in Chapter 7.

IT Operations and Exception Handling

Effective IT operations require that IT personnel understand and properly carry out operational tasks according to established processes and procedures. Personnel must also be trained to recognize exceptions and errors and respond accordingly. The tasks that may be included in IT operations are as follows:

- Running jobs according to the job schedule

- Monitoring jobs and allocating resources to jobs based on priority

- Restarting failed jobs and processes

- Facilitating backup jobs by loading or changing backup media, or by ensuring the readiness of target storage systems

- Monitoring systems, applications, and networks for availability and adequate performance
- Performing after-hours maintenance activities such as equipment cleaning and system restarts

IT organizations often employ a *production schedule*, a list of activities or tasks carried out periodically (daily, weekly, monthly, quarterly, and so on). Scheduled activities consist of system-borne activities such as backups and human-performed activities such as access reviews, reconciliations, and month-end close. Scheduled activities in systems may be automatically scheduled or manually invoked.

Larger organizations may have a **network operations center (NOC)** and a **security operations center (SOC)**, staffed by personnel who monitor activities in the organization's security devices, networks, systems, and applications. Some or all these activities are often outsourced to a managed security service provider (MSSP).

Exceptions and errors within IT operations are typically handled according to ITSM incident management and problem management processes, which were discussed in the preceding section.

IT Service Level Management

IT departments are service organizations, and their customers are the departments and business units in the business. It makes sense, then, that IT departments ought to establish service level targets, measure their service levels, and adjust where they fall short.

Service level management is composed of activities that confirm whether IS operations are providing adequate services to customers, achieved through continuous monitoring and periodic review of IT service delivery.

An IT department often plays two different roles in service level management. As a provider of service to its own customers, the IT department will measure and manage the services it provides directly. Also, many IT departments directly or indirectly manage services provided by external service providers. Thus, many IT departments are both service provider and customer, and often, the two are interrelated. This is depicted in Figure 4.1.

Service level agreements (SLAs) are formal, written statements describing response time, availability, and other performance measurements. Table 4.1 depicts common measurements that are the subject of SLAs.

TABLE 4.1 Example service level agreement measurements

Service level	How measured
Service desk live support hours	Days and times (e.g., M–F 0700–1800)
Service desk callback during support hours	Hours or minutes, varies by severity

Service level	How measured
System uptime	Percent, or maximum, downtime in hours or minutes, varies by system criticality
Incident management executive update	Frequency in minutes or hours, varies by severity level
Security patching	Time in hours or days from availability to installation, varies by severity and asset classification
After action review (AAR) scheduling	Time in days from incident closure to AAR occurrence

FIGURE 4.1 The different perspectives on the delivery of IT services

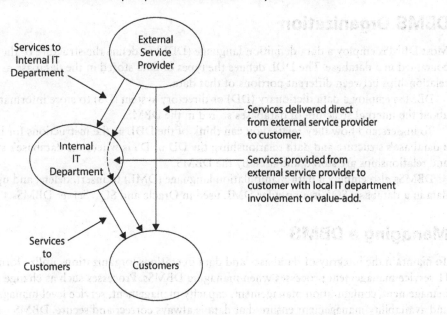

Service level agreements are often negotiated between the IT department and its customers. But in some cases, IT departments unilaterally publish their service levels without soliciting customer input—we consider this a poor practice.

There is the possibility that service levels will vary based on context. Departments or systems deemed critical may have different service levels than departments and systems that are less critical.

Effective service level management requires that SLAs be measured and published. In cases where IT exceeds service level targets, IT may be required to develop and implement a plan to correct these deficiencies. Organizations employing IT charge-back may incur financial penalties when IT fails to meet its SLAs.

Database Management Systems

A *database management system (DBMS)* is a software program or collection of programs that facilitates the storage and retrieval of potentially large amounts of structured information. A DBMS contains methods for inserting, updating, and removing data; computer programs and software applications can use these functions. A DBMS also usually contains authentication and access control, thereby permitting control over which users may access what data.

Database management systems are managed by a database administrator (DBA) in cooperation with personnel who manage the business applications and those who manage the underlying infrastructure (operating systems, storage systems, networks, etc.).

DBMS Organization

Most DBMSs employ a data definition language (DDL) to define the structure of the data contained in a database. The DDL defines the types of data stored in the database as well as relationships between different portions of that data.

DBMSs employ a data dictionary (DD) or directory system (DS) to store information about the internal structure of databases stored in the DBMS.

To understand how they relate, you can think of the DDL as the instructions for building a database's structure and data relationships; the DD or DS is where the database's structure and relationships are stored and used by the DBMS.

DBMSs also employ a data manipulation language (DML) to insert, delete, and update data in a database. SQL is a popular DML used in Oracle and SQL Server DBMSs.

Managing a DBMS

To maintain the integrity of databases and data operations, organizations utilize formal IT service management processes when managing DBMSs. Processes such as change management, configuration management, capacity management, service level management, and availability management ensure that data is always correct and secure. DBMS management should also be integrated with the SDLC process to ensure that applications and databases are always in sync.

DBMS Structure

There are three principal types of DBMSs in use today: relational, object, and hierarchical. Each is described in this section.

Relational Database Management Systems

Relational database management systems (RDBMSs) represent the most popular model used for DBMSs. A relational database permits the design of a structured, logical representation of information.

Many relational databases are accessed and updated through the SQL (Structured Query Language) computer language. Standardized in ISO/IEC and ANSI standards, SQL is used in many popular relational DBMS products, including Oracle Database, Microsoft SQL Server, MySQL, and IBM DB2.

RDBMS Basic Concepts

A relational database consists of one or more *tables*. A table can be considered a simple list of records, like lines in a data file. The records in a table are often called *rows*. The different data items that appear in each row are usually called *fields*.

A table often has a *primary key*, one of the table's fields whose values are unique. For example, a table of health care patients' names can include each patient's identification number, which can be the primary key for the table.

One or more *indexes* can be built for a table. An index facilitates rapid searching for specific records in a table based on the value of one of the fields. For instance, a table that contains a list of assets and their serial numbers can have an index of the table's serial numbers, permitting a rapid search for a record containing a specific serial number; without the index, RDBMS software would have to examine every record in the table sequentially until the desired records are found. Note that the table's primary key field is often used as an index.

One of the most powerful features of a relational database is the use of *foreign keys*. A foreign key is a field in a record in one table that can reference a primary key in another table. For example, a table that lists sales orders includes fields that are foreign keys, each of which references records in other tables. This is shown in Figure 4.2.

Relational databases can enforce *referential integrity*, meaning the database will not permit a program (or user) to delete a row from a table if there are records in other tables whose foreign keys reference the row to be deleted. The database instead will return an error code that will signal to the requesting program that there are rows in other tables that would be "stranded" if the row was deleted. Using the example in Figure 4.2, a relational database will not permit a program to delete salesperson #2 or #4 since there are records in the sales order table that reference those rows.

The power of relational databases comes from their design and from SQL. Queries are used to find one or more records from a table using the SELECT statement. An example statement is:

```
SELECT * FROM Orders WHERE Price > 100 ORDER BY Customer
```

One powerful feature in relational databases is a special query called a *join*, where records from two or more tables are searched in a single query. An example join query is:

```
SELECT Salesperson.Name, count(*) AS Orders FROM Salesperson JOIN
Salesperson_Number
ON Salesperson.Number = Orders.Salesperson GROUP BY Salesperson.Name
```

This query will produce a list of salespersons and the number of orders they have sold.

FIGURE 4.2   Fields in a sales order table point to records in other tables.

Orders Table

date	cust #	salesperson #
09152009	461	④
09152009	277	④
09152009	⑯	8
09152009	129	9
09162009	849	④
09162009	97	②

Customers Table

cust #	last name	first name
15	Jones	Christopher
⑯	Turner	Dell
17	Freeland	Brad
18	Green	Byron

Salesperson Table

salesperson #	last name	first name
②	Crawford	Bill
3	Ramos	Tom
④	Tavernia	Paul

Relational Database Security

Relational databases in commercial applications need to have some security features. Three primary security features are:

- **Access controls:** Most relational databases have access controls at the table and field levels, meaning a database can permit or deny a user the ability to read data from or write data to a specific table or field. To enforce access controls, the database must authenticate users to know the identity of each user making access requests. DBMSs employ a data control language (DCL) to control access to data in a database.

- **Encryption:** Sensitive data such as financial or medical records may need to be encrypted. Some relational databases provide field-level database encryption that permits a user or application to specify certain fields that should be encrypted. Encryption protects the data by making it difficult to read if an intruder can obtain the contents of the database by some illicit means.

- **Audit logging:** DBMSs provide audit logging features that permit an administrator or auditor to view some or all activities that take place in a database. Audit logging can show precisely the activities, including details of database changes and the user who made those changes. The audit logs themselves can be protected to resist tampering, making it difficult for someone to change data and erase their tracks.

Database administrators can also create *views*, which are virtual tables created via stored queries. Views can simplify viewing data by aggregating or filtering data. They can improve security by exposing only certain records or fields to users.

NoSQL

NoSQL DBMSs are nonrelational and designed to support large, sometimes disparate data-sets across multiple systems. Several types of NoSQL databases are in use, including column, document, key-value, and graph.

The motivation for using NoSQL databases is primarily applicability and usefulness; relational databases are not always the best choice for a DBMS in every application. NoSQL databases are often used in "big data" implementations where datasets must be derived from multiple large databases with varying formats, structures, and data types.

Object Database Management Systems

An *object database* (or object database management system [ODBMS]) is a database where information is represented as objects used in object-oriented programming languages. Object-oriented databases are used for data that does not require static or predefined attrib-utes, such as a fixed-length field or defined data structure. The data can even be of varying types. The data that is contained in an object-oriented database is unpredictable in nature.

Unlike the clean separation between programs and data in the relational database model, object databases make database objects appear as programming language objects. Both the data and the programming method are contained in an object. Object databases are just the mechanisms used to store data that are inherently part of the basic object-oriented program-ming model. Thus, when a data object is accessed, it will contain functions (methods), negating the requirement for a query language such as SQL.

Object databases are not widely used commercially. They are limited to a few applications requiring high-performance processing of complex data.

Relational databases are starting to look a little more like object databases through the addition of object-oriented interfaces and functions; object-oriented databases are starting to look a little more like relational databases through query languages such as Object Query Language (OQL).

Hierarchical Database Management Systems

A *hierarchical database* is so named because its data model is a top-down hierarchy, with parent records and one or more child records in its design. The dominant hierarchical data-base management system product in use today is IBM's IMS (Information Management System) that runs on mainframes in nearly all the larger organizations in the world.

A *network database* is like a hierarchical database, extended somewhat to permit lateral data relationships (like the addition of "cousins" to the parent and child records). Figure 4.3 illustrates hierarchical and network databases.

FIGURE 4.3   Hierarchical and network databases

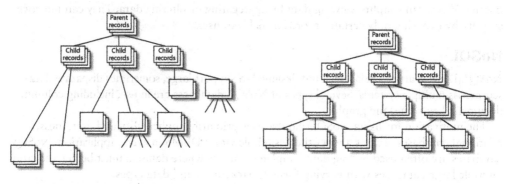

Hierarchical Database Structure   Network Database Structure

Data Management and Governance

Data management is the set of activities related to data acquisition, processing, storage, use, and disposal.

Arguably, the most important activity in data management is planning. Like most human endeavors, data management activities have far better outcomes when planning precedes action. Mainly, this is related to data architecture, which is the set of activities related to the design of databases and the flow of information between databases, systems, and organizations.

ISACA defines *data governance* as "Setting direction on data use through prioritization and decision making, and ensuring alignment with agreed-on direction and objectives." In other words, data governance represents senior management's directives on the collection and use of data, which is carried out by IT and other departments with DBAs and other personnel.

Data Life Cycle

The *data life cycle* is the set of activities that take place throughout the use of data in an organization. The phases of the data life cycle are:

- **Planning:** Before the creation or acquisition of data, the organization needs to understand its structure, sensitivity and value, use, and eventual destruction.

- **Design:** This is the actual process of creating the structure and protection of data. Typical activities at this stage include the creation of a database schema and configuring physical and logical storage systems that will store databases.

- **Build/acquire:** In this phase, data is created or imported from another system.

- **Operations:** In this phase, data is processed, shared, and used.
- **Monitoring:** This includes examination of the data itself as well as activities related to the access and use of data to ensure that the data retains its quality and is protected from misuse and harm.
- **Archival:** This is related to any long-term data storage for legal or historical purposes.
- **Disposal:** This is related to the discarding or erasure process that takes place at the end of the useful life of a set of data.

 DAMA International is a professional organization for people in the data management profession. Information is available at https://dama.org.

Data Quality Management

Data quality management encompasses several activities to ensure data confidentiality, integrity, and completeness. Activities in data quality management include:

- **Application controls:** Measures to ensure that applications enforce the integrity and completeness of data. This topic is covered in Chapter 4.
- **Systems development:** Measures to ensure that applications that are developed or acquired enforce the integrity and completeness of data. This topic is also covered in Chapter 4.
- **Systems integrity:** Measures to ensure that information systems enforce the confidentiality and integrity of data. This topic is covered in Chapter 6.

Other IT Service Management Topics

Several additional activities are a part of a standard ITSM program, according to ITIL and ISO/IEC 20000:2018. They are discussed briefly here.

Financial Management

Financial management for IT services consists of several activities, including:

- Budgeting
- Capital investment
- Expense management
- Project accounting and project return on investment (ROI)

IT financial management is the portion of IT management that considers the financial value of IT services that support organizational objectives.

Quality Assurance

Quality assurance (QA) ensures that changes to software applications, operating system configuration, network device configuration, and other information systems components are performed properly. Primarily, this is carried out through independent work verification.

QA can be carried out within most IT processes, including but not limited to the following:

- Software development
- Change management
- Configuration management
- Service management
- Incident management
- Problem management
- Business process development

As a result of QA activities, improvements in accuracy and efficiency are sought, and processes and systems are changed.

Security Management

Information *security management* is the collection of high-level activities that ensure an organization's information security program adequately identifies and addresses risks and operates properly. An information security management program usually consists of several activities:

- Development of security policies, processes, procedures, and standards
- Risk assessment and risk management
- Vulnerability management
- Incident management
- Security awareness training

In some organizations, security management includes disaster recovery and business continuity planning.

These topics are discussed in detail in Chapter 7.

Media Control

Security standards and privacy laws have highlighted the need for formal processes to ensure the proper management of digital media, including its protection and the destruction of data that is no longer needed. These processes are usually associated with data retention and purging procedures so that needed data is adequately protected with physical and logical security controls, and data no longer needed is effectively discarded and erased. Procedures related to the disposal of media that is no longer needed now include steps to erase data on that media or make the data on that media irretrievable in another way.

Media that should be considered in scope for media management and destruction policies and procedures include:

- Backup media
- Virtual tape libraries
- Optical media
- Hard drives and solid-state drives
- Flash memory in computers, network devices, disk drives, workstations, mobile devices, and portable USB storage devices
- Hard drives in printers, copiers, and scanners
- Hard copy

Policies and procedures for media sanitization need to be included in service provider contracts and recordkeeping to track media destruction over time.

Media control is closely related to data management, discussed in the next subsection.

Auditing IT Service Management and Operations

Auditing IT operations requires considerable technical expertise for the auditor to fully understand the technology they are examining. If an auditor lacks technical knowledge, interviewed subjects may offer explanations that can evade vital facts that the auditor should know. Auditors must be familiar with hardware, operating systems, database management systems, networks, IT operations, and monitoring.

Auditing Computer Operations

The auditor should examine computer operational processes, including:

- **System configuration standards:** The auditor should examine configuration standards that specify the detailed configuration settings for each type of system used in the organization.
- **System build procedures:** The auditor should examine the procedures used to install and configure the operating system.
- **System recovery procedures:** The procedures used to recover systems from various failures should be examined. Usually, this will include reinstalling and configuring the operating system, restoring software and data from backup, and verifying system recovery.

- **System update procedures:** The auditor should examine procedures used for making system changes, including configuration and component upgrades.

- **Patch management:** The auditor should examine the procedures for receiving security advisories, risk analysis, and decisions regarding when new security patches should be implemented. Procedures should also include testing, implementation, and verification.

- **Daily tasks:** Daily and weekly operating procedures for systems should be examined, which may include data backup, log review, log file cycling, review of performance logs, and system capacity checks.

- **Backup and replication:** The auditor should examine procedures and records for file and database backup, backup verification, replication, recovery testing, backup media control and inventory, and off-site media storage.

- **Media control:** Media control procedures should be examined, which include backup media retirement procedures, disk media retirement procedures, media custody, and off-site storage.

- **Monitoring:** Computer monitoring is discussed in detail later in this section.

Auditing File Management

The IS auditor should examine file management policies and procedures, including:

- **Filesystem standards:** The auditor should examine filesystem standards that specify file-system architecture, directory-naming standards, and technical settings that govern disk utilization and performance.

- **Access controls:** The auditor should examine filesystem access control policies and procedures, the configuration settings that control which users and processes can access directories and files, and log files that record access control events such as permission changes and attempted file accesses, including any procedures followed when such events occur.

- **Capacity management:** The settings and controls used to manage the capacity of filesystems should be examined, including logs that show filesystem utilization, procedures for adding capacity, and records of capacity-related events.

- **Version control:** In filesystems and data repositories that contain documents under version control, the auditor should examine version control configuration settings, file update procedures, and file recovery procedures and records.

Auditing Data Entry

The IS auditor should examine data entry standards and operations, including:

- **Data entry procedures:** This may include document control, input procedures, and error recovery procedures.

- **Input verification:** This may include automatic and manual controls used to ensure that data has been entered properly into forms.

- **Batch verification:** This may include automatic and manual controls used to calculate and verify batches of records that are input.
- **Correction procedures:** This may include controls and procedures used to correct individual forms and batches when errors occur.

Auditing Lights-Out Operations

A *lights-out operation* is any production IT environment that runs without on-site operator intervention, such as computers in a data center. The term "lights out" means that the computers can be in a room with the lights out since no personnel need to attend to them.

Audit activities of a lights-out operation will fall primarily into the other categories of audits discussed in this chapter, plus a few specific activities, including:

- Remote administration procedures
- Remote monitoring procedures

Auditing Problem Management Operations

The auditor should examine the organization's problem management operations, including:

- **Problem management policies and processes:** The auditor should examine policy and procedure documents that describe how problem management is supposed to be performed.
- **Problem management records:** A sampling of problems and incidents should be examined to determine whether problems are properly managed.
- **Problem management timelines:** The time spent on each problem should be examined to see whether the resolution falls within the SLA.
- **Problem management reports:** The auditor should examine management reports to ensure management is aware of all problems.
- **Problem resolution:** The auditor should examine a sample of problems to see which ones require changes in other processes. The other process documents should be examined to determine if they were changed. The auditor should also examine records to see if another party has verified the fixes.
- **Problem recurrence:** The auditor should examine problem records to ensure that the same problems are not repeated.

Auditing Monitoring Operations

The IS auditor needs to audit system monitoring operations to ensure that they are effective, including:

- **Monitoring plan:** The auditor should review any monitoring plan documents that describe the organization's monitoring program, tools, and processes.

- **Response plans:** The auditor should review response plans and records of responses.

- **Problem logs:** Monitoring problem logs should be reviewed to see what problems are being recorded. The auditor should determine whether all devices and systems are represented in problem logs.

- **Preventive maintenance:** The auditor should examine monitoring results, monitoring plans, and preventive maintenance records, and determine whether the level of preventive maintenance is adequate and effective.

- **Reporting:** Auditors should examine any reported and published monitoring reports to confirm their suitability, accuracy, and completeness.

- **Management review and action:** Any monitoring reports, meeting minutes, and decision logs should be examined to see whether management is reviewing monitoring reports and whether management actions are being carried out.

Auditing Procurement

The auditor should examine hardware, software, and services procurement processes, procedures, and records to determine whether the following activities are being performed:

- **Requirements definition:** All stakeholders (both technical and business, as appropriate) must develop functional, technical, and security requirements. Each requirement must be approved and used to scrutinize candidate products and services. Each candidate supplier's responses must be scored based on their ability to meet requirements. This entire process needs to be transparent and documented. Auditors must examine procurement policies, procedures, and records from selected procurement projects.

- **Feasibility studies:** Many service requests will require an objective feasibility study designed to identify the economic and business benefits that may be derived from the requested service. Auditors must examine selected feasibility study documents and policy and procedure documents to perform feasibility projects.

Auditing Database Management Systems

DBMSs are as complex as operating systems. This complexity requires considerable auditor scrutiny in several areas, including:

- **Security configuration:** Security-related configuration settings of DBMSs should effectively reduce the likelihood and impact of intrusions. Configuration settings should be formally documented.

- **Configuration management:** The configuration of DBMSs should be centrally controlled and tracked in larger organizations to ensure consistency among systems. Individual DBMSs and configuration management records should be compared.

- **Change management:** Databases are used to store not only information, but also software in many cases. The auditor should examine DBMS change management processes and records to determine whether changes are being performed consistently and systematically. All changes should be requested, reviewed, approved by management, tested, implemented, and recorded. Software changes should be examined in coordination with an audit of the organization's software development life cycle.

- **Capacity management:** The availability and integrity of supported business processes require sufficient capacity in all underlying databases. The auditor should examine procedures and records related to capacity management to see whether management ensures sufficient capacity for business data.

- **Access management:** Access controls determine which users and systems can access and update data. The auditor should examine access control configurations, access requests, access logs, access provisioning and deprovisioning, and access reviews.

- **Resilience:** Databases should be periodically backed up with suitable tools and techniques. The ability to recover data from backup should be tested occasionally. Availability metrics should be developed and published.

- **Staff competence:** The qualifications of DBAs and other personnel should be sufficient to give the organization (and auditors) confidence that the DBAs will keep databases in good working order.

Summary

All activities in the IT department should be managed, controlled, and monitored. Activities performed by operations personnel should be a part of a procedure or process approved by management. Processes, procedures, and projects should have sufficient recordkeeping to facilitate measurements.

IT operations should be structured in a service management model aligned with the IT Infrastructure Library (ITIL) or the COBIT framework of processes. These frameworks ensure that comprehensive coverage of activities will likely occur in most IT organizations.

IT systems performance management consists of availability management, capacity management, and system monitoring, to ensure that IT systems will have the maximum possible availability and have sufficient capacity to perform all expected work.

Problem and incident management processes strive to reduce system malfunctions and outages to a minimum. Incident management focuses on one event at a time, while problem management seeks the root cause of chronic incidents.

Change, configuration, release, and patch management processes ensure that changes to IT systems are controlled and approved, resulting in improved resilience.

Service level management ensures that IT systems operate correctly and are available according to set parameters related to uptime and response time to incidents.

Data management is the purposeful management of the input, processing, output, storage, retrieval, and retention of data in an organization.

Auditing IT systems and operations is fairly straightforward, and requires considerable knowledge of the workings of typical IT systems, networks, and associated technologies.

Exam Essentials

Be able to explain why IT operations processes should be formalized.   IT operations processes and procedures should be written down and periodically reviewed. They should also be measured and reported so management can better understand ongoing IT operations.

Know the methods used to manage and measure system performance.   Key processes, including availability and capacity management, ensure that IT systems' availability is measured and as high as needed. Capacity management ensures that IT systems have sufficient resources for IT systems and applications have sufficient capacity to continue operating without exhausting critical resources such as CPU, storage, and network throughput.

Know how system monitoring helps IT personnel be aware of anomalies and incidents.   System monitoring helps IT personnel be informed of anomalies, malfunctions, system health, and capacity issues. An IT department should be aware of these issues through tooling and monitoring, instead of relying on end users to inform them.

Understand the common types of security monitoring.   Security monitoring of devices, including firewalls, intrusion prevention systems, data loss prevention systems, file integrity monitoring systems, and many others provide security personnel with a continuous awareness of the environment's security posture.

Be able to explain how incident and problem management are related.   Incident management is related to individual events representing malfunctions, outages, and other anomalies. When any incident becomes chronic, problem management seeks to identify the root cause and stop it from occurring.

Know the critical nature of change and configuration management.   Change management is the life cycle process through which all changes to IT systems are processed in a formal request, review, approve, implement, verify, and closure process. Configuration management is a process that catalogs the configuration settings of all IT systems and devices.

Be able to explain vulnerability and patch management.   Vulnerability management is a highly critical life cycle process that ensures that exploitable vulnerabilities in systems and devices are remediated promptly and effectively. Effective vulnerability management greatly reduces the likelihood and impact of break-ins that exploit known vulnerabilities.

Know the value of log management in IT and security operations.   Log management is another cornerstone activity for organizations to quickly be aware of attacks, attempted intrusions, and employee misbehavior. It is important to understand all the types of available logs, and the vital elements that should be a part of every log entry.

Understand the value of service level management.　Service level management helps IT management understand the degree to which the IT department performs according to its service level agreements (SLAs).

Understand the structure and management of database management systems (DBMSs).　Database management systems are the backend of virtually every business application, even those running on mobile devices. DBMSs are nearly as complex as operating systems, with broad and complex configurability, user management, log management, and access control.

Know about data governance and management.　Data governance is an oversight function that ensures data is used in agreed-on ways. Data governance is vital for the protection of intellectual property as well as privacy. Data management consists of various processes used to carry out data governance directives. This differs from data quality, which covers the completeness and accuracy of the data and processes around ensuring that the data is reliable so that management can rely upon it.

Review Questions

1. A web application is displaying information incorrectly, and many users have contacted the IT service desk. This matter should be considered a(n):

   A. Incident

   B. Problem

   C. Bug

   D. Outage

2. An IT organization is experiencing many cases of unexpected downtime caused by unauthorized changes to application code and operating system configuration. Which process should the IT organization implement to reduce downtime?

   A. Configuration management

   B. Incident management

   C. Change management

   D. Problem management

3. An IT organization manages hundreds of servers, databases, and applications, and is having difficulty tracking changes to the configuration of these systems. What process should be implemented to remedy this?

   A. Configuration management

   B. Change management

   C. Problem management

   D. Incident management

4. In an audit of configuration management, an auditor should request all the following artifacts *except*:

   A. System-hardening standards

   B. CMDB procedures

   C. Change management procedures

   D. Check-out/check-in logs

5. A database administrator has been asked to configure a database management system so that it records all changes made by users. What should the database administrator implement?

   A. Audit logging

   B. Triggers

   C. Stored procedures

   D. Journaling

6. The purpose of vulnerability scanning is all of the following, *except*:

   A. A quality assurance step to ensure that security configurations and patches are in place

   B. An operational step to direct IT personnel to correct configuration errors and install patches

   C. The first activity in a penetration test to identify easily exploited vulnerabilities

   D. To identify security-related defects in application source code

7. The best definition of release management is:

   A. A quality process to ensure that end users have signed off on application changes

   B. A gate process to ensure that all problems have been fixed in a new application

   C. A management process to control the promotion of updated applications to production

   D. A compliance process stipulated by HIPAA

8. All of the following are a part of patch management, *except*:

   A. Subscribe to vendor security advisories.

   B. Subscribe to non-vendor security advisories.

   C. Conduct vulnerability scans.

   D. Perform risk analysis to determine risk to the organization.

9. A typical security log entry should contain all of the following, *except*:

   A. Checksum

   B. Time and date of occurrence

   C. Location

   D. User ID

10. For too long, employees in an organization have complained that the IT service desk takes too long to assist. What is the first thing management should put in place to remedy this?

   A. End user bill of rights

   B. Acceptable use policy (AUP)

   C. Service level agreement (SLA)

   D. Automated callback

11. An IT department is putting an SLA in place to determine the maximum time taken to install security patches. Which of the following should not be included in this effort?

   A. Develop separate SLAs based on exploitability.

   B. Develop separate SLAs based on system location.

   C. Develop separate SLAs based on system criticality.

   D. Develop separate SLAs based on compliance context.

12. Why should audit logs be read-only for all personnel, including system administrators?

  A. Necessary for referential integrity

  B. Supports nonrepudiation

  C. Improves system performance

  D. Prevents the concealment of disallowed actions

13. A system administrator has received a security advisory from a vendor that describes a critical vulnerability that can be escalated by a remote actor who does not require login credentials. How should the system administrator categorize this advisory for Internet-connected systems?

  A. High

  B. Critical

  C. Moderate

  D. Informational

14. What is the distinction between vulnerability management and patch management?

  A. Patch management is a part of vulnerability management.

  B. Vulnerability management is a part of patch management.

  C. Vulnerability management and patch management are separate, unrelated processes.

  D. Organizations are free to implement vulnerability management or patch management.

15. In configuration management, what is meant by a configuration item?

  A. An individual system administrator

  B. An individual asset

  C. An individual configuration setting in a system or device

  D. A request to change a configuration setting in a system or device

16. Which of the following is not a required item in a typical IT department change request?

  A. Verification procedure

  B. Backout procedure

  C. Root cause analysis

  D. Description of the change

17. Which of the following event types is not typically sent to a SIEM?

  A. Hard drive fault

  B. Successful login attempt

  C. Unsuccessful login attempt

  D. Creation of a new privileged user

18. A security analyst works in a small enterprise with a dozen on-premises servers. The analyst manually reviews security logs on the servers every few days. What, if any, improvement is needed for this activity?

    A. Send all security log entries to a SIEM.

    B. Send all security log entries to a Syslog server.

    C. Use a search tool to look for keywords in the security logs.

    D. Implement a SIEM on each of the servers.

19. An IS auditor is auditing an IT department's operational log monitoring system. Which of the following is likely not a part of the auditor's examination?

    A. Résumés of personnel who examine logs

    B. Request for monitoring procedures

    C. Request for a list of monitored systems

    D. Request for operational event logs

20. How should an IT department manage emergency changes in its change management process?

    A. Wait until business hours to submit the change request and make the change.

    B. Obtain approval from designated management, then perform the change.

    C. Make the required change and submit a change request after the fact.

    D. Make the required change and tell the change manager about it.

Chapter 5

IT Infrastructure

THE CERTIFIED INFORMATION SYSTEMS AUDITOR (CISA) OBJECTIVES REPRESENT 26% OF THE MATERIAL COVERED ON THE EXAM AND INCLUDE:

✓ **Domain 4: Information Systems Operations & Business Resilience**

    A. Information Systems Operations

        1. Common Technology Components

        2. IT Asset Management

        3. Job Scheduling and Production Process Automation

        4. System Interfaces

        5. End-User Computing

    Supporting Tasks

        21. Conduct periodic review of information systems and enterprise architecture.

        23. Evaluate IT maintenance practices to determine whether they are controlled effectively and continue to support the organization's objectives.

        28. Evaluate end-user computing to determine whether the processes are effectively controlled.

        32. Evaluate data classification practices for alignment with the organization's policies and applicable external requirements.

        33. Evaluate policies and practices related to asset lifecycle management.

Together, the topics in Chapter 4, "IT Service Management," Chapter 6, "Business Continuity and Disaster Recovery," and this chapter represent 26 percent of the CISA examination.

In addition to being familiar with IT business processes, IS auditors need to have a keen understanding of the workings of computer hardware, operating systems, and network communications technology. This knowledge will help the auditor better understand many aspects of service management and operations.

Information Systems Hardware

Hardware is the elemental basis of information systems. It consists of circuit boards containing microprocessors and memory; other components connected through circuitry, such as hard disk drives or solid-state drives; and peripherals such as keyboards, printers, monitors, and network connections.

IS auditors need to understand at least the basic concepts of computer hardware architecture, maintenance, and monitoring so that they can properly assess an organization's use and care of information systems hardware. A lack of knowledge in this area could result in the auditor overlooking or failing to understand important aspects of an organization's operations.

The macro trend toward the use of cloud computing infrastructure versus on-premises computer hardware does not preclude the need to be familiar with the concepts of computing hardware. Although contact with computer hardware is absent when an organization is managing virtual workloads, organizations utilizing cloud-based infrastructure still need to be familiar with hardware concepts; this is applied through the configuration of virtual servers and the resources they use. Further, computer hardware is still used by end users in the form of desktop and laptop computers as well as tablet computers and smartphones.

Computer Usage

Computers are manufactured for various purposes and contexts and are used for many different purposes. They can be classified by their capacity, throughput, size, use, or the operating system or software they use.

Types of Computers

From a business perspective, computers are classified according to their size and portability. In this regard, the types of computers are:

- **Supercomputer:** These are the largest computers in terms of the number and/or power of their central processing units (CPUs). Supercomputers are generally employed for scientific applications such as weather and climate forecasting, seismology, and other computer-intensive applications.

- **Mainframe:** These business workhorse computers are designed to run large, complex applications that connect to enormous databases or support vast numbers of users. When computing began, mainframes were the only kind of computer; most of the other types were derived from the mainframe. Today, mainframes are still commonly used for larger financial transaction systems and other large-scale applications such as airline reservation systems.

- **Midrange:** These computers are not as large and powerful as mainframe computers, but they are larger or more powerful than small servers. There are no hard distinctions between these sizes of computers, only vague, rough guidelines.

- **Server:** If mainframe computers are the largest business servers, the ordinary server is the smallest. In terms of its hardware complement and physical appearance, a server can be indistinguishable from a user's desktop computer.

- **Blade server:** In this style of hardware design, servers are modules that plug into a cabinet. Each module contains all the internal components of a stand-alone computer. The cabinet itself will contain power supplies and network connectors.

- **Virtual server:** This is a cloud-based server that exists in a hypervisor environment, whether in an on-premises private cloud or a public cloud.

- **Appliance:** This type of computer typically comes with one or more tools or applications preinstalled. The term *appliance* is sometimes used to connote the fact that little or no maintenance is required on the system.

- **Desktop:** This is a computer used by an individual worker. Its size makes it fairly easy to move from place to place, but it is not considered portable. The desktop computers of today are more powerful in many ways than the mainframe computers of a few decades ago. Desktop computers used to be called microcomputers, but the term is seldom used now.

- **Laptop/notebook:** This computer is portable in every sense of the word. It is self-contained, equipped with a battery, and folds for storage and transport. Functionally, desktop and laptop computers are nearly identical; they may run the same operating system and programs.

- **Mobile:** These computers come in the form of smartphones and tablet devices.

- **Embedded:** These computers are built into products such as televisions, automobiles, medical devices, surveillance cameras, personal digital assistants, wearable devices, and many other industrial and consumer devices.

Uses for Computers

Aside from the sizes and types of computers discussed in the previous section, computers may also be used for several reasons, including the following:

- **Application server:** This computer—usually a mainframe, midrange, or server—runs application-server software. An application server contains one or more application programs that run on behalf of users. Data used by an application server may be stored on a database server that contains a database management system.

- **Web server:** This is a server that runs a web server program to make web pages available to users. A web server will usually contain both the web server software and the content ("pages") that are requested by and sent to users' web browser programs. A web server can also be linked to an application server or database server to permit the display of business information, such as order forms and reports.

- **Database server:** Also a mainframe, midrange, or small server, a database server runs specialized database management software that controls the storage and processing of large amounts of data that reside in one or more databases.

- **Gateway:** A server that performs some manner of data transformation—for instance, converting messages from one format to another—between two applications.

- **File server:** This computer is used to provide a central location for the storage of commonly used files. File servers may be used by application servers or by a user community.

- **Print server:** In an environment that uses shared printers, a print server typically receives print requests from users or applications and stores them temporarily until they are ready to be printed.

- **Production server/test server:** The terms *production server* and *test server* denote whether a server supports actual business use (a production server) or is a separate server that can be used to test new programs or configurations (a test server). Most organizations will have at least one test server for every type of production server so that any new programs, configurations, patches, or settings can be tested on a test server, with little or no risk of disrupting actual business operations.

- **Thick client:** A thick client is a user's computer (of the desktop or laptop variety) that contains a fully functional operating system and one or more application programs. Purists will argue that a thick client is only a thick client if the system contains one or more software application client programs. This is a reasonable distinction between a thick client and a workstation, described later.

- **Thin client:** A thin client is a user's workstation that contains a minimal operating system and little or no data storage. Thin-client computers are often used in businesses where users run only application programs that can be executed on central servers and data is displayed on the thin client's screen. A thin client may be a desktop or laptop computer with thin-client software installed, or it may be a specialized computer with no local storage other than flash memory.

- **Workstation:** This is a user's laptop or desktop computer. For example, a PC running the Windows operating system and using Microsoft Office word processor and spreadsheet programs, a Firefox browser, and Skype messenger would be considered a workstation.

- **Virtual desktop:** This workstation operating system physically resides on a central server and is displayed by and used on a user's desktop computer.

- **Mobile device:** A user's smartphone or tablet is considered a mobile device. Indeed, the lines between laptops and tablets are blurring as larger tablets, particularly with companion keyboards, function like laptops. Laptop operating systems are also appearing on larger tablet devices.

 NOTE Computers are generally designed for general use so that they may perform any of the functions listed here.

Computer Hardware Architecture

Computers made since the 1960s share common characteristics in their hardware architecture: They have one or more central processing units, a bus (or more than one), main memory, and secondary storage. They also have some means for communicating with other computers or with humans, usually through communications adapters.

This section describes computer hardware in detail.

Mobile Devices, the New and Disruptive Endpoint

Much is said about endpoints being the weak link in IT infrastructure. But historically speaking, these proclamations are more about laptop computers, which can, for the most part, be well managed by enterprises.

Mobile devices are a different matter entirely. They are turning all the rules about endpoint computing on their head. Principally:

- End users choose which models to purchase and own them outright.

- End users can install any application they choose.

- Mobile devices can be easily connected to corporate email without any help (or consent) from the IT department.

- Few, if any, antimalware or other anti-tampering tools are available.

- Mobile devices are easily lost and more easily broken into than laptop computers.

- Mobile device manufacturers have published application interfaces, thereby enabling the creation of malware that can steal data and alter the device's operation.

IS auditors need to understand how organizations are addressing the mobile device dilemma.

Central Processing Unit

The *central processing unit (CPU)* is the main hardware component of a computer system. The CPU is the component that executes instructions in computer programs.

Each CPU has an arithmetic logic unit (ALU), a control unit, and a small amount of memory. The memory in a CPU is usually in the form of registers, which are memory locations where arithmetic values are stored.

The CPU in modern computers is wholly contained in a single large-scale integration integrated circuit (LSI IC), more commonly known as a microprocessor. A CPU is attached to a computer circuit board (often called a motherboard on a personal computer) by soldering or a plug-in socket. A CPU on a motherboard is shown in Figure 5.1.

FIGURE 5.1   A CPU that is plugged into a computer circuit board

Image courtesy of Fir0002/Flagstaffotos

CPU Architectures

A number of architectures dominate the design of CPUs. Two primary architectures that are widely used commercially are:

- **CISC (complex instruction set computer):** This CPU design has a comprehensive instruction set, and many instructions can be performed in a single cycle. This design philosophy claims superior performance over RISC. Well-known CISC CPUs include Intel x86, VAX, PDP-11, Motorola 68000, and System/360.

- **RISC (reduced instruction set computer):** This CPU design uses a smaller instruction set (meaning fewer instructions in its "vocabulary"), with the idea that a small instruction set will lead to a simpler microprocessor design and better computer performance.

Well-known RISC CPUs include Alpha, MIPS, PowerPC, and SPARC. None of these is produced today, but they are still found in some environments.

Another aspect of CPUs that is often discussed is their power requirements. Typically, the CPUs used for laptop computers and mobile devices are known as low-power CPUs, while other CPUs are used in desktop, server, and mainframe systems, where performance and speed are more important considerations than power consumption.

Computer CPU Architectures

Early computers had a single CPU. However, it became clear that many computing tasks could be performed more efficiently if computers had more than one CPU to perform them. Some of the ways that computers have implemented CPUs are:

- **Single CPU:** In this design, the computer has a single CPU. This simplest design is still prevalent, particularly among small servers and personal computers.

- **Multiple CPUs:** A computer design can accommodate multiple CPUs, from as few as 2 to as many as 128 or more. There are two designs for multi-CPU computers: symmetric and asymmetric. In the symmetric design, all CPUs are equal in terms of how the overall computer's architecture uses them. In the asymmetric design, one CPU controls all others. Virtually all multi-CPU computers made today are symmetric.

- **Multicore CPUs:** A change in the design of CPUs themselves has led to multicore CPUs, in which two or more central processors occupy a single CPU chip. The benefit of multicore design is the ability for software code to be executed in parallel, leading to improved performance. Many newer servers and personal computers are equipped with multicore CPUs, and some are equipped with multiple multicore CPUs.

Bus

A *bus* is an internal component in a computer that provides the means for the computer's other components to communicate with one another. A computer's bus connects the CPU with its main and secondary storage as well as to external devices.

Most computers also utilize electrical connectors that permit the addition of small circuit boards that may contain additional memory, a communications device or adapter (e.g., a network adapter or a modem), a storage controller (e.g., a SCSI [Small Computer Systems Interface] or ATA [AT Attachment] disk controller), or an additional CPU.

Several industry standards for computer buses have been developed. Notable standards include:

- **Universal Serial Bus (USB):** This standard connects external peripherals such as storage devices, printers, and mobile devices. It operates at data rates up to 40.0 Gbit/sec and is discussed in more detail later in this chapter.

- **Serial ATA (SATA):** This standard is used mainly to connect mass storage devices such as hard disk drives, optical drives, and solid-state drives.

- **PCI Express (PCIe):** This bus standard replaced older standards such as PCI and PCI-X and employs data rates from 250 Mbyte/sec to 128 Gbyte/sec.

- **Thunderbolt:** This hardware interface standard is a combination of PCI Express and DisplayPort (DP) in a single serial signal.

- **PC Card:** Formerly known as PCMCIA, the PC Card bus is prevalent in laptop computers and is commonly used to add specialized communication devices.

- **ExpressCard:** Also developed by the PCMCIA, this bus standard replaces the PC Card standard.

It is not uncommon for a computer to have more than one bus. For instance, many PCs have an additional front-side bus (FSB), which connects the CPU to a memory controller hub, as well as a high-speed graphics bus, a memory bus, and the low pin count (LPC) bus that is used for low-speed peripherals such as parallel and serial ports, keyboard, and mouse.

Main Storage

A computer's *main storage* is used for short-term information storage. Main storage is usually implemented with electronic components such as random-access memory (RAM), which is relatively expensive but also relatively fast in terms of accessibility and transfer rate.

A computer uses its main storage for several purposes:

- **Operating system:** The computer's running operating system uses main storage to store information about running programs, open files, logged-in users, in-use devices, active processes, and so on.

- **Buffers:** Operating systems and programs set aside a portion of memory as a "scratch pad" to temporarily store information retrieved from hard disks or information being sent to a printer or other device. Buffers are also used by network adapters to store incoming and outgoing information temporarily.

- **Storage of program code:** Any program that the computer is currently executing will be stored in main storage so that the CPU can quickly access and read any portion of the program as needed. Note that the program in main storage is only a working copy of the program, used by the computer to reference instructions quickly in the program.

- **Storage of program variables:** When a program is being run, it will store intermediate results of calculations and other temporary data. This information is stored in main storage, where the program can quickly reference portions of it as needed.

Main storage is typically volatile, which means that the information stored in it should be considered temporary. If electric power were suddenly removed from the computer, the contents of main storage would vanish and not be easily recovered, if at all.

Different technologies are used in computers for main storage:

- **DRAM (dynamic RAM):** In the most common form of semiconductor memory, data is stored in capacitors that require periodic refreshing to keep them charged—hence the term *dynamic*.

- **SRAM (static RAM):** This form of semiconductor memory does not require periodic refresh cycles like DRAM.

A typical semiconductor memory module is shown in Figure 5.2.

FIGURE 5.2   Typical RAM module for a laptop, workstation, or server

Source: Sassospicco / Wikimedia Commons / CC BY-SA 2.5

Secondary Storage

Secondary storage is the permanent storage used by a computer system. Unlike primary storage (which is usually implemented in volatile RAM modules), secondary storage is persistent and can last many years.

This type of storage is usually implemented using hard disk drives or solid-state drives with capacities ranging from gigabytes to terabytes.

Secondary storage represents an economic and performance trade-off from primary storage. It is usually far slower than primary storage, but the unit cost for storage is far less costly. As of this writing, the price paid for about 16 GB of RAM could also purchase a 2 TB hard disk drive, which makes RAM (primary) storage more than 1,000 times more expensive than hard disk (secondary) storage. A hard disk drive from a desktop computer is shown in Figure 5.3.

FIGURE 5.3   Typical computer hard disk drive

Source: Robert Jacek Tomczak / Wikimedia Commons / Public domain

A computer uses secondary storage for several purposes:

- **Program storage:** The programs that the computer executes are contained in secondary storage. When a computer begins to execute a program, it makes a working copy of the program in primary storage.

- **Data storage:** Information read into, created by, or used by computer programs is often stored in secondary storage. Secondary storage is usually used when information is needed for use later.

- **Computer operating system:** The set of programs and device drivers that are used to control and manage the computer's use is stored in secondary storage.

- **Temporary files:** Many computer programs need to store information for temporary use that may exceed the capacity of main memory. Secondary storage is often used for this purpose. For example, a user wants to print a data file onto a nearby laser printer; software on the computer will transform the stored data file into a format that is used by the laser printer to make a readable copy of the file; this "print file" is stored in secondary storage temporarily until the printer has completed printing the file for the user, and then the file is deleted.

- **Virtual memory:** This is a technique for creating a main memory space that is physically larger than the actual available main memory. Virtual memory (which should not be confused with virtualization) is discussed in detail later in this chapter in the section "Computer Operating Systems."

While secondary storage is usually implemented with hard disk drives, many newer systems use semiconductor flash memory in solid-state drives (SSDs). Flash is a nonvolatile semiconductor memory that can be rewritten and requires no electric power to preserve stored data.

Although secondary storage technology is persistent and highly reliable, hard disk drives and even SSDs are known to fail from time to time. For this reason, important data in secondary storage is often copied to other storage devices, either on the same computer or on a different computer, or it is copied onto computer backup tapes that are designed to store large amounts of data for long periods at low cost. This practice of data backup is discussed at length in the section "Information Systems Operations" in Chapter 4.

Firmware

Firmware is special-purpose storage that is used to store the instructions needed to start a computer system. Typically, firmware consists of low-level computer instructions that are used to control the various hardware components in a computer system and to load and execute components of the operating system from secondary storage. This process of system initialization is known as an initial program load (IPL), or bootstrap (or just "boot").

Read-only memory (ROM) technology is often used to store a computer's firmware. Several available ROM technologies are in use:

- **ROM:** The earliest forms of ROM are considered permanent and can never be modified. The permanency of ROM makes it secure, but it can be difficult to carry out field upgrades. For this reason, ROM is not often used.

- **PROM (programmable read-only memory):** This is also a permanent and unchangeable form of storage. A PROM chip can be programmed only once, and it must be replaced if the firmware needs to be updated.

- **EPROM (erasable programmable read-only memory):** This type of memory can be written to with a special programming device and then erased and rewritten later. EPROM chips are erased by shining ultraviolet (UV) light through a quartz window on the chip; the quartz window is usually covered with a foil label, although sometimes an EPROM chip does not have a window at all, which effectively makes it a PROM device.

- **EEPROM (electrically erasable programmable read-only memory):** This is similar to EPROM, except that no UV light source is required to erase and reprogram the EEPROM chip; instead, signals from the computer in which the EEPROM chip is stored can be used to reprogram or update the EEPROM. Thus, EEPROM was one of the first types of firmware that could be updated by the computer on which it was installed.

- **Flash:** This memory is erasable, reprogrammable, and functionally like EEPROM, in that the contents of flash memory can be altered by the computer that it is installed in. Flash memory is the technology used in popular portable storage devices such as USB memory devices, Secure Digital (SD) cards, Compact Flash, and Memory Stick.

A well-known use for firmware is the ROM-based BIOS (basic input/output system) on Intel-based personal computers.

I/O and Networking

Regardless of their specific purpose, computers nearly always must have some means for accepting input data from some external source as well as for sending output data to some external destination. Whether this input and output are continuous or infrequent, computers usually have one or more methods for transferring data. These methods include:

- **Input/output (I/O) devices:** Most computers have external connectors to permit the attachment of devices such as keyboards, mice, monitors, scanners, printers, and cameras. The electrical signal and connector-type standards include PS/2 (for keyboards and mice), USB, parallel, serial, and Thunderbolt. Some types of computers lack these external connectors; instead, special adapter cards can be plugged into a computer's bus connector. Early computers required reprogramming and/or reconfiguration when external devices were connected, but newer computers are designed to recognize when an external device is connected or disconnected and will adjust automatically.

- **Networking:** A computer can be connected to a local or wide area data network. Then, one of a multitude of means for inbound and outbound data transfer can be configured to use the networking capability. Some computers will have built-in connectors or adapters, but others will require the addition of internal or external adapters that plug into bus connectors such as PC Card, ExpressCard, or PCI.

Multicomputer Architectures

Organizations that use several computers have a lot of available choices. Not so long ago, organizations that required several servers would purchase individual server computers. Now there are choices that can help to improve performance and reduce capital, including:

- **Blade computers:** This architecture consists of a main chassis component that is equipped with a central power supply, cooling, network, and console connectors, with several slots fitted with individual CPU modules. The advantage of blade architecture is the lower-than-usual unit cost for each server module since it consists of only a circuit board. The costs of power supply, cooling, and so on, are amortized among all the blades. A typical blade system is shown in Figure 5.4.

FIGURE 5.4 Blade computer architecture

Source: Robert Kloosterhuis / Wikimedia Commons / CC BY-SA 2.0

- **Grid computing:** The term *grid computing* describes a large number of loosely coupled computers used to solve a common task. Computers in a grid may be near each other or scattered over a wide geographic area. Grid computing is a viable alternative to supercomputers for solving computationally intensive problems.

- **Server clusters:** A *cluster* is a tightly coupled collection of computers that is used to solve a common task. In a cluster, one or more servers actively perform tasks, while zero or more computers may be in a "standby" state, ready to assume active duty should the need arise. Clusters usually give the appearance of a single computer to the perspective of outside systems. Clusters usually operate in one of two modes: active-active and active-passive. In active-active mode, all servers perform tasks; in active-passive mode, some servers are in a standby state, waiting to become active in an event called a failover, which usually occurs when one of the active servers has become incapacitated.

These options give organizations the freedom to develop a computer architecture that will meet their needs in terms of performance, availability, flexibility, and cost.

Virtualization Architectures

Virtualization refers to the set of technologies that permits two or more running operating systems (of the same type or different types) to reside on a single physical computer. Virtualization technology enables organizations to use computing resources more efficiently.

Before I explain the benefits of virtualization, I should first state one of the principles of computer infrastructure management. It is a sound practice to use a server for one single purpose. Using a single server for multiple purposes can introduce several problems, including:

- Tools or applications that reside on a single computer may interfere with one another.

- Tools or applications that reside on a single computer may interact with one another or compete for common resources.

- Although rarely, a tool or application on a server could cause the entire server to stop running; on a server with multiple tools or applications, this could cause the other tools and applications to stop functioning.

Prior to virtualization, the most stable configuration for running many applications and tools was to run each on a separate server. This would, however, result in a highly inefficient use of computers and of capital, as most computers with a single operating system spend much of their time in an idle state.

Virtualization permits IT departments to run many applications or tools on a single physical server, each within its own respective operating system, thereby making more efficient use of computers (not to mention electric power and data center space). Virtualization software emulates computer hardware so that an operating system running in a virtualized environment does not know that it is actually running on a virtual machine. Virtualization software, known as a *hypervisor*, includes resource allocation configuration settings so that each guest (a running operating system) will have a specific amount of memory, hard disk space, and other peripherals available for its use. Virtualization also facilitates the sharing of peripheral devices such as network connectors so that many guests can use an individual network connector, although each will have its own unique IP address.

Virtualization is the basis of cloud-based infrastructure-as-a-service (IaaS) services such as Amazon AWS, Google Cloud, and Microsoft Azure.

Virtualization software provides security by isolating each running operating system and preventing it from accessing or interfering with others. This is like the concept of process isolation within a running operating system, where a process is not permitted to access resources used by other processes.

A server running virtual machines is depicted in Figure 5.5.

FIGURE 5.5 Virtualization

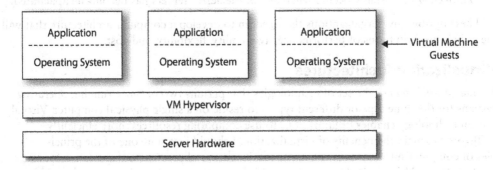

Many security issues need to be considered in a virtualization environment:

- **Access control:** Access to virtualization management and monitoring functions should be restricted to those personnel who require it.

- **Resource allocation:** A virtualization environment needs to be carefully configured so that each virtual machine is given the resources it requires to function correctly and perform adequately.

- **Logging and monitoring:** Virtual environments need to be carefully monitored so that any sign of security compromise will be quickly recognized and acted on.

- **Hardening:** Virtual environments need to be configured so that only necessary services and features are enabled, and all unnecessary services and features are either disabled or removed.

- **Vulnerability management:** Virtualization environments need to be monitored as closely as operating systems and other software so that the IT organization is aware of newly discovered security vulnerabilities and available patches.

Another form of virtualization, containerization, is the practice of running multiple application instances within a single operating system. Each application instance runs independently in a container, and each is protected from the others, so software running in one container cannot access information in any other container.

Hardware Maintenance

In comparison to computer hardware systems that were manufactured through the 1980s, today's computer hardware requires little or no preventive or periodic maintenance.

And with today's popular cloud-based computing, some organizations have little or no data center hardware to maintain at all.

Computer hardware maintenance is limited to periodic checks to ensure that the computer is free of dirt and moisture. From time to time, a systems engineer will need to open a computer system cabinet and inspect it for dust and dirt accumulation. They may need to remove this debris with a vacuum cleaner or filtered compressed air. Depending on the cleanliness of the surrounding environment, inspection and cleaning may be needed as often as every few months or as seldom as every few years.

Maintenance may also be carried out by third-party service organizations that specialize in computer maintenance.

Hardware maintenance should be monitored when required. Qualified service organizations should be hired to perform maintenance at appropriate intervals. If periodic maintenance is required, management should establish a service availability plan that includes planned downtime when such operations take place.

Automated hardware monitoring tools can provide information that will help determine whether maintenance is needed. Automated monitoring is discussed in the next section.

Hardware Monitoring

Automated *hardware monitoring* tools can be used to keep a continuous watch on the health and utilization of server and network hardware. In an environment with many servers, this capability can be centralized so that the health of many servers and network devices can be monitored using a single monitoring program.

Hardware monitoring capabilities may vary among different makes of computer systems, but can include any or all of the following:

- **CPU:** Monitoring will indicate whether the system's CPU is operating properly and whether its temperature is within normal range.

- **Power supply:** Monitoring will show whether the power supply is operating properly, including input voltage, output voltage and current, cooling fans, and temperature.

- **Internal components:** Monitoring will specify whether other internal components, such as storage devices, memory, chipsets, controllers, adapters, and cooling fans, are operating properly and within normal temperature ranges.

- **Resource utilization:** Monitoring will measure the amount of resources in use, including CPU, memory, disk storage, and network utilization.

- **Asset management:** Many monitoring systems can track assets in the environment, giving management an electronic asset inventory capability.

- **External environment:** Monitoring is usually considered incomplete unless the surrounding environment is also monitored. This usually includes temperature, humidity, the presence of water, and vibration in locales where earthquakes are common. Monitoring can also include video surveillance and access door alarms.

Centralized monitoring environments typically utilize the local area network to transmit information from systems to a central console. Many monitoring consoles can send alert messages to the personnel who manage the systems being monitored. Reports can often show monitoring statistics over time so that personnel can identify trends that could indicate impending failure.

Public cloud IaaS vendors perform hardware monitoring on behalf of their customers.

Hardware monitoring is often included in network device and network traffic monitoring performed by network operations center (NOC) personnel.

Information Systems Architecture and Software

This section discusses computer operating systems, data communications, filesystems, database management systems, media management systems, and utility software.

Computer Operating Systems

Computer operating systems (which are generally known as operating systems, or OSs) are large, general-purpose programs that are used to control computer hardware and facilitate the use of software applications. Operating systems perform the following functions:

- **Access to peripheral devices:** The operating system controls and manages access to all devices and adapters connected to the computer, including storage devices, display devices, and communications adapters.

- **Storage management:** The operating system provides for the orderly storage of information on storage hardware. For example, operating systems provide filesystem management for the storage of files and directories on SSDs or hard drives.

- **Process management:** Operating systems facilitate the existence of multiple processes, some of which will be computer applications and tools. Operating systems ensure that each process has private memory space and is protected from interference and eavesdropping by other processes.

- **Resource allocation:** Operating systems facilitate the sharing of computer resources such as memory, communications, and display devices.

- **Communication:** Operating systems facilitate communications with users via peripheral devices and with other computers through networking. They typically have drivers and tools to facilitate network communications.

- **Security:** Operating systems restrict access to protected resources through process, user, and device authentication.

Examples of popular operating systems include Linux, Solaris, macOS, Android, iOS, Chrome OS, and Microsoft Windows.

The traditional context of the relationship between operating systems and computer hardware is this: One copy of a computer operating system runs on a computer at any given time. Virtualization, however, has changed all of that. Virtualization was discussed earlier in this chapter.

Server Clustering

Using special software, a group of two or more computers can be configured to operate as a cluster. This means that the group of computers will appear as a single computer for the purpose of providing services. Within the cluster, one computer will be active, and the other computer(s) will be in passive mode; if the active computer experiences a hardware or software failure and crashes, the passive computer(s) will transition to active mode and continue to provide service. This is known as *active-passive* mode. The transition is called a *failover*.

Clusters can also operate in *active-active* mode, in which all computers in the cluster provide service; in the event of one computer's failure, the remaining computer(s) will continue providing service.

Grid Computing

Grid computing is a technique for distributing a problem or task to several computers at the same time, taking advantage of each computer's processing power to solve the problem or complete the task in less time. It is a form of distributed computing, but in grid computing, the computers are coupled more loosely, and the number of computers participating in solving a problem can be dynamically expanded or contracted at will.

Cloud Computing

Cloud computing refers to dynamically scalable and usually virtualized computing resources that are provided as a service. Cloud computing services may be rented or leased so that an organization can have scalable application environments without the need for supporting hardware or a data center. Cloud computing may also include networking, computing, and even application services in a software-as-a-service (SaaS) or platform-as-a-service (PaaS) model. Cloud computing is discussed in more detail in Chapter 4.

Data Communications Software

The prevalence of network-centric computing has resulted in networking capabilities being included with virtually every computer and being built into virtually every computer operating system. Almost without exception, computer operating systems include the ability for the computer to connect with networks based on the TCP/IP suite of protocols, enabling the computer to communicate on a home network, enterprise business network, or the global Internet.

Data communications is discussed in greater detail later in this chapter in the section "Network Infrastructure."

Filesystems

A *filesystem* is a logical structure that facilitates the storage of data on a digital storage medium such as a hard drive, SSD, CD/DVD-ROM, or flash memory device. The structure of the filesystem facilitates the creation, modification, expansion and contraction, and deletion of data files. A filesystem may also be used to enforce access controls to control which users or processes are permitted to access, alter, or create files in a filesystem.

It can also be said that a filesystem is a special-purpose database designed for the storage and management of files.

Modern filesystems employ a storage hierarchy that consists of two main elements:

- **Directories:** A directory is a structure that is used to store files. A filesystem may contain one or more directories, each of which may contain files and subdirectories. The topmost directory in a filesystem is usually called the "root" directory. A filesystem may exist as a hierarchy of information, in the same way that a building can contain several file rooms, each of which contains several file cabinets, which contain drawers that contain dividers, folders, and documents. Directories are called folders in some computing environments.

- **Files:** A file is a sequence of zero or more characters that are stored as a logical whole. A file may be a document, spreadsheet, image, sound file, computer program, or data that is used by a program. A file can be as small as zero characters in length (an empty file) or as large as many gigabytes (trillions of characters). A file occupies units of storage on storage media (which could be a hard disk, SSD, or flash memory device, for example) that may be called blocks or sectors; however, the filesystem hides these underlying details from the user so that the file may be known simply by its name, the directory in which it resides, and its contents.

Well-known filesystems in use today include:

- **FAT (File Allocation Table):** This filesystem has been used in MS-DOS and early versions of Microsoft Windows, and FAT is often used as the filesystem on portable media devices such as flash drives. Versions of FAT include FAT12, FAT16, and FAT32. FAT does not support security access controls, including specifying access permissions to files and directories. FAT also does not include any journaling features, making it more vulnerable to corruption if power is removed during write operations.

- **NTFS (New Technology File System):** This is used in newer versions of Windows, including desktop and server editions. NTFS supports file- and directory-based access control and filesystem journaling (the process of recording changes made to a filesystem; this aids in filesystem recovery).

- **ext3:** This journaled filesystem is used by the Linux operating system.

- **HFS (Hierarchical File System):** This filesystem is used on computers running the Apple macOS operating system.

- **APFS (Apple File System):** This filesystem is used on computers running the Apple macOS operating system.

- **Resilient File System (ReFS):** This filesystem is used on Windows Server 2012 and later versions and is intended to replace NTFS.

- **ISO/IEC 9660:** This filesystem is used by CD-ROM and DVD-ROM media.

- **UDF (Universal Disk Format):** This optical media filesystem is considered a replacement for ISO/IEC 9660. UDF is widely used on rewritable optical media.

Media Management Systems

Information systems may employ automated tape management systems (TMSs) or disk management systems (DMSs) that track the tape and disk volumes that are needed for application processing.

Disk and tape management systems instruct system operators to mount specific media volumes when they are needed. These systems reduce operator error by requesting specific volumes and rejecting incorrect volumes that do not contain the required data.

TMSs and DMSs are most often found as components of a computer backup system. Most commercial backup systems track which tape or disk volumes contain which backed-up files and databases. Coupled with automatic volume recognition (usually through barcode readers), backup systems maintain an extensive catalog of the entire collection of backup media and their contents. When data needs to be restored, the backup software (or the TMS or DMS) will specify which media volume should be mounted, verify that the correct media is available, and then restore the desired data as directed.

Significant reductions in the cost of storage, together with the trend toward cloud computing and cloud storage, have resulted in few new installations of TMSs and DMSs. Still, many organizations utilize these today, and IS auditors must be familiar with their function and operation.

Utility Software

Utility software comprises a broad class of programs that support the development or use of networks, information systems, operating systems, and applications. Utility software is most often used by IT specialists whose responsibilities include some aspect of system development, support, or operations. End users, on the other hand, most often use software applications instead of utilities.

Utility software can be classified into the following categories:

- **Software and data design:** This includes system, program, and data modeling tools that are used to design new applications or to model existing applications.

- **Software development:** These programs are used to facilitate the actual coding of an application (or another utility). Development tools can provide a wide variety of functions, including program language syntax checking, compilation, debugging, and testing.

- **Software testing:** In addition to unit testing that may be present in a development environment, dedicated software testing tools perform extensive testing of software functions. Automated testing tools can contain entire suites of test cases that are run against an application program, with the results stored for future reference.

- **Security testing:** Several different types of software tools are used to determine the security of software applications, operating systems, DBMSs, and networks. One type of security testing tool examines an application's source code, looking for potential security vulnerabilities. Another type runs the application program and inputs different forms of data to see if the application contains vulnerabilities in the way that it handles this data. Other security testing tools examine operating system and DBMS configuration settings. Still others send specially crafted network messages to a target system to see what types of vulnerabilities might exist that could be exploited by an intruder or a hacker.

- **Data management:** These utilities are used to manipulate, list, transform, query, compare, encrypt, decrypt, import, or export data. They may also test the integrity of data (e.g., examining an index in a relational database or the integrity of a filesystem) and possibly make repairs.

- **System health:** These utilities assess the health of an operating system by examining configuration settings, verifying the versions of the kernel, drivers, and utilities, and making performance measurements and tuning changes. Some system utilities also assess the health of system components, including the CPU, main memory, secondary storage, and peripherals.

- **Network:** These utilities examine the network to discover other systems connected to it, determine network configuration, and listen to network traffic.

Utilities and Security

Because some utilities are used to observe or change access controls or security, organizations should limit the use of utilities to personnel whose responsibilities require it. All other personnel should not be permitted to use them.

Because many utilities are readily available, simply posting a policy will not prevent their use. Instead, strict access controls should be established so that unauthorized users who do obtain utilities would derive little or no use from them. These controls are typically implemented through one of two methods:

- Remove local administrator privileges from end users on their workstations so that they are unable to install software packages or change the configuration of their workstations' operating systems.

- Employ software whitelisting software that prohibits all but strictly permitted software programs from running on users' workstations.

Software Licensing

Most organizations purchase many software components in support of their software applications and IT environments overall. For example, organizations often purchase operating systems, software development tools, DBMSs, web servers, network management tools, office automation systems, and security tools. Organizations need to be aware of the licensing terms and conditions for each of the software products that they lease or purchase.

To be effective, an organization should centralize its records and expertise in software licensing to avoid licensing issues that could lead to unwanted, potentially costly, and embarrassing legal actions. Some of the ways that an organization can organize and control its software usage include:

- **Developing policies:** The organization should develop policies that define acceptable and unacceptable uses of software.

- **Centralizing procurement:** This can help funnel purchasing through a group or department that can manage and control software acquisition and use.

- **Implementing software metering:** Automated tools installed on each computer (including user workstations) can alert IT of every software program installed and run in the organization. This can help raise awareness of new software programs being used and the number of copies of programs installed and in use.

- **Implementing concurrent licensing:** The organization can use dynamic license management to control the number of users who can use a program simultaneously. This can help reduce costs for expensive programs used infrequently by many employees.

- **Reviewing software contracts:** The person or group responsible for managing software licensing should be aware of the terms and conditions of use.

Digital Rights Management

The Internet has provided a means for easily distributing content to large numbers of people. This ability, however, sometimes runs afoul of legal copyright protection afforded to the owners of copyrighted work. This encompasses software programs as well as documents and media.

Organizations also face the problem of limiting the distribution of documents for privacy or intellectual property protection. For example, an organization may publish a technical white paper describing its services and desire that only its current customers be able to view the document.

Digital rights management (DRM) is a set of emerging technologies that permits the owner of digital information (such as documents) to control access to that information, even after it is no longer contained in the owner's environment. In some instances, these technologies are implemented in system hardware (such as ebook readers), and in other cases, they are implemented in software.

Whether implemented in hardware or software, the program or device displaying information will first examine the file to determine whether the information should be displayed. Some of the characteristics that the owner of a file may be able to set include:

- **Expiration:** The owner of a file may be able to set an expiration date, after which time the file cannot be viewed or used.

- **Registration:** The owner of a file may be able to require anyone viewing the file to register themself in a reliable way (such as through email address verification).

- **Authentication:** The owner of a file may be able to require that persons viewing a file first authenticate themselves.

Network Infrastructure

Networks are used to transport data from one computer to another, either within an organization or between organizations. Network infrastructure is the collection of devices and cabling that facilitates network communications among an organization's systems as well as among the organization's systems and those belonging to other organizations. This section describes the following network infrastructure topics:

- Enterprise architecture

- Network architecture

- Network-based services

- Network models

- Network technologies

- Local area networks

- Wide area networks

- Wireless networks

- The TCP/IP suite of protocols

- The global Internet

- Network management

- Networked applications

Enterprise Architecture

There are two distinct facets related to the term *enterprise architecture*. The first is the overall set of infrastructure that facilitates access to applications and information: the networks, whether wired or wireless, local or wide area, together with resilience, access controls, and monitoring; the systems with their applications and tools; and the data and where it is stored, transmitted, and processed. The second facet is the ongoing activity carried out by one or more persons with titles such as enterprise network architect, enterprise data architect, enterprise systems engineer, or enterprise security architect, any and all of whom are concerned with "big picture" aspects of the organization and its mission, objectives, and goals, and whether the organization's infrastructure contributes to their fulfillment.

Enterprise architecture, done correctly, requires standards: consistent ways of doing things, and consistency in the components that are used and how those components are configured.

The goals of enterprise architecture include:

- **Scalability:** Enterprise architects should design the whole enterprise and its components so that systems, networks, and storage can be easily expanded where needed.

- **Agility:** The overall design of the organization's infrastructure should be flexible enough to meet new goals and objectives.

- **Transparency:** High-level and detailed diagrams should be readily available and up-to-date. There should be no secrets.

- **Security:** The design of an organization's infrastructure should reflect its needs through means such as segmentation, the creation of security zones, monitoring, and the inclusion of security components, including firewalls and intrusion prevention systems.

- **Consistency:** The organization's infrastructure should reflect consistency using common components and configurations. This makes troubleshooting and upkeep more effective when engineers are familiar with micro architectures, components, and configurations. For example, an organization with retail stores or branch offices should employ identical architectures in each of those locations; this makes support and troubleshooting easier because engineers don't first need to figure out how a local network is configured—they're all the same, or nearly so.

- **Repeatability:** Consistency brings repeatability. In an organization with retail stores or branch offices, for instance, additions or changes are "cookie-cutter" instead of time-consuming "one-off" efforts.

- **Efficiency:** Repeatability and consistency yield efficiency. Upgrades, expansion, and configuration changes are consistent and repeatable, and troubleshooting takes less time.

- **Resilience:** Enterprise architects need to understand where resilience is required so that infrastructure will be continuously available even in the event of individual components' failure or maintenance.

The challenge facing many organizations is the temptation to cut corners and deviate from (or never implement) standard architectures. Short-term gains are almost sure to be smaller than long-term inefficiencies realized later. Vision and discipline are required to attain and maintain a consistent and effective enterprise architecture.

Network Architecture

The term *network architecture* has several meanings, all of which refer to the overall design of an organization's network communications. Like other aspects of its information technology, an organization's network architecture should support its mission, goals, and objectives.

The facets of network architecture include:

- **Physical network architecture:** This is concerned with the physical locations of network equipment and media. This includes, for instance, the design of a network cable plant (also known as structured cabling), as well as the locations and types of network devices. An organization's physical network architecture may be expressed in several layers. A high-level architecture may depict global physical locations or regions and their interconnectivity, while an in-building architecture will be highly specific regarding the types of cabling and locations of equipment.

- **Logical network architecture:** This is concerned with the depiction of network communications at local, campus, regional, and global levels. Here, the network architecture will include several related layers, including representations of network protocols, device addressing, traffic routing, security zones, and the utilization of carrier services.

- **Data flow architecture:** This is closely related to application and data architecture. Here, the flow of data is shown as connections among applications, systems, users, partners, and suppliers. Data flow can be depicted in nongeographic terms, although representations of data flow at local, campus, regional, and global levels are also needed, since geographic distance is often inversely proportional to capacity and throughput.

- **Network standards and services:** This is more involved with the services that are used on the network and less with the geographic and spatial characteristics of the network. Services and standards need to be established in several layers, including cable types, addressing standards, routing protocols, network management protocols, utility protocols (such as Domain Name System [DNS], Network Time Protocol [NTP], file sharing, printing, email, remote access, and many more), and application data interchange protocols, such as SOA (Service-Oriented Architecture), SOAP (Simple Object Access Protocol), and XML (eXtensible Markup Language).

- **Security architecture:** This includes the creation of trust zones, segmentation, and security controls such as firewalls, intrusion prevention systems (IPSs), web content filtering, proxy servers, gateways, and security monitoring.

Types of Networks

Computer networks can be classified in several different ways. The primary method of classification is based on the size of a network. By size, we refer not necessarily to the number of nodes or stations on the network, but to its physical or geographic size. These types are (from smallest to largest):

- **Personal area network (PAN):** Also known as a piconet, a PAN is generally used by a single individual. Its reach ranges from a few centimeters up to 3 meters and is used to connect peripherals and communication devices for use by an individual.

- **Local area network (LAN):** The original type of network, a LAN connects computers and devices together in a small building or a residence. The typical maximum size of a LAN is 100 meters, which is the maximum cable length for popular network technologies such as Ethernet.

- **Campus area network (CAN):** A CAN connotes the interconnection of LANs for an organization that has buildings in proximity.

- **Metropolitan area network (MAN):** A MAN spans a city or regional area. Usually, this type of network consists of two or more in-building LANs in multiple locations that are connected by telecommunications circuits (such as Multiprotocol Label Switching [MPLS], T1, Frame Relay, or dark fiber) or private network connections over the global Internet.

- **Wide area network (WAN):** A WAN's size can range from regional to international. An organization with multiple locations across vast distances will connect its locations together with dedicated telecommunications connections or protected connections over the Internet. It is noted that an organization will also call a single point-to-point connection between two distant locations a "WAN connection."

The classifications discussed here are not rigid, nor do they impose restrictions on the use of any specific technology from one to the next. Instead, they are simply a set of terms that enable professionals to speak easily about the geographic extent of their networks with easily understood terms.

The relative scale of these network terms is depicted in Figure 5.6.

FIGURE 5.6   A comparison of network sizes

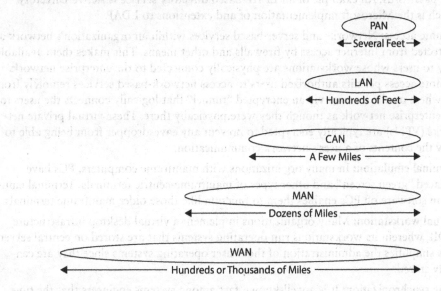

Network-Based Services

Network-based services are the protocols and utilities that facilitate system- and network-based resource utilization. In a literal sense, many of these services operate on servers; they are called network-based services because they facilitate or utilize various kinds of network communication.

Some of these services are:

- **Email:** Email servers collect, store, and transmit email messages from person to person. They accept incoming email messages from other users on the Internet and likewise send email messages over the Internet to email servers that accept and store email messages for distant recipients.

- **Print:** Print servers act as aggregation points for network-based printers in an organization. When users print a document, their workstation sends it to a specific printer queue on a print server. If other users are also sending documents to the same printer, the print server will store them temporarily until the printer is able to print them.

- **File storage:** File servers provide centralized storage of files for use among groups of users. Often, centralized file storage is configured so that files stored on remote servers logically appear to be stored locally on user workstations.

- **Directory:** These services provide centralized management of resource information. Examples include DNS, which provides translation between resource name and IP address, and Lightweight Directory Access Protocol (LDAP), which provides directory information for users and resources, and is often used as a central database of user IDs and passwords. An example of an LDAP-based directory service is Active Directory, which is the Microsoft implementation of and extensions to LDAP.

- **Remote access:** Network- and server-based services within an organization's network are protected from Internet access by firewalls and other means. This makes them available only to users whose workstations are physically connected to the enterprise network. Remote access permits authorized users to access network-based services remotely from anywhere on the Internet via an encrypted "tunnel" that logically connects the users to the enterprise network as though they were physically there. These virtual private networks (VPNs) are typically encrypted to prevent any eavesdropper from being able to view the contents of a user's network communication.

- **Terminal emulation:** In many organizations with mainframe computers, PCs have replaced "green screen" and other types of mainframe-centric terminals. Terminal emulation software on PCs enables them to function like those older mainframe terminals.

- **Virtual workstation:** Many organizations implement a virtual desktop infrastructure (VDI), wherein its workstations run operating systems that are stored on central servers. This simplifies the administration of those user operating systems since they are centrally stored.

- **Time synchronization:** It is a well-known fact among systems engineers that the time clocks built into most computers are not very accurate (some are, in fact, notoriously inaccurate). Distributed applications and network services have made accurate "timestamping" increasingly important. Time synchronization protocols enable an organization's time server system to ensure that all other servers' and workstations' time clocks are synchronized. And the time server itself will synchronize with one of several reliable Internet-based time servers, GPS-equipped time servers, or time servers that are attached to international standard atomic clocks.

- **Network connectivity and authentication:** Many organizations have adopted one of several available methods that authenticate users and workstations before logically connecting them to the enterprise network. This helps to prevent non-organization–owned or noncompliant workstations from being able to connect to an internal network, which is a potential security threat. Users or workstations that are unable to authenticate are connected to a "quarantine" network, where users can obtain information about the steps they need to take to get connected to enterprise resources. Network-based authentication can even quickly examine an organization's workstation, checking it for proper security settings (antimalware, firewall, security patches, security configuration, and so on), and allow it to connect logically only if the workstation is configured properly. Various protocols and technologies that are used to connect, verify, and authenticate devices to a network include Dynamic Host Configuration Protocol (DHCP), 802.1X, and network access control (NAC).

- **Web security:** Most organizations have a vested interest in having some level of control over the choice of Internet websites that their employees choose to visit. Websites that serve no business purpose (for example, online gambling, porn, and online games) can be blocked so that employees cannot access them. Further, many Internet websites (even legitimate ones) host malware that can be automatically downloaded to user workstations. Web security appliances can examine incoming content for malware, in much the same way that a workstation checks incoming files for viruses.

- **Cloud access control:** Many organizations utilize a cloud access security broker (CASB) system to monitor and control access to cloud-based services, as a part of an overall data management and data protection program. A CASB can prevent users from uploading sensitive internal information to a nonsanctioned cloud storage service, for instance.

- **Antimalware:** Malware (viruses, worms, Trojan horses, and so on) remains a significant threat to organizations. Antivirus software on each workstation is still an important line of defense. Because of the complexity of antimalware, many organizations have opted to implement advanced antimalware solutions along with centralized management and control. Using a central antimalware console, security engineers can quickly spot workstations under attack, as well as those whose antimalware is not functioning, and they can force new antimalware updates to some or all user workstations. They can even force user workstations to commence an immediate whole-disk scan for malware if an outbreak has started. Centralized antimalware consoles can also receive virus infection alerts from workstations and keep centralized statistics on virus updates and outbreaks, giving security engineers a vital "big picture" status.

- **Network management:** Larger organizations with too many servers and network devices to administer manually often turn to network management systems. These systems serve as a collection point for all alerts and error messages from vital servers and network devices. They can also be used to configure network devices centrally, making wide-scale configuration changes possible by a small team of engineers working in a NOC. Network management systems also measure network performance, throughput, latency, and outages, giving network engineers vital information on the health of the enterprise network.

Network Models

Network models are the archetype of the actual designs of network protocols. While a model is often a simplistic depiction of a more complicated reality, the Open Systems Interconnection (OSI) and TCP/IP network models accurately illustrate what is actually happening in a network. It is fairly difficult to see the components of the network in action; the models help us to understand how they work.

These models were developed to build consensus among the various manufacturers of network components (from programs to software drivers to network devices and cabling) to improve interoperability between different types of computers. In essence, it was a move toward networks with "interchangeable parts" that would facilitate data communications on a global scale.

The two dominant network models that are used to illustrate networks are OSI and TCP/IP. Both are described in this section.

The OSI Network Model

The first widely accepted network model is the Open Systems Interconnection (OSI) model. The OSI model was developed by the International Organization for Standardization (ISO) and the International Telecommunication Union (ITU). The working groups that developed the OSI model ignored the existence of the TCP/IP model, which was gaining in popularity around the world and has become the de facto world standard.

The OSI model consists of seven layers. Messages that are sent on an OSI network are encapsulated; a message that is constructed at layer 7 is placed inside layer 6, which is then placed inside layer 5, and so on. This is not figurative—this encapsulation literally takes place and can be viewed using tools that show the detailed contents of packets on a network. Encapsulation is illustrated in Figure 5.7.

The layers of the OSI model are, from bottom to top:

- Physical
- Data link
- Network
- Transport
- Session
- Presentation
- Application

Because it is difficult for many people to memorize a list such as this, there are some memory aids to help remember the sequence of these layers, including the following:

- Please Do Not Throw Sausage Pizza Away
- Please Do Not Touch Steve's Pet Alligator
- All People Seem To Need Data Processing
- All People Standing Totally Naked Don't Perspire

The layers of the OSI model are explained in more detail in the remainder of this section.

FIGURE 5.7   Encapsulation of packets in the OSI network model

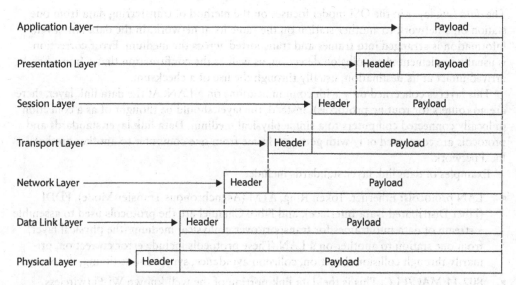

OSI Layer 1: Physical

The *physical* layer in the OSI model is concerned with electrical and physical specifications for devices. This includes communications cabling, voltage levels, and connectors, as well as some of the basic specifications for devices that would connect to networks. At the physical layer, networks are little more than electric signals flowing in wires or radio frequency airwaves.

At this layer, data exists merely as bits; there are no frames, packets, or messages here. The physical layer also addresses the modulation of digital information into voltage and current levels in the physical medium.

Examples of OSI physical layer standards include:

- **Cabling:** 10BASE-T, 100BASE-TX, 1000BASE-X, twinaxial, and fiber optics, which are standards for physical network cabling

- **Communications:** RS-232, RS-449, and V.35, which are standards for sending serial data between computers

- **Telecommunications:** T1, E1, SONET (Synchronous Optical Networking), DSL (Digital Subscriber Line), and DOCSIS (Data Over Cable Service Interface Specification), which are standards for common carrier communications networks for voice and data

- **Wireless communications:** Asynchronous Connection-Less (ACL) used by Bluetooth, 802.11a PHY (meaning the physical layer component of 802.11), and other wireless local area network (WLAN) airlink standards

- **Wireless telecommunications:** LTE (Long-Term Evolution), WiMAX (Worldwide Inter-operability for Microwave Access), CDMA (Code Division Multiple Access), W-CDMA, CDMA2000, TDMA (Time Division Multiple Access), and UMTS (Universal Mobile Tele-communications Service), which are airlink standards for wireless communications between cell phones and base stations (these standards also include some OSI layer 2 features)

OSI Layer 2: Data Link

The *data link* layer in the OSI model focuses on the method of transferring data from one station on a network to another station on the same local network. In the data link layer, information is arranged into frames and transported across the medium. Error correction is usually implemented as collision detection, as well as the confirmation that a frame has arrived intact at its destination, usually through the use of a checksum.

This layer is concerned only with communications on a LAN. At the data link layer, there are no routers (or routing protocols). Instead, the layer should be thought of as a collection of locally connected computers to a single physical medium. Data link layer standards and protocols are concerned only with getting a frame from one computer to another on that local network.

Examples of data link layer standards include:

- **LAN protocols:** Ethernet, Token Ring, ATM (Asynchronous Transfer Mode), FDDI (Fiber Distributed Data Interface), and Fibre Channel are the protocols used to assemble a stream of data into frames for transport over a physical medium (the physical layer) from one station to another on a LAN. These protocols include error correction, primarily through collision detection, collision avoidance, synchronous timing, or tokens.

- **802.11 MAC/LLC:** This is the data link portion of the well-known Wi-Fi (wireless LAN) protocols.

- **Common carrier packet networks:** MPLS and Frame Relay are packet-oriented standards for network services provided by telecommunications carriers. Organizations that required point-to-point communications with various locations would often obtain an MPLS or Frame Relay connection from a local telecommunications provider. Frame Relay is being replaced by MPLS and is rapidly declining in use.

- **ARP (Address Resolution Protocol):** This protocol is used when one station needs to communicate with another, and the initiating station does not know the receiving station's network link layer (hardware) address. ARP is prevalent in TCP/IP networks but is used in other network types as well.

- **Point-to-Point (PPP) and Serial Line Internet Protocol (SLIP):** These protocols are used to transport TCP/IP packets over point-to-point serial connections (usually RS-232). SLIP is now obsolete, and PPP is generally seen only in remote access connections that utilize dial-up services.

- **Tunneling:** PPTP (Point-to-Point Tunneling Protocol), L2TP (Layer 2 Tunneling Protocol), and other tunneling protocols were developed to extend TCP/IP (among others) from a centralized network to a branch network or a remote workstation, usually over a dial-up connection.

In the data link layer, stations on the network must have an address. Ethernet and Token Ring, for instance, use MAC (Media Access Control) addresses, which are considered hardware addresses. Most other multistation protocols also utilize some form of hardware addressing for each device on the network.

OSI Layer 3: Network

The purpose of the OSI *network* layer is the delivery of messages from one station to another via one or more networks. The network layer can process messages of any length and will "fragment" messages so that they are able to fit into packets that the network is able to transport.

The network layer is concerned with the interconnection of networks and the packet routing between networks. Network devices called routers are used to connect networks. Routers are physically connected to two or more logical networks and are configured with (or have some ability to learn) the network settings for each network. Using this information, routers can make routing decisions that will enable them to forward packets to (or closer to) the correct network, moving them closer to their ultimate destination.

Examples of protocols at the network layer include:

- **IP (Internet Protocol):** This network layer protocol is used in the TCP/IP suite of protocols. IP is concerned with the delivery of packets from one station to another, whether the stations are on the same network or on different networks. IP has the IP address scheme for assigning addresses to stations on a network; this is entirely separate from link layer (hardware) addressing such as Ethernet's MAC addressing. IP is the basis for the global Internet.

- **IPsec (Internet Protocol Security):** This protocol is used to authenticate, encapsulate, and encrypt IP traffic between networks. This protocol is often used for VPNs facilitating secure remote access.

- **ICMP (Internet Control Message Protocol):** This communications diagnostics protocol is also a part of the TCP/IP suite. One of its primary uses is the transmission of error messages from one station to another; these error messages are usually related to problems encountered when attempting to send packets from one station to another.

- **IGMP (Internet Group Management Protocol):** This protocol is used to organize multicast group memberships between routers. IGMP is a part of the multicast protocol family.

- **Logical link control and adaptation protocol (L2CAP):** This is the network layer used by Bluetooth.

- **AppleTalk:** This original suite of protocols was developed by Apple Computer for networking the Apple brand of computers. The suite of protocols includes the transmission of messages from one computer over interconnected networks, as well as routing protocols. AppleTalk has since been deprecated in favor of TCP/IP.

OSI Layer 4: Transport

The *transport* layer in the OSI model is primarily concerned with the reliability of data transfer between systems. The transport layer manages the following characteristics of data communications:

- **Connection orientation:** At the transport layer, communications between two stations can take place in the context of a connection. Here, two stations will initiate a unique, logical context (called a connection) under which they can exchange messages until a later time when the stations agree to end the connection. Stations can have two or more unique connections established concurrently; each is uniquely identified.

- **Guaranteed delivery:** Protocols at the transport layer can track individual packets to guarantee delivery. For example, the TCP uses something like a return receipt for each transported packet to confirm that each sent packet was successfully received by the destination.

- **Sequence of delivery:** The transport layer includes protocols that can track the sequence in which packets are delivered. Typically, each transported packet will have a serialized number that the receiving system will use to make sure that packets on the receiving system are delivered in proper order. When coupled with guaranteed delivery, a receiving system can request retransmission of any missing packets, ensuring that none are lost.

The protocols at the transport layer are doing the heavy lifting by ensuring the integrity and completeness of messages that flow from system to system. The ability for data communications to take place over the vast worldwide network that is the global Internet is made possible by the characteristics of protocols in the transport layer.

Examples of transport layer protocols include:

- **TCP (Transmission Control Protocol):** This is the "TCP" in the TCP/IP protocol suite. TCP is connection-oriented due to the formal establishment (three-way handshake) and maintenance (sequence numbers and acknowledgments) of a connection, using flags to indicate connection state. When a system sends a TCP packet to another system on a specific port, that port number helps the operating system direct the message to a specific program. For example, port 25 is used for inbound email, ports 20 and 21 are used for FTP (File Transfer Protocol), and ports 80 and 443 are used for HTTP (Hypertext Transfer Protocol) and HTTPS (HTTP Secure), respectively. Hundreds of preassigned port numbers are the subject of Internet standards. TCP employs guaranteed delivery and guaranteed order of delivery.

- **UDP (User Datagram Protocol):** This is the other principal protocol used by TCP/IP in the OSI transport layer. Unlike TCP, UDP is a lighter-weight protocol that lacks connection orientation, order of delivery, and guaranteed delivery. UDP consequently has less computing and network overhead, which makes it ideal for some protocols that are less sensitive to occasional packet loss. Examples of protocols that use UDP are DNS (Domain Name System), TFTP (Trivial File Transfer Protocol), and VoIP (Voice over IP). Like TCP, UDP also employs port numbers so that incoming packets on a computer can be delivered to the right program or process. Sometimes UDP is called "unreliable data protocol," a memory aid that is a reference to the protocol's lack of guaranteed delivery.

The TCP/IP suite of protocols is described in more detail later in this chapter.

OSI Layer 5: Session

The *session* layer in the OSI model is used to control connections that are established between applications on the same, or different, systems. This involves connection establishment, termination, and recovery.

In the OSI model, connection control takes place in the session layer. This means that the concept of the establishment of a logical connection between systems is a session layer function. However, TCP—which is generally thought of as a transport layer protocol—handles this on its own.

Examples of session layer protocols include:

- **Interprocess communications:** Sockets and named pipes are some of the ways that processes on a system (or on different systems) exchange information.

- **SIP (Session Initiation Protocol):** SIP is used to set up and tear down VoIP and other communications connections.

- **RPC (Remote Procedure Call):** This is another interprocess communication technology that permits an application to execute a subroutine or procedure on another computer.

- **NetBIOS (Network Basic Input/Output System):** This permits applications to communicate with one another using the legacy NetBIOS API.

OSI Layer 6: Presentation

The *presentation* layer in the OSI model is used to translate or transform data from lower layers (session, transport, and so on) into formats that the application layer can work with. Examples of presentation layer functions include:

- **Character set translation:** Programs or filters are sometimes needed to translate character sets between ASCII and EBCDIC (Extended Binary Coded Decimal Interchange Code), for instance.

- **Encryption/decryption:** Communications may be encrypted if data is to be transported across unsecured networks. Example protocols are SSL (Secure Sockets Layer), TLS (Transport Layer Security), and MIME (Multipurpose Internet Mail Extensions).

- **Codecs:** Protocols such as MPEG (Moving Picture Experts Group) use codecs to encode/decode or compress/decompress audio and video data streams.

OSI Layer 7: Application

The *application* layer in the OSI model contains programs that communicate directly with the end user. This includes utilities that are packaged with operating systems, as well as tools and software applications.

Examples of application layer protocols include:

- **Utility protocols:** DNS, SNMP (Simple Network Management Protocol), DHCP, and NTP

- **Messaging protocols:** SMTP (Simple Mail Transfer Protocol), NNTP (Network News Transfer Protocol), HTTP, VoIP, X.400, and X.500

- **Data transfer protocols:** NFS (Network File System) and FTP

- **Interactive protocols:** Telnet, IRC (Internet Relay Chat), SSH

End-user applications that communicate over networks do so via OSI layer 7.

OSI: A Model That Has Never Been Implemented—or Has It?

The OSI network model is a distinguished tool for teaching the concepts of network encapsulation and the functions taking place at each layer. However, the problem is that no actual, living network protocol environments have ever been built that contain all the layers of the OSI model, and it is becoming increasingly apparent that none ever will. The world's dominant network standard, TCP/IP, is a layered protocol stack that consists of four layers, and it's not likely that TCP/IP's model will ever be increased to seven layers.

As the OSI model was being developed and socialized by ISO (and is now defined by ISO/IEC 7498-1), the rival TCP/IP model was quickly becoming the world's standard for data network communications. OSI has been relegated to a teaching tool, and the model itself is more of an interesting museum piece that represents an idea that never came to fruition.

There is a different and equally valid point of view regarding the implementation of the OSI model: it can be said that all the modern encapsulated network protocols—TCP/IP, IPX/SPX (Internetwork Packet Exchange/Sequenced Packet Exchange), AppleTalk, and Token Ring—are implementations, albeit incomplete, of the OSI model. Technology philosophers and historians should take up this topic.

The TCP/IP Network Model

The TCP/IP network model is one of the basic design characteristics of the TCP/IP suite of protocols. The network model consists of four "layers," where each layer is used to manage some aspect of the transmission, routing, or delivery of data over a network. In a layered model, each layer receives services from the next lowest layer and provides services to the next higher layer.

Like OSI, the TCP/IP network model utilizes encapsulation. This means that a message created by an application program is encapsulated within a transport layer message, which in turn is encapsulated within an Internet layer message, which is encapsulated in a link layer message, which is delivered to a network adapter for delivery across a physical network medium. This encapsulation is depicted in Figure 5.8.

The layers of the TCP/IP model, from bottom to top, are:

- Link
- Internet
- Transport
- Application

These layers are discussed in detail in this section.

FIGURE 5.8   Encapsulation in the TCP/IP network model

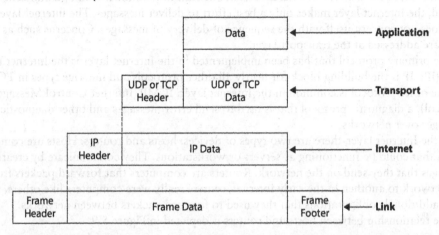

One of the primary purposes of the layered model (in both the OSI and TCP/IP models) is to permit abstraction. This means that each layer needs to be concerned only with its own delivery characteristics, while permitting other layers to manage their own matters. For instance, the order of delivery is managed by the transport layer; at the Internet and link layers, the order of delivery is irrelevant. Also, the link layer is concerned with just getting a message from one station to another and with collisions and the basic integrity of the message as it is transported from one device to another. But the link layer has no concept of a logical connection or order of delivery, which are addressed by higher layers.

TCP/IP Link Layer

The *link layer* is the lowest layer in the TCP/IP model. Its purpose is the delivery of messages (usually called frames) from one station to another on a local network. Being the lowest layer of the TCP/IP model, the link layer provides services to the transport layer.

The link layer is the physical layer of the network and is usually implemented in the form of hardware network adapters. TCP/IP can be implemented on top of any viable physical medium that has the capacity to transmit frames from one station to another. Examples of physical media used for TCP/IP include those from standards such as Ethernet, ATM, USB, Wi-Fi, Bluetooth, GPRS (General Packet Radio Service), DSL, ISDN (Integrated Services Digital Network), and fiber optics.

The link layer is only concerned with delivering messages from one station to another on a local network. At this layer, there is no concept of neighboring networks or routing; these are handled at higher layers in the model.

TCP/IP Internet Layer

The *Internet layer* of the TCP/IP model is the foundation layer of TCP/IP. The purpose of this layer is the delivery of messages (packets) from one station to another on the same network or on different networks. The Internet layer receives services from the link layer and provides services to the transport layer.

At this layer, the delivery of messages from one station to another is not guaranteed. Instead, the Internet layer makes only a best effort to deliver messages. The Internet layer also does not concern itself with the sequence of delivery of messages. Concerns such as these are addressed at the transport layer.

The primary protocol that has been implemented in the Internet layer is the Internet Protocol (IP). IP is the building block for nearly all other protocols and message types in TCP/IP. One other protocol is common in the Internet layer: ICMP (Internet Control Message Protocol), a diagnostic protocol that is used to send error messages and other diagnostic messages over networks.

At the Internet layer, there are two types of devices: hosts and routers. Hosts are computers that could be functioning as servers or workstations. They communicate by creating messages that they send on the network. Routers are computers that forward packets from one network to another. In the early Internet, routers really were computers like others, with some additional configurations that they used to forward packets between networks.

The relationship between hosts and routers is depicted in Figure 5.9.

FIGURE 5.9   Hosts and routers at the Internet layer

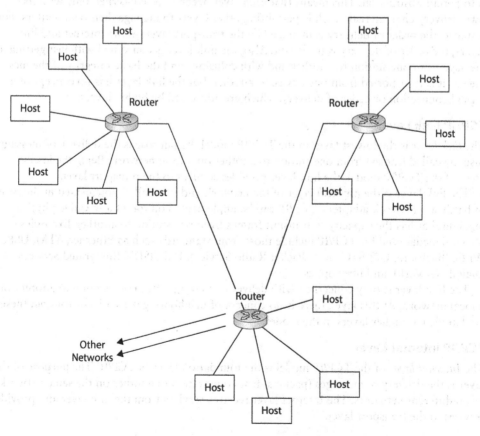

TCP/IP Transport Layer

The *transport layer* in the TCP/IP model consists of two main packet transport protocols, TCP and UDP, as well as a few other protocols that were developed after the initial design of TCP/IP. The transport layer receives services from the Internet layer and provides services to the application layer.

Several features are available at the transport layer for packet delivery, including:

- **Reliable delivery:** This involves two characteristics: integrity of the packet contents and guaranteed delivery. TCP includes these two features that ensure confirmation that a packet sent from one station will be delivered to its destination and that the contents of the packet will not be altered along the way.

- **Connection orientation:** This involves the establishment of a persistent logical "connection" between two stations. This is particularly useful when a station is communicating on many simultaneous "conversations" from one or more source stations. When a connection is established, the requesting system communicates on an arbitrary source port, to the destination system on standard ports (HTTP port 80, DNS port 53, and so on). The two stations will negotiate and agree on arbitrary high-numbered ports (channels) that will make each established connection unique.

- **Sequence of delivery:** The sequence of packet delivery can be guaranteed to match the order in which they were sent. This is implemented using sequence numbers, which are used by the receiving system to deliver packets in the correct order to the receiving process.

- **Flow control:** This means that the delivery of packets from one station to another will not overrun the destination station. For example, transferring a large file from a faster system to a slower system could overrun the slower system, unless the latter has a way to pause the transfer (flow control) periodically so that it can keep up with the inbound messages.

- **Port number:** A message on one station may be sent to a specific port number on a destination station. A port number essentially signifies the type of message that is being sent. A "listener" program can be set up on a destination system to listen on a preassigned port and then process messages received on that port number. The primary advantage of port numbers is that a destination system does not need to examine the contents of a message to discern its type; instead, the port number defines the purpose. There are many standard port numbers established, including 23 = Telnet, 25 = email, 53 = Domain Name System, 80 = HTTP, and so on.

Note that not all transport layer protocols utilize all these features. For instance, UDP utilizes flow control, but none of the other features are listed.

TCP/IP Application Layer

The *application layer* is the topmost layer of the TCP/IP model. This layer interfaces directly with applications and application services. The application layer receives services from the transport layer and may communicate directly with end users.

Application layer protocols include DNS, SNMP, DHCP, NTP, SMTP, NNTP, HTTP, HTTPS, NFS, FTP, and Telnet. There are many more.

The TCP/IP and OSI Models

The *TCP/IP model* was not designed to conform to the seven-layer OSI network model. However, the models are similar in their use of encapsulation and abstraction, and some layers between the two models are similar. Figure 5.10 shows the TCP/IP and OSI models side by side and how the layers in one model correspond to the other.

FIGURE 5.10   The TCP/IP and OSI network models side by side

OSI	TCP/IP
Application Presentation Session	Application
Transport	Transport
Network	Internet
Data Link Physical	Link

Exam Tip

Mapping TCP/IP and OSI models to each other has no practical purpose except to understand their similarities and differences. There is no unanimous agreement on the mapping of the models. It is easy to argue for some small differences in the way that they are conjoined.

Network Technologies

Many *network technologies* have been developed over the past several decades. Some, such as Ethernet, DSL, and TCP/IP, are found practically everywhere, while other technologies, such as ISDN, Frame Relay, and AppleTalk, have had shorter life spans.

The IS auditor needs to be familiar with network technologies, architectures, protocols, and media so that they may examine an organization's network architecture and operation. The following sections describe network technologies at a level of detail that should be sufficient for most auditing needs:

- **Local Area Networks:** This section discusses LAN topologies, cabling, and transport protocols (including Ethernet, ATM, Token Ring, USB, and FDDI).

- **Wide Area Networks:** This section discusses WANs, including transport protocols MPLS, SONET, T-carrier, Frame Relay, and ISDN.

- **Wireless Networks:** This section discusses wireless network standards Wi-Fi, Bluetooth, Wireless USB, NFC, and IrDA.

- **TCP/IP Protocols and Devices:** This section discusses TCP/IP protocols in the link layer, Internet layer, transport layer, and application layer.

- **The Global Internet:** This section discusses global Internet addressing, DNS, routing, and applications.

- **Network Management:** This section discusses the business function, plus the tools and protocols used to manage networks.

- **Networked Applications:** This section discusses the techniques used to build network-based applications.

Local Area Networks

Local area networks exist within a relatively small area, such as a floor in a building, a lab, a storefront, an office, or a residence. Because of electrical signaling limitations, a LAN is usually several hundred feet in length or less.

Physical Network Topology

Wired LANs are transported over network cabling that runs throughout a building. Network cabling is set up in one of three physical topologies:

- **Star:** A separate cable is run from a central location to each computer. This is the way that most networks are wired today. The central location might be a wiring closet or a computer room, where all the cables from each computer would converge at one location and be connected to network equipment such as a switch or hub.

- **Ring:** Cabling runs from one computer to the next. Early Token Ring and Ethernet networks were often wired this way. Where the network cable was attached to a computer, a "T" connector was used: one part connected to the computer itself, and the other two connectors were attached to the network cabling.

- **Bus:** A central cable, with connectors along its length that facilitate "branch" cables connected to individual computers. Like the ring topology, this was used in early networks but is seldom used today.

These three topologies are depicted in Figure 5.11.

FIGURE 5.11   Network physical topologies: star, ring, and bus

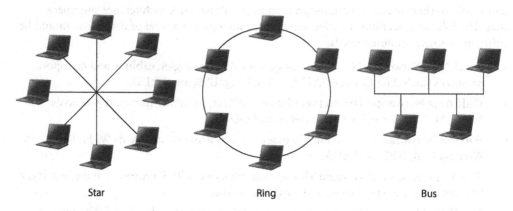

Star   Ring   Bus

Note that the logical function and physical topology of a network may vary. For instance, a Token Ring network may resemble a physical star (with all stations connected to a central device), but it will function logically as a ring. An Ethernet network functions as a bus, but it may be wired as a star, bus, or ring, depending on the type of cabling used (and, as indicated earlier, star topology is prevalent). The point is that logical function and physical topology often differ from each other.

Cabling Types

Several types of cables have been used in LANs over the past several decades. This section will focus on the types in use today but will mention those that have been used in the past, which may still be in use in some organizations.

Twisted-Pair Cable

Twisted-pair cabling is a thin cable that contains four pairs of insulated copper conductors, all surrounded by a protective jacket. Several varieties of twisted-pair cabling are suitable for various physical environments and provide various network bandwidth capabilities.

Because network transmissions can be subject to interference, network cabling may include shielding that protects the conductors from interference. Some of these types are:

- **Shielded twisted-pair (U/FTP or STP):** This type of cable includes a thin metal shield that protects each pair of conductors from electromagnetic interference (EMI), making it more resistant to interference.

- **Screened unshielded twisted-pair (S/UTP):** Also known as foiled twisted-pair (FTP), this type of cable has a thin metal shield that protects the conductors from EMI.

- **Screened shielded twisted-pair (S/STP or S/FTP):** This type of cable includes a thin layer of metal shielding surrounding each twisted-pair of conductors, plus an outer shield that protects all the conductors together. This is all covered by a protective jacket.

- **Unshielded twisted-pair (UTP):** This type of cable has no shielding and consists only of the four pairs of twisted conductors and the outer protective jacket.

The abbreviations for twisted-pair cable have recently changed in compliance with international standard ISO/IEC 11801, "Information technology — Generic cabling for customer premises." The new standard takes the form X/YTP, where X denotes whether the entire cable has shielding, and Y indicates whether individual pairs in the cable are shielded. Table 5.1 shows the old and new names and their meanings. The old names are likely going to be in common use for many years, as office buildings and residences around the world are wired with twisted-pair cabling that is labeled with the old names; this wiring will likely last for decades in many locations.

TABLE 5.1 Old and new twisted-pair cabling abbreviations and meaning

Old name	New name	Cable shielding	Pair shielding
UTP	U/UTP	None	None
FTP	F/UTP	Foil	None
STP	U/FTP	None	Foil
S-FTP	SF/UTP	Foil, braiding	None
S-STP	S/FTP	Braiding	Foil

Twisted-pair network cabling is also available with different capacity ratings to meet various bandwidth requirements. The common ratings include:

- **Category 5:** Cat-5 cabling grade has been in common use since the mid-1990s and is suitable for 10 Mbit, 100 Mbit, and 1000 Mbit (1 Gbit) Ethernet over distances up to 100 meters (328 ft.). Cat-5 cable is typically made from 24-gauge copper wire with three twists per inch. A newer grade, Category 5e, has better performance for Gigabit Ethernet networks.

- **Category 6:** This is the cabling standard for Gigabit Ethernet networks. Cat-6 cabling greatly resembles Cat-5 cabling, but Cat-6 has more stringent specifications for cross-talk and noise. Cat-6 cable is typically made from 23-gauge copper. Cat-6 cabling is "backward compatible" with Cat-5 and 5e cabling, which means that Cat-6 cables can be used for 10 Mbit and 100 Mbit Ethernet networks as well as 1000 Mbit (1 Gb or 1 Gbit).

- **Category 7:** This cable standard has been developed to permit 10 Gbit Ethernet over 100 meters of cabling. Cat-7 cabling is almost always made from S/FTP cabling to provide maximum resistance to EMI. A newer grade, Category 7a, is designed to have telephone, cable TV, and 1 GB networking in the same cable. This newer grade is still under development.

- **Category 8:** This is a new cable standard designed for high-speed networking over short distances, intended for use in data centers.

Twisted-pair cable ratings are usually printed on the outer jacket of the cable. Figure 5.12 shows a short length of Category 5 cable with the rating and other information stamped on it.

FIGURE 5.12   Category 5 twisted-pair cable

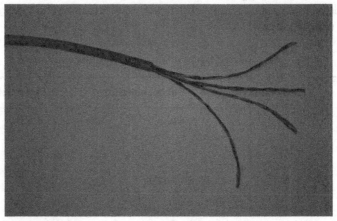

Image courtesy of Rebecca Steele

Fiber-Optic Cable

Fiber-optic cable is the transmission medium for fiber-optic communications, a method of transmitting information using pulses of light instead of electric signals through metal cabling. The advantages of fiber-optic cable are its much higher bandwidth, lower loss, and compact size. Because communications over fiber-optic cable are based on light instead of electric current, they are immune from EMI.

In LANs, multimode-type fiber-optic cable can carry signals up to 10 Gbit/sec up to 600 meters (and distances up to a few kilometers at lower bandwidths), sufficient for interconnecting buildings in a campus-type environment. For longer distances, single–mode fiber-optic cable is used, usually by telecommunications carriers, to interconnect cities for voice and data communications.

Compared to twisted-pair and other network cable types, fiber-optic cable is relatively fragile and must be treated with care. It can never be pinched, bent, or twisted—doing so will break the internal fibers. For this reason, fiber-optic cabling is usually limited to data centers requiring high bandwidths between systems, where network engineers will carefully route fiber-optic cabling from device to device, using guides and channels that will prevent the cable from being damaged. However, the advantage of fiber-optic cabling is its high capacity and freedom from EMI.

Figures 5.13 and 5.14 show fiber-optic cable and connectors.

FIGURE 5.13   Fiber-optic cable with its connector removed to reveal its interior

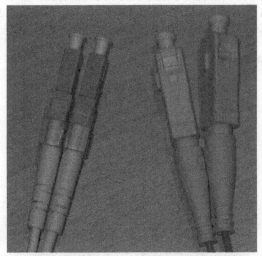

Source: Poil / Wikimedia Commons / CC BY-SA 3.0

FIGURE 5.14   Connectors link fiber-optic cable to network equipment.

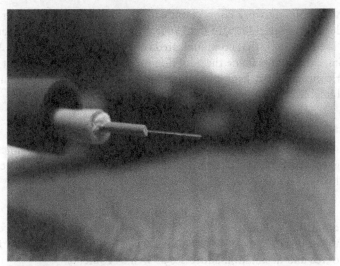

Source: Hhedeshian / Wikimedia Commons / CC BY 3.0

Other Types of Network Cable

Twisted-pair and fiber-optic cable are the dominant LAN cable types. However, older types of cable have been used and are still found in many installations, including:

- **Coaxial:** Cable A coaxial cable consists of a solid inner conductor surrounded by an insulating jacket and a metallic shield. A plastic jacket protects the shield. Coaxial cables were used in early Ethernet networks with cable types such as 10BASE5 and 10BASE2. Twist-lock or threaded connectors were used to connect coaxial cable to computers or network devices. This is fundamentally the type of cable also used for "TV cable." A typical coaxial cable is shown in Figure 5.15.

FIGURE 5.15   Coaxial cable

- **Serial:** Point-to-point network connections can be established over USB or RS-232 serial cables. In the case of serial lines, in the 1980s, many organizations used central computers and user terminals that communicated over RS-232 serial cabling. At that time, these existing cable plants made the adoption of SLIP (Serial Line Internet Protocol) popular for connecting workstations and minicomputers to central computers using existing cabling. SLIP is all but obsolete now, displaced by USB.

Network Transport Protocols

Many protocols or standards have been developed to facilitate data communications over network cabling. Ethernet, ATM, Token Ring, USB, and FDDI protocols are described in detail in the following sections.

Ethernet

Ethernet is the dominant standard used in LANs. It uses a frame-based protocol, which means that data transmitted over an Ethernet-based network is placed into a "frame" that has places for source and destination addresses as well as contents.

Shared Medium   Ethernet is a "broadcast" or "shared medium" type of protocol. This means that a frame that is sent from one station on a network to another station may be physically received by all stations that are connected to the network medium. When each station receives the frame, the station will examine the destination address of the frame to determine whether the frame is intended for that or another station. If the frame is destined for another station, the station will simply ignore the frame and do nothing. The destination station will accept the frame and deliver it to the operating system for processing.

Collision Detection   Ethernet networks are asynchronous—a station that needs to transmit a frame may do so at any time. However, Ethernet also employs a "collision detection" mechanism whereby a station that wants to broadcast a frame will begin transmitting and also listen to the network to see if any other stations are transmitting at the same time. If another station is transmitting, the station that wants to transmit will "back off" and wait for a short interval and then try again (in a 10 Mbit Ethernet, the station will wait for 9.6 microseconds). If a collision (two stations transmitting at the same time) does occur, both transmitting stations will stop, wait a short interval (the length of the interval is based on a randomly generated number), and then try again. The use of a random number as a part of the "back-off" algorithm ensures that each station has a statistically equal chance to transmit its frames on the network. This is essential for large networks with numerous stations.

Ethernet Addressing   On an Ethernet network, each station on the network has a unique address called a Media Access Control (MAC) address, expressed as a 6-byte hexadecimal value. A typical address is displayed in a notation separated by colons or dashes, such as F0:E3:67:AB:98:02.

The Ethernet standard dictates that no two devices in the entire world will have the same MAC address; this is established through the issuance of ranges of MAC addresses that are allocated to each manufacturer of Ethernet devices. Typically, each manufacturer will be issued a range, which consists of the first 3 bytes of the MAC address; the manufacturer will then assign consecutive values for the last 3 bytes to each device that it produces.

For example, suppose a company is issued the value A0-66-01 (called its Organizationally Unique Identifier [OUI]). The devices that the company produces will have that value as the first 3 bytes of their MAC address and assign 3 additional bytes to each device that it produces, giving addresses such as A0-66-01-FF-01-01, A0-66-01-FF-01-02, A0-66-01-FF-01-03, and so on. This will guarantee that no two devices in the world will have the same address.

Ethernet Frame Format   An Ethernet frame consists of a header segment, a data segment, and a checksum. The header segment contains the destination MAC address, the source MAC address, and a 2-byte Ethernet-type field. The data segment ranges from 46 to 1,500 bytes in length—the maximum for any particular network is known as the maximum transmission unit (MTU). The checksum field is 4 bytes in length and is a CRC (cyclic redundancy check) checksum of the entire frame. An Ethernet frame is shown in Figure 5.16.

FIGURE 5.16   An Ethernet frame consists of a header, data, and checksum

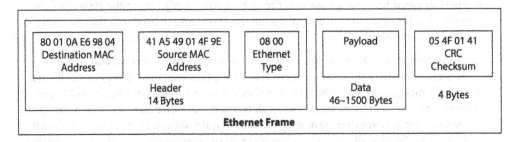

Network Devices   Network devices must not only facilitate the transmission of frames on Ethernet networks, but they must support all other network standards as well. These devices include:

Network Adapter   A network adapter, commonly known as a network interface card (NIC), is a device that is directly connected to a computer's bus and contains one or more connectors to which an Ethernet network cable may be connected. Often, a computer's NIC is integrated with the computer's motherboard, but a NIC may also be a separate circuit card that is plugged into a bus connector.

Hub   Organizations realized that ring and bus topology networks were problematic regarding cable failures. This gave rise to the star topology as a preferred network architecture because a cable problem would affect only one station instead of many or all stations. A multiport repeater would be used to connect all the devices to the network. Over time, this device became known as a hub. Like repeaters, Ethernet hubs propagate packets to all stations on the network.

Gateway   A gateway is a device that acts as a protocol converter or performs some other type of message transformation.

Repeater   A repeater is a device that receives and retransmits the signal on an Ethernet network. Repeaters are useful for situations in which cable lengths exceed 100 meters, or to interconnect two or more Ethernet networks. A disadvantage of repeaters is that they propagate collisions, errors, and other network anomalies to all parts of the network. Repeaters as stand-alone devices are seldom used in Ethernet networks today; more modern devices have absorbed their functions.

Bridge   A bridge is a device used to interconnect Ethernet networks. For example, an organization may have an Ethernet network on each floor of a multistory building; a bridge can be used to interconnect each of the separate Ethernet segments. A bridge is like a repeater, except that a bridge does not propagate errors such as collisions, but instead propagates only well-formed packets. Bridges also, as stand-alone devices, are seldom seen in today's Ethernet networks.

Switch   An Ethernet switch is like a hub, but with one important difference: a switch will listen to traffic and learn the MAC address(es) associated with each port (connector) and will send packets only to destination ports. The result is potentially greater network throughput, because each station on the network will be receiving only the frames that are specifically addressed to it. When only one station is connected to each port on an Ethernet switch, theoretically, collisions will never occur. Switches are the dominant method for contemporary networks.

Devices such as routers, layer 3 switches, layer 4 switches, and layer 4–7 switches are discussed in the section "TCP/IP Protocols and Devices," later in this chapter.

ATM

ATM (Asynchronous Transfer Mode) is a link-layer network protocol developed in the 1980s in response to the need to unify telecommunications and computer networks. ATM has been a dominant protocol in the core networks of telecommunications carriers, although IP is becoming more dominant.

Messages (called cells) on an ATM network are transmitted in synchronization with a network-based time clock. Stations on an Ethernet, on the other hand, transmit as needed, provided the network is quiet at the moment.

ATM cells are fixed at a length of 53 bytes (5-byte header and 48-byte payload). This small frame size improves performance by reducing jitter, which is a key characteristic of networks that are carrying streaming media such as broadcast television, VoIP, or video.

ATM is a connection-oriented link-layer protocol. This means that two devices on an ATM network that want to communicate with each other will establish a connection through a virtual circuit. A connection also establishes a Quality of Service (QoS) setting that defines its priority and sensitivity.

Cells transmitted from one station to another are transported through one or more ATM switches. The path that a cell takes is established when the virtual circuit is established. An ATM switch is used even when two stations on the same LAN are communicating with each other.

Like Ethernet, ATM can be used to transport TCP/IP messages. TCP/IP packets that are larger than 48 bytes in length are transmitted over ATM in pieces and reassembled at the destination.

Token Ring

Token Ring is a LAN protocol that was developed by IBM in the 1980s. Historically, Token Ring was prevalent in organizations that had IBM mainframe or midrange computer systems. However, as TCP/IP and Ethernet grew in popularity, Token Ring declined and it is rarely found today.

Token Ring networks operate through the passage of a 3-byte token frame from station to station on the network. If a station needs to send information to another station on the network, it must first receive the token; then it can place a frame on the network that includes the token and the message for the destination station. When the token frame reaches the destination station, the destination station will remove the message from the token frame and then pass an empty token (or a frame containing the token and a message for another station) to the next station on the network.

The principal Token Ring device is the multistation access unit (MAU). A MAU contains several Token Ring cable connectors and connects network cables from the MAU to each station on the network. A typical MAU contains as many as eight connectors; if a Token Ring network is to contain more than eight stations, MAUs can be connected using their ring-in/ring-out connectors. Figure 5.17 shows small and large Token Ring networks.

FIGURE 5.17   Token Ring network topologies

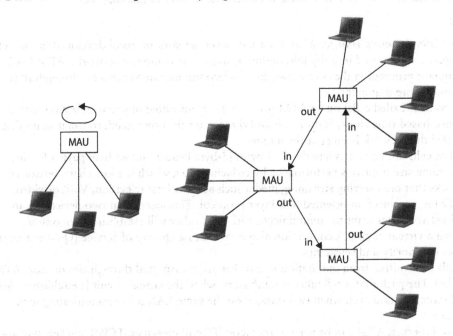

The design of Token Ring technology makes collisions impossible, since no station can transmit unless it possesses the token. A disadvantage of this design occurs if the station with the token encounters a malfunction that causes it not to propagate the token. This results in a momentary pause until the network goes into a recovery mode and regenerates a token.

Universal Serial Bus

Universal Serial Bus (USB) is not typically considered a network technology, but rather a workstation bus technology. This is primarily because USB is used to connect peripherals such as mice, keyboards, storage devices, printers, scanners, cameras, microphones, and network adapters. However, the USB specification indeed contains full networking capabilities, which makes use of those small USB hubs possible.

USB data rates are shown in Table 5.2.

TABLE 5.2   USB data rates

USB version	Data rate
1.0	12 Mbit/sec
2.0	480 Mbit/sec
3.0	5.0 Gbit/sec
4.0	40 Gbit/sec

The length of a USB cable is restricted to 5 meters. The maximum number of devices on a USB network is 127.

One of the valuable characteristics of USB technology is the ability to "hot plug" devices. This means that USB devices can be connected and disconnected without the need to power down the workstation they are connected to. This is achieved primarily through the design specification for devices and device drivers that tolerate plugging and unplugging. This does not mean, however, that all types of USB devices may be plugged and unplugged at will. USB mass storage devices, for instance, should be logically "dismounted" to ensure the integrity of the filesystem on the device.

FDDI

Fiber Distributed Data Interface (FDDI) is a LAN technology whose range can extend up to 200 kilometers over optical fiber. FDDI is a "dual ring" technology that utilizes redundant network cabling and counter-rotating tokens, which together make FDDI highly resilient. Each ring has a 100 Mbit/sec data rate, making the entire network capable of 200 Mbit/sec.

FDDI has been largely superseded by 100 Mbit/sec and 1 Gbit/sec Ethernet and is no longer common in commercial networks.

Wide Area Networks

Wide area networks (WANs) can extend for miles to thousands of miles between stations. The term WAN is generally used in two ways: to connote an organization's entire regional or global data network and as the label for the long-distance network connections used to join individual networks together. In the second usage, the terms "WAN link" and "WAN connection" are used.

Wide Area Transmission Modes

Before we discuss specific WAN protocols, it is important that you understand the basics of message transmission techniques used in WANs.

The basic problem of wide area communications is the need to route communications efficiently from many different endpoints to several destinations without constructing dedicated connections between all possible communication sources and destinations. Instead, some scheme for sharing a common communication medium is needed. These methods are:

- **Circuit-switched:** Here, a dedicated, end-to-end communications channel is established that lasts for the duration of a connection. The best-known example of circuit-switched technology is the old public-switched telephone network, where a telephone call from one telephone to another occupied a dedicated circuit that was assigned at the onset of the call and used until the call was finished.

- **Packet-switched:** Communications between endpoints takes place over a stream of packets, which are routed through switches until they reach their destination. Frame Relay and the TCP/IP Internet are good examples of packet-switched networks. While landline telephone calls still have the appearance of being circuit-switched, telephone conversations are actually converted into packets for transmission through the core of a digital telecommunications network.

- **Message-switched:** Each message is switched to its destination when a communications path is available. An example of message switching is the transmission of individual email messages between servers on the Internet.

- **Virtual circuit:** A logical communications channel is established between two endpoints on a packet-switched network. This channel may be known as a permanent virtual circuit (PVC) or a switched virtual circuit (SVC). Virtual circuits are used in ATM and Frame Relay networks, and VPNs can also be thought of as virtual circuits.

Wide Area Network Protocols

This section describes several well-known protocols used in WANs.

FTTH

Fiber to the home (FTTH) is the delivery of broadband services through fiber-optic cable to customer premises. FTTH can deliver Internet data, voice, and cable TV services to residents and businesses. A typical FTTH connection is made to a node on the customer's premises that provides Ethernet LAN connectivity. U.S. broadband providers offering FTTH include Google Fiber, Verizon Fios, and Ziply Fiber. A typical FTTH node is shown in Figure 5.18.

MPLS

Multiprotocol Label Switching (MPLS) is a variable-length, packet-switched network technology. In an MPLS network, each packet has one or more labels affixed to it that contain information that helps MPLS routers to make packet-forwarding decisions, without having to examine the contents of the packet itself (for an IP address, for instance).

MPLS can be used to carry many types of traffic, including Ethernet, ATM, SONET, and IP. It is often used to trunk voice and data networks over WAN connections between business locations in an enterprise network. One of the strengths of MPLS is its QoS (Quality of Service) properties, which facilitate the rapid transfer of packets using time-sensitive protocols such as VoIP and H.323.

FIGURE 5.18 A typical terminating node for a fiber to the home (FTTH) connection

MPLS employs two types of devices: label edge routers (LERs) and label switch routers (LSRs). Label edge routers are used at the boundaries of an MPLS network; LERs push a label onto incoming packets that enter the network. LSRs make packet-forwarding decisions based on the label's value. When a packet leaves the MPLS network, another LER pops the label off the packet and forwards it out of the MPLS network.

DOCSIS

Data Over Cable Service Interface Specification (DOCSIS) is a packet-switched network technology built on "cable TV" carrier infrastructure. DOCSIS is delivered to customers using a cable modem, a device that converts digital signals in the cable TV infrastructure into Ethernet and connects to a LAN. The DOCSIS standard defines data rates up to 10 Gbit/sec.

SONET

Synchronous Optical Networking (SONET) is a class of telecommunications network transport technologies transmitted over fiber-optic networks. It is a multiplexed network technology that can be used to transport voice and data communications at very high speeds over long distances.

SONET networks are almost exclusively built and operated by telecommunications network providers that sell voice and data connectivity services to businesses. Often, the end-point equipment for SONET networks provides connectivity using a native technology such as MPLS, Ethernet, or T1.

Telecommunications service providers often encapsulate older services, such as DS0, DS1, T1, and Frame Relay, over SONET networks.

The data rates available in SONET networks are shown in Table 5.3. Rates are expressed using the term optical carrier (OC) level.

TABLE 5.3 SONET OC levels

SONET OC level	Data rate
OC-1	51,840 Kbit/sec
OC-3	155,520 Kbit/sec
OC-12	622,080 Kbit/sec
OC-24	1,244,160 Kbit/sec
OC-48	2,488,320 Kbit/sec
OC-192	9,953,280 Kbit/sec
OC-768	39,813,120 Kbit/sec
OC-3072	159,252,240 Kbit/sec

T-carrier

The term *T-carrier* refers to a class of multiplexed telecommunications carrier network technologies developed to transport voice and data communications over long distances using copper cabling.

The basic service in T-carrier technology is known as DS0, which is used to transport a single voice or data circuit. The data rate for a DS0 is 64 Kbit/sec. Another basic T-carrier service is the DS1, also known as T1. DS1 contains 24 channels, each a DS0. The total speed of a DS1 is 1,544 Kbit/sec. There are additional services, all of which are shown, together with their respective data rates and channels, in Table 5.4. These services are unique to North America.

TABLE 5.4 T-carrier data rates and channels in North America

T-carrier class	Data rate	Number of DS0 channels
DS0	64 Kbit/sec	1
DS1 (T1)	1,544 Kbit/sec	24
DS2	6,312 Kbit/sec	96
DS3 (T3)	44,736 Kbit/sec	672
DS4	274,176 Kbit/sec	4,032
DS5	400,352 Kbit/sec	5,760

In Europe, T-carrier circuits are known instead as E1 and E3, which multiplex 32 and 512 64 Kbit/sec circuits, respectively. The European E-carrier standards are based on multiples of 32 circuits, whereas North American standards are based on multiples of 24 circuits. Otherwise, there isn't much practical difference between them. E-carrier services are shown in Table 5.5.

TABLE 5.5   E-carrier services

E-carrier class	Data rate
E1	2,048 Kbit/sec
E2	8 Mbit/sec
E3	34 Mbit/sec
E4	140 Mbit/sec

T-carrier and E-carrier protocols are synchronous, which means that packets transported on a T-carrier or E-carrier network are transmitted according to the pulses of a centralized clock that is usually controlled by the telecommunications carrier. This is contrasted with Ethernet, which is asynchronous, meaning a station on an Ethernet may transmit a frame at any time of its choosing (provided the network is not busy at that exact moment).

Organizations that use a T-carrier or E-carrier service to carry data can utilize individual DS0 channels (which are the same speed as a dial-up connection) or an entire T1 (or E1) circuit without multiplexing. This enables the use of the entire 1,544 Kbit/sec (T1) or 2,048 Kbit/sec (E1) as a single resource.

Frame Relay

Frame Relay is a carrier-based, packet-switched network technology. It is most often used to connect remote data networks to a centralized network; for example, a retail store chain might use Frame Relay to connect each of its retail store LANs to the corporate LAN.

Frame Relay is often more economical than dedicated DS0 or DS1/T1 circuits. By their nature, Frame Relay backbone networks are shared, in the sense that they transport packets for many customers.

Connections between locations using Frame Relay are made via a permanent virtual circuit (PVC), which is not unlike a VPN, except that the payload is not encrypted. For purposes of security and privacy, PVCs are generally considered private, like a T1 circuit.

Frame Relay has all but superseded the older X.25 services. Correspondingly, MPLS is rapidly overtaking Frame Relay.

ISDN

Integrated Services Digital Network (ISDN) is best described as a digital version of the public-switched telephone network. In many regions of the United States, ISDN was the first "high-speed" Internet access available for residential and small business subscribers.

A subscriber with ISDN service will have a digital modem with one connection to a digital ISDN voice telephone and one connection (typically Ethernet) to a computer. The speed of the computer connection in this configuration is 64 Kbits/sec. Alternatively, the ISDN modem could be configured in a "bonded" state with no voice telephone and only a computer connection at 128 Kbits/sec. Both configurations use a BRI (basic rate interface) type of connection.

Higher speeds, up to 1,544 Kbits/sec, are also available, and these are known as primary rate interface (PRI) connections.

ISDN utilizes a separate, but similar, environment where an ISDN modem "dials" a phone number, like dial-up Internet service.

ISDN has been replaced by Digital Subscriber Line (DSL) and other broadband technologies.

Wide Area Network Devices

This section describes devices used to connect WAN components to each other and to an organization's internal network.

Modem

A modulator-demodulator unit, also known as a modem, is a device used to connect a telecommunications carrier network to a computer or a LAN. Early modems consisted of an analog telephone connector for connecting to the public telephone network and a serial port for connecting to a computer. Later versions connect to ISDN, cable, and DSL networks and include an Ethernet port for connecting to a single computer or a LAN.

Multiplexer

A *multiplexer* connects several separate signals and combines them into a single data stream. There are four basic types of multiplexing:

- **Time division:** Separate signals are combined into a pattern, where each individual signal occupies a separate dedicated time slot.

- **Asynchronous time division multiplexing:** Separate signals are allocated into time slots of varying sizes depending on need.

- **Frequency division multiplexing:** Separate signals are combined into a single stream, where each separate signal occupies a nonoverlapping frequency.

- **Statistical multiplexing:** Separate signals are inserted into available time slots. This is different from time division multiplexing, where input signals are assigned to time slots. In statistical multiplexing, input signals are dynamically assigned to available time slots.

Channel Service Unit/Data Service Unit

Also known as a CSU/DSU, this device connects a telecommunications circuit (typically a T1 line) to a device such as a router. It is essentially a modem for T1 and similar telecom technologies.

WAN Switch

WAN *switch* is a general term that encompasses several types of WAN switching devices, including ATM switches, Frame Relay switches, MPLS switches, and ISDN switches. See the respective sections on these technologies earlier in this chapter.

Router

A *router* is a device used to connect two or more logical local (occupying the same subnet) networks together. In the context of WANs, a router would be used to connect two or more WANs to each other.

See also the discussion of routers in the "TCP/IP Protocols and Devices" section later in this chapter.

Wireless Networks

Several types of wireless technologies are available to organizations that want to implement data communications without constructing or maintaining a wiring plant. Furthermore, wireless networks permit devices to move from place to place, even outside of buildings, facilitating highly flexible and convenient means for high-speed communications.

The technologies discussed in this section are the type that an organization would set up on its own, without any services required from a telecommunications service provider.

Wi-Fi

Wi-Fi describes several similar standards developed around the IEEE 802.11a/b/g/ac/ax/be/n standards. Wi-Fi, or WLAN, permits computers to communicate with each other wirelessly at high speeds over moderate distances from each other. The term *Wi-Fi* is a trademark of the Wi-Fi Alliance for certifying products as compatible with IEEE 802.11 standards. The generic term describing networks based on IEEE 802.11 standards is wireless LAN, or WLAN, although this term is not often used.

Wi-Fi Standards

The various Wi-Fi standards are outlined in Table 5.6.

TABLE 5.6 Comparison of Wi-Fi standards

Standard	Year introduced	Maximum data rate	Indoor range
802.11a	1999	54 Mbit/sec	35 m
802.11b	1999	11 Mbit/sec	38 m
802.11g	2003	54 Mbit/sec	38 m
802.11n	2009	150 Mbit/sec	70 m
802.11ac	2013	780 Mbit/sec	35 m
802.11ax	2021	9.608 Gbit/sec	30 m
802.11be	Expected 2024	23.059 Gbit/sec	35 m

Wi-Fi Security

Wi-Fi networks can be configured with several security features that protect the privacy as well as the availability of the Wi-Fi network. Available features include:

- **Authentication:** Individual stations that want to connect with a Wi-Fi network can be required to provide an encryption key. Furthermore, the user may be required to provide a user ID and password. Without this information, a station is unable to connect to the Wi-Fi network and communicate with it. Wi-Fi access points can contain a list of user IDs and passwords, or they can be configured to utilize a network-based authentication service such as RADIUS, LDAP, or Active Directory. Use of the latter generally makes more sense for organizations that want to centralize user authentication information; this also makes access simpler for employees, who do not need to remember yet another user ID and password.

- **Access control:** A Wi-Fi network can be configured to permit only stations with known MAC addresses or specific digital certificates to connect to it. Any station without a permitted address or certificate will not be able to connect.

- **Encryption:** A Wi-Fi network can use encryption to protect traffic from interception through over-the-air eavesdropping. It can encrypt with the WEP (Wired Equivalent Privacy; now deprecated and should not be used), WPA (Wi-Fi Protected Access), WPA2, or WPA3 method. A Wi-Fi network can also be configured not to use encryption, in which case another station may be able to eavesdrop on any communications on the wireless network. When a Wi-Fi network uses encryption, only the airlink communications are encrypted; network traffic from the Wi-Fi access point to other networks will not be encrypted.

- **Network identifier:** A Wi-Fi access point is configured with a service set identifier (SSID) that identifies the network. For organizations that provide network access only for their own personnel, it is recommended that the SSID not be set to a value that makes the ownership or identity of the access point obvious. Using a company name, for instance, is not a good idea. Instead, a word—even a random set of characters—that does not relate to the organization's identity should be used. The reason for this is that the SSID will not itself identify the owner of the network, which could, in some circumstances, invite outsiders to attempt to access it. An exception to this is a "public hot spot" used to provide free network access, where the SSID will clearly identify the establishment providing access.

- **Broadcast:** A Wi-Fi access point can be configured to broadcast its SSID, making it easier for users to discover and connect to the network. However, broadcasting SSIDs also alerts outsiders to the presence of the network, which can compromise network security by encouraging someone to attempt to connect to it. However, turning off the SSID broadcast does not make the network absolutely secure: a determined intruder can obtain tools that will enable them to discover the presence of a Wi-Fi network that does not broadcast its SSID.

- **Signal strength:** The transmit signal strength of a Wi-Fi access point can be configured so that radio signals from the access point do not significantly exceed the service area. Often, signal strength of access points will be set to maximum, which provides persons outside the physical premises with a strong signal. Instead, transmit signal strength should be turned down so that as small a signal as possible leaves the physical premises. This is a challenge in shared-space office buildings, however, and thus cannot be used as a Wi-Fi network's only security control.

> Because a Wi-Fi network uses radio signals, an untrusted outsider can intercept those signals, which could provide enough information for that outsider to penetrate the network. It is for this reason that all the controls discussed in this section should be utilized to provide effective defense-in-depth security protection.

WiMAX

WiMAX (Worldwide Interoperability for Microwave Access) is a set of wireless telecommunications protocols that provides data throughput from 30 Mbit/sec to 1 Gbit/sec. WiMAX is an implementation of the IEEE 802.16 standard.

WiMAX networks were in service in the 2000s but have been largely discontinued in favor of LTE.

LTE

LTE (Long-Term Evolution) is a telecommunications standard for wireless voice and data communications for smartphones, mobile devices, and wireless broadband modems. LTE is a shared-medium technology that provides data rates up to 300 Mbit/sec.

5G

5G represents the latest generation of telecommunications standards for wireless voice and data for mobile devices. Like LTE, 5G is a shared-medium protocol capable of throughput up to 10 Gbit/sec.

LEOS

Low earth orbit satellite (LEOS) services provide Internet access to customers using satellites in low earth orbit. LEOS services are popular for customers located in rural areas not served by terrestrial broadband services such as DSL, DOCSIS, and FTTH. LEOS providers include Starlink, OneWeb, and Project Kuiper.

Bluetooth

Bluetooth is a short-range airlink standard for data communications between computer peripherals and low-power consumption devices. Designed as a replacement for short-range cabling, Bluetooth also provides security via authentication and encryption.

Applications using Bluetooth include:

- Mobile phone ear sets
- In-car audio for smartphones
- Data transfer between smartphones and computers
- Music player headphones
- Computer mice, keyboards, and other low-power and low-speed peripherals
- Printers and scanners

Bluetooth is a lower-power standard, which supports the use of very small devices, such as mobile phone ear sets. And yet, a new standard, Bluetooth Low Energy (BLE), uses far less power for devices such as security tokens. The Bluetooth standard includes one-time authentication of devices using a process called pairing. Communications over Bluetooth can also be encrypted so that any eavesdropping is made ineffective. Data rates range from 1 to 24 Mbit/sec.

WUSB

Wireless USB (WUSB) is a short-range, high-bandwidth wireless protocol used for personal area networks (PANs). Data rates range from 110 to 480 Mbit/sec. WUSB is typically used to connect computer peripherals that would otherwise be connected with cables.

WUSB can be thought of as a competitor to Bluetooth, and due to Bluetooth's success, WUSB is not widely used.

NFC

Near-Field Communication (NFC) is a standard of extremely short-distance radio frequencies that are commonly used for merchant payment applications. The typical maximum range for NFC is 10 centimeters (4 in.).

NFC supports two types of communications: active-active and active-passive. In active-active mode, the base station and the wireless node electronically transmit messages over the NFC airlink. In active-passive mode, the wireless node has no active power supply and instead behaves more like an RFID (radio frequency identification) card. Throughput rates range from 106 to 848 Kbit/sec.

Common applications of NFC include merchant payments using a mobile phone or credit card–sized card, and advanced building access control systems.

TCP/IP Protocols and Devices

TCP/IP, the technology that the Internet is built upon, contains numerous protocols. This section discusses many of the well-known protocols, layer by layer. First, link layer protocols are discussed, followed by Internet layer protocols, then transport layer protocols, and finally application layer protocols. This is followed by a discussion of network devices that are used to build TCP/IP networks.

Link Layer Protocols

The *link layer* (sometimes referred to as the network access layer) is the lowest logical layer in the TCP/IP protocol suite. Several protocols have been implemented as link layer protocols, including:

- **ARP (Address Resolution Protocol):** This protocol is used when a station on a network needs to find another station's MAC address when it knows its Internet layer (IP) address. Basically, a station sends a broadcast on a local network, asking, in effect, "What station on this network has IP address xx.xx.xx.xx?" If any station on the network does have this IP address, it responds to the sender. When the sending station receives the reply, the receiving station's MAC address is contained in the reply, and the sending station can now send messages to the destination station since it knows its MAC address. Another type of ARP message is known as a gratuitous ARP message that informs other stations on the network of the station's IP and MAC addresses, regardless of whether it was requested to do so or not. Gratuitous ARP messages can be used in network attacks and are often blocked by the switch.

- **RARP (Reverse Address Resolution Protocol):** This protocol is used by a station that needs to know its own Internet layer (IP) address. A station sends a broadcast on a local network, asking, "This is my MAC address (xx.xx.xx.xx.xx.xx). What is my IP address supposed to be?" If a station configured to respond to RARP requests exists on the network, it will respond to the querying station with an assigned IP address. RARP has been largely superseded by BOOTP (Bootstrap Protocol) and later by DHCP.

- **OSPF (Open Shortest Path First):** This routing protocol is implemented in the TCP/IP Internet layer. The purpose and function of routing protocols are discussed in detail later in this section.

- **L2TP (Layer 2 Tunneling Protocol):** This tunneling protocol is implemented in the link layer. The purpose and function of tunneling protocols are discussed later in this section.

- **PPP (Point-to-Point Protocol):** This packet-oriented protocol is used mainly over point-to-point physical connections such as RS-232 or HSSI (High-Speed Serial Interface) between computers.

- **Media Access Control (MAC):** This is the underlying communications standard used by various media such as Ethernet, DSL, MPLS, and ISDN.

Internet Layer Protocols

Internet layer protocols are the fundamental building blocks of TCP/IP. The Internet layer is the lowest layer where a frame or packet is uniquely TCP/IP.

Protocols in the TCP/IP Internet layer include:

- IP
- ICMP
- IGMP
- IPsec

IP

IP is the principal protocol used by TCP/IP at the Internet layer. The main transport layer protocols (discussed in the next section), TCP and UDP, are built on IP. The purpose of IP is to transport messages over internetworked networks. IP is the workhorse of the TCP/IP protocol suite: most communications used on the Internet are built on it.

Characteristics of IP include:

- **IP addressing:** At the IP layer, nodes on networks have unique addresses. IP addressing is discussed in detail later in this section.

- **Best-effort delivery:** IP does not guarantee that a packet will reach its intended destination.

- **Connectionless:** Each packet is individual and not related to any other packet.

- **Out-of-order packet delivery:** No assurances for order of delivery are addressed by IP. Packets may arrive out of order at their destination.

Higher-layer protocols such as TCP address reliability, connections, and sequence of delivery.

Multicast

Multicast is a method for sending IP packets to multiple stations in a one-to-many fashion. This enables a sender to send a single packet to any number of receivers. Multicast traffic originates from the IP network range 224.0.0.0/24.

Network infrastructure, such as switches and routers, take care of the task of receiving individual multicast packets and relaying them to all receivers.

The list of receivers for any given multicast is maintained in multicast groups. Group membership can change in real time without involvement from the originator of the multicast traffic. The protocol used to manage group membership is the Internet Group Management Protocol (IGMP).

ICMP

ICMP is used by systems for diagnostic purposes. Primarily, ICMP messages are automatically issued whenever there are problems with IP communications between two stations. For example, if one station attempts to send a message to another station, and a router on the network knows that there is no existing route to the destination station, the router will send an ICMP Type 3, Code 1 "No route to host" diagnostic packet back to the sending station to inform it that the destination station is not reachable.

ICMP message types are shown in Table 5.7.

TABLE 5.7 ICMP message types

ICMP message type	Definition
0	Echo reply
1	(reserved)

ICMP message type	Definition
2	(reserved)
3	Destination unreachable (contains 14 subcodes that describe the reason in detail)
4	Source quench
5	Redirect message (with 4 subcodes)
6	Alternate host address
7	(reserved)
8	Echo request
9	Router advertisement
10	Router solicitation
11	Time exceeded (with 2 reason subcodes)
12	Parameter problem: bad IP header (with 3 reason subcodes)
13	Time stamp
14	Time stamp reply
15	Information request
16	Information reply
17	Address mask request
18	Address mask reply
19–29	(reserved)
30	Traceroute
31–255	(seldom used or reserved for future use)

The well-known ping command uses the ICMP 8 Echo request packet type. If the target station is reachable, it will respond with ICMP 1 Echo reply packets. The ping command is used to determine whether a particular system is reachable from another system over a TCP/IP network.

NOTE The absence of a response to a ping message does not necessarily mean that the system does not exist or is not communicating. Some organizations block ICMP Echo request messages at their network boundaries for security purposes.

IGMP

IGMP provides a type of communications called multicast. Multicast is discussed earlier in this section.

IPsec

The *IPsec* suite of protocols is used to secure IP-based communication. The security that IPsec provides is in the form of authentication and encryption.

IPsec authentication is used to confirm the identity of a station on a network. This is used to prevent a rogue system from easily masquerading as another, real system. Authentication is achieved through the establishment of a security association (SA) between two nodes, which permits the transmission of data from the originating node to the destination node. If the two nodes need to send messages in both directions, two SAs need to be established. The Internet Key Exchange (IKE) protocol is used to set up associations.

IPsec has two primary modes of operation:

- **Transport mode:** Only the payload of an incoming packet is authenticated or encrypted. The original IP header is left intact. The original headers are protected with hashes; if the headers are altered, the hashes will fail, and an error will occur.

- **Tunnel mode:** Each entire incoming packet is encapsulated within an IPsec packet. The entire incoming packet can be encrypted, which protects the packet against eavesdropping. This mode is often used for protecting network traffic that traverses the Internet, thereby creating a VPN between two nodes, between two networks, or between a remote node and a network. IPsec tunnel mode is shown in Figure 5.19.

FIGURE 5.19   IPsec tunnel mode protects all traffic between two remote networks.

Internet Layer Node Addressing: IPv4

To specify the source and destination of messages, TCP/IP utilizes a numeric address scheme. In TCP/IP, a station's address is known as an "IP address." On a given network, no two stations will have the same IP address; this uniqueness permits any station to communicate directly with any other station.

The TCP/IP address scheme also includes a subnet mask, which permits a station to determine whether any particular IP address resides on the same subnetwork. Furthermore, an IP address plan usually includes a default gateway, a station on the network that can forward messages to stations on other subnets or networks.

IP Addresses and Subnets

The notation of an IP address is four sets of integers, separated by periods. The value of each integer may range from 0 through 255; hence, each integer is an 8-bit value. A typical IP address is 141.204.13.240. The entire IP address is 32 bits in length.

Each station on a network is assigned a unique IP address. Uniqueness permits any station to send messages to any other station; the station needs to know only the IP address of a destination station.

A larger organization may have hundreds, thousands, or even tens of thousands of stations on many networks. Typically, a network is the interconnection of computers within a single building or even part of a building. Within a larger building or collection of buildings, the individual networks are called subnetworks, or subnets. Those subnets are joined together by network devices such as routers or switches; they function as gateways between networks.

Subnet Mask

A *subnet mask* is a numeric value that determines which portion of an IP address is used to identify the network and which portion is used to identify a station on the network.

For example, an organization has the network 141.204.13. On this network the organization can have up to 256 stations, numbered 0 through 255. Example station IP addresses on the network are 141.204.13.5, 141.204.13.15, and 141.204.13.200.

A subnet mask actually works at the bit level. A "1" signifies that a bit in the same position in an IP address is the network identifier, whereas a "0" signifies that a bit in the same position is part of the station's address. In the previous example, where the first three numbers in the IP address signify the network, the subnet mask would be 255.255.255.0. This is illustrated in Figure 5.20.

FIGURE 5.20   A subnet mask denotes which part of an IP address signifies a network and which part signifies a station on the network.

Station IP Address	141.204.13.15	10001101.11001100.00001101.00001111
Subnet Mask	255.255.255.0	11111111.11111111.11111111.00000000
Network Portion	141.204.13.0	10001101.11001100.00001101.00000000
Station Portion	0.0.0.15	00000000.00000000.00000000.00001111

Network Address   Station Address

Default Gateway

Networks are usually interconnected so that a station on one network can communicate with a station on any other connected network (subject to any security restrictions). When a station wants to send a packet to another station, the sending station will examine its own network ID (by comparing its IP address to the subnet mask) and compare that to the IP address of the destination. If the destination station is on the same network, the station may simply send the packet directly to the destination station.

If, however, the destination station is on a different network, the sending station cannot send the packet to it directly. Instead, the sending station will send the packet to a node called the default gateway—usually a router that has knowledge of neighboring and distant networks and is capable of forwarding packets toward their destination. Any network that is interconnected to other networks will have a default gateway, which is where all packets for "other" or "unknown" networks are sent. The default gateway will forward the packet closer to its ultimate destination. A default gateway can be thought of as "the way out of this network to all other networks."

For example, suppose a station at IP address 141.204.13.15 wants to send a packet to a station at IP address 141.204.21.110. The sending station's subnet mask is 255.255.255.0, which means it is on network 141.204.13. This is a different network from 141.204.21.110, so the sending station will send the packet instead to the default gateway at 141.204.13.1, a router that can forward the packet to 141.204.21.110.

When the packet reaches a router that is connected to the 141.204.21 network, that router can send the packet directly to the destination station, which is on the same network as the router.

Classful Networks

The original plan for subnets and subnet masks allowed for the network/node address boundary to align with the decimals in IP addresses. This was expressed in several classes of networks, shown in Table 5.8.

TABLE 5.8   Classes of networks

Class	Subnet mask	Number of stations per network
A	255.0.0.0	16,777,216
B	255.255.0.0	65,536
C	255.255.255.0	256

The matter of the shortage of usable IP addresses in the global Internet is related to classful networks. This is discussed later in this chapter in the section, "The Global Internet."

Classless Networks

It became clear that the rigidity of Class A, Class B, and Class C networks as the only ways to create subnets was wasteful. For instance, the smallest subnet available was a Class C network with its 256 available addresses. If a given subnet had only one station on it, the other 255 addresses were wasted and unused. This situation gave rise to classless networks, where subnet masks could divide networks at any arbitrary boundary.

Classless networks don't have names like the classful networks' Class A, Class B, and Class C. Instead, they just have subnet masks that help to serve the purpose of preserving IP addresses and allocating them more efficiently. The method, classless inter-domain routing (CIDR), is used to create subnets with any arbitrary subnet mask.

Table 5.9 shows some example subnet masks that can be used to allocate IP addresses to smaller networks.

TABLE 5.9 Classless network subnet masks

Subnet mask (decimal)	Subnet mask (binary)	CIDR notation	Number of nodes
255.255.255.254	11111111.11111111.11111111.11111110	/31	2
255.255.255.252	11111111.11111111.11111111.11111100	/30	4
255.255.255.248	11111111.11111111.11111111.11111000	/29	8
255.255.255.240	11111111.11111111.11111111.11110000	/28	16
255.255.255.224	11111111.11111111.11111111.11100000	/27	32
255.255.255.192	11111111.11111111.11111111.11000000	/26	64
255.255.255.128	11111111.11111111.11111111.10000000	/25	128
255.255.255.0	11111111.11111111.11111111.00000000	/24	256

A more rapid way of expressing an IP address with its accompanying subnet mask has been developed, where the number of bits in the subnet mask follows the IP address after a slash. For example, the IP address 141.204.13.15/26 means the subnet mask is the first 26 bits (in binary) of the IP address, or 255.255.255.192. This is easier than expressing the IP address and subnet mask separately.

Virtual Networks (VLANs)

In the preceding discussions of IP addresses and subnets, the classic design of TCP/IP LANs specifies that LANs are physically separate. Each LAN will have its own physical cabling and devices.

Virtual networks (VLANs) are logically separate networks that occupy the same physical network. VLANs are made possible through advanced configuration of network devices, including switches and routers.

The primary advantage of VLAN technology is the cost savings realized using fewer network cables and devices. Another advantage of VLAN technology is the ability to divide a single network into logically separate networks, thereby creating smaller broadcast domains and reducing the potential for information leakage.

The main disadvantage is that, though they are logically separate, VLANs occupy a single physical medium: Traffic on one VLAN has the potential to disrupt traffic on other VLANs, since they must share the physical network. Even with QoS capabilities, a given physical network has finite bandwidth that all VLANs must share.

Special IP Addresses

Other IP addresses are used in IP that have not been discussed thus far. These other addresses and their functions are:

- **Loopback:** The IP address 127.0.0.1 (or any other address in the entire 127 address block) is a special "loopback" address that is analogous to earlier technologies, where a physical loopback plug would be connected to a network connector to confirm communications within a system or device. The 127.0.0.1 loopback address serves the same function. If a system attempts to connect to a system at IP address 127.0.0.1, it is essentially communicating with itself. A system that can connect to itself through its loopback address is testing its IP drivers within the operating system; during network troubleshooting, it is common to issue a ping 127.0.0.1 or similar command to verify whether the computer's IP software is functioning correctly.

- **Broadcast:** The highest numeric IP address in an IP subnet is its broadcast address. When a packet is sent to a network's broadcast address, all active stations on the network will logically receive and potentially act on the incoming message. For example, in the network 141.204.13/24, the broadcast address is 141.204.13.255. Any packet sent to that address would be sent to all stations. A ping command sent to a network's broadcast address will cause all stations to respond with an Echo reply.

Internet Layer Node Addressing: IPv6

The IP version IPv4 had several shortcomings, namely in the total number of available IP addresses for use in the global Internet. The new version, IPv6, takes care of the problem of available addresses, as well as other matters.

The total number of IP addresses available in IPv4 is 2^{32}, or 4,294,967,296 addresses. Because IP was originally designed prior to the proliferation of network-enabled devices, over 4 billion available IP addresses seemed more than sufficient to meet world demand. The number of IP addresses available in IPv6 is 2^{128}, or about 3.4×10^{38} addresses.

Many new network-enabled devices support IPv6, which is enabling organizations to slowly migrate their networks. However, it is expected that IPv4 will be with us for many years. Network devices today support "dual-stack" networks where IPv4 and IPv6 coexist on the same network medium.

The format of an IPv6 address is eight groups of four hexadecimal digits, separated by colons. For example:

2001:0db8:0000:0042:0000:07cc:1028:1948

Unlike IPv4 with its various schemes of subnetting, the standard size of an IPv6 subnet is 64 bits. Protocols for assigning addresses to individual nodes, such as stateless address auto-configuration, generally work with /64 networks.

Transport Layer Protocols

The two principal protocols in TCP/IP's transport layer are TCP and UDP. Many Internet communications are based on these. This section explores TCP and UDP in detail.

TCP and UDP support the two primary types of Internet-based communication: that which requires highly reliable and ordered message delivery, and that which has a high tolerance for lost messages, respectively. TCP and UDP are uniquely designed for these two scenarios.

TCP

TCP is a highly reliable messaging protocol that is used in situations where high-integrity messaging is required. The main characteristics of TCP-based network traffic are:

- **Unique connections:** TCP utilizes a connection between two stations. TCP supports several concurrent connections between any two stations, potentially numbering in the tens of thousands.

- **Guaranteed message integrity:** TCP performs checks on the sent and received segments to ensure that the segments arrived at their destination fully intact. If the checksum indicates that the segment was altered in transit, TCP will handle retransmission.

- **Guaranteed delivery:** TCP guarantees message delivery. This means that if an application sends a message to another application over an established TCP connection and the function sending the message receives a "success" code from the operating system, then the message was successfully delivered to the destination system. This is contrasted with the message delivery used by UDP, which is discussed later in this section.

- **Guaranteed delivery sequence:** Segments sent using TCP include sequence numbers so that the destination system can assemble arriving segments into the correct order. This guarantees that an application receiving segments from a sending application over TCP can be confident that segments are arriving in the same order in which they were sent.

UDP

UDP is a lightweight messaging protocol used in situations where speed and low overhead are more important than guaranteed delivery and delivery sequence.

Unlike the connection-oriented TCP, UDP is connectionless. This means that UDP does not need to set up a connection between sending and receiving systems before datagrams can be sent; instead, the sending system just sends its datagrams to the destination system. Like TCP, datagrams can be sent to a specific port number on a destination system.

UDP does nothing to assure order of delivery. Hence, it is entirely possible that datagrams may arrive at the destination system out of order. In practice, this is a rarity, but the point is that UDP does not make any effort to reassemble datagrams into their original order upon arrival.

One might ask, why use UDP with all these shortcomings? The answer is efficiency and throughput. Without the overhead of connections and acknowledgment for every packet, UDP is simpler and requires far less bandwidth than TCP.

Protocol Data Units (PDUs)

In the telecommunications and network industry, discrete terms are used to signify the messages that are created at various layers of encapsulated protocols such as TCP/IP. These terms include:

Technology	PDU
Network cable	Bit
Ethernet	Frame
ATM	Cell
TCP	Segment
UDP	Datagram
IP	Packet

Frequently, the term *packet* is used to signify messages at every layer, although it is useful to know the specific terms used for each.

Furthermore, not only does UDP not guarantee the sequence of delivery, it also does not even guarantee that the destination system will receive a datagram. In UDP, when an application sends a message to a target system, the "success" error code returned by the operating system means only that the datagram was sent. The sending system receives no confirmation that the datagram was received by the destination system.

Application Layer Protocols

Scores of protocols have been developed for the TCP/IP application layer. Several are discussed in this section; they are grouped by the type of service that they provide.

- **FTP (File Transfer Protocol):** An early and still widely used protocol for batch transfer of files or entire directories from one system to another. FTP is supported by most modern operating systems, including Unix, macOS, and Windows. One drawback of FTP is that the login credentials (and all data) are transmitted unencrypted, which means that anyone eavesdropping on network communications can easily intercept them and reuse them for potentially malicious purposes.

- **FTPS (File Transfer Protocol Secure, or FTP-SSL):** This is an extension of the FTP protocol in which authentication and file transfer are encrypted using SSL or TLS.

- **SFTP (SSH File Transfer Protocol):** This is an extension to the FTP protocol where authentication and file transfer are encrypted using SSH.

- **SCP (Secure Copy Protocol):** This is a file transfer protocol that is like rcp (remote copy), but which is protected using SSH.

- **rcp (remote copy):** This is an early Unix-based file transfer protocol that is used to copy files or directories from system to system. The main drawback with rcp is the lack of encryption of credentials for transferred data.

- **SMTP (Simple Mail Transfer Protocol):** This is the protocol used to transport virtually all email over the Internet. SMTP is used to route email messages from their source over the Internet to a destination email server. It is an early protocol that lacks authentication and encryption. It is partly for this reason that people should consider their email to be nonprivate.

- **SMTPS (Simple Mail Transfer Protocol Secure):** This is a security-enhanced version of SMTP that incorporates TLS. It is sometimes known as "SMTP over TLS."

- **POP (Post Office Protocol):** This is a protocol used by an end-user email program to retrieve messages from an email server. POP is not particularly secure because user credentials and messages are transported without encryption; POP version 3 (POP3) can utilize encryption and is preferred over earlier versions.

- **IMAP (Internet Message Access Protocol):** Like POP, this protocol is used by an end-user program to retrieve email messages from an email server.

- **NNTP (Network News Transfer Protocol):** This is the protocol used to transport Usenet news throughout the Internet, and from news servers to end users using news-reading programs. Usenet news has been largely deprecated by web-based applications.

- **NFS (Network File System):** This protocol was developed to make a disk-based resource on another computer appear as a logical volume on a local computer. The NFS protocol transmits the disk requests and replies over the network.

- **RPC (Remote Procedure Call):** This protocol is used to permit a running process to make a procedure call to a process running on another computer. RPC supports a variety of functions that permit various types of client-server computing.

- **Telnet:** This is an early protocol that is used to establish a command-line session on a remote computer. Telnet does not encrypt user credentials as they are transmitted over the network.

- **rlogin:** This is an early Unix-based protocol used to establish a command-line session on a remote system. Like Telnet, rlogin does not encrypt authentication or session contents.

- **SSH (Secure Shell):** This protocol provides a secure channel between two computers whereby all communications between them are encrypted. SSH can also be used as a tunnel to encapsulate and thereby protect other protocols.

- **HTTP (Hypertext Transfer Protocol):** This protocol is used to transmit web page contents from web servers to users who are using web browsers.

- **HTTPS (Hypertext Transfer Protocol Secure):** This is like HTTP in its use for transporting data between web servers and browsers. HTTPS is not a separate protocol, but instead is the instance where HTTP is encrypted with SSL or TLS.

- **RDP (Remote Desktop Protocol):** This proprietary protocol from Microsoft is used to establish a graphical console interface to another computer.

- **SNMP (Simple Network Management Protocol):** This protocol is used by network devices and systems to transmit management messages indicating a need for administrative attention. SNMP is used to monitor networks and their components; SNMP messages are generated when events warrant attention by network engineers or system engineers. In larger organizations, SNMP messages are collected by a network management system that displays the network topology and devices that require attention.

- **NTP (Network Time Protocol):** This protocol is used to synchronize the time-of-day clocks on systems, using time-reference standards. The use of NTP is vital because the time clocks in computers often drift (run too fast or too slow), and it is important for all computers' time clocks in an organization to be precisely the same so that complex events can be more easily managed and correlated.

- **DNS (Domain Name System):** This is a vital Internet-based service that is used to translate domain names (such as www.isecbooks.com) into IP addresses. A call to a DNS server is a prerequisite for system-to-system communications where one system wants to establish a communications session with another system and where it knows only the domain name for the target system.

- **LDAP (Lightweight Directory Access Protocol):** This protocol is used as a directory service for people and computing resources. LDAP is frequently used as an enterprise authentication and computing resource service. Microsoft Active Directory is an adaptation of LDAP.

- **X.500:** This protocol is a functional predecessor to LDAP that provides directory services.

TCP/IP Network Devices

Network devices are required to facilitate the transmission of packets among TCP/IP networks. These devices include:

- **Router:** This device is used to connect two or more separate TCP/IP networks to each other. A router typically has two or more network interface connectors, each of which is connected to a separate network. A router that is used to connect LANs is typically equipped with Ethernet interfaces, whereas a router used to connect LANs with WANs will have one or more Ethernet connectors and one or more connectors for WAN protocols such as SONET or MPLS. A router may also have an access control list (ACL, which is functionally like a firewall) that the router uses to determine whether packets passing through it should be permitted to proceed to their destination.

- **Firewall:** This device is used to control which network packets are permitted to cross network boundaries. Typically, a firewall will block or permit packets to pass based on their source IP address, destination IP address, and protocol. Firewalls are typically used at an organization's network boundary to protect it from unwanted network traffic from the Internet but still permit traffic to the organization's email and web servers, for instance.

- **Application firewall:** This device is used to control packets being sent to an application server, blocking those that contain unwanted or malicious content. An application firewall can help to protect a web server from attacks such as SQL injection or buffer overflow.

- **Intrusion prevention system (IPS):** This device is used to detect and potentially block network packets that may be malicious.

- **Proxy server:** This device is typically used to control end-user access to websites on the Internet. A proxy server typically controls access according to policy.

- **Layer 3 switch:** This device routes packets between different VLANs. Functionally, this is the same as a router; a router performs network routing using software running on a microprocessor, whereas a layer 3 switch performs this routing using a dedicated application-specific integrated circuit (ASIC), giving it much better performance than a router.

- **Layer 4 switch:** This device is used to route packets to destinations based on TCP and UDP port numbers.

- **Layer 4–7 switch:** Also known as a content switch, web switch, or application switch, this device routes packets to destinations based on their internal content. Layer 4–7 switches can intelligently route incoming network traffic to various servers based on policy, performance, or availability.

Interestingly, the names of layer 3, layer 4, and layer 4–7 switches are based on their OSI network model layers even though these are TCP network devices.

Other network devices such as hubs, switches, and gateways are discussed in the section, "Ethernet," earlier in this chapter.

Software-Defined Networking

Software-defined networking (SDN) is a new class of capabilities where network infrastructure is created, configured, and managed in the context of virtualization. In SDN, routers, firewalls, switches, IPSs, and other network devices are no longer physical devices but software programs that run in virtualized environments.

SDN gives organizations greater agility regarding their network infrastructure: instead of procuring additional network devices as network infrastructure needs grow and change, virtual network devices are instantiated and deployed immediately.

Organizations and groups of organizations are developing SDN standards, such as Open-Flow, to build consistent practices to SDN.

The Global Internet

The TCP/IP networks owned by businesses, government, military, and educational institutions are interconnected; collectively this is known as the global Internet—or just the Internet. It is in the context of the global Internet that TCP/IP topics such as node addressing, routing, domain naming, and other matters are most relevant.

IP Addressing

The allocation of routable IP addresses is coordinated through a central governing body known as the Internet Assigned Numbers Authority (IANA). This coordination is necessary so that duplicate addresses are not allocated, which would cause confusion and unreachable systems.

The original IP address allocation scheme appears in Table 5.10.

TABLE 5.10   Internet IP address allocation

Addresses	Name	Total number of networks available	Addresses per network
1.0.0.0–126.255.255.255	Class A networks	126	16,777,124
128.0.0.0–191.255.255.255	Class B networks	16,384	65,532
192.0.0.0–223.255.255.255	Class C networks	2,097,152	254

When TCP/IP was established, the entire IP address space (that is, the entire range of possible addresses from 1.1.1.1 through 255.255.255.255) appeared to be far more than would ever be needed. However, it soon became apparent that the original IP address allocation scheme was woefully inadequate. This led to the establishment of ranges for private networks and rules for their use. Private address ranges are listed in Table 5.11.

TABLE 5.11   Private address ranges

Address range	Available addresses
10.0.0.0–10.255.255.255	16,777,214
172.16.0.0–172.31.255.255	1,048,576
192.168.0.0–192.168.255.255	131,072

The availability of a sufficient number of publicly routable IP addresses has been addressed with IPv6. See the sidebar on IPv6 earlier in this chapter.

 NOTE The number of available addresses does not take network IDs and broadcast addresses into account, which will lower the number of actual addresses. This will vary based on how networks are subnetted.

The private addresses listed in Table 5.11 are not "routable." This means that no router on the Internet is permitted to forward a packet with any IP address within any of the private address ranges. These IP addresses are intended for use wholly within organizations to facilitate communication among internal systems. When any system with a private address needs to communicate with a system on the Internet, its communication is required to pass through a gateway that will translate the internal IP address to a public routable IP address. The NAT (Network Address Translation) method is often used for this purpose.

Domain Name System

The Internet utilizes the *Domain Name System (DNS)*, a centrally coordinated domain name registration system. Several independent domain registrars are licensed to issue new domain names to individuals and corporations in exchange for modest fees. These domain registrars often also provide DNS services on behalf of each domain name's owner.

New and changed domain names are periodically uploaded to the Internet's "root" DNS servers, enabling users to access services by referring to domain names such as www.myblogsite.com.

Network Routing

Routers used by Internet service providers (ISPs) receive and forward IP traffic to and from any of the millions of systems that are connected to the Internet. These big routers exchange information on the whereabouts of all publicly reachable networks in large "routing tables" that contain rules about the topology of the Internet and the addresses and locations of networks. Internet routers exchange this information with routing protocols, which are "out-of-band" messages that contain updates to the topology and IP addressing of the Internet. Some of these protocols are:

- BGP (Border Gateway Protocol)
- OSPF (Open Shortest Path First)
- IGRP (Interior Gateway Routing Protocol)
- EIGRP (Enhanced Interior Gateway Routing Protocol)
- EGP (Exterior Gateway Protocol, now obsolete)
- IS-IS (Intermediate System to Intermediate System)
- RIP (Routing Information Protocol; this is one of the earliest protocols and no longer used for Internet routing)

Organizations with several internal networks also use one or more of these routing protocols so that their routers can keep track of the changing topology and addressing of their networks.

Global Internet Applications

Applications are what make the Internet popular. From electronic banking to e-commerce, entertainment, news, television, and movies, applications on the Internet have made it possible for people anywhere to view or receive virtually any kind of information and content.

The World Wide Web

The *World Wide Web* encompasses all the world's web servers, which are accessible from workstations of many types that use web browser programs. Requests to web servers, and content returned to browsers, are issued using HTTP and HTTPS. Content sent to browsers consists primarily of text written in HTML, as well as rich text, including images and dynamic content such as audio and video.

The World Wide Web rapidly gained popularity because information and applications could be accessed from anywhere without any special software. Readily available tools simplified the publication of many types of data on the web.

The most critical service that supports the World Wide Web is DNS. This service translates server domain names into IP addresses. For example, if a user wants to visit www.wiley.com, the operating system running the user's browser will make a request to a local DNS server for the IP address corresponding to www.wiley.com. After the DNS server responds with the server's IP address, the user's browser can issue a request to the server (at 172.64.145.177) and then receive content from the server.

Web servers can act as application servers. Authenticated users can receive menus, data entry screens and forms, query results, and reports, all written in HTML, all with only web browser software. Web servers that function as application servers have built-in protocols to communicate with backend application servers and database management systems.

Email

Electronic mail was one of the Internet's first applications. Although email existed before the Internet, it was implemented on the Internet to send messages not only within organizations but also between them. The SMTP, POP, and IMAP protocols were developed and adopted early on and are still widely used today. SMTP remains the backbone of Internet email transport. Organizations are increasingly using SMTPS to protect the contents of email messages.

Instant Messaging

Email, while far more rapid than postal-delivered letters, can still be slow at times. Instant messaging (IM), originally developed on DEC PDP-11 computers in the 1970s and on Unix in the early 1980s, was adapted to the Internet in the early 1990s. Like all other Internet applications, IM is based on the TCP/IP protocol suite and enables people all over the world to communicate in real time via text, voice, and video.

Messaging and Collaboration

Numerous *messaging and collaboration* tools have been developed and are used that help groups, teams, and departments work together more effectively. These tools include Microsoft Teams, Slack, and Discord.

Web Conferencing

Web and videoconferencing platforms facilitate remote meetings. These platforms greatly eased what would otherwise be considered communication friction during the COVID-19 pandemic, when most office workers and students were directed to work from home for months at a time. These tools include Zoom, BlueJeans, Microsoft Teams, Google Meet, Webex, and GoTo Meeting. These and other platforms feature videoconferencing, breakout rooms, screen and file sharing, polls, whiteboards, and other features.

Network Tunneling

Tunneling refers to protocols that permit communications between two endpoints to be encapsulated in a logical "tunnel." Often, a tunnel is used to protect communications containing sensitive data that is transported over public networks such as the Internet. Packets in a tunnel can be encrypted, which hides the true endpoint IP addresses as well as the message contents, to prevent any intermediate system from eavesdropping on those communications. Tunnels are frequently called virtual private networks (VPNs), because they provide both security (through encryption and authentication) and abstraction (by hiding the details of the path between systems).

VPNs are frequently used for end-user remote access to an organization's network. When an end user wants to connect to an organization's internal network, the network establishes a session with a VPN server and provides authentication credentials. An encrypted tunnel is then established that gives the end user the appearance and functionality of being connected to the internal network.

Network Management

Network management is the function of ensuring that a data network continues to support business objectives. Activities include monitoring network devices, identifying problems, and applying remedies as needed to restore network operations.

Network management is the continued reliable operation of an organization's data network. A properly functioning data network, in turn, supports business applications that support critical business processes.

Network Management Tools

Network management requires tools that are used to monitor, troubleshoot, and maintain data networks. This permits an IT organization to ensure the continuous operation of its data network so that it has sufficient capacity and capability to support applications and services vital to the organization's ongoing business operations.

The tools that are used to fulfill this mission include:

- **Network management system:** This software application collects network management messages that are sent from network devices and systems. These messages alert the management system that certain conditions exist on the device, some of which may require intervention. Some network management systems also contain the means for network administrators and engineers to diagnose and correct conditions that require attention.

- **Network management report:** Network management systems generate reports showing key metrics such as network availability, utilization, response time, and downtime. Reports from helpdesk systems or incident management systems also help communicate the health of an organization's networks.

- **Network management agent:** An agent is a small software module that resides on managed network devices and other systems. It monitors operations on the device or system and transmits messages to a centralized network management system when needed.

- **Incident management system:** This is a general-purpose ticketing engine that captures and tracks individual incidents and reports on an organization's timely response to them. Often, network management systems and incident management systems can be integrated together so that conditions requiring attention in the network can automatically create a ticket that will be used to track the course of the incident until it is closed.

- **Sniffer:** This software program can be installed on a network-attached system or a separate hard device to capture and analyze network traffic.

- **Security information and event management (SIEM) system:** A SIEM (pronounced "sim") system collects, correlates, analyzes, reports on, and creates actionable alerts based on the individual error and event messages generated by the systems and devices in an environment.

Organizations employing network management tools often implement a NOC staffed with personnel who monitor and manage network devices and services. Often this function is outsourced to a managed security service provider (MSSP).

Networked Applications

Other than simple end-user tools on a business workstation, business applications are rarely installed and used within the context of an individual computer. Instead, many applications are centrally installed and used by many people who are often in many locations. Data networks facilitate the communications between central servers and business workstations. The applications discussed in the following sections are client-server, web-based, and middleware.

Client-Server

Client-server applications are a prior-generation technology used to build high-performance business applications. They consist of one or more central application servers, database servers, and business workstations. The central application servers contain some business logic—primarily the instructions to receive and respond to requests sent from workstations. The remainder of the business logic will reside on each business workstation; primarily this is the logic used to display and process forms and reports for the user.

When a user is using a client-server application, they are typically selecting functions to input, view, or change information. When information is input, application logic on the business workstation will request, analyze, and accept the information and then transmit it to the central application server for further processing and storage. When viewing information, a user will typically select a viewing function with, perhaps, criteria specifying which information they want to view. Business logic on the workstation will validate this information and then send a request to the central application server, which in turn will respond with information that is then sent back to the workstation and transformed for easy viewing.

The performance of client-server applications was improved by removing all application display logic from the central computer and placing that logic on each individual workstation. This scheme succeeded in principle but failed in practice for two principal reasons:

- **Network performance:** Client-server applications often overburdened the organization's data network, and application performance failed when many people were using it at once. A typical example is a database query issued by a workstation that results in thousands of records being returned to the workstation over the network.

- **Workstation software updates:** Keeping the central application software and the software modules on each workstation in sync proved to be problematic. Often, updates required that all workstations be upgraded at the same time. Invariably, some workstations are down or otherwise unavailable for updates (powered down by end users or taken home if they are laptop computers), potentially resulting in application malfunctions for those users.

Organizations that did implement full-scale client-server applications were often dissatisfied with the results. And at nearly the same time, the World Wide Web was invented and soon proved to be a promising, simpler alternative.

Client-server application design has enjoyed a revival with the advent of smartphone and tablet applications, or apps, which are often designed as client-server.

Web-Based Applications

With client-server applications declining in favor, web-based applications were the only way forward. The primary characteristics of web-based applications that make them highly favorable include:

- **Centralized business logic:** All business logic resides on one or more centralized servers. There are no longer issues related to pushing software updates to workstations since they run web browsers that rarely require updating.

- **Lightweight and universal display logic:** Display logic, such as forms, lists, and other application controls, is easily written in HTML, a simple markup language that displays well on workstations without any application logic on the workstation.

- **Lightweight network requirements:** Unlike client-server applications that would often send large amounts of data from the centralized server to the workstation, web applications send mainly display data to workstations.

- **Workstations requiring few, if any, updates:** Workstations require only browser software. Updates to applications themselves are entirely server-based.

- **Fewer compatibility issues:** Instead of requiring a narrow choice of workstations, web-based applications can run on nearly every kind of workstation, including Unix, Windows, macOS, Chrome OS, or Linux.

Middleware

Middleware is a component used in some client-server or web-based application environments to control the processing of communications or transactions. Middleware manages the interaction between major components in larger application environments.

Some of the common types of middleware are:

- **Transaction processing (TP) monitors:** A TP monitor manages transactions between application servers and database servers to ensure the integrity of business transactions among a collection of database servers.

- **RPC gateways:** These systems facilitate communications through the suite of RPC protocols between various components of an application environment.

- **Object request broker (ORB) gateways:** An ORB gateway facilitates the execution of transactions across complex, multiserver application environments that use CORBA (Common Object Request Broker Architecture) or Microsoft COM/DCOM technologies.

- **Message servers:** These systems store and forward transactions between systems and ensure the eventual delivery of transactions to the right systems.

Middleware is typically used in a large, complex application environment, particularly when there are multiple technologies (operating systems, databases, and languages) in use. Middleware can be thought of as glue that helps the application environment operate more smoothly.

Asset Inventory and Classification

Information assets fall into two basic categories: information and information systems. Information consists of software, tools, and every type of data. Information system is an inclusive term that encompasses servers, workstations, mobile devices, network devices, gateways, appliances, and almost every other kind of IT hardware that is used.

Information and information systems both need to be inventoried. This helps management continue to be aware of their existence so that they can be properly managed and protected. The inventory of sensitive data supports an organization's privacy program.

Information and information systems also need to be classified. This will ensure that they will be properly handled according to their criticality, sensitivity, importance, and other criteria. A classification scheme may be developed as a result of a risk assessment, as well as regulations and standards such as the Health Insurance Portability and Accountability Act (HIPAA), General Data Protection Regulation (GDPR), and the Payment Card Industry Data Security Standard (PCI DSS).

Hardware Asset Inventory

An IT organization that is responsible for the management of information and information systems must have a means for knowing what all those assets are. More than that, IT needs to acquire and track several characteristics about every hardware asset, including:

- **Identification:** This includes make, model, serial number, asset tag number, logical name, and any other means for identifying the asset.
- **Value:** Initially, this may signify the purchased value, but it may also include its depreciated value if an IT asset management program is associated with the organization's financial asset management program.
- **Location:** The asset's location needs to be specified so that its existence may be verified in a periodic inventory.
- **Condition:** The asset's current capability needs to be noted—for example, whether it is operational or down for upgrades or maintenance.
- **Security classification:** Security management programs almost always include a plan for classifying the sensitivity of information and/or information systems. Example classifications include secret, restricted, confidential, and public.
- **Asset group:** IT assets may be classified into a hierarchy of asset groups. For example, any of the servers in a data center that support a large application may be assigned to an asset group known as "Application X Servers."
- **Configuration:** Every asset's configuration must be managed and known according to established standards and in compliance with applicable regulations and standards.
- **Owner:** This is usually the person or group responsible for the operation of the asset.
- **Custodian:** Occasionally, the ownership and operations of assets will be divided into two bodies, where the owner owns them, but a custodian operates or maintains them.

Because hardware assets are installed, moved, and eventually retired, it is important to verify the information periodically in the asset inventory by physically verifying the existence of the physical assets. Depending on the value and sensitivity of systems and data, this inventory "true-up" may be performed as often as monthly or as seldom as once per year. Discrepancies in actual inventory must be investigated to verify that assets have not been moved without authorization or stolen.

Information Assets

Sometimes overlooked because it is intangible, information stored in systems should be treated as an asset. In almost all cases, information such as software and databases has tangible value and should be included in the list of IS assets.

Operating systems and subsystems such as database management systems or applications that reside in virtual machines are considered assets. Like physical assets, these may have tangible value and should be inventoried periodically.

Emerging privacy laws, including the GDPR, the California Consumer Privacy Act (CCPA), and the California Privacy Rights Act (CPRA), are compelling organizations to improve their knowledge and control of information assets, particularly those containing sensitive information about individuals.

Data Classification Overview

In most organizations, various types and sets of information will have varying degrees of sensitivity. These levels of sensitivity will implicitly dictate that information at different levels should be handled accordingly. For instance, the most sensitive information should be encrypted whenever stored or transmitted and should be accessible only to those individuals who have a justified need to use it.

Would it be easier to handle all information the same way that the most sensitive information in the organization is handled? Although it would be easier to remember how to handle and dispose of all information, it might also be an onerous task, particularly if all information is handled at the level warranted for the organization's most sensitive or critical information. Encrypting everything and shredding everything would be a wasteful use of resources. That said, it is incumbent on an organization to build a simple data classification program that is easy to understand and follow. Too many levels of classification would be burdensome and difficult for users to understand and follow.

Data Classification Details

In most organizations, a data classification program can be defined in detail in less than a dozen pages, and the practical portions of it could almost fit on a single page. For many organizations, a simple four-level classification program is a good place to start. The four levels could be labeled as secret, restricted, confidential, and public. Any information in the organization would be classified into one of these four levels.

Example handling procedures for each of these levels are found in Table 5.12.

TABLE 5.12   Example of information handling guidelines

	Secret	Restricted	Confidential	Public
Example Information Types	Passwords, merger and acquisition plans and terms	Credit card numbers, bank account numbers, Social Security numbers, detailed financial records, detailed system configuration, vulnerability scan reports	System documentation, end-user documentation, internal memos, network diagrams	Brochures, press releases

	Secret	Restricted	Confidential	Public
Storage on Server	Must be encrypted; store only on servers labeled sensitive	Must be encrypted	Access controls required	Access controls required for update
Storage on Mobile Device	Must never be stored on mobile device	Must be encrypted	Access controls required	No restrictions
Storage in the Cloud	Must never be stored in the cloud	Must be encrypted	Access controls required	Access controls required for update
Email	Must never be emailed	Must be encrypted	Authorized recipients only	No restrictions
Website	Must never be stored on any web server	Must be encrypted	Access controls required	No restrictions
Fax	Encrypted, attended fax only	Manned fax only, no email-based fax	Attended fax only	No restrictions
Courier and Shipment	Double-wrapped; signature and secure storage required	Signature and secure storage required	Signature required	No restrictions
Hard Copy Storage	Double-locked in authorized locations only	Double-locked	Locked	No restrictions
Hard Copy Distribution	Only with owner permission; must be registered	To authorized parties only; only with owner permission	To authorized parties only	No restrictions
Hard Copy Destruction	Cross-cut shred; make a record of destruction	Cross-cut shred	Cross-cut shred or secure waste bin	No restrictions

TABLE 5.12   Example of information handling guidelines *(continued)*

	Secret	Restricted	Confidential	Public
Soft Copy Destruction	Erase with DoD 5220.22-M spec tool	Erase with DoD 5220.22-M spec tool	Delete and empty recycle bin	No restrictions

The classification and handling guidelines presented in Table 5.12 are meant as an example to illustrate the differences in various forms of data handling for various classification levels. However, the contents of Table 5.12 can serve as a starting point for an actual data classification and handling procedure.

Job Scheduling and Production Process Automation

Modern business applications and information systems are integrated with other systems for the purpose of exchanging data files in one or both directions. These file transfers serve as data updates, so that systems are working with the latest data. Some examples of these file transfers include:

- An updated list of all employees copied from the HR system to other systems, such as Active Directory, financial accounting, and ticketing systems.
- An updated list of employees and their managers, copied from the HR system to other systems that need to know the identity of each employee's manager, for approval purposes. For instance, an expense management system needs to know to whom an expense report should be sent for manager approval.
- An updated list of projects, copied from the financial accounting system to the time management system, for employees who charge their work hours to one or more projects.
- Updates to a city's geographic information system (GIS) sent to commercial map and navigation systems, to update the layout of highways, roads, and speed limits.

To ensure the completeness and integrity of these file transfers, IT departments generally employ commercial job scheduling systems to manage all the details. These systems permit IT administrators to set up and monitor these file transfer jobs; the systems track and report on each job's success and failure so that personnel can be confident of job success and troubleshoot errors.

To ensure the completeness and integrity of transferred files, the file transfer process may perform some type of "batch total" calculation. For example, a software program would count the number of records in a transferred file on both the sending and receiving systems. Comparing the number of records confirms whether the receiving system received the correct number of records.

Other types of jobs that are automatically scheduled include:

- Backups
- Scheduled reboots
- Storage system maintenance
- Database maintenance, such as refreshing indices and moving transactions to a data warehouse or data lake
- Vulnerability scans
- Network discovery scans

A less obvious aspect of job scheduling is related to data entry. Many organizations still perform manual data entry, although in far lower volume than in generations past. Data entry should be considered a formal scheduled IT task (regardless of whether IT personnel, or persons in other departments perform data entry). Data entry requires recordkeeping for IT personnel and auditors to know that data entry is being performed correctly and completely.

System Interfaces

System interfaces are the means through which information flows into and out of information systems. Interactive end-user interfaces are certainly included in system interfaces, although the bulk of our discussion centers on automated interfaces.

Formally, a system interface is called an *application programming interface (API)*, which is used for the automated transfer of data files as well as individual transactions in real time. APIs facilitate data transfer between applications and systems.

APIs are defined by application software programs that contain detailed specifications specifying data formats and other rules. APIs are protected by several safeguards, including:

- Data controls, to ensure that only data with acceptable characters and data ranges are permitted into systems
- Access controls, so that only authorized systems and programs are permitted to access them
- Firewalls, so that only authorized systems are permitted to establish communications with APIs

- Web application firewalls (WAFs), to reduce the threat of tampering, corrupted data, and injection attacks
- Audit logs, to record all successful and unsuccessful activities
- Security scans and penetration tests, performed periodically to ensure there are no exploitable vulnerabilities in APIs that would permit an attacker to steal information or compromise systems
- Encryption controls, to ensure transferred data is encrypted in transit and while stored on intermediate systems such as file transfer servers

End-User Computing

A critical portion of an IT organization's function is the services it renders to organization personnel to facilitate their access and use of IT systems and applications. Operational models for supporting end-user computing include:

- **Organization-provided hardware and software:** The organization provides all computing devices (typically, laptop or desktop computers and perhaps mobile computing devices such as tablets or smartphones) and software.
- **Personnel-provided hardware and software:** The organization provides network infrastructure and instructions on how end users may configure their computing devices to access the organization's IT applications and systems. Some organizations provide a stipend to its personnel to pay for all or part of the costs of end-user computers.
- **Hybrid models:** Many organizations employ a hybrid of the organization and personnel models. Often, an organization provides laptop or desktop computers, and employees are permitted to access email and some organization applications via personally owned devices such as home computers, tablets, and smartphones.

Usually, the organization will employ enterprise management tools to facilitate efficient and consistent management of end-user computers. Typically, end-user computers are "locked down," which limits the amount of and types of configuration changes that end users may perform on their devices, including:

- Operating system configuration
- Patch installation
- Software program installation
- Use of external data storage devices

Such restrictions may be viewed by end users as an inconvenience. However, these restrictions not only help to ensure greater security of end-user devices and the entire organization's IT environment, but they also promote greater consistency, which leads to reduced support costs.

Some organizations employ a zero-trust model for end-user computing. This approach is sometimes used in conjunction with BYOD (bring your own device), where end users provide their own computing devices.

Shadow IT

Shadow IT is defined by ISACA as "The use of systems, services, hardware or software on an enterprise network or within an enterprise's infrastructure without proper vetting and approval from the IT or cybersecurity department." Shadow IT takes on many forms, including:

- **Disintermediation of IT:** The most prominent example of shadow IT is the practice of groups, teams, departments, and business units acquiring IT systems and services directly, bypassing corporate IT.

- **Bring your own device (BYOD):** As a violation of corporate policy, personnel conduct organization business on personally owned IT devices such as laptops, tablets, and smartphones, in addition to (or instead of) business-issued and owned devices. When personnel use their own devices, the organization lacks visibility into data storage and usage, and lacks protective measures such as the enterprise antimalware software, enterprise managed firewalls, and other endpoint safeguards.

- **Bring your own tools:** As a violation of corporate policy, personnel may install additional software tools on company-managed devices. This practice introduces risks associated with the claimed and actual behavior of these tools, potentially resulting in the compromise of business information and the endpoint itself.

- **Bring your own service:** Similar to bring your own tools, bring your own service involves personnel using cloud-based services that are not a part of IT-supported applications and services. This practice results in the loss of visibility of company information, with the possibility of violations of privacy and/or data sovereignty laws.

- **Bring your own generative AI:** Like bring your own tools, personnel may use their favorite generative AI tools, rather than those permitted by the organization (if any).

While it is possible in some circumstances, shadow IT can be difficult and costly to prevent in all cases. Thus, IS auditors need to be aware of the general reasons why shadow IT exists.

Auditing IT Infrastructure

Auditing infrastructure requires considerable technical expertise for the auditor to fully understand the technology that they are examining. If an auditor lacks technical knowledge, interviewed subjects may offer explanations that can evade vital facts that the auditor should be aware of. Auditors need to be familiar with hardware, operating systems, database management systems, networks, IT operations, monitoring, and DRP.

Auditing Information Systems Hardware

Auditing hardware requires attention to several key factors and activities, including:

- **Standards:** The auditor should examine hardware procurement standards that specify the types of systems the organization uses. These standards should be periodically reviewed and updated. A sample of recent purchases should be examined to determine whether standards are being followed. The scope of this activity should include servers, workstations, network devices, and other hardware used by IT.

- **Maintenance:** Maintenance requirements and records should be examined to determine whether any required maintenance is being performed. If service contracts are used, they should be examined to ensure that all critical systems are covered.

- **Capacity:** The auditor should examine capacity management and planning processes, procedures, and records. This will help the auditor to understand whether the organization monitors its systems' capacity and does any planning for future expansion.

- **Change management:** Change management processes and records should be examined to determine whether hardware changes are being performed in a life cycle process. All changes that are made should be requested and reviewed in advance, approved by management, and recorded.

- **Configuration management:** The auditor should examine configuration management records to determine whether the IT organization is tracking the configuration of its systems in a centralized and systematic manner.

 Audits of these aspects of hardware are applicable to public cloud environments as well.

Auditing Operating Systems

Auditing operating systems, whether on-premises or cloud-based, requires attention to many different details, including:

- **Standards:** The auditor should examine written standards to determine whether they are complete and up-to-date. They should then examine a sampling of servers and workstations to ensure that they comply with the organization's written standards.

- **Maintenance and support:** Business records should be examined to see whether the operating systems running on servers or workstations are covered by maintenance or support contracts.

- **Change management:** The auditor should examine operating system change management processes and records to determine whether changes are being performed in a systematic manner. All changes should be requested and reviewed in advance, approved by management, and recorded.

- **Configuration management:** Operating systems are enormously complex; in all but the smallest organizations, configuration management tools should ensure consistency of configuration among systems. The auditor should examine configuration management processes, tools, and recordkeeping.

- **Security management:** The auditor should examine security configurations on a sample of servers and workstations and determine whether they are "hardened" or resemble manufacturer default configurations. This determination should be made considering the relative risk of various selected systems. An examination should include patch management and administrative access.

Auditing Filesystems

Filesystems containing business information must be examined to ensure that they are properly configured. An examination should include:

- **Capacity:** Filesystems must have adequate capacity to store all the currently required information, plus room for future growth. The auditor should examine any file storage capacity management tools, processes, and records.

- **Access control:** Files and directories should be accessible only by personnel with a business need. Records of access requests should be examined to see if they correspond to the access permissions observed.

Auditing Database Management Systems

DBMSs are as complex as operating systems. This complexity requires considerable auditor scrutiny in several areas, including:

- **Configuration management:** The configuration of DBMSs should be centrally controlled and tracked in larger organizations to ensure consistency among systems. Individual DBMSs and configuration management records should be compared.

- **Change management:** Databases store information and software in many cases. The auditor should examine DBMS change management processes and records to determine whether changes are being performed consistently and systematically. All changes should be requested and reviewed in advance, approved by management, tested, implemented, and recorded. Changes to software should be examined in coordination with an audit of the organization's systems/software development life cycle.

- **Capacity management:** The availability and integrity of supported business processes requires sufficient capacity in all underlying databases. The auditor should examine procedures and records related to capacity management to see whether management ensures sufficient capacity for business data.

- **Access management:** Access controls determine which users and systems can access and update data. The auditor should examine access control configurations, access requests, and access logs.

Auditing Network Infrastructure

The IS auditor needs to perform a detailed study of the organization's network infrastructure and underlying management processes. An auditor's scrutiny should include:

- **Enterprise architecture:** The auditor should examine enterprise architecture documents. There should be overall and detailed schematics and standards.

- **Network architecture:** The auditor should examine network architecture documents, including schematics, topology and design, data flow, routing, and addressing. Auditors should also look for network segmentation, including why and how it was implemented.

- **Virtual architecture:** The auditor should examine all aspects of network infrastructure that is implemented in public cloud environments.

- **Security architecture:** Security architecture documents should be examined, including critical and sensitive data flows, network security zones, access control devices and systems, security countermeasures, intrusion detection and prevention systems, firewalls, screening routers, gateways, antimalware, and security monitoring.

- **Standards:** The auditor should examine standards documents and determine whether they are reasonable and current. Selected devices and equipment should be examined to see whether they conform to these standards.

- **Change management:** All changes to network devices and services should be governed by a change management process. The auditor should review change management procedures and records and examine a sample of devices and systems to ensure that changes are being performed according to the change management policy.

- **Capacity management:** The auditor should determine how the organization measures network capacity, whether capacity management procedures and records exist, and how capacity management affects network operations.

- **Configuration management:** The auditor should determine whether any configuration management standards, procedures, and records exist and are used. They should examine the configuration of a sampling of devices to see whether configurations are consistent from device to device.

- **Administrative access management:** Access management procedures, records, and configurations should be examined to see whether only authorized persons are able to access and manage network devices and services.

- **Network components:** The auditor should examine several components and their configuration to determine how well the organization has constructed its network infrastructure to support business objectives.

- **Log management:** The auditor should determine whether administrative activities performed on network devices and services are logged. They should examine the configuration of logs to see if they can be altered. The logs themselves should be examined to determine whether any unauthorized activities are taking place.

- **User access management:** Often, network-based services provide organizationwide user access controls. The auditor should examine these centralized services to see whether they conform to written security standards. Examination should include user ID convention, password controls, inactivity locking, user account provisioning, user account termination, and password reset procedures.

Auditing Network Operating Controls

The IS auditor needs to examine network operations to determine whether the organization is operating its network effectively. Examinations should include:

- **Network operating procedures:** The auditor should examine procedures for normal activities for all network devices and services. These activities will include login, startup, shutdown, upgrade, and configuration changes.

- **Restart procedures:** Procedures for restarting the entire network (and portions of it for larger organizations) should exist and be tested periodically. A network restart would be needed in the event of a massive power failure, network failure, or significant upgrade.

- **Troubleshooting procedures:** The auditor should examine network troubleshooting procedures for all significant network components. Procedures that are specific to the organization's network help network engineers and analysts quickly locate problems and reduce downtime.

- **Security controls:** Operational security controls should be examined, including administrator authentication, administrator access control, logging of administrator actions, protection of device configuration data, security configuration reviews, and protection of audit logs.

- **Change management:** All changes to network components and services should follow a formal change management life cycle, including request, review, approval by management, testing in a separate environment, implementation, verification, and complete recordkeeping. The auditor should examine change management policy, procedures, and records.

Auditing IT Operations

Auditing IT operations involves examining the processes used to build, maintain, update, and repair computing hardware, operating systems, and network devices. Audits will cover processes, procedures, and records, as well as examinations of information systems.

Auditing Job Scheduling and Production Process Automation

The IS auditor should examine job scheduling and production process automation, including:

- **Version of job scheduling system:** This may include verifying whether this software is the latest version, and that any functionality and security patches are installed and current.

- **Access to job scheduling system:** Auditors should determine who has access to the job scheduling system, and what functions are permitted by each person.

- **Access to production applications:** Auditors need to follow the trail of control by job scheduling systems by seeing how they are authenticated to managed systems.

- **Contents of scheduled jobs:** Auditors need to examine the list of scheduled jobs, to see whether these align with the needs of the organization. Further, auditors need to examine the change control process to see how changes to scheduled jobs are reviewed and approved.

- **Job completion logs:** Auditors need to determine whether job completion logs are complete and accurate and whether IT personnel are alerted when job failures occur. Auditors should note what assurance mechanisms are in place to ensure complete and accurate file transfers, such as batch totals.

- **Exception processing:** Auditors should determine how exceptions and errors are handled, and whether linkages to other processes such as change and configuration management are sound.

Auditing System Interfaces

IS auditors should examine system interfaces, including:

- **Vulnerability management:** Auditors need to determine what vulnerability management procedures are in place to ensure that APIs are free of exploitable vulnerabilities.

- **Access control:** This includes management access to APIs, as well as access controls for systems that access APIs.

- **Activity logs:** This includes records of API activities, errors, and configuration changes.

- **Error response:** The procedures IT personnel follow when errors are detected in APIs, and the records for that response, should be examined.

- **Encryption:** Auditors need to understand encryption algorithms in place, and determine whether encryption was implemented properly.

- **Key management:** This is related to in-transit and at-rest encryption, whether keys are adequately protected, and who has access to them.

Summary

IS auditors need to have a thorough understanding of information systems hardware and software and how they work to support business objectives. This includes knowing how computer hardware functions; how operating systems are installed, configured, operated, and monitored; how networks and network models are designed, how they work, and how they are monitored and managed; how end users' workstations are provisioned, managed, and used; and how software applications are designed, licensed, monitored, and operated. Because newer technologies are not always implemented properly at first, IS auditors need to understand technologies such as virtualization, containerization, virtual desktops, software-defined networking, and mobile devices to ensure that the organization is not incurring unnecessary risk through their use.

The more that IS auditors understand information technology, from the very small to the very large, the more likely it is that they will recognize risky practices.

Asset management is among the most critical practices in information technology. Organizations that practice substandard asset management for their hardware, software, and data cannot excel at effective management or protection.

All activities in the IT department should be managed, controlled, monitored, and documented. Activities performed by operations personnel should be a part of a procedure or process that is approved by management. Processes, procedures, and projects should have sufficient recordkeeping to facilitate measurements.

Job scheduling and production automation are a critical part of IT operations. Modern business applications exchange data, in batches and in real time, with other business applications and with external service providers. It is imperative that these processes and their underlying technology be closely managed and well documented.

End-user computing represents a highly critical part of information technology overall. The desktops, laptops, tablets, and smartphones in the hands of end users facilitate and support numerous business processes. Because they are so powerful, end-user computers are the target of attacks by cybercriminals.

Shadow IT represents many forms of unsanctioned uses of computers and technologies, away from the management of safeguards and visibility from IT, cybersecurity, legal, and more. The nature of information technology makes it difficult to prevent all forms of shadow IT.

Exam Essentials

Understand the functions of information technology. From the very small (operating systems, network concepts) to the very large (architectures, how the Internet works), IS auditors need to have the best possible understanding of the functionality of computer components, operating systems, filesystems, storage systems, networks, applications, and interfaces). Gaps in this knowledge can mean that unsafe practices may be overlooked.

Understand the management of information technology. IS auditors need to understand how information technology should be managed, to ensure that IT environments are trusted and reliable.

Be able to explain the OSI and TCP/IP network models. IS auditors must be familiar with OSI and TCP/IP network models, including encapsulation, protocols, and how they contribute to network technology. Auditors with this knowledge will be more likely to detect unsafe practices.

Understand the intricacies of the global Internet. Virtually all organizations are connected to the global Internet, and rely on that connection for some (if not all) of their IT systems to function. Thus, it's imperative that IS auditors understand Internet functionality in detail, to help identify both good and bad practices.

Be able to explain why asset management is critical.   IS auditors must have a solid understanding of asset inventory and asset management, including knowledge of the other IT- and cybersecurity-related processes which rely on sound asset management. Asset management is not only hardware, but software, data, workers, vendors, service providers, work centers, and more.

Be familiar with job processing, automation, and interfaces.   It's critical for IS auditors to understand how modern job processing (scheduled jobs for backup, file transfer, and other maintenance) is managed in IT organizations. Much job processing involves IT systems and business applications communicating with systems and applications outside the organization; hence, IS auditors need to understand how this communication is managed and protected.

Know how end-user endpoints are managed and used.   End-user computing is a vital part of information technology. Without end-user computing, we would not be able to access and use business applications. IS auditors need to understand modern endpoint management tools and practices to ensure they do not introduce risks to the organization. Lacking mature enterprise management controls and antimalware tools, and being small enough to easily lose, mobile devices are a popular attack target. The IS auditor needs to understand how the organization addresses these matters.

Be able to recognize shadow IT.   Shadow IT, the unsanctioned use of computers, software, and cloud services, lurks in nearly every organization. IS auditors must understand management's approach to shadow IT and any safeguards that are in place to prevent it.

Review Questions

1. What is the portion of a computer that performs most calculations?
   A. CISC
   B. CPU
   C. GPU
   D. Math coprocessor

2. An IT administrator is describing a problem to a colleague and refers to main storage. What is the main storage on a computer system?
   A. SSD
   B. ROM
   C. RAM
   D. HDD

3. The practice of having multiple OS instances running on a single system is known as:
   A. Virtualization
   B. Containerization
   C. Clustering
   D. Hypervisor

4. What are a computer's CPU, memory, and peripherals connected to each other through?
   A. Kernel
   B. FireWire
   C. Pipeline
   D. Bus

5. _____ is the term used to describe multiple application instances running in a single operating system.
   A. Containerization
   B. Serverless
   C. Virtualization
   D. Vectoring

6. What are the layers of the TCP/IP reference model?
   A. Link, Internet, transport, application
   B. Physical, link, Internet, transport, application
   C. Link, transport, Internet, application
   D. Physical, data link, network, transport, session, presentation, application

7. What is the purpose of the Internet layer in the TCP/IP model?

    A. Encapsulation

    B. Packet delivery on a local network

    C. Packet delivery on a local or remote network

    D. Order of delivery and flow control

8. What is the purpose of the DHCP protocol?

    A. To control flow on a congested network

    B. To query a station to discover its IP address

    C. To assign an IP address to a station

    D. To assign an Ethernet MAC address to a station

9. An IS auditor is examining a Wi-Fi network and has determined that the network uses WEP encryption. What action should the auditor take?

    A. Recommend that encryption be changed to WPA2/WPA3.

    B. Recommend that encryption be changed to EAP.

    C. Request documentation for the key management process.

    D. Request documentation for the authentication process.

10. What is 126.0.0.1 an example of?

    A. MAC address

    B. Loopback address

    C. Class A address

    D. Subnet mask

11. Hardware monitoring measures all of the following *except*:

    A. Disk errors

    B. Ambient temperature

    C. Resource utilization

    D. System health

12. An organization has implemented an application architecture consisting of multiple identical servers that service incoming transactions. What server architecture is in use?

    A. Enclave

    B. Processing group

    C. Hypervisor

    D. Cluster

13. What technology would be used to store a large number of unstructured data files?
    A. Database management system
    B. Filesystem
    C. Server cluster
    D. Hypervisor

14. An organization needs to implement a mechanism to enforce data retention policy within documents, no matter where they reside. What technology should be used?
    A. Digital rights management
    B. Server clustering
    C. Data clustering
    D. Tokenization

15. Which of the following statements about virtual server hardening is true?
    A. The configuration of the host operating system will automatically flow to each guest operating system.
    B. Each guest virtual machine needs to be hardened separately.
    C. Guest operating systems do not need to be hardened because they are protected by the hypervisor.
    D. Virtual servers do not need to be hardened because they do not run directly on computer hardware.

16. What is the distinction between a network's physical structure and its logical structure?
    A. Physical structure refers to cabling, whereas logical structure refers to data flow.
    B. Logical structure refers to cabling, whereas physical structure refers to data flow.
    C. Physical structure refers to frames, whereas logical structure refers to packets.
    D. Logical and physical structure are the same.

17. What are email, directory, file storage, and time synchronization examples of?
    A. Data labels
    B. Applications
    C. Utilities
    D. Network services

18. Which of the following is *not* a layer of the TCP/IP model?
    A. Data link
    B. Physical
    C. Presentation
    D. Application

19. What is the most common cabling type in modern LANs?

    A. Thinnet

    B. Twisted-pair

    C. Fiber

    D. Coax

20. Asset inventory is critical for all of the following activities *except*:

    A. Static code analysis

    B. Vulnerability scanning

    C. License management

    D. Server hardening

Chapter

6

Business Continuity and Disaster Recovery

THE CERTIFIED INFORMATION SYSTEMS AUDITOR (CISA) OBJECTIVES REPRESENT 26% OF THE MATERIAL COVERED ON THE EXAM AND INCLUDE:

✓ **Domain 4: Information Systems Operations & Business Resilience**

    B. Business Resilience

        1. Business Impact Analysis (BIA)

        2. System Resiliency

        3. Data Backup, Storage, and Restoration

        4. Business Continuity Plan (BCP)

        5. Disaster Recovery Plans (DRP)

    Supporting Tasks

        13. Evaluate the organization's ability to continue business operations.

Business Continuity
and Disaster
Recovery

Chapters 4 "IT Service Management," and 5 "IT Infrastructure," cover the balance of subject matter in CISA Domain 4. Together, the topics in those chapters and this chapter represent 26 percent of the CISA examination.

In the age of digital transformation (DX), organizations are more dependent than ever on information technology for executing core business processes. This, in turn, changes the business resilience conversation and increases the emphasis on business continuity and disaster recovery planning, which has moved to this domain in the 2024 CISA job practice.

Business Resilience

In the context of information systems, *business resilience* concerns the resilience of IT systems and business applications that support critical business processes. It ensures the organization's ongoing viability and survival in the event of a major disaster. Given the phenomenon of digital transformation (DX), which represents an increasing dependency of business processes on information technology, ensuring the resilience of IT systems is even more important. The two primary activities within business resilience are business continuity planning and disaster recovery planning.

Business Continuity Planning

Business continuity planning (BCP) is a business activity that is undertaken to reduce risks related to the onset of disasters and other disruptive events. BCP activities identify the most critical activities and assets in an organization. They identify risks and mitigate those risks through changes or enhancements in technology or business processes so that the impact of disasters is reduced and the time to recovery is lessened. The primary objective of BCP is to improve the chances that the organization will survive a disaster without incurring costly or even fatal damage to its most critical activities.

The activities of BCP development scale for any size organization. BCP has the unfortunate reputation of existing only in the stratospheric, thin air of the largest and wealthiest organizations. This misunderstanding hurts most organizations that are too timid to begin any kind of BCP effort at all because they believe that these activities are too costly and disruptive. The fact is that any size organization, from a one-person home office to a multinational conglomerate, can successfully undertake BCP projects that will bring about immediate benefits as well as take some of the sting out of disruptive events that do occur.

Organizations can benefit from BCP projects, even if a disaster never occurs. The steps in the BCP development process usually bring immediate benefit in the form of process and technology improvements that increase the resilience, integrity, and efficiency of those processes and systems.

Exam Tip

Business continuity planning is closely related to disaster recovery planning—both are concerned with the recovery of business operations after a disaster.

Disasters

I always tried to turn every disaster into an opportunity.

— John D. Rockefeller

In a business context, disasters are unexpected and unplanned events that result in the disruption of business operations. A disaster could be a regional event spread over a wide geographic area, or it could occur within the confines of a single room. The impact of a disaster will also vary, from a complete interruption of all company operations to a mere slowdown. (The question invariably comes up: When is a disaster a *disaster*? This is somewhat subjective, like asking, "When is a person sick?" Is it when they are too ill to report to work, or if they just have a sniffle and a scratchy throat? We'll discuss disaster declaration later in this chapter.)

Types of Disasters

BCP professionals broadly classify disasters as natural or human-made, although the origin of a disaster does not greatly affect how we respond to it. Let's examine the types of disasters.

Natural Disasters

Natural disasters are phenomena that occur in the natural world with little or no assistance from humankind. They are a result of the natural processes that occur in, on, and above the earth.

Examples of natural disasters include:

- **Earthquakes:** Sudden movements of the earth with the capacity to damage buildings, houses, roads, bridges, and dams; to precipitate landslides and avalanches; and to induce flooding and other secondary events.

- **Volcanoes:** Eruptions of magma, pyroclastic flows, steam, ash, and flying rocks that can cause significant damage over wide geographic regions. Some volcanoes, such as Kilauea in Hawaii, produce a nearly continuous and predictable outpouring of lava in a limited area, whereas others, such as the Mount St. Helens eruption in 1980 in Washington State, caused an ash fall over thousands of square miles that brought many metropolitan areas to a standstill for days and blocked rivers and damaged roads. Figure 6.1 shows a volcanic eruption viewed from space.

FIGURE 6.1   Mount Etna volcano in Sicily

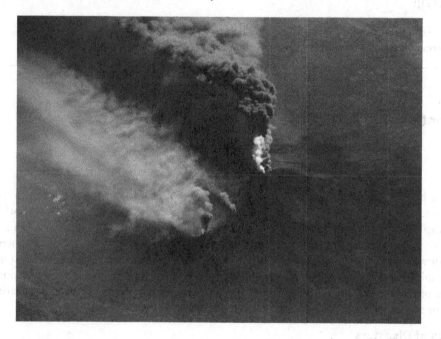

Source: NASA / Public Domain

- **Landslides:** Sudden downhill movements of earth, usually down steep slopes, can bury buildings, houses, roads, and public utilities and cause secondary (although still disastrous) effects such as the rerouting of rivers.

- **Avalanches:** Sudden downward flows of snow, rocks, and debris on a mountainside can damage buildings, houses, roads, and utilities, resulting in direct or indirect damage affecting businesses. A slab avalanche consists of the movement of a large, stiff layer of compacted snow. A loose snow avalanche occurs when the accumulated snowpack exceeds its shear strength. A power snow avalanche is the largest type and can travel in excess of 200 mph and exceed 10 million tons of material.

- **Wildfires:** Fires in forests, chaparral, and grasslands are part of the natural order. However, fires can also damage power lines, buildings, equipment, homes, and entire communities, and cause injury and death.

- **Tropical cyclones:** The largest and most violent storms are known in various parts of the world as hurricanes, typhoons, tropical cyclones, tropical storms, and cyclones. Tropical cyclones consist of strong winds that can reach 190 mph, heavy rains, and storm surges that can raise the level of the ocean by as much as 20 feet. All of these can result in widespread coastal flooding, damage to buildings, houses, roads, and utilities, and significant loss of life.

- **Tornadoes:** These violent rotating columns of air can cause catastrophic damage to buildings, houses, roads, and utilities when they reach the ground. Most tornadoes can have wind speeds from 40 to 110 mph and travel along the ground for a few miles. Some tornadoes can exceed 300 mph and travel for dozens of miles.

- **Windstorms:** While generally less intense than hurricanes and tornadoes, windstorms can nonetheless cause widespread damage, including damage to buildings, roads, and utilities. Widespread electric power outages are common, as windstorms can uproot trees that can fall into overhead power lines.

- **Lightning:** Atmospheric discharges of electricity occur during thunderstorms, dust storms, and volcanic eruptions. Lightning can start fires, damage buildings and power transmission systems, and cause power outages.

- **Ice storms:** Ice storms occur when rain falls through a layer of colder air, causing raindrops to freeze onto whatever surface they strike. When ice forms on power lines, the resulting weight causes them to collapse, causing widespread power outages. A notable example is the Great Ice Storm of 1998 in eastern Canada, which resulted in millions being without power for as long as two weeks and in the virtual immobilization of the cities of Montreal and Ottawa. It also affected people in the northeastern U.S.

- **Hail:** This form of precipitation consists of ice chunks ranging from 5mm to 150mm in diameter. An example of a damaging hailstorm is the April 1999 storm in Sydney, Australia, where hailstones up to 9.5cm in diameter damaged 40,000 vehicles, 20,000 properties, and 25 airplanes, and caused one direct fatality. The storm caused $1.5 billion in damage.

- **Flooding:** Standing or moving water spills out of its banks, flows into and through buildings, and causes significant damage to roads, buildings, and utilities. Flooding can be a result of locally heavy rains, heavy snowmelt, a dam or levee break, tropical cyclone storm surge, or an avalanche or landslide that displaces lake or river water.

- **Tsunamis:** This series of waves usually results from the sudden vertical displacement of a lakebed or ocean floor, but a tsunami can also be caused by landslides, asteroids, or explosions. A tsunami wave can be barely noticeable in open, deep water, but as it approaches a shoreline, the wave can grow to a height of 50 feet or more. Recent notable examples are the 2004 Indian Ocean tsunami and the 2011 Japan tsunami. Coastline damage from the Japan tsunami is shown in Figure 6.2.

FIGURE 6.2 Damage to structures caused by the 2011 Japan tsunami

Source: United States Navy / Public Domain

- **Pandemic:** The spread of infectious disease can occur over a wide geographic region, even worldwide. Pandemics have regularly occurred throughout history and are likely to continue occurring, despite advances in sanitation and immunology. A pandemic is the rapid spread of any type of disease, including typhoid, tuberculosis, bubonic plague, or influenza. Pandemics in the 20th century include the 1918–1920 Spanish flu, the 1956–1958 Asian flu, the 1968–1969 Hong Kong "swine" flu, the 2009–2010 swine flu, and the 2020–2022 COVID pandemics. Figure 6.3 shows an auditorium that was converted into a hospital during the 1918–1920 Spanish flu pandemic.

- **Extraterrestrial impacts:** This category includes meteorites and other objects that may fall from the sky from way, way up. Sure, these events are extremely rare, and most organizations don't even include them in their risk analysis, but we've included them here to round out the types of natural events.

FIGURE 6.3 An auditorium was used as a temporary hospital during the 1918 flu pandemic.

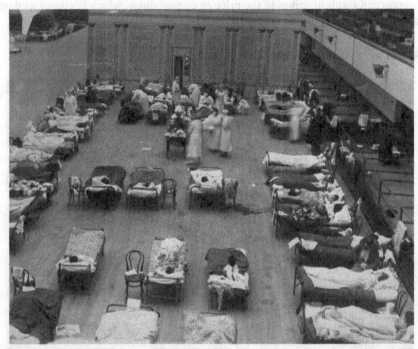

Source: Edward A. "Doc" Rogers / Oakland Public Library

Human-Made Disasters

Human-made disasters are events directly or indirectly caused by human activity through action or inaction. They result in the same way as natural disasters: localized or widespread damage to businesses that results in potentially lengthy interruptions in operations.

Examples of human-made disasters include:

- **Civil disturbances:** These can include protests, demonstrations, riots, strikes, work slowdowns and stoppages, looting, and resulting actions such as curfews, evacuations, or lockdowns.

- **Utility outages:** Failures in electric, natural gas, district heating, water, communications, and other utilities can be caused by equipment failures, sabotage, or natural events such as extreme weather, landslides, or flooding.

- **Service outages:** Failures in IT equipment, software programs, and online services can be caused by faulty or damaged hardware, software bugs, or misconfiguration.

- **Materials shortages:** Interruptions in the supply of food, fuel, supplies, and materials can have a ripple effect on businesses and the services that support them. Readers who are old enough may remember the petroleum shortages of the mid-1970s, including lines at gas stations. The 2020 COVID pandemic triggered numerous goods shortages; Figure 6.4 shows a shortage of baby formula in a grocery store in Washington State. Shortages can result in spikes in the price of commodities, which is almost as damaging as not having any supply at all.

FIGURE 6.4   Baby formula shortages hit the United States in 2021.

Source: John Crowley / Wikimedia Commons / CC BY-SA 2.0

- **Fires:** As contrasted to wildfires, human-made fires originate in or involve homes, buildings, equipment, and materials.

- **Hazardous materials spills:** Many created or refined substances can be dangerous if they escape their confines. Examples include petroleum substances, gases, pesticides and herbicides, medical substances, and radioactive substances.

- **Transportation accidents:** This broad category includes plane crashes, railroad derailments, bridge collapses, and the like.

- **Terrorism and war:** Whether they are actions of a nation, nation-state, or group, terrorism and war can have devastating but usually localized effects in cities and regions. Often, terrorism and war precipitate secondary effects such as materials shortages and utility outages.

- **Security events:** The actions of a lone hacker or a team of organized cybercriminals can bring down one system, one network, or many networks, which could result in widespread interruption in services. The hackers' activities can directly result in an outage, or an organization can voluntarily (although reluctantly) shut down an affected service or network to contain the incident.

It is important to remember that real disasters are usually complex events that involve more than just one type of damaging event. For instance, an earthquake directly damages buildings and equipment, but it can also cause fires and utility outages. A hurricane also brings flooding, utility outages, and sometimes even hazardous materials events and civil disturbances such as looting.

How Disasters Affect Organizations

Disasters have a wide variety of effects on an organization. Many disasters have direct effects, but sometimes it is the secondary effects of a disaster event that are most significant from the perspective of ongoing business operations.

A risk analysis is a part of the BCP process (discussed in the next section) that will identify the ways in which disasters are likely to affect a particular organization. During the risk analysis, the primary, secondary, and downstream effects of likely disaster scenarios need to be identified and considered. Whoever is performing this risk analysis will need to have a broad understanding of the interdependencies of business processes and IT systems, as well as the ways in which a disaster will affect ongoing business operations. Similarly, personnel who are developing contingency and recovery plans also need to be familiar with these effects so that those plans will adequately serve the organization's needs.

Disasters, by our definition, interrupt business operations in some measurable way. An event that has the appearance of a disaster may occur, but if it doesn't affect a particular organization, then we would say that no disaster occurred, at least for that organization.

It would be shortsighted to say that a disaster affects only operations. Rather, it is appropriate to understand the longer-term effects that a disaster has on the organization's image, brand, reputation, and ongoing financial viability. The factors affecting image, brand, and reputation have as much to do with how the organization communicates to its customers, suppliers, and shareholders, as how the organization handles a disaster in progress.

Here are some of the ways that a disaster affects an organization's operations:

- **Direct damage:** Events such as earthquakes, floods, and fires directly damage an organization's buildings, equipment, or records. The damage may be severe enough that no salvageable items remain, or it may be less severe, where some equipment and buildings may be salvageable or repairable.

- **Utility interruption:** Even if an organization's buildings and equipment are undamaged, a disaster may affect utilities such as power, natural gas, or water, which can incapacitate some or all business operations. Significant delays in refuse collection can result in unsanitary conditions.

- **Transportation:** A disaster may damage or render transportation systems such as roads, railroads, shipping, or air transport unusable for a period. Damaged transportation systems will interrupt supply lines and personnel.

- **Services and supplier shortage:** Even if a disaster does not directly affect an organization, critical suppliers affected by a disaster can have an undesirable effect on business operations. For instance, a regional baker that cannot produce and ship bread to its corporate customers will soon result in sandwich shops and restaurants without a critical resource.

- **Staff availability:** A community-wide or regional disaster that affects businesses is also likely to affect homes and families. Depending on the nature of a disaster, employees will place a higher priority on the safety and comfort of family members. Also, workers may not be able or willing to travel to work if transportation systems are affected or if there is a significant materials shortage. Employees may also be unwilling to travel to work if they fear for their personal safety or that of their families.

- **Customer availability:** Various types of disasters may force or dissuade customers from traveling to business locations to conduct business. Many of the factors that keep employees away may also keep customers away.

WARNING   The kinds of secondary and tertiary effects that a disaster has on a particular organization depend entirely on its unique set of circumstances that constitute its specific critical needs. A risk analysis should be performed to identify these specific factors.

The Business Continuity Planning Process

The proper way to plan for disaster preparedness is to know what kinds of disasters are likely and what possible effects they may have on the organization. That is, plan first, act later.

The business continuity planning process is a life cycle process. In other words, business continuity planning (and disaster recovery planning) is not a one-time event or activity. It's a set of activities that results in the ongoing preparedness for disaster that continually adapts to changing business conditions and that continually improves.

The elements of the BCP process life cycle are:

- Develop BCP policy.
- Conduct business impact analysis (BIA).
- Perform criticality analysis (CA).
- Establish and finalize recovery targets.

- Develop recovery and continuity strategies and plans.
- Train personnel.
- Test recovery and continuity plans and procedures.
- Maintain strategies, plans, and procedures through periodic reviews and updates.

Figure 6.5 shows the BCP life cycle, which is described in detail throughout this chapter.

FIGURE 6.5 The BCP process life cycle

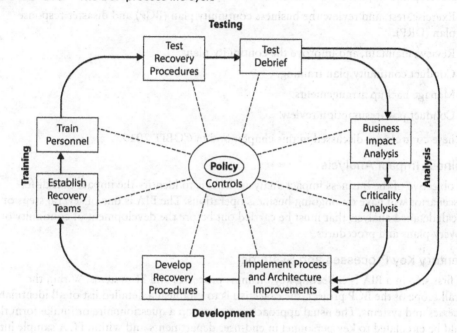

BCP Policy

Like any strategic activity, a formal BCP effort must flow from the existence of a formal policy and be included in the overall governance model that is the topic of this chapter. BCP should be an integral part of the IT control framework; it should not lie outside of it. Therefore, BCP policy should include or cite specific controls that ensure that key activities in the BCP life cycle are performed appropriately.

BCP policy should also define the scope of the BCP strategy. This means that the specific business processes (or departments or divisions within an organization) included in the BCP effort must be defined. Sometimes, the scope will include a geographic boundary. In larger organizations, it is possible to "bite off more than you can chew" and define a scope that is too large for a BCP project, so limiting the scope to a smaller, more manageable portion of the organization can be a good approach.

BCP and COBIT 2019 Controls

The specific *COBIT 2019 controls* that are involved with BCP are contained within DSS04—Managed Continuity. DSS04 has eight specific controls that constitute the entire BCP life cycle:

- Define the business continuity policy, objectives, and scope.
- Maintain business resilience.
- Develop and implement a business continuity response.
- Exercise, test, and review the business continuity plan (BCP) and disaster response plan (DRP).
- Review, maintain, and improve the continuity plans.
- Conduct continuity plan training.
- Manage backup arrangements.
- Conduct post-resumption review.

These controls are discussed in this chapter and in COBIT 2019.

Business Impact Analysis

The objective of the business impact analysis (BIA) is to identify the impact that different scenarios will have on ongoing business operations. The BIA is one of several steps of critical, detailed analysis that must be carried out before the development of continuity or recovery plans and procedures.

Inventory Key Processes and Systems

The first step in a BIA is collecting key business processes and IT systems. Within the overall scope of the BCP project, the objective is to establish a detailed list of all identifiable processes and systems. The usual approach is to develop a questionnaire or intake form that would be circulated to key personnel in end-user departments and within IT. A sample intake form is shown in Figure 6.6.

Typically, the information that is gathered on intake forms is transferred to a multicolumned spreadsheet, where information on all the organization's in-scope processes can be viewed together. This will become even more useful in subsequent phases of the BCP project, such as the criticality analysis.

The use of an intake form is not the only accepted approach when gathering information about critical processes and systems. It's also acceptable to conduct one-on-one interviews or group interviews with key users and IT personnel to identify critical processes and systems. We recommend the use of an intake form (whether paper-based or electronic), even if the interviewer uses it only as a framework for note-taking.

FIGURE 6.6 BIA sample intake form for gathering data about key processes

Process or system name	
Interviewee	
Title	
Department	
Contact info	
Date	
Process owner	
Process operator(s)	
Process description	
Customer-facing (Y or N)	
IT system(s) used	
Key suppliers	
Communications needed	
Assets needed	
Process dependencies	
Other dependencies	
Documentation location	
Records location	

Planning Precedes Action

IT personnel are often eager to get to the fun and meaty parts of a project. Developers are anxious to begin coding before design; system administrators are eager to build systems before they are scoped and designed; and BCP personnel fervently desire to begin designing more robust system architectures and to tinker with replication and backup capabilities before key facts are known. In the case of business continuity and disaster recovery planning, completion of the BIA and other analyses is critical, as the analyses help to define the systems and processes most needed before getting to the fun part.

Statements of Impact

When processes and systems are being inventoried and cataloged, it is also vitally important to obtain one or more statements of impact for each. A statement of impact is a qualitative or quantitative description of the impact on the business if the process or system were incapacitated for a time.

For IT systems, you might capture the number of users and the names of departments or functions that are affected by the unavailability of a specific IT system. Include the geography of affected users and functions if appropriate. Here are some example statements of impact on IT systems:

- Three thousand customer support users in France and Italy will be unable to access customer records.
- All users in North America will be unable to read or send email.

Statements of impact for business processes may cite the business functions that would be affected. Here are some examples:

- Accounts payable and accounts receivable functions will be unable to process.
- The legal department will be unable to access contracts and addendums.

Statements of impact for revenue-generating and revenue-supporting business functions could quantify financial impact per unit of time (be sure to use the same units of time for all functions so that they can be easily compared with one another). Here are some examples:

- The inability to place orders for appliances will cost at the rate of $12,000 per hour.
- Delays in payments will cost $45,000 per day in interest charges.

As statements of impact are gathered, it may make sense to create several columns in the main worksheet so that like units (names of functions, numbers of users, financial figures) can be sorted and ranked later.

A complete BIA will have the following information about each process and system:

- Name of the system or process
- Who is responsible for it
- A description of its function
- Dependencies on systems
- Dependencies on suppliers
- Dependencies on key employees
- Quantified statements of impact in terms of revenue, users affected, and/or functions impacted

You're almost home.

Criticality Analysis

When all the BIA information has been collected and charted, the criticality analysis (CA) can be performed.

The criticality analysis is a study of each system and process, a consideration of the impact on the organization if it is incapacitated, the likelihood of incapacitation, and the estimated cost of mitigating the risk or impact of incapacitation. In other words, it's a somewhat special type of risk analysis that focuses on key processes and systems.

The criticality analysis needs to include or reference a threat analysis. A threat analysis is a risk analysis that identifies every threat that has a reasonable probability of occurrence, plus one or more mitigating controls or compensating controls, and new probabilities of occurrence with those mitigating/compensating controls in place. In case you're having a little trouble imagining what this looks like (we're writing the book and are having trouble seeing this!), look at Table 6.1, which is a lightweight example of what we're talking about.

TABLE 6.1   Example threat analysis, which identifies threats and controls for critical systems and processes

System	Threat	Probability	Event cost est.	Mitigating control	Mitigation cost	Mitigated probability
Application Server	Denial of service	0.1%	$200,000	High-performance filtering router	$60,000	0.01%
	Malware	1%	$20,000	Antivirus	$200	0.1%
	Storage failure	2%	$60,000	RAID-5	$20,000	0.01%
	Administrator error	15%	$100,000	Configuration management tools	$10,000	1%
	Hardware CPU failure	5%	$10,000	Server cluster	$15,000	1%
	Application software bug	5%	$30,000	Source code reviews	$10,000	2%
	Extended power outage	25%	$300,000	UPS	$12,000	2%
				Electric generator	$40,000	0.5%
	Flood	2%	$500,000	Relocate data center	$200,000	0.1%

In this threat analysis, notice the following:

- Multiple threats are listed for a single asset. In the table, we mentioned just eight threats. For all the threats but one, we listed only a single mitigating control. For the extended power outage threat, we listed two mitigating controls.
- Cost of downtime is estimated. For systems or processes where you have a cost per unit of time for downtime, you'll need to include it here, along with some calculations to show the payback for each control.

- Some mitigating controls can benefit more than one system. That may not have been obvious in this example, but in the case of a UPS (uninterruptible power supply) and an electric generator, many systems can benefit, so the cost for these mitigating controls can be allocated across many systems, thereby lowering the cost for each system. Another example is a high-availability storage area network (SAN) located in two different geographic areas; while initially expensive, many applications can use the SAN for storage, and all will benefit from replication to the counterpart storage system.

- Threat probabilities are arbitrary. In Table 6.1, the probabilities were for a single occurrence in an entire year, so 5 percent means the threat will be realized once every 20 years.

- The length of the outage was not included. You may need to include this also, particularly if you are quantifying downtime per hour or another unit of time.

It is probably becoming obvious that a threat analysis, and the corresponding criticality analysis, can get complicated. The rule here should be this: The complexity of the threat and criticality analyses should be proportional to the value of the assets (or revenue, or both). For example, in a company where application downtime is measured in thousands of dollars per minute, it's probably worth taking a few weeks or even months to work out all the likely scenarios and a variety of mitigating controls, and to work out which ones are the most cost-effective. On the other hand, for a system or business process where the impact of an outage is far less costly, a good deal less time might be spent on the supporting threat and criticality analysis.

Exam Tip

Test-takers should ensure that any question dealing with BIA and CA places the business impact analysis first. Without this analysis, criticality analysis is impossible to evaluate in terms of likelihood or cost-effectiveness in mitigation strategies. The BIA identifies strategic resources and provides value to their recovery and operation, which is, in turn, consumed in the criticality analysis phase. If presented with a question identifying BCP at a particular stage, make sure that any answers you select facilitate the BIA and then the CA before moving on toward objectives and strategies.

Determine Maximum Tolerable Downtime

The next step for each critical process is to establish a metric called maximum tolerable downtime (MTD). This is a theoretical time interval measured from the onset of a disaster, after which the organization's very survival is at risk. Establishing MTD for each critical process is an important step that aids in the establishment of key recovery targets, discussed next.

Establishing Key Recovery Targets

When the cost or impact of downtime has been established, and the cost and benefit of mitigating controls have been considered, some key targets can be established for each critical process. These objectives determine how quickly key systems and processes should be made available after the onset of a disaster and the maximum tolerable data loss that results from the disaster. The two key recovery targets are:

- **Recovery time objective (RTO):** This refers to the maximum period that elapses from the onset of a disaster until the resumption of service.

- **Recovery point objective (RPO):** This refers to the maximum acceptable data loss from the onset of a disaster.

- **Recovery capacity objective (RCapO):** This refers to the transaction processing capacity of the recovery system, usually expressed as a percentage of the processing capacity of the primary system.

- **Recovery consistency objective (RCO):** This refers to the consistency or completeness of the recovery system, usually expressed as a percentage as compared to the primary system.

- **Service delivery objective (SDO):** This typically refers to some aspect of service delivery, such as SLAs.

Once these target objectives are known, the disaster recovery (DR) team can begin to build system recovery capabilities and procedures that will help the organization economically realize these targets. This is discussed in detail later in this chapter.

Developing Continuity Plans

In the previous section, we discussed the notion of establishing recovery targets and the development of architectures, processes, and procedures. The processes and procedures are related to the normal operation of those new technologies as they will be operated in normal day-to-day operations. When those processes and procedures have been completed, business continuity recovery strategies (actions that will take place during and immediately after a disaster) to continue the delivery of products and services can be developed.

For example, an organization has established RPO, RTO, RCapO, RCO, and SDO targets for its critical applications. These targets necessitated the development of server clusters and storage area networks with replication. While implementing those new technologies, the organization developed the operations processes and procedures in support of those new technologies that would be carried out every day during normal business operations. As a separate activity, the organization would then develop the procedures to be performed when a disaster strikes the primary operations center for those applications; those procedures would include all the steps that must be taken so that the applications can continue operating in an alternate location or in the public or private cloud.

The procedures for operating critical applications during a disaster are a small part of the entire body of procedures that must be developed. Several other sets of procedures must also be developed, including:

- Personnel safety procedures
- Disaster declaration procedures
- Responsibilities
- Contract information
- Recovery procedures
- Continuing operations
- Restoration procedures

All of these are required so that an organization will be adequately prepared in the event a disaster occurs.

Personnel Safety Procedures

When a disaster strikes, measures to ensure the safety of personnel are a top priority and need to be taken immediately. If a disaster has occurred or is about to occur in a building, personnel may need to be evacuated as soon as possible. Arguably, however, in some situations, evacuation is exactly the wrong thing to do; for example, if a hurricane or tornado is bearing down on a facility, the building itself may be the best shelter for personnel, even if it incurs some damage. The point here is that personnel safety procedures need to be carefully developed, and possibly more than one set of procedures will be needed, depending on the event.

 The highest priority in any disaster or emergency is the safety of human life.

Personnel safety procedures need to take many factors into account, including:

- Ensuring that all personnel are familiar with evacuation and sheltering procedures
- Ensuring that visitors know how to evacuate the premises and know the location of sheltering areas
- Posting signs and placards that indicate emergency evacuation routes and gathering areas outside of the building
- Locating emergency lighting to aid in evacuation or sheltering in place
- Providing fire extinguishment equipment (portable fire extinguishers and so on)
- Ensuring that people can communicate with public safety and law enforcement authorities, including in situations where communications and electric power have been cut off and when all personnel are outside of the building
- Caring for injured personnel

- Training in CPR and emergency first aid
- Providing safety personnel who can assist in the evacuation of injured and disabled persons
- Providing the ability to account for visitors and other nonemployees
- Providing emergency shelter in extreme weather conditions
- Providing emergency food and drinking water
- Conducting periodic tests to ensure that evacuation procedures will be adequate in the event of a real emergency

Local emergency management organizations may have additional information available that can assist an organization with its emergency personnel safety procedures.

Disaster Declaration Procedures

Disaster response procedures are initiated when a disaster is declared. However, there needs to be a procedure for the declaration itself so that there will be little doubt as to the conditions that must be present.

Why is a disaster declaration procedure required? Primarily because it's not always clear whether a situation is a real disaster. Sure, a 7.5 earthquake or a major fire is a disaster, but overcooking popcorn in the microwave and setting off a building's fire alarm system might not be. Many "in-between" situations may or may not be considered disasters. A disaster declaration procedure must state some basic conditions that will help determine whether a disaster should be declared.

Further, who has the authority to declare a disaster? What if senior management personnel frequently travel and may not be around? Who else can declare a disaster? And, finally, what does it mean to declare a disaster—and what happens next? The following points constitute the primary items that organizations need to consider for their disaster declaration procedure.

Form a Core Team

A *core team* of personnel needs to be established, all of whom will be familiar with the disaster declaration procedure, as well as the actions that must take place once a disaster has been declared. This core team should consist of middle and upper managers who are familiar with business operations, particularly those that are critical. This core team must be large enough so that a requisite few of them are on hand when a disaster strikes. In organizations that have second-shift, third-shift, and weekend workers, some of the core team members should be in supervisory positions during those times. However, some of the core team members can be personnel who work "business hours" and are not on-site all the time.

Declaration Criteria

The *declaration* procedure must contain some tangible criteria that a core team member can consult to guide them down the "Is this a disaster?" decision path. A declaration procedure can include criteria in operational areas such as finance, customer service, operations, legal, compliance, and reputation, optionally with severity scores (low, medium, high) in organizations that want to quantify the situation in detail.

The criteria for declaring a disaster should be related to the availability and viability of ongoing critical business operations. Example criteria include any one or more of the following:

- Forced evacuation of a building containing or supporting critical operations that is likely to last for more than four hours

- Hardware, software, or network failures that result in a critical IT system being incapacitated or unavailable for more than four hours

- A major, prolonged outage by an Internet service provider or cloud service provider

- Any security incident that results in a critical IT system being incapacitated for more than four hours (security incidents could involve malware, break-in, attack, sabotage, and so on)

- Any event causing employee absenteeism or supplier shortages that, in turn, results in one or more critical business processes being incapacitated for more than eight hours

- Any event causing a communications failure that results in critical IT systems being unreachable for more than four hours

The preceding examples are a mostly complete list of criteria for many organizations. The duration periods will vary from organization to organization. For instance, a large, pure online business such as Salesforce.com would probably declare a disaster if its main websites were unavailable for more than a few minutes. However, in an organization where computers are far less critical, an outage of four hours might not be considered a disaster.

Activating the Plan

When disaster declaration criteria are met, the disaster should be declared. The procedure for disaster declaration could permit any single core team member to declare the disaster, but it may be better to have two or more core team members agree on whether a disaster should be declared. Whether an organization should use a single-person declaration or a group of two or more is each organization's choice.

Disaster declaration will trigger the crisis management plan and assemble the crisis management team. Often, this is a broad cross-section of IT, security, BCDR, and business leaders to work the event overall.

All core team members empowered to declare a disaster should always have the procedure on hand. In most cases, the criteria should fit on a small, laminated wallet card that each team member can always keep close. For organizations that use the consensus method for declaring a disaster, the wallet card should include the names and contact numbers of other core team members so that each will have a way of contacting others.

Next Steps

Declaring a disaster will activate the start of one or more other response procedures, but not necessarily all of them. For instance, if a disaster is declared because of a serious computer or software malfunction, there is no need to evacuate the building. While this example may be obvious, not all instances will be this clear. Either the disaster declaration procedure itself or each of the subsequent response procedures should contain criteria that will help determine which response procedures should be enacted.

False Alarms

Probably the most common cause of personnel not declaring a disaster is the fear that an actual disaster is not taking place. Core team members empowered with declaring a disaster should not necessarily hesitate. Instead, core team members could convene with additional core team members to reach a firm decision, provided this can be done quickly.

If a disaster has been declared and later it is clear that it has been averted (or did not exist in the first place), the disaster can simply be called off and declared over. Response personnel can be contacted and told to cease response activities and return to their normal activities.

 Depending on the level of effort in the opening minutes and hours of disaster response, the consequences of declaring a disaster when none exists may or may not be significant. In the spirit of continuous improvement, any organization that has had a few false alarms should seek to improve its disaster declaration criteria or procedures. Well-trained and experienced personnel can usually reduce the frequency of false alarms.

Disaster Responsibilities

During a disaster, many important tasks must be performed to evacuate or shelter personnel, assess damage, recover critical processes and systems, and carry out many other functions that are critical to the survival of the enterprise.

About 20 different responsibilities are described here. In a large organization, each responsibility may be staffed with a team of two, three, or several individuals. In small organizations, a few people may have many responsibilities, switching from role to role as the situation warrants.

All these roles should be staffed by people who are available. It is important to remember that many of the "ideal" persons to fill each role may be unavailable during a disaster for several reasons, including the following:

- **Injured, ill, or deceased:** Some regional disasters will inflict widespread casualties that will include some proportion of response personnel. Those who are injured, ill (in the case of a pandemic, for instance, or who are recovering from a sickness or surgery when the disaster occurs), or who are killed by the disaster are clearly not going to show up to help.

- **Caring for family members:** Some types of disasters may cause widespread injury or require mass evacuation. In these situations, many personnel will be caring for family members whose immediate safety needs will take priority over the needs of the workplace.

- **Unavailable transportation:** Some types of disasters include localized or widespread damage to transportation infrastructure, which may result in many persons who are willing to be on-site to help with emergency operations being unable to travel to the worksite.

- **Out of the area:** Some disaster response personnel may be away on business travel or on vacation and be unable to respond. However, some persons being away may be opportunities in disguise; unaffected by the physical impact of the disaster, they may be able to help in other ways, such as communications with suppliers, customers, or other personnel.

- **Communications:** Some types of disasters, particularly those that are localized (versus widespread and obvious to an observer), require that disaster response personnel be contacted and asked to help. If a disaster strikes after hours, some personnel may be unreachable.

- **Fear:** Some types of disasters (such as pandemics, terrorist attacks, and floods) may instill fear for safety on the part of response personnel who may disregard the call to help and stay away from the worksite.

Response personnel in all disciplines and responsibilities will need to be able to piece together whatever functionality they are called on to do, using whatever resources are available—this is part art and part science. Although response and contingency plans may make certain assumptions, personnel may find themselves with fewer resources than they need, requiring them to do the best they can with the resources available.

Each role will be working with personnel in many other roles, often working with unfamiliar persons. An entire response and recovery operation may be operating almost like a brand-new organization in unfamiliar settings and with an entirely new set of rules. In typical organizations, teams work well when team members are familiar with, and trust, one another. In a response and recovery operation, the stress level is much higher because the stakes—company survival—are higher, and often the teams are composed of persons who have little experience with one another and these new roles. This will cause additional stress that will bring out the best and worst in people, as illustrated in Figure 6.7.

Emergency Response

These are the first responders during a disaster. Their top priorities include personnel evacuation or sheltering, first aid, triage of injured personnel, and possibly firefighting.

Command and Control (Emergency Management)

During disaster response operations, someone must be in charge. In a disaster, resources may be scarce, and many matters will vie for attention. Someone needs to fill the role of decision maker to keep disaster response activities moving and to handle situations that arise. This role may need to be rotated among various personnel, particularly in smaller organizations, to counteract fatigue. In times of disaster, it is crucial to prioritize the well-being of responders. Establishing resource plans that account for their needs and prevent overworking is essential.

FIGURE 6.7 Stress is compounded by the pressure of disaster recovery and the formation of new teams in times of chaos.

Although the first person on the scene may be the person in charge initially, that will change as qualified assigned personnel show up and take charge and as the nature of the disaster and response solidifies. The leadership roles may then be passed among key personnel already designated to be in charge. Some organizations establish a command-and-control structure that designates roles such as Commander, Operations, Logistics, Planning, Finance, and Communications and Public Information. This ensures clear lines of responsibility and effective coordination of the response efforts.

Documentation

It's vital that one or more persons continually document the important events during disaster response operations. From decisions to discussions to status to roll calls, these events must be written down (and later recorded digitally) so that the details of disaster response can be pieced together afterward. This will help the organization better understand how disaster response unfolded, how decisions were made, and who performed which actions, all of which will help the organization be better prepared for future events.

Internal and External Communications

In many disaster scenarios, personnel may be stripped of many or all their normal means of communication, such as desk phone, voicemail, email, smartphone, and instant messaging. Yet never are communications as vital as during a disaster, when nothing is going according to plan. Internal communications are needed so that the status of various activities can be sent to command and control and so that priorities and orders can be sent to disaster response personnel.

People outside of the organization also need to know what's going on when a disaster strikes. There's a potentially long list of parties who want or need to know the status of business operations during and after a disaster, including:

- Customers
- Suppliers
- Partners
- Shareholders
- Neighbors
- Regulators
- Local government
- Media
- Law enforcement and public safety authorities

These different audiences need different messages, as well as messages in different forms.

Legal and Compliance

Several needs may arise during a disaster that require the attention of inside or outside legal counsel. Disasters present unique situations that need legal assistance, such as:

- Interpretation of regulations
- Interpretation of contracts with suppliers and customers
- Management of matters of liability to other parties

Typical legal matters need to be resolved before the onset of a disaster, and this information should be included in disaster response procedures since legal staff members may be unavailable during a disaster.

Damage Assessment

Whether a disaster is a physically violent event, such as an earthquake or volcano, or instead involves no physical manifestation, such as a serious security incident, one or more experts are needed who can examine affected assets and accurately assess the damage. Because most organizations own many different types of assets (buildings, equipment, and information), qualified experts are needed to assess each asset type involved. It is not necessary to call upon all available experts—only those whose expertise matches the type of event that has occurred need to be consulted.

Some expertise may go well beyond the skills present in an organization, such as a building structural engineer who can assess potential earthquake damage. In such cases, it may be sensible to retain the services of an outside engineer who will respond and provide an assessment of whether a building is safe to occupy after a disaster. In fact, it may make sense to retain more than one, in case one or more of them is affected by a disaster.

Salvage

Disasters destroy assets that the organization uses to make products or perform services. When a disaster occurs, someone (either a qualified employee or an outside expert) needs to examine assets to determine which are salvageable; then, a salvage team needs to perform the actual salvage operation at a pace that meets the organization's needs.

In some cases, salvage may be a critical-path activity, where critical processes are paralyzed until salvage and repairs or replacements to critically needed machinery can be performed. In other cases, the salvage operation is performed on inventory of finished goods, raw materials, and other items so that business operations can be resumed. Occasionally, when it is obvious that damaged equipment or materials are a total loss, the salvage effort involves selling the damaged items or materials to another organization.

Assessment of damage to assets may be a high priority when an organization files an insurance claim. Insurance may be a primary source of funding for the organization's recovery effort.

WARNING   Salvage operations may be a critical-path activity or one that can be carried out well after the disaster. To the greatest extent possible, this should be decided in advance. Otherwise, the command-and-control function will need to decide the priority of salvage operations.

Physical Security

After a disaster, the organization's usual physical security controls may be compromised. For instance, fencing, walls, and barricades could be damaged, or video surveillance systems may be disabled or without electricity. These and other failures could lead to an increased risk of loss or damage to assets and personnel until those controls can be restored. Also, security controls in temporary quarters such as hot/warm/cold sites and temporary work centers may be inadequate compared to those in primary locations.

NOTE   Another physical security control example during a disaster is the concept of fail-safe and fail-secure. During a power failure, fail-safe locks automatically unlock doors. Fail-safe locks are essential for situations where reentry should be unrestricted. Fail-secure locks remain locked when the power goes out and are key for protecting high-value assets such as IT equipment rooms.

Supplies

During emergency and recovery operations, personnel will require supplies of many kinds, from food and drinking water, writing tablets, and pens, to smartphones, portable generators, and extension cords. This function may also be responsible for ordering replacement assets, such as servers and network equipment for a cold site.

Transportation

When workers are operating from a temporary location and/or if regional or local transportation systems have been compromised, many arrangements for all kinds of transportation may be required to support emergency operations. These can include transportation of replacement workers, equipment, or supplies by truck, car, rail, sea, or air. The transportation function could also be responsible for arranging for temporary lodging for personnel.

Networks

This technology function is responsible for damage assessment to the organization's voice and data networks, building/configuring networks for emergency operations, or both. This function may require extensive coordination with external telecommunications service providers, who may be suffering the effects of a local or regional disaster as well.

Network Services

This function is responsible for network-centric services such as Domain Name System (DNS), Simple Network Management Protocol (SNMP), virtual private network (VPN), network routing, and authentication.

Systems

This function is responsible for building, loading, and configuring the servers and systems that support critical services, applications, databases, and other functions. Personnel may have other resources, such as virtualization technology, to enable additional flexibility.

Database Management Systems

For critical applications that rely on database management systems, this function is responsible for building databases on recovery systems and for restoring or recovering data from backup media, replication volumes, or e-vaults onto recovery systems. Database personnel will need to work with systems, network, and applications personnel to ensure that databases are operating properly and are available as needed.

Data and Records

This function is responsible for accessing and re-creating electronic and paper business records. It supports critical business processes and works with database management personnel and, if necessary, data entry personnel to rekey lost data.

Applications

This function is responsible for recovering application functionality on application servers. This may include reloading application software, performing configuration, provisioning roles and user accounts, and connecting the application to databases, network services, and other application integration issues.

Access Management

This function creates and manages user accounts for network, system, and application access. Personnel with this responsibility may be especially susceptible to social engineering and tempted to create user accounts without proper authority or approval.

Information Security and Privacy

Personnel who serve in this capacity are responsible for ensuring that proper security controls are being carried out during recovery and emergency operations. They will be expected to identify risks associated with emergency operations and to require remedies to reduce risks.

Security personnel will also be responsible for enforcing privacy controls to ensure that employee and customer personal data is not compromised, even as business operations are affected by the disaster.

Off-site Data Storage

This function is responsible for managing the effort of retrieving backup media from off-site storage facilities and for protecting that media in transit to the scene of recovery operations. If recovery operations take place over an extended period (more than a couple of days), data at the recovery site will need to be backed up and sent to an off-site media storage facility to protect that information should a disaster occur at the hot/warm/cold site (and what bad luck that would be!).

User Hardware

In many organizations, little productive work gets done when employees don't have their workstations, printers, scanners, copiers, and other office equipment. Thus, a user hardware function is required to provide, configure, and support the variety of office equipment required by end users working in temporary or alternate locations. This function, like most others, will have to work with many others to ensure that workstations and other equipment are able to communicate with applications and services as needed to support critical processes.

Training

During emergency operations, when response personnel and users are working in new locations (and often on new or different equipment and software), some personnel may need training so that their productivity can be quickly restored. Training personnel will need to be familiar with many disaster response and recovery procedures so that they can help people in those roles understand what is expected of them. This function will also need to be able to dispense emergency operations procedures to these personnel.

Restoration

This function comes into play when IT is ready to migrate applications running on hot/warm/cold site systems back to the original (or replacement) processing center.

Contract Information

This function is responsible for understanding and interpreting legal contracts. Most organizations are a party to one or more legal contracts that require them to perform specific activities, provide specific services, and communicate status if service levels have changed. These contracts may or may not have provisions for activities and services during disasters, including communications regarding any changes in service levels.

This function is vital not only during the disaster planning stages but also during actual disaster response. Customers, suppliers, regulators, and other parties need to be informed according to specific contract terms.

Recovery Procedures

Recovery procedures are the instructions that key personnel use to bootstrap services (such as IT systems and other business-enabling technologies) that support the critical business functions identified in the BIA and CA. The recovery procedures should work together with the technologies that may have been added to IT systems to make them more resilient.

An example would be useful here: A fictitious company, Acme Rocket Boots, determines that its order-entry business function is highly critical to the ongoing viability of the business and sets recovery objectives to ensure that order entry would be continued within no more than 48 hours after a disaster. Acme determined that it needs to invest in storage, backup, and replication technologies to make a 48-hour recovery possible. Without these investments, IT systems supporting order entry would be down for at least 10 days until they could be rebuilt from scratch. Acme cannot justify the purchase of systems and software to facilitate an auto-failover of the order-entry application to hot-site DR servers. Instead, the recovery procedure would require that the database be rebuilt from replicated data on cloud-based servers. Other tasks, such as installing recent patches, would also be necessary to make recovery servers ready for production use. All the tasks required to prepare the systems constitute the body of recovery procedures needed to support the business order-entry function.

This example is, of course, an oversimplification. Actual recovery procedures could potentially require dozens of pages of documentation. Procedures would also be necessary for network components, end-user workstations, network services, and other supporting IT services required by the order-entry application. Those are the procedures needed to get the application running again. More procedures would be needed to keep the applications running properly in the recovery environment.

Continuing Operations Procedures

Procedures for continuing operations involve more business processes than IT systems. However, the two are related since the procedures for continuing critical business processes must fit together with the procedures for operating supporting IT systems that may also (but not necessarily) be operating in a recovery or emergency mode.

Let us clarify that last statement: It is entirely conceivable that a disaster could strike an organization with critical business processes that operate in one city but that are supported by IT systems located in another city. A disaster could strike the city with the critical business function, which means that personnel may have to continue operating that business function in another location, on the original, fully featured IT application. It is also possible that a disaster could strike the city with the IT application, forcing it into an emergency/recovery mode in an alternate location, while users of the application are operating in a mostly business-as-usual mode. And, of course, a disaster could strike both locations (or a disaster could strike in one location where both the critical business function and its supporting IT applications reside), throwing both the critical business function and its supporting IT applications into emergency mode. Any organization's reality could be even more complex than this: just add dependencies on external application service providers, applications with custom interfaces, or critical business functions that operate in multiple cities. If you wondered why disaster recovery and business continuity planning were so complicated, perhaps your appreciation has grown after reading this passage.

Restoration Procedures

When a disaster has occurred, IT operations may need to take up residence temporarily in an alternate processing site while repairs are performed on the original site. Once those repairs are completed, IT operations would need to be transitioned back to the main (or replacement) processing facility. You should expect that the procedures for this transition will also be documented (and tested—testing is discussed later in this chapter).

> Transitioning applications back to the original processing site is not necessarily just a second iteration of the initial move to the cloud/hot/warm/cold site. Far from it; the recovery site may have been a skeleton (in capacity, functionality, or both) of its original self. The objective is not necessarily to move the functionality at the recovery site back to the original site, but to restore the original functionality to the original site.

Let's continue the Acme Rocket Boots example: The company's order-entry application at the DR site had only basic, not extended, functions. For instance, customers could not look at order history or place custom orders; they could only order off-the-shelf products. However, when the application is moved back to the primary processing facility, the history of orders accumulated on the DR application needs to be merged into the main order history database, which was not a part of the DR plan.

Considerations for Continuity and Recovery Plans

If continuity and recovery plans are to be effective, they must involve considerable detailed planning and logistics.

Availability of Key Personnel

An organization cannot depend on every member of its regular expert workforce to be available in a disaster. As discussed earlier in this chapter in more detail, personnel may be unavailable for several reasons, including:

- Injury, illness, or death
- Caring for family members

- Unavailable transportation
- Damaged transportation infrastructure
- Being out of the area
- Lack of communications
- Fear related to the disaster and its effects

 An organization must develop thorough and accurate recovery and continuity documentation as well as cross-training and plan testing. When a disaster strikes, an organization has one chance to survive, and survival depends on how well the available personnel can follow recovery and continuity procedures and keep critical processes functioning properly.

A successful disaster recovery operation requires available personnel who are located near company operations centers. While the primary response personnel may consist of the individuals and teams responsible for day-to-day corporate operations, others need to be identified. In a disaster, some personnel will be unavailable for many reasons.

Key personnel, as well as their backup persons, must be identified. Backup personnel can consist of employees who have familiarity with specific technologies, such as operating system, database, and network administration, and who can cover for primary personnel if needed. Sure, it would be desirable for these backup personnel also to be trained in specific recovery operations, but at the very least, if these personnel have access to specific detailed recovery procedures, having them on a call list is probably better than having no available personnel during a disaster.

In the event of a disaster, many other parties need to be notified, including employees. Outside parties should be aware of the disaster and basic changes in business conditions.

In a regional disaster such as a hurricane or earthquake, nearby parties will certainly be aware of the disaster and that your organization is involved in it somehow. However, those parties may not be aware of the status of business operations immediately after the disaster: a regional event's effects can range from complete destruction of buildings and equipment to no damage at all and business-as-usual conditions. Unless key parties are notified of the status, they may have no other way to know for sure.

Parties who need to be contacted may include:

- **Key suppliers:** This may include electric and gas utilities, fuel delivery, and materials delivery. In a disaster, an organization will often have to impart special instructions to one or more suppliers, requesting delivery of extra supplies or temporary cessation of deliveries.

- **Key customers:** Many organizations have key customers whose relationships are valued above most others. These customers may depend on a steady delivery of products and services that are critical to their own operations; in a disaster, those customers may have a dire need to know whether such deliveries will be able to continue or not and under what circumstances.

- **Public safety:** Police, fire, and other public safety authorities may need to be contacted, not only for emergency operations such as firefighting, but also for any required inspections or other services. It is important that "business office" telephone numbers for these agencies be included on contact lists, as 911 and other emergency lines may be flooded by calls from others.

- **Insurance adjusters:** Most organizations rely on insurance companies to protect their assets from damage or loss in a disaster. Because insurance adjustment funds are often a key part of continuing business operations in an emergency, it's important to be able to reach insurers as soon as possible after a disaster has occurred.

- **Regulators:** In some industries, organizations are required to notify regulators of certain types of disasters. While regulators obviously may be aware of noteworthy regional disasters, they may not immediately know of an event's specific effects on an organization. Further, some types of disasters are highly localized and may not be newsworthy, even in a local city.

- **Local government:** Organizations may want to notify the local city, county, or other government entity, particularly when its citizens are directly or indirectly affected by the disaster.

- **Media:** Media outlets such as newspapers and television stations may need to be notified to quickly reach the community or region with information about the effects of a disaster on organizations.

- **Shareholders:** Organizations are usually obliged to notify their shareholders of any disastrous event that affects business operations. This may be the case whether the organization is publicly or privately held.

The persons or teams responsible for communicating with these outside parties should include all the individuals and organizations in a list of parties to contact. This information should also be included in emergency response procedures.

Wallet cards containing emergency contact information should be prepared for core team personnel for the organization as well as for members in each department who would be actively involved in disaster response. Wallet cards are advantageous, because most personnel will have a wallet, notebook, or purse nearby always, even when away from home, running errands, traveling, or on vacation. Information on the wallet card should include contact information for fellow team members, a few of the key disaster response personnel, and any conference bridges or emergency call-in numbers that are set up. An example wallet card is shown in Figure 6.8.

Emergency Supplies

The onset of a disaster may cause personnel to be stranded at a work location, possibly for several days. This can be caused by several reasons, including inclement weather that makes travel dangerous or a transportation infrastructure that is damaged or blocked with debris.

Emergency supplies should be laid up at a work location and made available to personnel stranded there, regardless of whether they are supporting a recovery effort (it's also possible that severe weather or a natural or human-made event could make transportation dangerous or impossible).

FIGURE 6.8   Example laminated wallet card for core team participants with emergency contact information and disaster declaration criteria

Emergency Contacts
Joe Phillips, VP Ops: 213-555-1212 h, 415-555-1212 m
Marie Peterson, CFO: 206-555-1212 h, 425-555-1212 m
Mark Woodward, IT Ops: 360-555-1212 h, 253-555-1212 m
Gary Doan, VP Facilities: 509-555-1212 h, 702-555-1212 m
Jeff Patterson, IT Networks: 760-555-1212 h, 310-555-1212 m
Documentation at briefcase.yahoo.com: Userid = wunderground, password = L0c43Dupt1te
Emergency conference bridge: 1-800-555-1212, host code 443322, PIN 0748
Disaster declaration criteria: 8-hr outage anticipated on critical systems, 2 core members vote, then initiate call tree procedure to notify other response personnel

Off-site media storage vendor: 719-555-1212
Telecommunications and network service provider: 312-555-1212
Local emergency response authorities: 714-555-1212
Local health authorities: 702-555-1212
Local law enforcement authorities: 512-555-1212
Local hospitals: 808-555-1212, 913-555-1212
National weather service hotline: 602-555-1212
Regional transportation authority hotline: 312-555-1212
Local building inspectors: 414-555-1212

A disaster can also prompt employees to report to a work location (at the primary location or at an alternate site), where they may remain for days at a time, even around the clock if necessary. A situation like this may make the need for emergency supplies less critical, but making supplies available to support recovery personnel may still be beneficial to the recovery effort.

An organization stocking emergency supplies at a work location should consider including the following items:

- Drinking water
- Food rations
- First aid supplies
- Blankets
- Flashlights
- Battery or crank-powered radio

Local emergency response authorities may recommend other supplies be kept at a work location as well.

Communications

Communications within organizations, as well as with customers, suppliers, partners, shareholders, regulators, and others, are vital under normal business conditions. During a disaster and subsequent recovery and restoration operations, such communications are more important than ever, as many of the usual means of communication may be impaired.

Disaster response procedures should include a call tree. This method involves the first personnel involved in a disaster notifying others in the organization, informing them of the developing disaster, and enlisting their assistance. Just as the branches of a tree originate at the trunk and are repeatedly subdivided, a call tree is most effective when each person in the tree can make just a few phone calls. Not only will the notification of important personnel proceed more quickly, but each person will not be overburdened with many calls.

Remember that in a disaster, a significant portion of personnel may be unavailable or unreachable. Therefore, a call tree should be structured to provide sufficient flexibility and assurance that all critical personnel will be contacted. Figure 6.9 shows an example call tree.

FIGURE 6.9   Example call tree structure

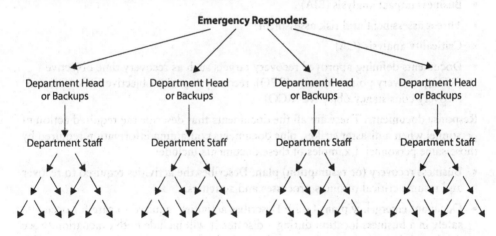

An organization can also use an automated outcalling system such as Everbridge or PagerDuty to notify critical personnel of a disaster. Such a system can play a prerecorded message or request that personnel call an information number to hear a prerecorded message. Most outcalling systems keep a log of which personnel have been successfully reached.

An automated calling system should not be located in the same geographic region as the disaster. A regional disaster could damage the system or make it unavailable during a disaster. The system should be Internet accessible so that response personnel can access it to determine which personnel have been notified and to make any needed changes before or during a disaster.

Transportation

Some types of disasters may make certain modes of transportation unavailable or unsafe. Widespread natural disasters, such as earthquakes, volcanoes, hurricanes, and floods, can immobilize virtually every form of transportation, including highways, railroads, boats, and airplanes. Other types of disasters may impede one or more types of transportation, which could result in overwhelming demand for the available modes. High volumes of emergency supplies may be needed during and after a disaster, but damaged transportation infrastructure often makes the delivery of those supplies difficult.

Components of a Business Continuity Plan

The complete set of business continuity plan documents will include the following:

- **Supporting project documents:** These will include the documents created at the beginning of the business continuity project, including the project charter, project plan, statement of scope, and statement of support from executives.

- **Analysis documents:** These include:
  - Business impact analysis (BIA)
  - Threat assessment and risk assessment
  - Criticality analysis (CA)
  - Documents defining approved recovery targets such as recovery time objective (RTO), recovery point objective (RPO), recovery capacity objective (RCapO), and recovery consistency objective (RCO)

- **Response documents:** These are all the documents that describe the required action of personnel when a disaster strikes, plus documents containing information required by those same personnel. Examples of these documents include:
  - **Business recovery (or resumption) plan:** Describes the activities required to recover and resume critical business processes and activities.
  - **Occupant emergency plan (OEP):** Describes activities required to care for occupants safely in a business location during a disaster. It will include both evacuation procedures and sheltering procedures, each of which may be required, depending on the type of disaster that occurs.
  - **Emergency communications plan:** Describes the types of communications imparted to many parties, including emergency response personnel, employees in general, customers, suppliers, regulators, public safety organizations, shareholders, and the public.
  - **Contact lists:** Contains names and contact information of emergency response personnel, critical suppliers, customers, and other parties.
  - **Disaster recovery plan:** Describes the activities required to restore critical IT systems and other critical assets, whether in alternate or primary locations.

- **Continuity of operations plan (COOP):** Describes the activities required to continue critical and strategic business functions at an alternate site.

- **Cybersecurity incident response plan (CIRP):** Describes the steps required to deal with a security incident that could reach disastrous proportions.

- **Test and review documents:** This is the entire collection of documents related to testing all of the business continuity plans, as well as reviews and revisions to documents.

Testing Recovery and Continuity Plans

> It's surprising what you can accomplish when no one is concerned about who gets the credit.
>
> — Ronald Reagan

Business continuity (BC) and disaster recovery (DR) plans may look elegant and even ingenious on paper, but their true business value is unknown until their worth is proven through testing.

The process of testing BC and DR plans uncovers flaws not only in the plans, but also in the systems and processes that they are designed to protect. For example, testing a system recovery procedure may point out the absence of a critically needed hardware component, or a recovery procedure may contain a syntax or grammatical error that misleads the recovery team member and results in recovery delays. Testing is designed to uncover these types of issues.

BC and DR plans must be tested to prove their viability. Without testing, an organization has no way of really knowing whether its plans are effective. With ineffective plans, an organization has a far smaller chance of surviving a disaster.

BC and DR plans have built-in obsolescence—not by design but by virtue of the fact that technology and business processes in most organizations are constantly changing and improving. Thus, it is imperative that newly developed or updated plans be tested as soon as possible to ensure their effectiveness.

Types of tests range from lightweight and unobtrusive to intense and disruptive and include the following:

- Document review
- Walk-through
- Simulation
- Parallel test
- Cutover test

These tests are described in more detail in this section.

 NOTE Usually, an organization performs less intensive tests first to identify the most obvious flaws and then follows with tests that require more effort.

Each type of test requires advanced preparation and recordkeeping. Preparation will consist of several activities, including:

- **Participants:** The organization should identify personnel who will participate in an upcoming test. It is important to identify all relevant skill groups and department stakeholders so that the test will include a full slate of contributors.

- **Schedule:** The availability of each participant must be confirmed so that the test will include participation from all stakeholders.

- **Facilities:** For all but the document review test, proper facilities need to be identified and set up. This might consist of a large conference room or training room. If the test will take place over several hours, one or more meals and/or refreshments may also be needed.

- **Scripting:** The simulation test requires some scripting, usually in the form of one or more documents that describe a developing scenario and related circumstances. Scenario scripting can make parallel and cutover tests more interesting and valuable, but this can be considered optional.

- **Recordkeeping:** For all the tests except the document review, one or more persons should take good notes that can be collected and organized after the test is completed.

- **Contingency plan:** The cutover test involves the cessation of processing on primary systems and the resumption of processing on recovery systems. This is the highest-risk plan, and things can go wrong. A contingency plan to get primary systems running again in case something goes wrong during the test should be developed.

These preparation activities are shown in Table 6.2.
The various types of tests are discussed next.

TABLE 6.2   Preparation activities required for each type of BC/DR test

	Document review	Walk-through	Simulation	Parallel test	Cutover test
Participants	Yes	Yes	Yes	Yes	Yes
Schedule	Yes	Yes	Yes	Yes	Yes
Facilities		Yes	Yes	Yes	Yes
Scripting			Yes	Optional	Optional
Recordkeeping	Yes	Yes	Yes	Yes	Yes
Contingency plan					Yes

Document Review

A *document review* test involves reviewing some or all business continuity and disaster recovery plans, procedures, and other documentation. Individuals typically review these documents on their own, at their own pace, but within whatever time constraints or deadlines have been established.

The purpose of a document review test is to review the accuracy and completeness of document content. Reviewers should read each document with a critical eye, point out any errors, and annotate the document with questions or comments that can be sent back to the document's author(s), who can make any necessary changes.

If significant changes are needed in one or more documents, the project team may want to include a second round of document review before moving on to more resource-intensive tests.

The owner or document manager for the organization's BC and DR planning project should document which persons review which documents and perhaps even include the review copies or annotations. This practice will create a more complete record of the activities related to the development and testing of important BCP planning and response documents. It will also help to capture the true cost and effort of developing and testing BCP capabilities in the organization.

Walk-through

A *walk-through* is like a document review; it's a review of just the BCP documents. However, while a document review is carried out by individuals working independently, a walk-through is performed by a group of individuals in a live discussion.

A walk-through is usually facilitated by a leader who guides the participants through each document page by page. The leader may read sections of the document aloud, describe various scenarios where information in a section might be relevant, and take comments and questions from participants.

A walk-through is likely to take considerably more time than a document review. One participant's question on some minor point in the document could spark a worthwhile and lively discussion that could last a few minutes to an hour. The group leader or another person will need to take careful notes to record any deficiencies found in any of the documents as well as issues to be handled after the walk-through. The leader will also need to control the pace of the review so that the group does not get unnecessarily hung up on minor points. Some discussions will need to be cut short or tabled for a later time or for an offline conversation among interested parties.

FEMA offers Exercise Evaluation Guide (EEG) templates to help organizations map exercise results to objectives, capabilities, recovery targets, and critical tasks for further analysis and assessment. Groups can easily adapt and make use of these tools to efficiently gather observations and action items for plan improvements. These templates are available from https://preptoolkit.fema.gov/web/hseep-resources/eegs.

Even if major revisions are needed in recovery documents, it probably will be infeasible to conduct another walk-through with updated documents. However, follow-up document reviews are probably warranted to ensure that the documents were updated appropriately, at least in the opinion of the walk-through participants. Executing the BCP life cycle can easily overlook addressing gaps and improvements identified during exercises. It is important to track findings and monitor their closure.

WARNING   Participants in the walk-through should carefully consider that the potential audience for recovery procedures may be persons who are not as familiar as they are with systems and processes. They need to remember that the ideal personnel may not be available during a real disaster. Participants also need to realize that the skill level of recovery personnel might be a little below that of the experts who operate systems and processes in normal circumstances. Finally, walk-through participants need to remember that systems and processes undergo almost continuous change, which could render some parts of the recovery documentation obsolete or incorrect all too soon. Hence, operational policy may include the requirement of keeping DRPs up-to-date when system changes are made.

Simulation

A *simulation* is a test of BC and DR procedures in which the participants participate in a "mock disaster" to add some realism to the process of actively practicing their response procedures.

A simulation could be an elaborate and choreographed walk-through test, where a facilitator reads from a script and describes a series of unfolding events in a disaster, such as a hurricane or an earthquake. This type of simulation could almost be viewed as "playacting," where the script is the set of emergency response documentation. By stimulating the imagination of simulation participants, it's possible for participants to imagine that a disaster is taking place, which may help them better understand what real disaster conditions could be like. It will help tremendously if the facilitator has experienced one or more disaster scenarios so that he or she can add more realism when describing events.

To make the simulation more credible and valuable, the chosen scenario should have a reasonable chance of occurring in the local area. Good choices would include an earthquake in San Francisco or Los Angeles, a volcanic eruption in Seattle, or an avalanche in Switzerland. A poor choice would be a hurricane or tsunami in central Asia because these events would never occur there.

A simulation can also go a few steps further. For instance, it can take place at an established emergency operations center (EOC), the same place where emergency command and control would operate in a real disaster. The facilitator could also change some of the participants' roles to simulate the real absence of certain key personnel to see how the remaining personnel might conduct themselves in a real emergency.

The facilitator of a simulation is limited only by their own imagination when organizing a simulation. One important fact to remember, though, is that a simulation does not actually affect any live or DR systems—it's all as pretend as the make-believe cardboard televisions and computers in furniture stores.

Parallel Test

A *parallel test* is an actual test of BC and DR plan procedures and their supporting IT systems. The purpose of a parallel test is to evaluate the ability of personnel to follow procedures in plans—verify the actual DR system capabilities. In a parallel test, personnel set up the IT systems that would be used in an actual disaster and operate those IT systems with real business transactions to determine whether the IT systems correctly perform the processing.

The outcome of a parallel test is threefold:

- It evaluates the accuracy of response procedures.
- It evaluates the ability of personnel to follow the emergency response procedures correctly.
- It evaluates the ability of IT systems and other supporting apparatus to process real business transactions properly.

A parallel test is so named because live production systems continue to operate, while backup IT systems process business transactions in parallel to see if they process them the same way as the live production systems do.

Setting up a valid parallel test is complicated in many cases. In effect, you need to insert a logical "Y cable" into the business process flow so that the information flow will split and flow both to production systems (without interfering with their operation) and to backup systems. The results of transactions need to be compared. Personnel must be able to determine whether the backup systems would be able to output correct data without actually having them do so. In many complex environments, you would not want the DR system to actually feed information back into a live environment, because that may cause duplicate events to occur someplace else in the organization (or with customers, suppliers, or other parties). For instance, in a travel reservations system, you would not want a DR system to book actual travel, because that would cost real money and consume available space on an airline or other mode of transportation. However, it is important to know whether the DR system will be able to perform those functions. Somewhere along the line, it will be necessary to "unplug" the DR system from the rest of the environment and manually examine the results to see if they appear to be correct.

Organizations that want to see if their backup/DR systems can manage a real workload can perform a cutover test, which will be discussed next.

Cutover Test

A *cutover test* is the most intrusive type of disaster recovery test. However, it also provides the most reliable results in answering the question of whether backup systems have the capacity and correct functionality to shoulder the real workload properly.

The consequences of a failed cutover test, however, might resemble an actual disaster; if any part of the cutover test fails, then real, live business processes will be going without the support of IT applications as though a real outage or disaster were in progress. But even a failure like this would show you that "No, the backup systems won't work in the event a real disaster were to happen later today."

In some respects, a cutover test is easier to perform than a parallel test. A parallel test is a little trickier since business information is required to flow to the production system and to the backup system, which means that some artificial component has been somehow inserted into the environment. However, with a cutover test, business processing takes place on the backup systems only, which can often be achieved through a simple configuration somewhere in the network or the systems layer of the environment.

Not all organizations perform cutover tests, because they take a lot of resources to set up and they are risky. Many organizations find that a parallel test is sufficient to determine whether backup systems are accurate, and the risk of an embarrassing incident is almost zero with a parallel test.

Documenting Test Results

Every type and every iteration of DR plan testing needs to be documented. It's not enough to say, "We did the test on September 10, 2023, and it worked." First, no test goes perfectly—opportunities for improvement are always identified. The most important part of testing is to discover what parts of the test still need work so that those parts of the plan can be fixed before the next test (or a real disaster).

As with any well-organized project, success is in the details. The road to success is littered with big and small mistakes, and all the things identified in every sort of BC/DR test need to be detailed so that the next iteration of the test will give better results.

Recording and comparing detailed test results from one test to the next will also help the organization to measure progress. By this, we mean that the quality of the BC/DR plan should steadily improve from year to year. Simple mistakes of the past should not be repeated, and the only failures in future tests should be in new and novel parts of the environment that wasn't well thought out to begin with. And even these should diminish over time.

Debriefing to Improve Recovery and Continuity Plans

Every test of response and recovery plans should include a debrief or review so that participants can discuss the test's outcome: what went well, what went wrong, and how things should be done differently next time. Someone who will be responsible for making changes to relevant documents should collect all this information. The updated documents should be circulated among the test participants, who can confirm whether their discussion and ideas are properly reflected in the document.

Training Personnel

The value and usefulness of a high-quality set of emergency response, business continuity, and disaster recovery plans and procedures will be greatly diminished if those responsible for carrying them out are unfamiliar with them.

A person cannot learn to ride a bicycle by reading even the most detailed how-to instructions on the subject, so it's equally unrealistic to expect personnel to be able to carry out response procedures properly if they are inexperienced in those procedures.

Several forms of training can be made available for the personnel who are expected to be available if a disaster strikes, including:

- **Document review:** Personnel can carefully read procedure documents to familiarize them with the nature of the recovery procedures. But, as mentioned earlier, this alone may be insufficient.
- **Participation in walk-throughs:** People who are familiar with specific processes and systems that are the subject of walk-throughs should participate in them. Exposing personnel to the walk-through process will not only help to improve the walk-through and recovery procedures but will also provide a learning experience for participants.
- **Participation in simulations:** Taking part in simulations will similarly benefit the participants by giving them the experience of actively role-playing a disaster.
- **Participation in parallel and cutover tests:** Other than experiencing an actual disaster and its recovery operations, no experience is quite like participating in parallel and cutover tests. Here, participants will gain actual hands-on experience with critical business processes and IT environments by performing the actual procedures that they would in the event of a disaster. When a disaster strikes, those participants can draw upon their memory of having performed those procedures in the past instead of just the memory of having read and simulated through role-playing recovery procedures.

You can see that all the tests that need to be performed to verify the quality of response plans also provide personnel with training opportunities. The development and testing of disaster-related plans and procedures provide a continuous learning experience for all the personnel involved.

Making Plans Available to Personnel When Needed

When a disaster strikes, one of the effects is often no access to even the most critical IT systems. Given a 40-hour workweek, there is roughly a 25 percent likelihood that critical personnel will be at the business location when a disaster strikes (at least the violent type of disaster that strikes with no warning, such as an earthquake—other types of disasters, such as hurricanes, may afford the organization a little bit of time to anticipate the disaster's impact). The point is that chances are very good that the personnel who are available to respond may be unable to access the procedures and other information that they will need, unless special measures are taken.

WARNING   Complete BCP documentation often contains details of key systems, operating procedures, recovery strategies, and even vendor and model identification of in-place equipment. If available to unauthorized personnel, this information can be misused, so the mechanism selected for ensuring availability must include planning to prevent inadvertent disclosure.

Response and recovery procedures can be made available to personnel during a disaster in several ways:

- **Hard copy:** Although many have grown accustomed to the paperless office, emergency response, business continuity, and disaster recovery documentation should be available in hard-copy form. Copies, even multiple copies, should be available for each responder, with a copy at the workplace and another at home, and possibly even a set in the responder's vehicle.

- **Soft copy:** Traditionally, soft-copy documentation is kept on file servers, but as you might expect, those file servers might be unavailable in a disaster. Soft copies should be available on responders' portable devices (laptops, tablets, and smartphones). An organization can also consider issuing documentation on memory sticks and cards. Depending on the type of disaster, it can be difficult to know what resources will be available to access documentation, so making it available in more than one form will ensure that at least one copy of it will be available to the personnel who need access to it.

- **Alternate work/processing site:** Organizations that utilize a hot/warm/cold site for the recovery of critical operations can maintain hard copies and/or soft copies of recovery documentation there. This makes perfect sense; personnel working at an alternate processing site or worksite will need to know what to do, and having those procedures on-site will facilitate their work.

- **Online:** Soft copies of recovery documentation can be archived on an Internet-based site that includes the ability to store data. Almost any type of online service that includes authentication and the ability to upload documents could be suitable for this purpose.

- **Wallet cards:** It's unreasonable to expect to publish recovery documentation on a laminated wallet card, but those cards could store the contact information for core response team members as well as a few other pieces of information, such as conference bridge codes, passwords to online repository of documentation, and so on. An example wallet card appears earlier in this chapter, in Figure 6.8.

Maintaining Business Continuity and Disaster Recovery Plans

Business processes and technology undergo almost continuous change in most organizations. A BCP that is developed and tested is liable to be outdated within months and obsolete within a year. If much more than a year passes, a plan in some organizations may approach uselessness. This section discusses how organizations need to keep their DR plans up-to-date and relevant.

A typical organization needs to establish a schedule whereby the principal plans will be reviewed. Depending on the rate of change, this could be as frequently as quarterly or as seldom as every two years.

Further, every change, however insignificant, in business processes and information systems should include a step to review, and possibly update, relevant BC/DR documents. That is, a review of, and possibly changes to, relevant documents should be a required step in every business, engineering, or information systems change process, and should be a key component of the organization's systems development life cycle (SDLC). If this is done faithfully, then you would expect that the annual review of BC/DR documents would conclude that few (if any) changes were required, although it is still a good practice to perform a periodic review, just to be sure.

Periodic testing of BC/DR documents and plans, discussed in detail in the previous section, is another vital activity. Testing validates the accuracy and relevance of plans, and any issues or exceptions in the testing process should precipitate updates to appropriate documents.

Sources for Best Practices

It is unnecessary to begin BCP and DRP by first inventing a practice or methodology. BCP and DRP are advanced professions with several professional associations, professional certifications, international standards, and publications. Any or all of these are, or can lead to, sources of practices, processes, and methodologies:

- **U.S. Cybersecurity & Infrastructure Security Agency (CISA):** This branch of the U.S. Department of Homeland Security (DHS) is concerned with cybersecurity and resilience. The CISA website is at www.cisa.gov.

- **U.S. Federal Emergency Management Agency (FEMA):** FEMA is part of the Department of Homeland Security (DHS) and is responsible for emergency disaster relief planning information and services. FEMA's most visible activities are its relief operations after hurricanes and floods in the United States. Its website is at www.fema.gov.

- **Federal Financial Institutions Examination Council (FFIEC) Business Continuity Management booklet:** This booklet provides guidance to assist examiners in evaluating financial institutions and service provider's risk management processes to ensure the availability of critical financial services. The FFIEC Business Continuity Management Handbook can be downloaded at https://ithandbook.ffiec.gov/it-booklets/business-continuity-management.

- **U.S. National Fire Protection Agency (NFPA):** NFPA has developed a pre-incident planning standard, NFPA 1620, which addresses the protection, construction, and features of buildings and other structures. It also requires the development of pre-incident plans that emergency responders can use to deal with fires and other emergencies. The NFPA website is at www.nfpa.org.

- **U.S. National Institute of Standards and Technology (NIST):** This branch of the U.S. Department of Commerce is responsible for developing business and technology standards for the federal government. The quality of the standards developed by NIST is exceedingly high, and as a result, many private organizations all over the world are adopting them. The NIST website is at www.nist.gov.

- **Business Continuity Institute (BCI):** This membership organization is dedicated to the advancement of business continuity management. BCI has more than 8,000 members in almost 100 countries. BCI holds several events around the world, prints a professional journal, and it has developed a professional certification, the Certificate of the BCI (CBCI). Its website is at www.thebci.org.

- **Disaster Recovery Institute International (DRI International):** This professional membership organization provides education and professional certifications for DRP professionals. Its website is at https://drii.org. Its certifications include:
  - Associate Business Continuity Professional (ABCP)
  - Certified Business Continuity Vendor (CBCV)
  - Certified Functional Continuity Professional (CFCP)
  - Certified Business Continuity Professional (CBCP)
  - Master Business Continuity Professional (MBCP)
  - Certified Business Continuity Auditor (CBCA)
  - Certified Business Continuity Lead Auditor (CBCLA)

- **Business Continuity Management Institute (BCM Institute):** This professional association specializes in education and professional certification. BCM Institute is a co-organizer of the World Continuity Congress, an annual conference that is dedicated to business continuity and disaster recovery planning. Its website is at www.bcm-institute.org. Certifications offered by BCM Institute include:
  - Business Continuity Certified Expert (BCCE)
  - Business Continuity Certified Specialist (BCCS)
  - Business Continuity Certified Planner (BCCP)
  - Business Continuity Certified Auditor (BCCA)
  - Business Continuity Certified Lead Auditor (BCCLA)
  - Disaster Recovery Certified Planner (DRCP)
  - Disaster Recovery Certified Expert (DRCE)
  - Disaster Recovery Certified Specialist (DRCS)
  - Crisis Management Certified Planner (CMCP)
  - Crisis Management Certified Specialist (CMCS)
  - Crisis Management Certified Expert (CMCE)
  - Crisis Communication Certified Planner (CCCP)
  - Crisis Communication Certified Specialist (CCCS)

- Crisis Communication Certified Expert (CCCE)
- Operational Resilience Certified Planner (ORCP)
- Operational Resilience Certified Specialist (ORCS)
- Operational Resilience Certified Expert (ORCE)

Disaster Recovery Planning

DRP is undertaken to reduce risks related to the onset of disasters and other events and is closely related to BCP. The groundwork for DRP begins in BCP activities such as business impact analysis, criticality analysis, establishment of recovery objectives, and testing. The outputs from these activities are the key inputs to DRP:

- The business impact and criticality analyses help prioritize which business processes (and, therefore, which IT systems) are the most important.

- Key recovery targets specify how quickly specific IT applications are to be recovered. This guides DRP personnel as they develop new IT architectures that make IT systems compliant with those objectives.

- Testing of DR plans can be performed in coordination with testing of BCP plans to more accurately simulate real disasters and disaster response.

Disaster Recovery Team Roles and Responsibilities

Disaster recovery plans need to specify the teams that are required for disaster response, as well as each team's roles and responsibilities. Table 6.3 describes several teams and their roles.

TABLE 6.3   Disaster response teams' roles and responsibilities

Team	Responsibilities
Emergency Management	Coordinates the activities of all other response teams
First Responders	Usually outside personnel such as police, fire, and rescue who help to extinguish fires, evacuate personnel, and provide emergency medical aid
Communications	Coordinates communication among teams, as well as between teams and outside entities
Damage Assessment	Examines equipment, supplies, furnishing, and assets to determine what can be used immediately in support of critical processes and what will need to be handed off to salvage teams
Salvage	Examines equipment, supplies, furnishings, and other assets to determine what can be salvaged for immediate or long-term reuse

TABLE 6.3   Disaster response teams' roles and responsibilities *(continued)*

Team	Responsibilities
Network Engineering	Establishes and maintains electronic (voice and data) communications in support of critical services during a disaster
Systems Engineering	Establishes and maintains systems as needed to support critical applications and services
Database Engineering	Establishes and maintains database management systems as needed to support critical applications; performs data recovery, using local or remotely stored media as needed
Application Support	Establishes and maintains critical applications in support of critical business processes
Application Development	Makes changes to critical applications as needed during the recovery effort
End-User Computing	Establishes and maintains end-user computing facilities (desktop computers, laptop computers, mobile devices, etc.) as needed in support of critical applications and services
Systems Operations	Performs routine and nonroutine tasks such as backups to keep critical applications running
Transportation	Coordinates transportation of personnel to recovery sites
Relocation	Acquires lodging and other resources needed by personnel who are working at remote operations centers
Security	Coordinates physical and logical security activities to ensure the continuous protection of staff, assets, and information
Finance	Facilitates the availability of financial resources as needed to commence and continue emergency response operations

Some of the roles in Table 6.3 may overlap with the responsibilities defined in the organization's BCP. BC and DR planners will need to work together to ensure that the organization's overall response to disaster is appropriate and does not overlook vital functions. Also, because of variations in organizations' disaster response plans, some of these teams will not be needed in some organizations.

Recovery Objectives

During the business impact analysis and criticality analysis phases of a BC/DR project, the speed with which each business activity (with its underlying IT systems) needs to be restored after a disaster is determined. The objectives discussed here are:

- Recovery time objective (RTO)
- Recovery point objective (RPO)
- Recovery capacity objective (RCapO)
- Recovery consistency objective (RCO)
- Service delivery objective (SDO)

Recovery Time Objective

Recovery time objective (RTO) is the period from the onset of an outage until the resumption of service. RTO is usually measured in hours or days. Each process and system in the BIA should have an RTO value.

RTO does not mean that the system (or process) has been recovered to 100 percent of its former capacity. Far from it—in an emergency, management may determine that a DR server in another city with, say, 60 percent of the capacity of the original server is adequate. That said, an organization could establish two RTO targets, one for partial capacity and one for full capacity.

> For a given organization, it's probably best to use one unit of measure for recovery objectives for all systems. That will help to avoid any errors that would occur during a rank-ordering of systems so that, for example, two days does not appear to be a shorter period than four hours.

Further, a system that has been recovered in a disaster situation might not have 100 percent of its functionality. For instance, an application that lets users view transactions that are more than two years old may, in a recovery situation, only contain 30 days' worth of data. Again, such a decision is usually the result of a careful analysis of the cost of recovering different features and functions in an application environment. In a larger, complex environment, some features might be considered critical, while others are less so.

> Senior management should be involved in any discussion related to recovery system specifications in terms of capacity, integrity, or functionality.

Recovery Point Objective

A *recovery point objective (RPO)* is the greatest acceptable period for which recent data may be irretrievably lost in a disaster. Like RTO, RPO is usually measured in hours or days. However, for critical transaction systems, RPO could even be measured in minutes or seconds.

RPO is usually expressed as a worst-case figure; for instance, a transaction processing system RPO will be two hours or less.

The value of a system's RPO is usually a direct result of the frequency of data backup or replication. For example, if an application server is backed up once per day, the RPO is going to be at least 24 hours (or one day, whichever way you like to express it). Maybe it will take three days to rebuild the server, but once data is restored from backup, no more than the last 24 hours of transactions are lost. In this case, the RTO is three days, and the RPO is one day.

Recovery Capacity Objective

A *recovery capacity objective (RCapO)* is generally expressed as a percentage. If any incident or disaster results in the organization switching to a temporary or recovery process or system, the capacity of that temporary or recovery process or system may be less than that used during normal business operations. For example, in the event of a communications outage, cashiers in a retail location will hand-write sales receipts, which may take more time than the use of point-of-sale terminals. The manual process may mean cashiers can process 80 percent as much work; this is the RCapO.

For economic reasons, an organization may elect to build a recovery site that has less processing or storage capacity than the primary site. Management may agree that a recovery site with reduced processing capacity is an acceptable trade-off, given the relatively low likelihood that a failover to a recovery site would occur. For instance, an online service may choose to operate its recovery site at 80 percent of the processing capacity of the primary site. In management's opinion, the relatively low decrease in capacity is worth the cost savings.

In an emergency, management may determine that a disaster recovery server in another city with, say, 60 percent of the capacity of the original server is adequate. In that case, the organization could establish two RTO targets: one for partial capacity and one for full capacity. In other words, the organization needs to determine how quickly a lower-capacity system should be running and when a full-capacity system should be running.

Recovery Consistency Objective

A *recovery consistency objective (RCO)* measures the consistency and integrity of processing at a recovery site compared to the primary processing site.

RCO is calculated as:

$$1 - (\text{number of inconsistent objects}) / (\text{number of objects})$$

A system that has been recovered in a disaster situation may no longer have 100 percent of its functionality. For instance, an application that lets users view transactions that are more than two years old may, in a recovery situation, contain only 30 days' worth of data. The RCO decision is usually the result of a careful analysis of the cost of recovering different features and functions in an application environment. In a larger, complex environment, some features may be considered critical, while others are less so.

For example, suppose an organization's online application is used to calculate the current and future costs of a household budget. While the primary site uses inputs and performs calculations based on 12 external data sources, the recovery site performs calculations based on only 8 external data sources. Economic considerations compelled management to accept the fact that the recovery site will calculate results based on fewer inputs, and that this is an acceptable trade-off between higher licensing fees for the use of some external sources and small variations in the results shown to users of the site.

The RCO comes into play in organizations that decide to scale back the replication of features and functionality at a recovery site versus the primary processing site. For instance, a recovery site may lack detailed reporting capabilities because of the cost of software or service licensing. An organization may have to pay for a second, expensive license for a recovery site that would rarely be used. Instead, management may decide that users or customers can go without those or other functions at a recovery site, instead focusing on core functions.

Service Delivery Objective

A *service delivery objective (SDO)* is a measure of the agreed-upon level or quality of service at an alternate processing site. Depending on the nature of the business process in question, SDO may be measured in transaction throughput, service quality, response time, available capabilities and features, or something else that is measurable.

Publishing Recovery Targets

If an application's storage system takes a snapshot every hour, the RPO could be one hour unless the storage system itself was damaged in a disaster. If the snapshot is replicated to another storage system four times per day, then the RPO might be better expressed as six to eight hours.

The last example brings up an interesting point. There may not be one "golden" RPO figure for a given system. Instead, the severity of a disrupting event or a disaster will dictate the time to get systems running again (RTO) with a certain amount of data loss (RPO). Here are some examples:

- A server's CPU or memory fails and is replaced and restarted in two hours. No data is lost. The RTO is two hours, and the RPO is zero.

- The storage system supporting an application suffers a hardware failure that results in the loss of all data. Data is recovered from a snapshot on another server taken every six hours. The RPO is six hours in this case.

- The database in a transaction application is corrupted and must be recovered. Backups are taken twice daily. The RPO is 12 hours. However, it takes 10 hours to rebuild indexes on the database, so the RTO is closer to 22–24 hours since the application cannot be returned to service until indexes are available.

 NOTE When publishing RTO and RPO figures to customers, it's best to publish the worst-case figures: "If our data center burns to the ground, our RTO is X hours, and the RPO is Y hours." Saying it that way would be simpler than publishing a chart that shows RPO and RTO figures for various types of disasters.

Pricing Recovery Capabilities

Generally, the shorter the RTO or RPO and the higher the RCO and RCapO for a given system, the more expensive it will be to achieve the target. Table 6.4 depicts a range of RTOs along with the technologies needed to achieve them and their relative cost.

TABLE 6.4 The lower the RTO, the higher the cost to achieve it

RTO/ RPO	Technologies needed	Cost
2 weeks	Backup media; purchase a server if the original server has burned or floated away	$
1 week	Backup media; replacement server on hand	$$
2 days	Backup media; application software installed on replacement server	$$
12 hours	Backup media or replication; application server installed and running on replacement server	$$$
1 hour	Server cluster with auto or manual failover; near real time replication	$$$$
5 minutes	Load balancing or rapid failover server cluster; real time replication	$$$$$

The BCP project team needs to understand the relationship between the time required to recover an application and the cost required to recover the application within that time. A shorter recovery time is more expensive, and this relationship is not linear. This means that reducing RPO from three days to six hours may mean that the equipment and software investment might double, or it might increase eightfold. There are so many factors involved in the supporting infrastructure for a given application that the BCP project team must just knuckle down and develop the cost for a few different RTO and RPO figures. Similarly, the capacity and consistency of the recovery system compared with the primary system will directly impact the cost of developing and implementing the recovery system. Once costs have been analyzed and approved, the actual DR capabilities can be designed and implemented.

The business value of the application itself is the primary driver in determining the amount of investment that senior management is willing to make to reach any arbitrary RTO, RPO, RCapO, RCO, and other figures. This business value may be measured in local currency if the application supports revenue. However, the loss of an application during a disaster may harm the organization's reputation. Again, management will have to decide on how much it will be willing to invest in DR capabilities that bring RTO, RPO, RCapO, RCO, and other figures to acceptable levels. Figure 6.10 illustrates these relationships.

FIGURE 6.10   Aim for the sweet spot and balance the costs of downtime and recovery.

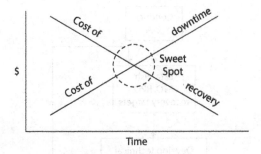

Developing Recovery Strategies

When management has chosen specific RPO and RTO (and, optionally, RCapO and RCO) targets for a given system or process, the BCP project team can roll up its sleeves and devise ways to meet these targets. This section discusses the technologies and logistics associated with various recovery strategies. This will help the project team decide which strategies are best suited for their organization.

Developing recovery strategies to meet specific recovery targets is an iterative process. The project team will develop a strategy to reach specific targets for a specific cost; senior management could well decide that the cost is too high, and they are willing to increase RPO and/or RTO targets, and lower RCapO and RCO targets, accordingly. Similarly, the project team could also discover that it is less costly to achieve specific recovery targets, and management could respond by lowering those targets. This is illustrated in Figure 6.11.

Site Recovery Options

In a worst-case disaster scenario, the site where information systems reside is partially or completely destroyed. In most cases, the organization cannot afford to wait for the damaged or destroyed facility to be restored, as this could take weeks or even months. If an organization can take that long to recover an application, you'd have to wonder whether it is needed at all. The assumption has got to be that in a disaster scenario, critical applications will be recovered in another location. This other location is called a recovery site. There are two dimensions to the process of choosing a recovery site: The first is the speed at which the application will be recovered at the recovery site; the second is the location of the recovery site itself. Both are discussed here.

As you might expect, speed costs. If a system is to be recovered within a few minutes or hours, the costs will be much higher than if the system can be recovered in 5 days.

Various types of facilities are available for rapid or not-too-rapid recovery. These facilities are called hot sites, warm sites, and cold sites. As the names might suggest, hot sites permit rapid recovery, while cold sites provide a much slower recovery. The costs associated with these are somewhat proportional as well, as illustrated in Table 6.5.

FIGURE 6.11   Recovery objective development flowchart

```
            ┌──────────────┐
            │   Conduct    │
            │     BIA      │
            └──────────────┘
                   │           ┌──────────────┐
                   ▼           │              │
            ┌──────────────┐   │
            │   Establish  │   │
            │   RTO, RPO   │   │
            │recovery targets│ │
            └──────────────┘   │
                   │           │
                   ▼           │
         ┌──────────────────┐  │
         │ Develop technical│  │
         │ architecture and │  │
         │processes to support│
         │ recovery targets │  │
         └──────────────────┘  │
                   │           │
                   ▼           │
                 ╱ Are ╲       │
               ╱ technologies ╲  Y
              ╲ too expensive? ╱────── Start over
                 ╲       ╱
                   │ N
                   ▼
         ┌──────────────────┐
         │Implement technologies│
         │and processes to support│
         │ recovery targets │
         └──────────────────┘
```

NOTE   The use of a private or public cloud, although not explicitly included in Table 6.5, offers varying degrees of recovery site readiness that can be established in the cloud, which includes both hot and warm sites.

The details about each type of site are discussed in the remainder of this section.

TABLE 6.5   Relative costs of recovery sites

Site Type	Speed to recovery	Cost
Hot	0–24 hours	$$$$
Warm	24 hours–7 days	$$$
Cold	More than 7 days	$$
Mobile	2–7 days	$$$–$$$$

Hot Sites

A *hot site* is an alternate processing center where backup systems are already running in a near readiness state to assume production workload. The systems at a hot site most likely have application and database management software already loaded and running, perhaps even at the same patch levels as the systems in the primary processing center.

A hot site is the best choice for systems whose RTO targets range from zero to several hours, perhaps as long as 24 hours.

A hot site may consist of infrastructure in a private or public cloud, or leased rack space (or even a cage for larger installations) at a colocation center. If the organization has its own processing centers, then a hot site for a given system would consist of the required rack space to house the recovery systems. Recovery servers will be installed and running, with the same version and patch level for the operating system, database management system (if used), and application software.

Systems at a hot site require the same level of administration and maintenance as the primary systems. When patches or configuration changes are made to primary systems, they should be made to hot site systems at the same time or very shortly afterward.

Because systems at a hot site need to be at or very near a state of readiness, a strategy needs to be developed regarding a method for keeping the data on hot standby systems current. This is discussed in detail in the later section, "Recovery and Resilience Technologies."

Systems at a hot site should have full network connectivity. A method for quickly directing network traffic toward the recovery servers should be worked out in advance so that a switchover can be accomplished. This is also discussed in the "Recovery and Resilience Technologies" section.

When setting up a hot site, the organization will need to send one or more technical staff members to the site to set up systems. However, once the systems are operating, much or all of the system- and database-level administration can be performed remotely. However, in a disaster scenario, the organization may need to send the administrative staff to the site for day-to-day management of the systems. This means that the workspace for these personnel needs to be identified so that they can perform their duties during the recovery operation.

> **NOTE** Site planning needs to consider work (desk) space for on-site personnel. Some colocation centers provide limited work areas, but these areas are often shared and often have little privacy for in-person or video meetings. Also, transportation, hotel, and dining accommodations need to be arranged, possibly in advance, if the hot site is in a different city from the primary site.

Warm Sites

A *warm site* is an alternate processing center where recovery systems are present, but at a lower state of readiness than recovery systems at a hot site. For example, while the same version of the operating system may be running on the warm site system, it may be a few patch levels behind primary systems. The same could be said about the versions and patch levels of database management systems (if used) and application software; they may be present, but they're not as up-to-date as they are on the primary systems. Like a hot site, a warm site can be implemented in a private or public cloud, a colocation center, or an organization's own alternate processing center.

A warm site is appropriate for an organization whose RTO figures range from roughly 1 to 7 days. In a disaster scenario, recovery teams would travel to the warm site and work to bring the recovery systems to a state of production readiness and bring them up-to-date with patches and configuration changes to bring them into a state of complete readiness.

A warm site is also used when the organization is willing to take the time necessary to recover data from tape or other backup media. Depending on the size of the database(s), this recovery task can take several hours to a few days.

The primary advantage of a warm site is that its costs are lower than those of a hot site, particularly in the effort required to keep the recovery system up-to-date. The site may not require expensive data replication technology, but instead, data can be recovered from backup media.

Cold Sites

A *cold site* is an alternate processing center where the degree of readiness for recovery systems is low. At the very least, a cold site is nothing more than an empty rack or allocated space on a computer room floor. It's just an address in someone's data center or colocation site where computers can be set up and used at some future date. A cold site could also exist in the form of an enterprise account established at a public cloud organization, but where no infrastructure has been created and configured.

Often, there is little or no equipment at a cold site. When a disaster or other highly disruptive event occurs in which the outage is expected to exceed 7 to 14 days, the organization will order computers from a manufacturer or perhaps have computers shipped from some other business location, so that they can arrive at the cold site soon after the disaster event has begun. Then, personnel would travel to the site and set up the computers, operating systems, databases, network equipment, and so on, and get applications running within several days.

The advantage of a cold site is its low cost. The main disadvantage is the cost, time, and effort required to bring it to operational readiness in a short period. However, for some organizations, a cold site is exactly what is needed.

Table 6.6 shows a comparison of hot, warm, and cold recovery sites and a few characteristics of each.

TABLE 6.6   Detailed comparison of cold, warm, and hot sites

	Cold	Warm	Hot
Computers	Ship to site	On-site	Running and ready
Application Software	To be installed	Installed	Running and ready

	Cold	Warm	Hot
Data	To be recovered	To be recovered	Continuously updated
Connectivity	To be established	Ready to go	Already connected
Support Staff	Travel to site	Travel to site	On-site or remotely managed
Cost	Lowest	Moderate	Highest

Mobile Sites

A *mobile site* is a portable recovery center that can be delivered to almost any location in the world. A viable alternative to a fixed-location recovery site, it can be transported by semi-truck and may even have its own generator, communications, and cooling capabilities.

IBM have mobile sites installed in semitruck trailers that can be shipped by truck, rail, ship, or air to nearly any location in the world.

Cloud Sites

Organizations are increasingly using cloud hosting services as their recovery sites. Such sites charge for the utilization of servers and devices in virtual environments. Hence, capital costs for recovery sites are near zero, and operational costs come into play as recovery sites are used.

As organizations become accustomed to building recovery sites in the cloud, they are increasingly moving their primary processing sites to the cloud as well.

Reciprocal Sites

A *reciprocal* recovery site is a data center that is operated by another company. Two or more organizations with similar processing needs will draw up a legal contract that obligates one or more of the organizations to house another party's systems temporarily in the event of a disaster.

Often, a reciprocal agreement pledges not only floor space in a data center, but also the use of the reciprocal partner's computer system. This type of arrangement is less common, but it is used by organizations that use mainframe computers and other high-cost systems.

With the wide use of public cloud and Internet colocation centers, reciprocal sites have fallen out of favor. Still, they may be ideal for organizations with mainframe computers that are otherwise too expensive to deploy to a cold or a warm site.

Geographic Site Selection

The location of the recovery site is a critical factor in the selection process. The distance between the main processing site and the recovery site is vital and may heavily determine the viability and success of a recovery operation.

A recovery site should not be in the same geographic region as the primary site. A recovery site in the same region may be involved in the same regional disaster as the primary site and may be unavailable for use or be suffering from the same problems present at the primary site.

> "Geographic region" refers to a location that will likely experience the effects of the same regional disaster that affects the primary site. No arbitrarily chosen distance (such as 100 miles) guarantees sufficient separation. In some locales, 50 miles is plenty of distance; in other places, 300 miles is too close—it all depends on the nature of disasters that are likely to occur in these areas. Information on regional disasters should be available from local disaster preparedness authorities or from local disaster recovery experts.

Considerations When Using Third-Party Disaster Recovery Sites

Since most organizations cannot afford to implement their own secondary processing site, the only other option is to use a disaster recovery site that is owned by a third party. This could be a colocation center, a disaster services center, or a public cloud provider. An organization considering such a site needs to ensure that its services contract addresses the following:

- **Disaster definition:** The definition of disaster needs to be broad enough to meet the organization's requirements.

- **Equipment configuration:** IT equipment must be configured as needed to support critical applications during a disaster.

- **Availability of equipment during a disaster:** IT equipment needs to be available during a disaster. In the case of disaster service providers, the organization needs to know how the disaster service provider will allocate equipment if many of its customers suffer a disaster simultaneously.

- **Customer priorities:** The organization needs to know whether the disaster services provider has any customers (government or military, for example) whose priorities may exceed its own.

- **Data communications:** There must be sufficient bandwidth and capacity for the organization and other customers who may be operating at the disaster provider's center simultaneously.

- **Testing:** The organization needs to know what testing it is permitted to perform on the service provider's systems so that it can test its ability to recover from a disaster in advance.

- **Right to audit:** The organization should have a "right to audit" clause in its contract so that it can verify the presence and effectiveness of all key controls in place at the recovery facility. Note, however, that a right to audit is generally not an option for public cloud providers.

- **Privacy and data sovereignty:** Privacy and data protection regulations often include stipulations concerning the location of the storage and processing of sensitive data, including PII. These restrictions may be a primary consideration during the search for suitable disaster recovery sites.
- **Security and environmental controls:** The organization needs to know what security and environmental controls are in place at the disaster recovery facility.

Acquiring Additional Hardware

Many organizations elect to acquire their own server, storage, and network hardware for disaster recovery purposes. How an organization goes about acquiring hardware depends on its high-level recovery strategy:

- **Cold site:** An organization will need to be able to purchase hardware as soon as the disaster occurs.
- **Warm site:** An organization probably will need to purchase hardware before the disaster, but it may be able to purchase hardware when the disaster occurs. The choice will depend on the recovery time objective.
- **Hot site:** An organization will need to purchase its recovery hardware in advance of the disaster.
- **Cloud:** An organization will not need to purchase hardware, as this is provided by the cloud infrastructure provider.

Table 6.7 lists the pros and cons of these strategies. A warm site strategy is not listed since an organization could purchase hardware either in advance of the disaster or when it occurs. However, because cold, hot, and cloud sites are deterministic, they are included in the table.

TABLE 6.7   Hardware acquisition pros and cons for hot, cold, and cloud recovery sites

Strategy	Advantages	Disadvantages
Hot/ Warm	Hardware already purchased and ready for use	Capital tied up in equipment that may never be used Higher cost to continue maintaining recovery systems
Cold	Capital spent only if needed Lower costs (until a disaster occurs)	Appropriate equipment may be difficult to find and purchase Difficult to test recovery strategy unless hardware is purchased, leased, or borrowed
Cloud	Zero capital costs Operational costs incurred as cloud-based infrastructure used	Infrastructure owned by a third party

The main reasons for choosing a cloud hosting provider are to eliminate capital costs and to rapidly develop and deploy virtual infrastructure. The cloud hosting provider provides all hardware and charges organizations when the hardware is used.

Dual-Purpose Infrastructure

The primary business reason for not choosing a hot site is the high capital cost required to purchase disaster recovery equipment that may never be used. One way around this obstacle is to put those recovery systems to work every day. For example, recovery systems could be used for the development or testing of the same (or different) applications that are used in production. This way, systems that are purchased for recovery purposes are being well utilized for other purposes, and they'll be ready in case a disaster occurs.

When a disaster occurs, the organization will be less concerned about development and testing and more concerned about keeping critical production applications running. Forgoing development or testing (or whatever low-criticality functions are using the DR hardware) during a disaster will be a small sacrifice.

Recovery and Resilience Technologies

Once recovery targets have been established, the next major task is to survey and select technologies to enable recovery time, recovery point, recovery capacity, and recovery consistency objectives to be met. Here are several important factors to consider:

- Does the technology help the information system achieve the RTO, RPO, and other targets?
- Does the cost of the technology meet or exceed budget constraints?
- Can the technology be used to benefit other information systems (thereby lowering the cost for each system)?
- Does the technology fit well into the organization's current IT operations?
- Will operations staff require specialized training on the technology used for recovery?
- Does the technology contribute to the simplicity of the overall IT architecture, or does it complicate it unnecessarily?

These questions are designed to help determine whether a specific technology is a good fit, from a technology perspective as well as from process and operational perspectives.

RAID

Redundant array of independent disks (RAID) is a family of technologies used to improve the reliability, performance, or size of disk-based storage systems. From a disaster recovery or systems resilience perspective, the feature of RAID that is of particular interest is reliability. RAID is used to create virtual disk volumes over an array (pun intended) of disk storage devices and can be configured so that the failure of any individual disk drive in the array will not affect the availability of data on the disk array.

RAID is usually implemented on a hardware device called a disk array, which is a chassis in which several hard disks can be installed and connected to a server. The individual disk drives can usually be "hot swapped" in the chassis while the array is still operating. When the array is configured with RAID, a failure of a single disk drive will have no effect on the disk array's availability to the server to which it is connected. A system operator can be alerted to the disk's failure, and the defective disk drive can be removed and replaced while the array is still fully operational.

There are several options, or levels, for RAID configuration:

- **RAID-0:** This is known as a striped volume, where a disk volume splits data evenly across two or more disks to improve performance.

- **RAID-1:** This creates a mirror, where data written to one disk in the array is also written to a second disk in the array. RAID-1 makes the volume more reliable through the preservation of data, even when one disk in the array fails.

- **RAID-4:** This level of RAID employs data striping at the block level by adding a dedicated parity disk. The parity disk permits the rebuilding of data in the event one of the other disks fails.

- **RAID-5:** This is like RAID-4 block-level striping, except that the parity data is distributed evenly across all the disks instead of being dedicated on one disk. Like RAID-4, RAID-5 allows for the failure of one disk without losing information.

- **RAID-6:** This is an extension of RAID-5, where two parity blocks are used instead of a single parity block. The advantage of RAID-6 is that it can withstand the failure of any two disk drives in the array, instead of a single disk, as is the case with RAID-5.

Several nonstandard RAID levels have been developed by various hardware and software companies. Some of these are extensions of RAID standards, while others are entirely different.

Storage systems are hardware devices that are entirely separate from servers—their only purpose is to store a large amount of data and to be highly reliable using redundant components and the use of one or more RAID levels. Storage systems generally come in two forms:

- **Storage area network (SAN):** This stand-alone storage system can be configured to contain several virtual volumes and to connect to several servers through fiber-optic cables. The servers' operating systems will often consider this storage to be "local," as though it consists of one or more hard disks present in the server's own chassis.

- **Network attached storage (NAS):** This stand-alone storage system contains one or more virtual volumes. Servers access these volumes over the network using the NFS or Server Message Block/Common Internet File System (SMB/CIFS) protocols, common on Unix and Windows operating systems, respectively.

In public cloud environments, the physical implementation of storage is an abstraction.

Replication

Replication is an activity whereby data written to a storage system is also copied over a network to another storage system. The result is the presence of up-to-date data that exists on two or more storage systems, each of which could be in a different geographic region.

Replication can be handled in several ways and at different levels in the technology stack:

- **Disk storage system:** Data-write operations that take place in a disk storage system (such as a SAN or NAS) can be transmitted over a network to another disk storage system, where the same data will be written to the other system.

- **Operating system:** The operating system can control replication so that updates to a particular filesystem can be transmitted to another server, where those updates will be applied locally on that other server.

- **Database management system:** The database management system (DBMS) can manage replication by sending transactions to a DBMS on another server.

- **Transaction management system:** The transaction management system (TMS) can manage replication by sending transactions to a counterpart TMS located elsewhere.

- **Application:** The application can write its transactions to two different storage systems. This method is not often used.

- **Virtualization and containerization:** Virtual machine and container images can be replicated to recovery sites to speed up the recovery of applications.

Replication can take place from one system to another system in primary-backup replication. This is the typical setup when data on an application server is sent to a distant storage system for data recovery or disaster recovery purposes.

Replication can also be bidirectional, between two active servers, called multiprimary. This method is more complicated, because simultaneous transactions on different servers could conflict with one another (such as two reservation agents trying to book two passengers in the same seat on an airline flight). Some form of concurrent transaction control would be required, such as a distributed lock manager.

In terms of the speed and integrity of replicated information, there are two types of replication:

- **Synchronous replication:** Writing data to a local and to a remote storage system is performed as a single operation, guaranteeing that data on the remote storage system is identical to data on the local storage system. Synchronous replication incurs a performance penalty, as the speed of the entire transaction is slowed to the rate of the remote transaction.

- **Asynchronous replication:** Writing data to the remote storage system is not kept in sync with updates on the local storage system. Instead, there may be a time lag, and you have no guarantee that data on the remote system is identical to data on the local storage system. However, performance is improved, because transactions are considered complete when they have been written to the local storage system only. Bursts of local updates to data will take a finite period to replicate to the remote server, subject to the available bandwidth of the network connection between the local and remote storage systems.

Replication is often used for applications where the RTO is smaller than the time necessary to recover data from backup media. For example, if a critical application's RTO is established to be two hours, then recovery from backup media is probably not a viable option, even if backups are performed every two hours. While more expensive than recovery from backup media, replication ensures that up-to-date information is present on a remote storage system that can be brought online in a short period.

Server Clusters

A *cluster* is a collection of two or more servers that appears as a single server resource. Clusters are often the technology of choice for applications that require a high degree of availability and a very small RTO, measured in minutes.

When an application is implemented on a cluster, even if one of the servers in the cluster fails, the other server (or servers) in the cluster will continue to run the application, usually with no user awareness that a failure occurred.

There are two typical configurations for clusters: active-active and active-passive. In active-active mode, all servers in the cluster are running and servicing application requests. This is often used in high-volume applications where many servers are required to service the application workload.

In active-passive mode, one or more servers in the cluster are active and servicing application requests, while one or more servers in the cluster are in "standby" mode; they can service application requests but won't do so unless one of the active servers fails or goes offline for any reason. When an active server goes offline and a standby server takes over, this event is called a failover.

A typical server cluster architecture is shown in Figure 6.12.

FIGURE 6.12 Application and database server clusters

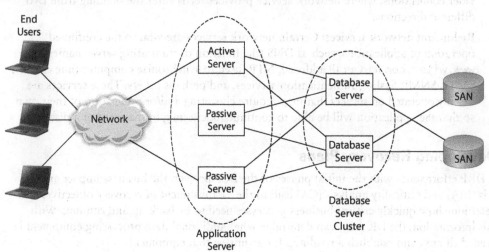

A server cluster is typically implemented in a single physical location, such as a data center. However, a cluster can also be implemented where great distances separate the servers in the cluster. This type of cluster is called a geographic cluster, or *geo-cluster*. Servers in a geo-cluster are connected through a WAN connection. A typical geographic cluster architecture is shown in Figure 6.13.

FIGURE 6.13   Geographic cluster with data replication

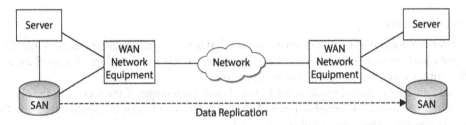

Network Connectivity and Services

An overall application environment that is required to be resilient and have recoverability must have those characteristics present within the network that supports it. A highly resilient application architecture that includes clustering and replication would be of little value if it had only a single network connection that was a single point of failure.

An application that requires high availability and resilience may require one or more of the following in the supporting network:

- **Redundant network connections:** These may include multiple network adapters on a server, but also a fully redundant network architecture with multiple switches, routers, load balancers, and firewalls. They could also include physically diverse network provider connections, where network service provider feeds enter the building from two different directions.

- **Redundant network services:** Certain network services are vital to the continued operation of applications, such as DNS (the function of translating server names like www.wiley.com into an IP address), NTP (used to synchronize computer time clocks), SMTP, SNMP, Syslog, authentication services, and perhaps others. These services are usually operated on servers that may require clustering and/or replication of their own so that the application will be able to continue functioning in the event of a disaster.

Developing Recovery Plans

A DRP effort starts with the initial phases of the BCP project: the business impact analysis (BIA) and criticality analysis (CA) lead to the establishment of recovery objectives that determine how quickly critical business processes need to be back up and running. With this information, the DR team can determine what additional data processing equipment is needed (if any) and establish a roadmap for acquiring that equipment.

The other major component of the DR project is the development of recovery plans. These are the process and procedure documents that will be vital when a disaster has been declared. These processes and procedures will instruct response personnel on how to establish and operate business processes and IT systems after a disaster has occurred. It's not enough to have all the technology ready if personnel don't know what to do.

Most DR plans are going to have common components:

- **Disaster declaration procedure:** This needs to include criteria for how a disaster is determined and who has the authority to declare a disaster.

- **Roles and responsibilities:** DR plans should specify what activities need to be performed and specify which persons or teams are best equipped to perform them.

- **Emergency contact lists:** Response personnel need contact information for other personnel so that they may establish and maintain communications as the disaster unfolds and recovery operations begin. These contact lists should include several different ways of contacting personnel, since some disasters have an adverse impact on regional telecommunications infrastructure.

- **Communication plans:** These are the detailed types and frequencies for keeping key persons informed of disaster recovery efforts. Some organizations utilize detailed playbooks containing prewritten notifications and update messages that will need only minor tailoring for any disaster situation.

- **System recovery procedures:** These are the detailed steps for getting recovery systems up and running. These procedures will include a lot of detail describing obtaining data, configuring servers and network devices, confirming that the application and business information is healthy, and starting business applications.

- **System operations procedures:** These are detailed steps for operating critical IT systems while they are in recovery mode. These detailed procedures are needed because the systems in recovery mode may need to be operated differently from their production counterparts; further, they may need to be operated by personnel who have not been doing this before.

- **System restoration procedures:** These are the detailed steps to restore IT operations back to the original production systems.

NOTE Business continuity and disaster recovery plans work together to get critical business functions operating again after a disaster. Because of this, BC and DR teams need to work closely when developing their respective response procedures to ensure that all activities are covered but without unnecessary overlap (or gaps).

DR plans need to consider the likely disaster scenarios that may occur in an organization. Understanding these scenarios can help the DR team take a more pragmatic approach when creating response procedures. The added benefit is that not all disasters result in the entire loss of a computing facility. Most are more limited in their scope, although all of them can result in a complete inability to continue operations. Some of these scenarios are:

- Complete loss of network connectivity
- Sustained electric power outage
- Loss of a key system (this could be a server, storage system, or network device)
- Extensive data corruption or data loss

These scenarios are probably more likely to occur than a catastrophe, such as a major earthquake or hurricane (depending on where your data center is located).

Data Backup and Recovery

Disasters and other disruptive events can damage information and information systems. It's essential that fresh copies of this information exist elsewhere in a form that enables IT personnel to load this information easily into alternative systems so that processing can resume as quickly as possible.

 Testing backups is important; testing recoverability is critical. In other words, performing backups is only valuable to the extent that backed-up data can be recovered in the future.

Backup to Tape and Other Media

In organizations still utilizing their own IT infrastructure, backup to tape is giving way to virtual tape libraries (VTLs) (discussed later) and cloud storage. From a DR perspective, however, the issue probably is not whether the organization has backup capabilities, but whether its current backup capabilities are adequate in the context of disaster recovery. An organization's backup capability may need to be upgraded if:

- The current backup system is difficult to manage.
- Whole-system restoration takes too long.
- The system lacks flexibility regarding DR (for instance, how difficult it would be to recover information onto a different type of system).
- The technology is old or outdated.
- Confidence in the backup technology is low.

Many organizations may consider backup as a means for restoring files or databases when errors have occurred, and they may have confidence in their backup system for that purpose. However, the organization may have somewhat less confidence in its backup system and its ability to recover all its critical systems accurately and in a timely manner.

While tape has been the default medium since the 1960s, using hard drives as backup media is growing in popularity: hard disk transfer rates are far higher, and disk is a random-access medium, whereas tape is a sequential-access medium. A VTL is a type of data storage technology that sets up a disk-based storage system with the appearance of tape storage, permitting existing backup software to continue to back up data to "tape," which is really just more disk storage.

E-vaulting is another viable option for system backup. E-vaulting permits organizations to back up their systems and data to an off-site location, which could be a storage system in another data center or a third-party service provider. This accomplishes two important objectives: reliable backup and off-site storage of backup data.

Backup Schemes

There are three main schemes for backing up data:

- **Full backup:** This is a complete copy of a dataset.
- **Incremental backup:** This is a copy of all data that has changed since the last full or incremental backup.
- **Differential backup:** This is a copy of all data that has changed since the last full backup.

The precise nature of the data to be backed up will determine which combination of backup schemes is appropriate for the organization. Some of the considerations for choosing an overall scheme are as follows:

- Criticality of the dataset
- Size of the dataset
- Frequency of change of the dataset
- Performance requirements and the impact of backup jobs
- Recovery requirements

An organization that is creating a backup scheme usually starts with the most common scheme, which is a full backup once per week and an incremental or differential backup every day. However, as stated previously, various factors will influence the design of the final backup scheme, such as the following:

- A small dataset could be backed up more than once a week, whereas an especially large dataset might be backed up less often.
- A more rapid recovery requirement may induce the organization to perform differential backups instead of incremental backups.
- If a full backup takes a long time to complete, it should probably be performed during times of lower demand or system utilization.

Backup Media Rotation

Organizations will typically want to retain backup media for as long as possible to provide a greater range of choices for data recovery. However, the desire to maintain a large library of backup media will be countered by the high cost of media and the space required to store it. Although legal or statutory requirements may dictate that backup media be kept for some minimum period, the organization may be able to find creative ways to comply with such requirements without retaining several generations of such media.

Some examples of backup media rotation schemes are discussed next.

First In, First Out (FIFO)

In this scheme, there is no specific requirement for retaining any backup media for long periods (such as one year or more). The method in the FIFO rotation scheme specifies that the oldest available backup media is the next one to be used.

This scheme's advantage is its simplicity. However, it has a significant disadvantage; any corruption of backed-up data needs to be discovered quickly (within the period of media rotation), or else no valid set of data can be recovered. Hence, only low-criticality data without any lengthy retention requirements should be backed up using this scheme.

Grandfather-Father-Son

The most common backup media rotation scheme, grandfather-father-son creates a hierarchical set of backup media that provides for greater retention of backed-up data while remaining economically feasible. In the most common form of this scheme, full backups are performed once per week and incremental or differential backups are performed daily.

Daily backup media used on Monday will not be used again until the following Monday. Backup media used on Tuesday, Wednesday, Thursday, Friday, and Saturday are handled in the same way.

Full backups created on Sunday are kept longer. Media used on the first Sunday of the month are not used again until the first Sunday of the following month. Similarly, media used on the second Sunday are not reused until the second Sunday of the following month, and so on for each week's media for Sunday.

For even longer retention, for example, media created on the first Sunday of the first month of each calendar quarter can be retained until the first Sunday of the first month of the next quarter. Backup media can be kept for even longer if needed.

Towers of Hanoi

The *Towers of Hanoi* backup media retention scheme is complex but results in a more efficient scheme for producing a lengthier retention of some backups. Patterned after the Towers of Hanoi puzzle, the scheme is most easily understood visually, as shown in Figure 6.14 in a five-level scheme.

FIGURE 6.14   Towers of Hanoi backup media rotation scheme

Day of Cycle

Backup Set to Use	1	2	3	4	5	6	7	8	9	10	11	12	13	14	15	16	17	18	19	20
		A		A		A		A		A		A		A		A		A		A
			B				B				B				B				B	
					C								C							
									D								D			
	E																			

Backup Media Storage

Backup media that remains in the same location as backed-up systems is adequate for data recovery purposes but completely inadequate for disaster recovery purposes; any event that physically damages information systems (such as fire, smoke, flood, hazardous chemical spill) is also likely to damage backup media. To provide disaster recovery protection, backup media must be stored off-site in a secure location. Selection of this storage location is as important as the selection of a primary business location; in the event of a disaster, the survival of the organization may depend on the protection measures in place at the off-site storage location.

Exam Tip

CISA exam questions relating to off-site backups may include details for safeguarding data during transport and storage, mechanisms for access during restoration procedures, media aging, and retention, or other details that may aid you during the exam. Watch for question details involving the type of media, geo-locality (distance, shared disaster spectrum [such as a shared coastline], and so on) of the off-site storage area and the primary site, or access controls during transport and at the storage site, including environmental controls and security safeguards.

The criteria for the selection of an off-site media storage facility are like the criteria for the selection of a hot/warm/cold/cloud recovery site discussed earlier in this chapter. If a media storage location is too close to the primary processing site, it is more likely to be involved in the same regional disaster, which could result in damage to backup media. However, if the media storage location is too far away, it might take too long for a delivery of backup media, which would result in a recovery operation that runs unacceptably long.

Another location consideration is the proximity of the media storage location and the hot/warm/cold recovery site. If a hot site is being used, chances are there is some other near real time means (such as replication) for data to get to the hot site. However, a warm or cold site may be relying on the arrival of backup media from the off-site media storage facility, so it might make sense for the off-site facility to be near the recovery site. If the public cloud is used as an alternate recovery site, then a different means than tape backup will need to be used to get data to the public cloud, such as e-vaulting or replication.

An important factor when considering off-site media storage is the method of delivery to and from the storage location. Chances are that the backup media is being transported by a courier or a shipping company. It is vital that the backup media arrive safely and intact and that the opportunities for interception or loss be reduced as much as possible. Not only can lost backup media make recovery more difficult, but it can also cause an embarrassing security incident if knowledge of the loss were to become public. From a confidentiality/integrity perspective, encryption of backup media is a good idea, although this digresses somewhat from disaster recovery (concerned primarily with availability).

 The requirements for off-site storage are a little less critical than those for a hot/warm/cold recovery site. All you must do is be able to get your backup media out of that facility. This can occur even if there is a regional power outage, for instance.

Backup media that must be kept on-site should be stored in locked cabinets or storerooms that are separate from the rooms where backups are performed. This will help to preserve backup media if a relatively small fire (or similar event) breaks out in the room containing computers that are backed up.

Backup Media Records and Destruction

To ensure the ability to restore data from backup media, organizations need meticulous records that list all backup volumes in place, where they are located, and which data elements are backed up on them. Without these records, it may prove impossible for an organization to recover data from its backup media library.

Protecting Portable Backup Media with Encryption

Information security and data privacy laws are expanding data protection requirements by requiring encryption of portable backup media in many cases. This is a sensible safeguard, especially for organizations that utilize off-site backup media storage. There is a risk of loss of backup media when it is being transported back and forth from an organization's primary data center and the backup media off-site storage facility.

Laws and regulations may specify maximum periods that specific information may be retained. Organizations need to have good records management that helps them track which business records are on which backup media volumes. When it is time for an organization to stop retaining a specific set of data, those responsible for the backup media library need to identify the backup volumes that can be recycled. If the data on the backup media is sensitive, the backup volume may need to be erased prior to use. Any backup media that is being discarded needs to be destroyed so that no other party can possibly recover data on the volume. Records of this destruction need to be kept.

Testing Disaster Recovery Plans

Disaster recovery plans need to be accurate and complete if they are going to result in a successful recovery. It is recommended that recovery plans be thoroughly tested.

The types of recovery tests are:

- Document review
- Walk-through
- Simulation
- Parallel test
- Cutover test

These test methods are described in detail earlier in this chapter.

Incident Response Communications

Security incident response, in its details, is far from straightforward; while timely communication with specific parties is essential, organizations must take care not to overcommunicate an incident's details. Sometimes, the organization should limit communications about the existence of an incident only to authorized parties rather than to the entire organization.

The incident response team should also consider using out-of-band communications if normal communications channels are suspected to be compromised. For instance, if the team believes that corporate email and/or instant messaging is compromised, an entirely different system should be used for communication until the incident has been closed.

Crisis Management and Communications

Many organizations employ crisis management and/or crisis communications personnel and procedures. Both exist to improve responses to various business emergencies, including business interruptions of every kind. If they exist, these capabilities should be incorporated into security incident response plans.

Organizations use the crisis management process to respond to various business emergencies. One could liken crisis management to a general mobilization plan for business leaders and others to come together to respond quickly and effectively to disruptive events. Given that disasters and security incidents fall into the category of disruptive events, a security incident response plan, business continuity plan, and disaster recovery plan should use crisis management capabilities.

Why would an organization develop a similar, parallel capability instead of using what it already has? Crisis management does not exist to take over or control business continuity, disaster recovery, or security incident response. Rather, crisis management can provide templates and techniques for communications and escalation. Crisis management should help simplify the overall effort of responding to all kinds of business emergencies.

Crisis communications is a subset of the overall public relations function used to inform internal and external parties of the proceedings of business emergencies. A crisis communications person or team often prepares for a variety of business emergencies through prewritten press releases and prepared remarks that can be tailored for each event.

Crisis communications often establish relationships with internal and external parties such as investor relations, public safety, and news media. Policy related to crisis management and crisis communications should define the personnel authorized to communicate with external parties. But even then, an organization's top executives may often be required to approve individual external communications.

Communications in the Incident Response Plan

Communications procedures, including identifying the specific parties to be involved in incident communications, should be sufficiently detailed so that incident responders will know who to inform, what to say (and not say), and how often to communicate. Personnel doing the communicating, as well as personnel receiving communication, need to understand the serious and sensitive nature of incident communications and limit communications to the fewest possible personnel.

Limiting Communications to a Few Authorized Persons

Few security incidents should be discussed organizationwide. Rather, communications about an incident should involve the fewest possible numbers of personnel. Each of those persons needs to understand explicitly any obligations regarding the need to keep the lid on news and details about a security incident.

Regulatory Requirements

Internal secrecy must be balanced with regulatory requirements for reporting security incidents to regulators and affected parties. Organizations must have a detailed understanding of regulatory requirements and proceed accordingly. However, security leaders and incident responders must determine how to describe incidents without providing details that could enable other attackers to understand specific weaknesses that could be exploited in further attacks.

Law Enforcement Proceedings

Organizations sometimes choose to involve local, regional, or national law enforcement when an incident occurs. Law enforcement organizations can be outstanding business partners in these situations, sometimes making cyber-incident experts available to help the organization understand what happened. It is a good practice to determine the key points of contact for various agencies with which your organization is most likely to interact during an incident. This helps ensure that lines of communication are already established, which can shorten the time for an agency to engage with the organization.

Often, a law enforcement organization will request that the organization refrain from publicly disclosing details about the incident, sometimes requiring that the organization say nothing to the public. This is understandable, particularly if the law enforcement agency is attempting to identify the perpetrator(s) in the incident to apprehend and charge them with a crime. In these cases, organizations must keep detailed records so that all members of the incident response team know what information is known about the incident, what has been communicated with law enforcement, and what has been communicated publicly.

 The FBI Cybercrime division has a site dedicated to reporting cyber events at https://www.ic3.gov.

Shaping Public Opinion

Experienced cybersecurity professionals often recognize good and bad examples of organizations' handling of security breaches. Better organizations quickly acknowledge a security incident and provide useful information to affected parties and the public. Other organizations handle these matters poorly, either with outright denial, whitewashing, or minimizing the scope or impact of an incident, disclosing it gradually when forced.

Organizations need to be keenly aware of how their announcements and updates of a security incident will be interpreted. For instance, "There is no evidence of actual data exfiltration" is often code for "We don't have logging turned on, so if the attacker stole data, we have no way of knowing one way or the other." Such a statement can be damning and difficult to undo.

Auditing Business Continuity Planning

Audits of an organization's business continuity plan are especially difficult, because it is impossible to prove whether the plans will work unless a real disaster occurs. The IT auditor has quite a task when it comes to auditing an organization's business continuity. The lion's share of the audit results hinges on the quality of documentation and walk-throughs with key personnel.

As is typical with most audit activities, an audit of an organization's BC program involves a top-down analysis of key business objectives, a review of documentation, and interviews to determine whether the BC strategy and program details support those key business objectives. This approach is depicted in Figure 6.15.

The objectives of an audit of BCP should include the following activities:

- Obtain documentation that describes current business strategies and objectives. Obtain high-level documentation (for example, strategy, charter, objectives) for the BC program, and determine whether the BC program supports business strategies and objectives.

- Obtain the most recent BIA and accompanying threat analysis, risk analysis, and criticality analysis. Determine whether these documents are current and complete, and that they support the BC strategy. Also, determine whether the scope of these documents covers those activities considered strategic according to high-level business objectives. Finally, determine whether the methods in these documents represent good practices for these activities.

- Determine whether key personnel are ready to respond during a disaster by reviewing test plans, training plans, and results. Find out where emergency procedures are stored and whether key personnel have access to them.

- Verify whether there is a process for regularly reviewing and updating BC documentation. Evaluate the process's effectiveness by reviewing records to see how frequently documents are reviewed.

These activities are described in more detail in the following sections.

FIGURE 6.15   Top-down approach to an audit of business continuity

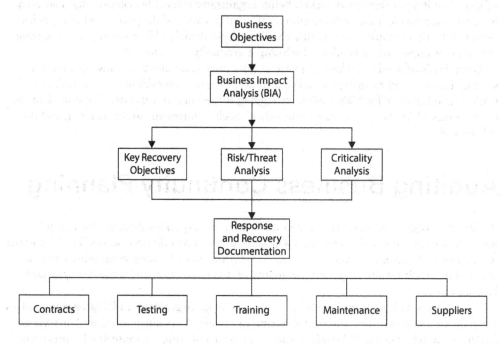

Auditing Business Continuity Documentation

The bulk of an organization's business continuity plan lies in its documentation, so it should be of little surprise that the bulk of the audit effort will lie in the examination of this documentation. The following steps will help the auditor to determine the effectiveness of the organization's BC plans:

- Obtain a copy of business continuity documentation, including response procedures, contact lists, and communication plans.

- Examine samples of distributed copies of BC documentation, and determine whether they are up-to-date. These samples can be obtained during interviews with key response personnel, which are covered in this procedure.

- Determine whether all documents are clear and easy to understand, not just for primary responders, but for alternate personnel who may have specific relevant skills but less familiarity with the organization's critical products, services, business processes, and applications.

- Examine documentation related to declaring a disaster and activating the business continuity plan. Determine whether the declaration methods are likely to be effective in a disaster scenario.

- Obtain emergency contact information and contact some of the personnel to see whether the contact information is accurate and up-to-date. Also, determine whether all response personnel are still employed in the organization and are in the same or similar roles in support of disaster response efforts.

- Contact some or all the response personnel who are listed in emergency contact lists. Interview them to see how well they understand their disaster response responsibilities and whether they are familiar with disaster response procedures. Ask each interviewee if they have a copy of these procedures. See if their copies are current.

- Determine whether a process exists for the formal review and update of business continuity documentation. Examine records to see how frequently, and how recently, documents have been reviewed and updated.

- Determine whether response personnel receive any formal or informal training on response and recovery procedures. Determine whether personnel are required to receive training and whether any records are kept that show which personnel received training and at what time.

Reviewing Prior Test Results and Action Plans

The effectiveness of business continuity plans relies, to a great degree, on the results and outcomes of tests. An IS auditor needs to examine these tests carefully to determine their effectiveness and to what degree they are used to improve procedures and to train personnel. The following procedure will help the IS auditor determine the effectiveness of business continuity testing:

- Determine whether there is a strategy for testing business continuity procedures. Obtain records for past tests and a plan for future tests. Determine whether prior tests and planned tests are adequate for establishing the effectiveness of response and recovery procedures.

- Examine records for tests performed over the past year or two. Determine the types of tests performed. Obtain a list of participants for each test. Compare the participants to lists of key recovery personnel. Examine test workpapers to determine the level of participation by key recovery personnel.

- Determine whether there is a formal process for recording test results and for using those results to make improvements in plans and procedures. Examine workpapers and records to determine the types of changes that were recommended in prior tests. Examine BC documents to see whether these changes were made as expected.

- Considering the types of tests that were performed, determine the adequacy of testing as an indicator of the effectiveness of the BC program. Did the organization perform only document reviews and walk-throughs, for example, or did the organization also perform parallel or cutover tests?

- If tests have been performed for two years or more, determine whether there's a trend showing continuous improvement in response and recovery procedures.

- If the organization performs parallel tests, determine whether the tests are designed to effectively determine the actual readiness of standby systems. Also, determine whether parallel tests measure the capacity of standby systems or merely their ability to process correctly but at a lower level of performance.

Interviewing Key Personnel

The knowledge and experience of key personnel are vital to the success of any DR operation. Interviews will help the IT auditor determine whether key personnel are prepared and trained to respond during a disaster. The following procedure will guide the IT auditor in interviews:

- Obtain the name, title, tenure, and full contact information for each person interviewed.

- Ask the interviewee to summarize his or her professional experience and training and current responsibilities in the organization.

- Ask the interviewee whether they are familiar with the organization's business continuity and disaster recovery programs.

- Determine whether the interviewee is among the key response personnel expected to respond during a disaster.

- Ask the interviewee if they have been issued a copy of any response or recovery procedures. If so, ask to see those procedures and determine whether they are current versions. Ask if the interviewee has additional sets of procedures in any other locations (residence, for example).

- Ask the interviewee if they have received any training. Request evidence of this training (certificate, calendar entry, and so on).

- Ask the interviewee if they have participated in any tests or evaluations of recovery and response procedures. Ask the interviewee whether the tests were effective, whether management takes the tests seriously, and whether any deficiencies in tests resulted in any improvements to test procedures or other documents.

Reviewing Service Provider Contracts

No organization is an island. Every organization has critical suppliers, and without them, it cannot carry out its critical functions. The ability to recover from a disaster also frequently requires the support of one or more service providers or suppliers. The IT auditor should examine contracts for all critical suppliers and consider the following guidelines:

- Does the contract support the organization's requirements for the delivery of services and supplies, even in the event of a local or regional disaster?
- Does the service provider have its own disaster recovery capabilities that will ensure its ability to deliver critical services during a disaster?
- Is recourse available should the supplier be unable to provide goods or services during a disaster?

Reviewing Insurance Coverage

The IT auditor should examine the organization's insurance policies related to the loss of property and assets supporting critical business processes. Insurance coverage should cover the actual cost of recovery or a lesser amount if the organization's executive management has accepted a lower amount. The IT auditor should obtain documentation that includes cost estimates for various DR scenarios, including equipment replacement, business interruption, and the cost of performing business functions and operating IT systems in alternate sites. These cost estimates should be compared with the value of insurance policies.

Visiting Media Storage and Alternate Processing Sites

The IT auditor should identify and visit remote sites used for storage of backup media and alternate processing. This will permit the auditor to confirm their existence, verify features and functions of these sites to see if they correspond to details in continuity and recovery plans, and to discover any risks.

Auditing Disaster Recovery Planning

The objectives of an audit of disaster recovery planning should include the following activities:

- Determine the effectiveness of planning and recovery documentation by examining previous test results.
- Evaluate the methods used to store critical information off-site (which may consist of off-site storage, alternate data centers, or e-vaulting).
- Examine environmental and physical security controls in any off-site or alternate sites and determine their effectiveness.
- Note whether off-site or alternate-site locations are within the same geographic region— which could mean that both the primary and alternate sites may be involved in common disaster scenarios.

Auditing Disaster Recovery Plans

The following steps will help the auditor determine the effectiveness of the organization's DR plans:

- Obtain a copy of DR documentation, including response procedures, contact lists, and communication plans.

- Examine samples of distributed copies of DR documentation and determine whether they are up-to-date. These samples can be obtained during interviews with key response personnel, which are covered in this procedure.

- Determine whether all documents are clear and easy to understand, not just for primary responders, but for alternate personnel who may have specific relevant skills but less familiarity with the organization's critical applications.

- Obtain contact information for off-site storage providers, hot site facilities, and critical suppliers. Determine whether these organizations are still providing services to the organization. Call some of the contacts to determine the accuracy of the documented contact information.

- For organizations using third-party recovery sites such as cloud infrastructure providers, obtain contracts that define organization and cloud provider obligations, service levels, and security controls.

- Obtain logical and physical architecture diagrams for key IT applications that support critical business processes. Determine whether BC documentation includes recovery procedures for all components that support those IT applications. See whether documentation includes recovery for end users and application administrators.

- If the organization uses a hot site, examine one or more systems to determine whether they have the proper versions of software, patches, and configurations. Examine procedures and records related to the tasks in support of keeping standby systems current. Determine whether these procedures are effective.

- If the organization has a warm site, examine the procedures used to bring standby systems into operational readiness. Examine warm site systems to see whether they are in a state where readiness procedures will likely be successful.

- If the organization has a cold site, examine all documentation related to the acquisition of replacement systems and other components. Determine whether the procedures and documentation are likely to result in systems capable of hosting critical IT applications within the period required to meet key recovery objectives.

- If the organization uses a cloud service provider's service as a recovery site, examine the procedures used to prepare and bring cloud-based systems to operational readiness. Examine procedures and configurations to see whether they are likely to support the organization successfully during a disaster.

- Determine whether any documentation exists regarding the relocation of key personnel to the hot/warm/cold processing site. See whether the documentation specifies which personnel are to be relocated and what accommodations and supporting logistics are provided. Determine the effectiveness of these relocation plans.

- Determine whether backup and off-site (or replication or e-vaulting) storage procedures are being followed. Examine systems to ensure that critical IT applications are being backed up and that proper media are being stored off-site (or that the proper data is being e-vaulted). Determine whether data recovery tests are ever performed and, if so, whether the results of those tests are documented, and problems are properly dealt with.

- Evaluate procedures for transitioning processing from the alternate processing facility back to the primary processing facility. Determine whether these procedures are complete and effective.

- Determine whether a process exists for the formal review and update of business continuity documentation to ensure continued alignment with DR planning. Examine records to see how frequently, and how recently, documents have been reviewed and updated. Determine whether this is sufficient and effective by interviewing key personnel to understand whether significant changes to applications, systems, networks, or processes are reflected in recovery and response documentation.

- Determine whether response personnel receive any formal or informal training on response and recovery procedures. Determine whether personnel are required to receive training, and whether any records are kept that show which personnel received training and at what time.

- Examine the organization's change control process. Determine whether the process includes any steps or procedures that require personnel to determine whether any change has an impact on DR documentation or procedures.

Reviewing Prior DR Test Results and Action Plans

The effectiveness of DR plans relies on the results and outcomes of tests. The IS auditor needs to examine these plans and activities to determine their effectiveness. The following will help the IS auditor audit DR testing:

- Determine whether there is a strategy for testing DR plans. Obtain records for past tests and a plan for future tests.

- Examine records for tests that have been performed over the past year or two. Determine the types of tests that were performed. Obtain a list of participants for each test. Compare the participants to lists of key recovery personnel. Examine test workpapers to determine the level of participation by key recovery personnel.

- Determine whether there is a formal process for recording test results and for using those results to make improvements in plans and procedures. Examine workpapers and records to determine the types of changes that were recommended in prior tests. Examine DR documents to see whether these changes were made as expected.

- Considering the types of tests that were performed, determine the adequacy of testing as an indicator of the effectiveness of the DR program. Did the organization perform only document reviews and walk-throughs, for example, or did the organization also perform parallel or cutover tests?

- If tests have been performed for two years or more, determine whether there's a trend showing continuous improvement in response and recovery procedures.

- If the organization performs parallel tests, determine whether tests are designed in a way that effectively determines the actual readiness of standby systems. Also, determine whether parallel tests measure the capacity of standby systems or merely their ability to process correctly but at a lower level of performance.

- Determine whether any tests included the retrieval of backup data from off-site storage or e-vaulting facilities.

Evaluating Off-site Storage

Storage of critical data and other supporting information is a key component in any organization's DR plan. Because some types of disasters can completely destroy a business location, including its vital records, it is imperative that all critical information is backed up and copies moved to an off-site storage facility. The following procedure will help the IS auditor determine the effectiveness of off-site storage:

- Obtain the location of the off-site storage or e-vaulting facility. Determine whether the facility is in the same geographic region as the organization's primary processing facility.

- If possible, visit the off-site storage facility. Examine its physical security controls as well as its safeguards to prevent damage to stored information in a disaster. Consider the entire spectrum of physical and logical access controls. Examine procedures and records related to the storage and return of backup media and other information that the organization may store there. If it is not possible to visit the off-site storage facility, obtain copies of audits or other attestations of control effectiveness.

- Take an inventory of backup media and other information stored at the facility. Compare this inventory with a list of critical business processes and supporting IT systems to determine whether all relevant information is, in fact, stored at the off-site storage facility.

- Determine how often the organization performs its own inventory of the off-site facility and whether steps to correct deficiencies are documented and remedied.

- Examine contracts, terms, and conditions for off-site storage providers or e-vaulting facilities, if applicable. Determine whether data can be recovered at the original processing center and recovered to alternate processing centers within a period that will ensure that DR can be completed within RTOs.

- Determine whether the appropriate personnel have current access codes for off-site storage or e-vaulting facilities and whether they can recover data from those facilities.

- Determine what information, in addition to backup data, exists at the off-site storage facility. Information stored off-site should include architecture diagrams, design documentation, operations procedures, and configuration information for all logical and physical layers of technology and facilities supporting critical IT applications, operations documentation, and application source code.

- Obtain information related to the way backup media and copies of records are transported to and from the off-site storage or e-vaulting facility. Determine the adequacy of controls protecting transported information.
- Obtain records supporting the transport of backup media and records to and from the off-site storage facility. Examine samples of records and determine whether they match other records, such as backup logs.

Evaluating Alternate Processing Facilities

The IS auditor should examine alternate processing facilities to determine whether they are sufficient to support the organization's BC and DR plans. The following procedure will help the IS auditor to determine whether an alternate processing facility will be effective:

- Obtain addresses and other location information for alternate processing facilities. These will include hot sites, warm sites, cold sites, cloud-based services, and alternate processing centers owned or operated by the organization. Note that the exact locations of cloud services are often unavailable for security reasons.
- Determine whether alternate facilities are located within the same geographic region as the primary processing facility and the probability that the alternate facility will be adversely affected by a disaster that strikes the primary facility.
- Perform a threat analysis on the alternate processing site. Determine which threats and hazards pose a significant risk to the organization and its ability to carry out operations effectively during a disaster.
- Determine the types of natural and human-made events likely to take place at the alternate processing facility. Determine whether there are adequate controls to mitigate the effect of these events.
- Examine all environmental controls and determine their adequacy. This should include environmental controls (HVAC), power supply, uninterruptible power supply (UPS), line conditioners, power distribution units (PDUs), and electric generators. Also, examine fire detection and suppression systems, including smoke detectors, pull stations, fire extinguishers, sprinklers, and inert gas suppression systems.
- If the alternate processing facility is a separate organization, obtain the legal contract and all exhibits. Examine these documents and determine whether the contract and exhibits support the organization's recovery and testing requirements.

Cloud-based service providers often do not permit on-site visits. Instead, they may have one or more external audit reports available through standard audits such as SOC 1, SOC 2, ISO, or PCI. Auditors will need to determine whether any such external audit reports may be relied on, and whether there are any controls that are not covered by such external audits.

Summary

Natural and human-made disasters can damage business facilities, assets, and information systems, thus threatening the viability of the organization by halting its critical processes. Even without direct effects, many secondary or indirect effects from a disaster, such as crippled transportation systems, damaged communications systems, and damaged public utilities, can seriously harm an organization. The development of business continuity plans helps an organization be better prepared to act when a disaster strikes. A vital part of this preparation is the development of alternative means for continuing the most critical activities, usually in alternate locations that are not damaged by a disaster.

There is an accepted methodology for BC and DR planning, which begins with the development of a BCP policy, a statement of the goals and objectives of a planning effort. This is followed by a BIA, a study of the organization's business processes to determine which are the most critical to the organization's ongoing viability. For each critical process, a statement of impact is developed, which is a brief description of the effect on the organization if the process is incapacitated for any significant period. The statement of impact can be qualitative or quantitative.

Next, a criticality analysis is performed, where all in-scope business processes are ranked in order of criticality. Ranking can be strictly quantitative, qualitative, or even subjective. The maximum tolerable downtime (MTD) is established for each critical business process. This drives the development of recovery targets.

Next, recovery targets for each critical business process are developed. The key targets are RTO and RPO, which specify time to system restoration and maximum data loss, respectively. When these targets have been established, the project team can develop plans that include changes to technical architecture and business processes that will help achieve these established recovery objectives. Other targets include RCapO, RCO, and SDO.

Continuity plans are then developed. These consist of procedures for personnel safety and disaster declaration, together with definitions of responsibilities, contact information for key personnel, and procedures for recovery, continuity of operations, and restoration of assets.

The effectiveness of business continuity plans can be determined only by testing. There are five types of tests: document review, walk-through, simulation, parallel test, and cutover test. These five tests represent progressively more complex (and risky) means for testing procedures and IT systems to determine whether they will be able to support critical business processes in a real disaster. The parallel test involves the use of backup IT systems in a way that enables them to process real business transactions while primary systems continue to perform the organization's real work. The cutover test transitions business data processing to backup IT systems, where they will process actual business workload for a period.

Response personnel need to be carefully chosen from available staff to ensure that enough personnel will be available in a real disaster. Some personnel may be unable to respond for a variety of reasons related to the disaster itself. As a result, some of the personnel who respond in an actual disaster may not be as familiar with the systems and procedures required to recover and maintain them. This makes training and accurate procedures critical for effective disaster recovery.

Recovery and continuity plans need to be periodically updated to reflect changes in information systems, and distributed to or made available to response and recovery personnel.

Auditing an organization's BC capabilities involves examining BCP policies, plans, procedures, contracts, and technical architectures. The IT auditor also needs to interview response personnel to gauge their readiness and visit off-site media storage and alternate processing sites to identify risks present there.

Once acceptable architectures and process changes have been determined during a DRP project, the organization sets out to make investments in these areas to bring its systems and processes closer to the recovery objectives. Procedures for recovering systems and processes are also developed at this time, as well as procedures for other aspects of disaster response, such as emergency communications plans and evacuation plans.

Some of the investment in IT system resilience may involve the establishment of an alternate processing site, where IT systems can be resumed in support of critical business processes. There are several types of alternate sites, including a hot site, where IT systems are in a continual state of near-readiness and can assume production workload within an hour or two; a warm site, where IT systems are present but require several hours to a day of preparation; a cold site, where no systems are present but must be acquired, which may require several days of preparation before those replacement systems are ready to support business processes; and a cloud-based site, in which virtual machines are provided on an on-demand basis, and where the organization will establish a hot, warm, or cold capability therein. Virtual infrastructure in a public cloud can serve as a hot or warm site.

Some of the technologies that may be introduced in IT systems to improve recovery targets include RAID, a technology that improves the reliability of disk storage systems; replication, a technique for copying data in near real time to an alternate (and usually distant) storage system; e-vaulting, where data is copied to a cloud-based e-vaulting service; and clustering, a technology whereby several servers (including some that can be located in another region) act as one logical server, enabling processing to continue even if one or more servers are incapacitated or unreachable.

Organizations developing BC and DR plans should become familiar with their crisis management and crisis communications processes and capabilities, and utilize them when possible, providing consistency of approach for all kinds of business emergencies.

Exam Essentials

Understand the business impact analysis (BIA) process and its relationship with BC and DR planning. Business impact analysis (BIA) is used to determine the dependencies of business processes and information systems and their relative criticality. One output of a BIA is a set of recovery targets (RTO, RPO, RCapO, RCO, etc.) that determine how quickly a system should be recovered.

Be able to explain how BC planning and DR planning complement each other.   Business continuity (BC) planning involves the continuation of critical business processes with alternate systems, alternate work locations, alternate personnel, or any combination of these. Disaster recovery (DR) planning involves the assessment and recovery of processing systems, including the implementation of recovery (alternate) systems, the recovery of the primary system, and the eventual resumption of processing on the primary system (or a replacement if it is damaged beyond repair).

Know how recovery targets (RTO, RPO, RCapO, RCO, etc.) function.   Recovery time objective (RTO) is the maximum period that elapses from the onset of a disaster until the resumption of service. Recovery point objective (RPO) is the maximum data loss from the onset of a disaster. Recovery capacity objective (RCapO) is the transaction or storage capacity of the recovery system as compared to the primary system. Recovery consistency objective (RCO) refers to the consistency or completeness of the recovery system, as compared to the primary system. Service delivery objective (SDO) refers to some aspect of service delivery such as SLAs.

Understand how BC and DR plans are tested.   BC and DR plans must be tested to validate effectiveness through document review, walk-through, simulation, parallel testing, or cutover testing practices. Regular testing must take place to ensure new objectives and procedures meet the requirements of a living enterprise environment. Participation in these tests provides familiarity and training for engaged operational staff members, raising understanding and awareness of requirements and responsibilities.

Be able to explain resilient IT architecture and resilient devices.   Resilient IT architecture often involves the use of redundant systems and data paths, so that the complete failure of any individual system or device will not result in the cessation of processing. Resilient devices have redundant components such as power supplies, network interfaces, storage devices, and processors. Many resilient devices permit a "hot swap" of individual components that do not interrupt the system's processing.

Be able to explain various data replication and data backup technologies.   Data can be replicated from one storage system to another, whether located in the same facility or in another location. It can also be backed up to tape, virtual tape libraries (VTLs), hard drives, or e-vaulted (stored in the cloud). Various backup media rotation schemes are used to efficiently back up data at several points in time.

Understand crisis management and its relationship with BC and DR planning.   Crisis management is used by organizations to respond to various business emergencies. It can provide templates and techniques for communications and escalation, helping to simplify the overall effort of responding to all kinds of business emergencies.

Review Questions

1. Which of the following is the best choice for backing up a department file server?
    A. Replication
    B. VTL
    C. Mirroring
    D. RAID

2. The discipline that is related to the resilience of business processes is known as:
    A. Redundancy
    B. Disaster recovery planning
    C. Business continuity planning
    D. Contingency planning

3. What is the proper sequence of the following activities?
    A. BIA, CA, BCP, DRP
    B. CA, BIA, BCP, DRP
    C. BIA, CA, DRP, BCP
    D. BCP, DRP, CIA, CA

4. Which of the following statements is correct regarding disaster response?
    A. Organizations utilize industry sector disaster response templates for all disaster types.
    B. Organizations develop disaster response plans when a disaster is declared.
    C. Organizations use different procedures for responding to natural disasters versus human-caused disasters.
    D. Organizations use the same procedures for responding to disasters of all types.

5. Which of the following is the correct sequence of DRP tests in order of difficulty and impact?
    A. Walk-through, simulation, parallel test, cutover test
    B. Parallel test, cutover test, simulation
    C. Cutover test, simulation, walk-through, parallel test
    D. On-site test, remote test, cloud test

6. A disaster recovery manager is performing an after-action review of a recent BC plan walk-through. One of the participants suggested that future walk-throughs be made more realistic. What kind of a test can be performed in the future to meet this need?
    A. Simulation
    B. Parallel test
    C. Cutover test
    D. Document review

7. What is the purpose of a criticality assessment in a business resilience program?

    A. Separate critical business processes from noncritical business processes.

    B. Determine the relative criticality of disaster response personnel.

    C. Determine the relative criticality of in-scope business processes.

    D. Determine the relative criticality of service providers.

8. What is the result of a system whose RPO is 24 hours and RTO is 1 hour?

    A. In a disaster, the system will be recovered within 24 hours, with as much as 25 hours of lost data.

    B. In a disaster, the system will be recovered within 24 hours, with a potential for as much as 1 hour of lost data.

    C. In a disaster, the system will be recovered within 1 hour, with the potential for as much as 24 hours of lost data.

    D. In a disaster, the recovery team has 1 hour to begin recovery work, which will take no more than 24 hours.

9. An IS auditor is examining a business continuity plan (BCP) and has observed that the BCP was last reviewed 2 years earlier. What can the auditors conclude from this?

    A. The plan may be outdated since it has not been reviewed within the past year.

    B. The plan is outdated since it has not been reviewed within the past year.

    C. Nothing can be concluded, based on the information provided.

    D. This is a low-criticality business process.

10. An organization has designed a DR site for a critical business application. From the information given, what type of a recovery site is this?

    A. Offline

    B. Hot

    C. Cold

    D. Warm

11. What is the most important consideration when selecting a hot site?

    A. Time zone

    B. Geographic location in relation to the primary site

    C. Proximity to major transportation

    D. Natural hazards

12. An organization has established a recovery point objective of 14 days for its most critical business applications. Which recovery strategy would be the best choice?

    A. Mobile site

    B. Warm site

    C. Hot site

    D. Cold site

13. What technology should an organization use for its application servers to provide continuous service to users?

   A. Dual power supplies

   B. Server clustering

   C. Dual network feeds

   D. Transaction monitoring

14. An organization currently stores its backup media in a cabinet next to the computers being backed up. A consultant told the organization to store backup media at an off-site storage facility. What risk did the consultant most likely have in mind when they made this recommendation?

   A. A disaster that damages computer systems can also damage backup media.

   B. Backup media rotation may result in loss of data backed up several weeks in the past.

   C. Corruption of online data will require rapid data recovery from off-site storage.

   D. Physical controls at the data processing site are insufficient.

15. An IT department has designed and implemented a hot recovery site with all of the features and half of the transaction throughput of the primary site. What is the value of RCO and RCapO targets in this case?

   A. RCO is 50% and RCapO is 100%.

   B. RCO is 100% and RCapO is 50%.

   C. RCO and RCapO are 50%.

   D. RCO is 100% and RCapO is 150%.

16. Who are the best persons to develop a DRP for a critical business application?

   A. The most senior IT experts on the business application

   B. The most senior users of the business application

   C. The most senior experts on the type of business application

   D. Consultants

17. A regional disaster has occurred, and the BC and DR plans have just been activated. One of the first responders has arrived at the data center to assess damage. At the data center, they have observed that the most recent backup media is in the data center, as well as hard-copy response procedures, and that one worker has been injured by a falling object. Which of the following should the responders do first?

   A. Assess damage to the most critical systems.

   B. Remove the disaster response procedures before they are damaged.

   C. Remove the backup media before it is damaged.

   D. Tend to the injured worker.

18. An organization's business continuity plan requires the consensus of any three of the organization's top executives to declare a disaster. What risk is associated with this stipulation in a regional disaster scenario?

- **A.** Regulators should be included in disaster declarations.
- **B.** Top executives are the wrong personnel to declare a disaster.
- **C.** Lacking hands-on knowledge, top executives are not going to be able to recover critical systems.
- **D.** It may be difficult to find three of the organization's top executives, leading to a delay in disaster declaration.

19. What is the consequence of an organization that declared a disaster they later learned did not exist?

- **A.** No consequence, since there was no disaster
- **B.** High consequence in the form of sanctions or fines from regulators
- **C.** Little consequence, other than the marshaling of resources in preparation for disaster response
- **D.** High consequence, resulting in a considerable waste of time

20. A nationwide organization with numerous offices and processing centers employs local resources in each region for disaster response. A consultant has suggested that personnel in other regions should also be trained in response procedures. Why would a consultant make this recommendation?

- **A.** Local personnel in the affected region may not be available for disaster response.
- **B.** Personnel in other regions should be given a chance to help.
- **C.** To improve the quality of the disaster response procedures.
- **D.** To perform disaster response exercises more frequently.

Chapter

7

Information Security Management

THE CERTIFIED INFORMATION SYSTEMS AUDITOR (CISA) OBJECTIVES REPRESENT 26% OF THE MATERIAL COVERED ON THE EXAM AND INCLUDE:

✓ **Domain 5: Protection of Information Assets**

  A. Information Asset Security and Control

    1. Information Asset Security Frameworks, Standards, and Guidelines

    2. Privacy Principles

    5. Network and End-Point Security

    6. Data Classification

    7. Data Encryption and Encryption-Related Techniques

    8. Public Key Infrastructure (PKI)

    9. Web-Based Communication Techniques

    10. Virtualized Environments

    11. Mobile, Wireless, and Internet-of-Things (IoT) Devices

  B. Security Event Management

    1. Security Awareness Training and Programs

    2. Information System Attack Methods and Techniques

    3. Security Testing Tools and Techniques

    4. Security Monitoring Tools and Techniques

    5. Incident Response Management

    6. Evidence Collection and Forensics

Supporting Tasks

11. Evaluate IT management and monitoring of controls.

29. Evaluate the organization's information security and privacy policies and practices.

34. Evaluate the information security program to determine its effectiveness and alignment with the organization's strategies and objectives.

35. Perform technical security testing to identify potential threats and vulnerabilities.

The topics in this chapter and Chapter 8 "Identity and Access Management," combine to cover Domain 5 of the CISA exam, which represents 26 percent of the CISA examination.

Information assets consist of information and information systems. *Information* includes software, tools, and data. *Information system* is an inclusive term that encompasses servers, workstations, mobile devices, network devices, gateways, appliances, IoT devices, and applications. An information system can be a single device or a collection of systems that work together for some business purpose.

Information Security

When most people think of cybersecurity, they imagine hackers trying to break into an organization's system and steal sensitive information, ranging from Social Security numbers and credit cards to top secret military information. Although protecting sensitive information from unauthorized disclosure is certainly one element of a cybersecurity program, it is important to understand that cybersecurity actually has three complementary objectives, as shown in Figure 7.1.

FIGURE 7.1 The three key objectives of cybersecurity programs are confidentiality, integrity, and availability.

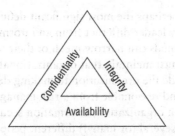

Confidentiality ensures that unauthorized individuals are not able to gain access to sensitive information. Cybersecurity professionals develop and implement security controls, including firewalls, access control lists, and encryption, to prevent unauthorized access to information. Attackers may seek to undermine confidentiality controls to achieve one of their goals: the unauthorized disclosure of sensitive information.

Integrity ensures that there are no unauthorized modifications to information or systems, either intentionally or unintentionally. Security professionals use integrity controls, such as hashing and integrity monitoring solutions, to enforce this requirement. Integrity threats may come from attackers actively seeking the alteration of information without authorization, or they may result from human error, mechanical failure, or environmental conditions, such as a power spike corrupting information.

Availability ensures that information and systems are ready to meet the needs of legitimate users at the time those users request them. Security professionals use availability controls, such as fault tolerance, clustering, and backups, to ensure that legitimate users gain access as needed. Similar to integrity threats, availability threats may come from attackers actively seeking the disruption of access, or they may come from human error, mechanical failure, or environmental conditions, such as a fire destroying a data center that contains valuable information or services.

Cybersecurity analysts often refer to these three goals, known as the CIA Triad, when performing their work. They often characterize risks, attacks, and security controls as affecting one or more of the three CIA Triad goals when describing them.

Role of the Information Security Manager

Information security managers are responsible for safeguarding the confidentiality, integrity, and availability of the information and systems used by their organization. But they must achieve these goals within the context of the organization's day-to-day activities and strategic objectives. The information security manager must wear two hats: that of a cybersecurity subject matter expert and that of a business leader engaged with the organization's mission.

This "dual-hattedness" is perhaps the most significant defining characteristic of what makes an information security leader different from an information security professional. Information security professionals can narrow much of their focus to cybersecurity matters. Leaders, on the other hand, must maintain that organizational focus at the same time and use their expertise to help guide the organization to making decisions that are both sound from a business perspective and reasonable from a risk management perspective.

Depending on the size of an organization, information security management and leadership may be a role shared by several (or many!) different people, a consolidated role held by a single person, or even a partial role filled by someone who also bears other responsibilities within the organization. There is no one-size-fits-all answer to sizing the information security function for an organization—the selection is highly dependent on the nature of the organization's security requirements, the complexity of their operating environment, and the team they have in place.

Chief Information Security Officer

The most senior information security leader within an organization often bears the title of chief information security officer (CISO). The CISO is a senior business executive who is responsible for overseeing all information security efforts within the organization. The CISO title is commonly accepted as the standard for an organization's information security leader, although some organizations may use different titles, including these:

- Vice president for information security (or assistant/associate vice president)
- Director of information security
- Information security manager

Many people believe that the use of these alternative titles indicates diminished status in the organization and a lack of prioritization for cybersecurity. In many cases, there is some truth behind this perception. In some cases, the use of the term *officer* may also imply that the individual bearing the title is an officer of the corporation or nonprofit organization. This has specific legal consequences that affect the CISO's responsibility and personal liability. However, it is important to note that just because someone has the title of CISO does not automatically make them an officer of the organization. Election or appointment as an officer is a formal process that requires the consent of the governing board.

Lines of Authority

The *lines of authority* for the CISO also convey the role that cybersecurity plays in the organization, both the number and the type of people reporting to the CISO and the person to whom the CISO reports. It is quite common for the CISO to report to the chief information officer (CIO), who leads the IT function. This CISO/CIO reporting relationship clearly places responsibility for information security issues within the IT organization. In other cases, the CISO may report to other executives, such as:

- Chief executive officer (CEO)
- Chief risk officer (CRO)
- Chief security officer (CSO) (this role includes oversight of information security, physical security, and other security concerns)
- Chief operating officer (COO)
- Chief audit executive (CAE)

The nature of this reporting relationship signals the importance that the organization places on the cybersecurity function as well as the perceived role of cybersecurity within the organization. For example, placing the information security function underneath a chief risk or chief security officer signals that the organization views information security risks within the context of a broader enterprise risk management or security program. As with titling, there is no "correct" placement of the CISO within the organizational structure, but organizations should be cognizant of the message they send to the security team and other employees based on their selection.

Although there are strong arguments for placing information security in several different parts of the organization, one general principle that should almost always be observed is that information security should not be buried underneath another function. This is particularly true when doing so may create a conflict of interest. For example, an organization might decide to place the information security function under a director of technology infrastructure who reports to the CIO. This approach is problematic for several reasons:

- It indicates that information security is not as important to the organization as other technology functions.

- It creates a potential conflict of interest when the information security team disagrees with an approach endorsed by the director to whom they report or when the security team is expected to report unflattering results of audits or tests performed on assets owned by that individual.

- It creates difficulties when the cybersecurity team has a conflict with another technology team that resides in a different part of the IT organization.

Organizing the Security Team

The CISO bears ultimate responsibility for protecting the confidentiality, integrity, and availability of the information and systems used by the organization. The specific controls and techniques used to achieve those goals will vary greatly, depending on the nature of the organization and its security requirements.

In almost every case, a team of information security professionals supports the CISO in their work, providing subject matter expertise and operational talents to achieve the organization's security objectives.

Roles and Responsibilities

Responsibility for different information security functions may be spread among a team and across the organization. For example, consider an organization's response to a cybersecurity incident. The organization may decide that the CISO has overall accountability for the incident response effort. However, the CISO does not do this on their own. They are supported by a variety of stakeholders who play different roles. The incident response team leader and members report to the CISO and carry out the actual response. Legal counsel provides valuable input on compliance issues and responsibilities. The CEO may need to be kept informed of incident progress. Tracking all of these stakeholders is crucial to ensuring that items don't slip through the cracks.

The RACI matrix is a common management tool used to specify how roles and responsibilities are shared throughout an organization. The matrix shows various security responsibilities and roles and then includes one of four letters indicating the level of involvement each role has in that responsibility. The options for filling in the RACI matrix are as follows:

- *Responsible (R)* roles are those who actually carry out the work involved. There must be at least one role assigned as responsible for each responsibility, although there may be more than one.

- *Accountable (A)* roles bear ultimate and final responsibility for achieving the objective. Consider this the "buck stops here" role for the responsibility. Each responsibility in the matrix must have one, and only one, accountable role.

- *Consulted (C)* roles are those who provide input that affects the responsibility because of their subject matter expertise.

- *Informed (I)* roles are those who are provided with regular updates on the status of the effort. They may need this information to complete their work, oversee the organization, or perform other tasks, but the key characteristic is that, unlike consulted roles, informed roles receive updates but do not provide input.

Figure 7.2 shows an abbreviated example of a RACI matrix for a few security roles in an organization.

FIGURE 7.2 RACI matrix for information security

	Incident Response	Privacy Compliance	Security Leadership
CEO	I		I
CIO	I	A	C
CISO	A	R	A
IR Leader	R	C	R
IR Team	R	C	
Compliance Leader	C	R	R
Compliance Team		R	
SOC Leader	C	I	R
SOC Team	C		
Legal Counsel	C	R	
Public Relations	C		

Information Security Risks

Security incidents occur when an organization experiences an adverse impact to the confidentiality, integrity, and/or availability of information or information systems. These incidents may occur as the result of malicious activity, such as an attacker targeting the organization and stealing sensitive information; as the result of accidental activity, such as an employee leaving an unencrypted laptop in the back of a rideshare; or as the result of natural activity, such as an earthquake destroying a data center.

Security professionals are responsible for understanding these risks and implementing controls designed to manage those risks to an acceptable level. To do so, they must first understand the effects that an incident might have on the organization and the impact it might have on an ongoing basis.

The DAD Triad

Earlier in this chapter, we introduced the CIA Triad, used to describe the three main goals of cybersecurity: confidentiality, integrity, and availability. Figure 7.3 shows a related model: the DAD Triad. This model explains the three important threats to cybersecurity efforts: disclosure, alteration, and denial. Each of these three threats maps directly to one of the main goals of cybersecurity.

FIGURE 7.3 The three key threats to cybersecurity programs are disclosure, alteration, and denial.

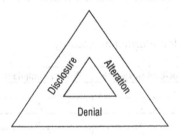

- *Disclosure* is the exposure of sensitive information to unauthorized individuals, otherwise known as data loss. Disclosure is a violation of the principle of confidentiality. Attackers who gain access to sensitive information and remove it from the organization are said to be performing data exfiltration. Disclosure may also occur accidentally, such as when an administrator misconfigures access controls or an employee loses a device.

- *Alteration* is the unauthorized modification of information and is a violation of the principle of integrity. Attackers may seek to modify records contained in a system for financial gain, such as adding fraudulent transactions to a financial account. Alteration may occur as the result of natural activity, such as a power surge causing a "bit flip" that modifies stored data. Accidental alteration is also a possibility, if users unintentionally modify information stored in a critical system as the result of a typo or other unintended activity.

- *Denial* is the disruption of an authorized user's legitimate access to information. Denial events violate the principle of availability. This availability loss may be intentional, such as when an attacker launches a distributed denial-of-service (DDoS) attack against a website. Denial may also occur as the result of accidental activity, such as the failure of a critical server, or as the result of natural activity, such as a natural disaster impacting a communications circuit.

The CIA and DAD triads are very useful tools for cybersecurity planning and risk analysis. Whenever you find yourself tasked with a broad goal of assessing the security controls used to protect an asset or the threats to an organization, you can turn to the CIA and DAD triads. For example, if you're asked to assess the threats to your organization's website, you may apply the DAD Triad in your analysis:

- Does the website contain sensitive information that would damage the organization if disclosed to unauthorized individuals?

- If an attacker were able to modify information contained on the website, would this unauthorized alteration cause financial, reputational, or operational damage to the organization?

- Does the website perform mission-critical activities that could damage the business significantly if an attacker were able to disrupt the site?

That's just one example of using the DAD Triad to inform a risk assessment. You can use the CIA and DAD models in almost any situation to serve as a helpful starting point for a more detailed risk analysis.

Incident Impact

The impacts of a security incident may be wide-ranging, depending on the nature of the incident and the type of organization affected. We can categorize the potential impact of a security incident using the same categories that businesses generally use to describe any type of risk: financial, reputational, strategic, operational, and compliance.

Let's explore each of these risk categories in greater detail.

Financial Risk

Financial risk is, as the name implies, the risk of monetary damage to the organization as the result of a data breach, service disruption, or other security incident. This may be very direct financial damage, such as the costs of rebuilding a data center after it is physically destroyed or the costs of contracting experts for incident response and forensic analysis services.

Financial risk may also be indirect and come as a second-order consequence of the breach. For example, if an employee loses a laptop containing plans for a new product, the organization suffers direct financial damages of a few thousand dollars from the loss of the physical laptop. However, the indirect financial damage may be more severe—competitors may get ahold of those product plans and beat the organization to market, resulting in potentially significant revenue loss.

Reputational Risk

Reputational risk occurs when the negative publicity surrounding a security breach causes the loss of goodwill among customers, employees, suppliers, and other stakeholders. It is often difficult to quantify reputational damage, since these stakeholders may not directly say that they will reduce or eliminate their volume of business with the organization as a result of the security breach. However, the breach may still have an impact on their future decisions about doing business with the organization.

Strategic Risk

Strategic risk is the risk that an organization will become less effective in meeting its major goals and objectives as a result of the breach. Consider again the example of an employee losing a laptop that contains new product development plans. In addition to the financial impact discussed earlier, this incident may pose strategic risk to the organization in two different ways. First, if the organization does not have another copy of those plans, they may be unable to bring the new product to market or may suffer significant product development delays. Second, if competitors gain hold of those plans, they may be able to bring competing products to market more quickly or even beat the organization to market, gaining first-mover advantage. Both of these effects demonstrate strategic risk to the organization's ability to carry out its business plans.

Operational Risk

Operational risk is risk to the organization's ability to carry out its day-to-day functions. Operational risks may slow down business processes, delay delivery of customer orders, or require the implementation of time-consuming manual workarounds to normally automated practices.

Operational risk and strategic risk are closely related, so it might be difficult to distinguish between them. Think about the difference in terms of the nature and degree of the impact on the organization. If a risk threatens the very existence of an organization or the ability of the organization to execute its business plans, that is a strategic risk that seriously jeopardizes the organization's ongoing viability. On the other hand, if the risk only causes inefficiency and delay within the organization, it fits better into the operational risk category.

Compliance Risk

Compliance risk occurs when a security breach causes an organization to run afoul of legal or regulatory requirements. For example, the Health Insurance Portability and Accountability Act (HIPAA) requires that health care providers and other covered entities protect the confidentiality, integrity, and availability of protected health information (PHI). If an organization loses patient medical records, they run afoul of HIPAA requirements and are subject to sanctions and fines from the U.S. Department of Health and Human Services. That's an example of compliance risk.

Organizations face many different types of compliance risks in today's regulatory landscape. The nature of those risks depends on the jurisdictions where the organization operates, the industry that the organization functions within, and the types of data that the organization handles.

Risks Often Cross Categories

Don't feel like you need to shoehorn every risk into one and only one of these categories. In most cases, a risk will cross multiple risk categories. For example, if an organization suffers a data breach that exposes customer PII to unknown individuals, the organization will likely suffer reputational damage due to negative media coverage. However, the organization may also suffer financial damage. Some of this financial damage may come in the form of lost business due to the reputational damage. Other financial damage may come as a consequence of compliance risk if regulators impose fines on the organization. Still more financial damage may occur as a direct result of the breach, such as the costs associated with providing customers with identity protection services and notifying them about the breach.

Building an Information Security Strategy

Perhaps the most important responsibility of an information security leader is the creation, implementation, and maintenance of an information security strategy for the organization. This strategy begins with an assessment of the current state of the organization and a comparison to the desired state of security based on the organization's control objectives. It then outlines a plan for working from that current state to achieve the desired state through clearly articulated goals.

Threat Research

Developing a cybersecurity strategy requires a strong understanding of the threat environment facing cybersecurity professionals. A strategy is only effective if it combats the threats that pose the greatest risk to the organization. These threats may be described using two important factors:

- *Threat actors* are the individuals or groups seeking to undermine the security of an organization.
- *Threat vectors* are the tactics, tools, and techniques used by threat actors to achieve their objectives.

Cybersecurity threat actors differ significantly in their skills, capabilities, resources, and motivation. Protecting your organization's information and systems requires a solid understanding of the nature of these different threats so that you may develop a set of security controls that comprehensively protect your organization against them.

SWOT Analysis

SWOT analysis is a technique commonly used by organizations to assess their current state and develop their forward-looking strategy. SWOT is an acronym describing the four major elements of the analysis:

- *Strengths* are internal characteristics of the organization that provide it with an advantage toward achieving its goals/mission. For example, a cybersecurity team might consider its cybersecurity awareness program as a strength if it is particularly effective.

- *Weaknesses* are internal characteristics of the organization that place it at a disadvantage toward achieving its goals/mission. For example, a cybersecurity team might identify the lack of application security skills as a weakness.

- *Opportunities* are external factors that the organization might exploit to better achieve its goals/mission. For example, a cybersecurity team might consider the use of managed service providers as an opportunity to relieve the burden on the team and focus their work on value-added activities.

- *Threats* are external factors that might jeopardize the organization's ability to achieve its goals/mission. For example, a hacktivist group targeting the organization would be an external threat.

The SWOT analysis may be conducted at any level of the organization. Senior leaders may conduct a SWOT analysis that analyzes the business overall. The CISO may conduct a SWOT analysis for the broad information security function, whereas the director of the incident response team may conduct a SWOT analysis for that specific function.

Organizations typically develop a SWOT analysis through a collaborative process that seeks inputs from all levels of the team, from individual contributors to senior management. The exercise of creating a SWOT analysis helps the organization think critically about its current position and how it will be affected by both internal and external forces moving forward.

A SWOT analysis may be quite detailed, but teams usually document the result of their work in a generalized chart similar to the one shown in Figure 7.4. This matrix organizes positive factors (strengths and opportunities) on the left side and negative factors (weaknesses and threats) on the right side. Similarly, internal factors (strengths and weaknesses) appear on the top, and external factors (opportunities and threats) appear on the bottom.

Gap Analysis

After identifying the risks that they face, organizations define their security requirements by writing a series of control objectives that describe how they plan to manage those risks. These control objectives are described from a strategic perspective in a general manner and provide a basis for the evaluation of the organization's current information security program against its desired state.

FIGURE 7.4 Cybersecurity SWOT analysis example

	Positive	Negative
	Strengths	**Weaknesses**
Internal	1. Experienced team 2. Strong technology infrastructure 3. Ability to innovate	1. Incident response skills 2. Disorganized vendor management process 3. Lack of consolidated logging
	Opportunities	**Threats**
External	1. Managed service provider offerings 2. Vendor-provided training	1. New state-level compliance requirements 2. Security failures at service providers

In many cases, organizations draw these control objectives from industry standard frameworks, such as the Control Objectives for Information Technologies (COBIT). Developed by ISACA, COBIT provides broad objective statements that apply to any IT organization. For example, the COBIT control objective for managed security states:

> Keep the impact and occurrence of information security incidents within the enterprise's risk appetite levels.

Chapter 2, "The Audit Process," discussed the COBIT framework and other approaches to developing control objectives.

With those control objectives in hand, cybersecurity managers can conduct an assessment of the current state of their controls and determine the degree to which they are achieving their control objectives. This process, known as a *gap analysis*, identifies areas of deficiency and opportunities for improvement that, if prioritized for remediation, may become the basis for goals in the organization's information security strategy.

Alignment with Business Strategy

Information security functions exist for only one purpose: to serve the business. Certainly, security teams are focused on protecting the confidentiality, integrity, and availability of that business's information and systems, but information security managers must remain constantly aware that they do so in service of the organization achieving its business goals and objectives.

This is often one of the most important challenges facing leaders of cybersecurity teams. It's easy for technical subject matter experts to get lost in the weeds of their work and come to think of cybersecurity as an end in and of itself, but cybersecurity is only effective when it facilitates the achievement of organizational goals and objectives. Information security efforts must align with the business's goals, objectives, functions, processes, and practices.

Cybersecurity Responsibilities

You've heard the old adage: security is everybody's responsibility. There's wisdom in that old saying—cybersecurity professionals aren't the only ones who must protect the organization's information and information systems. As you build your information security strategy, be sure to clearly document the roles of major contributors. These include three critical roles in data governance: data owners, data stewards, and data custodians.

Data owners are the senior-level officials who bear overall responsibility for particular datasets. The data owner sets policies and guidelines for data use and data security and has the authority to make final decisions regarding a dataset. Data owners are usually the business leaders who have responsibility for the mission area most closely related to the dataset. For example, an organization's vice president for human resources might be the data owner for employment information.

Practically speaking, most individuals who are senior enough to hold the position of data owner do not have the time available to get involved in the daily decisions of data governance. They usually delegate that responsibility to a *data steward*. The data steward handles the implementation of the high-level policies set by the data owner. For example, a data steward might make day-to-day decisions about who may access a dataset. In the case of the employee dataset, if the data owner is the vice president for human resources, that vice president might delegate data stewardship responsibility to a director for HR information services. In most cases, there is a reporting relationship between the data owner and the data steward.

Data custodians are the individuals who actually store and process the information in question. IT staff often find themselves in the position of data custodian because of their roles as system owners and administrators. Technologists are rarely data owners or data stewards, but they are usually data custodians for almost all of the data in the organization due to the nature of their jobs. Data stewards ensure that appropriate data protections are in place, including encryption, backups, access controls, and other mechanisms that meet the requirements set forth by data owners and stewards.

Data processors are third-party organizations that handle data on behalf of a data owner. For example, if the IT team at an organization stores data in a cloud service, that cloud service provider is a data processor.

Consider an example that helps tie these terms together. If your bank collects financial information from you to process loan applications and an IT administrator at the bank uses a cloud service to store those records, we have several roles at play. You are the data subject, because the records are about you. The bank, as an organization, is responsible for that data and likely designates a senior officer, such as the vice president of loans, as the data owner.

The IT administrator who handles the records is a data custodian, and the cloud service they use is a data processor.

Individual users also bear responsibility for protecting the security of information and systems that they use and access. Cybersecurity responsibility training should be provided to all end users but should also have a particular focus on two categories of users:

- *High-risk users* who are the likely targets of cyberattacks. This may be because they are high-profile individuals likely to attract attention or because they engage in activities that place them at higher risk, such as frequently traveling to high-risk destinations.

- *Privileged users* who would pose a higher-than-average risk if their accounts were compromised. This includes technologists with administrative access to systems, finance professionals with the ability to initiate funds transfers, executives with access to sensitive information, and other similar highly privileged groups.

Strong cybersecurity programs clearly define the responsibilities of each of these groups, communicate with them regularly, and monitor their progress toward achieving security objectives.

Implementing Security Controls

As an organization analyzes its risk environment, technical and business leaders determine the level of protection required to preserve the confidentiality, integrity, and availability of their information and systems. They express these requirements by writing the control objectives that the organization wishes to achieve. These control objectives are statements of a desired security state, but they do not, by themselves, actually carry out security activities. Security controls are specific measures that fulfill the security objectives of an organization.

Security Control Categories

Security controls are categorized based on their mechanism of action: the way that they achieve their objectives. There are three different categories of security control:

- *Technical controls* enforce confidentiality, integrity, and availability in the digital space. Examples of technical security controls include firewall rules, access control lists, intrusion prevention systems, and encryption.

- *Operational controls* include the processes that we put in place to manage technology in a secure manner. These include user access reviews, log monitoring, and vulnerability management.

- *Managerial controls* are procedural mechanisms that focus on the mechanics of the risk management process. Examples of administrative controls include periodic risk assessments, security planning exercises, and the incorporation of security into the organization's change management, service acquisition, and project management practices.

Organizations should select a set of security controls that meets their control objectives based on the criteria and parameters that they either select for their environment or have imposed on them by outside regulators. For example, an organization that handles sensitive information might decide that confidentiality concerns surrounding that information require the highest level of control. At the same time, they might conclude that the availability of their website is not of critical importance. Given these considerations, they would dedicate significant resources to the confidentiality of sensitive information while perhaps investing little, if any, time and money protecting their website against a denial-of-service attack.

Many control objectives require a combination of technical, operational, and management controls. For example, an organization might have the control objective of preventing unauthorized access to a data center. They might achieve this goal by implementing biometric access control (technical control), performing regular reviews of authorized access (operational control), and conducting routine risk assessments (managerial control).

Security Control Types

We can also divide security controls into types, based on their desired effect. The types of security control include the following:

- *Preventive controls* intend to stop a security issue before it occurs. Firewalls and encryption are examples of preventive controls.

- *Detective controls* identify security events that have already occurred. Intrusion detection systems are detective controls.

- *Corrective controls* remediate security issues that have already occurred. Restoring backups after a ransomware attack is an example of a corrective control.

- *Deterrent controls* seek to discourage an attacker from attempting to violate security policies. Vicious guard dogs and barbed wire fences are examples of deterrent controls.

- *Physical controls* are security controls that impact the physical world. Examples of physical security controls include fences, perimeter lighting, locks, fire suppression systems, and burglar alarms.

- *Compensating controls* are controls designed to mitigate the risk associated with exceptions made to a security policy.

Information security management is the collection of policies, processes, and procedures that ensures an organization's security program is effective. Security management is composed of a number of distinct and interrelated processes, including policy development and enforcement, risk management, security awareness training, user access management, security incident management, vulnerability management, third-party risk management, encryption, network access management, environmental controls, and physical access controls. Ongoing executive support is key to the success of a security management program.

These and other processes should be periodically audited to confirm their effectiveness. Control failures and exceptions should be documented and action plans developed to improve processes and systems.

Endpoint Security

Endpoint devices, such as laptop and desktop computers, mobile phones, and tablets, are the front lines in cybersecurity defensive strategies. They're at a high level of risk because they rest in the hands of end users who may intentionally or accidentally undermine the security mechanisms that protect these devices. For this reason, cybersecurity professionals pay careful attention to managing the secure configuration, monitoring, and management of endpoint systems.

Malware Prevention

Malicious software, or malware, is one of the most common threats to endpoints. Malicious software may invade a network, spreading under its own power, or it may arrive on a system when a user clicks a malicious link or installs unsafe software. Once it has a foothold on a system, malware may be used to gain control of system resources and to steal sensitive information.

Antimalware software uses two different mechanisms to protect systems against malicious software:

- Signature detection uses databases of known malware patterns and scans the files and memory of a system for any data matching the pattern of known malicious software. If it finds suspect contents, it can then remove the content from the system or quarantine it for further analysis. When you're using signature detection, it is critical that you frequently update the virus definition file to ensure that you have current signatures for newly discovered malware.

- Heuristic detection takes a different approach. Instead of using patterns of known malicious activity, these systems attempt to model normal activity and then report when they discover anomalies—activity that deviates from that normal pattern.

Administrators typically install antimalware software on all the systems in their organization and then take advantage of centralized consoles to ensure the software remains updated and to receive incident reports from managed endpoints.

Endpoint Detection and Response

Today, virtually every system out there has basic malware protection installed. Organizations are now deploying more sophisticated tools, known as endpoint detection and response (EDR) platforms. EDR extends traditional malware protection to include four important capabilities:

- Detecting security incidents
- Containing incidents that are detected
- Investigating contained incidents
- Remediating endpoints back to their pre-compromised state

That's a tall order and these solutions aren't perfect, but they go a long way toward automating an organization's endpoint security capabilities and incident response workflow.

Data Loss Prevention

Data loss prevention (DLP) solutions provide technology that helps an organization enforce information handling policies and procedures to prevent data loss and theft. They search systems for stores of sensitive information that might be unsecured and monitor network traffic for potential attempts to remove sensitive information from the organization. They can act quickly to block the transmission before damage is done and alert administrators to the attempted breach.

DLP systems work in two different environments:

- Host-based DLP uses software agents installed on a single system that search the system for the presence of sensitive information. These searches often turn up Social Security numbers, credit card numbers, and other sensitive information in the most unlikely places! Detecting the presence of stored sensitive information allows security professionals to take prompt action to either remove it or secure it with encryption. Taking the time to secure or remove information now may pay handsome rewards down the road if the device is lost, stolen, or compromised. Host-based DLP can also monitor system configuration and user actions, blocking undesirable actions. For example, some organizations use host-based DLP to block users from accessing USB-based removable media devices that they might use to carry information out of the organization's secure environment.

- Network-based DLP systems monitor outbound network traffic, watching for any transmissions that contain unencrypted sensitive information. They can then block those transmissions, preventing the unsecured loss of sensitive information. DLP systems may simply block traffic that violates the organization's policy, or, in some cases, they may automatically apply encryption to the content. This automatic encryption is commonly used with DLP systems that focus on email.

DLP systems also have two different types of detection mechanisms that they use to identify sensitive data:

- Pattern matching watches for the telltale signs of sensitive information. For example, if the DLP sees a number that is formatted like a credit card or Social Security number, it can automatically trigger an alert based on that pattern. Similarly, the DLP may contain a database of sensitive terms, such as "Top Secret" or "Business Confidential," and trigger when it sees those terms in a transmission.

- Watermarking allows systems or administrators to apply electronic tags to sensitive documents and then the DLP system can monitor systems and networks for unencrypted content containing those tags.

DLP systems may also operate as cloud-based managed security services. The service provider operates a DLP system that customers access in the cloud. This service delivery model relieves customers of the burden of operating and maintaining the DLP system themselves.

Change and Configuration Management

Configuration management tracks the way that specific endpoint devices are set up. Configuration management tracks both operating systems settings and the inventory of software installed on a device. Change management programs provide organizations with a formal process for identifying, requesting, approving, and implementing changes to configurations.

Baselining is an important component of configuration management. A baseline is a snapshot of a system or application at a given point in time. It may be used to assess whether a system has changed outside of an approved change management process. System administrators may compare a running system to a baseline to identify all changes to the system and then compare those changes to a list of approved change requests.

Version control is also a critical component of change management programs, particularly in the areas of software and script development. Versioning assigns each release of a piece of software an incrementing version number that may be used to identify any given copy.

Configuration management should also create artifacts that may be used to help understand system configuration. For example, diagrams often play an important role in helping security professionals understand how a system was designed and configured. These can be crucial when performing time-sensitive troubleshooting or incident investigations.

Together, change and configuration management allow technology professionals to track the status of hardware, software, and firmware, ensuring that change occurs when desired but in a controlled fashion that minimizes risk to the organization.

Patch Management

Applying patches to operating systems is critical because it ensures that systems are not vulnerable to security exploits discovered by attackers. Each time an operating system vendor discovers a new vulnerability, they create a patch that corrects the issue. Promptly applying patches ensures a clean and tidy operating system.

In Windows, the Windows Update mechanism is the simplest way to apply security patches to systems as soon as they are released. On Linux systems, administrators may take advantage of a variety of update mechanisms depending on their specific Linux distributions and organizational practices.

As a security administrator, you should not only ensure that your systems are configured to receive updates, you should also analyze the output of patch management processes to ensure that those patches are applied. Configuration management tools can assist you with automating this work. They also help you keep track of patches to the applications that you run in your organization.

System Hardening

System hardening involves analyzing the default settings of your operating system and removing services and components that are not required to meet your business needs.

As you perform system hardening, you should accomplish a few important tasks:

- Remove unnecessary software and operating system components to configure the system for the least functionality required to perform its function. This is an activity known as reducing the attack surface. The fewer things you have installed on a system, the fewer opportunities for an attacker to exploit.

- Lock down the host firewall to only allow access to those open ports and services that are intended for use by other systems.

- Disable any default accounts and passwords that came with the operating system or applications you installed. These default accounts provide attackers with a starting point for brute-force attacks and, when configured with default passwords, will be quickly compromised if exposed to the Internet.

- Verify that system configuration settings match best practices. On Windows systems, this may mean modifying Registry settings to configure your system to meet minimum security requirements. On Linux systems, you may need to modify configuration files to perform similar hardening tasks.

Mobile, Wireless, and Internet of Things Devices

Mobile, wireless, and Internet of Things (IoT) devices introduce unique security challenges due to their varied use cases, diverse operating environments, and increased potential for exposure to threats. Ensuring the security of these devices requires specialized approaches.

Mobile Devices

Mobile devices such as smartphones and tablets are ubiquitous and often used for both personal and professional tasks, making them prime targets for cyberattacks. Key strategies for securing mobile devices include:

- **Device encryption:** Encrypting the data stored on mobile devices to protect sensitive information in the event of loss or theft.

- **Mobile device management (MDM):** Using MDM solutions to enforce security policies, remotely wipe lost or stolen devices, and ensure that devices are running the latest security updates.

- **Application control:** Implementing application whitelisting and blacklisting to control which apps can be installed and run on the device, preventing the installation of malicious software.

Wireless Networks

Wireless networks provide flexibility and mobility but also introduce vulnerabilities due to their broadcast nature. Securing wireless networks involves:

- **Strong encryption:** Using robust encryption protocols such as WPA3 to protect data transmitted over wireless networks.
- **Network segmentation:** Creating separate networks for different types of devices (e.g., guest networks, IoT networks) to contain potential security breaches.
- **Access control:** Implementing strict access controls and regularly updating network credentials to prevent unauthorized access.

Internet of Things (IoT) Devices

The *Internet of Things (IoT)* is an approach that connects physical devices to the Internet, allowing them to collect and share data. IoT devices are often deployed in environments with minimal security oversight, making them attractive targets for attackers. Enhancing IoT security involves:

- **Firmware updates:** Ensuring that IoT devices are regularly updated with the latest firmware to patch known vulnerabilities.
- **Secure configuration:** Configuring devices securely by disabling unnecessary features, changing default passwords, and implementing network-level security measures.
- **Monitoring and analytics:** Utilizing IoT security platforms to monitor device behavior and detect anomalies that could indicate a security incident.

Network Security Controls

Networks also play a crucial role in an organization's cybersecurity program. Endpoints, servers, and other devices all rely on the network to communicate with one another. Networks are often trusted to carry sensitive information within an organization. Cybersecurity professionals use a variety of controls to ensure the security of their networks.

Network Segmentation

Well-designed networks group systems into network segments based on their security level. This approach limits the risk that a compromised system on one network segment will be able to affect a system on a different network segment. It also makes it more difficult for a malicious insider to cause the organization damage.

Firewalls

Network firewalls serve as the security guards of a network, analyzing all attempts to connect to systems on a network and determining whether the request should be allowed or denied according to the organization's security policy. They also play an important role in network segmentation.

Firewalls often sit at the network perimeter, in between an organization's routers and the Internet. From this network location, they can easily see all inbound and outbound connections. Traffic on the internal network may flow between trusted systems unimpeded, but anything crossing the perimeter to or from the Internet must be evaluated by the firewall.

Typical border firewalls have three network interfaces because they connect three different security zones together, as shown in Figure 7.5.

FIGURE 7.5   Network firewalls divide networks into three zones.

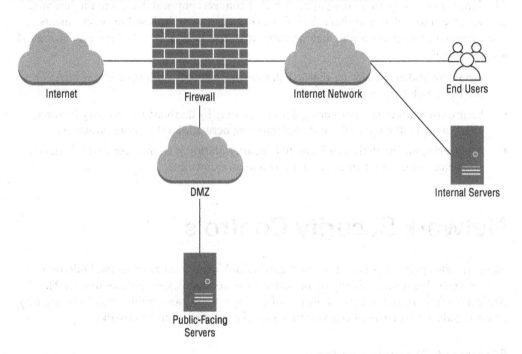

One interface connects to the Internet, or another untrusted network. This is the interface between the protected networks and the outside world. Generally speaking, firewalls allow many different kinds of connections out to this network when initiated by a system on more trusted networks, but they block most inbound connection attempts, allowing only those that meet the organization's security policy.

A second interface connects to the organization's intranet. This is the internal network where most systems reside. This intranet zone may be further subdivided into segments for endpoint systems, wireless networks, guest networks, data center networks, and other business needs. The firewall may be configured to control access between those subnets, or the organization may use additional firewalls to segment those networks.

The third interface connects to the DMZ network. Short for "demilitarized zone," the DMZ is a network where you can place systems that must accept connections from the outside world, such as a mail or web server. Those systems are placed in a separate security zone because they have a higher risk of compromise. If an attacker compromises a DMZ system, the firewall still blocks them from breaching the intranet. This approach is also known as a screened subnet.

Network designs using this philosophy often created an implicit trust in systems based on their network security zone. This approach is now going out of style in favor of a security philosophy known as zero-trust. Under the zero-trust approach, systems do not gain privileges based solely on their network location.

Virtual LANs

Virtual LANs (VLANs) are an important network security control. VLANs allow you to logically group together related systems, regardless of where they normally exist on the network.

When you create diagrams of your desired network layouts, you typically place different functional groups in different network locations. Users in the accounting department all share a network that is separate from users in the sales department and those in the IT department.

If your building and floor layout matched those network diagrams exactly, you'd be all set. More often than not, though, you usually wind up in a situation where users from different departments are mingled together and departments are spread across buildings. That's where virtual LANs come into play. You can use them to connect people who are on different parts of the network to one another and also separate them from other users who might be geographically close.

Network Device Security

Networks carry all types of data over distances short and far. Whether it's a transatlantic videoconference or an email across the room, many different networks carry the 1s and 0s that make communications work. Routers and switches are the core building blocks of these networks and require special security attention.

Switches

Network engineers use switches to connect devices to networks. They are simple-looking devices that contain a large number of network ports. Switches may be very small, with 8 or fewer ports, or they can be quite large, with 500 or more ports.

Switches are normally hidden away inside wiring closets and other secure locations. Each switchport is connected to one end of a network cable. Those cables then disappear into special pipes known as conduits for distribution around a building.

When the cable reaches the final destination, it usually terminates in a neat-looking wall faceplate. This provides a way for users and technicians to connect and disconnect computers from the network easily without damaging the cables inside the wall or having unsightly unused wires lying about the room.

Some devices directly connect to switchports through the use of wired networks. Many other devices don't use wires but instead depend on radio-based wireless networks. These networks are created by wireless access points (APs). These APs contain radios that send and receive network signals to mobile devices. The AP itself has a wired connection back to the switch, allowing the wireless devices to connect to the rest of the network.

Port security is a switch security control that protects against attackers disconnecting an authorized device from the wired network and replacing it with a rogue device that may eavesdrop on other users or attempt to access secure network resources. Port security works by limiting the MAC addresses that may be used on a particular switchport and requiring administrator intervention to change out a device. Port security works in two modes:

- In *static* mode, the administrator manually configures each switchport with the allowable MAC addresses. This is very time-consuming, but this MAC filtering approach is the most secure way to implement port security.

- In *dynamic*, or "sticky" mode, the administrator enables port security and then tells the switch to memorize the first MAC address that it sees on any given port and then restrict access to that MAC address. This makes configuration much faster but can be risky if you have unused but active switchports.

Routers

Routers play a higher-level role, connecting networks together by serving as a central aggregation point for network traffic heading to or from a large network. The router makes decisions about the best paths for traffic to follow as it travels to its final destination. The router plays a role on the network that is similar to the way an air traffic controller organizes planes in the sky, sending them to their correct destination.

Routers also play an important role in network security. They are often located both physically and logically between the firewall and another network. Because they see traffic before network firewalls, they can perform filtering that reduces the load on the network firewall. Routers aren't great at performing complex filtering, but network administrators can configure them to perform basic screening of network traffic. Routers share some common functionality with firewalls, but they are definitely not a substitute for firewall technology. Firewalls differ from routers in a number of ways:

- Firewalls are purpose-specific devices and are much more efficient at performing complex filtering than routers.

- Firewalls have advanced rule capabilities. They allow you to create rules that are conditional upon the time of day, users involved, and other criteria.

- Firewalls offer more advanced security functionality. They can incorporate threat intelligence, perform application inspection, and integrate with intrusion prevention systems to provide enhanced protection to a network.

Firewalls do offer advanced security protection, but administrators may still choose to place some access control lists at the router level to filter traffic before it reaches the firewall to reduce the burden on downstream devices.

Routers also allow you to configure Quality of Service (QoS) controls that provide guaranteed bandwidth to high-priority applications. For example, you might prioritize videoconferencing traffic over routine file transfers.

Network Security Tools

In addition to using routers, switches, and firewalls to carry out security functions, network engineers take advantage of several dedicated security tools, including virtual private networks, content filters, intrusion detection and prevention systems, and distributed denial-of-service (DDoS) protection systems.

Virtual Private Networks

Virtual private networks (VPNs) provide two important network security functions to IT administrators. First, site-to-site VPNs allow the secure interconnection of remote networks, such as connecting branch offices to a corporate headquarters or one another. Second, remote access VPNs provide mobile workers with a mechanism to securely connect from remote locations back to the organization's network.

VPNs work by using encryption to create a virtual tunnel between two systems over the Internet. Everything that enters one end of the tunnel is encrypted, and then it is decrypted when it exits the other end of the tunnel. From the user's perspective, the network appears to function normally, but if an attacker gains access to traffic between the two secure networks, all they see is encrypted information that they can't read.

VPNs require an endpoint on the remote network that accepts VPN connections. Many different devices may serve as VPN endpoints, such as a firewall, router, server, or a dedicated VPN concentrator. All of these approaches provide secure VPN connections, but organizations that have high volumes of VPN often choose to use a dedicated VPN concentrator because these devices are efficient at handling VPN connections and can manage high-bandwidth traffic with ease.

If you don't have a high volume of VPN traffic, you might choose to use the firewall, router, or server approach. If you go that way, be warned that VPN traffic requires resource-intensive encryption, and that unlike VPN concentrators, firewalls, routers, and servers usually don't contain specialized hardware that accelerates encryption. Using them as VPN endpoints can cause performance issues.

For many years, most VPNs used a protocol called IPsec, short for Internet Protocol Security, to create these encrypted tunnels. Administrators looking to run VPN connections that support traffic at the data link layer could also run the Layer 2 Tunneling Protocol L2TP over an IPsec connection.

IPsec and L2TP provide robust, secure transport, but they are often difficult to configure and may be blocked by firewalls. For that reason, IPsec is often used for static, site-to-site VPN tunnels but is becoming less common for remote user VPNs.

Remote user VPNs now often rely on Transport Layer Security (TLS) technology, which works at the application layer. These VPNs work on any system with a web browser and use port 443 for communications, a port that is typically allowed through almost every firewall. HTML5 VPNs provide a web-based interface that allows users to work with internal network resources without actually establishing a presence on the internal network and instead using the web server in a proxying role.

When implementing a remote access VPN, administrators must choose from two different tunneling approaches:

- In a full-tunnel VPN, any traffic leaving the remote device is sent through the VPN back to the home network and protected by encryption. This includes not only traffic headed back to the corporate network, but all web browsing and other activity as well.

- The alternative is to use a split-tunnel VPN. In this approach, some traffic is sent through the VPN while other traffic is sent out through the user's local network. The routing policy is set by the VPN administrator. In most cases, they configure the split tunnel to send traffic headed for corporate systems through the VPN while allowing regular Internet traffic to go directly to the destination over the local network. This approach was set up to reduce the burden on VPNs and to conserve bandwidth.

Today, most security experts discourage the use of split-tunnel VPNs. End users generally don't understand the difference and assume that, if they connect to a VPN, all of their network traffic is secure. This provides them with a false sense of security because some of their traffic is actually being sent directly over the Internet and may be subject to eavesdropping.

Another emerging trend is the Always-On VPN. In this strategy, all corporate mobile devices are configured to automatically connect to the VPN whenever they are powered on. This takes control away from the end user and ensures that traffic leaving the device is always protected by strong encryption.

Intrusion Detection and Prevention

Intrusion detection systems (IDSs) and intrusion prevention systems (IPSs) play an extremely important role in the defense of networks against hackers and other security threats. Intrusion detection systems sit on the network and monitor traffic, searching for signs of potentially malicious traffic.

For example, an intrusion detection system might notice that a request bound for a web server contains a SQL injection attack, a malformed packet is attempting to create a denial of service, a user's login attempt seems unusual based on the time of day and prior patterns, or a system on the internal network is attempting to contact a botnet command-and-control server.

All of these situations are examples of security issues that administrators would obviously want to know about. IDSs identify this type of situation and then alert administrators to the issue for further investigation.

In many cases, administrators are not available to immediately review alerts and take action or are simply overwhelmed by the sheer volume of alerts generated by an IDS.

That's where intrusion prevention comes into play. Intrusion prevention systems are just like intrusion detection systems but with a twist: They can take immediate corrective action in response to a detected threat. In most cases, this means taking action to remove the potentially malicious traffic from the network before it reaches endpoint systems. IPSs can achieve this goal through many different mechanisms of action. They might isolate network traffic, close network ports, automatically suspend compromised user accounts, or perform other remediation actions.

 Although many references treat intrusion detection systems (IDSs) and intrusion prevention systems (IPSs) as different technologies, the reality today is that the same products fill both functions. Any IPS can be set in "alert only" mode that tells it to act as an IDS.

IDS/IPS Errors

Intrusion detection and prevention systems can make mistakes. Two different types of errors are caused by these systems, and monitoring those errors is an important part of security analytics.

- *False positive errors* occur when the system alerts administrators to an attack but the attack does not actually exist. This is an annoyance to the administrator, who wastes time investigating the alert, and may lead to administrators ignoring future alerts.

- *False negative errors* occur when an attack actually takes place but the intrusion detection system does not notice it.

IDS/IPS Detection Techniques

Intrusion detection and prevention systems use two different technologies to identify suspicious traffic. The most common, and most effective, method is called signature detection. This approach works in a manner similar to antivirus software.

Signature-based systems contain very large databases containing patterns of data (or signatures) known to be associated with malicious activity. When the system spots network traffic matching one of those signatures, it triggers an intrusion alert. This approach is also known as rule-based detection.

The downside is that a signature-based system cannot detect a previously unknown attack. If you're one of the first victims of a new attack, it will sneak right past a signature-detection system. The upside is that if the signatures are well designed, these systems work very well, with a low false positive rate. Signature detection is reliable, time-tested technology.

The second method is known as anomaly detection. This model takes a completely different approach to the intrusion detection problem. Instead of trying to develop signatures for all possible malicious activity, the anomaly detection system tries to develop a model of normal activity and then report deviations from that model as suspicious.

For example, an anomaly detection system might notice that a user who normally connects to the VPN from home during the early evening hours is suddenly connecting from Asia in the middle of the night. The system can then either alert administrators or block the connection, depending on the policy. The models developed by these IDSs and IPSs are often application-aware and understand how to dissect the application protocols in use during a network session.

Anomaly detection does have the potential to notice new attack types, but it has a high false positive error rate and is not widely used by security administrators.

Many modern intrusion detection and prevention systems combine signature detection and anomaly detection capabilities in the same product.

IDS/IPS Configurations

There are also differences in the way that intrusion detection and prevention systems are set up and configured on the network. The two major approaches are in-band and out-of-band deployments.

In an in-band deployment, the IPS sits directly on the network path and all communications must pass through it on their way to their final destination. In this approach, the IPS can block suspicious traffic from reaching its final destination. In-band deployments are also known as inline deployments. Although this approach allows an active response, it also adds the risk that an issue with the IPS can disrupt all network communications because the in-band IPS is a single point of failure.

In an out-of-band deployment, the IPS is not in the network path but sits outside the flow of network traffic. It is connected to a SPAN port on a switch, which allows it to receive copies of all traffic sent through the network to scan, but it cannot disrupt the flow of traffic. This approach is also known as *passive mode*, because the IPS can still react by sending commands to block future traffic from offending systems, but it cannot stop the initial attack from entering the network because it only learns about that traffic after it has been sent.

DDoS Prevention

Most of the attack techniques used by hackers focus on undermining the confidentiality or integrity of data. One of the common goals of attackers is to steal sensitive information, such as credit card numbers or Social Security numbers, or alter information in an unauthorized fashion, such as increasing bank account balances or defacing a website.

Some attacks, however, focus on disrupting the legitimate use of a system. Unlike other attacks, these target the availability leg of the CIA triad. We call these attacks denial-of-service (DoS) attacks. These attacks make a system or resource unavailable to legitimate users by sending thousands or millions of requests to a network, server, or application, overwhelming it and making it unable to answer any requests. It is difficult to distinguish well-executed DoS attack requests from legitimate traffic.

There are two significant issues with this basic DoS approach from the attacker's perspective:

- *DoS attacks require large amounts of bandwidth.* Sending lots of requests that tie up the server requires a large network connection. It becomes a case of who has the bigger network connection.
- *DoS attacks are easy to block.* Once the victim recognizes they are under attack, they can simply block the IP addresses of the attackers.

Distributed denial-of-service (DDoS) attacks overcome these limitations by using botnets to overwhelm their target. The attack requests come from many different network locations, so it is difficult to distinguish them from legitimate requests.

DDoS attacks are a serious threat to system administrators because these attacks can quickly overwhelm a network with illegitimate traffic. Defending against them requires security professionals to understand them well and implement blocking technology on the network that identifies and weeds out suspected attack traffic before it reaches servers. This is often done with the cooperation of Internet service providers (ISPs) and third-party DDoS protection services.

Cloud Computing Security

Cloud computing can be an intimidating term, but the fundamental idea is straightforward: Cloud service providers deliver computing services to their customers over the Internet. This could be as simple as Google providing their Gmail service to customers in a web browser or Amazon Web Services (AWS) providing virtualized servers to corporate clients who use them to build their own technology environment. In each of these cases, the provider builds an IT service and uses the Internet to deliver that service to its customers.

Here's a more formal definition of cloud computing from the National Institute of Standards and Technology (NIST):

> Cloud computing is a model for enabling ubiquitous, convenient, on-demand network access to a shared pool of configurable computing resources (e.g., networks, servers, storage, applications, and services) that can be rapidly provisioned and released with minimal management effort or service provider interaction.

Let's walk through some of the components of that definition. Cloud computing is ubiquitous and convenient. The resources provided by the cloud are available to customers wherever they may be. If you have access to the Internet, you can access the cloud. It doesn't matter whether you're sitting in your office or on the beach.

Cloud computing is also on demand. In most cases, you can provision and deprovision cloud resources in a few minutes with a few clicks. You can acquire new cloud resources almost immediately when you need them, and you can turn them off quickly (and stop paying for them!) when they are no longer required.

Many of the key benefits of the cloud derive from the fact that it uses a shared pool of resources that may be configured for different purposes by different users. This sharing allows oversubscription because not everyone will use all their resources at the same time, and it achieves economies of scale. The fact that many different users share resources in the same cloud infrastructure is known as *multitenancy*. In a multitenant environment, the same physical hardware might support the workloads and storage needs of many different customers, all of whom operate without any knowledge of or interaction with their fellow customers.

The cloud offers a variety of configurable computing resources. We'll talk about the different cloud service models later in this chapter, but you can acquire infrastructure components, platforms, or entire applications through cloud service providers and then configure them to meet your needs.

The rapid provisioning and releasing of cloud services also takes place with minimal management effort and service provider interaction. Unlike with on-premises hardware acquisition, you can provision cloud services yourself without dealing with account representatives and order processing times. If you need a new cloud server, you don't need to call up Microsoft, Amazon, or Google. You just click a few buttons on their website and you're good to go. From the perspective of most users, the cloud presents seemingly infinite capacity.

Benefits of the Cloud

As organizations consider the appropriate role for the cloud in their technology infrastructure, the essential question that they seek to answer is the appropriate balance of on-premises versus cloud/off-premises resources. The correct balance will vary from organization to organization. Understanding some of the major benefits provided by the cloud is helpful to finding that correct balance:

- **On-demand self-service computing:** Cloud resources are available when and where you need them. This provides developers and technologists with incredible agility, reducing cycle times and increasing the speed of deployment.

- **Scalability:** As the demand for a cloud-based service increases, customers can manually or automatically increase the capacity of their operations. In some cloud environments, the cloud service provider may do this in a manner that is completely transparent to the customer, scaling resources behind the scenes. Cloud providers achieve scalability in two ways:

  - *Vertical scaling* increases the capacity of existing servers, as shown in Figure 7.6(a). For example, you might change the number of CPU cores or the amount of memory assigned to a server. In the physical world, this means opening up a server and adding physical hardware. In the cloud, you can just click a few buttons and add memory or compute capacity.

  - *Horizontal scaling* adds more servers to a pool of clustered servers, as shown in Figure 7.6(b). If you run a website that supports 2,000 concurrent users with two servers, you might add a new server every time your typical usage increases another

1,000 users. Cloud computing makes this quite easy, since you can just replicate your existing server with a few clicks.

FIGURE 7.6   (a) Vertical scaling vs. (b) horizontal scaling

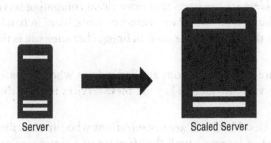

(a) Vertical Scaling

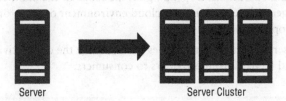

(b) Horizontal Scaling

- **Elasticity:** Elasticity and scalability are closely related. Scalability is focused on rapidly increasing capacity. Elasticity says that capacity should expand *and contract* as needs change to optimize costs. If your website starts to experience a burst in activity, elasticity allows you to automatically add servers until that capacity is met and then remove those servers when the capacity is no longer needed.

- **Measured service:** Everything you do in the cloud is measured by the provider. Providers track the number of seconds of processing time you consume, the amount of storage you occupy, the number of log entries that you generate, and many other measures. They use this information to be able to assess charges based on your usage. You pay for exactly what you request—no more and no less.

- **Agility and flexibility:** The speed to provision cloud resources and the ability to use them for short periods of time lends tremendous agility and flexibility to technology organizations. Developers and engineers who wish to try a new idea can rapidly spin up a test environment, evaluate the approach, and decide whether to move it into production with minimal effort and cost.

Cloud Roles

In any cloud computing environment, different organizations take on different roles. There are five important roles in the cloud:

- *Cloud service providers* are the firms that offer cloud computing services to their customers. They may build their own data centers or work hand in hand with other cloud providers to deliver their service, but their defining characteristic is they offer a cloud service for sale.

- *Cloud consumers* are the organizations and individuals who purchase cloud services from cloud service providers. They use these services to meet their own business requirements.

- *Cloud partners* (or cloud brokers) are organizations who offer ancillary products or services that support or integrate with the offerings of a cloud service provider. Cloud partners may offer training or consulting to help customers make use of a cloud service, provide software development and integration services, or perform any other service that facilitates the use of a cloud offering.

- *Cloud auditors* are independent organizations who provide third-party assessments of cloud services and operations. Depending on the scope of the audit engagement, they may provide a general assessment of a cloud environment or focus on security controls for a narrow scope of operations.

- *Cloud carriers* serve as the intermediaries who provide the connectivity that allows the delivery of cloud services from providers to consumers.

 The same organization may take on multiple roles. For example, if an organization purchases cloud infrastructure components from a cloud service provider, they are a cloud consumer. If they use those infrastructure components to build a cloud software application that they offer to their own customers, then they are also a cloud service provider themselves!

Cloud Service Models

We categorize the types of services offered by cloud service providers into several buckets based on the nature of the offering. The wide variety of services available in the cloud are often described as "anything-as-a-service" or the acronym XaaS, where X indicates the nature of the specific service. Although there are many different types of cloud services, we often describe them using three major service models: infrastructure-as-a-service (IaaS), software-as-a-service (SaaS), and platform-as-a-service (PaaS).

Infrastructure-as-a-service (IaaS)

Infrastructure-as-a-service (IaaS) offerings allow customers to purchase and interact with the basic building blocks of a technology infrastructure. These include computing, storage, and networks. Customers then have the flexibility to configure and manage those services in any way they like to meet their own business needs. The customer doesn't need to worry about the management of the underlying hardware, but they do have the ability to customize components to meet their needs. In the IaaS model, the cloud service provider is responsible for managing the physical facilities and the underlying hardware. The provider must also implement security controls that prevent customers from eavesdropping on each other or interfering with each other's use of the infrastructure environment.

Software-as-a-service (SaaS)

Software-as-a-service (SaaS) offerings provide customers with access to a fully managed application running in the cloud. The provider is responsible for everything from the operation of the physical data centers to the performance management of the application itself, although some of these tasks may be outsourced to other cloud service providers. In the SaaS model, the customer is only responsible for limited configuration of the application itself, the selection of what data they wish to use with the cloud solution, and the use of application-provided access controls to limit access to that data.

Platform-as-a-service (PaaS)

Platform-as-a-service (PaaS) offerings fit into a middle ground between SaaS and IaaS solutions. In a PaaS offering, the service provider offers a platform where customers may run applications that they have developed themselves. The cloud service provider builds and manages the infrastructure and offers customers an execution environment, which may include code libraries, services, and tools that facilitate code execution.

Cloud Deployment Models

Cloud deployment models describe how a cloud service is delivered to customers and whether the resources used to offer services to one customer are shared with other customers.

Public Cloud

When we think of "the cloud," we commonly first think of public cloud offerings. Public cloud service providers deploy infrastructure and then make it accessible to any customers who wish to take advantage of it in a multitenant model. A single customer may be running workloads on servers spread throughout one or more data centers, and those servers may be running workloads for many different customers simultaneously.

The public cloud supports all cloud service models. Public cloud providers may offer IaaS, PaaS, and SaaS services to their customers. The important distinction is that those services do not run on infrastructure dedicated to a single customer but rather on infrastructure that is available to the general public. AWS, Microsoft Azure, and Google Compute Engine all offer the public cloud model.

Private Cloud

The term *private cloud* is used to describe any cloud infrastructure that is provisioned for use by a single customer. This infrastructure may be built and managed by the organization that will be using the infrastructure, or it may be built and managed by a third party. The distinction here is that only one customer uses the environment. For this reason, private cloud services tend to have excess unused capacity to support peak demand and, as a result, are not as cost-efficient as public cloud services.

Hybrid Cloud

Hybrid cloud is a catch-all term used to describe cloud deployments that blend public, private, and/or community cloud services together. It is not simply purchasing both public and private cloud services and using them together. Hybrid cloud requires the use of technology that unifies the different cloud offerings into a single coherent platform.

For example, a firm might operate their own private cloud for the majority of their workloads and then leverage public cloud capacity when demand exceeds the capacity of their private cloud infrastructure. This approach is known as public cloud bursting.

Shared Responsibility Model

In some ways, cybersecurity work in a cloud-centric environment is quite similar to on-premises cybersecurity. No matter where our systems are hosted, we still need to think about the confidentiality, integrity, and availability of our data and implement strong access controls and other mechanisms that protect those primary objectives.

However, cloud security operations also differ significantly from on-premises environments because cloud customers must divide responsibilities between one or more service providers and the customers' own cybersecurity teams. This type of operating environment is known as the shared responsibility model. Figure 7.7 shows the common division of responsibilities in IaaS, PaaS, and SaaS environments.

In some cases, this division of responsibility is straightforward. Cloud providers, by their nature, are always responsible for the security of both hardware and the physical data center environment. If the customer were handling either of these items, the solution would not fit the definition of cloud computing.

The differences in responsibility come higher up in the stack and vary depending on the nature of the cloud service being used. In an IaaS environment, the customer takes over security responsibility for everything that isn't infrastructure—the operating system, applications, and data that they run in the IaaS environment.

FIGURE 7.7   Shared responsibility model for cloud computing

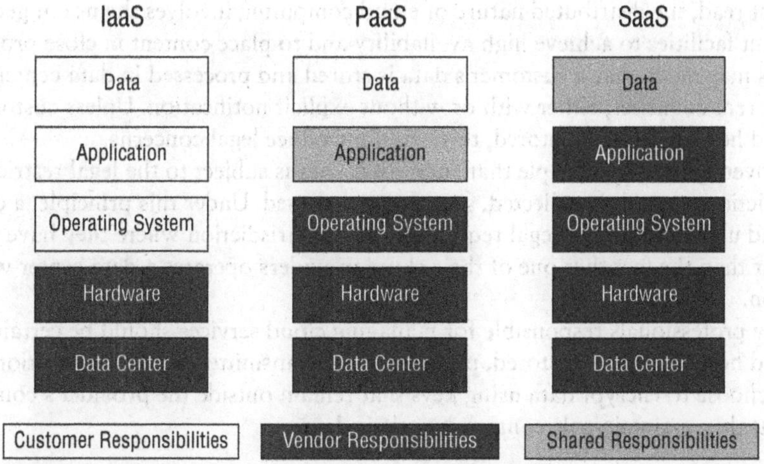

In a PaaS solution, the vendor also takes on responsibility for the operating system, whereas the customer retains responsibility for the data being placed into the environment and configuring its security. Responsibility for the application layer is shared between the service provider and the customer, and the exact division of responsibilities shifts based on the nature of the service. For example, if the PaaS platform provides runtime interpreters for customer code, the cloud provider is responsible for the security of those interpreters.

In an SaaS environment, the provider takes on almost all security responsibility. The customer retains some shared control over the data that they place in the SaaS environment and the configuration of access controls around that data, but the SaaS provider is being paid to take on the burden of most operational tasks, including cybersecurity.

Cloud Security Issues

The cloud brings tremendous operational and financial advantages to organizations, but those advantages also come with new security issues that arise in cloud environments.

Availability

Availability issues exist in cloud environments, just as they do in on-premises settings. One of the major advantages of the cloud is that cloud providers may operate in many different geographic regions, and they often provide simple mechanisms for backing up data across those regions and/or operating in a high-availability mode across diverse zones. For example, a company operating a web server cluster in the cloud may choose to place servers on each major continent to serve customers in those regions and also to provide geographic diversity in the event of a large-scale issue in a particular geographic region.

Data Sovereignty

As you just read, the distributed nature of cloud computing involves the use of geographically distant facilities to achieve high availability and to place content in close proximity to users. This may mean that a customer's data is stored and processed in data centers across many different countries, either with or without explicit notification. Unless customers understand how their data is stored, this could introduce legal concerns.

Data sovereignty is a principle that states that data is subject to the legal restrictions of any jurisdiction where it is collected, stored, or processed. Under this principle, a customer might wind up subject to the legal requirements of a jurisdiction where they have no involvement other than the fact that one of their cloud providers operates a data center within that jurisdiction.

Security professionals responsible for managing cloud services should be certain that they understand how their data is stored, processed, and transmitted across jurisdictions. They may also choose to encrypt data using keys that remain outside the provider's control to ensure that they maintain sole control over their data.

Virtualization Security

Virtual machine escape vulnerabilities are the most serious issue that may exist in a virtualized environment, particularly when a device is running several virtual systems of differing security levels. In an escape attack, the attacker has access to a single virtual guest system and then manages to leverage that access to intrude upon the resources assigned to a different virtual machine. The hypervisor is supposed to prevent this type of access by restricting a virtual machine's access to only those resources assigned to that machine. Escape attacks allow a process running on the virtual machine to "escape" those hypervisor restrictions.

Virtual machine sprawl occurs when IaaS users create virtual service instances and then forget about them or abandon them, leaving them to accrue costs and accumulate security issues over time. Organizations should maintain instance awareness to avoid VM sprawl issues.

Cloud Application Security

Cloud applications depend heavily on the use of application programming interfaces (APIs) to provide service integration and interoperability. In addition to implementing secure coding practices, security analysts responsible for API-based applications should implement API inspection technology that scrutinizes API requests, looking for requests that pose security issues. These capabilities are often found in web application firewall (WAF) solutions.

Secure web gateways (SWGs) also provide a layer of application security for cloud-dependent organizations. SWGs monitor web requests made by internal users and evaluate them against the organization's security policy, blocking requests that violate these requirements. SWGs are commonly used to block access to potentially malicious content but may also be used to enforce content filtering restrictions.

Governance and Auditing

Technology governance efforts guide the work of IT organizations and ensure that they are consistent with organizational strategy and policy. These efforts should also guide the establishment and maintenance of cloud vendor relationships. Cloud governance efforts assist with the following:

- Vetting vendors being considered for cloud partnerships

- Managing vendor relationships and monitoring for early warning signs of vendor stability issues

- Overseeing an organization's portfolio of cloud activities

Auditability is an important component of cloud governance. Cloud computing contracts should include language guaranteeing the right of the customer to audit cloud service providers. Customers may choose to perform these audits themselves or engage a third party to perform an independent audit. The use of auditing is essential to providing customers with the assurance that the provider is operating in a secure manner and meeting its contractual data protection obligations.

Cloud Security Controls

Cloud providers and third-party organizations offer a variety of solutions that help organizations achieve their security objectives in the cloud. Organizations may choose to adopt cloud native controls offered by their cloud service provider, third-party solutions, or a combination of the two.

Controls offered by cloud service providers have the advantage of direct integration with the provider's offerings, often making them cost-effective and user-friendly. Third-party solutions are often more costly, but they bring the advantage of integrating with a variety of cloud providers, facilitating the management of multicloud environments.

Cloud Access Security Brokers

Most organizations use a variety of cloud service providers for different purposes. It's not unusual to find that a large organization purchases cloud services from dozens, or even hundreds, of different providers. This is especially true when organizations use highly specialized SaaS products. Managing security policies consistently across these services poses a major challenge for cybersecurity analysts.

Cloud access security brokers (CASBs) are software tools that serve as intermediaries between cloud service users and cloud service providers. This positioning allows them to monitor user activity and enforce policy requirements. CASBs operate using two different approaches:

- Inline CASB solutions physically or logically reside in the connection path between the user and the service. They may do this through a hardware appliance or an endpoint agent that routes requests through the CASB. This approach requires configuration of the network and/or endpoint devices. It provides the advantage of seeing requests before they are sent to the cloud service, allowing the CASB to block requests that violate policy.

▪ API-based CASB solutions do not interact directly with the user but rather interact directly with the cloud provider through the provider's API. This approach provides direct access to the cloud service and does not require any user device configuration. However, it also does not allow the CASB to block requests that violate policy. API-based CASBs are limited to monitoring user activity and reporting on or correcting policy violations after the fact.

Resource Policies

Cloud providers offer resource policies that customers may use to limit the actions that users of their accounts may take. Implementing resource policies is a good security practice to limit the damage caused by an accidental command, a compromised account, or a malicious insider.

For example, a resource policy might prohibit affected users from using any resources outside of specific geographic regions and restrict the services that they may use. Policies may also limit users to only launching smaller server instances in an effort to control costs.

Hardware Security Modules

Hardware security modules (HSMs) are special-purpose computing devices that manage encryption keys and also perform cryptographic operations in a highly efficient manner. HSMs are expensive to purchase and operate, but they provide an extremely high level of security when configured properly. One of their core benefits is that they can create and manage encryption keys without exposing the keys to a single human being, dramatically reducing the likelihood that the keys will be compromised.

Cloud service providers often use HSMs internally for the management of their own encryption keys and also offer HSM services to their customers as a secure method for managing customer keys without exposing them to the provider.

Cryptography

Cryptography is the practice of encoding information in a manner that it cannot be decoded without access to the required decryption key. Cryptography consists of two main operations: *encryption*, which transforms plaintext information into ciphertext using an encryption key, and *decryption*, which transforms ciphertext back into plain text using a decryption key.

Goals of Cryptography

Security practitioners use cryptographic systems to meet four fundamental goals: confidentiality, integrity, authentication, and nonrepudiation. Achieving each of these goals requires the satisfaction of a number of design requirements, and not all cryptosystems are intended to achieve all four goals. In the following sections, we'll examine each goal in detail and give a brief description of the technical requirements necessary to achieve it.

Confidentiality

Confidentiality ensures that data remains private in three different situations: when it is at rest, when it is in transit, and when it is in use.

Confidentiality is perhaps the most widely cited goal of cryptosystems—the preservation of secrecy for stored information or for communications between individuals and groups. Two main types of cryptosystems enforce confidentiality:

- *Symmetric cryptosystems* use a shared secret key available to all users of the cryptosystem.
- *Asymmetric cryptosystems* use individual combinations of public and private keys for each user of the system.

When developing a cryptographic system for the purpose of providing confidentiality, you must think about data in three states:

- *Data at rest,* or stored data, is that which resides in a particular location awaiting access. Examples of data at rest include data stored on hard drives, backup tapes, cloud storage services, USB devices, and other storage media.
- *Data in motion,* or data on the wire, is data being transmitted between two systems. Data in motion might be traveling on a corporate network, a wireless network, or the public Internet.
- *Data in use* is data that is active in a computer system where it may be accessed by a process running on that system.

Each of these situations poses different types of confidentiality risks. For example, data in motion may be susceptible to eavesdropping attacks, whereas data at rest is more susceptible to the theft of physical devices. Data in use may be accessed by unauthorized processes if the operating system does not properly implement process isolation.

Obfuscation is a concept often confused with confidentiality. It is the practice of making it intentionally difficult for humans to understand how code or security mechanisms work. This technique is often used to hide the inner workings of software, particularly when it contains sensitive intellectual property.

Integrity

Integrity ensures that data is not altered without authorization. If integrity mechanisms are in place, the recipient of a message can be certain that the message received is identical to the message that was sent. Similarly, integrity checks can ensure that stored data was not altered between the time it was created and the time it was accessed. Integrity controls protect against all forms of alteration, including intentional alteration by a third party attempting to insert false information, intentional deletion of portions of the data, and unintentional alteration by faults in the transmission process.

Message integrity is enforced through the use of encrypted message digests, known as *digital signatures*, created upon transmission of a message. The recipient of the message simply verifies that the message's digital signature is valid, ensuring that the message was not altered in transit. Integrity can be enforced by both public and secret key cryptosystems.

Authentication

Authentication verifies the claimed identity of system users and is a major function of cryptosystems. For example, suppose that Bob wants to establish a communications session with Alice and they are both participants in a shared-secret communications system. Alice might use a challenge-response authentication technique to ensure that Bob is who he claims to be.

Figure 7.8 shows how this challenge-response protocol would work in action. In this example, the shared secret code used by Alice and Bob is quite simple—the letters of each word are simply reversed. Bob first contacts Alice and identifies himself. Alice then sends a challenge message to Bob, asking him to encrypt a short message using the secret code known only to Alice and Bob. Bob replies with the encrypted message. After Alice verifies that the encrypted message is correct, she trusts that Bob himself is truly on the other end of the connection.

FIGURE 7.8 Challenge-response authentication protocol

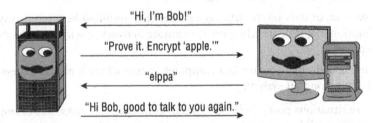

"Hi, I'm Bob!"

"Prove it. Encrypt 'apple.'"

"elppa"

"Hi Bob, good to talk to you again."

Nonrepudiation

Nonrepudiation provides assurance to the recipient that the message was originated by the sender and not someone masquerading as the sender. It also prevents the sender from claiming that they never sent the message in the first place (also known as *repudiating* the message). Secret key, or symmetric key, cryptosystems (such as simple substitution ciphers) do not provide this guarantee of nonrepudiation. If Jim and Bob participate in a secret key communication system, they can both produce the same encrypted message using their shared secret key. Nonrepudiation is offered only by public key, or asymmetric, cryptosystems, a topic discussed later in this chapter.

Symmetric Key Algorithms

Symmetric key algorithms rely on a "shared secret" encryption key that is distributed to all members who participate in the communications. This key is used by all parties to both encrypt and decrypt messages, so the sender and the receiver both possess a copy of the shared key. The sender encrypts with the shared secret key and the receiver decrypts with it. When large-sized keys are used, symmetric encryption is very difficult to break. It is primarily employed to perform bulk encryption and provides only for the security service of confidentiality. Symmetric key cryptography can also be called *secret key cryptography* and *private key cryptography*. Figure 7.9 illustrates the symmetric key encryption and decryption processes.

FIGURE 7.9 Symmetric key cryptography

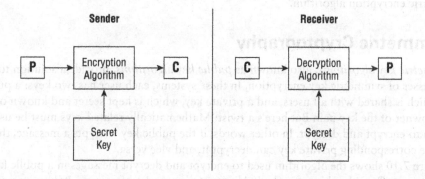

 The use of the term *private key* can be tricky because it is part of three different terms that have two different meanings. The term *private key* by itself always means the private key from the key pair of public key cryptography (aka asymmetric). However, both *private key cryptography* and *shared private key* refer to symmetric cryptography. The meaning of the word *private* is stretched to refer to two people sharing a secret that they keep confidential. (The true meaning of *private* is that only a single person has a secret that's kept confidential.) Be sure to keep these confusing terms straight in your studies.

Symmetric key cryptography has several weaknesses:

Key distribution is a major problem.   Parties must have a secure method of exchanging the secret key before establishing communications with a symmetric key protocol. If a secure electronic channel (such as the use of digital certificates) is not available, an offline key distribution method must often be used (that is, out-of-band exchange).

Symmetric key cryptography does not implement nonrepudiation.   Because any communicating party can encrypt and decrypt messages with the shared secret key, there is no way to prove where a given message originated.

The algorithm is not scalable.   It is extremely difficult for large groups to communicate using symmetric key cryptography. Secure private communication between individuals in the group could be achieved only if each possible combination of users shared a private key.

Keys must be regenerated often.   Each time a participant leaves the group, all keys known by that participant must be discarded.

The major strength of symmetric key cryptography is the great speed at which it can operate. Symmetric key encryption is very fast, often 1,000 to 10,000 times faster than asymmetric algorithms. By nature of the mathematics involved, symmetric key cryptography also naturally lends itself to hardware implementations, creating the opportunity for even higher-speed operations.

The Advanced Encryption Standard (AES) is the most commonly used example of a symmetric encryption algorithm.

Asymmetric Cryptography

Asymmetric key algorithms, also known as *public key algorithms*, provide a solution to the weaknesses of symmetric key encryption. In these systems, each user has two keys: a public key, which is shared with all users, and a private key, which is kept secret and known only to the owner of the key pair. But here's a twist: Mathematically related keys must be used in tandem to encrypt and decrypt. In other words, if the public key encrypts a message, then only the corresponding private key can decrypt it, and vice versa.

Figure 7.10 shows the algorithm used to encrypt and decrypt messages in a public key cryptosystem. Consider this example. If Alice wants to send a message to Bob using public key cryptography, she creates the message and then encrypts it using Bob's public key. The only possible way to decrypt this ciphertext is to use Bob's private key, and the only user with access to that key is Bob. Therefore, Alice can't even decrypt the message herself after she encrypts it. If Bob wants to send a reply to Alice, he simply encrypts the message using Alice's public key, and then Alice reads the message by decrypting it with her private key.

FIGURE 7.10   Asymmetric key cryptography

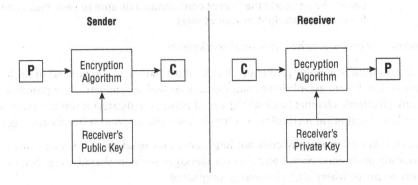

Asymmetric key algorithms also provide support for digital signature technology. Basically, if Bob wants to assure other users that a message with his name on it was actually sent by him, he first creates a message digest by using a hashing algorithm (you'll find more on hashing algorithms in the next section). Bob then encrypts that digest using his private key. Any user who wants to verify the signature simply decrypts the message digest using Bob's public key and then verifies that the decrypted message digest is accurate.

The following is a list of the major strengths of asymmetric key cryptography:

The addition of new users requires the generation of only one public/private key pair. This same key pair is used to communicate with all users of the asymmetric cryptosystem. This makes the algorithm extremely scalable.

Users can be removed far more easily from asymmetric systems. Asymmetric cryptosystems provide a key revocation mechanism that allows a key to be canceled, effectively removing a user from the system.

Key regeneration is required only when a user's private key is compromised. If a user leaves the community, the system administrator simply needs to invalidate that user's keys. No other keys are compromised and therefore key regeneration is not required for any other user.

Asymmetric key encryption can provide integrity, authentication, and nonrepudiation. If a user does not share their private key with other individuals, a message signed by that user can be shown to be accurate and from a specific source and cannot be later repudiated.

Key distribution is a simple process. Users who want to participate in the system simply make their public key available to anyone with whom they want to communicate. There is no method by which the private key can be derived from the public key.

No preexisting communication link needs to exist. Two individuals can begin communicating securely from the moment they start communicating. Asymmetric cryptography does not require a preexisting relationship to provide a secure mechanism for data exchange.

The major weakness of public key cryptography is its slow speed of operation. For this reason, many applications that require the secure transmission of large amounts of data use public key cryptography to establish a connection and then exchange a symmetric secret key. The remainder of the session then uses symmetric cryptography.

Hash Functions

Later in this chapter, you'll learn how cryptosystems implement digital signatures to provide proof that a message originated from a particular user of the cryptosystem and to ensure that the message was not modified while in transit between the two parties. Before you can completely understand that concept, we must first explain the concept of *hash functions*.

We will explore the basics of hash functions and look at several common hash functions used in modern digital signature algorithms.

Hash functions have a very simple purpose—they take a potentially long message and generate a unique output value derived from the content of the message. This value is commonly referred to as the *message digest*. Message digests can be generated by the sender of a message and transmitted to the recipient along with the full message for two reasons.

First, the recipient can use the same hash function to recompute the message digest from the full message. They can then compare the computed message digest to the transmitted one to ensure that the message sent by the originator is the same one received by the recipient. If the message digests do not match, that means the message was somehow modified while in transit. It is important to note that the messages must be *exactly* identical for the digests to match. If the messages have even a slight difference in spacing, punctuation, or content, the message digest values will be completely different. It is not possible to tell the degree of difference between two messages by comparing the digests. Even a slight difference will generate totally different digest values.

Second, the message digest can be used to implement a digital signature algorithm.

There are five basic requirements for a cryptographic hash function:

- They accept an input of any length.

- They produce an output of a fixed length, regardless of the length of the input.

- The hash value is relatively easy to compute.

- The hash function is one-way (meaning that it is extremely hard to determine the input when provided with the output).

- The hash function is *collision* free (meaning that it is extremely hard to find two messages that produce the same hash value).

The Secure Hash Algorithm (SHA) versions 2 and 3 (SHA-2 and SHA-3) are government standard hash functions promoted by the National Institute of Standards and Technology (NIST).

Digital Signatures

Once you have chosen a cryptographically sound hashing algorithm, you can use it to implement a *digital signature* system. Digital signature infrastructures have two distinct goals:

- Digitally signed messages assure the recipient that the message truly came from the claimed sender. They enforce nonrepudiation (that is, they preclude the sender from later claiming that the message is a forgery).

- Digitally signed messages assure the recipient that the message was not altered while in transit between the sender and recipient. This protects against both malicious modification (a third party altering the meaning of the message) and unintentional modification (because of faults in the communications process, such as electrical interference).

Digital signature algorithms rely on a combination of the two major concepts already covered in this chapter—public key cryptography and hashing functions.

If Alice wants to digitally sign a message she's sending to Bob, she performs the following actions:

1. Alice generates a message digest of the original plaintext message using one of the cryptographically sound hashing algorithms, such as SHA-3.

2. Alice then encrypts only the message digest using her private key. This encrypted message digest is the digital signature.

3. Alice appends the signed message digest to the plaintext message.

4. Alice transmits the appended signature and message to Bob.

When Bob receives the digitally signed message, he reverses the procedure, as follows:

1. Bob decrypts the digital signature using Alice's public key.

2. Bob uses the same hashing function to create a message digest of the full plaintext message received from Alice.

3. Bob then compares the decrypted message digest he received from Alice with the message digest he computed himself. If the two digests match, he can be assured that the message he received was sent by Alice. If they do not match, either the message was not sent by Alice or the message was modified while in transit.

 Digital signatures are used for more than just messages. Software vendors often use digital signature technology to authenticate code distributions that you download from the Internet, such as applets and software patches.

Note that the digital signature process does not provide any privacy in and of itself. It only ensures that the cryptographic goals of integrity, authentication, and nonrepudiation are met. However, if Alice wanted to ensure the privacy of her message to Bob, she could add a step to the message creation process. After appending the signed message digest to the plaintext message, Alice could encrypt the entire message with Bob's public key. When Bob received the message, he would decrypt it with his own private key before following the steps just outlined.

Digital Certificates

Digital certificates provide communicating parties with the assurance that the people they are communicating with truly are who they claim to be. Digital certificates are essentially endorsed copies of an individual's public key. When users verify that a certificate was signed by a trusted certificate authority (CA), they know that the public key is legitimate.

Digital certificates contain specific identifying information, and their construction is governed by an international standard—X.509. Certificates that conform to X.509 contain the following certificate attributes:

- Version of X.509 to which the certificate conforms

- Serial number (from the certificate creator)

- Signature algorithm identifier (specifies the technique used by the certificate authority to digitally sign the contents of the certificate)

- Issuer name (identification of the certificate authority that issued the certificate)

- Validity period (specifies the dates and times—a starting date and time and an expiration date and time—during which the certificate is valid)

- Subject's *Common Name (CN)* that clearly describes the certificate owner (e.g., "certmike.com")

- Certificates may optionally contain *subject alternative names (SANs)* that allow you to specify additional items (IP addresses, domain names, and so on) to be protected by the single certificate.

- Subject's public key (the most important data in the certificate—the actual public key the certificate owner used to set up secure communications)

Certificates may be issued for a variety of purposes. These include providing assurance for the public keys of:

- Computers/machines

- Individual users

- Email addresses

- Developers (code-signing certificates)

Certificate Authorities

Certificate authorities (CAs) are the glue that binds the public key infrastructure together. These neutral organizations offer notarization services for digital certificates. To obtain a digital certificate from a reputable CA, you must prove your identity to the satisfaction of the CA.

Certificate authorities do not need to be third-party service providers. Many organizations operate internal CAs that provide *self-signed certificates* for use inside an organization. These certificates won't be trusted by the browsers of external users, but internal systems may be configured to trust the internal CA, saving the expense of obtaining certificates from a third-party CA.

Certificate Management

The technical concepts behind the public key infrastructure are relatively simple. In the following sections, we'll cover the processes used by certificate authorities to create, validate, and revoke client certificates.

Certificate Creation

When you want to obtain a digital certificate, you must first prove your identity to the CA in some manner; this process is called *enrollment*. As mentioned in the previous section, this sometimes involves physically appearing before an agent of the certification authority with the appropriate identification documents. Some certificate authorities provide other means of verification, including the use of credit report data and identity verification by trusted community leaders.

Once you've satisfied the certificate authority regarding your identity, you provide them with your public key in the form of a *certificate signing request (CSR)*. The CA next creates an X.509 digital certificate containing your identifying information and a copy of your public key. The CA then digitally signs the certificate using the CA's private key and provides you with a copy of your signed digital certificate. You may then safely distribute this certificate to anyone with whom you want to communicate securely.

Certificate authorities issue different types of certificates depending upon the level of identity verification that they perform. The simplest, and most common, certificates are *domain validation (DV) certificates*, where the CA simply verifies that the certificate subject has control of the domain name. *Extended validation (EV) certificates* provide a higher level of assurance and the CA takes steps to verify that the certificate owner is a legitimate business before issuing the certificate.

Certification Validation

When you receive a digital certificate from someone with whom you want to communicate, you *verify* the certificate by checking the CA's digital signature using the CA's public key. Next, you must check and ensure that the certificate was not revoked using a *certificate revocation list* (CRL) or the Online Certificate Status Protocol (OCSP). At this point, you may assume that the public key listed in the certificate is authentic, provided that it satisfies the following requirements:

- The digital signature of the CA is authentic.
- You trust the CA.
- The certificate is not listed on a CRL.
- The certificate actually contains the data you are trusting.

The last point is a subtle but extremely important item. Before you trust an identifying piece of information about someone, be sure that it is actually contained within the certificate. If a certificate contains the email address (billjones@foo.com) but not the individual's name, you can be certain only that the public key contained therein is associated with that email address. The CA is not making any assertions about the actual identity of the billjones@foo.com email account. However, if the certificate contains the name Bill Jones along with an address and telephone number, the CA is vouching for that information as well.

Digital certificate verification algorithms are built into a number of popular web browsing and email clients, so you won't often need to get involved in the particulars of the process. However, it's important to have a solid understanding of the technical details taking place behind the scenes to make appropriate security judgments for your organization. It's also the reason that, when purchasing a certificate, you choose a CA that is widely trusted. If a CA is not included in, or is later pulled from, the list of CAs trusted by a major browser, it will greatly limit the usefulness of your certificate.

Certificate Revocation

Occasionally, a certificate authority needs to *revoke* a certificate. This might occur for one of the following reasons:

- The certificate was compromised (e.g., the certificate owner accidentally gave away the private key).

- The certificate was erroneously issued (e.g., the CA mistakenly issued a certificate without proper verification).

- The details of the certificate changed (e.g., the subject's name changed).

- The security association changed (e.g., the subject is no longer employed by the organization sponsoring the certificate).

You can use three techniques to verify the authenticity of certificates and identify revoked certificates:

Certificate Revocation Lists   Certificate revocation lists (CRLs) are maintained by the various certificate authorities and contain the serial numbers of certificates that have been issued by a CA and that have been revoked along with the date and time the revocation went into effect. The major disadvantage to certificate revocation lists is that they must be downloaded and cross-referenced periodically, introducing a period of latency between the time a certificate is revoked and the time end users are notified of the revocation.

Online Certificate Status Protocol (OCSP)   This protocol eliminates the latency inherent in the use of certificate revocation lists by providing a means for real time certificate verification. When a client receives a certificate, it sends an OCSP request to the CA's OCSP server. The server then responds with a status of valid, invalid, or unknown. The browser uses this information to determine whether the certificate is valid.

Certificate Stapling   The primary issue with OCSP is that it places a significant burden on the OCSP servers operated by certificate authorities. These servers must process requests from every single visitor to a website or other user of a digital certificate, verifying that the certificate is valid and not revoked.

Certificate stapling is an extension to the Online Certificate Status Protocol that relieves some of the burden placed on certificate authorities by the original protocol. When a user visits a website and initiates a secure connection, the website sends its certificate to the end user, who would normally then be responsible for contacting an OCSP server to verify the certificate's validity. In certificate stapling, the web server contacts the OCSP server itself and receives a signed and time-stamped response from the OCSP server, which it then attaches, or staples, to the digital certificate. Then, when a user requests a secure web connection, the web server then sends the certificate with the stapled OCSP response to the user. The user's browser then verifies that the certificate is authentic and also validates that the stapled OCSP response is genuine and recent. Because the CA signed the OCSP response, the user knows that it is from the certificate authority and the time stamp provides the user with assurance that the CA recently validated the certificate. From there, communication may continue as normal.

The time savings come when the next user visits the website. The web server can simply reuse the stapled certificate, without recontacting the OCSP server. As long as the time stamp is recent enough, the user will accept the stapled certificate without needing to contact the CA's OCSP server again. It's common to have stapled certificates with a validity period of 24 hours. That reduces the burden on an OCSP server from handling one request per user over the course of a day, which could be millions of requests, to handling one request per certificate per day. That's a tremendous reduction.

Exploring Cybersecurity Threats

Cybersecurity threat actors differ significantly in their skills, capabilities, resources, and motivation. Protecting your organization's information and systems requires a solid understanding of the nature of these different threats so that you can develop a set of security controls that comprehensively protect your organization against their occurrence.

Classifying Cybersecurity Threats

Before we explore specific types of threat actors, let's examine the characteristics that differentiate the types of cybersecurity threat actors. Understanding our adversary is crucial to defending against them.

Internal vs. External   We most often think about the threat actors who exist outside our organizations: competitors, criminals, and the curious. However, some of the most dangerous threats come from within our own environments. We'll discuss the insider threat later in this chapter.

Level of Sophistication/Capability   Threat actors vary greatly in their level of cybersecurity sophistication and capability. As we explore different types of threat actors in this chapter, we'll discuss how they range from the unsophisticated script kiddie simply running code borrowed from others to the advanced persistent threat (APT) actor exploiting vulnerabilities discovered in their own research labs and unknown to the security community.

Resources/Funding   Just as threat actors vary in their sophistication, they also vary in the resources available to them. Highly organized attackers sponsored by criminal syndicates or national governments often have virtually limitless resources, whereas less organized attackers may simply be hobbyists working in their spare time.

Intent/Motivation   Attackers also vary in their motivation and intent. The script kiddie may be simply out for the thrill of the attack, whereas competitors may be engaged in highly targeted corporate espionage. Nation-states seek to achieve political objectives; criminal syndicates often focus on direct financial gain.

As we work through this section, we'll explore different types of threat actors. As we do so, take some time to reflect back on these characteristics. In addition, you may wish to reference them when you hear news of current cybersecurity attacks in the media and other sources. Dissect those stories and analyze the threat actors involved. If the attack came from an unknown source, think about the characteristics that are most likely associated with the attacker. These can be important clues during a cybersecurity investigation. For example, a ransomware attack seeking payment from the victim is more likely associated with a criminal syndicate seeking financial gain than a competitor engaged in corporate espionage.

Threat Actors

Now that we have a set of attributes that we can use to discuss the different types of threat actors, let's explore the most common types that security professionals encounter in their work.

Script Kiddies

The term *script kiddie* is a derogatory term for people who use hacking techniques but have limited skills. Often such attackers rely almost entirely on automated tools they download from the Internet. These attackers often have little knowledge of how their attacks actually work, and they are simply seeking convenient targets of opportunity.

You might think that with their relatively low skill level, script kiddies are not a real security threat. However, that isn't the case for two important reasons. First, simplistic hacking tools are freely available on the Internet. If you're vulnerable to them, anyone can easily find tools to automate denial-of-service (DoS) attacks, create viruses, make a Trojan horse, or even distribute ransomware as a service. Personal technical skills are no longer a barrier to attacking a network.

Second, script kiddies are plentiful and unfocused in their work. Although the nature of your business might not find you in the crosshairs of a sophisticated military-sponsored attack, script kiddies are much less discriminating in their target selection. They often just search for and discover vulnerable victims without even knowing the identity of their target. They might root around in files and systems and only discover who they've penetrated after their attack succeeds.

In general, the motivations of script kiddies revolve around trying to prove their skill. In other words, they may attack your network simply because it is there. Secondary school and university networks are common targets of script kiddies' attacks because many of these attackers are school-age individuals.

Fortunately, the number of script kiddies is often offset by their lack of skill and lack of resources. These individuals tend to be rather young, they work alone, and they have very few resources. And by resources, we mean time as well as money. A script kiddie normally can't attack your network 24 hours a day. They usually have to work a job, go to school, and attend to other life functions.

Hacktivists

Hacktivists use hacking techniques to accomplish some activist goal. They might deface the website of a company whose policies they disagree with. Or a hacktivist might attack a network due to a political issue. The defining characteristic of hacktivists is that they believe they are motivated by the greater good, even if their activity violates the law.

Their activist motivation means that measures that might deter other attackers will be less likely to deter a hacktivist. Because they believe that they are engaged in a just crusade, they will, at least in some instances, risk getting caught to accomplish their goals. They may even view being caught as a badge of honor and a sacrifice for their cause.

The skill levels of hacktivists vary widely. Some are only script kiddies, whereas others are quite skilled, having honed their craft over the years. In fact, some cybersecurity researchers believe that some hacktivists are actually employed as cybersecurity professionals as their "day job" and perform hacktivist attacks in their spare time. Highly skilled hacktivists pose a significant danger to their targets.

The resources of hacktivists also vary somewhat. Many are working alone and have very limited resources. However, some are part of organized efforts. The hacking group Anonymous is the most well-known hacktivist group. They collectively decide their agenda and their targets. Over the years, Anonymous has waged cyberattacks against targets as diverse as the Church of Scientology, PayPal, Visa and Mastercard, Westboro Baptist Church, and even government agencies.

Hacktivists tend to be external attackers, but in some cases, internal employees who disagree strongly with their company's policies engage in hacktivism. In those instances, it is more likely that the hacktivist will attack the company by releasing confidential information. Government employees and self-styled whistleblowers fit this pattern of activity, seeking to bring what they consider unethical government actions to the attention of the public.

For example, many people consider Edward Snowden a hacktivist. In 2013, Snowden, a former contractor with the U.S. National Security Agency, shared a large cache of sensitive government documents with journalists. Snowden's actions provided unprecedented insight into the digital intelligence gathering capabilities of the United States and its allies.

Criminal Syndicates

Organized crime appears in any case where there is money to be made, and cybercrime is no exception. The ranks of cybercriminals include links to traditional organized crime families in the United States, outlaw gangs, the Russian mafia, and even criminal groups organized specifically for the purpose of engaging in cybercrime.

The common thread among these groups is motive and intent. The motive is simply illegal financial gain. Organized criminal syndicates do not normally embrace political issues or causes, and they are not trying to demonstrate their skills. In fact, they would often prefer to remain in the shadows, drawing as little attention to themselves as possible. They simply want to generate as much illegal profit as they possibly can.

Advanced Persistent Threats

In recent years, a great deal of attention has been given to state actors hacking into either foreign governments or corporations. The security company Mandiant created the term advanced persistent threats (APTs) to describe a series of attacks that they first traced to sources connected to the Chinese military. In subsequent years, the security community discovered similar organizations linked to the government of virtually every technologically advanced country.

The term *APT* tells you a great deal about the attacks themselves. First, they use advanced techniques, not simply tools downloaded from the Internet. Second, the attacks are persistent, occurring over a significant period of time. In some cases, the attacks continue for years as attackers patiently stalk their targets, awaiting the right opportunity to strike.

The APT attacks that Mandiant reported are emblematic of *nation-state attacks*. They tend to be characterized by highly skilled attackers with significant resources. A nation has the labor force, time, and money to finance ongoing, sophisticated attacks.

The motive can be political or economic. In some cases, the attack is done for traditional espionage goals: to gather information about the target's defense capabilities. In other cases, the attack might be targeting intellectual property or other economic assets.

Zero-Day Attacks

APT attackers often conduct their own security vulnerability research in an attempt to discover vulnerabilities that are not known to other attackers or cybersecurity teams. After they uncover a vulnerability, they do not disclose it but rather store it in a vulnerability repository for later use.

Attacks that exploit these vulnerabilities are known as zero-day attacks. Zero-day attacks are particularly dangerous because they are unknown to product vendors, and therefore, no patches are available to correct them. APT actors who exploit zero-day vulnerabilities are often able to easily compromise their targets.

Insiders

Insider attacks occur when an employee, contractor, vendor, or other individual with authorized access to information and systems uses that access to wage an attack against the organization. These attacks are often aimed at disclosing confidential information, but insiders may also seek to alter information or disrupt business processes.

An insider might be of any skill level. They could be a script kiddie or very techni-cally skilled. Insiders may also have differing motivations behind their attacks. Some are motivated by certain activist goals, whereas others are motivated by financial gain. Still others may simply be upset that they were passed over for a promotion or slighted in some other manner.

An insider will usually be working alone and have limited financial resources and time. However, the fact that they are insiders gives them an automatic advantage. They already have some access to your network and some level of knowledge. Depending on the insider's job role, they might have significant access and knowledge.

Behavioral assessments are a tool used to identify possible insider threats. Cybersecurity teams should work with human resources partners to identify insiders exhibiting unusual behavior and intervene before the situation escalates.

The Threat of Shadow IT

Dedicated employees often seek to achieve their goals and objectives through whatever means allows them to do so. Sometimes, this involves purchasing technology services that aren't approved by the organization. For example, when file sharing and synchronization services first came on the market, many employees turned to personal Dropbox accounts to sync work content between their business and personal devices. They did not do this with any malicious intent. On the contrary, they were trying to benefit the business by being more productive.

This situation, where individuals and groups seek out their own technology solutions, is a phenomenon known as shadow IT. Shadow IT poses a risk to the organization because it puts sensitive information in the hands of vendors outside of the organization's control. Cybersecurity teams should remain vigilant for shadow IT adoption and remember that the presence of shadow IT in an organization means that business needs are not being met by the enterprise IT team. Consulting with shadow IT users often identifies acceptable alterna-tives that both meet business needs and satisfy security requirements.

Competitors

Competitors may engage in corporate espionage designed to steal sensitive information from your organization and use it to their own business advantage. This may include theft of customer information, stealing proprietary software, identifying confidential product development plans, or gaining access to any other information that would benefit the competitor.

Threat Vectors

Threat actors targeting an organization need some means to gain access to that organiza-tion's information or systems. Threat vectors are the means that threat actors use to obtain that access.

Email and Social Media

Email is one of the most commonly exploited threat vectors. Phishing messages, spam messages, and other email-borne attacks are a simple way to gain access to an organization's network. These attacks are easy to execute and can be launched against many users simultaneously. The benefit for the attacker is that they generally need to succeed only one time to launch a broader attack. Even if 99.9 percent of users ignore a phishing message, the attacker needs the login credentials of only a single user to begin their attack.

Social media may be used as a threat vector in similar ways. Attackers might directly target users on social media, or they might use social media in an effort to harvest information about users that may be used in another type of attack.

Direct Access

Bold attackers may seek to gain direct access to an organization's network by physically entering the organization's facilities. One of the most common ways they do this is by entering public areas of a facility, such as a lobby, customer store, or other easily accessible location, and sitting and working on their laptops, which are surreptitiously connected to unsecured network jacks on the wall.

Alternatively, attackers who gain physical access to a facility may be able to find an unsecured computer terminal, network device, or other system. Security professionals must assume that an attacker who is able to physically touch a component will be able to compromise that device and use it for malicious purposes.

Wireless Networks

Wireless networks offer an even easier path to an organization's network. Attackers don't need to gain physical access to the network or your facilities if they are able to sit in the parking lot and access your organization's wireless network. Unsecured or poorly secured wireless networks pose a significant security risk.

Removable Media

Attackers also commonly use removable media, such as USB drives, to spread malware and launch their attacks. An attacker might distribute inexpensive USB sticks in parking lots, airports, or other public areas, hoping that someone will find the device and plug it into their computer, curious to see what it contains. As soon as that happens, the device triggers a malware infection that silently compromises the finder's computer and places it under the control of the attacker.

Cloud

Cloud services can also be used as an attack vector. Attackers routinely scan popular cloud services for files with improper access controls, systems that have security flaws, or accidentally published API keys and passwords. Organizations must include the cloud services that they use as an important component of their security program.

The vulnerabilities facing organizations operating in cloud environments bear similarities to those found in on-premises environments, but the controls often differ.

Third-Party Risks

Sophisticated attackers may attempt to interfere with an organization's IT supply chain, gaining access to devices at the manufacturer or while the devices are in transit from the manufacturer to the end user. Tampering with a device before the end user receives it allows attackers to insert backdoors that grant them control of the device once the customer installs it on their network. This type of third-party risk is difficult to anticipate and address.

Other issues may also arise in the supply chain, particularly if a vendor fails to continue to support a system that the organization depends on, provide required system integrations, or provide adequate security for outsourced code development or data storage. Strong vendor management practices can identify these issues quickly as they arise and allow the organization to address the risks appropriately.

Privacy

Cybersecurity professionals are responsible for protecting the confidentiality, integrity, and availability of all information under their care. This includes personally identifiable information (PII) that, if improperly disclosed, would jeopardize the privacy of one or more individuals.

When privacy breaches occur, they clearly have a negative impact on the individuals whose information was lost in the breach. Those individuals may find themselves exposed to identity theft and other personal risks. Privacy breaches also have organizational consequences for the business that loses control of personal information. These consequences may include reputational damage, fines, and the loss of important intellectual property that may now fall into the hands of a competitor.

Organizations seeking to codify their privacy practices may adopt a privacy notice that outlines their privacy commitments. In some cases, laws or regulations may require that the organization adopt a privacy notice. In addition, organizations may include privacy statements in their terms of agreement with customers and other stakeholders.

Sensitive Information Inventory

Organizations often deal with many different types of sensitive and personal information. The first step in managing this sensitive data is developing an inventory of the types of data maintained by the organization and the places where it is stored, processed, and transmitted.

Organizations should include the following types of information in their inventory:

- Personally identifiable information (PII) includes any information that uniquely identifies an individual person, including customers, employees, and third parties.

- Protected health information (PHI) includes medical records maintained by health care providers and other organizations that are subject to the Health Insurance Portability and Accountability Act (HIPAA).

- Financial information includes any personal financial records maintained by the organization.

- Government information maintained by the organization may be subject to other rules, including the data classification requirements discussed in the next section.

Once the organization has an inventory of this sensitive information, it can begin to take steps to ensure that it is appropriately protected from loss or theft.

Data Classification

Information classification programs organize data into categories based on the sensitivity of the information and the impact on the organization should the information be inadvertently disclosed. For example, the U.S. government uses the following four major classification categories:

- *Top Secret* information requires the highest degree of protection. The unauthorized disclosure of Top Secret information could reasonably be expected to cause exceptionally grave damage to national security.

- *Secret* information requires a substantial degree of protection. The unauthorized disclosure of Secret information could reasonably be expected to cause serious damage to national security.

- *Confidential* information requires some protection. The unauthorized disclosure of Confidential information could reasonably be expected to cause identifiable damage to national security.

- *Unclassified* information is information that does not meet the standards for classification under the other categories. Information in this category is still not publicly releasable without authorization.

Businesses generally don't use the same terminology for their levels of classified information. Instead, they might use friendlier terms, such as Highly Sensitive, Sensitive, Internal, and Public.

Information classification decisions may then drive asset classification as well. When performing asset classification, managers identify the highest-level classification of information that is stored, processed, or transmitted by the device in question. The device is then assigned a classification level that may then be used to determine the appropriate security controls to apply to that device. This approach allows organizations to apply costly and time-consuming controls only when necessary, ensuring that measures taken to protect assets are proportional to their business value.

Information Life Cycle

Data protection should continue at all stages of the information life cycle, from the time the data is originally collected until the time it is eventually disposed of.

At the early stages of the data life cycle, organizations should practice data minimization, where they collect the smallest possible amount of information necessary to meet their business requirements. Information that is not necessary should either be immediately discarded or, better yet, not collected in the first place.

Although information remains within the care of the organization, the organization should practice purpose limitation. This means that information should be used only for the purpose that it was originally collected and that was consented to by the data subjects.

At the end of the life cycle, the organization should implement data retention standards that guide the end of the data life cycle. Data should be kept for only as long as it remains necessary to fulfill the purpose for which it was originally collected. At the conclusion of its life cycle, data should be securely destroyed.

Exam Tip

Reducing the amount of data that you retain is a great way to minimize your security risk. Remember this as you answer exam questions that ask you to identify the best or most effective strategy for reducing risk.

Privacy and Data Breach Notification

In the unfortunate event of a data breach, the organization should immediately activate its cybersecurity incident response plan. Organizations may also have a responsibility under national and regional laws to make public notifications and disclosures in the wake of a data breach. This responsibility may be limited to notifying the individuals involved or, in some cases, may require notification of government regulators and/or the news media.

In the United States, every state has a data breach notification law, with different requirements for triggering notifications. The European Union's GDPR also includes a breach notification requirement. The United States lacks a federal law requiring broad notification for all security breaches but does have industry-specific laws and requirements that require notification in some circumstances.

The bottom line is that breach notification requirements vary by industry and jurisdiction, and an organization experiencing a breach may be required to untangle many overlapping requirements. For this reason, organizations experiencing a data breach should consult with an attorney who is well versed in this field.

Security Awareness and Training

The success of a security program depends on the behavior (both action and inaction) of many different people. Security training and awareness programs help ensure that employees and other stakeholders are aware of their information security responsibilities and that those responsibilities remain top-of-mind. Information security managers are responsible for establishing, promoting, and maintaining an information security training and awareness program to foster an effective security culture in their organizations.

User Training

Users within your organization should receive regular security training to ensure that they understand the risks associated with your computing environment and their role in minimizing those risks. Strong training programs take advantage of a diversity of training techniques, including the use of computer-based training (CBT).

Not every user requires the same level of training. Organizations should use role-based training to make sure that individuals receive the appropriate level of training based on their job responsibilities. For example, a systems administrator should receive detailed and highly technical training, whereas a customer service representative requires less technical training with a greater focus on social engineering and pretexting attacks that they may encounter in their work.

Phishing attacks often target users at all levels of the organization, and every security awareness program should include specific antiphishing campaigns designed to help users recognize suspicious requests and respond appropriately. These campaigns often involve the use of phishing simulations, which send users fake phishing messages to test their skills. Users who click on the simulated phishing message are sent to a training program designed to help them better recognize fraudulent messages.

Security awareness training also commonly incorporates elements of gamification, designed to make training more enjoyable and help users retain the message of the campaign. Capture the flag (CTF) exercises are a great example of this. CTF programs pit technologists against one another in an attempt to attack a system and achieve a specific goal, such as stealing a sensitive file. Participants in the CTF exercise gain an appreciation for attacker techniques and learn how to better defend their own systems against similar attacks.

You'll also want to think about the frequency of your training efforts. You'll need to balance the time required to conduct training with the benefit of reminding users of their responsibilities. One approach used by many organizations is to conduct initial training whenever an employee joins the organization or assumes new job responsibilities and then use annual refresher training to cover the same material and update users on new threats and controls.

The team responsible for providing security training should review materials on a regular basis to ensure that the content remains relevant. Changes in the security landscape and the organization's business may require updating the material to remain fresh and relevant.

Role-Based Training

All users should receive some degree of security education, but organizations should also customize training to meet specific role-based requirements. For example, employees handling credit card information should receive training on PCI DSS requirements. Human resources team members should be trained on handling personally identifiable information. IT staffers need specialized skills to implement security controls. Training should be custom-tailored to an individual's role in the organization.

Ongoing Awareness Efforts

In addition to formal training programs, an information security program should include security awareness efforts. These are less formal efforts that are designed to remind employees about the security lessons they've already learned. Unlike security training, awareness efforts don't require a commitment of time to sit down and learn new material. Instead, they use posters, videos, email messages, and similar techniques to keep security top-of-mind for those who've already learned the core lessons.

Figure 7.11 shows an example of a security awareness poster developed by the U.S. Department of Energy.

FIGURE 7.11 Security awareness poster

Source: U.S. Department of Energy / Public Domain

Security Incident Response

Many IT professionals use the terms security event and security incident casually and interchangeably, but this is not correct. Members of a cybersecurity incident response team should use these terms carefully and according to their precise definitions within the organization. The National Institute for Standards and Technology (NIST) offers the following standard definitions for use throughout the U.S. government, and many private organizations choose to adopt them as well:

- An *event* is any observable occurrence in a system or network. A security event includes any observable occurrence that relates to a security function. For example, a user accessing a file stored on a server, an administrator changing permissions on a shared folder, and an attacker conducting a port scan are all examples of security events.

- An *adverse event* is any event that has negative consequences. Examples of adverse events include a malware infection on a system, a server crash, and a user accessing a file that they are not authorized to view.

- A *security incident* is a violation or imminent threat of violation of computer security policies, acceptable use policies, or standard security practices. Examples of security incidents include the accidental loss of sensitive information, an intrusion into a computer system by an attacker, the use of a keylogger on an executive's system to steal passwords, and the launch of a denial-of-service attack against a website.

 Every security incident includes one or more security events, but not every security event is a security incident.

Computer security incident response teams (CSIRTs) are responsible for responding to computer security incidents that occur within an organization by following standardized response procedures and incorporating their subject matter expertise and professional judgment.

Phases of Incident Response

Organizations depend on members of the CSIRT to respond calmly and consistently in the event of a security incident. The crisis-like atmosphere that surrounds many security incidents may lead to poor decision making unless the organization has a clearly thought-out and refined process that describes how it will handle cybersecurity incident response. Figure 7.12 shows the simple incident response process advocated by NIST.

Notice that this process is not a simple progression of steps from start to finish. Instead, it includes loops that allow responders to return to prior phases as needed during the response. These loops reflect the reality of responses to actual cybersecurity incidents. Only in the simplest of incidents would an organization detect an incident, analyze data, conduct a recovery, and close out the incident in a straightforward sequence of steps. Instead, the containment process often includes several loops back through the detection and analysis phase to identify whether the incident has been successfully resolved. These loops are a normal part of the cybersecurity incident response process and should be expected.

FIGURE 7.12   Incident response process

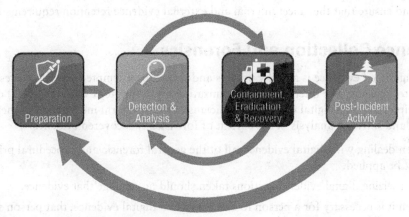

Preparation

CSIRTs do not spring up out of thin air. As much as managers may wish it were so, they cannot simply will a CSIRT into existence by creating a policy document and assigning staff members to the CSIRT. Instead, the CSIRT requires careful preparation to ensure that the CSIRT has the proper policy foundation, has operating procedures that will be effective in the organization's computing environment, receives appropriate training, and is prepared to respond to an incident.

Detection and Analysis

The detection and analysis phase of incident response is one of the trickiest to commit to a routine process. Although cybersecurity analysts have many tools at their disposal that may assist in identifying that a security incident is taking place, many incidents are only detected because of the trained eye of an experienced analyst.

Containment, Eradication, and Recovery

During the incident detection and analysis phase, the CSIRT engages in primarily passive activities designed to uncover and analyze information about the incident. After completing this assessment, the team moves on to take active measures designed to contain the effects of the incident, eradicate the incident from the network, and recover normal operations.

Post-Incident Activity

Security incidents don't end after security professionals remove attackers from the network or complete the recovery effort to restore normal business operations. Once the immediate danger passes and normal operations resume, the CSIRT enters the post-incident activity phase of incident response. During this phase, team members conduct a lessons-learned review and ensure that they meet internal and external evidence retention requirements.

Evidence Collection and Forensics

Collecting digital evidence is a tricky process and should be attempted only by professional forensic technicians. The International Organization on Computer Evidence (IOCE) outlines six principles to guide digital evidence technicians as they perform media analysis, network analysis, and software analysis in the pursuit of forensically recovered evidence:

- When dealing with digital evidence, all of the general forensic and procedural principles must be applied.

- Upon seizing digital evidence, actions taken should not change that evidence.

- When it is necessary for a person to access original digital evidence, that person should be trained for the purpose.

- All activity relating to the seizure, access, storage, or transfer of digital evidence must be fully documented, preserved, and available for review.

- An individual is responsible for all actions taken with respect to digital evidence while the digital evidence is in their possession.

- Any agency that is responsible for seizing, accessing, storing, or transferring digital evidence is responsible for compliance with these principles.

As you conduct forensic evidence collection, it is important to preserve the original evidence. Remember that the very conduct of your investigation may alter the evidence you are evaluating. Therefore, when analyzing digital evidence, it's best to work with a copy of the actual evidence whenever possible. For example, when conducting an investigation into the contents of a hard drive, make an image of that drive, seal the original drive in an evidence bag, and then use the disk image for your investigation.

Media analysis: Media analysis, a branch of computer forensic analysis, involves the identification and extraction of information from storage media. This may include magnetic media (e.g., hard disks and tapes) or optical media (e.g., CDs, DVDs, and Blu-ray discs).

Techniques used for media analysis may include the recovery of deleted files from unallocated sectors of the physical disk, the live analysis of storage media connected to a computer system (especially useful when examining encrypted media), and the static analysis of forensic images of storage media.

In-Memory analysis: Investigators often wish to collect information from the memory of live systems. This is a tricky undertaking, since it can be difficult to work with memory without actually altering its contents. When gathering the contents of memory, analysts should use trusted tools to generate a memory dump file and place it on a forensically prepared device, such as a USB drive. This memory dump file contains all of the contents collected from memory and may then be used for analysis. As with other types of digital evidence, the analyst collecting the memory dump should compute a cryptographic hash of the dump file to later prove its authenticity. Any analysis performed on the file should not touch the original collected dump but work from copies of that dump file.

Network analysis: Forensic investigators are also often interested in the activity that took place over the network during a security incident. This is often difficult to reconstruct due to the volatility of network data—if it isn't deliberately recorded at the time it occurs, it generally is not preserved.

Network forensic analysis, therefore, often depends on either prior knowledge that an incident is under way or the use of preexisting security controls that log network activity. These include:

- Intrusion detection and prevention system logs
- Network flow data captured by a flow monitoring system
- Packet captures deliberately collected during an incident
- Logs from firewalls and other network security devices

The task of the network forensic analyst is to collect and correlate information from these disparate sources and produce as comprehensive a picture of network activity as possible.

Software analysis: Forensic analysts may also be called on to conduct forensic reviews of applications or the activity that takes place within a running application. In some cases, when malicious insiders are suspected, the forensic analyst may be asked to conduct a review of software code, looking for backdoors, logic bombs, or other security vulnerabilities.

In other cases, forensic analysts may be asked to review and interpret the log files from application or database servers, seeking other signs of malicious activity, such as SQL injection attacks, privilege escalations, or other application attacks.

Hardware/Embedded device analysis: Finally, forensic analysts often must review the contents of hardware and embedded devices. This may include a review of:

- Personal computers
- Smartphones
- Tablet computers
- Embedded computers in cars, security systems, and other devices

Analysts conducting these reviews must have specialized knowledge of the systems under review. This often requires calling in expert consultants who are familiar with the memory, storage systems, and operating systems of such devices. Because of the complex interactions between software, hardware, and storage, the discipline of hardware analysis requires skills in both media analysis and software analysis.

Auditing Information Security Controls

Auditing information security controls requires substantial knowledge about IT, threats, vulnerabilities, countermeasures, and common asset protection practices. The IS auditor who lacks this knowledge will likely overlook threats or vulnerabilities that may be obvious to more knowledgeable auditors.

Auditing Security Management

Auditing security management activities requires attention to several key activities, including:

- **Policies, processes, procedures, and standards:** The auditor should request and examine information security policies to determine what processes are required. This should be followed by requests to examine process and procedure documentation for key processes that are cited in security policies. The IS auditor should review the entire body of information security policy to determine whether there is adequate coverage on every topic. Rather than examine the organization's security policy in a vacuum, it should be compared to an industry standard, such as current versions of ISO/IEC 27001 or NIST 800-53, to ensure that the organization has not omitted any topic that should be included in its security policy.

- **Records:** For security management processes that usually have associated recordkeeping, the auditor should examine business records to see whether processes are active.

- **Security awareness training:** The auditor should examine training materials, procedures, and records to determine the effectiveness of the organization's security awareness training program. In various walk-throughs on this and other topics, the IS auditor should ask questions related to security awareness training, such as the following: "Have you received security awareness training?" "Does your organization have a security policy?" A still better question is "What security procedures are required for laptop computers?" to determine whether employees can corroborate the effectiveness of the security awareness program.

- **Data ownership and management:** The IS auditor should inquire about the methodology used to determine ownership and management of business data. The key point with data ownership and management is accountability: When someone is responsible for the management of a given dataset, that person will ensure that only authorized parties have access to it and will take steps to ensure the continuing integrity of the data. The auditor should determine if there are companywide policies and procedures on data management, or whether this is a disorganized or undocumented activity.

- **Data custodians:** Often, business owners of information and systems delegate management to the IT department, who will manage access on their behalf. If an organization manages data in this way, the IS auditor should identify whether data custodians effectively carry out the wishes of the data owner or act on their own *as if* they were the owner.

- **Backup and media storage:** The IS auditor should examine policies to see what backup measures are required and how media is to be protected. Next, the IS auditor should examine records of backups and restoration requests and tests to determine the historical viability of backup. The IS auditor should examine inventory records and verify that selected media volumes exist and are in the correct location.

- **Security administrators:** Often, an IT department will handle the day-to-day responsibilities of managing access to, and integrity of, business data. The IS auditor should determine if IT staff are knowledgeable about these duties and qualified to carry them out.

- **New and existing employees:** Data management is implicitly every employee's responsibility. As individuals who are entrusted to access and use company data properly, individual employees are obligated to handle data properly, to keep data confidential, and to be alert for any misuse of data. The IS auditor should determine whether any policies exist on this topic and whether security awareness training covers this subject matter.

Auditing Network Security Controls

Auditing network security controls requires a thorough understanding of network technologies, network security techniques, and the architecture of the organization's network being audited. Any gaps in understanding may lead to insufficient scrutiny of the network, possibly resulting in a failure to identify serious deficiencies.

Performing an Architecture Review

The IS auditor needs to conduct a meticulous review of the organization's network architecture. This will require an examination of architecture diagrams and documents, walk-throughs with key systems and network staff, and inspection of many system and network device configuration files.

NOTE   The IS auditor needs to conduct an investigation into the available network paths, independent of any examination of documents, to discover any undocumented or unintended paths. This process is explained in more detail earlier in this section.

Auditing architecture requires attention to several key details, including:

- **Architecture diagrams:** The IS auditor should obtain and become familiar with high-level and detailed architecture diagrams that show the logical relationships between key network and system features.

- **Architecture documents:** Visual diagrams are usually accompanied by written documents that describe the purpose of various architectural features. The IS auditor should use these documents to supplement diagrams to get a more complete picture of the network architecture.

- **Support of business objectives:** The IS auditor should determine if the network's architecture supports key business objectives.

- **Compliance with security and privacy policy:** The IS auditor should determine if the network's architecture is compliant with the organization's security and privacy policy. This may include the logical segregation of business functions, protection of key assets, and separation of responsibilities between departments.

- **Comparisons of documented versus actual:** The IS auditor should examine several key points in the documented network architecture to see if the network's configuration actually reflects its documented design. The auditor should seek to understand any discrepancies found.

- **Change and review process:** The IS auditor should determine if the organization has any processes used to identify, review, and approve any network architecture changes, as well as updates to diagrams and documentation. This is described more fully in the next section.

Auditing Network Access Controls

Auditing network access controls requires attention to several key factors and activities, including:

User Authentication   In environments that employ network-centric user authentication (such as Microsoft Active Directory or LDAP), IS auditors need to apply the full range of a user access control audit.

Firewalls   The IS auditor should examine network architecture (described earlier in this section) and understand the role of firewalls in the network. With this understanding, the auditor should carefully examine network security policies, firewall access control lists, and configurations to determine if firewalls support security policy. The auditor should also examine change control records and firewall change records to determine if all firewall changes are approved and applied properly.

Segmentation and Microsegmentation   The IS auditor should examine security policy and network architecture to determine the network segmentation and microsegmentation that is required in the organization. This should include an understanding of the business drivers for segmentation, as well as techniques used to determine the effectiveness of segmentation.

Intrusion Detection and Prevention Systems   The IS auditor should examine network security policy and IDS/IPS settings and logs to see if they detect intrusions, malware, botnets, and other violations of security policy. IDSs/IPSs should be examined to see whether they perform malware detection and reputation filtering. The auditor should verify whether alerts from IDS/IPS are sent to a SIEM and whether alerts are produced there.

Web Content Filtering   The IS auditor should examine network security policy and web content filtering capabilities to see if they prohibit access to high-risk sites. Web-filtering systems should be examined to see whether they perform malware detection and reputation filtering.

Cloud Access Security Broker (CASB)   The IS auditor should determine whether CASB systems are in place to monitor and control access to cloud-based resources. The auditor should examine procedures and records to see whether appropriate action takes place when policy violations are detected.

Data Loss Prevention   The IS auditor should examine the DLP system to see whether it is properly configured to detect the storage and/or movement of sensitive data and whether there are procedures and records indicating that people do respond to alerts.

Remote Access   The IS auditor should examine remote access policy to determine acceptable remote access scenarios. The auditor should then examine remote access servers and some workstations to determine if remote access infrastructure supports and enforces policy. Some issues to consider when auditing remote access are:

- Whether user authentication is any more difficult (such as multifactor) over remote access than on the physical network
- Whether remote access clients allow split tunneling
- Whether remote access permits non–company-owned computers to access network resources remotely
- Whether workstations missing security patches are permitted to connect via remote access
- Whether workstations with nonfunctioning or out-of-date antimalware software are permitted to connect
- Whether workstations with noncompliant security configuration settings are permitted to connect
- Whether remote access backdoors exist, with tools such as GoToMyPC, for example

Jump Servers   The IS auditor should identify whether jump servers or other logical air gaps exist to protect critical systems and critical data from compromise. The IS auditor should determine whether jump servers can be bypassed and, if so, whether they can be used to exfiltrate data.

Wi-Fi Access Points   The IS auditor should determine whether Wi-Fi access points are used and, if so, how they are controlled. The auditor should determine whether there are any rogue (unapproved) access points in use and whether the organization routinely scans for them and takes action. The auditor should also determine whether guest access is permitted and, if so, how internal resources (including network bandwidth) are protected against users connecting as a guest.

Auditing Network Change Management

Auditing network change management requires attention to several key factors and activities, including:

- **Change control policy:** The IS auditor should examine the organization's change control policy to understand how change is supposed to be controlled and managed.
- **Change logs:** The IS auditor should determine if information systems contain automatic logs that contain all changes to systems and, if so, if these logs are reviewed by IT staff to ensure that only approved changes are being made to systems. The auditor should examine procedures and records to determine what actions are taken when unapproved changes are discovered.
- **Change control procedures:** The IS auditor needs to examine change control procedures and examine records to determine if procedures are effective and are being followed.
- **Emergency changes:** The IS auditor should examine change control policy, procedures, and records to see how emergency changes are handled and how they are approved.
- **Rolled-back changes:** The IS auditor should examine change control records to see what changes needed to be rolled back because of problems. The auditor should determine how these situations were handled.
- **Documentation:** The IS auditor should determine whether change control procedures and records include updates to documentation, including network operations procedures, architecture diagrams, and disaster recovery plans.
- **Linkage to system development life cycle (SDLC):** The IS auditor should understand how the organization's SDLC is integrated with its change management processes to ensure that only completed and properly approved software changes are proposed for promotion into production.

The IS auditor should examine all of these aspects of change management to understand whether the organization is really in control of its environment.

Auditing Vulnerability Management

Auditing vulnerability management requires attention to several key factors and activities, including:

- **System hardening:** The IS auditor should identify any system hardening standards in place. This includes seeing whether standards are periodically reviewed and updated, how standards were implemented, and how compliance to standards is verified.

- **Virtualization:** The IS auditor should examine the organization's virtualization and containerization architecture and standards, and then examine selected virtualization and containerization environments to determine how well these systems are managed and protected.

- **Alert management:** The IS auditor should determine if the organization actively searches for or subscribes to security alert bulletins. The auditor should examine procedures and records to see if any alert bulletins result in responsive actions such as applied security patches or configuration changes.

- **Infrastructure penetration testing:** The IS auditor should determine if the organization performs any penetration testing on its own network and system infrastructure. The auditor should examine procedures and records to determine if the organization's penetration testing program is effective. The auditor should see if vulnerabilities are mitigated and confirmed.

- **Application penetration testing:** The IS auditor should determine if the organization performs any application penetration testing on its software applications to identify vulnerabilities. The auditor should examine procedures and records to determine if the organization's application penetration testing process is effective.

- **Patch management:** The IS auditor should examine procedures and records to determine if the organization performs any patch management activities. These activities may consist of a periodic review of available security and functionality patches, whether any patches are applied to production systems, and whether any SLAs for patching are established and followed. The auditor should determine if patches are tested on nonproduction environment systems to understand their impact.

Complementary Penetration Testing

The IS auditor should consider the use of security scanning or penetration testing during a network security audit. This can help determine whether the organization's own penetration testing of infrastructure and applications is complete and effective.

Summary

Information security management is concerned with the identification and protection of valuable and sensitive assets. Security management begins with executive support of the organization's information security program, including the development and enforcement of an organizationwide information security policy. Several processes also support security management, including security monitoring, auditing, security awareness training, incident response procedures, data classification, vulnerability management, service provider management, and corrective and preventive action processes.

Security roles and responsibilities need to be explicitly developed and communicated. Managers and staff need to demonstrate knowledge of their roles and responsibilities through proper decisions and actions.

Computers are used as instruments of crimes, can be used to support criminal activity, and are the target of crimes. Criminal activities are a threat to organizations, whether the activity is espionage, data theft, fraud, or sabotage.

Several techniques are used to protect sensitive and valuable information from disclosure to unauthorized parties. These techniques include user access controls, network access controls, antimalware, intrusion detection/prevention systems, data loss prevention systems, cloud access security brokers, system and network hardening, and encryption. Many threats exist that require a variety of countermeasures, many of which require continuous vigilance and effort.

Exam Essentials

Know the role of endpoint security technologies in an enterprise cybersecurity program.   Antimalware software protects endpoint devices from many different threats. Antimalware software uses signature detection and heuristic detection to prevent malware infections. Endpoint detection and response (EDR) platforms manage the detection, containment, investigation, and remediation of endpoint security incidents. Data loss prevention (DLP) systems prevent the unauthorized exfiltration of sensitive data. Change and configuration management systems maintain secure system configurations, whereas patch management ensures that security updates are consistently applied. System hardening techniques close holes that might be exploited by an attacker.

Explain the role of network segmentation.   Network segmentation techniques place systems and users of different security levels on different network segments, containing the damage caused by a potential security incident. Firewalls provide segmentation of networks into security zones, whereas VLANs group users and devices by function.

Understand the security requirements for routers, switches, and other network devices.   Routers and switches must be protected against unauthorized physical access to avoid compromise. Switch security techniques include VLAN pruning, the prevention of VLAN hopping, and port security. Router security techniques include the use of access control lists to filter traffic and quality of service controls to prioritize important network use.

Explain the three major cloud service models.   In the anything-as-a-service (XaaS) approach to computing, there are three major cloud service models. Infrastructure-as-a-service (IaaS) offerings allow customers to purchase and interact with the basic building blocks of a technology infrastructure. Software-as-a-service (SaaS) offerings provide customers with access to a fully managed application running in the cloud. Platform-as-a-service (PaaS) offerings provide a platform where customers may run applications that they have developed themselves.

Describe the four major cloud deployment models. *Public cloud* service providers deploy infrastructure and then make it accessible to any customers who wish to take advantage of it in a multitenant model. The term *private cloud* is used to describe any cloud infrastructure that is provisioned for use by a single customer. A *community cloud* service shares characteristics of both the public and private models. Community cloud services do run in a multitenant environment, but the tenants are limited to members of a specifically designed community. *Hybrid cloud* is a catch-all term used to describe cloud deployments that blend public, private, and/or community cloud services together.

Understand the shared responsibility model of cloud security. Under the shared responsibility model of cloud security, cloud customers must divide responsibilities between one or more service providers and the customers' own cybersecurity teams. In an IaaS environment, the cloud provider takes on the most responsibility, providing security for everything below the operating system layer. In PaaS, the cloud provider takes over added responsibility for the security of the operating system itself. In SaaS, the cloud provider is responsible for the security of the entire environment, except for the configuration of access controls within the application and the choice of data to store in the service.

Understand the goals of cryptography. The four goals of cryptography are confidentiality, integrity, authentication, and nonrepudiation. Confidentiality is the use of encryption to protect sensitive information from prying eyes. Integrity is the use of cryptography to ensure that data is not maliciously or unintentionally altered. Authentication refers to uses of encryption to validate the identity of individuals. Nonrepudiation ensures that individuals can prove to a third party that a message came from its purported sender.

Explain the differences between symmetric and asymmetric encryption. Symmetric encryption uses the same shared secret key to encrypt and decrypt information. Users must have some mechanism to exchange these shared secret keys. The Diffie–Hellman algorithm provides one approach. Asymmetric encryption provides each user with a pair of keys: a public key, which is freely shared, and a private key, which is kept secret. Anything encrypted with one key from the pair may be decrypted with the other key from the same pair.

Explain how digital signatures provide nonrepudiation. Digital signatures provide nonrepudiation by allowing a third party to verify the authenticity of a message. Senders create digital signatures by using a hash function to generate a message digest and then encrypting that digest with their own private key. Others may verify the digital signature by decrypting it with the sender's public key and comparing this decrypted message digest to one that they compute themselves using the hash function on the message.

Understand the purpose and use of digital certificates.   Digital certificates provide a trusted mechanism for sharing public keys with other individuals. Users and organizations obtain digital certificates from certificate authorities (CAs), who demonstrate their trust in the certificate by applying their digital signature. Recipients of the digital certificate can rely on the public key it contains if they trust the issuing CA and verify the CA's digital signature.

Security events are occurrences that may escalate into a security incident.   An event is any observable occurrence in a system or network. A security event includes any observable occurrence that relates to a security function. A security incident is a violation or imminent threat of violation of computer security policies, acceptable use policies, or standard security practices. Every incident consists of one or more event, but every event is not an incident.

The cybersecurity incident response process has four phases.   The four phases of incident response are preparation; detection and analysis; containment, eradication, and recovery; and post-incident activities. The process is not a simple progression of steps from start to finish. Instead, it includes loops that allow responders to return to prior phases as needed during the response.

Review Questions

1. In what cloud security model does the cloud service provider bear the most responsibility for implementing security controls?

    A. IaaS

    B. FaaS

    C. PaaS

    D. SaaS

2. Helen would like to configure her organization's switches so that they do not allow systems connected to a switch to spoof MAC addresses. Which one of the following features would be helpful in this configuration?

    A. Loop protection

    B. Port security

    C. Flood guard

    D. Traffic encryption

3. Patricia is using a computer at a hotel business center and she is concerned that the operating system on the device may be compromised. What is the best way for her to use this computer in a secure fashion?

    A. Use live boot media.

    B. Connect to a VPN.

    C. Run a malware scan.

    D. Only access secure websites.

4. Karim is investigating an alert generated by his organization's NIDS. The system alerted to a distributed denial-of-service attack and Karim's investigation revealed that this type of attack did take place. What type of report has the system generated?

    A. False positive

    B. True negative

    C. True positive

    D. False negative

5. What type of security solution provides a hardware platform for the storage and management of encryption keys?

    A. HSM

    B. IPS

    C. SIEM

    D. SOAR

6. Ryan is investigating a security incident. He believes that the incident is originating from a single system on the Internet and targeting multiple systems on his network. What control could he put in place to stop the incident as quickly as possible?

    A. DDoS mitigation

    B. Host firewall rule

    C. Operating system update

    D. Network firewall rule

7. Howard is assessing the legal risks to his organization based on its handling of PII. The organization is based in the United States, handles the data of customers located in Europe, and stores information in Japanese data centers. What law would be most important to Howard during his assessment?

    A. Japanese law

    B. European Union law

    C. U.S. law

    D. All should have equal weight.

8. David would like to send Mike a message using an asymmetric encryption algorithm to provide confidentiality. What key should he use to encrypt the message?

    A. David's public key

    B. David's private key

    C. Mike's public key

    D. Mike's private key

9. When Mike receives the message that David encrypted for him in Question 8, what key should he use to decrypt the message?

    A. David's public key

    B. David's private key

    C. Mike's public key

    D. Mike's private key

10. If David wishes to digitally sign the message that he is sending Mike, what key would he use to create the digital signature?

    A. David's public key

    B. David's private key

    C. Mike's public key

    D. Mike's private key

11. When Mike receives the digitally signed message from David, what key should he use to verify the digital signature?

    A. David's public key

    B. David's private key

    C. Mike's public key

    D. Mike's private key

12. An auditor is examining an organization's data loss prevention (DLP) system. The DLP system is recording instances of sensitive information that is leaving the organization. There are no records of actions taken. What should the IS auditor recommend?

    A. That management appoint a party responsible for taking action when the DLP system detects that sensitive information is leaving the organization

    B. That management develop procedures for responding to DLP system alerts

    C. That management discontinue use of the DLP system since no one is taking action

    D. That the DLP system be reconfigured to stop issuing alerts

13. An IS auditor has discovered that an employee has installed a Wi-Fi access point in their cube. What action should the IS auditor take?

    A. The IS auditor should include this in their audit report.

    B. The IS auditor should immediately report this as a high-risk situation.

    C. The IS auditor should ask the employee to turn off the Wi-Fi access point when it is not being used.

    D. The IS auditor should test the Wi-Fi access point to see whether it properly authenticates users.

14. Matt is updating the organization's threat assessment process. What category of control is Matt implementing?

    A. Operational

    B. Technical

    C. Corrective

    D. Managerial

15. Jade's organization recently suffered a security breach that affected stored credit card data. Jade's primary concern is the fact that the organization is subject to sanctions for violating the provisions of the Payment Card Industry Data Security Standard. What category of risk is concerning Jade?

    A. Strategic

    B. Compliance

    C. Operational

    D. Financial

16. Chris is responding to a security incident that compromised one of his organization's web servers. He believes that the attackers defaced one or more pages on the website. What cyber-security objective did this attack violate?

    A. Confidentiality

    B. Nonrepudiation

    C. Integrity

    D. Availability

17. Tonya is concerned about the risk that an attacker will attempt to gain access to her organization's database server. She is searching for a control that would discourage the attacker from attempting to gain access. What type of security control is she seeking to implement?

    A. Preventive

    B. Detective

    C. Corrective

    D. Deterrent

18. Which one of the following individuals bears ultimate responsibility for protecting an organization's data?

    A. Data steward

    B. End users

    C. Data custodian

    D. Data owner

19. Tony is reviewing the status of his organization's defenses against a breach of their file server. He believes that a compromise of the file server could reveal information that would prevent the company from continuing to do business. What term *best* describes the risk that Tony is considering?

    A. Strategic

    B. Reputational

    C. Financial

    D. Operational

20. Which one of the following statements about cloud computing is incorrect?

    A. Cloud computing offers ubiquitous, convenient access.

    B. Cloud computing customers store data on hardware that is shared with other customers.

    C. Cloud computing customers provision resources through the service provider's sales team.

    D. Cloud computing resources are accessed over a network.

Chapter

8

Identity and Access Management

THE CERTIFIED INFORMATION SYSTEMS AUDITOR (CISA) OBJECTIVES REPRESENT 26% OF THE MATERIAL COVERED ON THE EXAM AND INCLUDE:

✓ **Domain 5: Protection of Information Assets**

  A. Information Asset Security and Control

   1. Physical Access and Environmental Controls

   2. Identity and Access Management

  Supporting Tasks

   30. Evaluate physical and environmental controls to determine whether information assets are adequately safeguarded.

   31. Evaluate logical security controls to verify the confidentiality, integrity and availability of information.

The topics in this chapter and Chapter 7 combine to cover Domain 5 of the CISA exam, which represents 26 percent of the CISA examination.

Access controls are the technical, physical, and administrative methods used to control access to an information-based resource. Access controls must be actively managed by staff members who are authorized to perform this function and trained to perform it properly. In this chapter, we explore both logical and physical access controls.

Logical Access Controls

Logical access controls are used to control whether and how subjects (usually persons, but also running programs and computers) are able to access objects (usually systems and/or data). Logical access controls work in a number of different ways:

- **Subject access**   A logical access control uses some means to determine the identity of the subject that is requesting access. Once the subject's identity is known, the access control performs a function to determine whether the subject should be allowed to access the object. If the access is permitted, the subject is allowed to proceed; if the access is denied, the subject is not allowed to proceed. An example of this type of access control is an application that first authenticates a user by requiring a user ID and password before permitting access to the application.

- **Service access**   A logical access control is used to control the types of messages that are allowed to pass through a control point. The logical access control is designed to permit or deny messages of specific types (and may possibly permit or deny based upon origin and destination) to pass. An example of this type of access control is a firewall, screening router, or IPS that makes pass/block decisions based upon the type of traffic, its origin, and its destination.

An analogy of these two types of access is a concert hall with a parking garage. The parking garage (the "service access") permits cars, trucks, and motorcycles to enter but denies oversized vehicles from entering. Upstairs at the concert box office (the "subject access"), persons are admitted if they possess a photo identification that matches a list of prepaid attendees. Certain persons are granted "backstage access" if they possess the required credentials and are not carrying dangerous objects such as firearms.

Access Control Concepts

In discussions about access control, security professionals often use terms that are not used in other IS disciplines.

- *Subject, object* These nouns refer to access control situations. A *subject* is usually a person, but it could also be a running program, device, or computer. In typical security parlance, a subject is someone (or some*thing*) that wants to access something. An *object* (which could be a computer, application, database, file, record, or other resource) is the thing that the subject wants to access.

- *Fail open, fail closed* This refers to the behaviors of automatic access control systems when they experience a failure. For instance, if power is removed from a keycard building access control system, will all doors be locked or unlocked? The term *fail closed* means that all accesses will be denied if the access control system fails; the term *fail open* means that all accesses will be permitted upon failure. Generally, security professionals like access control systems to fail closed, because it is safer to admit no one than to admit everyone. But there will be exceptions now and then where fail open might be better; for example, building access control systems may need to fail open in some situations to facilitate emergency evacuation of personnel or entrance of emergency services personnel. Note that you may also hear fail closed and fail open referred to as *fail secure* and *fail safe*, respectively.

- *Least privilege* According to this concept, an individual user should have the lowest privilege possible that will still enable him or her to perform required tasks.

- *Segregation of duties* This concept specifies that single individuals should not have combinations of privileges that would permit them to conduct high-value operations on their own. The classic example is a business accounting department where the functions of creating a payee, requesting a payment, approving a payment, and making a payment should rest with two or more separate individuals. This will prevent any one person from being able to embezzle funds from an organization without notice. In the context of information technology, functions such as requesting user accounts and provisioning user accounts should reside with two different persons so that no single individual could create user accounts on his or her own.

- *Split custody* This is the concept of splitting knowledge of a specific object or task between two persons. One example is splitting the password for a critical encryption key between two parties: one person has the first half and the other has the second half. Similarly, the combination to a bank vault can be split so that two persons have the first half of the combination while two others have the second half.

Access Control Models

Several *access control models* have been developed since the 1970s. These models are simple mechanisms that are used to understand and build access control systems. The early models include Biba, Bell–LaPadula, Clark–Wilson, Lattice, Brewer and Nash, Take-Grant, and non-interference. The models that are of interest to the IS auditor include:

- *Mandatory Access Control (MAC)*   This access model is used to control access to objects (files, directories, databases, systems, networks, and so on) by subjects (persons, programs, and so on). When a subject attempts to access an object, the operating system examines the access properties of the subject and object to determine whether the access should be allowed. The operating system then permits or denies the requested access. Access is administered centrally, and users cannot override it.

- *Discretionary Access Control (DAC)*   In this access model, the owner of an object is able to determine how and by whom the object may be accessed. The discretion of the owner determines which subjects will be permitted access.

- *Rule-Based Access Control (RuBAC)*   This model grants or denies access to objects based on rules that are established by the system administrator. These rules are typically enforced by the system's security policy, and access decisions are made based on specific conditions such as time of access, location, or other contextual factors. Unlike discretionary or mandatory access control, the decisions in RuBAC are not influenced by the identities of the users but rather by predefined rules.

- *Role-Based Access Control (RBAC)*   In this model, access rights are assigned to roles rather than to individual users. Users are then assigned to these roles, thereby inheriting the access rights associated with the roles. This model simplifies management because instead of assigning permissions to each user individually, the system administrator assigns permissions to roles. For example, a "manager" role might have permissions to access certain files that an "employee" role does not.

- *Attribute-Based Access Control (ABAC)*   ABAC is a more dynamic model where access to objects is determined by evaluating a set of attributes related to the user (subject), the resource (object), and the environment. Attributes might include the user's role, department, location, or the time of day. This model allows for fine-grained access control policies and is well-suited for complex environments where access decisions need to take into account multiple factors.

Access Control Threats

Because access controls are often the only means of protection between protected assets and users, access controls are often attacked. Indeed, the majority of attacks against computers and networks containing valuable assets are against access controls in attempts to trick, defeat, or bypass them. Threats represent the intent and ability to do harm to an asset.

Threats against access controls include:

- *Malware*   This includes viruses, worms, Trojan horses, rootkits, and spyware. Malware is *malicious code* that is used to perform unauthorized actions on target systems. It is often successful because of known vulnerabilities that can be exploited. In the context of access control, malware presents one of two threats: the ability to record login credentials typed in by a user, and the ability to exploit a vulnerability in an access control system, thereby enabling an attacker to bypass an access control. Vulnerabilities are discussed in more detail in the next section.

- *Eavesdropping*   Attackers will install network- or system-based sniffing tools to listen to network communications to intercept key transmissions such as user IDs and passwords used to access sensitive or valuable information. Usually, attackers will need to use some means such as malware or social engineering to install sniffing tools on a target system. In some instances, however, attackers will have access to the physical network and can directly connect sniffing tools to the network cabling.

- *Logic bombs and back doors*   Computer instructions inserted by programmers or others in the systems development process can result in an application that contains unauthorized code. A *logic bomb* is a set of instructions designed to perform some damaging action when a specific event occurs; a popular example is a *time bomb* that alters or destroys data on a specified date in the future. Some developers install time bombs in code that they manage and periodically advance the date in the time bomb. If the developer is fired from his or her job, the time bomb will activate after termination, and the developer will have gotten revenge on the former employer. A *back door* is a section of code that permits someone to bypass access controls and access data or functions. Back doors are commonly placed in programs during development but removed before development is complete. Sometimes, however, back doors are deliberately planted so that the developer (or someone else) can access data and functions.

- *Scanning attacks*   An attacker performs active or passive scanning in an attempt to discover weak access controls. For example, an attacker can use a *port scanning tool* to discover open and possibly vulnerable ports on target systems. An attacker can search for unprotected modems through *war dialing*. Or an attacker can listen to Wi-Fi network traffic to look for vulnerable wireless access points in *war driving*.

- *Race conditions*   Also known as a time-of-check/time-of-use (TOC/TOU) attack, the attacker is attempting to exploit the small window of time that sometimes exists between the time that a resource is requested and when the resource is available for use.

 The potency and frequency of threats on a system are directly proportional to the perceived value of assets that the system contains or protects.

Access Control Vulnerabilities

Vulnerabilities are the weaknesses that may be present in a system that enable a threat to be more easily carried out or to have greater impact.

Vulnerabilities by themselves do not bring about actual harm. Instead, threats and vulnerabilities work together. Most often, a threat exploits a vulnerability, because it is easier to attack a system at its weakest point. Common vulnerabilities include:

- *Unpatched systems*   Security patches are designed to remove specific vulnerabilities. A system that is not patched still has vulnerabilities, some of which are easily exploited. Attackers can easily enter and take over systems that lack important security patches.

- *Default system settings*   Default settings often include unnecessary services that increase the chances that an attacker can find a way to break into a system. The practice of *system hardening* is used to remove all unnecessary services and to make security configuration changes on a system to make it as secure as possible.

- *Default passwords*   Some systems are shipped with default administrative passwords that make it easy for a new customer to configure the system. One problem with this arrangement is that many organizations fail to change these passwords. Hackers have access to extensive lists of default passwords for practically every kind of computer and device that can be connected to a network.

- *Incorrect permissions settings*   If the permissions that are set up for files, directories, databases, application servers, or software programs are incorrectly set, this could permit access—and even modification or damage—by persons who should not have access.

- *Vulnerabilities in utilities and applications*   System utilities, tools, and applications that are not a part of the base operating system may have exploitable weaknesses that could permit an attacker to compromise a system successfully.

- *Application logic*   Software applications—especially those that are accessible via the Internet—that contain inadequate session management, resource management, and input testing controls can potentially permit an intruder to take over a system and steal or damage information.

Familiarity with Technology Is Key to an Effective IS Audit

The IS auditor needs to be highly familiar with information technologies to be effective. Without in-depth knowledge of security threats, vulnerabilities, controls, and countermeasures, the IS auditor will not be able to detect as many unsafe practices in a technology environment. Furthermore, without a depth of understanding, IS auditors will not be able to ask probing questions in walk-throughs or be able to interpret evidence correctly.

The IS auditor must understand information technology in general, but he or she must also understand the technology architecture in the specific environment that is being examined. In an environment that has the appearance of being highly secure, a configuration error in a single device can betray that security like a traitor and expose the entire organization to considerable harm. Only an IS auditor with a thorough understanding of information technology would have a chance to detect such a weakness and interpret it correctly.

Access Points and Methods of Entry

Computing and network resources must be accessed in order to support business processes, thereby providing services and value. The majority of information-based resources are accessed via TCP/IP networks; some resources are accessed using other technologies, such as direct hardwired connections (as in the case of some mainframe computers) and non-TCP/IP network technologies. Then there are desktop computers that sometimes themselves contain information and resources.

Modern LAN environments are protected from outside threats with firewalls and other means. Many larger organizations also employ internal firewalls to segment their networks, creating separate zones of trust within the organization. But, generally speaking, LANs are a lot like highway systems within individual countries: once you pass a border checkpoint and show a passport or another credential, you can roam freely inside that country unhindered.

Points of Entry

The main *point of entry* in many organizations is the internal corporate LAN. A user who can connect to the corporate LAN is able to reach computing resources logically in the organization—subject to the access controls associated with each resource. This makes the notion of protecting corporate accesses by controlling access to the LAN a vital topic.

Increasingly, however, organizations have fewer and fewer internal resources, as a result of the mass migration away from on-premises resources to cloud-based resources. In these organizations, the internal LAN is little more than a means for connecting to a few resources such as printers and scanners, or is primarily a means of accessing the Internet and the organizations' primary business applications that are SaaS-based.

The ease of connectivity to the corporate LAN highlights a number of important security issues. Probably the biggest issue is the ability for nonorganization-owned computers to connect to the network and access network-based resources. By permitting nonorganization-owned systems to connect to the network, the organization is essentially giving up control of the network. Allowing any computer or device connect to the network creates risks, including:

- *Exposure to malware*   Any computer that is not actively managed by centralized anti-malware software could be carrying malware that would attempt to propagate itself inside the corporate network. Indeed, worms such as Nimda and Code Red were able to spread in just this way. Laptops that were the personal property of employees would become infected on home networks and then spread the infection inside the corporate LAN in "typhoid Mary" style. Many instances of malware being imported on vendor-owned computers (for "demo" purposes) are also known.

- *Eavesdropping*   While the IT department can exert some level of control over desktop and server computing by prohibiting (and even preventing) the installation of network-sniffing programs, IT cannot easily control whether nonorganization-owned computers have network-sniffing programs (or malware that does the same thing!).

- *Open access*   A corporate LAN that permits any device to connect will permit a wireless access point to connect to the network. This, in turn, may permit anyone with a Wi-Fi client to connect to the network.

Available technologies can be used to control the systems that are permitted to connect to the corporate LAN. Network access control (NAC) through a network access protocol such as 802.1X is used to control whether a system is permitted to connect to corporate network resources. NAC and 802.1X use an authentication mechanism to determine whether each new device is permitted to connect. If the device lacks the necessary credentials, it cannot connect.

Whether the device is actually able to physically connect is another story. Network switches play a role in NAC and 802.1X; if a device is not permitted onto the network, the workgroup switch will not route any packets from the denied workstation into the LAN. The workstation remains logically disconnected.

It's important to track the points of entry to a network because each of these points of entry offers additional opportunities for an attacker to infiltrate the network. The sum total of all of the possible points of entry is known as the *attack surface*.

> Many organizations employ cloud-based environments for many or even all of their applications. As a result, corporate LAN environments often have few or no local resources. Accordingly, organizations may shift their strategies for the protection of assets.

Remote Access

Remote access is defined as the means of providing remote connectivity to a corporate LAN through a data link. Remote access is provided by many organizations so that employees who are temporarily or permanently off-site can access LAN-based resources from their remote location.

Remote access was initially provided using dial-up modems that included authentication. Today, most remote access is provided over the Internet itself and typically uses an encrypted tunnel, or *virtual private network* (VPN), to protect transmissions from any eavesdroppers. VPNs are so prevalent in remote access technology that the terms *VPN* and *remote access* have become synonymous. A typical VPN architecture appears in Figure 8.1.

Two security controls are essential for remote access:

- *Authentication*   It is necessary to know who is requesting access to the corporate LAN. Authentication may consist of the same user ID and password that personnel use when on-site, or multifactor authentication may be required.

- *Encryption*   Many on-site network applications do not encrypt sensitive traffic because it is all contained within the physically and logically protected corporate LAN. However, because remote access provides the same function as being on the corporate LAN, and because the applications themselves usually do not provide encryption, the remote access service itself usually provides encryption.

FIGURE 8.1   VPN architecture

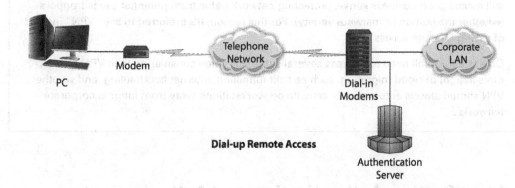

Dial-up Remote Access

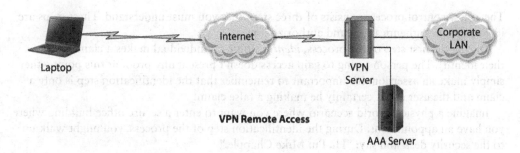

VPN Remote Access

These controls are needed because they are a substitute (or *compensating control*) for the physical access controls that are usually present to control which personnel may enter the building to use the on-site corporate LAN. When personnel are on-site, their identity is confirmed through keycard or other physical access controls. When personnel are off-site using remote access, because the organization cannot "see" the person on the far end of the remote access connection, the authentication used is the next best thing.

The migration of corporate resources from internal networks to cloud-based networks is changing the notion of remote access. As a result, organizations are incorporating multi-factor authentication for access to the organization's cloud-based resources, regardless of the location of users—whether they are on a corporate LAN, working from home, in the field, or traveling.

The New Remote Access Paradigm

As organizations migrate their business applications to colocation centers and cloud providers, and after the last internal resource is moved to the cloud, what is the point of remote access? Remote access to *what*?

> If we think about this in terms of VPN and the protection afforded through encryption, VPN still makes good business sense, protecting network traffic from potential eavesdroppers (whether the human or malware variety). For this reason, it's preferred to say "VPN" instead of saying "remote access."
>
> Organizations still need to address several subtopics when considering their VPN architectures in light of cloud migration, such as split tunneling, Internet backhauling, and whether VPN should always automatically activate on workstations away from internal corporate networks.

Identification, Authentication, and Authorization

The access control process consists of three steps that you must understand. These steps are identification, authentication, and authorization.

During the first step of the process, *identification*, an individual makes a claim about their identity. The person trying to gain access doesn't present any proof at this point—they simply make an assertion. It's important to remember that the identification step is only a claim and the user could certainly be making a false claim!

Imagine a physical world scenario where you want to enter a secure office building where you have an appointment. During the identification step of the process, you might walk up to the security desk and say: "Hi, I'm Mike Chapple."

Proof comes into play during the second step of the process: *authentication*. During the authentication step, the individual proves their identity to the satisfaction of the access control system. In our office building example, the guard would likely wish to see my driver's license to confirm my identity.

Simply proving your identity isn't enough to gain access to a system, however. The access control system also needs to be satisfied that you are allowed to access the system. That's the third step of the access control process: *authorization*. In our office building example, the security guard might check a list of that day's appointments to see if it includes my name.

Exam Tip

When you get ready for the exam, it's very important that you remember the distinction between the identification and authentication phases. Be ready to identify the phase associated with an example of a mechanism.

So far, we've talked about identification, authentication, and authorization in the context of gaining access to a building. Let's talk about how they work in the electronic world.

When we go to log in to a system, we most often identify ourselves using a username, most likely composed of some combination of the letters from our names.

When we reach the authentication phase, we're commonly asked to enter a password. There are many other ways to authenticate, and we'll talk about those later in this chapter.

Finally, in the electronic world, authorization often takes the form of access control lists that itemize the specific filesystem permissions granted to an individual user or group of users. Users proceed through the identification, authentication, and authorization processes when they request access to a resource.

Authentication Techniques

Computer systems offer many different authentication techniques that allow users to prove their identity. Let's take a look at three different authentication factors: something you know, something you are, and something you have.

Something You Know

Passwords are the most common example of a "something you know" authentication factor. The user remembers their password and enters it in a system during the authentication process.

Users should choose strong passwords consisting of as many characters as possible and combine characters from multiple classes, such as uppercase and lowercase letters, digits, and symbols.

Something You Are

The second authentication factor is *something you are*, otherwise known as *biometric authentication*. Biometrics measure one of your physical characteristics, such as a fingerprint, eye pattern, face, or voice. Using biometric authentication requires specialized readers, such as the retinal scanner shown in Figure 8.2(a) or the fingerprint reader shown in Figure 8.2(b).

Something You Have

The third authentication factor, *something you have*, requires the user to have physical possession of a device, such as a smartphone or authentication token key fob like the one shown in Figure 8.3.

Multifactor Authentication

When used alone, any one authentication factor provides some security for systems. However, they each have their own drawbacks. For example, an attacker might steal a user's password through a phishing attack. Once they have the password, they can then use that password to assume the user's identity. Other authentication factors aren't foolproof, either. If you use smartcard authentication to implement something you have, the user may lose the smartcard. Someone coming across it may then impersonate the user.

FIGURE 8.2 Biometric authentication with a (a) retinal scanner (b) fingerprint scanner

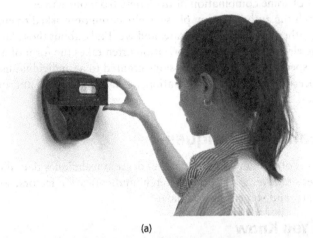

(a)

(b)

Source: (a) artiemedvedev/Adobe Stock Photos and (b) demphoto/Adobe Stock Photos

FIGURE 8.3 Authentication token

Source: Matteo F./Adobe Stock Photos

The solution to this problem is to combine authentication techniques from multiple factors, such as combining something you know with something you have. This approach is known as *multifactor authentication*.

Take the two techniques we just discussed: passwords and smartcards. When used alone, either one is subject to hackers either gaining knowledge of the password or stealing a smartcard. However, if an authentication system requires both a password (something you know) and a smartcard (something you have) it brings added security. If the hacker steals the password, they don't have the required smartcard, and vice versa. It suddenly becomes much more difficult for the attacker to gain access to the account. Something you know and something you have are different factors, so this is an example of multifactor authentication.

We can combine other authentication factors as well. For example, a fingerprint reader (something you are) might also require the entry of a PIN (something you know).

When evaluating multifactor authentication, remember that the techniques must be *different* factors. An approach that combines a password with the answer to a security question is *not* multifactor authentication because both factors are something you know.

Authentication Errors

The strength of an authentication mechanism may be measured by the number of errors that it generates. There are two basic types of errors in authentication systems.

False acceptance errors occur when the system misidentifies an individual as an authorized user and grants access that should be denied. This is a very serious error because it allows unauthorized access to the system, device, information, or facility. The frequency of these errors is measured by the *false acceptance rate (FAR)*.

False rejection errors occur when an authorized individual attempts to gain access to a system but is incorrectly denied access by the system. This is not as serious as a false acceptance because it does not jeopardize confidentiality or integrity, but it is still a serious error because it jeopardizes the availability of resources. The frequency of these errors is measured by the *false rejection rate (FRR)*.

The false acceptance rate and false rejection rate are not, by themselves, good measures of the strength of an authentication factor because they can be easily manipulated. On one extreme, administrators may configure the system to admit nobody at all, giving it a perfect false acceptance rate but also a very high false rejection rate. Similarly, if the system allows anyone access, it has a perfect false rejection rate but an unacceptably high false acceptance rate.

The solution to this is to use a balanced measure of strength called the *crossover error rate (CER)*. This is the efficacy rate that occurs when administrators tune the system to have equal false acceptance and false rejection rates. Figure 8.4 shows the relationship between the FAR, FRR, and CER. As you increase the sensitivity of a system, it increases the FRR but decreases the FAR. As you decrease the sensitivity of a system, it decreases the FRR but increases the FAR. In either case, the CER remains constant.

FIGURE 8.4   False acceptance rate (FAR), false rejection rate (FRR), and crossover error rate (CER)

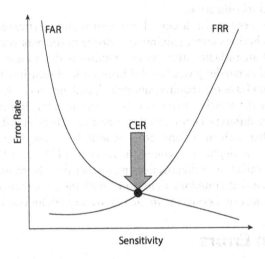

Single Sign-on and Federation

Federated identity management leverages the fact that a single individual may have accounts across a wide variety of systems. When organizations agree to federate their identity management systems, they share some of this information across the systems. This approach reduces the number of individual identities that a user must have and eases the burden on both the user and the organization.

You're probably already familiar with some federated identity management systems. When you log on to websites using your Google account, Facebook Connect, or Apple ID, you're using federated identity management.

Single sign-on (SSO) goes a step further and shares authenticated sessions across systems. Many organizations create SSO solutions within their organizations to help users avoid the burden of repeatedly authenticating.

In an SSO approach, users log on to the first SSO-enabled system they encounter and then that login session persists across other systems until it reaches its expiration. If the organization sets the expiration period to be the length of a business day, it means that users need to log in only once per day and then their single sign-on session will last the entire day.

Provisioning and Deprovisioning

Account administrators are responsible for managing the provisioning and deprovisioning of user accounts. When a new user joins the organization, administrators ensure that they go through the appropriate onboarding process and then provision a user account for that user. This involves creating authentication credentials and granting the user appropriate authorizations based on their job function.

When that user leaves the organization, administrators ensure that they go through an offboarding process that includes deprovisioning the account to remove their credentials and authorizations at the appropriate time. It is essential that administrators act quickly to remove the user's access from computer systems. This prevents the user from accessing sensitive information or resources after their departure and is especially important when a user leaves the organization under unfavorable circumstances.

Security professionals should ensure that the organization has a strong process designed to remove access, preferably in an automated or semiautomated fashion. This process may have several workflows.

The normal workflow, for a planned departure, should automatically begin when a supervisor informs the Human Resources department that an employee is resigning or retiring. The account administration team should configure the user's account to automatically expire on the date they are leaving the organization.

An emergency workflow may be used when a user is suddenly terminated. This may occur under adverse circumstances when a user is fired. In those cases, the IT department should carefully coordinate with Human Resources to time the account termination precisely.

If account administrators fail to precisely time the access revocation, two undesirable situations may occur. First, if the account is terminated before the employee is informed of their termination, the employee may gain advance notice of the impending termination and take retaliatory action against the employer. Second, if the account is not terminated immediately upon the user being informed of their termination, the user may gain access to the system after being fired and take retaliatory action.

Suspending and terminating accounts in a timely manner boosts enterprise security by reducing the risk of unauthorized access.

Account Monitoring

Security administrators must pay careful attention to the permissions and use of end-user accounts to protect against security incidents. Let's take a look at some account monitoring practices that organizations should put in place.

The first is inaccurate permissions assigned to accounts that either prevent a user from doing their work or violate the principle of least privilege. These permissions are often the result of privilege creep, a condition that occurs when users switch jobs and gain new permissions but never have their old permissions revoked.

To protect against inaccurate permissions, administrators should perform regular user account reviews in cooperation with managers from around the organization. During each of these manual reviews, the administrators should pull a listing of all the permissions assigned to each account and then review that listing with managers to ensure that it is appropriate for the user's role, making any necessary adjustments. Administrators should pay careful attention to users who switched jobs since the last account review.

Another issue is the unauthorized use of permissions either by someone other than the legitimate user accessing the account or by the user performing some illegitimate action. Protecting against unauthorized use of permissions is tricky because it can be hard to detect.

This requires the use of continuous account monitoring systems that watch for suspicious activity and alert administrators to strange actions.

For example, a continuous account monitoring system may flag violations of access policies, such as the following:

- Logons from strange geographic locations such as a user connecting from both the home office and a remote location in Eastern Europe at the same time; cases like this are known as impossible travel time logins and should be treated as risky logins.

- Logins from unusual network locations, such as a user who always logs in from the HR network suddenly appearing on a guest network.

- Logons at unusual times of day, such as a mail clerk logging into the system in the middle of the night.

- Deviations from normal behavior, such as users accessing files that they do not normally access.

- High volumes of activity that may represent bulk downloading of sensitive information. The specific circumstances that merit attention will vary from organization to organization but performing this type of behavior-based continuous account monitoring is an important security control.

Access Control Lists

Access control lists (ACLs) are a common means to administer access controls. ACLs are used by many operating systems and other devices such as routers as a simple means to control access to a resource such as a server or a network.

On many devices and systems, the list of packet-filtering rules (which give a router many of the characteristics of a firewall) is known as an ACL. In the Unix operating system, ACLs can control which users are permitted to access files, directories, and run tools and programs. ACLs in these and other contexts are often simple text files that can be edited with a text editor.

Protecting Stored Information

Information systems store information primarily in the form of databases and flat files. Operating systems and database management systems usually provide minimum protection of databases and files by default; organizations need to determine the correct level of protection that is pursuant to the value and sensitivity of information. The controls that may need to be enacted are discussed in this section.

Access Controls

Access controls are the primary means used to protect stored information from unauthorized accesses and unauthorized users.

Operating system access control settings (often in the form of ACLs) are used to determine which user IDs are permitted to access flat files (as well as the directories containing them). Following the principle of *least privilege*, all flat files containing sensitive information should have access restricted to only those users and processes that must be able to access them. No user or process that doesn't have a need to access specific files should be able to do so.

Access Logging

Operating systems and database management systems should be configured so that all access attempts to files and directories are logged. This practice promotes accountability and provides a trail of evidence in the event that a forensic investigation should be conducted in the future.

Access logs themselves must be highly protected—ideally, they should be stored in a different storage system than the one that stores the data whose access is being logged. Access logs should not be alterable, even by database administrators and system administrators, so that no one will be able to "erase his or her tracks" should someone decide to tamper with sensitive information and then attempt to hide the evidence afterward.

Access logging is effective only if someone actually examines the logs. Because this can be a time-consuming activity, many organizations utilize alert-generating tools such as a SIEM that sends alerts to key personnel when particular audit log entries (such as unauthorized access attempts) appear. These alerts permit personnel to act upon anomalous events when they occur.

Backup and Media Storage

Data stored on information systems can be lost or damaged. Some of the ways in which this can occur include:

- *Hardware failure* Many of the components in a storage system—particularly hard disks—are subject to failures, however rare they might be nowadays. These failures can result in data being irretrievable.

- *Administrator error* A system or database administrator can accidentally erase or alter information in a way that is not easily undone.

- *Software bug* An erroneous section of code in application software can inadvertently wipe out data in a database or in flat files. This can occur with an organization's own programs or with programs that are supplied by a software vendor.

Any of these possibilities should be reason enough for an IT operation to back up all critical data. Backing up data means making copies of it on other media in case the original media (or the system that it is stored on) fails. Then, after the original system is repaired, data can be copied from the backup media and processing can be resumed.

Backup Tools

Organizations often use backup tools that help the backup process be as efficient as possible. Some backup tools automatically manage backup media volumes and make data restoration easier than if it had to be done manually.

Protection of Backup Media

Because backup media is often transported from place to place, there are opportunities for media to be misplaced or lost in transit. For this reason, data on backup media should be encrypted so that any third party who happens to find a backup media volume will not be able to retrieve any data from it. When backup media is encrypted, a lost tape means only the loss of an inexpensive asset and not a potential compromise of sensitive information.

Off-site Backup Media Storage

To protect data from disasters, backup media should be stored at a location away from the original data. For example, if data from a server was backed up onto tape and the backup tapes are stored near the server, both server and backup media could be destroyed in an event such as a fire or flood. If backup media were stored in another location, however, then only the original server would be destroyed, but the system could be recovered using data on backup media at the other location.

Selecting an off-site media storage facility requires the organization to weigh several factors, including distance from the original data (too close means it may be destroyed in a regional disaster; too far away means it may take too long to obtain it when needed), security of the storage facility, security of the transportation of media back and forth between the original location and the off-site storage facility, and recordkeeping available so that it can easily be determined which media volumes are at the off-site facility at any given time. Security of the off-site storage facility should be at least as good as the security in the original location so that the protected information is not more vulnerable at the off-site facility.

E-vaulting

Many organizations are migrating away from tape backup to e-vaulting, where data is copied to a cloud-based e-vaulting service provider. While one disadvantage lies in the potential time it takes to copy a large dataset over the Internet, e-vaulting can reduce or eliminate the administrative burden of managing and protecting backup media. With e-vaulting, data can be restored directly over the Internet without having to transport backup media to a location where it is needed.

Restoration Testing

The organization should occasionally test backup media and data restoration software to make sure that data is actually being backed up onto the backup media and that it can be retrieved. I personally know of an organization that believed it was backing up its databases every day until it needed to restore one, only to find out that nothing was ever being written to the backup media. Clearly, the organization was not testing its backup system. Restoration tests should be scheduled and their results recorded.

Media Inventory

A periodic inventory of all backup media (whether physical in the form of backup tapes, or virtual in the form of e-vaulting volumes), including media at the off-site location, should be performed. This will ensure that all media volumes are being handled properly and that none has been lost or misplaced. The results of each inventory should be recorded and any anomalies corrected.

> The loss of one or more backup media volumes during an inventory would be considered a security incident, unless the media was known to be encrypted.

Patch Management

Patch management is an IT operational process whereby security and functionality patches are obtained, tested, and installed on information systems. The purpose of patch management is to keep systems running on currently supported vendor software and to ensure that all known security vulnerabilities are closed and software defects fixed.

Patch management is typically managed with tools that are quickly able to assess the "patch level" of many servers and then install patches en masse.

There are different points of view with regard to patches. Should all patches be installed, or just some patches? There are pros and cons to each approach. If all security patches are installed, then indeed all known vulnerabilities will be closed. However, some security patches may be unnecessary because specific components that are patched might not be used. If an organization chooses to install only the most critical patches, a security analyst will need to perform a risk analysis each time a security patch is released so that a formal determination of need can be established. And even if an organization does install all available security patches, a risk analysis can help to determine how quickly each patch needs to be installed.

The argument against installing patches is that each patch can add a tiny increment of instability to the system. Although the base operating system undergoes exhaustive testing, far less testing is performed on security patches before they are released. This is evidenced by the occasional security patch that breaks some other functionality—this does not happen often, but it does happen sometimes. This is another reason why organizations should first test patches (security and other) on test environments prior to installing them on production systems. Otherwise, there is a small chance that a new patch will cause unexpected problems that could be difficult to isolate.

Patch management is an integral part of the vulnerability management process, discussed next.

Vulnerability Management

The purpose of *vulnerability management* is to identify and manage vulnerabilities in IT applications and infrastructure. Vulnerabilities can result from errors in configuration, from flaws in the overall architecture, or from newly discovered weaknesses reported by security researchers.

Vulnerability management requires a number of distinct but connected activities.

Subscribing to Security Alerts

Most computer hardware and software manufacturers have a service whereby customers can be made aware of new vulnerabilities, weaknesses, threats, and the remedies for these. Often, the fixes for vulnerabilities, weaknesses, and threats are security patches or bulletins that advise changes in configuration. There are also some high-quality, nonvendor-related sources for security alerts, including Secunia, InfraGard, Full Disclosure, and US-CERT. Organizations should subscribe both to any available vendor sources as well as one or more of these nonvendor sources to get a full picture of new vulnerabilities as well as guidance on how to mitigate them.

System and Device Hardening

This is concerned with activities to design and implement standards for system and device configuration, to increase security and reduce the risk of compromise. Hardening is discussed in more detail later in this section.

Vulnerability Scanning and Penetration Testing

This involves the use of tools that scan or examine computers, network devices, or application programs with the purpose of finding any vulnerabilities. Organizations that have any computers or applications accessed over the Internet (including simple websites) should consider performing regular scans to make sure that those computers and applications are free of any high- or medium-risk vulnerabilities. An organization that does not remediate vulnerabilities faces the real threat of the computer or application being attacked and compromised, which could lead to a loss of sensitive information. Many commercial and open-source tools are available to inspect computers and applications for vulnerabilities; the better tools also rank findings by the level of risk and include instructions on how vulnerabilities can be fixed. Organizations also need to remember that scanning a system once and removing all vulnerabilities does not mean that there will never be new vulnerabilities in the future; this is because security researchers regularly find new vulnerabilities in programs and systems. A system that is secure today will most certainly be less secure tomorrow.

Patch Management

This is the process of responding to known vulnerabilities by installing security patches on target systems and devices. This process is described in detail in the preceding section. Patches should be applied proactively, and vulnerability scanning used as a step to confirm that all necessary patches have been installed on all systems.

Corrective Action Process

This is the process of recording vulnerabilities into an incident tracking process so that vulnerability remediation can be assigned to a person or team and be formally tracked. Corrective and preventive action processes are discussed earlier in this chapter.

System Hardening

System hardening is the process of changing the configuration of a system (which could be a server, subsystem, application, tool, or network device) so that it is more resistant to malfunctions and attacks. The principles behind system hardening are the endpoint security techniques discussed in Chapter 7, "Information Security Management."

Third-party Access Management

Nearly every organization relies on one or more third-party organizations in the development, support, or operations of its business processes. Often this takes the form of outsourced information systems or related services. Digital transformation has resulted in many organizations outsourcing some IT services that support critical business processes. There are so many specialties and subspecialties in IT that even the largest organizations need to utilize third-party organizations to build, support, or manage their IT environment.

Third Parties and Risk

The use of any third-party organization should not be permitted to result in an increase of overall risk to an organization, at least not without bringing some matching value. When considering outsourcing a service to a third party, a risk assessment should be performed to identify and characterize risks associated with this.

Some of the types of services that third-party service organizations provide include:

- Internet connectivity
- Internet hosting and colocation
- Cloud service, whether software-as-a-service (SaaS), infrastructure-as-a-service (IaaS), or platform-as-a-service (PaaS)
- Application services (for email, customer relationship management [CRM], enterprise resource planning [ERP], payroll, expense reporting, and other needs)
- Managed security services
- IT support
- Software development and testing
- Call centers
- Collection services
- Management and business consulting
- Auditors and security assessments
- Vendors that support hardware and software solutions
- Janitorial and other cleaning
- Shipping and receiving
- Building and equipment maintenance
- Temporary employee services

The primary risk with a third-party service provider is that the service provider will have access to some of the organization's sensitive information or to systems or networks containing or processing such information. Whether the service provider will have access to the organization's applications and data, or whether the organization will be sending data to the service provider, this overall risk needs to be broken down into each component and analyzed.

For each risk identified, remediation needs to be identified, typically so that the risk can be reduced to the same level as though the organization were performing the service on its own.

Types of Third-Party Access

Depending upon the type of service rendered, third-party service providers will have access to the organization's information in a variety of ways, including:

- Physical access to hard copy business records
- Physical access to information systems
- Physical access to storage media such as hard drives, solid-state drives, backup tapes, and optical drives
- Logical access to information systems, sensitive data, or source code

 A third-party service provider does not necessarily need access to sensitive business records to pose a risk. A service provider that is familiar with the organization's business practices can cause harm to the organization by interfering with business operations or disclosing business practices to outsiders such as customers, competitors, and others. Such interference or disclosure can occur through the action of an internal or external malicious actor or by innocent mistake.

Risks Associated with Third-Party Access

Knowing the type of access that a third-party service provider will have to an organization's information, the types of risks can be identified. Some of these risks include:

- Theft of business records
- Exposure of business records to unauthorized parties
- Alteration of business records
- Damage (both deliberate and accidental) to information systems hardware, software, or information
- Failure to perform services in a timely manner
- Failure to perform services accurately
- Failure to perform services professionally

Third-Party Access Countermeasures

As mentioned earlier in this section, the risks associated with a third-party service provider should be no different from associated risks if the organization were performing the service on its own. Even though new risks are introduced when transferring work to a service provider, countermeasures and compensating controls should be introduced that will keep the level of risk acceptably low.

Some of the countermeasures that can be used to mitigate risk include:

- Video surveillance with video recording
- Logging all data access and associated accesses to named individuals in the third-party organization
- Access controls that prevent the third party from accessing business records that it does not require in the performance of its services
- Logical access controls that limit the third party's access only to those data fields required to perform their services
- Vulnerability management tools and procedures
- Security awareness training
- Systems to block malware and its actions
- Security monitoring to detect and respond to security events
- Recording of voice or data communications sessions
- Periodic audits of the service provider's activities

Generally, an organization can require that a third-party service organization that has logical access to the organization's systems or stores any of the organization's data protect this data with the same (or higher) level of controls that the organization uses for its own data. This should result in the third-party service organization's *not* being in a situation where the organization's records are more vulnerable to theft, exposure, or compromise. For example, if an organization requires encryption of specific information when processed in your organization's systems, any service provider that processes the same information should also be required to encrypt it or to employ other means that result in the same level and type of protection.

 In any situation where treatment for a specific risk associated with a third-party service provider results in unavoidable residual risk, senior management will need to be made aware of the residual risk and determine whether they are willing to accept that risk.

When an organization is considering the use of a third-party service provider, the organization should require the service provider to answer a detailed questionnaire concerning security and other aspects of its operation. The organization should also ask whether the provider has had any external audits of its services; if so, the organization should request to see reports from those audits.

To validate information provided in questionnaires and other materials, an organization should consider requesting key pieces of evidence and perhaps a site visit to the service provider's offices and processing center(s).

Third-Party Security in Legal Agreements

The services performed by a third-party service provider should be succinctly described in a legal agreement. This will generally include a description of the services that are performed, measures of quantity and quality for services, service levels, remedies or penalties for failures in quality or quantity, rates and payments, and roles and responsibilities for both parties.

Legal agreements with service providers need to include several security provisions, including:

- A statement that all of the organization's information and knowledge of its business practices will be kept confidential
- Security- and privacy-related liabilities, roles, and responsibilities
- Security controls required to protect the organization's information
- Acceptable uses for the organization's information
- Persons who will be authorized to access the organization's information
- Background checks, nondisclosure agreements, and acceptable-use agreements for each person who is authorized to access the organization's information
- Required security training for persons authorized to access the organization's information
- Capabilities in place to log and respond to security-related events
- Steps to be taken if a security breach or suspected breach should occur
- Steps to be taken to reduce the likelihood of data loss caused by a natural or human-made disaster
- Identification of who is responsible for security and privacy in the third-party organization
- The right to inspect and audit the third-party organization's premises and operations on short notice
- Proof of compliance with all applicable laws and regulations
- Agreement to adequately destroy all copies of information on request or upon the termination of the agreement

Many additional security-related terms and conditions may be warranted, depending upon the nature of the services provided and the sensitivity and value of the information accessed and used by the service provider. Regulations imposed on the organization regarding the collection, handling, and use of relevant information may result in additional terms and conditions.

Third-Party Security in Security Policy

Many organizations provide cloud-based commercial applications, which are as easy to set up as filling in a registration form, paying with a credit card, and uploading sensitive data from an employee's workstation. These organizations operate as SaaS, PaaS, IaaS, or other cloud service models.

Often, the people in an organization have little idea about or regard for the security controls that are used by its service providers. Because of this, organizations can enact a security and business policy that forbids the use of any online service provider (SaaS, PaaS, IaaS, cloud, and so on) unless a risk assessment has first been performed for that service provider. Without such a policy, there is little to stop people from signing up with various online service providers and potentially putting the organization's sensitive data at risk.

An organization should have policies and processes in place to properly assess, measure, and monitor risks related to any third-party service provider.

Third-Party Risk Management Life Cycle

The *third-party risk management (TPRM)* process is a typical life cycle process. It starts with a decision to consider one or more third parties to perform a service to the organization. Even before selecting a service provider, the organization sends an appropriate questionnaire to each prospective service provider to understand the risk profile of each. Once a third party has been selected, the information gleaned from the questionnaire is used to determine the contents of the legal agreement; for instance, if a third party does not have a security awareness training program, a clause in the legal agreement would stipulate that the third party will implement such a program within a specific period of time. Annually, the organization will send a security questionnaire to each third party to reassess its security posture to ensure that its security programs continue to be acceptably effective.

Each third party represents a different level of risk and criticality to an organization. For this reason, organizations can develop risk levels or "tiers" that each third party is assigned to. For instance, three tiers corresponding to low, medium, and high risk are developed and third parties assigned to one of those tiers. Service providers at the highest tier are assessed with more rigor and at a higher frequency. Service providers at the lowest risk tier may be assessed at onboarding time and seldom thereafter. Each organization needs to determine the standards and procedures for each risk tier and the level and types of assessment performed at each.

Many security leaders build a third-party risk dashboard that depicts changes and trends in the risks associated with the entire portfolio of third parties. This dashboard can show risk "hot spots" and areas requiring more focus and attention. Information in the third-party risk program should be integrated with the organization's risk management life cycle and even with its ERM program if that exists.

Governance should also be a consideration in the TPRM life cycle. Some governance requirements, such as those that come from HIPAA, actually require that third-party service providers be appropriately vetted and must include certain security or privacy measures in their contracts.

Environmental Controls

Computers and networks operate in the physical world. Networks consist of devices such as routers, switches, and firewalls, plus cabling within and between buildings. Computer systems and network devices are designed to operate within a narrow band of temperature, humidity, moisture, and cleanliness. When they operate within these bounds, they are likely to provide years of service, but even brief periods outside these bounds can significantly shorten the life of many components.

Organizations that employ computers and networks to support vital business processes need to provide suitable environments for them. Failure to do so can result in higher operating costs and business disruptions resulting from more frequent unscheduled downtime due to environmental conditions. This section discusses the environmental systems and controls required to maintain a suitable environment for computers and networks.

Environmental Threats and Vulnerabilities

Computer systems require special facilities that include reliable electric power, environmental controls, and physical security. By their very nature, the controls that support and protect computer systems are complex and require periodic maintenance to provide reliable service. Redundant controls or systems are often needed for organizations intolerant of downtime.

This section discusses electric power, cooling and humidity controls, fire detection and suppression, and physical security.

Electric Power Vulnerabilities

Computer systems require a steady diet of clean electric power. The quality and delivery of electric power from virtually every public utility falls far short of the needs required by IT systems. Several power-related events threaten the health of computer equipment, including:

- *Spike or surge*   A sharp increase in voltage that lasts for only a fraction of a second
- *Inrush*   A sudden increase in current flowing to a device, usually associated with the startup of a large motor, which can cause a voltage drop that lasts several seconds
- *Noise*   The presence of other electromagnetic signals within incoming power
- *Dropout*   A momentary loss of power that lasts from a few milliseconds to a few seconds
- *Brownout*   A sustained drop in voltage that can last from several seconds to several hours
- *Blackout*   A complete loss of electric power for more than a few seconds

All of these phenomena can damage computer and network equipment by damaging internal components that make them fail outright or through latent damage that may shorten the life of an electronic component such as a power supply.

Physical Environment Vulnerabilities

Computer and network equipment is sensitive to changes in environmental conditions. The conditions that warrant discussion here are:

- *Temperature*   Computer and network equipment generate potentially large volumes of waste heat that must be continuously siphoned away. Even a brief interruption in environmental systems can cause sharp rises in temperature that can damage equipment. A temperature that is too low can cause condensation on equipment, which can invite corrosion and even cause short circuits when it occurs on electrical components.

- *Humidity*   Computer and network equipment must operate within a narrow band of humidity, usually 40 to 55 percent. When humidity drops below 40 percent, static buildup can occur that can damage sensitive electronics. Excessively high humidity can result in condensation, inviting corrosion and short circuits, causing the failure of computers and network equipment.

- *Dust and dirt*   Computer and network equipment is designed to be used in clean environments that are reasonably free of dust and dirt. Dust and dirt can accelerate wear in mechanical components and clog air filters, causing heat buildup.

- *Smoke and fire*   A fire that is in or near a data center can introduce smoke, which can damage computer and network equipment. Fire extinguishing agents such as water can also damage sensitive equipment. Fire departments often cut electric power to a building when there is a fire, so even equipment that is not threatened by the fire will suffer the effects of a power outage.

- *Sudden unexpected movement*   Earthquakes and landslides can violently shake equipment, pulling it away from its fastenings. Personnel moving equipment may accidentally bump into other devices or snag or damage loose cabling.

Environmental Controls and Countermeasures

Several environmental control systems are required to counteract the threats and vulnerabilities discussed in this section. When designed and operated correctly, these controls will contribute to high reliability and a good service record for IT equipment, which is sensitive to environmental conditions.

Electric Power

Because the quality of commercial utility electric power is usually insufficient for sensitive and critical computing equipment, several additional controls may be needed to improve the quality and/or quantity of available electric power. These controls are described in the following sections and depicted in Figure 8.5.

FIGURE 8.5 Components in a facility power system

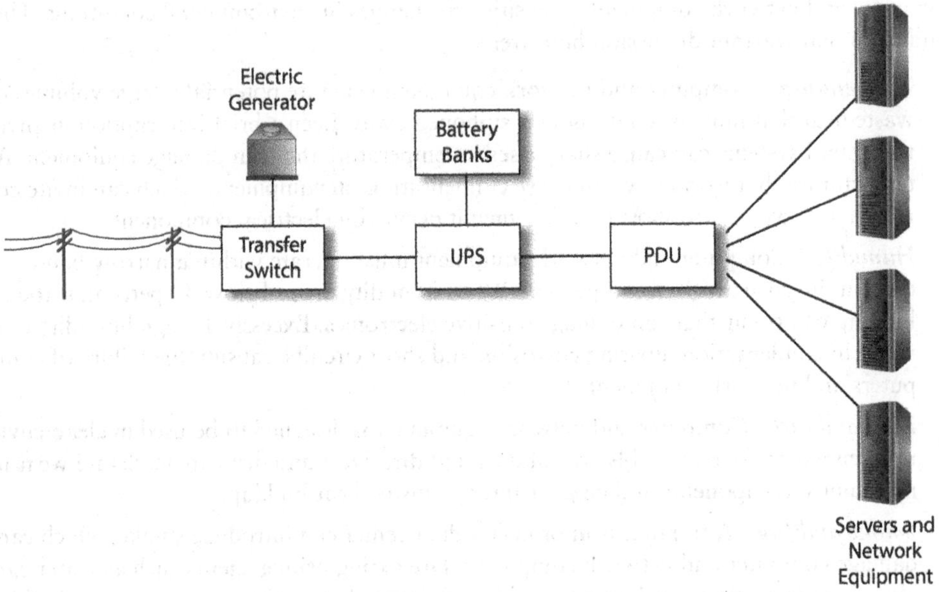

Uninterruptible Power Supply (UPS)

This is a system that filters incoming power from spikes and other noise and supplies power for short periods through a bank of batteries. A UPS is sufficient for power outages that last from a few minutes to as long as a few hours (provided there is sufficient battery capacity). A UPS provides a continuous supply of electricity; when there is a brownout or blackout, power delivered to computer systems is unaffected.

Electric Generator

This is a system consisting of an internal combustion engine powered by gasoline, diesel fuel, or natural gas that spins an electric generator. A generator can supply electricity for as long as several days, depending on the size of its fuel supply and whether it can be refueled.

Electric generators require several seconds to a few minutes to start up and provide emergency power. For this reason, electric generators are implemented in conjunction with a UPS system. In the event of a power failure, the UPS provides an uninterrupted flow of power and provides that power via its batteries until the generator has started and is producing electricity. Further, in a sustained power failure, many generators must be shut down for refueling (and indeed for any required maintenance); the UPS once again provides continuous power for this purpose.

Larger facilities employ multiple electric generators for larger workloads and greater overall reliability.

Dual Utility Power Feeds

An organization that is dependent on reliable electric power can consider using two separate electric utility power feeds that would ideally originate from separate utility substations. This safeguard helps to ensure a steady supply of electric power, even in the event of the outage of a utility company distribution line.

Transfer Switch

Facilities that use a UPS, one or more electric generators, and one or more public utility power feeds also employ a system of electrical switching equipment known as a *transfer switch*. A transfer switch automatically routes power among one or more public utility feeds, one or more generators, through one or more UPSs into the facility.

Power Distribution Unit

A *power distribution unit* (PDU) is a device that distributes electric power to a computer room or data center. A PDU may be large and supply dozens of separate power circuits or may be as small as a power strip. Some PDUs also have voltage step-down capabilities, converting higher input voltages into voltage levels used by computer equipment.

Multiple Power Feeds

Some organizations with high reliability requirements may build fully redundant power systems consisting of dual power feeds, dual transfer switches, generators, UPSs, and PDUs, delivering fully redundant power to each computer and network device. Organizations that utilize redundant power systems usually refer to their power systems as "A-side" and "B-side" systems. Computer and network equipment that utilizes dual power supplies can take advantage of redundant power systems by connecting one power supply to the A-side and one to the B-side. This permits systems to continue functioning, even in the event of a complete failure of any single component in the facility's power system. All such protected equipment will continue operating without interruption.

Power Planning

It is crucial to understand present and future electric power requirements so that the facility's electric power distribution components discussed here can be appropriately sized. Data centers generally size their power systems by calculating a minimum number of watts delivered to each square foot of data center space or to each cabinet. In the 1990s and early 2000s, data centers were generally configured to provide 40–100 watts per square foot, or as much as 3.125 kW per cabinet. However, with rapid advances in server technology, these figures have become inadequate. Modern data centers that need to get the most out of their IT equipment will plan for 150–200 watts per square foot, or as much as 6.250 kW per cabinet.

Data centers use different methods for calculating power requirements. Power figures often encompass an entire room or cage, which includes hot and cold aisles.

Planning for too high a power density will almost certainly result in excess electrical capacity, which is considered a waste of capital. Correspondingly, however, too small a figure per square foot or per cabinet will result in the data center running out of power before it runs out of space.

Many data centers that experience insufficient electric power are exploring ways of increasing their capacity. One solution is to use ambient air cooling instead of more expensive air conditioning. This is discussed in the next section.

Temperature and Humidity Controls

Because computing and network equipment sheds a large volume of waste heat, highly reliable and adequately sized HVAC (heating, ventilation, and air conditioning) systems are required.

The temperature in rooms containing computer and network equipment should range from 64.4° to 80.6°F (18° to 27°C), and humidity should range from 45 to 55 percent. In facilities with a considerable number of computer systems, this will require highly reliable and high-capacity HVAC systems.

It is recommended that facilities utilize an "N + 1" design, which means that there should be at least one additional HVAC system than is required to cool the facility continuously. For example, if a facility requires four HVAC systems for cooling, then at least five HVAC systems should be used. This permits adequate cooling to continue in the event one system fails or is being maintained.

Computer facilities should employ continuous temperature and humidity monitoring that regularly records readings and alerts personnel when readings exceed safe levels. Sensitive equipment should also have internal temperature monitoring capabilities that alert support personnel when readings exceed tolerance. Systems that are sensitive to variations in temperature should have auto-shutdown capabilities in the event that support personnel are unable to respond in time.

Many computer rooms and data centers employ a raised floor system consisting of removable tiles. The space under the tiles acts as an air plenum for air conditioning systems; tiles with holes in them are strategically placed to direct cold air into areas requiring it. Tiled floors are typically 80 to 100 cm (about 30 to 40 in.) above the floor beneath.

Data centers generally employ technology such as refrigeration or chilled water loops for controlling temperature. Many newer data centers employ ambient air cooling, which is less expensive as outside ambient air needs only to be filtered for dust. This approach has been adopted in many data centers trying to increase their power per square foot or power per cabinet figures by using less electric power for air cooling and therefore making more power available for IT equipment.

Fire Prevention, Detection, and Suppression Controls

Virtually every local government authority requires fire detection, prevention, and suppression controls. However, the minimum controls may be considered inadequate for facilities containing expensive computer and network equipment. For example, regulations requiring water-sprinkler suppression systems would certainly extinguish a fire in a data center, but the water would also cause considerable damage to equipment. For this reason, different types of detection and suppression systems are often used to protect valuable equipment from fire and suppression agent damage.

Fire Prevention

Measures that help to prevent fires in the first place contribute to a safer environment. Some measures include:

- *Combustibles*   Materials such as packing boxes and manuals should be stored away from computer equipment. Reductions in combustible materials make fires less likely to start or spread.

- *Cleanliness*   Dust can sometimes trigger highly sensitive smoke detectors; this is another reason to practice proper cleanliness measures in data centers.

- *Electrical equipment maintenance*   Maintenance activities such as soldering should not be done near computer equipment. Smoke from soldering can trigger smoke detectors and cause a discharge of fire suppression agents.

Fire Detection

Facilities can be equipped with more than the minimum required capabilities for smoke detection. Highly sensitive smoke and heat detection systems are available that can provide an earlier warning. This gives personnel an added opportunity to identify the cause of the fire and suppress it with limited-impact means such as fire extinguishers or simply cutting power to the offending device. Such measures help to avoid a larger fire that would require more aggressive suppression measures.

Commercial buildings also employ many manually operated fire alarms, often called "pull stations," where someone who sees a fire can pull the lever to set the alarm manually. In most cases, this causes fire alarms to sound but does not trigger fire suppression.

Fire Suppression

Most commercial facilities are required to have automatic or semiautomatic fire suppression systems. While the minimum is usually water-based sprinkler systems and a complement of hand-operated fire extinguishers, often an organization will make an investment in more sophisticated suppression systems that have less of an impact on computing equipment. But in some locations, even where advanced suppression systems are permitted, water-based systems are still required as a backup.

The types of centralized fire suppression systems include:

- *Wet pipe*   In this type of system, all sprinkler pipes are filled with water. Each sprinkler head is equipped with a fuse—a heat-sensitive glass bulb—that breaks upon reaching a preset temperature. When this occurs, water is discharged from just that sprinkler head, which is presumably located near a fire. When water begins to flow, an automatic sensor trips a fire alarm. This is the most common type of sprinkler system.

- *Dry pipe*   This type of system is used where ambient temperatures often drop below freezing. In this type of system, pipes are filled with compressed air. When sufficient heat causes one of the sprinkler head fuses to break, a control valve releases water into the piping. A delay of up to one minute occurs as water flows from the control valve to the sprinkler head.

- *Pre-action*   This type of system is used in areas with high-value contents such as data centers. A pre-action system is essentially a dry pipe system until a "preceding" event, such as a smoke detector alarm, occurs; at this time, the system is filled with water and essentially converted in real time to a wet pipe system. Then, if the ambient temperature at any of the sprinkler heads is high enough, those fuses break, releasing water to extinguish the fire. Pre-action systems are more expensive and complicated than wet pipe or dry pipe systems.

- *Deluge*   This type of system has dry pipes and all of the sprinkler heads are open. When the system is operated (for instance, when an alarm is triggered), water flows into the pipes and out of all of the sprinkler heads.

- *Inert gas*   This type of system is often the choice for use in computer centers because of its low impact on computing equipment and high effectiveness in fire suppression. Inert gas systems work by displacing oxygen from the room by bringing down the concentration of oxygen from the usual 21 percent to a lower figure, which slows the advancement of a fire. Through the 1980s, Halon 1301 was the substance of choice for inert gas systems. Declared a greenhouse gas in 1987, Halon 1301 has been replaced by other substances, such as FM-200.

In addition to centralized fire suppression systems, many commercial buildings are required to have hand-operated fire extinguishers. These come in a range of sizes, from 1 to 30 pounds and have fire retardants of several types, including:

- *Class A*   Suitable for ordinary solid combustibles such as wood and paper
- *Class B*   Suitable for flammable liquids and gases
- *Class C*   Suitable for energized electrical equipment
- *Class D*   Suitable for combustible metals
- *Class K*   Suitable for cooking oils and fats

The types listed here are U.S. standards. Different classifications are used in other countries.

Larger fire extinguishers are used in some facilities that have more than 50 pounds of fire retardant. These larger units are mounted on large-wheeled carts that can be pulled to the site of a fire.

The laws governing the use of fire detection and suppression systems vary from city to city. When planning a data center facility, it is crucial to understand precisely what is required in any specific location.

Cleaning

Facilities containing computing and network equipment need to be kept clean, with dirt, dust, and debris kept to a minimum. While computer rooms do not need to be kept clean to the same extent as "clean rooms" (facilities that manufacture disk drives, computer chips, and orbital satellites), they do need to be regularly cleaned to prevent the buildup of dust, dirt, and other particles that will clog filters and get inside computers and network devices, shortening their life span.

Lighting

While most modern data centers are generally staffed during business hours, and many more on a 24/7 basis, some private and commercial data centers are generally designed as "lights out" facilities. This means that they may not have personnel present during the business day, and likely not on a 24-hour basis. With that in mind, interior lighting is often turned down to conserve power. However, they do provide lighting to accommodate personnel who occasionally need to work on IT equipment. Such lighting is sometimes automatically controlled (through motion detection) or manually controlled through switches to activate lighting in areas where people are working.

Physical Security Controls

Physical security controls are primarily concerned with the protection of valuable or sensitive facilities (including those with computers and network devices) from unauthorized personnel. Controls are used to detect or prevent the entry of unwanted persons at these facilities. This section describes typical threats and vulnerabilities related to physical security and the controls and countermeasures that can be employed to protect a facility.

Physical Access Threats and Vulnerabilities

The threats and vulnerabilities in the realm of physical security are all associated with unwanted persons at business premises. A site without proper security controls may be subject to one or more threats, including:

- *Theft*   Persons who are able to enter a building may be able to steal equipment, records, or other valuable items.
- *Sabotage*   Persons who may enter a building or worksite may be able to damage or destroy valuable equipment or records.
- *Espionage*   Persons may conduct espionage to acquire information about the organization.

- *Covert listening devices*   Commonly known as *bugs*, these listening devices can be placed in a building to overhear conversations and transmit them to a receiver located in a remote location. Sometimes intruders plant bugs; they can also be hidden in articles that are delivered to a building (for example, in flower bouquets or gift baskets).

- *Tailgating*   When attempting to enter a building, an intruder follows an employee into the building without showing his or her security credentials (such as a keycard). This practice is also known as *piggybacking*.

- *Active shooter*   Many organizations are taking this increasingly prevalent threat seriously. An armed perpetrator may target a specific workplace and attempt to shoot multiple subjects who may or may not be specifically targeted.

While the active shooter threat is not directly related to information security, security leaders and auditors realize that workplace safety is of even higher importance than the protection of business equipment and IT equipment. Further, many of the controls that protect personnel also protect equipment. It is with these two objectives in mind that most workplace physical security plans are developed.

Several vulnerabilities can also increase risks, including:

- *Propped doors*   Sometimes a front, rear, or side door that is equipped with security controls will be propped open for various reasons, including hot weather (to permit a cooling breeze to enter and cool the building), frequent traffic moving in or out, or persons going out for a quick smoke who don't want the hassle of having to return to the building through another door.

- *Key-locked doors*   Some facilities still use doors locked with metal keys instead of (or in addition to) keycard entry and have not fully switched over to the exclusive use of keycards. This can result in the organization not knowing who is entering specific buildings or rooms.

- *Poorly managed keycard controls*   The lack of effective management of keycards can result in lost keycards and keycards issued to terminated personnel who are still able to access facilities.

- *Keycards displaying workplace*   Some organizations display their names on keycards. If such a keycard is lost or stolen, it's easy for someone to determine where the keycard can be used, inviting an intrusion. This weakness can be mitigated with PIN pads or biometric controls.

- *Poor visibility*   A facility may have exterior features that permit an unauthorized person to lurk about without being noticed. The person may be able to gain entry if he or she can discover a weakness before being noticed.

- *Inadequate video surveillance*   A facility lacking sufficient video surveillance may have one or more ingress/egress points, paths of approach, or corridors that are unwatched. This could invite intrusions by perpetrators who are able to identify these weaknesses.

- *Poorly protected Knox boxes*   The small metal safes used by fire departments for emergency entry into businesses are, in some cases, not well protected. Attackers may be able to remove them or force them open, giving attackers access to metal keys or keycards (often these are master keys that can open any door) that enable them to enter the building without signs of forced entry.

- *Poor security practices*   Team members with authorized access may also engage in insecure behaviors. The most common example of this is when an unauthorized person follows an authorized person into a secure facility. In some cases, this happens with the consent of the authorized person, who is simply being helpful by holding the door for someone who they assume is a fellow employee. This case is also known as a *piggybacking attack*. In other cases, the unauthorized individual catches the door before it closes behind the authorized person, without the authorized individual's knowledge. That case is known as a *tailgating attack*.

Physical Access Controls and Countermeasures

Several controls can be used to improve the physical security of a worksite, reducing the threat of intruders and resultant theft or damage. Some of these controls are:

- *Keycard systems*   Authorized persons are issued electronically activated ID cards that can be used to activate entry doors that are usually locked. These systems record the date and time that persons entered each door. Some keycard systems are also equipped with a PIN pad that requires the person to enter a numeric PIN before the door unlocks. This helps to prevent someone who finds a keycard from entering a facility. Keycard systems can also utilize biometrics such as palm scan, fingerprint scan, or iris scan. Note that older keycard system technology is vulnerable to keycard cloning, a technique used by an attacker to forge a copy of a keycard; this can occur if a keycard is momentarily located near a keycard cloning device that an attacker could carry and conceal.

- *Cipher locks*   These electronic or mechanical doors are equipped with combination locks. Only persons who know the combination may unlock the door. Some cipher locks can be equipped with different combinations for each person and also record each entry.

- *Fences, walls, and barbed wire*   These barriers are used to prevent unauthorized persons from approaching a building, keeping them at a safe distance away from the structure.

- *Bollards and crash gates*   These barriers prevent the entry of vehicles into protected areas. Some bollards can be retracted or removed when needed. Crash gates are hard barriers that lift into position, preventing the entry (or exit) of unauthorized vehicles, and can be lowered to permit authorized vehicles.

- *Video surveillance*   Video cameras, monitors, and recording systems can record the movement of persons in or near sensitive areas.

- *Visual notices*   This includes signs and placards that warn intruders that premises are monitored and protected.

- *Bug sweeping*   Because most covert listening devices emit radio frequency radiation, it is possible to detect them through the use of a bug sweeper.

- *Security guards*   These personnel control passage at entry points or roam building premises looking for security issues such as unescorted visitors.

- *Guard dogs*   Dogs assist security guards and can be used to apprehend and control trespassers.

A detailed risk analysis, including a study of physical facilities and access controls, should be used to determine which controls are appropriate for a facility for both workplace safety as well as protection of business and IT equipment.

Human Resources Security

The hearts of most organizations' business operations are not computers, machinery, or buildings, but people. People design and operate business processes; they design, build, and operate IT systems, and they support processes and systems and help to improve them over time. They interact, directly and indirectly, with vendors, partners, suppliers, and customers. And while people are an organization's greatest asset, they may also be a source of significant risk.

People are entrusted with access to sensitive information and entrusted to design and create information systems to manage sensitive information properly. But an employee in a position of trust can betray that trust and cause a significant amount of damage to the organization's operations and long-term reputation, whether acting out of ignorance, malice, or haste.

Trust is the key: organizations provide access to sensitive information, trusting that their employees will honor that trust and treat information properly. The trust is reciprocal: employees also trust that their employer will treat them with respect, pay them a fair salary, recognize their accomplishments, and give them opportunities to advance.

Organizations need to take several measures to mitigate human resource–related risks. These measures are described in the remainder of this section.

In nearly every case in this section, actions that organizations take regarding their employees should also apply to temporary and contract workers and to others who have access to their sensitive information.

Screening and Background Checks

Prior to hiring each employee, an organization should verify the facts that each candidate presents on his or her résumé or curriculum vitae. The confirmation of these and other important facts is commonly known as a background check, and may consist of:

- Verification of the candidate's identity
- Confirmation of the candidate's legal right to work in the employer's locale
- Verification of previous employment
- Verification of education
- Verification of professional licenses and certifications
- Investigation into the candidate's criminal history
- Investigation into the candidate's financial history
- Drug test
- Checks for associations with certain persons or groups (such as designated terrorist or hate groups)

Irregularities in any of these areas may be a signal to the employer that further investigation is required if the employer is still intent on hiring the candidate. The organization discovering irregularities in a candidate's background may also rescind a pending offer of employment or decide not to make an offer.

In addition to a background check, an employer will usually check references. This means that the employer will contact one or more professional colleagues to learn more about the candidate. The employer might also make inquiries through its network of professional acquaintances to gather intelligence about the candidate from people who are not references. For example, if a security manager is hiring a security analyst and receives a résumé from an employee at a local organization, the security manager could contact other known colleagues in the organization to determine whether any of them are familiar with the candidate. This can be a source of valuable information, since sometimes a candidate's references may be coached to say certain things or avoid certain topics.

WARNING   Employers frequently search professional and social networking sites such as LinkedIn, X, Instagram, and Facebook to gather additional intelligence on prospective employees. These and other networking sites often reveal more about a person's character than will be found on a résumé, application for employment, or references.

Another emerging trend in organizations is the practice of repeating background checks throughout an employee's tenure. This can help an employer discover certain facts about recent criminal convictions or significant financial events (such as judgments, collections, or bankruptcy) that may warrant action on the employer's part. Because of the cost associated with a background check, organizations that perform repeat background checks generally limit these checks to those vying for high-risk positions, such as those who handle or manage the use of financial resources.

> Organizations need to ensure that background screening is performed for temporary workers, contractors, and consultants. Some organizations perform these themselves, while others require that placement agencies or consulting firms screen their own candidates.

Job Descriptions

A *job description* is an employer's formal statement to an employee that says, "This is what we expect and require of you to perform this job." Employers should have formal job descriptions for each position in the organization. The main reason for this is to document formally the expectations that the organization has for each employee. These expectations should include:

- *Position title*   The job title (such as senior security auditor or database administrator)
- *Requirements*   The necessary education, skills, and work experience
- *Duties and responsibilities*   The tasks, projects, and other activities that the employee is expected to perform

The duties and responsibilities section should include a statement that says the employee is required to uphold all of the organization's policies (including security and privacy policies and code of ethics). The job description could list the major policies by name.

Employment Agreements

In locales that permit them, organizations should utilize written employment agreements with each employee. The employment agreement should clearly specify the terms and conditions of employment, including:

- *Duties*   The employment agreement should describe the employee's duties in his or her position. This may be similar to what is stated in the employee's job description.
- *Roles and responsibilities*   The employment agreement should define the employee's roles and responsibilities, as well as the responsibilities of the employer. This will be similar to what is in the job description.
- *Confidentiality*   The employee agrees to keep all company secrets confidential, even after termination of employment.
- *Compliance*   The employee must agree to comply with all applicable laws and regulations, as well as with all organization policies. The employment agreement should state the consequences of failing to comply with laws, regulations, and policies.
- *Termination*   The employment agreement should include the conditions and circumstances by which the organization or the employee can sever the agreement.

Some organizations require employees in certain positions to sign non-compete agreements as a way of protecting intellectual property and customer/supplier relationships.

Personnel Security Controls

Organizations need to enact several safeguards during the span of employment for each employee. These safeguards ensure that each employee's behavior is appropriate and that each employee is able to do only what is required of him or her. These safeguards include:

- *Periodic renewal of employment agreements* Documents signed at the time of hire, including nondisclosure, employment, security policy, code of conduct, and other agreements, should be renewed periodically. Organizations that employ this practice do this annually.

- *Repeat background checks* Occasionally, repeating background checks helps to ensure that each employee's background (criminal history in particular) is still acceptable. Some organizations do this only for higher-risk positions.

- *Access changes when transferred* Any employee who is transferred from one position to another should have his or her accesses for the former position removed. This helps to prevent the accumulation of privileges over time.

- *Awareness training* Employees should undergo periodic training on important topics, including security awareness training, so that they will continue to be aware of security procedures and requirements.

Policy and Discipline

During their service, employees, contractors, temps, and other workers are expected to comply with the organization's security policy and other policies. The organization's security management program needs to include monitoring and internal auditing to ensure that policies are adhered to. When policy violations occur, human resources will need to invoke its disciplinary action process as needed.

Disciplinary action that is related to security policy violations should not be treated differently from any other disciplinary matter. IT security may be asked to provide facts about the matter but should otherwise not be involved. Discipline is usually a matter between an employee's manager and the employee; human resources should be involved only if the matter is serious enough to warrant a letter in the employee's employment file, suspension, demotion, or termination of employment. The organization's legal department will be involved to protect the organization's treatment of the employee to respond when any employee's actions represent a violation of any law or legal agreement.

Equipment

Organizations should keep records regarding any equipment, software, licenses, or other assets that are entrusted to the employee, particularly when the asset will be used away from company premises, such as during travel or in the employee's home. Each time an asset is issued to an employee, a simple checkout document should be completed that describes the asset, the employee's name, the date issued, and an agreement that the asset will be returned to the employer on request. The employee should be required to sign this document, and a copy should be placed in his or her employment file.

If the employee transfers to another position or department or leaves the organization altogether, human resources should retrieve all equipment checkout forms and make sure that the employee returns each asset.

Transfers and Terminations

When employees are transferred from one position or department to another, they may be required to return certain assets entrusted to their care if they are no longer needed in the new role. Similarly, after transfer, an employee's access rights should be reviewed and any accesses from the old position that are not required in the new position should be removed. This is covered in more detail in the earlier section "Access Controls."

When an employee's employment is terminated, his or her access to information systems and business premises should be immediately revoked. All equipment, documents, software, and other assets in the employee's care should be returned and accounted for. The access badge and other identifying items should also be returned.

If an employee is being terminated for cause, the organization may elect to do a "look back" in electronic records to determine whether any recent activities represent risk to the organization. For example, a software developer who suspected an imminent termination may have appropriated a large cache of source code to be used in subsequent employment.

Auditing Access Controls

Auditing access controls requires a deep understanding of access controls, authentication mechanisms, and physical and environmental security. An IS auditor must be well-versed in these areas to effectively identify and mitigate potential security threats and vulnerabilities. This chapter provides comprehensive guidance on auditing logical access controls, network access paths, user access logs, and investigative procedures, ensuring that auditors can thoroughly evaluate and enhance the security posture of an organization.

Auditing Logical Access Controls

Auditing logical access controls requires attention to several key areas, including:

- Network access paths
- User access controls
- User access logs

- Investigative procedures
- Internet points of presence

These topics are discussed in depth in this section.

Auditing Network Access Paths

The IS auditor should conduct an independent review of the IT infrastructure to map out the organization's logical access paths. This will require considerable effort and may require the use of investigative and technical tools as well as specialized experts on IT network architecture. The reason for this is that the IT network may have undocumented access paths that are deliberately hidden from most personnel, or the network may have unexpected access paths resulting from incorrect configuration of even a single device. For instance, the IS auditor or a security specialist may discover a hidden, unauthorized Wi-Fi access point in an office or data center network, or the auditor may discover a network back door in the form of a firewall hole. The presence of deliberate or accidental back doors is a particular problem in larger organizations with highly complex network infrastructures that have many interconnections within the network and with external parties. Any of those connections could be a wide-open back door. Proving the absence of such a path is similar to the analogy of proving that there is no spider in the room where you are now.

The IS auditor should request network architecture and access documentation to compare what was discovered independently against existing documentation. The auditor will need to determine why any discrepancies exist.

Auditing Access Management

User access controls are often the only barrier between unauthorized parties and sensitive or valuable information. This makes the audit of user access controls particularly significant. Auditing user access controls requires keen attention to several key factors and activities in four areas:

- User access controls, to determine if the controls work as designed
- User access provisioning, to determine if provisioning processes are effective
- User access management, to determine if users have the correct level of access and that all permissions have been appropriately authorized
- Password management, to determine if passwords are effectively managed
- Employee transfers and terminations, to determine if accesses are managed and removed effectively

The IS auditor should not become so entrenched in the details of user access controls as to lose sight of the big picture. One of the responsibilities of the IS auditor is to continue to observe user access controls from the "big picture" perspective to determine if the entire set of controls *works together* to manage this important process effectively.

Auditing User Access Controls

Auditing user access controls requires attention to several factors, including:

- *Authentication*   The auditor should examine network and system resources to determine whether they require authentication or whether any resources can be accessed without first authenticating.

- *Authentication bypass*   The auditor should examine network and system resources to determine if it is possible to bypass user authentication methods. This may require the use of specialized tools or techniques. This needs to include penetration testing tools and application scanning tools to determine the presence of vulnerabilities that can be exploited to bypass authentication. For highly valued or sensitive data and applications that are Internet-accessible, hackers will certainly try these techniques in attempts to access and steal this information; the organization's security staff should regularly attempt to determine the presence of any such vulnerabilities.

- *Access violations*   The auditor should determine if systems, networks, and authentication mechanisms have the ability to log access violations. These usually exist in the form of system logs showing invalid login attempts, which may indicate intruders who are trying to log in to employee user accounts.

- *User account lockout*   The auditor should determine whether systems and networks have the ability to lock user accounts automatically that are the target of attacks. A typical system configuration will lock a user account after five unsuccessful login attempts within a short period. Such a control helps to thwart automated password-guessing attacks. Without such detective and preventive controls, intruders could write scripts to guess every possible password until a user's correct password is guessed correctly, thereby enabling an intruder to log in to a user account. Systems use different methods for unlocking such locked accounts: some will automatically unlock after a "cooling off period" (usually 30 minutes), or the user is required to contact the IT service desk and, after properly identifying him- or herself, get the account manually unlocked. The IS auditor should obtain policies, procedures, and records for this activity.

- *Intrusion detection and prevention*   The auditor should determine if there are any IDSs or IPSs that would detect authentication-bypass attempts. The auditor should examine these systems to determine whether they have up-to-date configurations and signatures, whether they generate alerts, and whether the recipients of alerts act upon them.

- *Dormant accounts*   The IS auditor should determine whether any automated or manual process exists to identify and close dormant accounts. Dormant accounts are user (or system) accounts that exist but are unused. These accounts represent a risk to the environment, as they represent an additional path between intruders and valuable or sensitive data. A dormant account could also be a back door, deliberately planted for future use. But chances are that most dormant accounts are user accounts that were assigned to persons who ended up not needing to access the environment or terminated employees whose accounts were never removed.

- *Shared accounts*   The IS auditor should determine if there are any shared user accounts; these are user accounts that are routinely (or even infrequently) used by more than one person. The principal risk with shared accounts is the inability to determine account-ability for actions performed with the account. Through the 1990s, information systems were routinely designed with shared user accounts, and many systems continue to use shared accounts. To the greatest extent possible, shared user accounts should be identified as audit exceptions and be replaced with individual user accounts.

- *System accounts*   The IS auditor should identify all system-level accounts on networks, systems, and applications. The purpose of each system account should be identified, and it should be determined whether each system account is still required (some may be artifacts of the initial implementation or of an upgrade or a migration). The IS auditor should determine who has the password for each system account, whether accesses by system accounts are logged, and who monitors those logs.

- *Jump servers*   The IS auditor should identify whether jump servers or other logical air gaps exist to protect critical systems and critical data from compromise. The IS auditor should determine who has access to jump servers, whether they can be bypassed, and whether they can be used to exfiltrate data.

Auditing Password Management

The IS auditor needs to examine password configuration settings on information systems to determine how passwords are controlled. Some of the areas requiring examination are:

- *Minimum length*   How many characters a password must have?

- *Complexity*   Whether passwords must contain various types of characters (lowercase alphabetic, uppercase alphabetic, numeric, symbols), whether dictionary words are permitted, and whether permutations of the user ID are permitted

- *Expiration*   How frequently passwords must be changed

- *History*   Whether former passwords may be used again

- *Minimum time between changes*   Whether users are permitted to change their passwords frequently (for instance, to cycle back to the familiar password they are used to)

- *Display*   Whether the password is displayed when logging in or when creating a new password

- *Transmission*   Whether the password is encrypted when transmitted over the network or is transmitted in plain text

- *Storage*   Whether the password is stored encrypted or hashed, or is stored in plain text; if the password is stored encrypted or in plain text, the IS auditor needs to determine who has access to it

In addition, auditing password management requires attention to several key technologies and activities:

- *Account lockout*   The IS auditor should determine whether systems automatically lock user accounts after a series of unsuccessful login attempts. The auditor should determine how locked user accounts are unlocked—whether automatically or manually—and whether these events are logged.

- *Access to encrypted passwords*   The IS auditor should determine if end users are able to access encrypted/hashed passwords, which would enable them to use password-cracking tools to discover other users' passwords and administrative passwords.

- *Password vaulting*   The IS auditor should determine if users are encouraged or required to use password vaulting tools for the safe storage of passwords and if administrative passwords are vaulted.

Auditing User Access Provisioning

Auditing the user access provisioning process requires attention to several key activities, including:

- *Access request processes*   The IS auditor should identify all user access request processes and determine if these processes are used consistently throughout the organization. The auditor should determine if there is one central user access request process, or if each environment has a separate process. The auditor should identify what data elements are required in a user access request—for instance, if the request specifies *why* and for *how long* the user needs this access. The auditor should examine business records to determine how access requests are documented.

- *Access approvals*   When studying the user access process, the IS auditor needs to determine how requests are approved and by what authority they are approved. The auditor should determine if system or data owners approve access requests, or if any accesses are ever denied (if no access requests are denied, the IS auditor should see if all requests are merely "rubber-stamped" without any real scrutiny). The auditor should examine business records to look for evidence of access approvals.

- *New employee provisioning*   The IS auditor should examine the new employee provisioning process to see how a new employee's user accounts are initially set up. The auditor should determine how a new employee's initial roles are determined: Does a new user have an established "template" of accesses, or do requests simply state, "Make John's access just like Susan's"? The auditor should determine if new employees' managers are aware of the access requests that their employees are given and if they are excessive. Furthermore, the auditor should determine if access to applications requires any initial training of the user of the application, or if the organization just "turns them loose" to figure out how the application is supposed to be used. The auditor also needs to determine how initial user credentials are communicated to the new employee and if the method is secure and reasonable.

- *Segregation of duties (SOD)*   The IS auditor should determine if the organization makes an effort to identify and mitigate segregation of duties issues. This may include whether there are any SOD matrices in existence and if they are actively used to make user access request decisions. Furthermore, the IS auditor should determine if the organization performs SOD reviews to identify persons who have access privileges within or among applications that would constitute SOD violations. The auditor should determine how violations are managed when they are found.

- *Access reviews*   The IS auditor should determine if there are any periodic access reviews and what aspects of user accounts are reviewed; this may include termination reviews, internal transfer reviews, SOD reviews, and dormant account reviews.

Auditing Employee Terminations

Auditing employee terminations requires attention to several key factors, including:

- *Termination process*   The IS auditor should examine the employee termination process and determine its effectiveness. This examination should include understanding how terminations are performed and how user account management personnel are notified of terminations. The auditor should identify specific security policies to determine how quickly user accounts should be terminated. The auditor should examine HR records to see if all employee terminations correspond to user account management termination records.

- *Timeliness*   The IS auditor should examine employee termination records and the records on individual information systems to determine if user accounts are locked or removed in a timely manner. Typically, user accounts should be locked or removed within one business day, but in environments with particularly valuable or sensitive information, employee terminations should be processed within minutes or hours to ensure that a departing employee cannot access systems immediately afterward (when passions often run high).

- *Access reviews*   The IS auditor should determine if any internal reviews of terminated accounts are performed, which would indicate a pattern of concern for effectiveness in this important activity. If such reviews are performed, the auditor should determine if any missed terminations are identified and if any process improvements are undertaken.

- *Contractor access and terminations*   In many organizations, a contractor's tenure is not managed by HR, so the IS auditor needs to determine how contractor access and termination is managed and if such management is effective. The classic problem with contractors is that it's sometimes difficult to determine precisely when a contractor no longer requires access to a system or network. The reason for this uncertainty lies in the nature of the contracted work: sometimes the contractor performs services sporadically or on request, and sometimes months or even years pass between these events. Furthermore, contractors are often hired and fired by internal managers without any notification to or tracking by HR. In light of these aspects, it can be difficult to determine the effectiveness of contractor-related access management.

Auditing Access Logs

Auditing access logs requires attention to several key points, including:

- *Access log contents* The IS auditor needs to determine what events are recorded in access logs. Events may include every user login and granular information, such as every program run and file accessed, or logs may include only invalid login attempts (or not even that). The IS auditor needs to understand the capabilities of the system being audited and determine if the right events are being logged, or if logging is suppressed on events that should and could be logged.

- *Centralized access logs* The IS auditor should determine whether the organization's access logs are aggregated or are stored on individual systems.

- *Access log protection* The IS auditor needs to understand access log protection mechanisms. Primarily, the auditor needs to determine if access logs can be altered, destroyed, or attacked to cause the system to stop logging events. For especially high-value and high-sensitivity environments, the IS auditor needs to determine if logs should be written to digital media that is unalterable, such as optical WORM (write once read many) media.

- *Access log review* The IS auditor needs to determine if there are policies, processes, or procedures regarding access log review. The auditor should determine if access log reviews take place, who performs them, how issues requiring attention are identified, and what actions are taken when necessary. Note that log reviews should be assigned to a particular role within the organization, preferably one that also does not have the ability to delete or alter logs. Conversely, anyone who might have the ability to delete or alter logs, such as someone with administrative privileges, should not be included in the log review role. This is a prime example of segregation of duties.

- *Access log retention* The IS auditor should determine how long access logs are retained by the organization and if they are backed up.

- *Access alerts* The IS auditor should determine whether automated mechanisms are in place that alert appropriate personnel of security alerts related to access logs. This includes but is not limited to alerts related to repeated unsuccessful attempts by a person to log in to a privileged account or instances where a critical system may not be able to log events any longer due to a malfunction, such as a filled disk, for example. The auditor should determine whether written procedures exist for such events, as well as records of their occurrence and response.

Auditing Incident and Investigative Procedures

Auditing incident management and investigative procedures requires attention to several key activities, including:

- *Investigation policies and procedures* The IS auditor should determine if there are any policies or procedures regarding security investigations. This would include who is responsible for performing investigations, where information about investigations is stored, and to whom the results of investigations are reported.

- *Computer crime investigations*   The IS auditor should determine if there are policies, processes, procedures, and records regarding computer crime investigations. The auditor should understand how internal investigations are transitioned to law enforcement.

- *Security incident response*   The IS auditor should examine security incident response policies, procedures, and plans to determine whether they are up-to-date. Interviewing incident responders to gauge their familiarity with incident response procedures can indicate the effectiveness of training and tabletop exercises. The auditor should examine some of the records from actual security incidents to see whether the responses were effective and whether the organization conducted post-incident reviews to identify process improvements.

- *Computer forensics*   The IS auditor should determine whether there are procedures for conducting computer forensics. The auditor should also identify tools and techniques that are available to the organization for the acquisition and custody of forensic data. The auditor should identify whether any employees in the organization have received computer forensics training and are qualified to perform forensic investigations. Because some organizations employ an outside firm for forensics assistance, the auditor should examine any contract in place to see whether this prearranged capability was properly established.

Auditing Internet Points of Presence

The IS auditor who is performing a comprehensive audit of an organization's system and network system needs to perform a "points of presence" audit to discover what technical information is available about the organization's Internet presence. Some of the aspects of this intelligence gathering including:

- *Search engines*   Google, Yahoo!, DuckDuckGo, Bing, and other search engines should be consulted to see what information about the organization is available. Searches should include the names of company officers and management, key technologists, and any internal-only nomenclature such as the names of projects.

- *Social networking sites*   Social networking sites such as LinkedIn, Facebook, Instagram, Glassdoor, and X should be searched to see what employees, former employees, and others are sharing about the organization. Any authorized or unauthorized "fan pages" should be searched as well.

- *Online sales sites*   Sites such as Craigslist and eBay should be searched to see if anything related to the organization is being sold online.

- *Domain names*   The IS auditor should verify contact information for known domain names as well as related domain names. For instance, for the organization *mycompany* . *com*, organizations should search for domain names such as *mycompany* . *net*, *mycompany* . *info*, and *mycompany* . *biz* to see if they are registered and what contents are available.

Justification of Online Presence

The IS auditor should examine business records to determine on what basis the organization established online capabilities such as email, Internet-facing websites, Internet e-commerce, Internet access for employees, and so on. These services add risk to the business and consume resources. The auditor should determine if a viable business case exists to support these services or if they exist as a "benefit" for employees.

Auditing Environmental Controls

Auditing environmental controls requires knowledge of building mechanical and electrical systems as well as fire codes. The IS auditor needs to be able to determine if such controls are effective and if they are *cost*-effective. Auditing environmental controls requires attention to these and other factors and activities, including:

- *Power conditioning*   The IS auditor should determine if power conditioning equipment, such as UPSs, line conditioners, surge protectors, or motor generators, are used to clean electrical anomalies such as noise, surges, sags, and so on. The auditor should examine procedures and records to see how frequently this equipment is inspected and maintained and if this is performed by qualified personnel.

- *Backup power*   The IS auditor should determine if backup power is available via electric generators or UPSs and how frequently they are tested. He or she should examine maintenance records to see how frequently these components are maintained and if this is done by qualified personnel.

- *Heating, ventilation, and air conditioning*   The IS auditor should determine if HVAC systems are providing adequate temperature and humidity levels and if they are monitored. Also, the auditor should determine if HVAC systems are properly maintained and if qualified persons do this.

- *Water detection*   The IS auditor should determine if any water detectors are used in rooms where computers are used. If so, the auditor should determine how frequently these are tested and if they are monitored.

- *Fire detection and suppression*   The IS auditor should determine if fire detection equipment is adequate, if staff members understand its function, and if the equipment is tested. The auditor should determine how frequently fire suppression systems are inspected and tested and if the organization has emergency evacuation plans and conducts fire drills. The auditor should examine the inspection tags on fire suppression equipment, including sprinkler valves and fire extinguishers, to see if their inspections are up-to-date. He or she should check the walls in data centers to ensure that they extend all the way to the real floor and ceiling and not merely down to the raised floor or up to the dropped ceiling.

- *Cleanliness*   The IS auditor should examine data centers for cleanliness. IT equipment air filters and the inside of some IT components should be examined to see if there is an accumulation of dust and dirt.

The IS auditor may need to consult with electrical and mechanical engineers to determine if power conditioning, backup power, HVAC systems, and fire detection and suppression equipment are in good working order and are adequately sized to meet the organization's needs.

Auditing Physical Security Controls

Auditing physical security controls requires knowledge of natural and human-made hazards, physical security controls, and access control systems.

Auditing Siting and Marking

Auditing building siting and marking requires attention to several key factors and features, including:

- *Proximity to hazards* The IS auditor should estimate the building's distance to natural and human-made hazards, such as:
    - Dams
    - Rivers, lakes, and canals
    - Natural gas and petroleum pipelines
    - Water mains and pipelines
    - Earthquake faults
    - Areas prone to landslides
    - Volcanoes
    - Severe weather such as hurricanes, cyclones, and tornadoes
    - Flood zones
    - Military bases
    - Airports
    - Railroads
    - Freeways

    The IS auditor should determine if any risk assessment regarding hazards has been performed and if any compensating controls that were recommended have been carried out.

- *Marking* The IS auditor should inspect the building and surrounding area to see if building(s) containing information-processing equipment identify the organization. Marking may be visible on the building itself but also on signs or parking stickers on vehicles.

Auditing Physical Access Controls

Auditing physical access controls requires attention to several key factors discussed in this section.

Physical Barriers

This category includes fencing, walls, barbed/razor wire, bollards, entry control points, and crash gates. The IS auditor needs to understand how these are used to control access to the facility and determine their effectiveness.

Surveillance

The IS auditor needs to understand how video and human surveillance are used to control and monitor access. He or she needs to understand how (and if) video is recorded and reviewed and if it is effective in preventing or detecting incidents.

Guards and Dogs

The IS auditor needs to understand the use and effectiveness of security guards and guard dogs. Processes, policies, procedures, and records should be examined to understand required activities and how they are carried out.

Keycard Systems

The IS auditor needs to understand how keycard systems are used to control access to the facility. Some points to consider include:

- *Controls*   Whether additional controls such as PIN pads or biometrics are utilized for critical locations
- *Work zones*   Whether the facility is divided into security zones and which persons are permitted to access which zones
- *Records*   Whether keycard systems record personnel movement
- *Provisioning*   What processes and procedures are used to issue keycards to employees (see the earlier section, "Auditing Logical Access Controls," for more details)
- *Monitoring*   What processes and records are in place to monitor the keycard system for access violations
- *Access reviews*   Whether the organization performs reviews of access logs and user access lists
- *Visitors*   How visitors are handled in terms of building access
- *Incidents*   What procedures are in place to respond to access incidents

Summary

Access management is a critical activity in a security management program. Access controls are often the only thing standing between valuable or sensitive information and parties who want to access it. Access management consists of several separate but related processes, including user access management, network access management, and access log review.

Physical and environmental controls are required to safeguard the physical safety and reliability of computing and network equipment. These controls include power system improvements; heating, cooling, and humidity controls; fire control systems; and physical access controls, such as keycard systems, fences, walls, and video surveillance.

Exam Essentials

Know the role of access controls in an enterprise cybersecurity program.   Access controls are technology-based methods of controlling access to an information-based resource. They must be actively managed by authorized staff. Logical access controls determine whether and how subjects (persons, programs, computers) can access objects (systems, data). Examples include user authentication (e.g., user ID and password) and service access controls (e.g., firewalls). Access control models include Mandatory Access Control (MAC) and Discretionary Access Control (DAC), each with its own advantages and disadvantages.

Explain access control threats and vulnerabilities.   Threats to access controls include malware, eavesdropping, logic bombs, back doors, scanning attacks, and race conditions. Vulnerabilities include unpatched systems, default system settings and passwords, incorrect permission settings, and vulnerabilities in utilities and applications. Organizations must mitigate these through practices like system hardening, regular patch management, and vulnerability scanning.

Describe the authentication process and techniques.   The authentication process includes identification (e.g., providing a username), authentication (e.g., entering a password), and authorization (e.g., checking permissions). Authentication techniques involve three factors: something you know (passwords), something you are (biometrics), and something you have (smartcards). Multifactor authentication combines techniques from different factors for added security.

Understand the importance of provisioning and deprovisioning user accounts.   Provisioning involves creating authentication credentials and granting appropriate authorizations for new users. Deprovisioning involves removing access when users leave or transfer roles. Effective processes prevent unauthorized access and potential security risks.

Explain the significance of account monitoring.   Regular user account reviews and continuous monitoring for suspicious activity are crucial. Practices include reviewing permissions for accuracy, detecting unauthorized use, and employing behavior-based monitoring to flag risky logins, unusual network locations, and deviations from normal behavior.

Explain third-party access management.   Managing third-party access involves assessing and mitigating risks associated with granting external entities access to sensitive information. Organizations should use detailed legal agreements, perform security assessments, and monitor third-party activities to maintain security.

Describe environmental and physical security controls. Environmental controls include reliable power, temperature and humidity controls, and fire detection and suppression systems. Physical security controls, such as keycard systems, surveillance, and barriers, prevent unauthorized access to facilities and protect valuable equipment and information.

Understand human resources security measures. Measures like background checks, job descriptions, employment agreements, and regular security training help ensure employees act responsibly and securely. Proper handling of employee transfers and terminations is essential to maintain security.

Explain auditing access controls. Auditing access controls involves evaluating logical access controls, user access provisioning, password management, and employee termination processes. Auditors must also review access logs, incident response procedures, and physical and environmental controls to ensure comprehensive security.

Review Questions

1. A fire sprinkler system has water in its pipes, and sprinkler heads emit water only if the ambient temperature reaches 220°F. What type of system is this?

   A. Deluge

   B. Post-action

   C. Wet pipe

   D. Pre-action

2. An organization is building a data center in an area that experiences frequent power outages. The organization cannot tolerate power outages. What power system controls should be selected?

   A. Uninterruptible power supply and electric generator

   B. Uninterruptible power supply and batteries

   C. Electric generator

   D. Electric generator and line conditioning

3. An auditor has discovered several errors in user account management: many terminated employees' computer accounts are still active. What is the best course of action?

   A. Improve the employee termination process.

   B. Shift responsibility for employee terminations to another group.

   C. Audit the process more frequently.

   D. Improve the employee termination process and audit the process more frequently.

4. An auditor has discovered that several administrators in an application share an administrative account. What course of action should the auditor recommend?

   A. Implement activity logging on the administrative account.

   B. Use several named administrative accounts that are not shared.

   C. Implement a host-based intrusion detection system.

   D. Require each administrator to sign nondisclosure and acceptable-use agreements.

5. Tom is building a multifactor authentication system that requires users to enter a passcode and then verifies that their face matches a photo stored in the system. What two factors is this system using?

   A. Something you know and something you have

   B. Something you have and somewhere you are

   C. Something you have and something you are

   D. Something you know and something you are

6. Frank is evaluating the effectiveness of a biometric system. Which one of the following metrics would provide him with the best measure of the system's effectiveness?

A. IRR

B. CER

C. FAR

D. FRR

7. Gary is logging in to a system and, after entering his username and password, is providing his fingerprint to gain access. What step of the identity and access management process is he performing?

A. Identification

B. Authorization

C. Authentication

D. Accounting

8. John is designing a system that will allow users from Acme Corporation, one of his organization's vendors, to access John's accounts payable system using the accounts provided by Acme Corporation. What type of authentication system is John attempting to design?

A. Single sign-on

B. Federated authentication

C. Transitive trust

D. Multifactor authentication

9. An auditor has reviewed the access privileges of some employees and has discovered that employees with longer terms of service have excessive privileges. What can the auditor conclude from this?

A. Employee privileges are not being removed when they transfer from one position to another.

B. Long-time employees are able to guess other users' passwords successfully and add to their privileges.

C. Long-time employees' passwords should be set to expire more frequently.

D. The organization's termination process is ineffective.

10. An organization needs to ensure the confidentiality and integrity of data being sent over the network. Which of the following methods would best achieve this?

A. Using strong passwords

B. Implementing encryption protocols

C. Regularly updating network hardware

D. Conducting frequent audits

11. What is the primary purpose of conducting regular user account reviews?
    A. To ensure compliance with company policies
    B. To provide user training on new software
    C. To identify and revoke unnecessary permissions
    D. To prepare for external audits

12. What is the most significant potential risk of not performing a thorough risk assessment before granting third-party access?
    A. Increased operational costs
    B. Reduced employee productivity
    C. Unauthorized data access and potential data breaches
    D. Overuse of system resources

13. An organization's remote access requires a user ID and one-time password token. What weakness does this scheme have?
    A. Someone who finds a one-time password token could log in as the user by guessing the password.
    B. Someone who finds a one-time password token could log in as the user by guessing the user ID.
    C. Someone who knows the user ID could derive the password.
    D. Someone who is able to eavesdrop on the authentication can log in later using a replay attack.

14. Which access control model is most suitable for an environment that requires strict control over who can access certain types of data, without the possibility of user modification?
    A. Discretionary Access Control (DAC)
    B. Role-Based Access Control (RBAC)
    C. Mandatory Access Control (MAC)
    D. Attribute-Based Access Control (ABAC)

15. An organization has hundreds of remote locations containing valuable equipment and needs to enact a secure access control system. The locations do not have electricity. What is the best choice for an access control method that can be implemented at these locations?
    A. Keycards
    B. Metal keys
    C. Cipher locks
    D. Video surveillance

16. Which type of malware is specifically designed to activate at a certain date and time, causing damage to data?

  A. Virus

  B. Worm

  C. Trojan horse

  D. Logic bomb

17. What is the primary purpose of the principle of least privilege in access control?

  A. To increase system performance

  B. To ensure users have enough privileges to perform any task

  C. To minimize the risk of unauthorized access

  D. To simplify the user access management process

18. Your organization needs to provide secure, remote access to employees who work at home. What technology can best assist with this need?

  A. VPN

  B. IPS

  C. CASB

  D. DLP

19. You are auditing a network firewall and determine that it is designed in a "fail open" configuration. What will happen if the firewall fails?

  A. It will allow any traffic to enter and leave the network.

  B. It will allow no traffic to enter or leave the network.

  C. It will continue to enforce its last known good configuration.

  D. It will alert administrators to the failure and await instructions.

20. Which environmental control is crucial for protecting data centers from fire damage while minimizing damage to equipment?

  A. Wet pipe sprinkler system

  B. Dry pipe sprinkler system

  C. Inert gas fire suppression system

  D. Portable fire extinguishers

Chapter 9

Conducting a Professional Audit

The goals and structure of this chapter are slightly different from the rest of this book. Whereas Chapters 1 through 6 convey information to the CISA candidate, in this chapter, the focus shifts to the professional world of the information systems (IS) auditor. It addresses the nature of different professional engagements common to IS auditors. We review the stages of, and responsibilities involved in, performing a risk-based IS audit for both internal and external auditors. This chapter also serves to introduce and frame examples of professional situations that may challenge an auditor.

This chapter reviews the process of performing an IS audit, and in doing so, it identifies how sections of the study materials in this book can be applied in the real world. By bringing the subject of conducting an IS audit "up a level," we provide associations between concepts found in the main chapters in this book so that you have real-life examples of a number of these concepts. These real-world descriptions should help solidify the material you learned from the rest of this book and should hopefully assist you in recalling information while studying and sitting for the test.

Further, you can use this chapter as a guide (or adapt it to create a checklist) when performing or participating in an IS audit. The material here is based on methods used in professional environments that have succeeded in achieving high client satisfaction ratings and delivering quality audits.

Finally, this chapter is designed to benefit both the auditor and the auditee. The more familiar the organization is with the audit process, the better the experience for everyone, and the better the outcome.

To employ an automotive metaphor, the study material in the main chapters of this book may teach you about how a vehicle functions and relates to the road, whereas this chapter teaches you about driving.

Understanding the Audit Cycle

The IS audit cycle is central to the profession of an IS auditor. The cycle itself could be executed by a single auditor, or the responsibilities could be distributed to individuals making up an audit team. In some professional situations, one or more sections discussed here may be unnecessary. The IS audit cycle described here is not the *only* cycle an IS auditor may perform, as the needs of different situations may require alternative procedures or approaches.

Candidates for the CISA exam will have had some experience with IS auditing, but not all candidates will have had visibility into the whole end-to-end business process. In this chapter, the stages of the cycle are illustrated as they would be considered by someone managing a professional audit.

For IS auditors early in their professional career, this chapter unveils some of the activities that their supervisors may perform. Understanding these phases will help new auditors see the big picture, deliver meaningful work, and hopefully hasten their advancement.

How the IS Audit Cycle Is Discussed

Some components of an IS audit cycle are uniform, regardless of the size of the client and the scope of the audit. Each stage discussed is a valid consideration while performing a moderately complex audit project. This chapter provides a relevant audit skeleton, regardless of whether the auditor serves as an internal auditor within an organization or is brought in from outside the organization being audited. This chapter is relevant for working on a variety of audit services, including PCI DSS, SOC 1/SOC 2, SOX, ISO, OMB Circular A-123 auditing, financial audits, internal audits, report writing, compliance audits, and other services.

Although the focus is on executing an audit involving control testing, many project stages will apply when performing other projects where an IS auditor's skills are required. It is not meant to be a complete reference when a project's needs go beyond the scope of this chapter. Additional procedures will be required to deliver services supporting other functions, such as enterprise-wide risk assessments, project life cycle evaluations, and disaster recovery planning.

For the sake of "telling the story," terms from outside of the CISA exam terminology are introduced in this chapter.

NOTE We will most often use the term "control testing," which is synonymous with auditing. "Testing" is the IS auditor's vernacular for auditing. It simply means to put a control to the test to see whether it is designed properly and operating to effectively manage business risks. The effectiveness of a control is the opinion that the IS auditor develops after performing one or more tests, and it can change year over year, depending on developing technologies, laws and regulations, and auditor judgment. The outcome of the test of a control will help the auditor know whether the control is being operated properly and that it contributes to the integrity of the control objective. Depending on the nature of the audit procedures being performed, a single instance of the control can be tested, or a sample of transactions could be audited to ensure that controls are consistently being executed.

"Client" and Other Terms in This Chapter

To ensure that the examples in this chapter are clear to the reader, this section explains how an experienced auditor's vernacular employs the versatile term "client" contextually. In this chapter, the terms "client" and "client organization" refer to the auditee business entity or departments within an audit project's scope.

- **Client:** The organization, department(s), and individual persons being audited.
- **Client organization:** The broader legal entity being audited; in some cases, this can be defined as subdepartments within a larger organization.

To say "in front of the client" can refer to being with the client outside the building, in a meeting, or sitting with a control owner (defined further later).

More specific terms are employed for parties encountered within client organizations. These terms will assist in this discussion of the IS auditing process. In this chapter, I use the following definitions to categorize client personnel as having the following roles:

- **Audit sponsor:** The person or committee within the client organization that has determined that the audit needs to be performed. When regulations require audits, the lead executive—commonly the CFO (chief financial officer), CIO (chief information officer), CAE (chief audit executive), CRO (chief risk officer), or CCO (chief compliance officer)—over the group being audited is most often the audit sponsor. If, however, an audit is required to fulfill a private legal obligation, such as a contract with a customer, the business unit leader, who is the auditee, may be the audit sponsor.
- **Audit audience:** The party that will review and employ the information contained in a report. In the case of an internal audit, this is most likely the organization's board of directors and/or audit committee, whereas for PCI DSS, or SOC 1/SOC 2 reporting purposes, this would more likely be the external auditors or customers of client organizations.
- **Primary contact:** The person who serves as the initial point of communication between the audit team and the client organization's control managers and owners. The primary contact has the authority to schedule meetings and address issues and may be provided with regular status reports. This individual does not need to be a control owner or manager, and most mature organizations will designate a primary contact to ensure an efficient and effective audit process.
- **Control owners:** The person(s) performing manual control activities or maintaining the successful performance of automated controls.
- **Control managers:** The members of management who oversee control owners. They are ultimately responsible for ensuring the successful execution of control activities and have a role in remediating issues discovered during testing, particularly when remediation calls for changes to business processes or additional resources.

"Client" as a Term for Internal Auditors

The term "client" usually implies that the auditee and auditor are not under the same roof. In this chapter, "client" means the auditee—whether an audit is performed by individuals external or internal to the organization. A department within a larger organization may be the audit "client." (As an example, in an audit focused on reviewing procurement practices, the procurement department is viewed as the "client.")

With internal auditing, though the audit cycle will lack a bidding process, contract negotiation, and engagement letters, an auditor within an organization is still an independent party. Within this chapter, if there are points in the auditing process where there is a recognizable difference between performing work internally as opposed to externally, the difference is noted.

Overview of the IS Audit Cycle

This section describes the IS audit cycle and covers background information that may be pertinent to an auditor's engagement. It includes a discussion on the origination of audits and some of the particularities of different engagement types. Different reasons are addressed regarding why a client organization may initiate a project requiring the assistance of an IS auditor.

The IS audit cycle is a standardized process, in that established steps are agreed upon as providing the basic structure for performing an IS audit. Common milestones have been established. IS audit projects will involve some, if not all, of these milestones, depending on the maturity of the organization and the resources available to support the audit. This chapter explores the details of these milestones and activities, but at a high level, they can be viewed as follows:

- Project origination
- Engagement letter or audit charter
- Ethics and independence
- New project launch
- Audit plan development
- Test plan development
- Pre-audit activities
- Resource planning
- Control testing activities
- Audit opinions development
- Audit recommendations development
- Supporting documentation management
- Audit results delivery
- Management response to audit findings

- Audit closure
- Audit follow-up

Each of these stages is covered in more detail in this section.

Project Origination

This section addresses the origination of IS audit projects. Project origination is the beginning of the IS audit cycle. The following service areas are included in this discussion, although some of these service areas are not fully covered in this chapter:

- External attestations
- Internal audits
- Incident response and disaster response
- Life cycle reviews
- Governance reviews
- Staffing arrangements

This chapter surveys how the need for audit work in each service area is identified and originates as a project, and it continues with a discussion of how an auditor's help is solicited and the auditor's common roles in supporting certain projects.

 Central to the risk-based audit approach is the determination of audit objectives, performance of a risk assessment, and determination of audit scope. In some situations, part or all of these stages are performed before an audit project is launched. If persons outside of this process are performing the audit project, audit team members should have a clear understanding of how these stages lead to the audit.

External Attestations

An *attestation* is a statement made by an auditor that certifies or affirms the results of an audit. Often, an attestation takes the form of a letter or report that is signed by an owner or partner in an auditing firm (or by the leader of the audit department in the case of an internal audit).

Many organizations are required to have an audit based on government regulations or contractual obligations. External auditors provide results free from the pressures of a management reporting relationship. Strict ethical and sometimes legal guidelines prohibit relationships that can impair independence, whether in fact or in appearance. These independence measures seek to remove obstacles to an auditor's objectivity when confirming the existence of practices and assessing the operation of controls within their organization—think of this like the idea of testing for conflicts related to the segregation of duties.

Examples of external attestations include:

- Financial audits
- Bank system control testing
- Lending or equity arrangements
- SOC 1/SOC 2 and other attestation audits
- Certifications such as ISO/IEC 27001, PCI DSS, and PA DSS

For external attestation services, a bid solicitation process is most commonly followed. The client organization issues a request for proposal (RFP) from external parties. The RFP will identify, at a high level, the scope of the work and some of the technologies involved. Proposals are collected and reviewed by the client organization, often including the audit sponsor and/or primary contact. Proposals are vetted for approach, skills, terms, fees, expenses, and other considerations. The party selected by this process is then brought in to negotiate a contract (discussed further in the section, "Engagement Letters and Audit Charters").

As an alternative to an RFP, an organization can issue a request for information (RFI) to solicit information from candidate audit firms to understand their capabilities and approach. This information can help an organization develop an RFP or proceed to an auditor selection.

Management's Need for an Independent Third Party

In addition to externally required attestations, the executive management of an organization can initiate projects for outside auditors. It is not uncommon for management to decide that an independent third party should handle a task due to internal resource limitations as well as a new or emerging risk and audit area. Management may have many reasons for hiring independent third parties to perform audits and reviews, some of which are:

- Freedom from institutional bias
- Fresh perspective (a new set of eyes)
- Professional perspective, if a certified or accredited auditor is employed
- Not employing the necessary skills in-house
- Answering inquiries by external parties (that is, performing agreed-upon procedures)
- Support management decision making (such as "buy versus build" and system selection decisions)
- Gain access to advice from outside professionals with deep industry experience

Projects requested by management are likely to report to a CFO, CIO, CAE, CRO, or CCO. Such projects may involve testing that supports goals that are not standard audit goals. It is important for auditors to be clear with clients regarding objectives and scope and how to address requests for additional work, including any independence concerns.

Internal Audits

Internal audit (IA) departments usually report to the organization's audit committee or board of directors (or a similar governing entity). The IA department usually has close ties with and a "dotted line" reporting relationship to finance leadership to manage day-to-day activities. This department will launch projects at the request and/or approval of the governing entity and, to a degree, members of executive management.

Regulation plays a large role in internal audit work. For example, public companies, banks, and government organizations are all subject to a great deal of regulation, much of which requires regular business controls and IS control testing. Management, as part of their risk management strategy, also requires this testing. External reporting of the results of internal auditing is sometimes necessary.

A common internal audit cycle consists of several categories of projects:

- Risk assessments and audit planning (typically annual in nature)
- Cyclical control testing (SOX and A-123, for example)
- Review of existing control structures
- Operational and IS audits

The central function of an internal audit department is the entity-wide risk assessment process. Annually, an attempt is made to identify and weigh all risks to an organization. This process results in ranking the organization's "areas of greatest risk" and is provided to the governing entity (commonly the audit committee) to review and determine the scope of the organization's internal audit function. Areas of greater risk warrant more attention by the governing entity. They may choose to have the scope of the IA department's work address these areas.

It is common for the IA department to maintain a multiyear plan (as discussed in Chapter 3, "IT Life Cycle Management"), in which it maintains a schedule or rotation of audits. The audit plan is shared with the governing entity, along with the risk assessment document, and the governing entity is asked to review and approve the IA department's plan annually. The governing entity may seek to include specific reviews in the IA department's audit plan at this point. When an audit plan is approved, the IA department's tasks for the year (and tentative tasks for future years) are determined.

The IIA (Institute of Internal Auditors) has excellent guidance for audit planning at https://na.theiia.org.

Even if the risk assessment is carried out by other personnel, IS auditors are often included in a formal risk assessment process. Specific skills are needed to communicate with an organization's IT personnel regarding technology risks. IS auditors will use information from management to identify, evaluate, and rank an organization's main business and technology risks. The outcome of this process may result in IT-related specific audits within the IA department's audit plan. The governing entity may select areas that are financial or operational and that are heavily supported by information systems.

Internal audits may be launched using a project charter, which formalizes the project to audit sponsors, the auditors, and the managers of the department(s) subject to the audit.

 Some governing entities may not have staff that understands technology risks. IS auditors may find they are educating governing entities on the nature of the risks they face.

Cyclical Control Testing

A great deal of effort has recently been expended getting organizations to execute a control testing cycle. Most frequently, these practices support the integrity of controls in financially relevant processes. Public corporations have needed to comply with Sarbanes–Oxley Section 404 requirements, and U.S. government organizations have been subject to OMB Circular A-123, compliance with the Federal Information Security Modernization Act (FISMA), and other similar requirements. Countries outside of the United States have instituted similar control testing requirements for publicly traded companies and governmental organizations. Many industries, such as banking, insurance, and health care, are likewise required to perform control testing due to industry-specific regulations.

Financial leadership is required to affirm that control testing cycles are operating successfully and that controls surrounding financial reporting are operating effectively. This requirement includes control testing by qualified and independent auditors (common regulations require that a portion of the control testing be conducted by an external IS auditor).

Organizations employ software tools to assist with tracking control testing. These systems track the execution and success of control tests performed as part of a testing cycle and can frequently manage to archive supporting evidence. Organizations may employ IS auditors to implement a system for tracking control testing.

Many organizations have functioning internal audit departments. Most internal auditors come from a financial background and have limited knowledge of the practice of IS auditing. Organizations that lack an existing internal audit department may outsource their whole internal audit function via the RFP process. IA departments may seek to augment their staff with IS auditors to cover internal shortcomings. Both staffing models are common, especially in less mature organizations and control environments.

Establishing Control Testing Cycles

Young or growing organizations may not have established or documented internal control testing cycles. IS auditors, working in conjunction with individuals focused on manual controls, will participate in the establishment of control testing. The auditor produces documentation of controls through a series of meetings with management. During the process, auditors will develop process and control documentation and confirm their accuracy with control owners through the performance of control walk-throughs.

These engagements are likely to occur when companies prepare to go public. Such companies need to comply with Sarbanes–Oxley Section 404 requirements, which involve documenting controls and performing a test of existence, also known as a "test set of 1/test of design" or a "walk-through," for each identified key control. Key controls are controls that would help to prevent and/or detect a material misstatement in an organization's financial processes, or said more plainly, these are the controls responsible for ensuring that the financial statements of public companies can be relied on.

Private companies often maintain SOX-equivalent documentation to retain the option of seeking public financing, or when lenders or private investors require it. Many organizations will find external resources to assist in the documentation and testing of applicable internal controls.

When auditors are bidding on engagements for establishing control testing cycles, there are uncertainties regarding the amount of time this process will take. Here are factors that may add unexpected amounts of time:

- Functions prove more complex or disorganized.

- Documentation provided by management could be out of date or nonexistent.

- Auditors may be needed to produce control procedures where none exist.

- Control weaknesses and failures may be uncovered, requiring unplanned remediation.

- Fraud may be uncovered, resulting in project interruptions and potential turnover of control owners.

If management has documented procedures or experience with control testing, auditors will need less effort to complete this process.

Budgets and fee arrangements for these engagements should keep in mind how the degree of effort required may not be uncovered until auditors are in the field.

Reviewing Existing Controls

Control structures change as an organization and the regulatory landscape change. Outside the organization, a change in regulations may change the focus of certain processes and control testing. Guidance covering SOX and A-123 auditing has changed over time. For example, changes over time by the American Institute of Certified Public Accountants (AICPA) and other organizations have allowed a greater degree of reliance on monitoring controls. Within an organization, business objectives may change, and with them the technologies and procedures. New systems or new lines of business may change which controls are most material. IS auditors are often asked to review and update the individual controls within a control testing cycle. They will update wording and may advise management on how to bring the control testing closer in line with external guidance.

Early SOX compliance efforts often led to long lists of control activities that would be considered excessive by today's standards. Older control structures predate more recent directives, causing an excessive operational and testing burden for the organization. Business, process, and technology changes may have left parts of a control structure obsolete or not yet included. Organizations often seek third-party assistance in performing control rationalization—updating and "streamlining" their list of key control activities to realign their controls with both current regulatory directives and recent risk assessments. IS auditors may be tasked with updating control documentation as an additional service while performing control tests.

Operational Audits

Operational audits are typically internal audits. These audits involve internal reporting to management and/or an organization's governing committees and can cover any area of the business. These reports are done at the request of a member of executive management or the governing entity and may originate from the discovery of an issue in the business, the annual risk assessment, or the established audit planning cycle. These audits often will be performed over a limited period, have a clearly specified scope, and result in issuing an internal audit report.

Operational audits require an auditor with experience in the function being audited. Many organizations will want to grow their internal audit function from within their ranks so their auditors have a functional knowledge of the departments they audit. If an organization lacks an internal audit function, they often will seek audit professionals with experience in their industry. Organizations will either hire additional auditors with skills in functions being audited or partake in a staff augmentation arrangement where the auditors with specific skills assist on a specific audit project.

Audits focused on operational elements will employ whatever methods of testing or analysis support the audit's objectives and may not include control testing. Examples of the objectives for operational and IS audits could include the following:

- Evaluate procedures within a department.
- Perform process reengineering within a complex function.
- Test compliance with policies.
- Prepare for a system implementation.
- Uncover internal inefficiencies.
- Perform data analysis for management decision making.
- Identify improvement opportunities for existing systems.
- Detect fraud and the risk of fraud.

When an operational area relies heavily on supporting systems, it is common for an IS auditor to own part or all of the cycle of performing operational audits. For certain operational audits, an IS auditor's background in the operation is important. Familiarity with the business of the department and the procedures performed is often required. A project could require an IS auditor with a financial background or experience with certain financial business processes.

Operational audits requested by management are more likely to experience scope expansion during the audit than other audits. The audit sponsor may determine that a more thorough analysis is needed. Both client and audit management may need to be made aware of resource constraints or competing priorities that may be deferred because of including additional work in the audit's scope.

Project Life Cycle Reviews

Project life cycles are a central function of an IT department, and project management practices can come under review as part of risk assessments and other projects. Areas frequently addressed in project life cycle reviews include:

- Tasks supporting implementing or upgrading existing software
- System development life cycle (SDLC) methodology
- Asset management
- Change management
- Patch management of critical systems
- Configuration management

IT projects often involve a great investment on the part of an organization. The success of these projects can be critical to an organization's future well-being and may have a bearing on members of management's future with an organization. Management has a strong interest in ensuring that their investment in the project goes well.

An IS auditor can assess life cycle reviews to cover an IT department from several different perspectives. SDLC reviews can cover segregation of duties of project personnel, quality assurance measures, or a review of issues tracking tools and associated controls. Reviews may be designed to assess whether certain project management best practices are followed, such as maintaining project plans and meeting minutes, performing and documenting appropriate user-level testing, and capturing approvals on customization design documents. These audits may assess compliance with management's policies in addition to looking at common industry practices.

Examples of possible life cycle projects include the following:

- An organization decided to implement new financial accounting software. Financial auditors determine the change to systems is material and seek to gain an understanding of controls in the process of implementation. An IS auditor is called in to review project documentation and speak with key project personnel. The auditor will review scope documents, approvals for customizations, segregation of duties/responsibilities, test plan records, issues tracking, completeness and accuracy of any data conversions, and other key records from the process. The IS auditor reports to the financial audit team whether the process is well controlled, and the audit team incorporates this information into their test plan development.

- An internal audit department may perform an IS review that addresses the controls in an organization's SDLC to ensure that proper review, approvals, version retention, and segregation of duties are performed according to control documentation.

- An organization is experiencing delays on an implementation project. Management is not sure whether this is due to the performance of the project manager or because of an underestimation of the project requirements. An independent reviewer is asked to speak with persons involved in the project and review project documents to provide feedback.

- A government agency is preparing to comply with new legislation and hopes to clarify the scope of compliance projects. The new legislation will result in increased traffic through their agency. Agency management seeks to learn whether procedures and technology are prepared for the increase in traffic. They don't have the bandwidth to task their staff with the review, so they hire outside reviewers to report on what changes are necessary and what changes may be desired.

- An organization's network security has been successfully compromised by ethical hackers ("ethical hackers" is a term signifying a professional services firm hired to test an organization's security controls). Management has committed to performing remediation activities to prevent future intrusions. IT management is strengthening existing controls and pursuing projects that aim to institute new control measures. IS auditors are brought in at the request of executive management to validate IT management's claims regarding the successful implementation of control measures.

 NOTE　Life cycle reviews may be covered in part by methods discussed in this chapter, but some reviews may require procedures not addressed here.

Implementation Problems

Problems from system implementations and data conversions are common, and management may be needed to remediate the issues. Client management may seek the help of IS auditors as additional "bandwidth."

Here is an example: A company is acquiring smaller competitors and migrating its information systems into one consolidated system. Attempts to report using migrated data show problems in the underlying data. Auditors are tasked with learning about the process and controls related to loading datasets onto the system correctly. The auditor will then test report data and attempt to identify the specific problems.

These tasks can be handled by IS auditing techniques. The more the task involves a consulting-style solution, the more the project is likely to stray from the standard IS audit process. When an IS auditor is brought into these situations, the auditor should be very clear about the scope of the work to be performed and ensure they have the appropriate skills to deliver on the task at hand.

IT and IS Governance Reviews

External regulations often require IT and IS governance reviews. These reviews are usually focused on management's risk management and performance measurement responsibilities. Financial auditing procedures also require governance evaluations. An auditor's risk analysis could identify information systems as an area material to an organization's control structure, such as within an e-commerce company.

Management's risk analysis could also identify areas of IT governance to review. Management could request that an internal audit department or external reviewers be requested to assess whether an IT department is aligned with a company's strategies or is delivering appropriate value for an organization's investment in IT.

Here are a few examples of IT governance projects:

- Management is facing some long-term budgeting decisions, possibly including eliminating positions. Rather than determining which positions to eliminate, management finds an independent party to provide an impartial perspective on the value each of the groups within the IT department provides. Management wants IS auditors to provide feedback on whether each group within IT is efficiently delivering value to the organization and is appropriately sized.

- A manufacturing company is preparing for growth. The IT department has not changed much since the company was small. Management wants an outside reviewer to recommend ways to "tune-up and tool-up" the IT department ahead of the expansion. Management hopes IS auditors will identify key IT risks facing expansion and work on developing an IT governance structure appropriate for a larger organization.

- Auditors are asked to review management's security policies and offer recommendations for improvement.

Organizations may seek the help of IS auditors to provide recommendations to strengthen their governance function.

Staff Augmentation

When an organization can oversee the work of an IS auditor but needs additional resources to accomplish the work, it may opt for outsourced or co-sourced staffing arrangements. It is not uncommon to temporarily requisition the help of a skilled IS auditor to support control testing or to serve on special teams (such as a computer/cyber incident response team [CIRT]). In this situation, the IS auditor reports directly to management in a client organization and the auditor may perform a limited part of the IS auditing cycle.

NOTE IS audit services will change over time. New audit practices are sure to be introduced with changes in technology, business, regulation, and the economy as other practices become obsolete or dated. Recent history includes the rapid emergence of SOX work as companies implement SOX compliance. There is still considerable work in this subject area, though it has decreased.

Engagement Letters and Audit Charters

Engagement letters define the terms of the audit engagement when external auditors are used. This section lists a few of the general terms and goes into more detail on a few subjects of interest to auditors. General subject areas addressed within the engagement letter include:

- Scope of work to be performed
- Distribution of the report
- Rates, time estimates, and fees

- Ownership of workpapers
- Terms for addendums
- Nondisclosure agreements
- Audit charters

Audit organizations and client organizations will both review the contract, and each party may require specific wording. Some contract negotiations can prove lengthy.

When audits are externally required, the party serving as audit sponsor may not be supportive of the audit. In these situations, the audit may not be welcomed by the primary contact or the control managers. Thus, it can be beneficial to give extra attention to the following:

- Audit terms on turnaround time for requests
- Availability of control owners and other key personnel
- The relationship with the primary contact
- Frequency and type of status reporting

This is not a legal discussion and does not claim to be legal advice; instead, it is a general discussion about the contents and nature of standard engagement letters. This book does not discuss additional legal clauses that may be required in an engagement letter.

Distribution of the Audit Report

The outcome of an audit is an *audit report*, a written explanation of the audit project, including the project's objectives, the controls tested, and the auditor's opinion of the effectiveness of each control. Most audit reports are solely for use by an organization's management and governing entities. Reports will contain language reflecting the limited distribution and use of the report. The audit organization will reply to inquiries regarding the report only with members of management and no other parties. For example, the cover sheet and the footer on each page of the report can include the following phrase: "This report is restricted to business use by management of XYZ Corporation and is not to be relied upon by any other party for any purpose."

Certain reports, such as SOC 1 or SOC 2 reports, are for distribution to third parties (but only for audit purposes and not for other purposes such as marketing). The engagement letter will state clearly the terms under which parties are permitted to receive these reports and will provide a process for getting permission from the audit organization if they seek to provide the report to another party.

As an example of contract terms surrounding a report, SOC 1 clients are forbidden from distributing a report to parties other than those using the control information in the SOC 1 report for management's review and to provide to their financial auditors. This stipulation means client organizations are not permitted to share this report with a *potential* client as a sales tool without express written permission from the audit organization. If management does distribute a report beyond the terms of the engagement letter, the audit organization is no longer responsible for the content of that report if relied on by a nonpermitted third party.

Rates, Time Estimates, and Fees

Part of an engagement letter will address the invoicing for services. Many attestation engagements are fixed-fee engagements, although additional invoices may be agreed upon with time budget overruns or changes in scope. Many nonattestation (in other words, professional services instead of audit) engagements will be billed based on hourly rates. Rates could be blended across teams or could identify individual rates for specific resources. The contract could identify the degree of detail the client will receive on their statement.

This section usually addresses expenses. Any conditions on expenses will be spelled out here. Clients may permit only certain kinds of expenses or ask for invoices with itemizations. Clients often select nearby audit firms that can provide resources without incurring travel or lodging expenses. Larger audits may draw resources from a wide area and may incur sizeable expense bills.

Ownership of Workpapers

For external auditors, ownership of workpapers is different in attestation and internal audit engagements.

When a certified professional is signing off on an audit, they retain ownership of workpapers because the auditor may be asked to defend their opinion with evidence. In some engagements, auditors may not have a problem providing a copy of part or all of the workpapers to management. Audit documentation of procedures is sometimes shared with management, and the documentation of test results beyond the report may be shared with management to support remediation efforts. In some external audits, ownership of audit workpapers is retained by the auditors, such as a bank requiring compliance testing from service providers.

Internal audit engagements are services done on behalf of management, and management retains ownership of audit documentation. IA departments commonly document their work in a combination of paper and electronic workpapers. Document retention requirements vary by industry and individual organization and should be clearly understood by internal auditors to ensure internal and/or external retention compliance.

The ownership, sharing, protection, and eventual disposal of workpapers can be addressed in the engagement letter.

Terms for Addendums

Most contracts prepare for the possibility of being extended with an addendum or change order. The addendum can increase or remove scope, extend deadlines, and add audit cycles based on the terms of the original engagement letter.

Nondisclosure Agreements

Because auditors gain access to proprietary information during the audit, they are almost always bound by nondisclosure agreements (NDAs). These may be signed by the individual auditors or by auditing firms, and they may be signed at an engagement level covering all team members. It is worth noting that NDAs usually do not cover disclosure to legal or regulatory authorities if fraud or other illegal activities are discovered during an audit. In some cases, an NDA is not signed but similar nondisclosure-type language is included in an engagement letter or contract.

Some audit firms sign blanket NDAs for their personnel. Audit firms using these often do not permit their auditors to sign individual nondisclosure forms. When auditors arrive at a client locale for the first time and are provided contracts to sign, they may need to address the requirement with audit management. Audit firm lawyers may want to avoid nonapproved language, as well as avoid having their auditors signing individual contracts with a client.

Audit Charters

Audit charters are used for projects internal to an organization. Internal audit projects will often employ an audit charter. They prove useful to ensure management's buy-in within an organization. Audit charters support the project by communicating and formalizing the following:

- Sponsorship by executive management
- The goals of the audit project
- The planned time frame for audit activities
- Obligations of auditor and auditee team members
- Expectations of auditor and auditee team members

Chartered projects often start with a kickoff meeting, which helps the team by enabling an introduction between team members in different departments. The event also promotes teamwork and reinforces the project's goals, obligations, and expectations.

When an outsourced IS audit resource is brought into a chartered audit project, it is important that the auditor become familiar with the audit charter. This will enable the auditor to understand what has been communicated to client management and control owners.

Systems implementation projects involving multiple departments may also employ a similar project charter. IS auditors may be brought into projects working under a project charter.

Ethics and Independence

It is important that the auditor maintain independence from the client organization in both fact and appearance. This chapter provides a few examples; for a comprehensive discussion of the subject, refer to the discussion of ethics, independence, and the ISACA Code of Professional Ethics in Chapter 2, "The Audit Process."

Independence in Fact

Avoiding issues of independence in "fact" is rather straightforward. An auditor may not audit their own work and may not report on testing if the subject of testing is a function owned or managed within the auditor's reporting relationship. The auditor may not design or be part of implementing controls and be called on to test those controls. Examples of this include the following:

- An auditor has had the responsibility of implementing the new AR (accounts receivable) module as part of the ERP (enterprise resource planning) implementation team; the auditor should not be performing control reviews on this system.

- An auditor has been tasked with monitoring the firewall log daily. The auditor may not test whether the firewall log is regularly monitored.

- An auditor reports to a control manager and may not test controls managed by that control manager.

In addition, the auditor should avoid testing the work of control owners or control managers when the auditor has family, intimate personal relationships, or external business relationships involved.

Independence in Appearance

Avoiding issues of independence in appearance is where an auditor faces additional challenges. Gifts from the client are one area where judgment can be required. Fortunately, an auditor often can lean upon workplace policies in such situations. Common workplace policies include forbidding gifts over certain values and getting permission to accept certain gifts (such as business dinners or tickets to a sporting event). Regardless of policies, an auditor must exhibit care when accepting gifts. A few examples are discussed here:

- The client organization's CFO offers the team coffee mugs with the company's new logo. Since this item has a limited cost, and marginal value, and is also a promotional tool for the company, there should not be an issue of independence in appearance.

- A control manager at the company offering to pay for a coffee may be a limited and acceptable gift.

- The CFO meets the audit team for dinner and covers the bill. This can be acceptable as a team-building event. The CFO then seeks to fund a night on the town with drinks and entertainment; this may be perceived as crossing the line.

- Small talk with a control owner about her office decorations leads to her offering the auditor a gift from her collection of sports memorabilia. The client could perceive this as impairing independence.

This is a subject of broad debate. An auditor should be aware of their audit organization's rules and guidelines regarding ethics, independence, and acceptable behavior. An internal auditor should apply the principles of gifts and influence with their audit clients, including internal company personnel.

Launching a New Project: Planning an Audit

A new audit project is on the table. The client wants auditors to start work soon, and so the process begins. Often in external audits, clients will limit the information provided until engagement letters and NDAs have been signed. Most external audit organizations severely limit the amount of work auditors are permitted to perform on a project before the client has signed the engagement letter. To ensure that valuable time is not wasted, management waits until both the audit firm and the client have a clear and formal understanding of the scope and purpose of the audit.

Planning for an internal audit with internal resources is similar to planning for an external audit but without the need to address cost and payment terms. Otherwise, most of the planning elements are nearly the same.

Understanding the Client's Needs

When a client organization decides that an audit is needed, they will usually describe their needs in writing and use a formal or informal selection process to choose an auditor. This selection process is centered on communication between the audit organization and the client about the client's needs. A client needing a signed attestation still looks for the best audit firm for their needs. A client has more than price to consider when selecting an audit firm. If an audit firm does not have experience in the client's industry or technologies, the auditors may not work effectively with management. If a client is the smallest in an auditor's book of business, the client may be concerned about the level of service they will receive. A firm may be selected because of experience with an area of a client's needs that is peripheral to the audit scope, and management's decision to perform such an audit could relate to these needs. Understanding the reasons behind an audit can be important for successful planning and meeting client expectations.

Once auditors are selected and NDAs are signed, a client organization may provide more specific reasons. Having such conversations with the primary contact or the audit sponsor early in the audit can provide valuable information to the audit team.

Examples of a client organization's needs that may factor into an audit include the following:

- Augment documentation of new or changed procedures
- Launch an internal audit function
- Update an outdated control infrastructure

- Assist in the education of a new executive
- Support a financing relationship
- Repair relationships damaged by a previous control failure
- Meet contract conditions by providing an audit report by a certain date

Knowing the reason behind management's decision to perform an audit will enable audit personnel to:

- Better understand the client's risk environment
- Provide more useful feedback on their control structure
- More accurately plan for the audit
- Focus extra testing on the most critical control objectives
- Meet client expectations and deadlines
- Provide meaningful reporting based on the results of the audit

IT managers frequently ask their auditors about how they compare with their peers.

Preliminary Discussions

Preliminary discussions between audit management and client management will set the stage for how well the parties will work together. It is important at this phase to anticipate challenges that may be faced during the audit. Common things to address in these initial discussions are:

- Clarifying scope by confirming an understanding of client needs and their risk environment
- Acquiring more detailed information on employed technology and a deeper understanding of how it supports the organization's objectives
- Establishing engagement procedures, such as scheduling control owner time and requesting control documentation
- Setting expectations, such as frequency and depth of status reports and review of testing exceptions

Both the client and the audit manager have an important investment in the success of this phase. The client organization hopes to maximize the benefit of the service, so it may identify areas where it would seek professional advice. The client representative may aim to minimize internal disruptions and ask the auditor to observe certain practices.

Understand the Technologies Employed

The audit manager uses information on employed technologies when developing the audit plan and when assigning resources to test controls.

When involving a third-party audit resource, a client's selection process will limit the amount of information they share publicly about their systems. If there is a bidding process, it may permit formal or informal Q&A, where answers will be provided in response to vendor inquiries to estimate effort. When the audit is launched and NDAs are signed, the client should be willing to share relevant documentation and information freely.

An audit manager also will be gathering information on the nature of testing that will be performed. Some questions an audit manager may consider include:

- What kind of security testing is required?
- What kind of process evaluation is required?
- What kind of application testing is required?
- What relevant customizations exist?
- Are any in-house–developed technologies employed?

In these preliminary discussions, the audit manager needs to gather more specific information on the technologies involved and the testing to be performed. The version numbers, implementation dates, and an idea of the transaction volumes are useful information. The audit manager will use such information during audit planning.

Performing a Risk Assessment

A *risk assessment* process considers the inherent risks of a certain operation and considers information from within the organization. Auditors will weigh information from several sources when performing a risk assessment, as illustrated in Figure 9.1.

FIGURE 9.1   Different considerations in a risk assessment

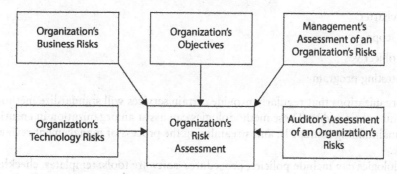

It is common to have financial information available for assessing the materiality of certain activities. Here are some examples:

- An organization may have extensive automated revenue transactions and very few assets tracked within its asset management system. Therefore, there is less inherent risk surrounding asset tracking, but thorough attention needs to be given to the systems supporting the revenue cycle. In the event of system failure, there could be a high risk of data redundancy or incomplete information capture.

- A debt collection service outsources the maintenance of its core collections-processing software to a software vendor. Therefore, risks relating to change management controls surrounding its core systems are reduced. However, because it is a high-transaction environment, data backup and restoration controls are elevated in criticality.

A risk assessment is arguably the most important aspect of an audit. Without a risk assessment, high-risk situations may not be identified and addressed sufficiently during an audit. Management may not realize the opportunity to reduce serious risks.

In certain situations, a financial auditor may need to participate in the risk assessment so that certain business risks that may not be obvious to the IS auditor can be identified. A financial auditor can help an IS auditor determine which systems controls are most material in a financially based risk assessment.

Audit Methodology

Audit methodologies are designed by audit management and standardize how parts of audits are performed. Methodologies are the procedures used by the audit team to perform an audit. They can be as simple as requiring audit scope to be documented and approved, to employing audit software and detailed procedures that govern the entire audit process.

ISACA considers the following items so central to the audit process that all audits will at least generate documented statements addressing them:

- Audit charter
- Audit scope
- Audit objectives
- Audit testing program

Audit organizations that regularly provide certain services will standardize methodologies for performing their audits. These methodologies can assist an organization in ensuring completeness, maintaining standards, and streamlining the process of management reviewing audit work.

Methodologies can include policies, procedures, software tools, templates, checklists, and other means of providing uniformity across the audit process. These methodologies are documented and taught to new members of the organization.

Documented methodologies can serve to govern many stages of the process, such as:

- Bidding on RFPs
- Risk assessments
- Scope
- Objectives
- Resource allocations

- Comprehensiveness of testing
- Sample method and size guidelines
- Report templates
- Completion checklists

Methodologies will provide a structure for achieving milestones within the audit process. Here are some examples:

- **Risk assessment:** An audit firm's risk assessment approach involves employing a spreadsheet predesigned to compute an aggregate score from several different risk measurements. Form letters may be used to communicate with management and collect their feedback on the client organization's risks. Management's feedback can be populated into the spreadsheet along with auditors' assessments, and the risks are ranked.

- **Budget:** A budget tracks time and rates incurred by auditors. A budget will be developed initially in the RFP process and updated in the planning process. Actual time incurred will be compared with the budget so audit management can better understand how to plan for future engagements.

- **Lead sheets:** Lead sheets are intake forms used by auditors to capture and organize test information. They provide a uniform method to represent test results and enable audit management to perform a formulaic review of test results.

- **Testing standards:** To maintain a rigorous standard of testing to support its reputation, an audit organization institutes testing standards. These standards require different testing methods to pass a control test. Testing methods are identified as follows: collaborative inquiry, observation, inspection, and reperformance. In addition, each control objective must be supported by one form of substantive testing.

- **Auditing software:** Large audit organizations frequently enforce their audit methodology with software that attempts to accommodate as much of the audit process as possible. These programs may accommodate most audit possibilities and enforce certain procedures to be executed by the audit team. They may even manage images of workpapers so that the software captures all audit documentation.

Methodologies used by audit firms may be designed to meet requirements published by regulatory organizations, such as the AICPA or the U.S. Office of Management and Budget.

Developing the Audit Plan

An audit plan is a project plan designed for performing an IS audit. Like a project plan, it is a tool for tracking tasks and forecasting the time and resource needs of the audit process. It will cite the audit methodology to be used and lay out milestones and sequential dependencies for the different tasks within the audit. The plan is updated with progress milestones and may be adjusted with certain audit changes.

In addition to serving as a high-level audit plan, the audit plan organizes the stages of risk assessment, audit objectives, and the initial assessment of client procedures in the beginning.

The audit plan does not track the details of audit testing—this is tracked in the audit testing matrix and the lead sheets.

Gathering Information: PBC Lists

A provided by client (PBC) list is a common tool used by auditors for managing information requested from the client. It provides a consolidated list that the auditor can use as a record of requests for process documents and records, and includes an effective checklist for tracking receipt of information. It will also help the primary contact manage the fulfillment of auditor information requests. Several PBC lists may be needed during an audit. PBC lists should be dated when they are delivered, and, if possible, they should document an agreed-upon delivery date.

Initial Information Requests

At the beginning of an audit, the auditor will require information about the organization's context. Common requests include:

- Organizational charts
- Company directory
- Control documentation
- System documentation
- Relevant reports or other information

This information will be used to prepare for and execute the audit. The list may also identify documents that a client has indicated exist, such as an information security policy.

A Client's Preparedness for an Audit

When an organization is facing its first audit, auditors frequently include an evaluation of the client's preparedness in their plans. A client may need an audit but may not be prepared. In attestation situations, the client organization may not yet be ready for an audit. A few possible examples of this are as follows:

- A company hopes to undergo an initial SOC 1 audit, but the control infrastructure is not yet in place or documented.
- A company has experienced significant growth. New ways have been devised to perform key processes. Procedures are inconsistent, and documentation is incomplete.
- Changes to business products, processes, and supporting technologies have left control documentation out of date.
- New control procedures have been only partially implemented.
- Logging in key systems hasn't been configured correctly, so audit information is inadequately captured or retained.
- There has been turnover of key control owners or control managers.

If a client organization's support for an audit is below par, the first order of business is housekeeping. If the engagement letter does not account for providing services to help the client prepare, it may be necessary to delay the start of the audit. Some challenges may be addressed by expanding the scope of the engagement letter to include the auditors aiding (such as with updating procedures) ahead of an audit. This approach is, however, a tricky issue; in an attestation or external audit, this is most frequently not possible or desirable due to independence or regulatory issues—auditors can't audit the structures they help to develop.

Developing Audit Objectives

An audit's objectives clarify the goals of the audit. Audit objectives also ensure the audit complies with applicable standards, laws, regulations, or other legal obligations. Objectives are clarified in a formal document and retained in project workpapers. The objectives provide a basis for measuring the success of testing and are central to an audit report's opinion.

Objectives are developed by considering several different sources:

- The engagement letter or audit charter addresses the nature of testing and the expectations of reporting. It provides a central pillar to an audit's objectives, which may focus on external security, operating effectiveness, compliance to a standard such as SOC 2, PCI DSS, or ISO/IEC 27001, or the correctness of transactions and processing.

- At this point, auditors will understand the nature of the client organization's business and have discussed the key processes at a high level.

- An overall understanding of the organization's risks from the risk assessment process will be incorporated.

- An understanding of a client's needs for launching the audit will also be considered. This understanding may reveal management's goals in conducting the audit or clarify the nature of a third party's interests in the report's outcome.

Statements of audit objectives may incorporate additional perspectives. Figure 9.2 illustrates how an audit objective is developed by considering many information sources.

FIGURE 9.2 Audit objectives are developed using information from several sources.

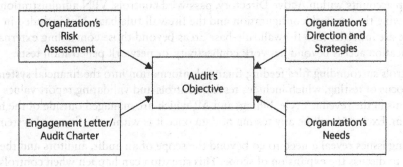

For example, an audit engagement letter identifies a client as needing control documentation and limited financial control testing. Auditors are aware of new financial systems. The risk assessment shows that financial auditors annually perform test procedures on manual and automated controls within the financial software of an organization. Conversations with management reveal that they hope to update documentation, confirm the success of their system implementation, and provide financial auditors with a report that shows system controls are operating effectively so that they can reduce the scope and cost of the financial audit. The objectives of the audit will be focused on updating procedure and control documentation for the new system and testing new software controls.

Developing the Scope of an Audit

An audit's scope is documented in a series of statements addressing the processes and/or systems to be reviewed and to what depth. It will also address how to implement the audit's objectives. Figure 9.3 illustrates the stages leading to the development of an audit's scope.

FIGURE 9.3   Audit objective and risk assessment help to determine audit scope.

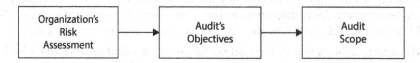

A risk assessment has identified the areas with the greatest risk within the overall scope, so an audit scope will be tailored to address these areas. For example, testing of low-risk areas may focus on a small number of key controls when more robust testing is called for in areas with greater risk.

Similar to casting a net, the scope statement will identify what is included under the net and set the boundaries of what is outside it. A well-defined scope will assist in the development of focused test plans.

Here are examples of project scope statements:

- Testing addresses internal and external access to key systems, including procedures to set up accounts within Active Directory, password controls, VPN administration, and reviewing the network configuration and the firewall rule base. Not included in the scope are inquiries into firewall rule-base areas beyond those controlling external access, application access beyond network connectivity, or network penetration tests.

- Controls surrounding files feeding financial information into the financial system are the focus of testing, which includes testing controls and validating report values from systems in the revenue cycle, billing, and AP, which are managed outside of the financial system. Excluded will be any testing of data once it is within the financial system.

If testing issues reveal a need to go beyond the scope of an audit, auditors and the client will need to discuss the expansion of scope. This situation can happen when controls fail and compensating controls need to be tested. When auditors are externally sourced, any augmentation of scope will need to be formalized through a signed addendum to the engagement letter.

> A client organization may set the audit scope rather than let an IS auditor determine it. An example of this is when auditors are brought in to perform an already-determined set of tests.

Prior Period Issues

When an audit fails a test, succeeding audits will retest the failed control and the effectiveness of any remediation efforts performed by management. When developing scope, audit reports from a prior period must be reviewed so auditors understand which issues require revisiting and additional scrutiny. An exception from a prior period may have been fixed, in which case audit documentation and testing plans may need to adjust to changes. Projects remediating issues to primary controls may be in process, so only secondary controls are available for testing.

Expanding Scope

In certain audits, such as internal audit reports, management may have some leeway in changing the scope during the reporting period. Understanding procedures or testing exceptions may reveal an area where management needs to dig deeper. It may be more economical to augment the current audit than to perform a procedure as part of a subsequent, currently unscheduled audit. Auditors are most likely available and are currently immersed in the procedures. Management may want to push deeper to get to the root of an issue immediately.

Developing a Test Plan

When an audit's scope has been approved, it's time to develop a test plan. This section covers the stages that go into developing the test plan. Audits that are performed on a previously established cycle may base much of their test plan work on plans used in prior audits. However, auditors must avoid any temptation to reuse a prior audit plan. It is very important that an auditor revisit audit objectives and reevaluate the scope of an audit for each audit cycle. Failure to do so can lead to serious audit problems when testing fails to satisfy audit objectives. Avoiding this practice is especially important in situations where new systems have been implemented, changes have occurred in the business, or control issues have been identified in the past.

Understanding the Control Environment

When an auditor prepares the test plan, information is drawn from several sources. If the audit is not in its initial year, documentation from previous audits will be available. Auditors who have performed the same audit in prior periods will have historical knowledge. Client management is consulted to update procedure and control documentation and identify the control owners.

When auditors collect information on the control environment, they often use PBC lists. Upon review, auditors may find that provided information falls short of an auditor's needs, requiring additional information requests. Shortfalls might be due to procedures that are new to the control structure or that have not been previously tested. It is common for auditors to meet with client management during this process.

Understanding the Client's Procedures

An auditor must understand the procedure to be tested before they can effectively plan and perform testing. Auditors begin by reviewing information provided by the client. Procedure documentation may be provided in several different forms:

- **Financial audit write-ups:** CFOs usually keep copies of the process documentation generated by financial auditors. It is common for a CFO to make these available to audit teams when areas are in scope. These could also include written procedures and systems-level documentation.

- **Internal audit documentation:** If the internal audit department tests controls on a cycle, it keeps procedure documentation regarding the controls it tests. When this documentation is within an audit's scope, other auditors can greatly benefit from it.

- **Management procedure documentation:** Management may have procedure documentation, such as instructional or reference material for employees (for example, desktop procedures). A department's policies may contain procedure documentation. Management may also retain procedure documentation from previous auditors.

- **Instruction manuals:** When management trains many people to perform the same procedures, a training department may provide instruction to employees. Training material may provide instruction on control procedures that are within the scope of the audit.

- **Checklists:** Management may oversee a process with a checklist. If a checklist is provided, it will offer a high-level understanding to auditors (as well as provide evidence of a controlled environment), but follow-up is likely to be required.

- **Walk-throughs:** Auditors may determine that they need to perform a walk-through of a process or transaction to document their understanding of the procedures used. The result of these walk-throughs can be a narrative of the process, flowcharts, or a control matrix that documents the control points in place.

Other sources may provide information on procedures as well.

An auditor must understand a procedure in the context of the audit. The impact of a procedure concerning the audit objectives is important when understanding controls within the procedure. This impact will affect the degree or depth of testing that should be employed.

Many auditors bring to the table experience with procedures performed (or technologies employed) at other organizations. An auditor who has experience elsewhere can often more quickly understand a similar procedure (or technology) in a new environment. Such experience can also assist by being available to a junior auditor who is responsible for a subject for the first time.

Understanding the Technology Environment

With an understanding of a business procedure, an auditor can then understand how technology is employed to support it. Procedure documentation will often identify existing systems at a high level. To develop an audit program, the audit team needs to "look under the hood." A PBC list may have been sent to the IT department. Conversations with IT personnel may be required to identify what kind of information they keep on their systems. Possible sources of information include:

- **Audit documentation:** Previous audits of different kinds may have documented certain processes within IT. Because many IT environments change quickly, information from an audit a few years back may no longer be relevant.

- **Network and system diagrams:** Information about network and data security can be provided in network diagrams. All network documentation should be dated, and auditors should inquire about its accuracy and completeness. Diagrams can help auditors quickly identify areas where they will need a greater depth of information.

- **Asset inventories:** An IT department may keep a consolidated list of the systems they support. System inventories are performed to different depths and may not contain exactly the information an auditor seeks, but they are often useful tools for drilling into that information. Auditors can review items on the list and inquire as to their relevance to procedures, or identify where a system's data resides, or whether it is on a standard backup schedule.

- **Configuration management database (CMDB):** An IT department may have a CMDB containing configuration information for systems and devices that auditors will examine. The auditors may need to examine the mechanisms by which configuration changes are made, the configurations themselves, or both.

- **Management's procedure documentation:** Management may have formalized certain procedures as part of developing a controlled environment. This information, when available, is often quite useful. Examples include change control procedures and system operation procedures.

- **Disaster recovery plans:** IT departments may have formalized within disaster recovery plans certain procedures to be performed in the event of an incident. At times these reflect common procedures performed by management. An auditor may find relevant procedures, technology, and control information by reviewing a disaster recovery plan.

It is important for an auditor to validate understandings based on documentation received from IT personnel.

In addition to being outdated, it is not uncommon for IT documentation to come up short of auditors' needs. Here are a couple of examples:

- Documentation may reveal that data entry and processing controls are employed within PeopleSoft, but it might not identify the Linux-hosted Oracle database on the backend, which should be included when testing data security.

- A written description of network security controls might identify the Cisco firewall, but might omit its use in series with an intrusion prevention system.

These clarifications are important for an understanding of key systems and how they are managed.

Changes to IT Environments

Technologies and technological procedures change regularly. If the auditors learn of changes, they should be sure to address them with client IT personnel. Conversations with IT should address the landscape of current IT projects and review whether they will impact testing controls.

New system implementations must be considered carefully when designing test procedures. When new systems are employed, there are many questions regarding the success of the deployment. Auditors may seek to review life cycle controls employed during a development process to determine if the system's implementation method introduces control risks. With new systems, there is a risk that documentation was not updated to reflect the use of a new system or that management shared documentation produced ahead of the system going live. "To-be" documentation could contain claims that certain controls exist that were omitted from the production launch.

Further, it is important to know of systems that are due to be implemented before or during a testing period. These can prove problematic to testing plans, as there could be an interruption or a change in control structures with a new system. Here's an example: A SOC 2 engagement is testing controls over a long period, typically 6 to 12 months. Control objectives are signed off by management ahead of the testing period, and they include performing weekly backups. Four months into the testing period, the IT department upgrades its backup software. In doing so, they change the cycle of backups. This situation introduces some problems:

- **Lack of testing evidence:** The old backup system may have housed records on the success and failure of backup jobs. If the system has been retired, records of backup success and failure may no longer be available when auditors request evidence.

- **Outdated control objectives:** Control objectives and control activities may be outdated as documented. The control objective reads that full backups are performed weekly, but the newly implemented practice performs daily incremental backups and full backups only every two weeks. This new practice could fail the stated control objective.

- **Outdated controls and control failures:** The IT department may have encountered problems with the new software performing backups on certain technologies, and may, for a period, fail to perform backups of systems hosted on certain critical servers.

Because of instances such as these, it is important for auditors to be included in communications about potential changes/updates. Without prior knowledge of changes like these, an auditor likely would report failures of control objectives, and client management would argue that failures should not be reported because they have a reasonable control structure in place. With a full understanding of IT plans, auditors can work with the client to accommodate the changes. Appropriate control language can be used, and coordination with management can be done to ensure the transition does not interfere with the audit.

Controls and Control Objectives

Controls are selected for testing because they support a control objective. The control objective is achieved when testing shows that tested controls are operating effectively. When building a test plan, auditors organize controls they will test by their support of control objectives.

Controls are implemented to mitigate risks within an organization. Multiple controls often work together to mitigate risks within a process or procedure. The control objective statement summarizes the risk-mitigation goals of controls within a procedure. The control objectives will collectively support the audit's objectives.

Control objectives and their supporting controls are listed in the test plan. Table 9.1 depicts an example of a control objective along with individual controls.

TABLE 9.1 Control objectives and their supporting controls

CO #	Control objective	Control #	Control description
1	Full data backups are performed weekly and securely stored off-site.	1.1	Backup system sends email alerts to the backup administrator when jobs are not successful. The backup administrator follows up on issues and records them in the issues tracking system.
		1.2	Backup media are numbered, and numbers are kept in the tape log. The location of backup media is tracked in the media log.
		1.3	Backup media is kept physically secure behind locked doors with limited access. When transferred to storage, backup media is locked in metal boxes.
		1.4	Backup media is stored securely off-site.

Though not all engagements will involve auditors developing lists of control objectives and control activities, many will involve auditors reviewing and providing the client organization feedback on existing controls. Lists such as the example in Table 9.1 can provide a great deal of assistance to individuals who are new to an audit or new to auditing in general, as these lists provide a connection between the individual control activities and the true purpose (or objective) for performing and testing those activities. This can be beneficial in helping to understand the "big picture" of why audits are being performed.

Developing Control Objectives and Supporting Controls

When developing their control environment, organizations will typically document control objectives and provide them to the auditor. However, when an auditor is tasked with developing the control objectives and the list of controls to test, they must keep the audit's objectives and scope in mind. It is important that control objectives be properly phrased both to reflect the actual control activities performed by management and to support the audit objectives. It is reasonable for an auditor to help develop control objectives as well as the list of controls. The only issue is if the auditor is asked to prescribe in detail how management should implement and operate the controls.

When examining existing control objectives and control activities, the auditor should determine whether each control activity supports the control objective. Control activities can exist within procedures that do not support, or poorly support, the control objective. Any such control activities should be removed from the list. A replacement control may need to be identified so that an objective is effectively supported. If an auditor experiences trouble in this area, they should consult upward within the organization.

With the list of supporting controls, the auditor should determine whether any of these controls ultimately perform the same function. If two control activities protect against the same problem, the auditor should determine which one should be selected as the key control and remove the other one from the list of controls to be tested. An auditor may want to learn which of these controls can be more efficiently tested before selecting equal controls as key. Management may agree that one of the controls is redundant and elect to cease performing it.

 Different methods can be used to arrive at sets of control objectives and control activities. Only one approach is conveyed here.

Key Controls and Compensating Controls

Compensating controls are valuable to identify during this phase of audit planning. When a control failure occurs, the organization relies on one or more compensating controls, a secondary measure designed to mitigate the same risks addressed by the key control. A good test to determine whether a control is a compensating control is whether a failure of the key control is revealed by the compensating control.

An example of a key control is a formal request and approval process for provisioning new user access. A request made by an individual's supervisor with approval by department management is key to ensure an individual's access levels match their job responsibilities. If access was provisioned outside of the normal process, a periodic (quarterly/annual) review of all user access may ensure that user access levels overall are appropriate.

In the event of the failure of a key control, a compensating control can be considered for testing to determine the materiality of the failure of the key control. Even for compensating controls, it is important for management to maintain a similar level of documentation to evidence that the control is occurring; otherwise, it may result in more remediation work for management if the compensating control is unable to be tested and validated by audit.

Reviewing Control Objectives and Supporting Controls

Over time, an organization will change elements of its control infrastructure. Control structures may evolve due to changes in the organization's business model, changes in management, or possibly in response to guidance from governing entities, such as how guidance on SOX control testing now emphasizes a greater focus on governance and monitoring.

When an auditor is tasked with reviewing a control structure, their goal is to make three key determinations:

- Do control activities correctly support management's activities?
- Do control activities support the control objectives?
- Do the control objectives effectively mitigate risks?

Auditors usually provide feedback to management on how the client can improve the wording of certain controls. Problems with the control structure could be identified, and management may need to institute additional control measures. Occasionally, auditors will determine and advise that two controls mitigate the same risk and one of them can be relegated to the level of compensating control, be omitted from testing, or even be eliminated from management's control structure altogether.

Helping a Client Understand and Identify Controls

Client management often has the obligation of writing and maintaining their control objectives and control activities. In these situations, auditors often still need to evaluate whether the provided control structure is sound and pertinent to the audit's goals and the organization's risk management strategies.

An IS auditor coming in to audit a new organization must keep in mind that not all organizations employ the skills to understand, identify, and document controls. Client organizations may be seeking the assistance of outside auditors to update or even write their control documentation. If this is the case, auditors should make sure the engagement letter identifies this service.

Certain engagements, such as SOC 2, agreed-upon procedures (AUPs), and outsourced or co-sourced SOX testing, presume management owns and maintains control documentation. If a client is seeking these services, the burden is on client management to have controls identified and documented. These engagements involve testing "management's controls." If management does not have a documented control structure (which happens), these engagements can run into problems. Consider the following examples:

- A company is undergoing its first SOC 2 audit. The company is responsible for providing the control structure for testing and writing "Section 3," which is management's description of controls. This is a small, growing company that doesn't have control experience in-house. They have agreed with a partner, acquiring company, or potential client that they will perform a SOC 2 audit. They figure the auditors they have hired will help them get through a process they have yet to understand.
- A bank has had trouble with an information system conversion. They have data problems, and outside parties have concerns. The bank hires a third-party auditor to perform agreed-upon procedures on converted data, but the auditor is not sure what needs to be tested.
- An internal audit department has relied upon external IS auditors. Since the last testing, a new ERP system has been implemented, but control documentation has not yet been updated to reflect current controls. Deadlines require testing to be completed soon, so auditors are lined up to perform the testing, though the controls are not current.

In these situations, the client may presume that the auditors will write the controls that will help them through the process. In the internal audit example, the burden of working with outdated controls may introduce problems in meeting the deadline and may introduce problems when attesting to controls over a defined period. Moreover, in the SOC 2 and AUP examples, there is a line an auditor must not cross. Auditors are not permitted to test controls they have designed. Feedback that does not involve writing control language can be provided.

Documenting Procedures

Certain projects require the IS auditor to generate systems and procedure documentation. Drafting these documents may take several meetings with client personnel before the documentation goals can be achieved. Providing draft documentation enables an auditor to communicate more effectively with control owners and managers to confirm an understanding of the subject matter.

The following are examples of documentation formats an auditor may use:

- Written text and lists
- Flowcharts
- Network diagrams
- Spreadsheets
- Data structure and data flow diagrams
- Screenshots
- Text files of command output

The task of creating documentation faces several challenges. When dealing with information systems, an auditor is often attempting to abstract complex concepts in an organized manner to the correct audience. It is common to rely on multiple visual tools to communicate processes and the systems that support them (see Figure 9.4).

When developing documentation, the auditor may find it useful to share documentation with control owners and managers. Control owners are often helpful when their area of expertise is being represented in new ways. It is also important for the success of testing that the auditor and control owner agree closely on what is being tested. Draft documentation proves a convenient tool for capturing accurate feedback, as notes and corrections can be written on the draft documentation.

Documentation frequently reflects a version number, the date of the latest update, the name of the person who created the document, and the name of the person who performed the last review and update.

 WARNING   Before a document's review is complete, an auditor should take care always to write "DRAFT" on any documentation that is not in final condition. "Final condition" would mean reviewed and accepted (and approved, if possible) by management and ready for inclusion in the audit workpapers. If an auditor has neglected to insert "DRAFT" onto a document before printing, this can simply be written with a pen before presenting it.

FIGURE 9.4   Different methods of diagramming can support IS auditing.

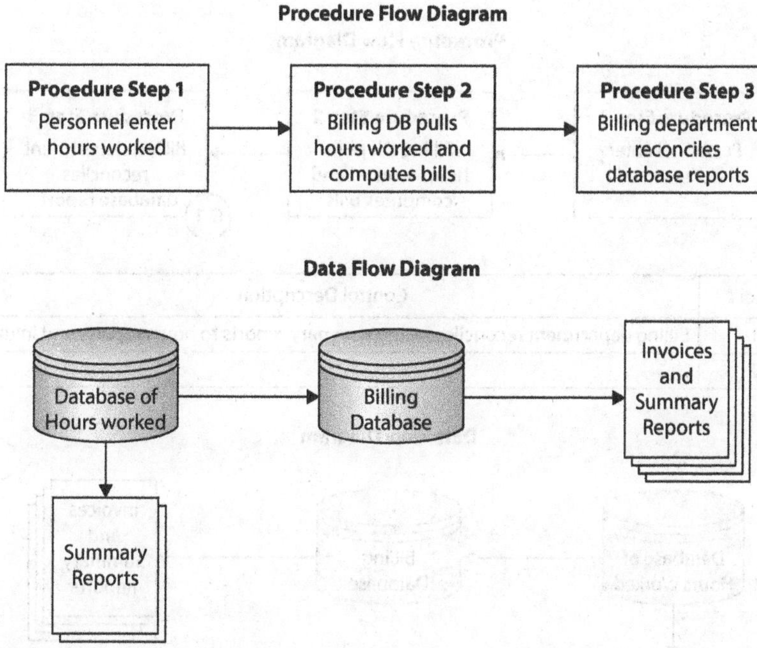

Procedure Flow Diagram

Procedure Step 1	Procedure Step 2	Procedure Step 3
Personnel enter hours worked	Billing DB pulls hours worked and computes bills	Billing department reconciles database reports

Data Flow Diagram

Database of Hours worked → Billing Database → Invoices and Summary Reports

Summary Reports

Mapping Controls to Documentation

For an auditor's purposes, individual control activities are often included in the procedure documentation. These may be cited within the text and repeated at the end of a section of writing, or they could be identified on a process or data flow diagram. This technique of mapping controls to process diagrams is shown in Figure 9.5.

One way to confirm that control documentation is complete is to examine a list of controls and verify that each control is reflected in supporting documentation.

If an IS auditor is developing documentation on behalf of a client, the client may have preferences regarding the technologies employed in its documentation. For example, a client may prefer that the documentation utilize certain flowcharting software, as the client may not have knowledge of the software in-house and/or may prefer to avoid purchasing a license to a new application.

Performing a Pre-Audit (or Readiness Assessment)

When audit management is unsure whether an audit program will be successful, they will often perform a preliminary review, which may be called a pre-audit, readiness assessment, or gap assessment. This is frequently employed when an organization is facing its initial audit, but it may be performed when employing new auditors or after significant changes to business processes or information systems.

FIGURE 9.5 Diagrammatic process mappings can visually overlay controls and tie them to control listings.

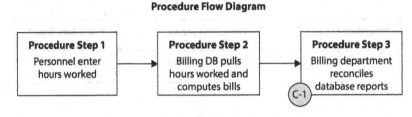

Procedure Flow Diagram

Procedure Step 1		Procedure Step 2		Procedure Step 3
Personnel enter hours worked	→	Billing DB pulls hours worked and computes bills	→	Billing department reconciles database reports

Control #	Control Description
C-1	Billing department reconciles billing summary reports to hours reports and initials …
C-2	…

Data Flow Diagram

Database of Hours Worked → Billing Database → Invoices and Summary Reports

Summary Reports

Control C-1: Billing department reconciles billing summary reports to hours-worked reports and initial billing reports. Billing reports are forwarded to finance.

The goals of a readiness assessment are to confirm that the control structure is correctly documented and that control activities are correctly represented. The readiness assessment should serve to avoid the embarrassment and disappointment of failed testing because of misunderstandings. It will determine whether control procedures are implemented as documented, and the goal is to confirm that documentary evidence needed for testing is available. The process involves auditors reviewing control documentation and conducting meetings with control owners. Auditors may perform some testing to the level of compliance, such as observing controls in walk-throughs, to confirm the existence of key controls.

If the engagement plans to test controls over a defined period, the pre-audit must be performed before the beginning of the test period. Adequate time after a pre-audit gives the client time to correct issues discovered in the pre-audit. Remediating a control issue may take time.

An example of this would be a company's first SOC 2 audit, when the client owns the audit program, and external auditors are to perform testing on management's stated controls. The auditor will confirm that they have learned management's procedures and controls and will determine whether the client is prepared for testing to begin.

This phase is in addition to procedures performed to generate an audit report, and no testing burden or required documentation is generated. Auditors will outline their observations and recommendations to management. Documentation gathered during this phase may contribute to procedure documentation in the audit workpapers but may never be used as documentation in support of testing. It will not serve to reduce any testing to be performed during the testing period because it is collected outside of the testing period.

 It is important to communicate to management how a pre-audit is different from testing. If the pre-audit has not been thoroughly explained to client personnel, control owners and managers may question why auditors hope to perform a confirmation of certain controls twice.

Presenting Pre-Audit Results

Any deficiencies identified are often presented to management in letter form. Any controls not in place also will be reported to management. The letter can address concerns at a number of different levels. Examples of feedback that may be delivered on a readiness assessment include:

- Control language requires updating or is inaccurate.

- Evidence of control activities is not captured.

- Certain transactional records are moved off-site monthly, but testing will require this information to be retained on-site for testing purposes.

- Control practices are not uniform in certain situations.

- Planned system changes will affect the performance or relevance of a control activity during a given period.

Some methodologies involve management agreeing in writing that they understand and will address any deficiencies in control descriptions or performance before the attestation period begins. If management lacks time for remediation, audit findings are likely. Management may accept an audit despite problems, perhaps citing that they accept the findings in a report and intend to have the issue fixed by the succeeding audit cycle.

Correcting Control Language

Most IS auditors are skilled at writing control language. When an auditor stumbles upon incorrect control wording, they should exhibit caution in some situations. Control language is the responsibility of management, and an auditor testing controls is forbidden from writing or altering it. Doing so would amount to auditors performing management's function and testing their own work. An auditor can report why a control statement is not accurate and can suggest that management reword the control to reflect the control activity correctly.

Client personnel may be unsure what the audit team is seeking, especially when management currently has limited experience with proper control language. This scenario has the potential to become frustrating for the client who is likely looking to expedite the audit progress. Audit management should clearly express to management why this separation of duties is important and can perhaps provide limited advice on what makes effective control language.

Organizing a Testing Plan

After the audit team has reviewed system and procedure documentation and has spoken with control owners about the control environment, they are familiar with the control environment. Once control wording is in its final form, the audit team is ready to assemble the audit's test program, sometimes referred to as the "test plan," "testing matrix," or abbreviated as the "matrix."

The test program is often in the form of a spreadsheet. Control activities are listed in the document, and auditors design a set of tests for each control. Depending on the control, there could be one to several test actions to perform, which could range from performing inquiries with control owners to complex substantive testing. Certain methodologies may require multiple types of testing to support the passing of each control. The degree of testing required for each control may consider the risk assessment, the audit objectives, and the project's budget.

A test plan outlines the testing down to the individual task level and provides a structure for capturing test results in a central document. The document ensures that the auditors perform testing completely. A test plan is an audit team's internal document. It helps auditors manage the testing process and track their progress.

 If you are working closely with financial auditors, the term "matrix" may refer to a central document in the joint financial–IS audit process.

Contents of a Test Plan

A test plan organizes a set of control objectives and controls within a spreadsheet. The test plan is designed to assist auditors in performing complete testing and tracking their progress, and it will contain many fields that will be populated later during testing. Certain fields will need to be populated before an auditor is ready to start testing, such as the following:

- Control number and name
- Control description
- Control objective supported
- Method of testing
- Date that testing will take place
- Test description
- Control owner
- Auditor resource assigned to test the control

Fields that are prepared by an auditor when developing a test plan include test results in narrative form. This part should provide an answer to a reviewer's question, "Was testing adequately performed?" and may include:

- Dates, names, titles, and contact info of people interviewed
- Short responses to inquiries when a full memo is not required
- Short description of the testing process
- Discussion of determinations made during testing
- References to supporting documentation
- Summary of test results
- Testing status
- Test results
- Residual risk
- Recommendations to management

Figure 9.6 illustrates an example test plan that documents a control as an entry in a testing plan.

The testing section of the test plan in Figure 9.6 is developed to capture test results even though testing has not yet occurred. Auditors could choose to expand this with sections for capturing residual risk and recommendations.

A good rule of thumb is that a test plan should contain enough information about the testing performed that an uninvolved third party could re-create/reperform the test if necessary.

Review of Test Plans

Before testing begins, audit management will approve the test plan. The review will consider the following:

- Do planned test procedures support a valid test of the control?
- Is the degree of testing appropriate to support each control objective and the audit's objective?
- Are all scope areas covered by testing?
- Do planned test procedures appear to fit in the planned time frame?
- Are auditors appropriately skilled to test their assigned controls?

The approved test plan document is placed in the audit's workpapers. Audit management may share this plan (or parts of it) with client personnel, or it may be kept internal to the audit team to protect the integrity of testing. If management knew precisely how each control was going to be tested, control owners could manipulate their controls to pass the audit even if they were not effective controls.

FIGURE 9.6   A test plan helps to organize the details of an IS audit.

Control objective #	2
Control objective	Accurate import of data files into system
Control #	2.3
Control activity	Reconciliation of validation totals upon file import
Description and control process	Users receive the file from the vendor and record key metrics relating to…
Risk	Data import results in inaccurate, incomplete, or improper transactions
Location performed	IT Department, Seattle, WA
Control validates for:	
Completeness	X
Existence	X
Accuracy	X
Presentation	
Validity	
Rights and obligations	
Cutoff	
Control type	Reconciliation
Control attribute	Preventative
Auto or manual	Manual
Documentary evidence generated	Initials on report
Testing	
Resource assigned to task	Michael, the auditor
Control tests	Manual
1.1	Existence of evidence containing initials
Test 1.1 result	*TBD*
1.2	Sample testing on population of initialed reports
Test 1.2 result	*TBD*
1.3	Corroborative inquiry regarding procedures being followed correctly
Test 1.3 result	*TBD*
1.4	Inquire regarding availability of procedure documentation
Test 1.4 result	*TBD*
Documentary evidence collected	*TBD*

Estimating Effort

Evaluating the time required for testing is important. When designing testing, the time it would take for an auditor to perform the task should be estimated and tracked. Estimates should include the amount of time to schedule meetings, perform interviews, review test materials, document testing results, update the test plan, and file documents. Experience is the best guide for estimating the amount of effort necessary to perform testing.

When reviewing a draft test plan, it can be helpful to review the estimated hours for each test, each control objective, and the overall plan. Plans should avoid spending too much time on less important controls or control objectives and ensure that testing for the most material control objectives is thorough.

It is important to compare test plan time estimates with the planned time budgets in the audit plan. If the testing plan is much larger than the time allotted, several issues could arise, such as:

- Testing is too ambitious, and there may need to be a reduction in test activities, control tests, or even control objectives.
- The scope of testing is appropriate and individual control tests are appropriately sized; however, testing time estimates were inaccurate. The client may agree to pay for the testing or may want to work with auditors to reduce the scope.

Time budgets for testing should build in some buffer time. Some technology tests sometimes don't reveal their magnitude until testing is performed. Issues with evidence delivered, unexpected test values, remediation of possible exceptions, and other interruptions could occur. When significant time budget overruns occur, they should be communicated to those responsible for governance.

Resource Planning for the Audit Team

Depending on how many audit professionals are available, resource planning will be more or less complex. For external engagements, the selection and bid solicitation process is the first place where an audit team assesses whether they have the skills available to perform an audit. After more detailed information is gathered from the primary contact, it is time to determine who will perform what work. The most efficient work will be performed by persons who have done testing on that technology (and the supported procedure) in the past. A project will be managed more efficiently with fewer persons involved; however, more hands on deck (with skilled supervision) can accelerate completion—to a point.

An auditor may find it useful to list the technologies in scope and assign audit resources to the technologies on the list. Such a list helps ensure that auditors have experience in the respective technologies they are assigned to.

If the audit organization has resources with "deep skills" in specific areas, those resources might not need to be included on the team in the field. A skilled auditor can meet with management to gather test materials and then "push down" specific testing tasks to persons with fewer skills. Without bringing them into the field, they can still contribute their skills, perhaps without requiring them to travel or meet with auditors.

Here is an example situation: Anne is reasonably familiar with Unix and available to the audit team, and Xavier is a Unix expert with limited availability. Anne can own several responsibilities on the audit team, including working with the Unix control owners. When information is gathered for the purposes of testing, Anne can pass the test materials, with detailed testing instructions, to Xavier. Xavier returns the test results to Anne, identifying the nature of any exceptions found. Anne is then able to address testing exceptions with the control owner and control manager. Anne has been freed up for other meetings, the testing has been performed by the most capable resource, and the audit has been expedited. Anne also gains valuable Unix testing experience.

Younger auditors who are mentored can develop technical skills and expand the experience base of the audit team. Exposure to new processes or technologies is best done when a more senior person is guiding them and able to serve as a backup. By doing so, an organization grows its skills from the inside.

Preparing Staff

Staff members are usually informed of the project when an engagement letter is signed. Details on a project's requirements may be scarce at the time, but management may share with staff a high-level summary of the engagement, the intended roles, and the planned hours per their proposal.

Once resource planning has been completed, it will be clear which personnel will be performing which tasks within an audit. When this occurs, it is important to meet with audit personnel to explain the project and define the roles of auditors during the project. During this meeting, audit management may provide resources or web links for auditors to use when researching the company and update their knowledge on technologies they will review. If audit team members will be tasked with technologies with which they have limited or outdated experience, this is the time to consider providing training.

Once schedules are set for resources visiting the client site, audit staff should be provided with guidelines on the logistics of traveling to their location and, if possible, finding acceptable lodging in the area. This is also a chance for audit personnel to raise questions about the audit. Frequently, dress code, guest Wi-Fi, and other auditee office norms are communicated at this time.

Performing Control Testing

Thorough preparation for testing will reap benefits when the audit team enters the testing phase. It may appear that the effort spent preparing is excessive compared to the task still at hand. Preparation's greatest benefit will be avoiding problems during testing, reviewing, and developing reports. Failure to include a few needed tests may set a team back several days. An error in objectives, scope, or understanding of the test environment can cause even greater problems.

A test plan developed with proper care will provide the audit team with a structure that facilitates effective and efficient testing. Testing is busy enough when it all goes well.

Control testing involves the execution of the test plan, consisting of interviews and evidence collection.

Project Planning with the Client

When the readiness assessment is complete and the client has addressed any preparedness issues, the attestation period is approaching. The primary contact will help the audit team plan and schedule testing. Table 9.2 is a quick summary of topics to address in this phase.

TABLE 9.2   Project planning to audit project planning

Subject	Common considerations
Dates	What schedule works for the client and the auditors? This will center on the availability of key resources and may consider busy periods in the client's cycle, such as financial closing cycles.
Availability of key resources	When will key control owners be away on training or vacation? Are there events or time periods to schedule around? Control managers are often asked to provide availability information on control owners.
Opening meetings	An audit traditionally starts with an opening meeting. In addition to audit management and the primary contact, it may include the audit sponsor, control managers, control owners, and staff auditors. Audit scope, schedules, procedures, permissions, and other subjects are discussed at this time.
Permission to access information	It should be clear to control owners what information they are permitted to provide to auditors and how they may provide it. Clients who manage sensitive information may follow risk-averse practices. For example, the client may forbid the use of flash drives or email to deliver audit evidence. Instead, the auditor and client will agree on a secure, online file sharing site that will be used. They may require approval prior to sharing certain documents or deliver information on a CD/DVD of which they later oversee the destruction.
Turnaround time guarantees	The time between when information is requested and when it is provided is sometimes an issue. Turnaround times can cause work bottlenecks for a client and can affect how quickly an auditor completes their work.
Learning procedures	How will an auditor get up to speed with the client's procedures? Are meetings with control owners required to confirm documentation is up-to-date? Is there a need to perform a walk-through of the controls before testing?

TABLE 9.2   Project planning to audit project planning *(continued)*

Subject	Common considerations
Scheduling testing	Do auditors coordinate with the control owners directly, or does the control manager want to manage their schedules? Also, remember the need for lead time, absences, and vacations.
Auditor workspace and Internet access	Where will auditors set up to do work? During what hours is the workspace accessible? Do auditors require the workspace to be locked? Do auditors require keycards or other means for accessing the client worksite? Is Internet access available? Will gaining access require accounts or passwords? Or training on client policies?

Gathering Testing Evidence

The process of gathering evidence should be orderly. Several common ways are used to request evidence:

- In person
- Email
- PBC (provided by client) lists
- File sharing sites

It is common when interviewing personnel to make in-person requests while discussing the control being tested. Direct requests may involve an auditor sitting with a control owner observing software controls and gathering screenshots and other electronic information as evidence. An auditor may confirm the availability of policies, procedures, and disaster recovery plans by asking someone to show where they are located. Direct requests may be made for information to be supplied later. An auditor might follow up a meeting with an email summarizing requested information and what is to be expected.

PBC lists are a tool that brings order to the process of gathering test information, but they're best employed when an auditor does not need to observe an activity directly. Concise and easy to understand, PBC lists are used by client management to track the information they are providing to auditors and by auditors to track what information they have requested and received. PBC lists are ideal for requesting transaction records, data, and process documents.

Depending on the testing being performed, there can be several phases of requests for information supporting testing. The audit team should be orderly regarding requests. If requests are made directly of control owners, the requests should be tracked.

Testing and providing test evidence can demand a great deal of time from client personnel, and a client may seek to minimize the impact. When gathering test evidence, the client contact may request that the team limit the frequency of information requests to their staff. Some requests may need to be made through the primary contact or their designee. Clients also may request liberal turnaround times so as not to overburden their personnel.

Sample Testing

Sample testing usually requires multiple rounds of requests. Initial requests are made by auditors for population sizes, from which auditors will select their test populations. Assuming the sample population information is correctly delivered (i.e., it provides a complete population to be sampled from) and understandable, auditors then submit a request for test evidence for the selected sample. Unless test results are successful, there could be requests for follow-up information. Unclear sample test results may require further investigation, resulting in requests for additional records or a live discussion with the control owner.

Security and HR Procedure Testing

Testing of information security often covers setup and removal of user account permissions. To determine whether access granting and removal procedures are operating, auditors will involve two key lists:

- Current employee listing
- List of employees terminated within a given period

These lists must be dated and should be provided at the same time. Lists should include (at a minimum) the employee's name, manager's name, department or title, employee hire date, and employee termination date. Testing surrounding HR procedures (such as hiring approvals) may require these lists as well. They may be requested early during testing or, in some cases (such as for a SOC 2), after some time has passed within a test period. These lists may also help auditors determine whether user account permissions are granted appropriately for their role. While there is a clear focus on employees, if the organization also utilizes the services of independent contractors, the same procedures should be performed for contract employees. Oftentimes this is a more difficult procedure due to differences in business processes for the onboarding and termination of independent contractors.

 It may be necessary to explain to a client why an IS audit requires auditors to speak with or make requests of HR personnel.

Using AI to Support an Audit

Artificial intelligence (AI) is being integrated into software products of every kind, and employees of every stripe are using generative AI (Gen AI) to assist with many kinds of tasks. We recognize that AI is a force multiplier that can make workers and systems more efficient, and auditors are no exception.

While we cannot anticipate every present and future use of AI, we are observing AI showing up in expected and unexpected places. As of this writing, the hype of AI is reaching manic proportions. We would not be surprised to see AI-powered electric toothbrushes, doorbells, and refrigerators. Some of these innovations are compelling, but others feel almost silly. The point is, IS auditors cannot escape the AI vortex and it's likely that IS auditors will see AI supplementing one or more of their tools.

Foremost, IS auditors must comply with the policies of their employer, whether an audit firm or a client organization. Whatever the business rules are—whether or not Gen AI is permitted, and under what circumstances—auditors must comply.

Because of the wide variety of potential uses of Gen AI in support of an audit, we take a principle-based approach to help IS auditors determine if, and how, AI can support audit operations. These principles include:

Confidentiality Any audit firm or customer organization data must be kept confidential. Thus, IS auditors must follow policies and business rules regarding information security and privacy. For instance, an auditor should not upload a customer's dataset to a public Gen AI system with a directive to analyze the dataset and provide the auditor with information about it; doing so would compromise the confidentiality of that dataset. If, however, the auditor's audit firm is a closed, private Gen AI system, then such an inquiry may be permissible.

Integrity Gen AI systems are known to "hallucinate," spoiling the integrity of the results of a query. It's also important to remember that Gen AI systems simply get things wrong from time to time. Thus, all results and outputs from an AI system must be confirmed for accuracy and completeness.

Human in the Loop When auditors employ an AI system to support their work, all outputs from an AI system must be confirmed for accuracy and completeness.

Explainability One of the foundational principles of an AI system is its explainability, which means that someone familiar with the inner workings of an AI system must be able to explain how an AI produced the output that it did. Note that not all AI systems are explainable; neural networks are a class of AI systems that are not always explainable, meaning that even the designers of a neural network may not be able to know how an AI produced a particular output. Given the high standards of integrity and transparency required of IS auditors, such a use in support of an audit and its conclusions would be inadvisable.

Safe, Legal, and Ethical Every use of an AI system, from simple queries to analysis of large datasets, must be safe, legal, and ethical. When we say "safe," we mean that the use of an AI system must be free of unanticipated consequences. By "legal," we mean that the use of any AI system must be legal and comply with applicable laws, regulations, and organizational policy. By "ethical," the use of an AI system must not rub up against auditors' professional codes of conduct and whatever it is that they stipulate.

An AI system is not intended to replace an IS auditor but instead can make them more efficient. For instance, an IS auditor may be auditing a business process that contains a large dataset from which she must choose samples. An AI system may help identify anomalous data in the dataset; anomalies can indicate unusual transactions, transaction errors, incomplete transaction data, and other outliers. Without an AI system, identifying anomalies could require additional time and effort.

Requests for Follow-up Information

Often, testing doesn't go precisely as planned. Certain information and documentation may be lacking from the provided evidence. This may occur when the course of business requires exceptions to standard procedures. An auditor may not learn of all these possibilities when meeting with a control owner, but instead, the auditor may find out later while examining evidence. Auditors usually need to make follow-up requests or have follow-up discussions to determine whether a notable occurrence during testing is an exception or is acceptable. If multiple follow-ups are needed for a particular control owner, it may be helpful for the IS auditor to consolidate the follow-ups in a precise manner to minimize any friction with client personnel and complete the audit in an efficient manner.

Launching the Testing Phase

Because the audit team and client personnel are ready for testing, it is time for auditors to begin. The availability of client personnel may determine the schedule of certain tests. Planning meetings will set expectations as to when auditors are expected to complete their work. Once schedules are set, logistics should be set for getting auditors into the field (such as securing transportation and lodging).

A testing period often starts with a series of kickoff meetings before interviews are scheduled with individual control owners. These meetings serve to introduce auditors to the control managers and their team of control owners and operators. This forum allows for:

- Auditors to meet personnel in person before testing launches
- Auditors to explain the scope of their audit and clarify testing expectations
- Control managers to frame the event for their personnel and to set rules and expectations
- Control owners to raise questions they may have about the process

Control owners may be experiencing some degree of nervousness, especially if they have not spoken with auditors before. Auditors will often find testing interviews work more smoothly when control owners have already met the auditor and have a deeper understanding of the scope and objectives of the audit. Gathering evidence will work more smoothly when control owners have had expectations set by management as to what they can expect during interviews and what they are permitted to provide auditors. In addition, explaining to control owners that the results of testing will be reviewed with them before they are reported will often help control owners relax when working with auditors.

Performing Tests of Control Existence

Tests of control existence determine whether a control is in place and operating effectively and whether the expected control activity occurs. Many controls will pass if a document simply exists or a software configuration setting is confirmed.

Control existence does not imply that a control is operating effectively over time, but whether it works when successfully operated. Existence tests are often performed using the following testing methods:

- **Inquiry and corroboration:** Auditor questions control owners about controls.

- **Observation:** Auditor views a control being performed.

- **Inspection:** Auditor reviews material evidencing compliance with stated control.

- **Reperformance:** Auditor performs control activity themself.

Many existence tests are performed when accompanying the control owner. Existence testing is a leading method of testing automated controls enforced by software.

Certain control testing engagements, such as SOX 302 testing and SOC 1 Type 1, test for a control's existence. A SOC 1 reports that at one moment in time these controls are in place. SOX 302 requirements also verify that the control environment is documented and that the controls have been tested once. In contrast, when the burden of control testing involves confirming operation over a given period, such as SOX 404 or a SOC 1 Type 2 report, control tests for existence may be performed multiple times during the test period.

Automated Controls

Automated controls are tested for existence. Many tests involve confirming that software configurations are set to specific values or observing whether systems enforce a rule.

Automated controls are most often observed in person by an auditor, and the auditor documents the occurrence for testing workpapers. Screenshots or other captured images provide evidence of software configurations. These images can be accompanied by an auditor's descriptive text for use as documentary evidence of the control test.

WARNING · In certain client situations, a control owner may ask to generate control evidence on their own. If possible, documentation of control settings should be gathered in the presence of the auditor, and preferably the first time an auditor asks to see it. Allowing a control owner to prepare evidence of controls can present certain issues, such as the control owner cutting corners and using images provided to previous auditors.

Governance Controls

Governance controls are often tested for existence as oftentimes policies, procedure documentation, committee meeting minutes, approvals, and other documents can be tested for existence. The provided documents may be subject to additional review per the test plan. If the evidence does not exist, additional test procedures will not be performed.

Further, governance controls are tested to ensure that executive management sets the "right tone at the top" when it comes to establishing a culture around various compliance, regulatory, and ethical considerations. Without the proper governance controls in place, it is difficult to have a proper control environment and pass the IS auditor standards for internal and external audits.

Testing Existence via Observation

Tests by observation are performed by an auditor witnessing whether a control activity is performed. This type of testing can involve the auditor looking over the shoulder of the control owner and requesting the owner perform certain tasks while demonstrating a procedure, or by viewing software settings within applications. Examples of observation testing include:

- Confirming that software requires and tracks approvals
- Observing physical and environmental controls for a server room
- Noting the existence of signed policies and a background report in an HR file
- Viewing system-generated alerts reaching a pager
- Reviewing a firewall rule base to confirm settings

Control tests by observation are recorded in writing in testing workpapers, or through retention of screenshots showing configurations. Recording observations should be sure to include the date and time, as well as the full name and title of the control owner. If observations can be supported by documentation beyond an auditor's recorded observations, this is preferable. Not all client or technology situations will provide such evidence.

 Client organizations may not permit their firewall rule base to be printed or carried off the premises. An auditor may have to observe the rule base and document their review as a test by observation. In cases such as this, it is important to include in workpaper documentation specific details of what was observed so that an uninvolved third party could reperform the observation and come to the same conclusion.

Testing by Inquiry and Corroborative Inquiry

Testing by inquiry involves asking questions of control owners. Inquiry is most commonly performed in person, over the phone, or via email. Some standards of testing require *corroborative inquiry*, meaning two persons with knowledge of a control must make reasonably agreeing statements. Discussions are documented, often in memos, and placed in the workpapers.

When documenting inquiries in workpapers or reports, the auditor must take care to phrase any statements by management as "representations" made by the client rather than facts. The wording might read, "Per the Unix system administrator, security logs are reviewed on a weekly basis," or "The CIO represented that spending is reviewed monthly."

The audit workpapers will include the record of the conversation and a memo addressing the result of the test.

Testing Existence by Inspection

Inspection is performed by reviewing the content of client-provided evidence. Testing may seek to analyze the nature of information discovered within the material being tested, which could be a report, policies, meeting minutes, or another document. Testing by inspection might seek to determine whether:

- Forms reflect the proper approval signatures
- Data backup software schedules and records match documented schedules
- Committee meeting minutes reflect management's discussion of the log file review
- Network and data flow diagrams are dated and current

The audit workpapers should include a memo addressing the results of testing, which identifies the inspected documents and copies of the documents. Any exceptions should be marked in the document and addressed in the memo.

Testing Existence Through Reperformance

Auditors may test security controls and automated controls via *reperformance*. In this type of test, auditors are taking information that is input to a control and performing tasks or calculations on their own to see if they achieve the same results that the control does. Examples of reperformance testing include:

- Attempting to set a password that is noncompliant with policies
- Confirming VPN authorization is required, and no guest account is enabled
- Checking whether specific employee keycards permit access to a restricted area
- Reproducing report values from business rules and raw data

 Reperformance can be used to perform substantive testing. Recomputing batch totals is a common audit procedure in financial audits.

The audit workpapers should include a description of the reperformance test. Workpapers for a reperformance test may then resemble other forms of testing, such as observation (VPN example) or sample testing (transaction records example).

Control Existence Failures

One possible result of testing is that a control being tested is not implemented. The absence of a control activity is often discovered during initial discussions with control owners or during a procedure walk-through. This absence can occur for several reasons:

- Documentation of controls has not been updated for new procedures. Effective controls may exist, but they are not included in testing programs.
- Changes in personnel resulted in a lack of ownership of the control process.
- Controls were documented as "to be implemented," or implementation was not successful.
- The organization never identified a standard industry practice as needing to be developed and performed.

When controls are found not to exist, they should be brought quickly to the client's attention. If it is possible (or prudent), validate the absence with a control manager before elevating the issue to the primary contact. A control manager may be able to clear up the confusion and prevent embarrassment, such as identifying a compensating control that could be tested to support audit objectives.

Performing Testing of Control Operating Effectiveness

Tests of control effectiveness confirm that a control activity's performance has been successful. Audits most often test control effectiveness over a defined period. To test for successful operation, evidence needs to indicate that a control repeatedly occurs correctly or appears to occur without interruption.

There are several methods of testing operating effectiveness, including inspection, reperformance, sample testing, continuous auditing/monitoring, and automated testing methods (not to be confused with testing of automated controls).

Testing Effectiveness by Inspection

Inspection can be used as a test of effectiveness as well as existence. Inspection can reveal that evidence indicates continued operation of a control activity. To test for control effectiveness, inspection is often used to review system log files or similar reports. Examples of how inspection methods are employed effectively for testing of reports or log files include:

- Confirming log entries were captured without interruption

- Reviewing changes to administrator passwords, confirming they are periodically changed in accordance with policy

- Reviewing changes to key settings, confirming that logs were not turned off and that settings were not changed at times during the testing period

Inspection may be employed as a method within sample testing as well. Testing may produce documents that are then tested by inspection.

 Gathering log file information for testing can be a challenge, as log files can be quite large and reviewing them may require special tools. A client may need to assist an auditor in interpreting the contents of the logs. If filtering is performed on a file before an auditor's inspection, it is best if the auditor observes the filtering operation and documents their observations. Some log files are overwritten on a periodic basis, limiting the availability of evidence.

Testing Effectiveness Through Reperformance

Effectiveness testing using *reperformance* can involve an auditor reproducing control activities performed by clients. This method can enable auditors to confirm that controls have been operating correctly because they can re-create the control activity themselves.

Reperformance can involve recomputing figures or confirming the reported values from source data. Examples of testing by reperformance include:

- Comparing a list of active system users against a list of terminated employees to see whether terminated employees' accounts were locked or removed.

- The control owner reconciles reports provided by two different systems and initials the documents before processing. To test that the reconciliation was performed correctly, an auditor reviews whether the figures match a sample of initialed documents.

- A billing application generates reports on hours worked by querying a database of hours worked on each project. An auditor seeks to validate that report totals are accurate. This data is imported into a database, and the auditor runs queries to attempt to reproduce the values generated by the billing application.

If the auditor is using a database or spreadsheet application to manipulate the data, workpapers may include evidence in electronic form. The auditor will need to take care not to alter the evidence. Workpapers should contain a memo discussing the testing methodology and identifying how and where (in the workpapers) the information is stored digitally.

Sample Testing

Sample testing is conducted when a control is performed on a regular basis and a record of the control activity exists. An auditor will select a population of control activity records to confirm that the control is being performed correctly. An auditor must review the population of control tests and then request the evidence supporting elements of that population. This technique often involves two rounds of requests from a control owner to gather a sample population and test evidence.

 It is important that an auditor perform procedures to ensure that the population provided by the client is complete and accurate. More importantly, though, the auditor should document processes or procedures performed by the client to understand how client personnel validate the completeness and accuracy of that information. This is a required test step even for reports that are generated directly from a system for both custom and canned reports.

Auditors may select sample populations by random test sets, or judgmentally select a population from the test set. Judgmental selection is often helpful when the materiality or criticality of transactions varies. Auditors might select transactions that relate to a company's largest clients or most critical systems. Judgmental selections may also seek to test a variety of transactions. Auditors might include different kinds of clients or applications hosted on different systems.

When an auditor performs sample testing, the audit workpapers should include:

- A written description of the testing process, including a discussion of how sample selection was performed and what sampling criteria were used

- A description of the sampling population, and how it was determined to be complete and accurate
- List of the test set population
- Test results
- At least one example of a successful test and each exception (if all test materials are not retained)

An auditor's workplace may have policies covering workpaper documentation requirements. Testing sometimes includes lengthy printed reports, and some places permit audit management to use their judgment regarding when retaining a sample of the report is sufficient evidence.

Continuous Auditing/Continuous Monitoring

In instances in which the volume of data is very large or the frequency of transactions is high, organizations may choose to utilize tools to perform continuous audits. This type of approach can be done with varying frequency (hourly, daily, weekly, monthly) based on the risk, volume, and type of data, and it incorporates the use of technology to perform an analysis of data/information. This analysis is designed with a level of precision such that anomalies in data are identified and reported upon for further detailed follow-up. Continuous auditing can both provide a greater level of assurance (since high-powered computers can audit 100 percent of a population in much less time than an IT auditor can manually audit a small sample) and make the audit program more efficient (as IT auditors are freed up to perform additional audit tasks, such as a follow-up on continuous audit findings, perform tests where the population or control type does not align with continuous audit techniques, and so on).

In instances related to testing IT general controls, technology may be used continuously to monitor items such as security provisioning. In that case, while there may not be a significant amount of activity over a period of time, tools can be put in place that will send an alert to a responsible party immediately if an unauthorized or inappropriate change in access is made. As mentioned, the use of such a tool can provide a high level of assurance and security, while at the same time enabling an organization to spend less time on periodic access reviews.

Continuous auditing should not be confused with automated testing or testing programs, described next. Although those techniques involve the use of technology, that technology is generally used at a particular point in time to assist in the performance of audit procedures.

Automated Testing

Automated testing can quickly provide an auditor with large amounts of critical system information. It often involves the use of testing programs (sometimes off-the-shelf programs) or test scripts. Test scripts may be designed by the audit organization, the software's manufacturer, or a third party. Running scripts should be done only in close cooperation with a control owner, such as a database administrator or operating system administrator, and approved by appropriate client personnel.

Testing programs and scripts may need to be run on a client's system. Many organizations will require that a script or testing program be reviewed before auditors are permitted to run it on their system. A client's review will usually confirm that a script is executing only inquiry commands. Special read-only user accounts may be enabled temporarily for test programs to run. The use of automated testing should be brought up early in conversations with the client, as approval and preparation for their use may take some time.

Testing Programs

Testing programs will often be developed by a software vendor. To assist a client's review of a software program, the client can be provided with the software make and version number, and, if possible, the auditor can provide software documentation.

Examples of automated testing programs include:

- Vulnerability scanning tools
- Segregation of duties analysis
- A program that runs on a network to identify all workstations connected to the domain and to confirm that antivirus definitions are current on all workstations
- Network analysis programs that review network components and the protocols enabled on network devices

Testing programs often provide organized reporting of the results of testing. An auditor's test consists of reviewing output reports from the test and recording the observations in a document. In addition to the output report and a record of an auditor's testing, the workpapers should include details on the testing program used, including name, manufacturer, version number, and relevant configuration settings used. The results of this analysis are then recorded in the testing matrix. Finally, a copy of the testing program should be retained.

Test Scripts

Scripts are programs that are run on systems and that usually generate a file showing the commands executed and the results. Scripts are written in scripting languages (such as JavaScript, /bin/sh, PowerShell, or SQL) that execute commands sequentially. Scripts can run a query and write query results into an output file. Test procedures will involve reviewing scripts' output files.

When a script is employed, an auditor should observe management running the script and collect the evidence without delay. The audit workpapers should include:

- Information on the system being tested, including version, current patches, and relevant configuration settings
- Text of the script itself, plus any information on the publisher, name of the product, and version number
- Output report from running the script
- Results of the auditor's review of the output report

Scripts designed for certain technologies have the issue of expiring as the technology becomes obsolete, so infrastructure is required to keep them current. Unless an auditor is an expert in a given scripting language, they should avoid writing or editing scripts. Automated tools are more common with large audit organizations and cutting-edge audit shops.

Discovering Testing Exceptions

Auditors will face problematic test results and will need to determine the nature of any exception. It may not be clear whether an unexpected result equates to a test failure. Despite preparation, an auditor may not immediately understand test results. A clear understanding of the procedure and the role of the control within that procedure is needed so that the auditor can determine whether a nonstandard test result amounts to an exception or simply a test that was run incorrectly. If an auditor reports prematurely on findings, it can lead to challenges with the client relationship and loss of professional integrity for the auditor. Auditors should attempt to confirm an understanding of how the test results amount to an exception.

An auditor should communicate an exception with audit management first. Audit managers will confirm their understanding as to why it appears to be an exception. Then the control manager and primary contact will be informed—perhaps at regular update meetings or more immediately if the finding is highly material.

When an exception is confirmed, it is documented in test matrices and the workpapers. If possible, the description of the exception should accompany the source document, including where it was identified. If the test was discovered in data testing or images of a screen, the evidence should be captured electronically (and perhaps printed), and a written description should be included.

Reporting exceptions in audit reports usually includes reporting to the client the residual risk and making recommendations.

Issues Requiring Follow-up

There can be several reasons why an auditor must return to the control owner for a clear understanding of test results and exceptions. Most often, this will be because a procedure, a control, or the evidence is not completely understood, possibly because control documentation is insufficient or outdated.

When following up with a control owner, the auditor, if email or a short conversation is not possible, should inform the primary contact and control manager that they will require more time with control owners. After completing follow-up with control owners, any clarifications the auditor acquires should be documented in the workpapers as support for the results of testing. In addition, procedure and control documentation could require updating. If follow-up confirms the exception is valid, it must be documented as such.

Confirming an exception with the control owner and control manager should prevent disagreements when an audit report is presented to a client organization.

Here's an example requiring follow-up that involves network security: Upon an initial review of the client's firewall rule base, the firewall appears to permit traffic that includes less secure protocols. The auditor does not yet know if this is an exception. Further inquiry is required for the auditor to learn whether compensating controls address the risk:

- Traffic could additionally be managed by a router, isolating it to specific servers.
- An intrusion prevention system (IPS) may be employed to isolate traffic that introduces security issues into the network.
- Valid business reasons may have led management to accept the risk of permitting this protocol. Staff may regularly monitor the activity.

Auditors may be told that management is aware of and accepts the risk of these protocols. Auditors would document management's communication in the workpapers, perhaps with an email or a memo recounting the conversation.

Discovering Incidents Requiring Immediate Attention

While testing, an auditor could discover information that requires immediate attention from the audit team, client management, or both. An auditor has a professional duty to be aware of possible indicators of illegal activities, fraud, hacking, or other improper actions. Situations that could require immediate attention include:

- Fraudulent evidence provided by client personnel
- Discovery of critical vulnerabilities that compromise the integrity of the environment being audited
- Improper, fraudulent, or unlawful actions on the part of client personnel
- Manipulation of financial figures reported to internal or external parties
- Requests made to auditors that could compromise the integrity of the audit process

An auditor must be sure to understand the nature of the discovery correctly. In many instances, auditors will not have a problem consulting with control owners to confirm their understanding; however, situations such as fraud could require a high degree of confidentiality if a proper investigation is required. If the audit team together is still unclear on how to handle a situation, it is best to consult audit management or certified professionals on how best to proceed.

Discovery of Fraud

If an auditor uncovers evidence of possible fraudulent or criminal activity, it is urgent that they address this with audit management. The auditor must begin thoroughly documenting all communications and should write a description of how the discovery was made. The auditor should confidentially consult with fellow auditors to confirm their interpretation of the evidence. If the team suspects a possible issue, they must then decide how to proceed.

If auditors agree that evidence appears to show fraudulent or criminal activity, the audit team will need to notify appropriate client personnel of the incident. The team should consider the nature of the incident and carefully consider which members of client management or the governing board are the most appropriate to inform.

In small to middle-sized organizations, the audit team may consider informing the CIO, CFO, legal counsel, internal audit director, or other members of executive management. In larger organizations, a level below executive management may prove more appropriate. In extreme situations, the chair of the audit committee or other governing board may need to be informed first. A meeting should be set up to discuss the evidence and see how the client would like to proceed.

The danger of informing someone in the client organization of fraud is that the person being notified may be the person committing, overseeing, or approving the fraud.

Handling Evidence of Fraud or Criminal Activity

If the auditor possesses documentary evidence of potentially fraudulent activity, they will need to isolate the document and establish a *chain of custody* for the potential evidence should criminal investigation proceedings occur. This chapter does not claim to be an authoritative resource on procedures to follow in the event of discovering fraud. If fraud is discovered, a professional investigator should be consulted immediately for guidance. The investigator will advise the audit team on how to act until an investigator is able to take over the chain of custody for evidence and continue the investigation.

An auditor may be required to handle evidence relating to the discovery of fraud or criminal activity. It is preferable to establish the chain of custody of evidence following the instructions of a certified professional. A certified professional may not be able to assume the chain of custody of evidence the day it is identified, so an auditor may be required to perform certain actions. The following points are important to consider when developing a chain of custody of evidence:

- Do not make any marks or additional marks on the evidence or disfigure it in any way (for example, don't punch any holes in it to insert it into a binder).

- Begin an evidence log spreadsheet that will track the location and possession of the evidence. The spreadsheet should be constructed to track the following information:

  - Evidence log number

  - Date and time evidence was received from the source

  - Information on the source of the evidence, including person, source system, report names, and other details

  - Name of person submitting evidence to custody

  - Date and time evidence is entered into the evidence log

  - A discussion of the information located within the documentary evidence that may indicate fraud

  - The method of storage of documentary evidence, which should be stored behind locked doors or in locked cabinets when not in the custodian's direct possession

  - The name of the person responsible for keeping documentary evidence secure and in their possession, and the time and date when the person accepted possession of the evidence; if the security of the evidence is transferred between members of the audit team, the date and time when this transfer of ownership occurs must be recorded

- If the evidence is a piece of paper that has information on only one side, some parties advise that one may write the following on the back of the page: document number, document revision date, and the source of the document, and sign and date it.
- Place the evidence into a tamper-evident envelope.
- Lock the evidence in a locked cabinet or safe.

If anyone on the audit team has experience with fraud investigations, this person should oversee this process, and as soon as possible a certified fraud investigator should be consulted. When a certified fraud investigator arrives, auditors will formally hand over custody of any documentary evidence and the evidence log to the investigator and record the transfer of custody in the evidence log.

Depending on the situation, size, and scope of the discovery, it may be advisable to have a trusted professional witness all evidentiary handling actions and use two-person integrity to handle the evidence throughout its life cycle.

WARNING   When collecting evidence that may later be used in a legal proceeding, strict forensic rules must be followed for collecting and protecting it. This situation often requires the services of a trained forensic specialist, who will follow these procedures to protect the evidence and its chain of custody. Consultation with legal counsel will also help determine if the audit and its associated evidence should be conducted under the purview of legal privilege.

Improper Actions by Management

Management may behave improperly during the audit, and client personnel may fear for their reputation with client management when auditors are around. Hence, client personnel may behave inappropriately as well. It is important for an auditor to maintain professional composure when client personnel act inappropriately. Less serious issues of inappropriate behavior can be addressed between audit management and the primary contact. More serious issues may require a meeting between control managers and audit sponsors.

Certain improper actions may be severe enough to interfere with the execution of the audit, such as:

- Refusing to provide test evidence
- Providing fraudulent or "doctored" evidence
- Attempting to explain away the evidence or cover up the activity
- Requesting audit personnel to act inappropriately
- Threatening audit personnel

Violations at this level will require action by the audit team. Auditors should document and communicate the incident immediately to audit management. Audit management and client management should then meet and address the issue.

Certain improper actions by management could strongly affect the audit execution and the final report. In some situations, refusal to provide evidence or providing fraudulent evidence can compel the audit team to suspend the audit.

In some jurisdictions, auditors may be required to promptly notify law enforcement of certain illegal activities, such as child porn. Auditors should consult with audit management to determine when and how this notification should be performed.

Materiality of Exceptions

The auditor employs judgment to assess the materiality of exceptions. During testing, an auditor will determine whether the exception is serious enough to warrant the immediate attention of management or whether it is a discrepancy of limited consequence. The question of materiality is addressed partly in the testing matrix, when an auditor assesses residual risk for a control that did not pass.

The materiality of controls and control failures is discussed in more detail in Chapter 2.

Audit management may not always agree with an auditor's assessment of materiality. Hopefully, this situation will be resolved quickly and a final determination can be made. A staff auditor may have a client-specific perspective, and management may have more insight into the nature of certain risks.

Assessing Residual Risk

After the nature of a control failure is confirmed, the auditor can assess its residual risk. Certain failures will introduce a relatively limited amount of risk, such as identifying low-access accounts that are not compliant with a password policy. Other failures can be highly material and require immediate attention. Following is an example of a material failure.

Auditors are performing tests of network security controls. When testing a requirement that employees use VPN for external access, auditors learn that RDP (Remote Desktop Protocol) traffic is permitted through the firewall and enabled on workstations. Inquiry reveals that some IT personnel work from home and that they access their workstations remotely using RDP, bypassing the VPN and its security controls. The residual risk is that unencrypted traffic, including authentications, is permitted through the firewall and is potentially visible to third parties. This situation is clearly a material breach of compliance with policies and compromises network security controls.

Table 9.3 depicts examples of how different exceptions from the same test could result in different levels of residual risk.

TABLE 9.3   Different kinds of exceptions and how residual risk is evaluated

Risk level	Exception	Residual risk
Low	No password policy is enforced on a shared account used in a lab for Internet access only.	Inappropriate persons may gain Internet access.
Medium	No password policy is applied to several user accounts with mid-level permissions.	Inappropriate persons may be able to compromise certain tasks within a procedure.
High	No password policy is applied to secure administrator- and executive-level accounts.	Inappropriate persons may gain access to executive-level accounts and perform inappropriate authorizations or access administrative accounts and compromise security administration.

In Table 9.3, the high-risk example would definitely be brought to the attention of the report's audience; however, it would be up to the auditor whether to bring medium- and low-risk exceptions to the attention of management.

Categorizing or Ranking Exceptions

In some reports, such as internal audit reports, the severity of exceptions may be weighted. Categorizations of materiality can be selected, such as:

- Ranked, most to least important
- Linear, such as low, medium, and high, or on a scale of 1 through 5 or 1 through 10
- Stoplight, with green (controls operating or compliant), yellow (requiring attention), and red (controls not operating or noncompliant)

Several parties can use weighted exceptions:

- Auditors may choose to present only the most material exceptions to the governing entity, again ranked by importance to the governing entity. Exceptions of lesser materiality are addressed with management.
- The IA department can use the ranking when scheduling any retesting of failed controls.
- Management may use the ranking to prioritize their remediation plans.

Weighted results lend effectively to diagrammatic representations of the residual risk. Weighted results help management better understand which residual risks are the most important.

Some situations may warrant the notification of those charged with governance of the volume of lesser materiality exceptions that could indicate a more pervasive issue at the organization.

Developing Audit Opinions

Auditors will develop opinions on individual control tests, control objectives, and at times, an audit as a whole. Reviewing test results and developing an opinion can be performed after all testing is complete, any follow-up with the control owner has been performed, and the test evidence is ready to be documented in the workpapers. In the event testing revealed exceptions, the control owner and the auditor would have already agreed to the facts relating to a performed test. An audit opinion is entered into the audit testing matrix.

 Agreeing on facts ahead of an opinion will reduce disagreements when reporting reveals the exceptions to management.

An auditor will conclude their opinions on all controls supporting a control objective before developing an opinion on a control objective.

Management Representation Letter

When certain licensed professionals are performing an external attestation, it is sometimes the practice to have client management sign a *management representation letter*. A management representation letter states that client personnel have provided truthful information throughout the audit process. By signing, management takes responsibility for the information provided to auditors. This attestation by the client provides an auditor with a degree of legal protection in the event the report's contents are subject to litigation. When this practice is followed, audit checklists require this letter before the delivery of a signed report to the audit client.

Control Activities

Developing opinions involves weighing the materiality of each exception, its residual risk, and its impact on control or audit objectives. Opinions on control activities will most often take the form of:

- Control passes
- Control passes with observations
- Control passes with notable but not material exceptions
- Control fails due to exceptions
- Control fails because the control activity is not performed

Tests that merely "pass" the planned test procedures are easy to handle. Passing controls are entered into the testing matrix and reflect simply that the test passed. There is no burden for the auditor to develop statements of residual risk or recommendations.

Testing observations are generated when a situation is uncovered during testing related to the control environment. Inquiry, for example, may reveal control weaknesses outside of the test plan scope. An auditor might also identify possible improvements to the control structure, or note that certain procedures are not always performed consistently.

When an audit test does identify exceptions, but the audit team considers the materiality of the exceptions to not constitute a control failure, the control may pass, but the exceptions may be brought to the attention of management. For example, an Active Directory control states that no shared accounts are permitted on the network. Inquiry confirms that setup of shared accounts is not permitted, but a review of accounts identifies several old shared accounts, though follow-up reveals the access granted to these accounts is appropriately limited and that the accounts were not used by personnel.

Testing a control activity could result in failure before all supporting tests are performed. In these situations, an auditor will need to decide whether to curtail any more testing of that control and conserve effort. An auditor decides whether additional tests of that control will benefit the client and whether the opinion of the control objective or the audit is influenced by these control activity test results.

Control Objectives

An auditor opines on control objectives once the opinions of all supporting control activities have been documented. Auditors will determine how the results of control testing support the control objective. Opinions on control objectives will state that controls pass with notable observations or fail. An audit's methodology may provide guidance in determining if a control objective passes or fails. Audit methodologies might provide guidance, such as:

- Each passed control objective must be supported by at least one substantive test confirming the effectiveness of supporting controls.

- A single control failure shouldn't fail a control objective unless the control is a key control or the auditor documents a clear justification. (Individual audit organizations each have their own tolerance for addressing control failures and any resultant additional testing that can be performed to determine whether a failure is an isolated incident.)

- A failure of two or more control activities should fail a control objective, unless an auditor documents a clear justification of their determination.

If auditors are weighing a control objective, when testing failures exist, auditors must consider how the control objective supports the audit's objectives. While developing an opinion on a control objective, auditors may determine that evidence is inconclusive, and that additional testing is needed before a determination can be finalized.

Final determinations on control objectives should be documented in the workpapers and approved by audit management.

Audit Opinions

Certain reports will deliver an opinion on the audit's results. An SSAE 18 Type 2 report will attest to whether controls appear to be operating effectively. To develop an audit opinion based on control objectives, the opinions on control objectives will be weighed against the audit's objectives. Audit opinions typically pass, pass with qualifying conditions, or fail. A statement supporting this determination should be approved and entered into the workpapers.

Developing Audit Recommendations

At the conclusion of an audit, it is common for an auditor to provide recommendations on improvements to a client's control environment. These recommendations can be delivered formally or informally.

Formal Recommendations

Auditors can provide formal recommendations to the client. This could take the form of internal audit reports or a letter accompanying the audit report. Recommendations included in a report are frequently accompanied by management's responses and possibly remediation plans.

Formal recommendations are carefully worded. Auditors must be careful to advise that management take action to remediate a weakness, avoiding statements that may appear that auditors are making decisions on the part of management. Wording is commonly along the lines of "management should consider" performing a certain action. Auditors may avoid highly specific recommendations, because there are often several options on how a control weakness can be mitigated and clients may argue specific methods rather than agree on a need to fix controls. In other words, auditors may advise a client on *what* to do, but will refrain from describing *how* to do it. However, depending on the audit rules of engagement, and if auditors are free to suggest mitigation approaches, they will often do so. When in doubt, it can't hurt to ask the auditor if they are permitted to advise their client on the remediation of audit findings.

Informal Recommendations

Auditors often discuss informal recommendations with control managers during testing. It is constructive for both the auditor and control managers to discuss improving an organization's controls. Executive management, such as an audit sponsor, may have some pointed questions they would like to ask auditors at the close of an audit. Like formal recommendations, auditors should phrase responses with care and maintain impartiality and professionalism in their answer.

Managing Supporting Documentation

In the process of auditing, an auditor will handle a significant volume of audit documents, process documentation, and testing evidence. Having a complete set of documentation is necessary to ensure the integrity of the audit process. In addition, having clear and organized documentation will benefit the execution of the audit. Some of these benefits include the following:

- Auditors will be able to answer detailed questions about test results.

- Audit managers will be able to confirm work is being done to expected standards.

- For auditors in accounting firms, the audit may be subject to a peer review, where other firms review a project's report and its workpapers and scrutinize the audit. An accounting firm may also be audited by the Public Company Accounting Oversight Board (PCAOB), in which case the auditor will be required to show all of the documentation that has been collected during the audit. Audits of systems according to the Payment Card Industry Data Security Standard (PCIDSS) and ISO standards have similar oversight structures, including "audits of audits" to ensure that audit procedures are followed and that minimum quality standards are met.

It is important that the format of testing documentation be finalized before staff auditors begin testing. Auditors also need to make sure that documentation keeps up with the progress of testing. Memos recording conversations should be inserted promptly into workpapers.

During the audit, it is often convenient to manage testing evidence in binders or electronic folders that are separate from audit documents.

Complete audit documentation will often have most or all of the following sections:

- Table of contents

- Engagement documentation, such as the signed engagement letter

- Contact information for all auditors and auditees

- Memos providing direction on understanding documentation

- Meeting minutes and memos from meetings between auditors and client personnel

- Procedure documentation and background information on key systems

- Testing matrices and lead sheets

- Supporting documentation generated during testing

- Checklists for audit completion

- Testing methods used

- Sample guidance

- Document review

Storing Electronic Documentation

It is increasingly common to retain as much as possible in the form of electronic versions of documentation. Electronic documentation can be stored as files within a filesystem, such as on a shared network or cloud-based data storage provider, but it is sometimes managed by supporting software.

In some engagements, outside auditors provide a copy of audit workpapers to the client. Sharing electronic versions of documentation can make this easy to do. When delivering electronic documentation, the auditor must confirm the preferred media and schedule of delivery with the client.

Electronic storage can introduce challenges if it is to be archived for a specific period. Storage media preferences evolve and could render documentation difficult to access if it is stored on outdated media. Another consideration is that certain media has a limited shelf life. Data that is to be stored for extended periods (generally, for more than 5 to 10 years) may need to be periodically rearchived onto newer media to ensure that the data can be retrieved if needed.

Data stored within audit management software risks becoming difficult to access in the distant future. Software can be expensive, and an organization could face software compatibility issues once the systems that generated the archive files have been upgraded, replaced, or are no longer supported.

Lead Sheets

One common practice for organizing testing documentation is to begin a documentation section for each control with a "lead sheet." Lead sheets often contain similar information to what was tracked in the testing matrix. They provide the reviewer with a tool for following the testing process and understanding the accompanying documentation. Lead sheets can also capture a reviewer's sign-off.

 Within most spreadsheet software, it is possible to populate information into lead sheets from the testing matrix.

Lead sheets typically end with the testing result clearly stated, as in Figure 9.7. Evaluations of residual risk, auditor opinions, and recommendations are often tracked in separate tools, but this is not necessary.

Delivering Audit Results

The audit's fieldwork has been completed, and control owners and managers have agreed to the facts of testing. Before delivering audit results, the auditor updates all matrices with test results, evaluates residual risks, and writes draft versions of audit opinions. The next task is to compose the results into a presentable form.

Typical presentations of audit results can include:

- Delivery of a formal report for review by the audit sponsors and other management
- Presentation of the report to the organization's audit committee of the board
- Publication for distribution to and review by third parties (such as SOC 2, PCI DSS, and ISO audits)
- Memo or letter summarizing audit results and reporting issues to control managers and/ or audit management

FIGURE 9.7   A testing lead sheet contains comprehensive information on the control and the testing performed.

Testing Lead Sheet Company ABC, Inc.	Control ID	2.3
	Tested by	Michael, the auditor
	Date completed	3/29/2025
	Reviewed by	

Control ID	2.3

Control Objective

Accurate import of data files into system

Control Activity

Reconciliation of validation totals upon file import

Tests Performed

Inquiry	X
Inspection	
Observation	
Re-performance	
Sample testing	X

Control Owner

Michael, the auditor

Sample Size

Approximately 440 file imports over the 6-month test period

Test Procedures Performed

1) Inquiry—Corroborate between two different department personnel

2) Sample testing—From a sample of reports, verify that the batch number of the import was recorded on the report and that import totals have been initialed and dated.

Workpaper Reference

2.3a—Memo describing sample selection process
2.3b—Test population
2.3c—Memo describing test results

Test Results

Inquiry
Inquired of file import manager Jane...

Sample Testing
Reviewed 40 out of 440 reviewed import reports and found initials

Conclusion

No exceptions noted

If IS audit procedures are a subset of a larger audit, IS audit results are communicated to audit management for inclusion in their report.

Discussions with audit sponsors and the primary contact will have clarified what a client expects for their deliverable at the beginning of the audit. The degree of formality will vary depending on client needs and the company culture.

> In the event of cyclical testing, such as SOX 404 or OMB A-123, the completed tests are often entered into a tracking system. After test completion, depending on the structure of testing and review, a limited amount of additional reporting may be requested. Internal audit management will prepare internal reporting for financial leadership so that they are comfortable signing off on controls supporting financial figures. This process includes a review of exceptions and their remediation projects.

Contributing to Larger Audit Reports

When an IS auditor is working for a team that includes non-IS auditors, typically audit management does not have an IS audit background. In this situation, the IS auditor may have a stronger understanding of the materiality of certain test results and the residual risks than the audit manager responsible for writing and delivering the report. This situation will require close coordination between the IS and non-IS auditors, which can be a challenge toward the end of an audit when time schedules are tight and several tasks are being pushed to completion. Ensuring that audit results are communicated correctly in final reports and during presentations can be a challenge. If audit reporting over- or underrepresents the materiality of information systems risks, it could have consequences for the audit relationship and the reputations of control managers or auditors.

IS auditors should participate in reviewing the report's representations. The audit manager should be receptive and allow this participation. This situation may be delicate because the audit team is balancing the success of its relationship with the audit manager with the needs of the audit organization and the client.

Audit Report Contents

Frequently, either the audit organization or the client organization will provide an audit report template. In the case of ISO and PCI DSS audits, audit report templates from governing organizations are used. At a high level, a report communicates scope, procedures, and conclusions. In audits involving numerous auditors, several parties may contribute content. Coordination between the report writer (frequently the audit manager or senior) and auditors who performed testing is standard during this time. The report writer will confirm with the field auditors that their statements correctly represent audit activities.

An audit report often includes the following:

- Standard language addressing the parties involved, audit scope, and auditing standards invoked during the audit
- Rules regarding the distribution of the report

- If applicable, the audit opinion
- If applicable, statements by client management regarding company history, financial activities, processing activities, and related controls
- Audit objectives
- Controls to be tested and how they support control objectives
- Test results and conclusions from testing, including exceptions, and evaluations of materiality and residual risk
- Auditor recommendations
- Client-provided feedback on exceptions, conclusions, or recommendations

During this process, audit staff and management review how to appropriately present the audit results. Younger auditors tend to experience mentoring, corrections, and rework during this phase.

Audit Management and Staff Disagreements

A staff auditor and an audit manager may draw different conclusions from test results. For an audit opinion to be defensible by audit management, the report and supporting detail must agree. During report writing and review, as audit management becomes familiar with test result details, a staff auditor's practices and judgment may face criticism. Disagreements can arise surrounding the assessments of the nature of an exception and the residual risks.

When a staff auditor's conclusion about an exception's residual risks differs from that of audit management, a discussion must follow. The following are several scenarios where disagreements may occur:

- A staff auditor may lack a thorough understanding of specific technologies or client procedures and may draw incorrect conclusions from test results.

- Staff auditors frequently have more familiarity with a procedure than audit management does, so their conclusions may be considered as-of-yet-undocumented knowledge of the situation. If an audit staff person does not thoroughly articulate the reasons for their conclusion, they may omit information critical to audit management's review and potentially be overruled. Audit management may require augmenting documentation when they come to understand the reasons behind their judgment.

- A staff auditor may be younger and less experienced with specific technologies than the control owner, and may prove impressionable in the presence of an "expert." A young staff auditor's judgment may be affected by the control owner's representations that an exception is not serious. Staff auditors may require mentoring on the nature of the exception and related risks.

Audit management may need to discuss exceptions with the client. Additional procedures may be required, such as increasing the test set size or testing a compensating control. Additional testing may prove frustrating to the client and audit team, as both client and audit team personnel are not expecting additional burdens on their schedules. This situation should be preventable through clear communication during audit procedures and regular oversight by management.

Writing the Report

Once test results are clear, writing the report should be a rather straightforward process. Most audit firms and IA departments have developed reporting templates; in some cases, clients will provide a report template; and sometimes, an audit template is provided through a standard such as PCI DSS. When no standard template is provided (or expected), the client may select a report from a similar engagement and benchmark. When developing the shell and structure of a report, the client may identify the parties responsible for providing content for the different sections of the report.

A report can be drafted in sections, even as testing progresses. As soon as a test has been captured fully in the workpapers, the section of a report relating to that test can be drafted for inclusion. It is common for the greatest amount of writing to be done to account for exceptions.

Attention to these few practices will deliver effective audit reports:

Write in the clearest way possible. This can mean breaking up long sentences into single statements using the fewest words. Although the auditor may be technically minded and trained, often it is better to compose the report in nontechnical terms so that client management can gain at least a basic understanding of findings.

It is often preferable to refer to control owners by their title. Each person can be listed with their title as a participant. A report will be meaningful to more people when individual names are avoided, however, and it will serve as a more effective tool for future management and reviewers.

If multiple writers are contributing report sections, employing uniform language throughout the report is essential but can prove challenging. If dissimilar language is used, more time may be required during review. It is handy to provide writing examples upon which the auditors writing each section can benchmark.

The testing matrix plays an important role in writing the report. Some reports, such as SOC 2, ISO, and PCI DSS audit reports, present results from the full testing matrix. Internal audits may focus reporting on the most material exceptions.

The report is not complete until the workpapers and testing matrix have been reconciled to the report detail. This requires that evidence in the workpapers is organized and supports the content of the report.

Auditors may want to sign the audit report digitally, both as a means of ensuring its authenticity and to protect it from tampering. Also, when delivering an audit report via email, auditors may consider encrypting the audit report to protect the contents from eavesdropping by other parties.

Management Response

When the conclusions of the audit report are clear to the audit team, the team sits down with the primary auditee contact, and possibly control managers, and delivers the results of testing. Presentations should share draft language of exceptions wording and audit opinions from testing, which will be included in the final report.

Some report formats seek management's responses to the results of testing. Client management will review the wording and the nature of the audit findings and compose responses. The auditor will include these responses in the final report.

Discussing the Auditor's Wording

Client management may choose to discuss the wording of exceptions or opinions. In some situations, the wording of the audit opinion could trigger confusion for the auditee organization or its customers. As long as a rewording doesn't affect the message or the nature of the opinion, audit management might agree to adjust certain wording.

Here are some examples of wording issues:

- Data backups have been a persistent problem, and the control objective of "daily incremental, weekly full" backups is not being met. Configuration problems existed within the backup software. Because resources were busy on other critical projects, the configuration problems were not addressed. IT management argues the successful weekly full backup is a mitigating factor not mentioned in test results or the opinion, though they agree the control failed, as worded.

- Partway through the audit period, an organization replaced a system that had been problematic due to a control issue. Per testing guidance, testing at different points during the period reveals material exceptions. Management impresses the point that the situation is now controlled effectively and argues that the audit report's description of test results does not fully reflect the effectiveness of their current and ongoing controls.

Auditors will have to consider these situations carefully. Client management may be seeking to avoid embarrassment for any exceptions, and an auditor must take special care not to give in to pressure or suggestions that result in misrepresenting exceptions or residual risks. If an auditor is unsure whether a change is appropriate, they should consult with higher levels of audit management regarding management's requests.

Management's Responses to Auditor Recommendations

Responses from client management about audit recommendations usually involve one of three responses:

- Management performs auditor-suggested remediation.

- Management seeks an alternate solution to their control weakness.

- Management believes no remediation action is necessary and assumes the risk of control failure.

Management may address the audit opinion in their written response to defend their position.

The auditor will then review management's responses and develop their own opinion on management's action plans. The auditor may believe that the response is appropriate and agree with management about the plans, but this is not always the case. When management responds by saying no action is necessary, an auditor may be compelled to report this inaction to regulators or governing entities or include in the report that management's responses do not satisfy the auditor's own concerns about the risks involved.

In some audits, management is required to develop a written plan (such as a plan of action and milestones [POA&M]) to remediate some or all audit findings. Then, the auditors, or others in authority, are required to review and approve the written plan. Progress will be ascertained in subsequent audits.

Report Audiences

The audience of an audit report will be defined at the beginning of the audit engagement. The report should be written in a language and at a level of depth appropriate to that audience.

Reports to Audit Committees

Reports presented to audit committees are written to communicate at a high level. Audit committees consist of members of the board of directors, who are usually removed from the day-to-day operations of an organization. Their main concern is whether there are problems that they need to be aware of.

Frequently a report will begin with a high-level executive summary. Language in the executive summary must be clear and direct without diving into details. For subjects warranting more thorough attention, additional pages provide supporting detail so that interested members can drill down further into a subject. Auditors will make sure that the issues of greatest concern get the attention of the committee.

Audit committee reports often make a point of:

- Clarifying the scope of the audit
- Drawing attention to significant issues
- Communicating management's response to issues

Reports attempting to describe mid-to-low–level operations are generally too detailed for the needs of an audit committee and likely to lose their attention or, in the worst case, confuse members. Be careful not to introduce confusion; this will waste valuable time and may strain the auditor/client relationship.

Audit management will frequently attend the meeting to present results and field any questions the committee may have about the report.

The report typically will be provided to committee members several days in advance of an audit committee meeting. Auditors will need to be aware of the committee's deadlines and procedures for submitting reports on time.

Reports to Client Management

Client management should have a high level of interest in the detailed results of an audit. Reports written for management will contain operational-level information with which they are familiar. The report's audience will include control managers and their directors. It is important that information in the report be accurate to ensure the report is deemed credible. Within the client organization, there may be parties with motives to discredit a report or the audit organization, so an auditor's diligence in presenting indisputable facts will protect their reputation.

Reports to management will often contain information on the results of each test performed. Exceptions will be addressed with more detail, and auditors will present their assessment of residual risk and will include recommendations.

In audit situations where management is tasked with providing their own responses addressing exceptions and recommendations, a report's completion can be held up by management's delay in responding. Auditors may need to engage their primary contact and perhaps their audit sponsor to ensure management delivers timely responses.

Frequently, when an audit is being presented to an audit committee, a second, more detailed, report is issued to client management. Providing a more detailed report to management before drafting the report to the audit committee will ensure that all communications with management are complete.

Depending on the organization, a senior executive may ask to sit with auditors and control managers to discuss the detailed report's findings.

Reports to Third Parties

Certain engagements involve presenting testing results to parties outside of the client organization. Here are a few examples of such audits:

- Organizations that provide services to third parties hire their own auditors to publish an audit report. Thus, a service organization avoids opening its doors to auditors hired by its customers. The final report is provided to customers and their auditors. An example of this is the transaction-based SOC 1 or SOC 2 reports governed by the AICPA.

- When two organizations agree to a partnering relationship or are considering a merger or acquisition, one party may request the results of an audit of the second party.

- Banks and other parties extending credit to an organization may require a set of procedures to be performed by auditors in terms of lending.

  Terms of an audit engagement should clarify what parties are permitted to review the report and under what conditions.

Reviewing the Draft Report

Once the report is in final draft form, it is subject to review by the head of audit management. This person will proofread the report for correct language and will tie the report back to the audit proposal and plan, testing matrix, and supporting workpapers. When a certified professional is signing a report, they will go through this process with great care before signing off on the report. Reviews often include reviewers initialing sections as complete during the review, such as initialing lead sheets when review of testing documentation has been completed.

Ideally, a review will go well; certain points of feedback will be delivered to improve the report, testing matrix, and workpapers; and the audit team will have a limited number of points of cleanup—opportunities for feedback and retesting may be required.

In lengthy audit projects, it may also be appropriate for auditors to conduct periodic reviews of audit results throughout the audit, instead of waiting until the end of the audit.

Some situations will lead to the testing workpapers not following the same structure as a report. If this occurs, it is important to include a description in the workpapers describing how they can be navigated to support the report.

Signed Reports

Certain reports must be signed by a certified professional. For example, a SOC 1 audit report must be signed by a certified public accountant (CPA) and a PCI DSS report on compliance (ROC) must be signed by a qualified security assessor (QSA) and by the auditee's management. The certified professional will have taken care to ensure that the audit process has complied with the standards set out by the certifying organization. The audit will have followed guidelines for documentation, review, sample size, internal review, and perhaps other areas. Checklists may be employed that must be completed before an audit may be signed.

Internal audits performed by outside parties may request that the audit report be signed by a certified professional or specialist. Client management can have reasons to seek a certified professional's sign-off on specific testing or internal audit reports. Here's an example: A company has had challenges with its fledgling internal audit department. Another company is seeking to partner with the company but has concerns, and places conditions on the partnership agreement that an outsourced certified internal audit firm provide a signed report.

Delivery of the Report

Audit management will clarify with the client how they would prefer to have the report delivered. Depending on the engagement, a report may be delivered during a closing meeting. Some clients expect a bound hard-copy report, while others will be happy with a printout or electronic file (this information should be agreed upon with the auditee at the commencement of the audit). Reports may be delivered at a formal occasion, such as a closing meeting or an audit committee meeting.

Reports delivered to management are often provided to specific personnel. Audit management will get a distribution list from the primary contact and provide sufficient copies.

Service providers often need to make their audit reports available to their customers' auditors. This is usually achieved by mailing hard-copy reports, sending electronic copies via email, or posting audit reports on a website.

Delivering Electronic Reports

If reports are delivered in electronic form, they should be prepared so that they cannot be altered. Additional controls, such as encrypting the report in transit, that prevent text or figures from being copied out of the report and prevent the report from being printed, may also be appropriate in some circumstances. These controls will help to prevent the original audit report from being misrepresented, abused, or distributed outside of its intended audience.

Additional Engagement Deliverables

A client organization, or the department being tested, could request additional information from an audit process, such as the following:

- Feedback on policies
- Suggestions for improving the control environment
- Test result information in greater detail than in the report
- The feasibility of control mitigation strategies

The client organization may have selected the contracted audit party because of the experience of its team members. Certain audit projects give an auditor a significant understanding of a client organization's environment. After testing, it is not uncommon for clients to ask the auditor how their systems and processes compare to those of their peers.

Auditors can be helpful when asked such questions, but they should be cautious in their responses. There are several potential pitfalls to avoid:

- Auditors should avoid making statements that go beyond their experience with the client and their personal areas of expertise.
- It would be problematic if a manager justifies a decision since "the auditor told me we should do it." An audit is usually not a consulting arrangement, and engagement letters often do not include disclaimers used by business advisors.
- An auditor should exhibit prudence when performing assessments of clients that are business competitors. An auditor should be careful not to reveal details of a competitor's systems. Even without identifying the party, providing certain information could be perceived as unethical and in violation of professional standards. If a client believes an auditor is overly liberal in sharing business information, they may fear that the auditor will treat their sensitive information similarly in dealing with other clients.

An auditor is in no way discouraged from providing advice to management but must do so in accordance with an engagement's requirements and in accordance with ethical and professional standards. Auditors may seek to avoid putting certain comments or advice in writing to protect them from exposure to liability or professional criticisms.

Audit Closing Procedures

The audit process concludes when reporting is finalized and workpapers are ready for storage. Methodologies may require certain checklists and approvals to be completed when wrapping up an audit.

Audit Checklists

Audit management may follow checklists for certain milestones during the audit. These may include requirements during the bidding and launching cycle, as well as closing procedures that make sure the audit is complete. Audit closing procedures may include the following:

- The report and workpapers have been reviewed.
- The report has been delivered.
- The signed management representation letter is in the workpapers.
- Workpapers are signed off on and archived.
- Final invoices have been sent.

Audit checklists are typically filed along with the engagement workpapers.

Closing Meetings

At some point after the delivery of reports, audit management and the client will discuss the performance of the audit. If the audit organization plans to continue performing audits for the client in the future, these inquiries help to develop business relationships as well as refine the performance of the audit. It is common to identify points of friction in the audit and seek ways to improve interactions. Clients may prefer to perform testing within certain calendar periods or may want to centralize requests for information. This occasion is a good opportunity to address changes in personnel. A client may choose to have another person serve as the primary contact, or the audit team may announce a change in staffing or management.

When auditors deliver these reports to management, these discussions frequently append the meeting in which reports are delivered. Auditors should be prepared to discuss such points at the end of the audit. It may prove best to address certain issues at a later time. For example, specific details of findings and recommendations for improvement may be best discussed with individual control owners, who may not be participants in the closing meeting.

Final Sign-off with the Client

Audit methodologies may involve formalizing the closing of an audit with a client. Audit organization management may seek closure to ensure that they can close the book on an audit. Auditors will know that all work on a project is complete, and no more hours will go against project budgets. Final invoicing can be processed, and the auditor can send a final invoice for audit services to the client.

One way of formalizing the end of an audit is to have management sign a letter accepting its completion. The client often signs a final document stating that the auditor has provided all services as contracted under the engagement letter. Such letters are placed in the engagement files.

Client Feedback and Evaluations

After an engagement is completed, the audit organization frequently will ask for feedback from client management. Some audit organizations track a complex set of feedback metrics. It is common to use this information for internal performance evaluations and bonuses.

An audit firm may follow up with clients with surveys. These surveys will solicit feedback on different parts of the audit. The client will provide the audit team with different "grades," which the audit firm may consider when seeking to improve service quality in the future. If a client is pleased with the service, this proves an opportunity for the audit firm to ask a client if they may serve as a reference client when the audit firm is bidding on services to a new client.

Some audit firms will bring the audit team together to review the client's feedback. If audits are performed on a regular schedule, the results of "what went well" and "potential improvements" in a prior audit may be discussed during kickoff meetings to ensure that focus is given to following up on feedback received.

Audit Follow-up

From an auditee's perspective, an audit is a part of an ongoing life cycle. After the initial growing pains of the "first time through," an organization usually experiences audits on a regular cadence. Control managers and owners are often familiar with the audit process, though specific testing practices may evolve to fit changes in business, technology, customer needs, and regulation.

A mature audit function will track issues over successive audit periods. The results of testing cycles or prior audit reports will have identified areas of improvement. Management will have agreed to certain remediation measures. The audit cycle provides an auditor with an opportunity to revisit controls that have failed in previous periods.

Follow-up on Management's Action Plans to Remediate Control Failures

Internal audit cycles will suggest improvements to control activities, and management will reply to these recommendations. Sometimes, management implements the auditor's recommendations; sometimes, they reply with alternative approaches to the issue. Often, a project is started by management as remediation and the planned completion date is provided with management's reply. Internal audit departments will track management's remediation plans on the calendar and will follow up with the project owner regarding completion. Testing will be reperformed on failed controls and may be performed on controls newly introduced by a project as well.

Retesting Issues in Succeeding Periods

Controls with audit exceptions will be retested either until improvements are made and the control passes, or the control is replaced with a new control activity. A test with repeated control failures will be shared with appropriate executive management and, depending on materiality, may be reported to a governing entity.

External Audit

External audit agreements often approve performing audits over several periods. The audit organization develops in-house knowledge of the client organization's issues. Audit recommendations aim to work with management to improve the control environment so testing failures in previous periods are avoided. It is standard to retest areas where previous tests have failed.

If tests continue to fail over successive periods, auditors will draw attention to the issues in their reports; audit reports will draw attention to issues that persist. In high-risk areas, audit management may deem the issue material enough to issue a qualified or adverse audit opinion.

When an audit organization is performing its first audit of a client, it will review previous periods' audit reports. These help the auditors evaluate the risk of different areas and include in-scope failed tests and management's remediation plans.

Internal Audit

Internal audit departments frequently track controls to be tested over cycles. Certain control testing cycles, OMB A-123, for example, will permit less-critical control testing on a less frequent basis. If a control has passed in previous testing, a risk evaluation may deem the control needs to be tested on a two- or three-year cycle only. However, control tests that have experienced exceptions, that have a high level of materiality/risk to an organization, or that include processes that have changed in previous periods probably will need to be retested on a more frequent basis.

Cyclical control testing is only a portion of internal audit work. An internal audit will, at the direction of the board of directors, pursue audits of different functions within an organization. Unlike internal audit testing cycles or external audits, audits of specific functions may be a one-time event. Issues discovered in these reports are tracked within the internal audit department. Internal audit management and the audit committee should allocate time each year to revisit the status of different issues uncovered in these audits.

Management Projects

Frequently, management will agree to remediate issues by initiating a project to solve the problem. Information systems projects end up in a priority queue, where they are allocated time based on available resources, complexity, relative importance, and other factors. Management is frequently cooperative in understanding the importance of a remediation project, but these are evaluated and prioritized among dozens, if not hundreds, of other IT projects. Auditors may find themselves pressing management on delayed projects relating to ongoing control issues.

Summary

This chapter has provided an in-depth study of the IS audit cycle, with the goal of providing a link between CISA study materials and the discipline of professional IS auditing. This material, which provides real-world associations for the subject materials addressed in this book, will benefit your recollection. After all, successfully passing the CISA audit exam requires more than being able to recite facts; it requires you to understand all aspects of IS auditing and many aspects of IT management and security.

An additional goal of this chapter has been to portray the "organic" challenges that auditors face in the field. Examples have illustrated scenarios that experience has shown are reasonable considerations during an audit.

We hope you have a better grasp of the IS auditing process and an awareness of the challenges encountered in the field. To the experienced auditor, it is frequently the case that as soon as one audit cycle ends, planning for the next period's audit is just around the corner. There are always opportunities to improve a current process, and experience will unveil more perspectives and stories.

Appendix A

Popular Methodologies, Frameworks, and Guidance

contain detailed information on practices
that contains that may assist you in your efforts. This appendix is intended to help you
make sense of these available resources and the terminology used in each section.

The appendix is divided into two major sections. The first section covers common
terms and concepts, whereas the second section describes the various methodologies, frameworks, and guidance available, and provides background information. Which portion of the book is the more relevant to be helpful to a CISA-certified professional?
If you are reading this for the first time, it is recommended that you proceed directly
to the first or most common Terms and Concepts, which provides the
basic terms relevant to be more prepared. Once you're done with the terminology
section and moving on to methodology, frameworks, and Guidance, you
must determine if you need some methodology, frameworks, A
through guidance, as you, in which a framework may be most relevant.

Read This

You will be interested on the use of the various frameworks processes
These resources. The above that employees of employing and professional
practices at tasks and techniques that may be required in an organization.

Common Terms and Concepts

This section was created for reference when working with one of
in the second section or another for educators in this book. Many
terms are referenced in this book as are several methodologies, frameworks, and
guidance. Many terms are referenced in this book, several methodologies, frameworks, and
guidance are referenced in this book, several methodologies, frameworks, and
guidance are referenced in this book, several methodologies, frameworks, and both of the
most common particular parts of each and each of the

Appendix

Popquist
Method-to-
Framework

Are you getting ready to develop, document, or audit IT controls? Several methodologies, frameworks, and guides contain detailed information on processes, control objectives, and controls that may assist you in your efforts. This appendix is dedicated to helping you make sense of these available resources and the terminology used within each of them.

The appendix is divided into two main sections. The first section focuses on common terms and concepts, whereas the second section describes the various methodologies, frameworks, and guides available and provides background information, high points, and a summary of why the resource may be helpful to a CISA-certified professional.

If you are reading this for the first time, it is recommended that you pay close attention to the first section, "Common Terms and Concepts," which provides you with a foundation from which to view the resources. Once familiar with the terminology, you can skip to the second section, "Frameworks, Methodologies, and Guidance," and find the resources that most directly apply to you and your organization's objectives. A table appears at the end of the appendix to guide you as to which frameworks may be most relevant to you.

Exam Tip

You will not be tested on details of the various frameworks discussed in the second section of this appendix. This appendix provides the aspiring and professional IS auditor with additional tools and techniques that may be required in an organization.

Common Terms and Concepts

This section was created for reference when working with one of the frameworks discussed in the second section (or another not addressed in this book). At some point, you may hear someone refer to one of the frameworks or methodologies described in this appendix or wonder if a particular framework or methodology may be valuable to you.

When looking for resources, consider the level and type of information you seek. Are you looking for information on implementing processes, control objective statements, or detailed guidance on specific controls? Are you developing a set of general IT controls, assessing a process, or writing particular policies and standards? Each of these activities may be covered in complementary resources; however, if you are in a time crunch, it is recommended that you first determine what you are looking for. Using the following standard terms and concepts should help you narrow down the type of information you are on an adventure to find.

Governance

Enterprise *governance* (or corporate governance) is defined as the responsibilities and practices followed by executive management and the board of directors to ensure that the enterprise's strategic goals and objectives are met, risks are managed, and resources are used responsibly.

ISACA defines governance as follows:

> Ensures that stakeholder needs, conditions and options are evaluated to determine balanced, agreed-on enterprise objectives to be achieved; setting direction through prioritization and decision making; and monitoring performance and compliance against agreed-on direction and objectives.

 NOTE See the ISACA online glossary for other definitions at www.isaca.org/ resources/glossary.aspx.

Examples of enterprise governance practices would be senior management providing direction and oversight, clearly identifying roles and responsibilities, coordinating initiatives, managing resources, identifying and assessing risks, and enforcing compliance. Integrity, ethical behavior, risk management, transparency, and accountability are just a few principles of enterprise governance. Enterprise governance is critical for increasing investor confidence and ensuring compliance and profitability.

IT governance is a vital part of enterprise governance and aims to ensure that IT is meeting strategic goals and managing risks, and that IT investments are generating business value. IT governance is the foundation for all IT strategic and tactical activities. It helps ensure that strategic goals and objectives are set and measured against; activities, resources, and investments are managed and prioritized; and IT risks are identified and managed.

Although IT governance is the focus of the *Certified in the Governance of Enterprise IT (CGEIT)* certification, it is essential to understand that IT governance is the foundation of IT management and may affect which processes and controls are prioritized or assessed at any given time.

Goals, Objectives, and Strategies

The terms "*goals*" and "*objectives*" are often used synonymously in documentation and planning. Both describe a desired end state, or what an organization intends to achieve. Strategies are the means or actions by which an organization intends to realize these goals.

One of the most popular terms in the IS world and control and process frameworks is "objective." Remember that an objective is what the enterprise is trying to achieve or the expected result of an activity. It is always set within a context. For example, the COBIT framework describes several IT processes and related objectives. In addition, the framework describes specific control objectives. COBIT is not an objective framework, but aligning IT processes with COBIT may help achieve objectives.

Business objectives, *process objectives*, and *control objectives* are different from each other. Business objectives are higher-level statements that guide the organization. Process objectives describe what the process activities intend to achieve, whereas control objectives describe what the implemented controls are trying to achieve or risks the controls are attempting to mitigate. It is essential to understand that the concept of objectives is widely used, and they need to be kept in the proper context. Some examples of different objectives are shown in Table A.1.

TABLE A.1   Examples of objectives

Type of objective	Context	Example objective
Business Objective	Supports business goal of managing IT-related business risks	Implement IT risk quarterly reporting by Q4.
Process Objective	Risk assessment and management process	Ensure all risk mitigation plans are updated by risk owners every quarter.
Control Objective	Risk response	Ensure the risk response process identifies risk strategies such as avoidance, reduction, acceptance, or sharing; determines risk responsibilities; and considers risk tolerance levels.

Detailed definitions of goals and objectives are provided in the *Business Motivation Model*, managed by the Object Management Group. In this publication, *goals* are seen as general statements that are ongoing, longer-term, and qualitative, whereas *objectives* are intended to be more specific, shorter-term, time-specific, and quantitative. In the same model, *strategies* are said to be the activities that are planned to channel efforts toward goals. The model provides an entire framework for developing mission, vision, goal, objective, strategy, tactic, and directive statements, just to name a few, for an organization.

Processes

Simply stated, *processes* are used to manage and organize activities, fulfill the organization's mission, and help meet organizational goals.

Each process represents a series of steps or activities designed to take one or more inputs and create some output(s) that deliver a service or product to meet specific expectations or desired objectives/goals for a particular group of customers. Usually, a process consists of one or more written procedures describing the actions of people (and/or systems). In summary, processes are put into place to guide how an organization works to produce value for customers.

Example Process

An example of a process would be the assessment and management of IT risks. The process would represent a set of activities and may look like this:

Determine the Context > Understand the Business Process > Identify Risks > Assess Risks > Prioritize > Respond > Monitor

- Potential inputs: Internal and external audit reports, business stakeholder interviews, vendor assessments, vulnerability scans
- Potential outputs: Risk registers, risk reports, mitigation tracking reports
- What business goal does this process meet? Manage IT-related business risks

Several frameworks describe the various IT processes, interdependencies, inputs, outputs, and metrics, most notably COBIT and IT Infrastructure Library (ITIL). These frameworks are discussed later in this appendix. For more detailed information on business process design or improvement, you may want to research business process modeling or methodologies and toolkits on the web, such as Rummler Brache (www.rummlerbrache.com/toolkit).

Capability Maturity Models

Initially developed by the Carnegie Mellon Software Engineering Institute as a software evaluation model, *capability maturity models (CMMs)* are used in several frameworks to determine and describe incremental maturity levels of business process and engineering capabilities.

The maturity of a process or system is rated on a scale from 0 to 5, with a level of 0 referring to a nonexistent process and a level of 5 equating to the greatest maturity in capability. The ideal maturity rating differs for each organization.

CMMs can assist organizations with developing process maturity baselines, benchmarking, prioritizing activities, and defining improvement. They can be helpful in conjunction with any process framework adopted. An example of a CMM is one that is used in the COBIT framework to describe the maturity of COBIT-identified processes.

Table A.2 provides an example of a maturity model and the ratings used to measure those processes outlined in COBIT. Figure A.1 represents how this maturity model can be used to show current and future desirable states and for benchmarking against competitors or industry standards.

TABLE A.2 Example process maturity model

Level	Label	Description
0	Nonexistent	Complete lack of any recognizable processes. The enterprise has not even recognized that there is an issue to be addressed.
1	Initial/ad hoc	There is evidence that the enterprise has recognized that the issues exist and need to be addressed. There are, however, no standardized processes; instead, ad hoc approaches tend to be applied on an individual or case-by-case basis. The overall approach to management is disorganized.
2	Repeatable but intuitive	Processes have developed to the stage where similar procedures are followed by different people undertaking the same task. There is no formal training or communication of standard procedures and responsibility is left to the individual. There is a high degree of reliance on the knowledge of individuals and, therefore, errors are likely.
3	Defined process	Procedures have been defined, documented, and communicated through training. It is mandated that these processes should be followed; however, it is unlikely that deviations will be detected. The procedures themselves are not sophisticated but are the formalization of existing practices.
4	Managed and measurable	Management monitors and measures compliance with procedures and takes action when processes appear not to be working effectively. Processes are under constant improvement and provide good practice. Automation and tools are used in a limited or fragmented way.
5	Optimized	Processes have been refined to a level of good practice, based on the results of continuous improvement and maturity modeling with other enterprises. IT is used in an integrated way to automate the workflow, providing tools to improve quality and effectiveness, and making the enterprise quick to adapt.

Other capability maturity models also exist and may be used to evaluate the overall maturity of functions such as an IT audit department, internal audit, or enterprise risk management.

FIGURE A.1   Rating scale for process maturity

Industry Average

Legend: 0 - No processes at all
1 - Processes are ad hoc and disorganized
2 - Consistent processes
3 - Documented processes
4 - Measured and managed processes
5 - Processes are continuously improved

Controls

Controls are how management establishes and measures processes by which organizational objectives are achieved. Controls may be established to improve effectiveness, efficiency, integrity of operations, and compliance with laws and regulations.

Control frameworks may represent collections of controls that work together to achieve an entire range of an organization's objectives. Because many organizations operate similarly, standard control frameworks have been established, which can be adopted in whole or in part. Some of these frameworks are discussed later in this appendix.

There are many ways in which the frameworks discuss controls:

- **Internal control:** This aggregate system is put into place in an organization to provide management with reasonable assurance that objectives are met. It refers to the many control objectives and related control activities in place to meet business objectives.

- **Control objectives:** Control objectives ensure that business objectives are achieved and that undesirable events are prevented, detected, and corrected.

- **Control activities/controls:** These are the specific policies, procedures, and activities in place to meet the control objectives. Controls may be implemented to help prevent or detect and correct undesired events in the organization.

There are two main types of controls: general controls and application controls. General controls support the functioning of the application controls—both are needed for complete and accurate information processing. General controls apply to all systems and the computing environment, whereas application controls handle application processing.

Some examples of IT general controls are:

- Access controls
- Change management
- Security controls

- Incident management
- System development life cycle (SDLC)
- Source code and versioning controls
- Disaster recovery and business continuity plans
- Monitoring and logging
- Vulnerability management
- Configuration management
- Event management

Examples of application controls are:

- Authentication
- Authorization
- Completeness checks
- Validation checks
- Input controls
- Output controls
- Identification/access controls

Tips for identifying and documenting controls include the following:

- When looking at processes, define potential risks/points of failure (what could go wrong in a process, or what would happen if this process fails?).
- Identify controls and examine whether they operate at a granularity level that makes them adequate in preventing or detecting errors and irregularities.
- Check to see if the control's strength is commensurate with the risk level the control intends to mitigate.
- The cost of implementing a control should not exceed the expected benefit.
- Well-designed internal controls can lead to operating efficiencies and sometimes reduction in costs and risks.
- Effective controls reduce risk, increase the likelihood of value delivery, and improve efficiency because of fewer errors and a consistent management approach.
- Auditors are responsible for the independent evaluation of internal controls and whether they are adequate.

The Deming Cycle

W. Edwards Deming developed a four-step quality control process known worldwide as the Deming Cycle, PDSA (Plan-Do-Study-Act) or PDCA (Plan-Do-Check-Act). The steps in the Deming Cycle are:

- **Plan:** Establish objectives to align with desired outcomes and predict results.
- **Do:** Execute the plan in a controlled manner.

- **Study/check:** Check the results regularly and compare with expectations.
- **Act:** Analyze the results and take corrective actions.

Many of the frameworks described in this appendix are based on this concept, which supports continuous quality monitoring and business process improvement. Each framework defines the processes and how they support the different steps. For example, specific processes are necessary in the project management frameworks for adequately planning, executing, and monitoring a project. Although each process is unique, they collectively contribute to continuous quality and improvement.

Projects

Virtually all technology professionals participate in projects. Projects are organized activities intended to develop a new process or system or a change to a process or system. Projects are generally thought of as unique, one-time, nonrepeated efforts. Examples of projects are:

- Design and development of a new software application
- Migration of an application from Windows to Linux
- Development of a new accounts payable process

Organizations usually utilize formal project management techniques in conjunction with software or system acquisition and implementation processes.

Here are a few things to keep in mind about projects and project management:

- Projects are a means to organize activities that are not addressed within normal operational limits. Often, projects are used to achieve an organization's strategic objectives.
- Project management consists of a set of processes.
- Projects are similar to operations in that they are performed by people, constrained by resources, planned, executed, and controlled.
- Operations are ongoing, while projects are temporary and unique.
- Project and operational objectives are different. Once project objectives are met, the project is considered complete. Operational objectives are ongoing and are in place to sustain business activities and goals. Once operational objectives are met, new ones are adopted and things keep moving forward.
- Controls exist in projects. Examples include comparing actual with planned budgets and time, analyzing variances, assessing trends to effect process improvements, evaluating alternatives, and recommending corrective actions.

There are frameworks available to assist you, should you be responsible for planning or managing a project. In addition, the information provided within these frameworks may be helpful if you are responsible for auditing the SDLC or assessing any related project documentation.

Frameworks, Methodologies, and Guidance

Creating appropriate processes and controls can be daunting. This is where industry frameworks, methodologies, and guidance can become valuable. Many internationally recognized organizations have already conducted the research and documented their conclusions, publishing several high-quality frameworks and methodologies.

Before re-creating the wheel, consider using these resources for your process and control discussions, audits, or project planning. Many documents available today are comprehensive and can save you much time and heartache. They often outline key processes and controls that can be implemented to meet specific business goals and objectives.

The following sections identify the most renowned and respected resources for managing IT governance, controls, processes, information security, and projects. The background and high points of each resource are described, as well as how each may be useful for a CISA-certified professional.

Remember that the following resources are merely structures of ideas formulated to solve or address complex issues, or outline possible courses of action to represent a preferred and reliable approach to an idea. They are not intended to be the sole source for your efforts. Use them to assist you as you build policies, controls, processes, or procedures.

Business Model for Information Security (BMIS)

Based on research conducted by the Institute for Critical Information Infrastructure Protection at the University of Southern California Marshall School of Business, the Business Model for Information Security (BMIS) was developed in 2009 by ISACA, mainly for use by security professionals. Primarily built on a foundation of systems theory, the business model is unique in that it tackles security issues from a systems perspective. The model is not intended to replace security program best practices but should be used to integrate security program components into one complete functioning system. As experienced cybersecurity professionals, we like to use BMIS as it helps them better understand the relationships between people, processes, technology, and the business.

BMIS Highlights

BMIS is a three-dimensional model, like a three-sided pyramid, composed of four elements and six dynamic connections, as shown in Figure A.2. The model requires balance and can be distorted should one of the elements not be addressed or appropriately managed. Using a business-oriented approach, the model explores the elements and the relationships between them in great detail.

The model's primary objective is to create an "intentional" security culture through instituting awareness campaigns, developing cross-functional teams (such as risk councils and steering committees), and obtaining management support and commitment. In addition, this intentional culture should aim to fulfill enterprise governance needs by ensuring the alignment of information security objectives to business objectives; instituting a risk-based approach to controls; instilling balance among the organization, people, process, and technology; and aligning security strategies across the enterprise.

FIGURE A.2   The Business Model for Information Security

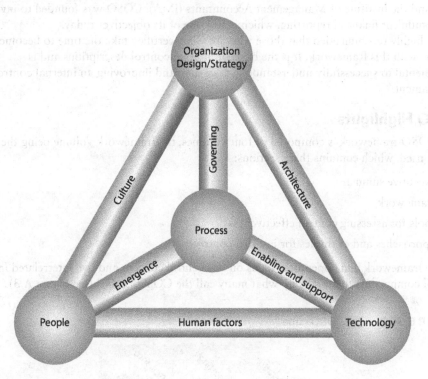

BMIS Value for the CISA

The model is helpful for senior executives, information security managers, those responsible for managing business risk, and those responsible for designing, implementing, monitoring, or improving an information security management system (ISMS).

In addition, the model is useful if you are looking for ways to align information security to privacy, risk, physical security, and compliance. It also provides a common language in discussions with business management about information security.

COSO Internal Control – Integrated Framework

Originally authored in 1992 by Coopers & Lybrand (now PWC) and updated in 2013, for the Committee of Sponsoring Organizations of the Treadway Commission (COSO), the COSO Internal Control – Integrated Framework is by far one of the most fundamental frameworks available to an IS auditor. It defines internal control and provides guidance for assessing and improving internal control systems. The term "internal control" stems from senior management's need to "control" and be "in control."

Formed in 1985, COSO is a private-sector group in the United States sponsored by the American Institute of Certified Public Accountants (AICPA), American Accounting Association (AAA), Financial Executives International (FEI), the Institute of Internal Auditors (IIA), and the Institute of Management Accountants (IMA). COSO was founded to investigate fraudulent financial reporting, which is still one of its objectives today.

It is highly recommended that those who are CISA-certified take the time to become familiar with this framework. It is the basis of internal control descriptions and is fundamental to successfully understanding, assessing, and improving an internal control environment.

COSO Highlights

The COSO framework is composed of four volumes, the framework volume being the most widely used, which contains these sections:

- Executive summary

- Framework

- Tools for assessing control effectiveness

- Approaches and examples for internal controls

The framework and appendices focus on one central concept and five interrelated internal control components that make up what many call the COSO "cube" (see Figure A.3).

FIGURE A.3   The COSO cube

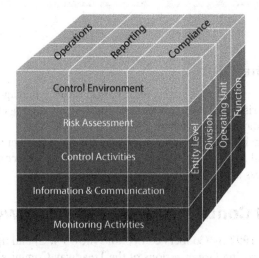

The COSO cube consists of three dimensions:

- Objectives
- Components
- Business units/areas

The central concept of the COSO framework is that internal control is a *process, affected by people*, designed to provide *reasonable assurance* that the entity is meeting its *objectives*:

- **Process:** A process is not one event, but a series of activities integrated into an organization.

- **Affected by people:** People across the organization establish objectives and ensure that controls are in place. At the same time, internal controls affect people's actions.

- **Reasonable assurance:** Internal control can provide only reasonable, not absolute, assurance that the organization is meeting its objectives, because of limitations such as human judgment and error, potential for controls to be circumvented through collusion, or controls being overridden by management.

- **Objectives:** Internal control helps organizations meet the following objectives, all of which are separate but may overlap:

  - Effectiveness and efficiency of operations: performance, profitability goals, safeguarding assets

  - Reliability of financial reporting: prepare reliable financial reports while preventing financial misstatements

  - Compliance with applicable laws and regulations

In addition, the framework describes the following five interrelated components of internal control:

- **Control environment:** This is the foundation of how the business operates, where individuals know that they are to conduct activities and carry out control responsibilities. A solid control environment is exhibited by integrity and ethical values, commitment to competence, dedicated board and audit committees, management's philosophy and operating style, the organizational structure, assignment of authority and responsibility, and human resources policies and practices.

- **Risk assessment:** The organization should establish mechanisms to identify, assess, and manage the risks to objectives. This component is evident through establishing entity-wide and activity-level objectives, identified risks, and how well the organization manages change.

- **Control activities:** Control policies and procedures are in place to ensure that the actions and controls needed to ensure objectives are met and that mitigating activities are carried out. Examples of control activities include approvals, authorizations, security of assets, segregation of duties, top-level reviews, information processing, physical controls, and performance indicators. Success in this area occurs when control activities are linked to meeting objectives and are deemed necessary to mitigate risks in meeting the objectives.

- **Information and communication:** Information about control activities should flow through the organization so that management knows whether its objectives are being met. It should be in a form and time frame that ensures people can respond. Information and communication can be considered successful when they flow up to management and down to employees in sufficient detail and in a timely manner, when established communication channels exist internally and with external parties, and when management is open and receptive to suggestions.

- **Monitoring activities:** The process should be monitored and modified as necessary through ongoing monitoring activities, separate evaluations, or a combination of both. Control deficiencies should be reported upstream, with critical issues communicated to the board or senior management. Management needs information to ensure that the internal control system is effective, to identify whether new risks have developed, and to determine if internal controls are still relevant. Monitoring is considered successful when it is ongoing and built into operations, separate evaluations are conducted, and deficiencies are reported on an open and timely basis.

When is an internal control system effective? When you've assessed and concluded that the five components are functioning successfully and the organization's objectives are being met:

- The board of directors and management understand whether operational objectives are being achieved.
- Financial reporting is prepared reliably.
- Laws and regulations are being complied with.

Making Sense of the COSO Cube

Each organization has three main types of objectives spanning all divisions and groups. The five interrelated internal control components must be in place to ensure these objectives are met. There must be a solid control environment, with risk assessments to confirm that adequate control activities are in place to mitigate risk and that risks to objectives are properly managed. In addition, information regarding risk, activities, and deficiencies should be reported through the organization and responded to promptly. Evaluation and monitoring of activities to ensure that objectives are met should occur continually, with corrective actions taken when necessary.

COSO Value for the CISA

COSO is the basis for most internal control discussions and process and control frameworks. Whether you are educating others on internal controls, as outlined in the ISACA Professional Code of Ethics, or evaluating or testing internal control effectiveness, COSO provides a foundation with which the CISA should be familiar. COSO is a great source for definitions and explanations. Due to the enterprise basis by which COSO has been developed, it is highly recommended that it serve as the foundation, and other frameworks, such as COBIT, ISO/IEC 27001/2, NIST 800-53, NIST CSF, PCI DSS, and ITIL, build upon this knowledge. Other COSO guidance includes ongoing updates to the Enterprise Risk Management – Integrated Framework and the Internal Control – Integrated Framework, such as *COSO in the Cyber Age*, which provides guidance for using frameworks to evaluate cybersecurity.

COBIT

The *COBIT* framework was created in 1992 by ISACA and the IT Governance Institute (ITGI). In 1996, the first edition of COBIT was released to the public. COBIT 2019 is the most current version available as of this writing. COBIT aligns with and meets COSO internal control requirements.

COBIT was developed to assist companies in maximizing the benefits derived through the strategic use of IT. Broad, yet detailed, the COBIT framework was designed for managers, auditors, and IT personnel and contains IT governance guidance. The framework aligns IT goals with general business goals; includes a comprehensive list of IT processes; and links related control objectives, metrics, and roles and responsibilities for carrying out process activities.

COBIT Highlights

The COBIT framework is covered in multiple documents:

- Executive summary
- COBIT 2019 Framework: Introduction and Methodology
- COBIT 2019 Framework: Governance and Management Objectives
- COBIT 2019 Design Guide: Designing an Information and Technology Governance Solution
- COBIT 2019 Implementation Guide: Implementing and Optimizing an Information and Technology Governance Solution
- COBIT 2019 Governance, Management Objectives, Practices, and Activities
- COBIT 2019 Management Awareness Diagnostic
- COBIT 2019 RACI by Role

Several publications related to COBIT are also available, including:

- Policy Template Library
- COBIT for DevOps Audit Program
- IT Control Objectives for Sarbanes–Oxley
- COBIT 2019 for Small and Medium Enterprises
- COBIT Focus Area: DevOps Using COBIT 2019

- COBIT Focus Area: Information and Technology Risk
- COBIT Focus Area: Information Security
- Implementing the NIST Cybersecurity Framework Using COBIT 2019

This complex framework requires dedicated individuals to implement and compile the elements. The framework is based on strong IT governance, stressing alignment with business strategy and goals.

As with many frameworks, COBIT is based on the Deming Cycle, with 40 IT processes falling into the following five domains:

- **Evaluate, Direct, and Monitor:** Processes in this domain are focused on the overall governance of IT.
- **Align, Plan, and Organize:** Processes in this domain are dedicated to ensuring that IT goals are strategically aligned with the business strategy and goals.
- **Build, Acquire, and Implement:** Processes for acquiring software, personnel, and external resources are covered in this domain, along with those processes needed to implement them.
- **Deliver, Service, and Support:** Operational managers can focus on these processes for delivering and supporting the resources utilized, including people, infrastructure, software, and third-party services.
- **Monitor, Evaluate, and Assess:** Processes ensure that the outcome is delivered and measured against initial expectations and that deviations are investigated and result in corrective actions.

COBIT Value for the CISA

The COBIT framework is ideal for those looking for a comprehensive framework to outline how IT goals and processes align with business goals, what processes IT should consider implementing, and related control objectives.

COBIT nicely ties general business goals to IT goals with a balanced scorecard, enabling you to see which IT processes are key in supporting specific IT goals and, ultimately, business goals.

For personnel implementing or evaluating a process, the COBIT framework provides an overview of general processes utilized to manage IT. Each process in COBIT includes key activities, control objectives, and metrics that should be in place.

COBIT is one of the most comprehensive and widely used frameworks available, which equates to the development of additional research and documentation being available. See the ISACA website for an extensive line of COBIT and COBIT-related documents. Not only will you find COBIT translated into more than eight foreign languages, but you also will find documents mapping popular frameworks with COBIT, a "quick start" guide to implementing COBIT, and guides for using COBIT within various focus areas (such as security, Sarbanes–Oxley, IT assurance, and service management).

GTAG

The *Global Technology Audit Guide (GTAG)* series of documents were developed by the IIA to help organizations with their IT control framework and audit practices. The guides are designed to assist with describing the importance of IT controls as part of the internal controls environment, establish the roles and responsibilities required to ensure controls are in place and assessed, and address the risks inherent in using and managing IT. The first GTAG was published in 2005 and updated in 2012.

Several groups aid in developing the guides, including an advanced technology committee and other professional organizations (ACIPA, FEI, ISSA, SANS Institute, and Carnegie Mellon Software Engineering Institute).

The GTAG documents are geared toward chief audit executives and other executives needing a high-level overview of the latest technology issues and how they affect the organization, the associated risks, and necessary IT controls.

GTAG Highlights

Dozens of GTAG documents have been published and are available through the IIA. These guides include:

- Auditing Mobile Computing
- Assessing Cybersecurity Risk
- Auditing IT Projects
- Business Continuity Management
- Auditing Insider Threat Programs
- Auditing IT Governance
- Data Analysis Technologies
- Continuous Auditing

GTAG Value for the CISA

Although GTAG documents primarily target the chief audit executive, IS auditors can use them to learn more about controls and to assist with describing IT risk and controls in executive terms.

GTAG documents can be downloaded by IIA members free from the IIA website at www .theiia.org. Hard copies of some guides can also be purchased should you choose to add the publications to your library.

ISF Standard of Good Practice for Information Security

The Standard of Good Practice for Information Security was first published in 1996 by the Information Security Forum (ISF). The ISF is a nonprofit organization dedicated to the development of information security good practices. Like ISACA, ISF is a paid membership organization with chapters worldwide. The standard was last updated in 2022 and is available from www.securityforum.org.

ISF Standard of Good Practice for Information Security Highlights

The Standard of Good Practice for Information Security contains guidance on security principles, control objectives, and controls in the following areas:

- Enterprise security management
- Critical business applications
- Computer installations
- Networks
- Systems development
- End-user environment

Although the document is divided into these main areas, there are reference tables so that specific control areas that may be present in more than one area can be found easily.

Standard of Good Practice Value for the CISA

The Standard of Good Practice for Information Security can provide information security control objective statements and describe the controls that should be in place. If you are looking for specific controls, such as access controls or controls around firewalls or emails, a reference guide can help point you to the proper section within each area.

ISO/IEC 27001 and 27002

Organizations facing privacy and information security concerns may decide to implement a formal ISMS to ensure that information security is managed, risks are assessed, and appropriate controls are put in place to mitigate risks to information security. Updated in 2022 by the International Organization for Standardization (ISO) and the International Electrotechnical Commission (IEC), ISO/IEC 27001 is a standard that organizations can use to develop, implement, control, and improve an ISMS. ISO/IEC 27001 provides the general framework for the ISMS, whereas ISO/IEC 27002 provides a more detailed list of control objectives and recommended controls. The controls presented within the document act as a guide for those responsible for initiating, implementing, or maintaining an ISMS.

Organizations may choose to be certified as compliant with ISO/IEC 27001 by an accredited certification body. Similar to other ISO management system certifications, there is a three-stage audit and certification process.

ISO/IEC 27001 and 27002 Highlights

The concept of an ISMS centers on the preservation of:

- **Confidentiality:** Ensuring that information is accessible only to those authorized to have access

- **Integrity:** Safeguarding the accuracy and completeness of information and processing methods
- **Availability:** Ensuring that authorized users have access to information and associated assets when required

The ISO/IEC standard contains an introductory section and a description of the risk management process framework needed around information security controls. Each organization must perform an information security risk assessment to determine which regulatory requirements must be satisfied before selecting appropriate controls.

The four main domains in ISO/IEC 27001 and 27002 are:

- Organizational controls
- People controls
- Physical controls
- Technological controls

Control objectives and controls for each section are listed in the standards and code of practice. ISO/IEC 27001 focuses on implementing controls throughout the Deming Cycle, whereas ISO/IEC 27002 lists the good practice controls an organization can implement.

ISO/IEC 27001 and 27002 Value for the CISA

Those involved with implementing or assessing information security controls or managing information security risk may find it helpful to look more closely into these standards. ISO/IEC standards documents can be purchased from the International Standards Organization.

NIST SP 800-53 and NIST SP 800-53A

NIST Special Publication 800-53 (NIST SP 800-53), Security and Privacy Controls for Information Systems and Organizations, provides a comprehensive catalog of security and privacy controls for U.S. federal organizations and information systems (and their suppliers) to support compliance with the mandatory federal standard FIPS Publication 200 Minimum Security Requirements for Federal Information and Information Systems. Revision 5 of SP 800-53 was published in September 2020.

The document NIST SP 800-53A, Assessing Security and Privacy Controls in Information Systems and Organizations, may be of particular interest to the IS auditor. A companion to NIST SP 800-53, this publication guides the IS audit for auditing all the controls in NIST SP 800-53. For each control in NIST SP 800-53, this document describes what the IS auditor should examine, who they should interview, and what to test. Control owners will also derive value as they know what would be expected of them in an audit, leading to better control design and operation.

NIST SP 800-53 Highlights

SP 800-53 revision 5 contains almost 1,000 controls across 20 control families. FIPS Publication 199 requires organizations to categorize information systems as low-impact, moderate-impact, or high-impact, in terms of criticality, based on the types of information they process. To support this framework, the NIST SP 800-53 has grouped minimum security control requirements security control baselines for low-impact, moderate-impact, and high-impact rated systems to provide a starting point for establishing expected control requirements.

The 20 control families in NIST SP 800-53R4 are:

- AC – Access Control
- AT – Awareness and Training
- AU – Audit and Accountability
- CA – Assessment, Authorization, and Monitoring
- CM – Configuration Management
- CP – Contingency Planning
- IA – Identification and Authentication
- IR – Incident Response
- MA – Maintenance
- MP – Media Protection
- PE – Physical and Environmental Protection
- PL – Planning
- PM – Program Management
- PS – Personnel Security
- PT – PII Processing and Transparency
- RA – Risk Assessment
- SA – System and Services Acquisition
- SC – System and Communications Protection
- SI – System and Information Integrity
- SR – Supply Chain Risk Management

NIST SP 800-53 Value for the CISA

Those establishing or auditing U.S. federal information systems and cybersecurity programs should be familiar with the NIST SP 800-53 control set. Moreover, IS auditors should also be familiar with NIST SP 800-53A, as this contains detailed guidance on auditing all the controls in NIST SP 800-53.

NIST Cybersecurity Framework

The *NIST Cybersecurity Framework (NIST CSF)* was published in 2014 as a response to the Presidential Executive Order 13636, Improving Critical Infrastructure Cybersecurity. The order directed NIST to work with stakeholders to develop a voluntary framework—based on existing standards, guidelines, and practices—for reducing cyber risks to critical infrastructure. The CSF is not intended to be another set of standards. Instead, the CSF is a body of work built around industry best practices and directly references internationally accepted cybersecurity and risk management standards.

NIST CSF was revised with the publication of NIST CSF 2.0 in 2024. The most noted and welcome change is the addition of the Govern function.

The NIST CSF comprises three main components: the *core, implementation tiers,* and *profiles.* The core is broken down into six functions, each including categories of cybersecurity outcomes and informative references providing guidance to standards and practices that illustrate methods to achieve the stated outcomes within each category. The implementation tiers provide context on how well an organization understands its cybersecurity risk and the processes to manage it. Finally, the profiles assist an organization in defining the outcomes it desires to achieve from the framework categories.

NIST CSF Highlights

The NIST CSF core is broken down into the following six functions:

- **Govern:** Establish, communicate, and monitor the organization's cybersecurity risk management strategy, expectations, and policy.

- **Identify:** Develop an understanding of the business context and resources that support critical operations to enable the organization to identify and prioritize cybersecurity risks that can impact operations.

- **Protect:** Implement appropriate safeguards to minimize the operational impact of a potential cybersecurity event.

- **Detect:** Implement capabilities to detect suspicious and malicious activities.

- **Respond:** Implement capabilities to respond to cybersecurity events properly.

- **Recover:** Maintain plans and activities to enable timely restoration of capabilities or services that might be impaired after a cybersecurity event.

Four tiers describe an organization's cybersecurity program capabilities supporting organizational goals and objectives. It is essential to highlight that the tiers do not represent maturity levels or how well capabilities are executed. The tiers are meant to describe and support decision-making about managing cybersecurity risk and resource prioritization. Here is a summary of the tiers:

- **Partial:** Cybersecurity program may not be formalized, and risks are managed in an ad hoc or reactive manner. There is limited awareness of cybersecurity risk across the organization.

- **Risk informed:** Cybersecurity program activities are approved by management and linked to organizational risk concerns and business objectives. However, cybersecurity considerations in business programs may not be consistent at all organizational levels.

- **Repeatable:** Cybersecurity program activities are formally approved and supported by policy. Cybersecurity program capabilities are regularly reviewed and updated based on risk management processes and changes in business objectives.

- **Adaptive:** There is a consistent organization-wide approach to managing cybersecurity risk through formal policies, standards, and procedures. Cybersecurity program capabilities are routinely updated based on previous and current cybersecurity events, lessons learned, and predictive indicators. The organization strives to adapt proactively to changing threat landscapes.

NIST CSF Value for the CISA

The CSF can enable the IS auditor to develop and use common terminology that is easier for nonsecurity professionals to comprehend. In addition, the informative reference feature makes the NIST CSF a powerful and flexible model to facilitate developing and auditing a cybersecurity program against defined objectives and outcomes.

Payment Card Industry Data Security Standard (PCI DSS)

If an organization stores, processes, or transmits credit card data, it is subject to the Payment Card Industry Data Security Standard (PCI DSS). In 2001, Visa launched its Cardholder Information Security Program (CISP), establishing security requirements for merchants and merchant service providers. Shortly after, other card brands launched their payment card security programs, such as the MasterCard Site Data Protection (SDP) Program, American Express Data Security Operating Procedures (DSOP), and the Discover Information Security & Compliance (DISC) program. Merchants and service providers that accepted multiple payment card types had to maintain compliance with multiple security programs. The PCI DSS grew from the need to standardize security requirements across the major card brand security programs. In 2004, the payment card companies established this comprehensive set of security requirements for merchants and service providers.

The PCI Security Standards Council (PCI SSC) is the independent group to oversee the standard going forward. An important distinction is that while the PCI SSC manages the technical and operational aspects of the standard, the compliance enforcement actions are the responsibility of the individual card brands. A top-down approach is taken from the card brands, which hold the card-issuing banks (banks that issue credit cards to consumers) and acquiring banks (banks that set up merchant accounts and enable merchants to accept credit card payments). The merchant agreement with acquiring banks will require the merchant to maintain compliance with the PCI DSS and requires all service providers that the merchant engages with to uphold those compliance requirements.

PCI DSS Highlights

PCI DSS v4.0 was released in March 2022. The standard comprises 260 control activities organized within six principles and 12 security requirements, shown in Table A.3.

TABLE A.3 PCI DSS Principles and Requirements

Principles	Requirements
Build and Maintain a Secure Network and Systems	1. Install and Maintain Network Security Controls. 2. Apply Secure Configurations to All System Components.
Protect Account Data	3. Protect Stored Account Data. 4. Protect Cardholder Data with Strong Cryptography During Transmission Over Open, Public Networks.
Maintain a Vulnerability Management Program	5. Protect All Systems and Networks from Malicious Software. 6. Develop and Maintain Secure Systems and Software.
Implement Strong Access Control Measures	7. Restrict Access to System Components and Cardholder Data by Business Need to Know. 8. Identify Users and Authenticate Access to System Components. 9. Restrict Physical Access to Cardholder Data.
Regularly Monitor and Test Networks	10. Log and Monitor All Access to System Components and Cardholder Data. 11. Test Security of Systems and Networks Regularly.
Maintain an Information Security Policy	12. Support Information Security with Organizational Policies and Programs.

Merchant Levels

Merchants and service providers are classified based on the number of credit card transactions they process. The classification levels dictate how the organization must certify compliance with the PCI DSS.

Although each card brand maintains its own table of merchant levels, a basic summary of merchant levels is as follows:

- Level 1: More than 6 million transactions annually
- Level 2: Between 1 and 6 million transactions annually
- Level 3: Between 20,000 and 1 million transactions annually
- Level 4: Less than 20,000 transactions annually

It is important to note that Visa, MasterCard, and Discover use similar criteria, while American Express and JCB have their classification criteria. Although American Express and

JCB have their criteria, it is generally accepted that if you are at a level for one provider, you will be considered the same for all.

Level 1 merchants are required to have quarterly external vulnerability scans performed by a PCI approved scanning vendor (ASV) and have an independent validation of compliance conducted by a qualified security assessor (QSA) who tests the implementation of the PCI DSS control activities and delivers a report on compliance (ROC). Level 2–4 merchants, depending on the acquirer's requirements, may simply be required to fill out a much shorter self-evaluation, called a self-assessment questionnaire (SAQ). Several versions of SAQs are provided for organizations using various payment acceptance methods. For instance, organizations with only stand-alone payment terminals would use the SAQ-B, which contains only the controls relevant to this type.

Service Provider Levels

A *service provider* or merchant may use a third-party service provider to store, process, or transmit cardholder data on its behalf, or a service provider may manage components such as routers, firewalls, databases, physical security, and/or servers.

Service providers are classified similarly to merchants. Although each card brand maintains its own table of service provider levels, a basic summary of merchant levels is as follows:

- **Level 1:** More than 300,000 transactions annually
- **Level 2:** Less than 300,000 transactions annually

Like level 1 merchants, Level 1 service providers are required to have quarterly internal and external vulnerability scans performed by a PCI ASV and have an independent validation of compliance conducted by a QSA who tests the implementation of the PCI DSS control activities and delivers a ROC that the service provider will submit to the respective payment brands.

Similar to merchant levels, it is generally accepted that if you are at a level for one provider, you will be considered the same for all.

PCI DSS Value for the CISA

The IS auditor may be called upon to assist in preparing an organization for a PCI DSS compliance assessment. The PCI DSS is a prescriptive standard by design and includes detailed testing procedures and guidance for each control activity. The PCI SSC publishes several supporting documents to enable consistent interpretation and implementation of the PCI DSS.

You can find more information regarding the PCI DSS and supporting documentation in the document library on the PCI SSC website: www .pcisecuritystandards.org.

CIS Critical Security Controls

The *Center for Internet Security (CIS) Critical Security Controls (CSC)* was first published in 2009 through a partnership with the U.S. National Security Agency, CIS, and SANS Institute to assist the Department of Defense with prioritizing its security initiatives. The working group used the premise that only actual attack information could be used to justify the control activities. Under this premise, the working group focused on gaining consensus on the control activities and the priority of control activities by sharing and analyzing cybersecurity attack experience and data. These exercises resulted in the 20 key control activities. The publication was originally owned by the SANS Institute and known as the SANS Top 20; ownership of the standard was transferred to CIS in 2015. The framework is now known as the CIS Controls.

Historically, the CIS Controls used the order of the controls as the implied order of prioritizing an organization's cybersecurity activities. This approach led to grouping the controls into Basic, Foundational, and Organizational categories. However, it has been observed that many of the practices found within the CIS Basic grouping of controls can be difficult to implement for organizations with limited resources. This difficulty highlighted an opportunity to provide recommended prioritization of specific control activities believed to provide the best risk mitigation based on the real-world attack data reviewed while balancing resource constraints and effective risk mitigation. This opportunity resulted in introducing implementation groups within version 8 of the controls. These groups are intended to assist organizations in focusing their security resources on specific objectives while leveraging the CIS Controls.

The three implementation group categories are:

- **Implementation Group 1:** An organization with limited resources and cybersecurity expertise available to implement subcontrols

- **Implementation Group 2:** An organization with moderate resources and cybersecurity expertise available to implement subcontrols

- **Implementation Group 3:** A mature organization with significant resources and cybersecurity expertise available to allocate to subcontrols

Version 8 was released in May 2021 and is the latest version as of this writing.

CIS CSC Highlights

The CIS Controls consist of 18 key activities, or critical security controls, that an organization can implement to mitigate cybersecurity attacks. The controls are described in a direct manner that is intended to be understandable by technical and nontechnical individuals:

- Inventory and Control of Enterprise Assets
- Inventory and Control of Software Assets
- Data Protection

- Secure Configuration of Enterprise Assets and Software
- Account Management
- Access Control Management
- Continuous Vulnerability Management
- Audit Log Management
- Email and Web Browser Protections
- Malware Defenses
- Data Recovery
- Network Infrastructure Management
- Network Monitoring and Defense
- Security Awareness and Skills Training
- Service Provider Management
- Application Software Security
- Incident Response Management
- Penetration Testing

CIS Controls Value for the CISA

The CIS Controls framework strives to provide a balance between providing descriptive, but not overly prescriptive, control activities that enable organizations to build cybersecurity program capabilities in a prioritized manner. The CIS Controls can enable the IS auditor to facilitate discussions using common terminology to describe control activities, simplifying audit planning and execution.

IT Assurance Framework

In 2006, the ISACA board of directors approved the IT Assurance Framework (ITAF) project to address the need for audit and assurance standards. As the project matured, additional needs, such as taxonomy and guidelines, were identified and addressed. In 2020, ISACA published the fourth and current edition of *ITAF™: A Professional Practices Framework for IT Audit.*

The ITAF establishes mandatory standards that address IT audit and assurance professionals' roles and responsibilities, knowledge, skills and diligence, conduct, and reporting requirements. The framework also provides nonmandatory guidance on design, conduct, and reporting on IT audit and assurance engagements and defines standard IT assurance terms and concepts.

ITAF Highlights

The document has three categories of audit and assurance standards: general, performance, and reporting.

General Standards

These are the guiding principles by which the profession operates. These standards deal with all IT audit and assurance activities conducted, and include:

- Audit charter
- Organizational independence
- Auditor objectivity
- Reasonable expectation
- Due professional care
- Proficiency
- Assertions
- Criteria

Performance Standards

These focus on the IT audit or assurance professional's conduct of assurance activities such as the design of audit and assurance activities, evidence, findings, and conclusions. ISACA IS Auditing Standards are the performance standards (current IS Auditing Standards are listed in more detail in Chapter 2, "The Audit Process"). These standards include topics such as:

- Risk assessment in planning
- Audit scheduling
- Engagement planning
- Performance and supervision
- Evidence
- Using the work of other experts
- Irregularity and illegal acts

Reporting Standards

These standards cover the report produced by the IT audit or assurance professional and address:

- Reporting
- Follow-up activities

The ITAF documentation also outlines guidelines for applying the standards. These guidelines assist the IT audit or assurance professional with understanding enterprise-wide issues and IT management processes as well as processes, procedures, methodologies, and approaches for conducting an IT audit and assurance engagement.

ITAF incorporates ISACA's IS auditing standards and the ISACA Code of Professional Ethics. In addition, all of the ISACA guidance is mapped to the framework. For more detailed information and to obtain your copy of the ITAF, see the ISACA website at www.isaca.org/itaf.

ITAF Value for the CISA

Compliance with the standards within ITAF is mandatory for all CISAs. It is recommended that all CISAs review the standards prior to certification and formulate good habits to ensure that standards are applied to any assurance work conducted. Although not mandatory, these guidelines, tools, and techniques can assist anyone needing to perform IT audits or assurance activities, and they can even help those on the receiving end of IT audit or assurance reports.

ITIL

In the 1980s, when the British government determined that the level of IT service quality provided to it was insufficient, it was clear that an IT control framework was needed. The Central Computer and Telecommunications Agency (CCTA) sponsored the development of the Information Technology Infrastructure Library (ITIL, pronounced *EYE-till*), which began guiding organizations on the efficient and financially responsible use of IT resources within public and private entities worldwide.

The current version of ITIL, known as ITIL v4, released in January 2019, consists of a collection of 34 management practices that contain guidelines for different aspects of good practice around IT service management (ITSM) and aligning IT services to business needs. When all volumes are combined, ITIL presents a comprehensive view of the proper provisioning and management of IT services.

ITIL Highlights

ITIL is a high-level, user-focused framework that defines a common language for ITSM processes. The framework describes the IT service organization that delivers agreed-upon services and maintains the infrastructure on which they are delivered. One of the critical components of ITIL is that the services and maintenance must be aligned and realigned according to business needs. To do this, the framework closely aligns its five volumes with the Deming Cycle:

- **ITIL Service Strategy:** This volume focuses on determining potential market opportunities concerning the delivery of IT services, with sections dedicated to service portfolio management and financial management.

- **ITIL Service Design:** This volume describes how to design proposed services with adequate processes and resources to support them. Availability management, capacity management, continuity management, and security management are key areas of service design.

- **ITIL Service Transition:** This volume describes the implementation of the design and creation or modification of the IT services. Key areas identified are change management, release management, configuration management, and service knowledge management.

- **ITIL Service Operation:** This volume provides guidance on the activities needed to operate IT services and maintain them according to service level agreements. It focuses on the key areas of incident management, problem management, event management, and request fulfillment.

- **ITIL Continual Service Improvement:** This volume focuses on ensuring that the IT services delivered to the business are continually improved through service reporting, service measurement, and service level management.

ITIL outlines the general IT processes needed to manage IT; the resources, outputs, and inputs used; and the controls that must be implemented to ensure business goals are met (such as policies and budgets).

ISO/IEC 20000

ISO/IEC 20000 is the international standard for IT service management and is considered the ISO version of ITIL. Like ISO/IEC 27001, organizations can voluntarily undergo ISO 20000 audits and earn a corporate certification.

ITIL Value for the CISA

Whether documenting, implementing, or assessing processes, the IS auditor can utilize the ITIL volumes for additional information on specific IT processes, such as change management or incident management. The framework outlines recommended controls to ensure IT services are delivered as promised. Several professional certifications in ITIL are available, including ITIL Foundation, ITIL Practice Manager, and ITIL 4 Master.

 The ITIL v4 volumes can be purchased online from AXELOS at www .axelos.com. ISO/IEC 20000 can be purchased online at www.iso.org.

PMBOK® Guide

A Guide to the Project Management Body of Knowledge (PMBOK® Guide) is a guide on project management fundamentals and practices. The guide is published by the Project Management Institute (PMI). It began as a whitepaper in 1987 and was published as a guide in 1996. The seventh edition was released in 2021.

Not only is PMBOK® a guide to project management, but it also is an internationally recognized standard on project management practices. Those interested in obtaining certification in this area may want to become certified as a Project Management Professional (PMP) through the PMI.

PMBOK Highlights

The PMBOK® Guide describes the many processes often used to manage projects. It consists of five process groups and ten knowledge areas.

Process Groups

Forty-seven processes are used by project teams. These processes fall into five groups, which are consistent with the Plan-Do-Check-Act activities of the Deming Cycle:

- **Initiating process group:** Defines the project/phase and gathers authorization
- **Planning process group:** Defines objectives and courses of action required to meet objectives and scope
- **Executing process group:** The work required to carry out the project management plan
- **Monitoring and controlling process group:** Regularly monitors progress and identifies variances from the plan; takes corrective actions
- **Closing process group:** Concludes that all objectives are met and the service, product, or result is accepted by the customer/sponsor; end of the project

The Project Management Knowledge Principles

Twelve principles are used in project management. Each principle guides project management actions. The 12 principles are:

- Pay Attention/Care (Stewardship)
- Team
- Stakeholders
- Value
- System thinking
- Leadership
- Tailoring
- Quality
- Complexity
- Opportunities and threats (Risk)
- Adaptability and resilience
- Change management

PMBOK™ Value for the CISA

As an IS auditor, you may be asked to take a closer look at the process for introducing new applications or systems into your organization. New applications and systems are often delivered via a system/software/solution delivery life cycle coupled with project management. Solutions are scoped and assessed, projects ensue, and much activity and documentation occurs throughout the process. Project management methodologies and frameworks can help you make sense of this madness.

In addition, project management skills can be valuable for an IS auditor. Being well-versed in project management can help ensure that your IS audit work remains in scope and on budget and that you are planning your time adequately. For example, you will want to give yourself enough time for audit planning and documentation and accommodate complex interview schedules.

The PMBOK® Guide can be purchased from booksellers worldwide or the PMI.

PRINCE2

PRojects IN Controlled Environments (PRINCE) is a structured project management standard covering project management fundamentals. The original standard was developed in 1989 by the U.K. Office of Government Commerce (OGC) specifically for IT project management. In 1996, PRINCE2 was released, representing a change in focus from beyond IT to general project management. In 2009, it was relaunched as PRINCE2:2009 Refresh (hereafter referred to as PRINCE2) and updated in 2017 and 2023. In addition to becoming the de facto standard for project management in the U.K., the standard has been adopted by organizations worldwide, although not as commonly in North America as some of the other frameworks described in this appendix. As with ITIL, an individual may pass an exam to become certified.

PRINCE2 Highlights

PRINCE2 consists of one main manual: *Managing Successful Projects with PRINCE2*. It is like the PMBOK® Guide, consisting of project management processes and components. However, it is different because it fully describes the methodology and implementation techniques. The central concept behind PRINCE2 is that projects should have an organized and controlled start, middle, and end. Although it is not as comprehensive as PMBOK®, PRINCE2 supplements general project management knowledge by explicitly describing how to manage projects in a controlled and organized manner.

PRINCE2 is a process-driven framework and integrates well with other processes and practices, such as Agile Scrum. The framework details 45 processes categorized into seven process groups. The process groups lead you through the project life cycle, similar to the Deming Cycle:

1. Starting up a project
2. Directing a project
3. Initiating a project
4. Controlling a stage
5. Managing product delivery
6. Managing stage boundaries
7. Closing a project

Key inputs, outputs, goals, and activities are defined for each process. In addition, a maturity model is available to measure project management capability maturity. Another bonus is that the entire framework can be tailored for each project, as every process has guidance on how to scale it for small or large projects. This results in a flexible, scalable, and fully described framework.

Similar to PMBOK® knowledge areas, PRINCE2 details seven "themes" that are deemed critical for project success:

- Business case
- Organization

- Quality
- Plans
- Risk
- Change
- Progress

PRINCE2 Value for the CISA

As an IS auditor, you may be asked to take a closer look at the process for introducing new applications or systems to your organization, including the software/system/solution delivery cycle and associated project management methodology and documentation. In addition, project management skills can be valuable for an IS auditor.

Like PMBOK®, PRINCE2 will provide general guidance on project management processes and controls. PRINCE2 is complementary to PMBOK® because it helps shape and direct the use of PMBOK® by introducing specific techniques. PMBOK® will lay a more comprehensive foundation, whereas PRINCE2 will describe how to start managing projects and put the pieces together.

Risk IT

Published in 2009 by ISACA and updated in 2020, Risk IT is the first comprehensive IT-specific risk framework developed. The framework is based upon enterprise risk management frameworks such as COSO ERM and ISO/IEC 31000, making it much easier to integrate the management of IT risks into overall enterprise risk management. Risk IT also complements COBIT. Risk IT provides guidance for managing all aspects of IT-related risks, including project, value delivery, compliance, security, availability, service delivery, and recovery risks.

Risk IT Highlights

ISACA has published two specifically significant documents: *the Risk IT Framework*, containing the principles, process details, management guidelines, and domain maturity models, and *the Risk IT Practitioner Guide*, which provides an overview of the Risk IT process model, how Risk IT links to COBIT, and describes in detail how to use the model.

To ensure the effective enterprise governance and management of IT risk, the Risk IT Framework is based on the following principles:

- Always align with business mission and objectives.
- Align IT risk management with enterprise risk management.
- Balance the costs and benefits of IT risk management.
- Promote ethical and open communication of IT risks.
- Establish the right tone from the top, while defining and enforcing accountability.
- Integrate risk practices into routine processes.
- Ensure a continuous process that is a part of daily activities.

The framework has three main domains: risk governance, risk evaluation, and risk response. Each of these domains is supported by three processes with various activities. Like COBIT, the guidance will provide a list of components, inputs and outputs, RACI charts, goals, and metrics for each process. The framework is depicted in Figure A.4.

FIGURE A.4   The Risk IT Framework

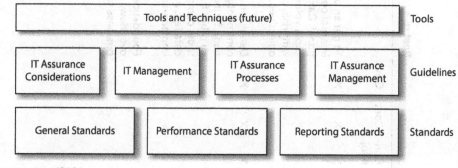

Image courtesy ISACA

In addition to the guiding principles and process model mentioned earlier, the Risk IT Framework contains good practice guidance, domain maturity models, reference materials, and a high-level comparison of risk frameworks.

For more detailed guidance on governing and managing risk, the Risk IT Practitioner Guide walks you through the entire process, from defining a risk universe, to developing risk appetite and risk tolerance, setting up risk scenarios, responding to risks, and prioritizing risks.

 You can find more information and download or purchase both documents at the ISACA website.

Risk IT Practice Value for the CISA

If you are being asked to audit an IT risk program or identify, govern, or manage IT-related risks, the Risk IT Framework and the Risk IT Practitioner's Guide will be of great value to you. They can also help assess risk and compare it against the organization's risk appetite and tolerance, or they can assist with integrating IT risk management within an existing enterprise risk management program.

Summary of Frameworks

Table A.4 contains a summary of the frameworks discussed in this appendix. The table indicates whether the framework is available for a fee, the primary focus of the framework, and the best uses for the framework.

TABLE A.4 Summary of frameworks

Title	Summary	Free Online/Hardcopy Cost	Primary focus						Best use
			DemCyc	Mat-Mod	Proc	Con-tObj	Cont	Gov	
COSO Internal Control – Integrated Framework	Provides a general overview of enterprise internal control.	No/$				X	X	X	To get an overview of what internal control is. Foundational. Can use Illustrative Tools volume to assist with risk, controls, and objectives.
COBIT 2019	Provides a detailed framework of IT processes and controls.	Yes*/$$	X	X	X	X	X	X	Details on processes, RACI, control objectives, and audit foundation. Links all other frameworks to it; most comprehensive/detailed. Audit and implementation.
GTAG	High-level overview of IT audit and controls.	Yes*/$			X				Foundational; provides overviews of IT controls in business terminology.

TABLE A.4 Summary of frameworks *(continued)*

Title	Summary	Free Online/ Hardcopy Cost	Primary focus			Best use
ISF Standard of Good Practice for Information Security	Overview of information security controls/domains.	No/$$		X		Excellent resource when implementing information security controls.
ISO/IEC 27001	Overview of information security governance/controls/ domains.	No/$$	X	X	X	Overview, details on information security. Control/activities. Use for audit and implementation of information security controls.
NIST SP 800-53	Detailed controls framework.	Yes/0		X	X	Government agencies and their suppliers; orgs that require more cybersecurity rigor.
NIST CSF		Yes/0	X	X	X	Orgs that need to formalize their cybersecurity efforts.
PCI DSS	Requirements for all orgs that process card-holder data.	Yes/0		X	X	Compliance for protection of cardholder data; also valuable for protecting other types of sensitive data.

TABLE A.4 Summary of frameworks *(continued)*

Title	Summary	Free Online/ Hardcopy Cost	Primary focus			Best use
CIS Critical Controls	Detailed controls framework.	Yes/0		X	X	Excellent controls framework for orgs just starting on cybersecurity controls.
ITAF	Standards and guidance for conducting IT audit and assurance activities.	Yes*/$				Fundamental framework for every CISA as it contains mandatory standards and several guidelines to assist with conducting IT audit and assurance activities.
ITIL	Service delivery standards.	No/$$	X	X		Overview. Use for guidance in improving service delivery processes.
PMBOK Guide	Enterprise project management.	No/$	X	X		Provides thorough guidance on managing projects: what to do.
PRINCE2	IT project management.	No/$$	X	X		Guidance on managing projects; how to do it.

TABLE A.4 Summary of frameworks *(continued)*

Title	Summary	Free Online/ Hardcopy Cost	Primary focus	Best use
RISK IT	IT-related business risk governance and management. Complements COBIT.	Yes*/$	X X	X Best used for developing or auditing IT risk processes and/or programs.

* Must be an ISACA or IIA member to download the documents free of charge

$ Denotes materials that can be purchased for less than $100.

$$ Denotes materials that can be purchased directly or through membership; more than $100.

Key to Primary Focus Areas:

DemCyc: Deming Cycle – continuous improvement

MatMod: Maturity model

Proc: Business process

ContObj: Control objectives

Cont: Controls

Gov: Governance

Pointers for Successful Use of Frameworks

Here are some tips for using the frameworks:

- Take time to learn the fundamentals of governance, controls, and processes. Become familiar with COSO, COBIT, PCI DSS, and NIST CSF.
- Keep in mind that no one single framework is the "right" framework.
- Much research has been done on governance, controls, and frameworks. Start here—don't reinvent the wheel.
- Use frameworks for guidance and tailor them to your unique organization.

Notes

We close this appendix with a few final thoughts:

- Goals and objectives define what the organization is trying to achieve.
- Organizations implement governance to identify and ensure the achievement of goals, objectives, and strategies.
- A process is a set of activities put in place to maximize the effectiveness and efficiency of operations. Organizations can manage operations through processes.
- Maturity models are often used to measure the maturity of process capabilities.
- The Deming Cycle focuses on continuous improvement by implementing various processes that address planning, execution, monitoring, and taking corrective actions.
- Control objectives are developed to ensure that business objectives are achieved.
- Control activities support control objectives and can be implemented within processes.
- Projects are temporary, unique, and have specific objectives and controls implemented.

This appendix focused on processes and internal controls, and described the various frameworks, methodologies, and guides available as resources. Now that we have examined the available resources, it is time to put all of this to use. For an overview of conducting professional audits, see Chapter 9, "Conducting a Professional Audit."

References

Some of the references in this appendix require user registration and/or payment for reference material.

Business Model for Information Security (BMIS); ISACA. `https://www.isaca.org/BMIS`

Business Motivation Model; Business Rules Group. `https://www.businessrulesgroup.org/bmm.shtml`

Certified in the Governance of Enterprise IT (CGEIT) certification; ISACA. https://www.isaca.org/cgeit

CIS Controls. https://www.cisecurity.org/controls

COBIT 2019; ISACA. https://www.isaca.org/COBIT

COSO Internal Control – Integrated Framework; Committee of Sponsoring Organizations of the Treadway Commission (COSO). https://www.coso.org/guidance-on-ic

Enterprise Risk Management – Integrated Framework (2004); COSO. https://www.coso.org/guidance-erm

Global Technology Audit Guides (GTAG); Institute of Internal Auditors. https://na.theiia.org

Guidance on Monitoring Internal Control Systems; COSO. https://www.coso.org/monitoring-internal-control-system

https://www.theiia.org/en/content/the-gait-series

A Guide to the Project Management Body of Knowledge (PMBOK®); Project Management Institute (PMI). https://www.pmi.org

Information Technology Assurance Framework (ITAF): A Professional Practices Framework for IT Assurance; ISACA. https://www.isaca.org/itaf

Information Technology Infrastructure Library (ITIL) 2011; AXELOS. https://www.axelos.com/best-practice-solutions/itil

Information security, cybersecurity and privacy protection — Information security controls (ISO/IEC 27002:2022); ISO. https://www.iso.org

Information security, cybersecurity and privacy protection — Information security management systems — Requirements (ISO/IEC 27001:2022); ISO. https://www.iso.org

Information technology — Service management — Part 1: Service management system requirements (ISO/IEC 20000:2018); ISO. https://www.iso.org

The ISF Standard of Good Practice for Information Security; Information Security Forum (ISF). https://www.securityforum.org/blog/standard-of-good-practice-for-information-security-2020-now-available-to-members

Managing Successful Projects with PRINCE2; AXELOS. https://www.axelos.com/best-practice-solutions/prince2

NACD Director's Handbook on Cyber-Risk Oversight; National Association of Corporate Directors (NACD). https://www.nacdonline.org/all-governance/governance-resources/governance-research/director-handbooks/nacd-directors-handbook-on-cyber-risk-oversight

NIST Cybersecurity Framework (CSF). `https://www.nist.gov/cyberframework`

NIST SP 800-53R5. `https://csrc.nist.gov/publications`

Payment Card Industry Data Security Standard (PCI DSS). `https://www.pcisecuritystandards.org`

Risk IT Framework and Risk IT Practitioner Guide; ISACA. `https://www.isaca.org/riskit`

The Rummler-Brache Toolkit; Rummler Brache. `https://www.rummlerbrache.com/toolkit`

Appendix B

Answers to Review Questions

Chapter 1: IT Governance and Management

Chapter 1: IT Governance and Management

1. C. IT governance is the mechanism through which IT strategy is established, controlled, and monitored through the balanced scorecard. Long-term and other strategic decisions are made in the context of IT governance.

2. A. Outsourcing is an opportunity for the organization to focus on its core competencies. When an organization outsources a business function, it no longer needs to be concerned about training employees in that function. Outsourcing does not always reduce costs, because cost reduction is not always the primary purpose for outsourcing in the first place.

3. D. The external auditor can only document the finding in the audit report. An external auditor is not in a position to implement controls.

4. D. An organization that opens a business office in another country and staffs the office with its own employees is insourcing, not outsourcing. Outsourcing is the practice of using contract labor, which is clearly not the case in this example. In this case, the insourcing is taking place at a remote location.

5. B. Conducting interviews with IT personnel and end users is the most appropriate initial action because it directly addresses the human factors contributing to high turnover, long wait times, and user discontentment. Interviews provide qualitative insights into the specific problems faced by both IT staff and end users, allowing for a more comprehensive understanding of the underlying issues.

   Reviewing the IT department's project management methodologies might help identify process inefficiencies but does not directly address staff turnover or user dissatisfaction.

   Analyzing the organization's hardware and software standards could reveal technical mismatches or outdated systems, but it doesn't address the human aspect of the problems.

   Evaluating the company's business continuity and disaster recovery plans is important for overall IT governance but is not directly relevant to addressing staff turnover or user satisfaction issues.

6. B. An organization that needs to understand whether a key process is effective should consider benchmarking the process. This will help the organization better understand whether its approach is similar to that of other organizations.

7. A. Annualized loss expectancy (ALE) is the annual expected loss allocated to an asset. It is calculated by multiplying the single loss expectancy (SLE—the financial loss experienced when the loss is realized one time) by the annualized rate of occurrence (ARO—the number of times that the organization expects the loss to occur).

8. B. The most difficult part of a quantitative risk analysis is determining the probability that a threat will actually be realized. It is relatively easy to determine the value of an asset and the impact of a threat event.

9. C. IT steering committee meeting agendas and minutes would most likely provide insight into the underlying causes of project dysfunctions such as aborted projects and budget over-runs. These documents would contain discussions and decisions about project priorities, resource allocations, risk assessments, and other strategic directives that impact project execution.

    IT procurement process records would primarily detail the acquisition of technology and ser-vices but wouldn't shed much light on project management or execution issues.

    The IT organization chart and job descriptions provide information about the structure and roles within the IT department but do not address project-specific decisions and issues.

    HR promotion policy documents are related to staff career progression and do not directly relate to project management challenges or budgetary issues.

10. D. The balanced scorecard is a tool that is used to quantify the performance of an organiza-tion against strategic objectives. The focuses of a balanced scorecard are financial, customer, internal processes, and innovation/learning.

11. B. An organization that has discovered that some employees have criminal records should have background checks performed on all existing employees, and it should also begin insti-tuting background checks (which should include criminal history) for all new employees. It is not necessarily required to terminate these employees; the specific criminal offenses may not warrant termination.

12. C. The options for risk treatment are the actions that management will take when a risk has been identified. The options are risk mitigation (where the risk is reduced), risk avoidance (where the activity is discontinued), risk transfer (where the risk is transferred to an insur-ance company), and risk acceptance (where management agrees to accept the risk as is).

13. C. IT standards that have not been reviewed for two years are out of date. If the IS auditor finds an IT policy that says that IT standards can be reviewed every two years, then there is a problem with IT policy as well; two years is far too long between reviews of IT standards.

14. A. Development of a business case is the most important step when considering the out-sourcing of a business function. The other items (measuring cost savings and changes in risk, and performing due diligence on service providers) are parts of development of a business case.

15. D. All employees should be required to sign a statement agreeing to support the policy. The other actions are important but less effective.

16. A. Charles is tracking a key performance indicator (KPI). A KPI is used to measure performance (and success). Without a definition of success, this would simply be a metric, but Charles is working toward a known goal and can measure against it. There is not a return investment calculation in this problem, and the measure is not a control.

17. D. Mandatory vacation programs require that employees take continuous periods of time off each year and revoke their system privileges during that time. The purpose of these required vacation periods is to disrupt any attempt to engage in the cover-up actions necessary to hide

fraud and result in exposing the threat. Separation of duties, least privilege, and defense-in-depth controls all may help prevent the fraud in the first place but are unlikely to hasten the detection of fraud that has already occurred.

18. C. Key risk indicators (KRIs) are measures that seek to quantify the security risk facing an organization. KRIs, unlike KPIs and KGIs, are a look forward. They attempt to show how much risk exists that may jeopardize the future security of the organization.

    Key performance indicators (KPIs) are metrics that demonstrate the success of the security program in achieving its objectives. KPIs are mutually agreed-upon measures that evaluate whether a security program is meeting its defined goals. Generally speaking, KPIs are a look back at historical performance, providing a measuring stick to evaluate the past success of the program.

    Key goal indicators (KGIs) are similar to KPIs but measure progress toward defined goals. For example, if an organization has a goal to eliminate all stored Social Security numbers (SSNs), a KGI might track the percentage of SSNs removed.

    KMIs are not a standard metric for cybersecurity programs.

19. B. When following the separation of duties principle, organizations divide critical tasks into discrete components and ensure that no one individual has the ability to perform both actions. This prevents a single rogue individual from performing that task in an unauthorized manner.

20. D. Key performance indicators (KPIs) are metrics that demonstrate the success of the security program in achieving its objectives. KPIs are mutually agreed-upon measures that evaluate whether a security program is meeting its defined goals. Generally speaking, KPIs are a look back at historical performance, providing a measuring stick to evaluate the past success of the program.

    Key goal indicators (KGIs) are similar to KPIs but measure progress toward defined goals. For example, if an organization has a goal to eliminate all stored Social Security numbers (SSNs), a KGI might track the percentage of SSNs removed.

    Key risk indicators (KRIs) are measures that seek to quantify the security risk facing an organization. KRIs, unlike KPIs and KGIs, are a look forward. They attempt to show how much risk exists that may jeopardize the future security of the organization.

    KMIs are not a standard metric for cybersecurity programs.

Chapter 2: The Audit Process

1. C. The IS auditor should conduct a risk assessment first to determine which areas have the highest risk, and then devote more testing resources to those high-risk areas.

2. A. When the IS auditor suspects fraud, they should conduct a careful evaluation of the matter and notify the audit committee. Because audit committee members are generally not involved in business operations, they will be sufficiently removed from the matter, and they will have the authority to involve others as needed.

3. D. Control risk is the term that signifies the possibility that a control will fail to prevent or detect unwanted actions.

4. A. The four categories of risk treatment are risk reduction (sometimes called risk mitigation, where risks are reduced through a control or process change), risk transfer (where risks are transferred to an external party such as an insurance company), risk avoidance (where the risk-bearing activity is discontinued), and risk acceptance (where management chooses to accept the risk).

5. D. The auditor should perform substantive testing, which is a test of transaction integrity.

6. C. The change log is the best evidence because it is objective and not subject to bias or hallucination.

7. B. Subjective sampling is used when the auditor concentrates on samples representing higher risk.

8. C. The IS auditor should immediately inform the auditee when any high-risk situation is discovered.

9. B. The IS auditor should act as a facilitator of a control self-assessment, and management should make any decisions regarding changes to controls.

10. D. Of the choices given, the organization history would be the least useful. The others will provide insight into the organization's mission and goals and how it sets out to achieve them.

11. C. If an auditor has discovered that automated workpapers could be updated by any personnel, the workpapers should not be trusted to contain complete and accurate information. Once this is fixed by eliminating write access, the auditor can rely on this data going forward but should not rely on the information prior to that point in time.

12. B. The auditor should determine that the process is effective and recommend that it be documented. Some regulations, however, may require that such a process be judged ineffective specifically because it lacks documentation.

13. A. An auditor who has determined that a key business process has been outsourced needs to determine effectiveness of that process by auditing that process or by relying on a separate audit report of that process.

14. D. An auditor would prefer bank statements over internal records because bank statements are produced by a bank, which is independent and objective. A bank is unlikely to alter its records to improve the audit outcome of one of its customers.

15. A. ISACA audit standards are mandatory for all ISACA certification holders, including those with the CISA certification. ISACA audit guidelines are optional.

16. C. The schedule, scope, and purpose of an audit should be established prior to the start of the audit. Sampling techniques should be established by auditors once they understand the nature of the systems and processes they are examining.

17. D. A financial services provider will often provide SOC 1 and SOC 2 Type II audit reports to a customer, providing its customer's auditor with the information they need to complete audits of the customer's financial accounting systems.

18. B. The auditor is using the discovery sampling technique, where the auditor is trying to find at least one exception in the population.

19. A. An IS auditor examining business records to look for evidence of fraud should employ discovery sampling. The auditor is examining a population in which even a single exception would represent a high-risk situation (such as embezzlement or fraud).

20. A. IS auditors may use AI/ML tools to examine large datasets, provided such use is permitted by policy and is both legal and ethical.

Chapter 3: IT Life Cycle Management

1. C. During the development phase, developers should perform only unit testing to verify that the individual sections of code they have written are performing properly.

2. A. Function point analysis (FPA) is used to estimate the effort required to develop a software program.

3. D. Critical path analysis helps a project manager determine which activities are on a project's "critical path."

4. C. When any significant change needs to occur in a project plan, a project change request should be created to document the reason for the change.

5. B. The phases of the systems development life cycle are a feasibility study, requirements definition, design, development, testing, implementation, and post-implementation.

6. B. Requirements need to be developed by several parties, including developers, analysts, architects, and users.

7. A. The requirements that are developed for a project should be the primary source for detailed tests.

8. B. The main purpose of change management is to review and approve proposed changes to systems and infrastructure. This helps to reduce the risk of unintended events and unplanned downtime.

9. D. A capability maturity model helps an organization to assess the maturity of its business processes, which is an important first step to any large-scale process improvement efforts.

10. D. Input validation checking is used to ensure that input values are within established ranges, of the correct character types, and free of harmful content.

11. C. In addition to business, functional, security, and privacy requirements, an organization considering cloud-based services needs to understand how the cloud services provider segregates the organization's data from that of its other customers.

12. D. When making an emergency change, personnel should first seek management approval, document the details of the change, and initiate an emergency change management procedure.

13. A. The migration to a new application can be done in several ways: parallel (running old and new systems side by side); geographic (migrating users in each geographic region separately); module by module (migrating individual modules of the application); or migrate all users, locations, and modules at the same time.

14. C. Developing risk tiers in third-party management helps an organization determine the level of due diligence for third parties at each risk tier. Because the level of risk varies, some third parties warrant extensive due diligence, whereas a lighter touch is warranted for low-risk parties.

15. B. Functional requirements should be measurable, because test cases should be developed directly from functional requirements. The same can be said about security and privacy requirements—all must be measurable because all should be tested.

16. D. In a matrix management approach, individuals have two different reporting relationships: a permanent one in their functional area and a temporary one to the project manager. This approach is commonly used when employees work on a project part-time while continuing their functional responsibilities.

17. C. The primary purpose of benchmarking is to compare key measurements in a business process to the same measurements performed by other organizations, particularly those considered to be top performers.

18. C. The Framework Core is a set of six security functions that apply across all industries and sectors: govern, identify, protect, detect, respond, and recover.

19. C. The team is conducting functional testing, which involves verifying that all functional requirements are met and that the application performs as expected according to the specifications.

20. B. The company is most likely aiming to achieve improved time-to-market by enabling faster and more frequent software releases through the adoption of a DevOps model. This approach enhances collaboration and streamlines workflows, unlike isolating environments or focusing on cost reduction. DevOps improves customer satisfaction by delivering timely updates, not by reducing features.

Chapter 4: IT Service Management

1. B. A problem is defined as a condition resulting from multiple incidents that exhibit common symptoms. In this example, many users are experiencing the effects of the application error.

2. C. Change management is the process of managing change through a life cycle process that consists of request, review, approve, implement, and verify.

3. A. Configuration management is the process (often supplemented with automated tools) of tracking configuration changes to systems and system components such as databases and applications.

4. D. Check-out/check-in logs are related to SDLC but not to configuration management.

5. A. The database administrator should implement audit logging, causing the database to record every change made to it.

6. D. The purposes of vulnerability scanning include confirming that proactive patching and proper configurations are in place, a good first step in a penetration test, and a means for directing IT to correct configuration errors and apply patches. Vulnerability scanning is not used to identify defects in application source code.

7. C. Release management is the step in the systems/software development life cycle (SDLC) to ensure that all requirements and steps before releasing software to production have been completed correctly and approved by management.

8. C. Vulnerability scans are not strictly necessary in patch management, as patches should be applied proactively because of vendor and non-vendor advisories.

9. A. Log entries do not need a checksum. A checksum is employed in lower-protocol layers.

10. C. The IT service desk needs to establish SLAs and begin measuring response time.

11. B. System location is less likely to be a driver for changes in SLA terms than the other choices.

12. D. Audit logs are set to read-only to prevent tampering, including the concealment of prohibited actions.

13. A. The advisory describes a critical vulnerability a threat actor can escalate remotely without login credentials. Such a vulnerability in externally facing systems should be addressed quickly.

14. A. Patch management is considered a part of vulnerability management. Vulnerability management is also concerned with security configuration settings.

15. B. In configuration management, a configuration item (CI) refers to an individual system or device.

16. C. Root cause analysis is not typically a part of a change request but instead is performed after an incident or problem.

17. A. Events such as hard drive faults, CPU utilization, and performance measures are generally monitored by a network monitoring system and not sent to a SIEM.

18. A. All security event logs should be sent to a SIEM, which can correlate events and generate alerts for further investigation and action.

19. D. An auditor is not likely to request the event logs themselves, as they would likely be large and cumbersome to deliver to the auditor. The other options are items likely requested for this audit.

20. B. Emergency changes should require management approval before the change is performed. Then, a change request should be filed, indicating that this was an emergency change already performed.

Chapter 5: IT Infrastructure

1. B. A computer's CPU, or central processing unit, performs most calculations.

2. C. RAM, or random-access memory, is the main storage on a computer system. Secondary storage is implemented with solid-state drives (SSDs) or hard disk drives (HDDs).

3. A. Virtualization permits several separate operating system instances to run on a single hardware platform.

4. D. A bus connects all the computer's internal components together, including its CPU, main memory, secondary memory, and peripheral devices.

5. A. Containerization is the technology that permits multiple application instances to run within a single operating system.

6. A. The layers of the TCP/IP model are (from lowest to highest) link, Internet, transport, and application.

7. C. The purpose of the Internet layer in the TCP/IP model is the delivery of packets from one station to another, on the same network or on a different network.

8. C. The DHCP protocol is used to assign IP addresses to computers on a network.

9. A. The WEP protocol has been seriously compromised and should be replaced with WPA2/WPA3 encryption.

10. C. Class A addresses are in the range 0.0.0.0 to 127.255.255.255. The address 126.0.0.1 falls into this range.

11. **B.** Hardware monitoring is used to measure numerous aspects of a running system, but ambient temperature is not measured. Internal temperature is measured and is an indicator of workload and cooling.

12. **D.** A cluster is a set of servers, which often appear as a single logical server to perform transactions.

13. **B.** A filesystem would be used to store unstructured data files. A database management system is typically used to store structured data.

14. **A.** Digital rights management (DRM) is the technology of choice for managing retention policy for documents when they reside outside of an organization's direct control.

15. **B.** In a virtualization environment, each guest operating system needs to be hardened; they are no different from operating systems running directly on server (or workstation) hardware.

16. **A.** Physical network structure refers to cabling and other hardware. Logical network structure refers to the inner workings of a network, in terms of protocols and data flow. For instance, an Ethernet network can be a physical star but operate like a logical bus.

17. **D.** Email, directory, file storage, and time synchronization are examples of network services, available to users via a network.

18. **C.** Presentation is not a layer of the TCP/IP model. The four layers of the TCP/IP model are link, Internet, transport, and application.

19. **B.** Twisted-pair cabling, such as Cat-5 and Cat-6, are the most common types of network cabling used in modern LANs.

20. **A.** Asset inventory is critical for many processes, including vulnerability management, license management, server hardening, data classification, system classification, and incident response. Asset inventory is not relevant to static code analysis.

Chapter 6: Business Continuity and Disaster Recovery

1. **B.** The best choice in this instance is to back up to a virtual tape library (VTL). Replication and mirroring are not suitable, as a ransomware attack may be able to encrypt file server data, and that encryption would be replicated or mirrored to alternate storage systems. RAID is not a backup solution but a storage resilience solution.

2. **C.** Business continuity planning is concerned with the resilience of business processes.

3. A. The correct sequence of activities in business resilience is business impact analysis (BIA), criticality analysis (CA), business continuity planning (BCP), then disaster recovery planning (DRP).

4. D. Organizations would use the same high-level disaster response procedures regardless of the nature of the disaster.

5. A. The progression of the types of DRP tests, in order of difficulty and impact, is walk-through (a meeting where the sequence of steps is discussed), simulation (like a walk-through but with a realistic scenario gradually revealed), parallel test (where recovery systems run in parallel with production systems), and cutover test (where recovery systems take over production work from production systems).

6. A. A simulation is like a walk-through, where a facilitator develops and provides periodic updates in a realistic scenario.

7. C. A criticality assessment, performed at the conclusion of a business impact analysis, determines the probability and impact of the incapacitation of business processes and information systems. This leads to a list of processes and systems in order of criticality.

8. C. RPO, or recovery point objective, is a measure of the maximum acceptable data loss. RTO, or recovery time objective, is a measure of the maximum time that a system or process will not be functioning.

9. A. Auditors generally consider documentation as outdated and invalid if it has not been formally reviewed within the past year.

10. C. Since the question describes only the design of a site, we can only conclude that this is a cold site, with no equipment and no readiness for processing transactions.

11. B. An important selection criterion for a hot site is the geographic location in relation to the primary site. If they are too close together, then a single disaster event may involve both locations.

12. D. An organization that has a 14-day recovery time objective (RTO) can use a cold site for its recovery strategy. Fourteen days is enough time for most organizations to acquire hardware and recover applications.

13. B. An organization that wants its application servers to be continuously available to its users needs to employ server clustering. This enables at least one server to always be available to service user requests.

14. A. The primary reason for employing off-site backup media storage is to mitigate the effects of a disaster that could otherwise destroy computer systems and their backup media.

15. B. RCO, or recovery consistency objective, generally addresses features and functionality. In this scenario, RCO is 100%. RCapO, or recovery capacity objective, measures the capacity of the recovery site as compared to the primary site. In this scenario, RCapO is 50%.

16. A. The best people to write a DRP for a critical business application are the IT personnel who are most senior and have the most knowledge of the system.

17. D. The safety of personnel always takes priority over all other considerations. In this scenario, the first responders on-site should tend to injured personnel before performing other tasks.

18. D. In a regional disaster scenario, telecommunications facilities are generally compromised and/or congested. Hence, it may be difficult to find three top executives who are reachable and can agree to activate disaster response proceedings.

19. C. The consequences of a "false positive," that of declaring a disaster and activating disaster response, are minimal. Disaster responders can resume their normal duties.

20. A. In a regional disaster scenario, local disaster response personnel may be unavailable to perform disaster response procedures; they may be tending to family members and securing their residences if they are damaged.

Chapter 7: Information Security Management

1. D. The cloud service provider bears the most responsibility for implementing security controls in an SaaS environment and the least responsibility in an IaaS environment. This is due to the division of responsibilities under the cloud computing shared responsibility model.

2. B. Port security restricts the number of unique MAC addresses that may originate from a single switchport. It is commonly used to prevent someone from unplugging an authorized device from the network and connecting an unauthorized device but may also be used to prevent existing devices from spoofing MAC addresses of other devices.

3. A. If Patricia's major concern is a compromised operating system, she can bypass the operating system on the device by booting it from live boot media and running her own operating system on the hardware. Running a malware scan may provide her with some information but may not detect all compromises and Patricia likely does not have the necessary permissions to correct any issues. Using a VPN or accessing secure sites would not protect her against a compromised operating system, as the operating system would be able to view the contents of her communication prior to encryption.

4. C. In a true positive report, the system reports an attack when an attack actually exists. A false positive report occurs when the system reports an attack that did not take place. A true negative report occurs when the system reports no attack and no attack took place. A false negative report occurs when the system does not report an attack that did take place.

5. A. Hardware security modules (HSMs) provide an effective way to manage encryption keys. These hardware devices store and manage encryption keys in a secure manner that prevents humans from ever needing to work directly with the keys.

6. D. The attack in question could be most quickly stopped with a network firewall rule blocking all traffic from the origin system. Host firewall rules would also address the issue but would be more time-consuming to create on every system. An operating system update would not stop attack traffic. There is also no indication that a DDoS attack is underway, so a DDoS mitigation service would not be helpful.

7. D. The principle of data sovereignty states that data is subject to the legal restrictions of any jurisdiction where it is collected, stored, or processed. In this case, Howard needs to assess the laws of all three jurisdictions.

8. C. When encrypting a confidential message using an asymmetric encryption algorithm, the person performing the encryption does so using the recipient's public key.

9. D. In an asymmetric encryption algorithm, the recipient of a confidential message uses their own private key to decrypt messages that they receive.

10. B. The sender of a message may digitally sign the message by encrypting a message digest with the sender's own private key.

11. A. The recipient of a digitally signed message may verify the digital signature by decrypting it with the public key of the individual who signed the message.

12. A. An organization using a DLP system should be acting on alerts that the DLP system generates in order to curb employee and system behavior.

13. B. Finding an unauthorized access point is a high-risk situation that the IS auditor should report immediately to management.

14. D. Managerial controls are procedural mechanisms that focus on the mechanics of the risk management process. Threat assessment is an example of one of these activities.

15. B. Jade is concerned about compliance risk because the issue involves violating the Payment Card Industry Data Security Standard (PCI DSS), which regulates the protection of credit card data. Compliance risk arises when an organization fails to follow laws, regulations, or standards that apply to its operations. Strategic risk involves decisions that affect the long-term goals or competitive position of the organization, which isn't the case here. Operational risk deals with internal processes, systems, or human errors, while financial risk involves the potential for financial loss, but neither of these risks directly relates to regulatory violations like PCI DSS.

16. C. The attack violated integrity because defacing a website alters its content, which means unauthorized changes were made to the website's data. Integrity ensures that information remains accurate and unaltered by unauthorized parties. Confidentiality refers to protecting sensitive information from unauthorized access, which isn't relevant in this scenario since the attackers modified visible content. Nonrepudiation ensures that actions or communications cannot be denied by the involved parties, but that doesn't relate to altering website content. Availability ensures systems are accessible when needed, which isn't affected by mere defacement unless the site becomes inaccessible.

17. D. Deterrent controls are designed to prevent an attacker from attempting to violate security policies in the first place. Preventive controls would attempt to block an attack that was about to take place. Corrective controls would remediate the issues that arose during an attack.

18. D. All individuals within an organization have some responsibility for protecting data. However, the data owner is the senior-most leader who bears ultimate responsibility for this protection. The data owner may delegate some authority and/or responsibility to data stewards, data custodians, and end users, but they still bear ultimate responsibility.

19. A. The risk that Tony is contemplating could fit any one of these categories. However, his primary concern is that the company may no longer be able to do business if the risk materializes. This is a strategic risk.

20. C. One of the important characteristics of cloud computing is that customers can access resources on-demand with minimal service provider interaction. Cloud customers do not need to contact a sales representative each time they wish to provision a resource but can normally do so on a self-service basis.

Chapter 8: Identity and Access Management

1. C. This is a wet pipe system because it involves water being constantly present in the pipes, and the sprinkler heads activate when the ambient temperature reaches a certain point, releasing the water. A deluge system, on the other hand, has open sprinkler heads and releases water through all heads simultaneously when a valve is opened, not requiring high ambient temperature. A post-action system doesn't exist, making it an incorrect option. A pre-action system requires an additional triggering mechanism before water fills the pipes, unlike the wet pipe system where water is already present.

2. A. The combination of an uninterruptible power supply (UPS) and an electric generator should be selected because the UPS provides immediate power to prevent any disruption during the transition, and the generator ensures long-term power availability during extended outages. A UPS with batteries would provide only short-term power and isn't sufficient for prolonged outages. An electric generator alone wouldn't prevent brief outages or surges before it starts. Electric generator and line conditioning would improve power quality but wouldn't ensure continuous power during outages.

3. D. The best course of action is to improve the employee termination process and audit the process more frequently. Improving the process ensures that terminated employees' accounts are promptly and correctly deactivated, addressing the root cause of the issue. Regular audits then ensure that the improvements are effective and that any future lapses are quickly identified. Simply shifting responsibility might not solve the underlying problem, and auditing more frequently without improving the process won't prevent the errors from occurring in the first place.

4. B. Using several named administrative accounts that are not shared should be recommended because it ensures accountability by associating actions with specific individuals. This prevents confusion over who performed certain actions and strengthens security. Implementing activity logging on a shared account could track actions but wouldn't solve the issue of identifying which administrator was responsible. A host-based intrusion detection system monitors for malicious activities but doesn't address the problem of shared accounts. Requiring nondisclosure and acceptable-use agreements focuses on behavior rather than resolving the issue of shared account use.

5. D. Facial recognition technology is an example of a biometric authentication technique, or "something you are." A passcode is an example of a knowledge-based authentication technique, or "something you know."

6. B. The false rejection rate (FRR) identifies the number of times that an individual who should be allowed access to a facility is rejected. The false acceptance rate (FAR) identifies the number of times that an individual who should not be allowed access to a facility is admitted. Both the FAR and FRR may be manipulated by changing system settings. The crossover error rate (CER) is the rate at which the FRR and FAR are equal and is less prone to manipulation. Therefore, the CER is the best measure for Fred to use. IRR is not a measure of biometric system effectiveness.

7. C. Gary is performing authentication, as he is verifying his identity by providing his fingerprint after entering his username and password. Identification occurs when he provides his username, establishing who he is. Authorization would happen after authentication, where the system determines what actions or resources Gary is allowed to access. Accounting involves tracking and logging Gary's activities within the system after he has gained access.

8. B. This type of authentication, where one domain trusts users from another domain, is called federated authentication. Federated authentication may involve transitive trusts, where the trusts may be followed through a series of domains, but this scenario only describes the use of two domains. The scenario only describes use of credentials for a single system and does not describe a multiple-system scenario where single sign-on would be relevant. There is no requirement described for the use of multifactor authentication, which would require the use of two or more diverse authentication techniques.

9. A. The auditor can conclude that employee privileges are not being removed when they transfer from one position to another. This situation often occurs when employees change roles within the organization and retain unnecessary privileges from their previous positions, leading to an accumulation of excessive privileges over time. The idea that long-time employees are guessing passwords is less likely and not directly related to the accumulation of privileges. Frequent password expiration would not address the root cause of privilege creep, and ineffective termination processes would result in former employees retaining access, not current ones with excessive privileges.

10. B. Implementing encryption protocols ensures the confidentiality and integrity of data sent over the network by encrypting the data, making it unreadable to unauthorized users, and using cryptographic methods to verify that the data has not been altered during transmission.

Using strong passwords enhances security for accessing systems but does not protect the data during transmission across the network.

Regularly updating network hardware may improve overall network performance and security but does not specifically protect the data's confidentiality and integrity while it is being transmitted.

Conducting frequent audits helps identify security weaknesses and ensure policies are followed, but it does not directly secure the data being transmitted over the network in real time.

11. C. Conducting regular user account reviews primarily serves to identify and revoke unnecessary permissions, ensuring that users have only the access they need and reducing the risk of unauthorized access to sensitive information.

Ensuring compliance with company policies is a secondary benefit of account reviews but not the primary purpose.

Providing user training on new software is unrelated to the objective of reviewing user accounts and their permissions.

Preparing for external audits might be a reason for conducting reviews, but it is not the primary goal, which is focused on maintaining appropriate access levels for users.

12. C. Unauthorized data access and potential data breaches are the most significant risks of not performing a thorough risk assessment before granting third-party access, as this could lead to sensitive information being exposed to unauthorized parties.

Increased operational costs are a potential concern but are less significant compared to the risk of data breaches.

Reduced employee productivity is not directly related to third-party access risk assessment and is less critical than data security issues.

Overuse of system resources might be an operational concern, but it does not pose as significant a threat as unauthorized data access and breaches.

13. B. The weakness in this scheme is that someone who finds a one-time password token could log in as the user by guessing the user ID. Since the one-time password token generates a new password for each login attempt, the attacker would only need to correctly guess the associated user ID to gain access. Guessing the password or deriving it from the user ID isn't feasible because the password changes frequently and isn't predictable. Eavesdropping and using a replay attack would not work because the password is valid for only a single use and typically has a very short life span.

14. C. Mandatory Access Control (MAC) is most suitable for environments requiring strict control over who can access certain types of data, as it enforces access policies set by a central authority and does not allow user modification of access permissions.

Discretionary Access Control (DAC) allows data owners to control access, which can lead to less strict enforcement and potential security risks if users modify permissions.

Role-Based Access Control (RBAC) assigns access based on roles, which provides good control but still allows some flexibility that might not meet the strictest requirements.

Attribute-Based Access Control (ABAC) grants access based on attributes and policies, offering flexibility but also complexity, which may not align with the need for strict, unmodifiable controls.

15. C. Cipher locks are the best choice for access control in this situation. They don't require electricity, making them ideal for locations without power, and they offer more flexibility and security than metal keys. Unlike metal keys, which can be difficult to manage across multiple locations, cipher locks can be easily reprogrammed if a combination needs to be changed, reducing the logistical challenges of key distribution and control. Keycards would require power, and video surveillance does not control access, so they are not viable options here.

16. D. A logic bomb is specifically designed to activate at a certain date and time, causing damage to data or other malicious activities upon the triggering condition being met.

A virus is a type of malware that attaches itself to a host file and spreads to other files and systems but does not necessarily activate based on a specific date and time.

A worm is a stand-alone malware that replicates itself to spread to other computers, typically through a network, but it does not activate based on a specific date and time.

A Trojan horse is a type of malware disguised as legitimate software, which may carry out various malicious activities once installed, but its activation is not specifically tied to a certain date and time.

17. C. The principle of least privilege in access control aims to minimize the risk of unauthorized access by ensuring users are granted only the permissions necessary to perform their specific tasks, thereby reducing potential security vulnerabilities.

Increasing system performance is not related to access control and least privilege directly focuses on security rather than performance.

Ensuring users have enough privileges to perform any task contradicts the principle of least privilege, which seeks to limit access to the minimum necessary.

Simplifying the user access management process is a secondary benefit, but the primary focus of the principle of least privilege is on reducing security risks rather than administrative simplicity.

18. A. A VPN (virtual private network) can best assist with providing secure, remote access to employees who work from home by encrypting the connection between the user's device and the organization's network, ensuring data security and privacy over the internet.

An IPS (intrusion prevention system) is designed to detect and prevent security threats within a network but does not facilitate remote access for employees.

A CASB (cloud access security broker) helps manage and secure the use of cloud services but is not primarily focused on providing remote network access.

A DLP (data loss prevention) system aims to prevent sensitive data from being lost, misused, or accessed by unauthorized users but does not provide remote access capabilities.

19. A. If the firewall is designed in a "fail open" configuration, it will allow any traffic to enter and leave the network if it fails. This configuration prioritizes availability, meaning that in the event of a failure, the firewall defaults to allowing all traffic through rather than blocking it, which could pose significant security risks. A "fail closed" configuration would prevent any traffic from passing through, ensuring security at the cost of availability. Continuing to enforce the last known good configuration or alerting administrators and awaiting instructions are not characteristics of a "fail open" configuration.

20. C. An inert gas fire suppression system is crucial for protecting data centers from fire damage while minimizing damage to equipment, as it extinguishes fires without using water, thereby avoiding potential harm to electronic equipment.

A wet pipe sprinkler system uses water to suppress fires, which can cause significant damage to data center equipment.

A dry pipe sprinkler system also uses water, though it is stored in pipes until needed, which still poses a risk of water damage to sensitive electronics.

Portable fire extinguishers can be useful for small, localized fires but are not sufficient for comprehensive protection of a data center and may not be suitable for automated response.

Index

O

S

U

V

Online Test Bank

To help you study for your CISA (Certified Information Systems Auditor) certification exam, register to gain one year of FREE access after activation to the online interactive test bank—included with your purchase of this book!

To access our learning environment, simply visit www.wiley.com/go/sybextestprep, follow the instructions to register your book, and instantly gain one year of FREE access after activation to:

- Hundreds of practice test questions, so you can practice in a timed and graded setting.
- Flashcards
- A searchable glossary